ALSO BY NATALIE ZEMON DAVIS

Slaves on Screen:
Film and Historical Vision

The Gift in Sixteenth-Century France

Women on the Margins:
Three Seventeenth-Century Lives

Fiction in the Archives:
Pardon Tales and Their Tellers in
Sixteenth-Century France

The Return of Martin Guerre

Society and Culture in Early Modern France

Trickster Travels

Trickster Travels

A Sixteenth-Century Muslim

Between Worlds

NATALIE ZEMON DAVIS

HILL AND WANG

A DIVISION OF FARRAR, STRAUS AND GIROUX

NEW YORK

Hill and Wang
A division of Farrar, Straus and Giroux
19 Union Square West, New York 10003

Distributed in Canada by Douglas & McIntyre Ltd.
Printed in the United States of America
First edition, 2006

Owing to limitations of space, illustration credits appear on pages 433–435.

Library of Congress Cataloging-in-Publication Data
Davis, Natalie Zemon, 1928–
    Trickster travels : a sixteenth-century Muslim between worlds / Natalie
Zemon Davis.— 1st ed.
        p.   cm.
    Includes bibliographical references and index.
    ISBN-13: 978-0-8090-9434-9 (hardcover : alk. paper)
    ISBN-10: 0-8090-9434-7 (hardcover : alk. paper)
    1. Leo Africanus, ca. 1492–ca. 1550.   2. Africanists—Europe—
Biography.   I. Title.

DT19.7.L46D385   2006
909′.5′092—dc22   2005017706

Designed by Cassandra J. Pappas

www.fsgbooks.com

1   3   5   7   9   10   8   6   4   2

For Chandler Davis, once again—as always

Contents

Note on Transliteration and Dates

Arabic names, book titles, and technical words are transcribed without diacritical marks beyond the hamza and the letter ʿayn. All precise dates concerning events and persons in the Islamic world in the medieval and early modern period are given in both the Muslim form, the lunar calendar dating from the Hijra, and the Christian form, or what we now call the form of the common era: thus, 897/1492 is the date for the Christian conquest of Muslim Granada, the edict expelling the Jews from Spain, and Christopher Columbus's departure from Cádiz for the Indies. All references to centuries will follow the common-era terminology: sixteenth century.

Trickster Travels

Introduction: Crossings

In 1514 King Manuel I of Portugal presented Pope Leo X with a white elephant from India. Paraded through the streets of Rome in an elaborate ceremony and named "Annone," or Hanno, by welcoming Romans, the elephant represented to the pope the king's intention to bring the realms that extended from North Africa to India into the Christian fold. Hanno survived in his pen for three years, a presence at public events and festivities and a favorite of the pope and the Roman populace. He was written about by poets, mythographers, and satirists, and imaged in drawings, paintings, and woodcuts; in fountain ornament, bas-relief, and majolica platter. Raphael designed his memorial fresco.[1]

In 1518 a Spanish pirate, fresh from successful raids against Muslim ships in the Mediterranean, presented the same pope with a captured North African traveler and diplomat from Fez named al-Hasan al-Wazzan. He would serve as a useful source of information, it was hoped, and as a symbol in the pope's desired crusade against the Ottoman Turks and the religion of Islam. Had not the Turks been an increased threat to Christendom since their conquest of Constantinople in 1453? The diplomat's arrival and imprisonment were noted in diaries and diplomatic correspondence. His baptism at St. Peter's fifteen months later was a grand ceremony. A librarian recorded his book-borrowing. But compared to Hanno, al-Hasan al-Wazzan's nine years in Italy went unrecorded by those who saw him, his presence unmemorialized by those whom he served or knew, his likeness not drawn and redrawn, his return to North Africa referred to only later and obliquely. Only a shred of his life remained in the memory of Europeans interested in Arabic letters and travel literature, to be passed on orally and reported years later.

In North Africa there are also baffling silences. During the years when al-Hasan al-Wazzan was serving as agent for the sultan of Fez in towns along Morocco's Atlantic coast, no mention of him was made by Portuguese military men and administrators in their chatty letters to King Manuel. During years when he had diplomatic duties in Cairo, no mention of him was made by a sharp-eyed observer who wrote in his journal of visitors to the court of the Mamluk rulers of Egypt and the Levant.

Yet al-Hasan al-Wazzan left behind in Italy several manuscripts, one of which, published in 1550, became a bestseller. Over the centuries his book attracted the curiosity of readers and scholars in many parts of the world. The mysteries about him and even his name began already with the first edition. Giovanni Battista Ramusio, the editor, entitled the book *La Descrittione dell'Africa* (The Description of Africa), called its author by his baptismal name, "Giovan Lioni Africano," and included a brief biography of him in his dedication. So he was known in the several subsequent editions of the book that were published in Venice as the first volume in Ramusio's series of *Navigations and Voyages*. And so he was known in the European translations that soon appeared: "Iean Leon, African [*sic*]" in French (1556); "Ioannes Leo Africanus" in Latin (1556); and "Iohn Leo, a More" in English (1600). Through the German translation (1805) of "Johann Leo der Africaner," his book continued to shape European visions of Africa, all the more strongly because it came from someone who had lived and traveled in those parts.[2]

Meanwhile a scholar at the Escorial library in Spain, himself a Maronite Christian from Syria, came upon an Arabic manuscript on another topic by al-Wazzan. It bore both his Muslim and his Christian names, which the librarian included in his published catalogue (1760–70). A century later, when the *Description* was enshrined in the *Recueil de voyages* (Collection of Voyages) by the important French Orientalist Charles Schefer, an Arabic name appeared in the introduction; and in the classic Hakluyt Society series of travel literature in England, the title page proclaimed: "by Al-Hassan Ibn-Mohammed Al-Wezaz Al-Fasi, a Moor, baptized as Giovanni Leone, but better known as Leo Africanus."[3]

Still its author remained a shadowy figure. Then in the early decades of the twentieth century, a few scholars approached the book and the man in new ways. In the context of the new French "colonial sciences" concerning the geography, history, and ethnography of Africa, the young Louis Massignon did his Sorbonne thesis on Morocco in the early sixteenth century as it had been described by "Léon l'Africain." From a close reading of the text (a technique that would flower in his later great publications on Sufi mysticism and poetry), Massignon extracted what he could not only about the geography of Morocco but also about al-Wazzan's life and travels, especially about his sources and methods of observing and classifying. The frame of al-Wazzan's book was "very Europeanized," Massignon opined, but "its core was very Arabic." Massignon's study was published in 1906, an important moment in France's steps toward establishing its protectorate of Morocco.[4]

The historical geographer Angela Codazzi knew Massignon's book well and took seriously his hope that an original manuscript of al-Wazzan's book would one day be found. Close to the collections in Italy's libraries, in 1933 she could announce that she had located an Italian manuscript of *The Description of Africa*, and it did indeed differ from the later printed edition of Ramusio. At the same time, Giorgio Levi della Vida, a remarkable scholar of Semitic languages and literatures, was making discoveries as well. Excluded from university teaching in 1931 as an antifascist, he was invited to catalogue the Arabic manuscripts at the Vatican Library. He left for the United States in 1939—an act of safety for a Jew—but not before putting the finishing touches on a book about the creation of the Oriental collections at the Vatican. Among its many riches, it had much to say about the reading, writing, and signing practices of al-Hasan al-Wazzan. Back in Italy after the war, Levi della Vida helped Codazzi interpret two manuscripts on other subjects that she had found by "Giovanni Leone Africano."[5]

The last important colonial presentation of Jean-Léon l'Africain was a new French translation and commentary prepared by Alexis Épaulard. During years in Morocco as a physician and military officer with the French protectorate, Épaulard had become impressed with "the exceptional value," both historical and geographical, of *The Description of Africa*. His book built upon the work of Massignon and Codazzi, without following their spirit. Épaulard used the Italian manuscript in Rome in 1939—and applauded Codazzi's plan to publish it one day (alas, unfulfilled)—but his *Description* is an amalgam of translations from Ramusio, occasional translations from the manuscript, and a modernized version of the sixteenth-century French translation. He ignored the possibility that the differences between the texts could reveal larger differences in viewpoint and cultural sensibility.

Like Massignon's book, the Épaulard edition confronted assertions made in the *Description* with evidence from outside its pages—from the distance between places to the unrolling of historical events—and corrected al-Wazzan when necessary. Geographical names were clarified, and Arab authors he cited were identified. To achieve this, Épaulard assembled a team of French scholars in sub-Saharan studies, two of them then based in Dakar at the Institut Français d'Afrique Noire, and consulted specialists in North African folklore and historiography. The notes are useful, but they did not address the question raised by Massignon about where the text or its author was positioned in regard to the world he was writing about and the world he was writing for. Differences were smoothed over again: Épaulard liked to think that "Jean Léon" had never left his Christian life in Italy.

Épaulard did not live to see the fulfillment of his project. The team finished it up, and the *Description* was published in Paris by the Institut des Hautes Études Marocaines in 1956, three years after Morocco became an independent state.[6]

The Épaulard team had particularly envisaged their readers as historians of Africa, and soon scholars of sub-Saharan Africa began to have their say about al-Wazzan's reliability as a witness. In the late decades of the century, specialists from Europe, Africa, and America compared his pages on Black Africa with other evidence and later accounts: some claimed he gave convincing, precious detail on little-known societies and kingdoms, others that he was reporting tall stories picked up in Timbuktu and had never traveled beyond its borders. Here a ruler verified, there a conquest found false, here a trading practice confirmed, there a fire mentioned by no one else but al-Wazzan. All these approaches—in worthy pursuit of "scrupulous care in handling" a primary source—broke the *Description* into fragments, rather than considering it as a whole or its author's literary practices.[7]

While the Africanists were arguing, a new generation arose of post-colonial readers of al-Hasan al-Wazzan. Most important was Oumelbanine Zhiri, whose own travels took her from her native Morocco to France to the United States. Her 1991 book, *L'Afrique au miroir de l'Europe: Fortunes de Jean Léon l'Africain à la Renaissance*, showed what impact the printed editions of Jean Léon's book had had on the European view of Africa's peoples, landscapes, and past. Her scope was wide—literary books, history books, and geographies—as she detailed what European writers had taken from, reshaped, and sometimes ignored in the *Description*. She inserted the non-European world into the consciousness of the Renaissance in a new way. In contrast with earlier studies of European attitudes toward the Turks, where all the imaging came from the European side, Zhiri's *Mirror* set up an interchange, with the North African Jean Léon making a difference. Zhiri has gone on to carry the story forward over the centuries and is now turning to issues in the manuscript itself.[8]

The second major study of Leo Africanus comes from a different part of the world and takes the story in different directions. Following his years as a German career officer and diplomat in Morocco and Tunisia, Dietrich Rauchenberger plunged deeply into research on the intriguing al-Hasan al-Wazzan. Among other stops, his quest led him to the Africa manuscript in Rome, the basis of his big *Johannes Leo der Afrikaner* (1999). Rauchenberger recounted the life, writings, and Italian milieu of Johannes Leo and uncovered the little-known resonance of his work among German scholars. The force of Rauchenberger's study is its remarkable treatment of al-Wazzan's controversial pages on sub-Saharan Africa. He used the manuscript and its divergences from the printed editions to assess al-Wazzan's reliability as an observer and traveler and placed this assessment in a richly drawn picture of the sub-Saharan region and its peoples. He concluded by quoting approvingly one of the African specialists on Épaulard's team: "'We are lucky that the work of Leo Africanus was directed to a European public in Europe. Had he written for an Arab public, many valuable details would doubtless have been left out because they would have been assumed known.'"[9]

Scholars in Arabic studies and Arab scholars based in Morocco have, in fact, increasingly turned to al-Hasan al-Wazzan and his Africa book. In 1995 Serafín Fanjul, a specialist in Arabic literature, translated anew a Ramusio edition of the *Description* into Spanish. In part he wanted to close the gap between Arabists and Europeanists; in part he wanted to claim "Juan León," who was born in Granada, and his book for the mixed "cultural patrimony" of Spain.[10]

Fanjul had his doubts about the sincerity of Juan León's conversion to Christianity, an act that was troubling from the beginning for scholars in Morocco. In a pioneering study of 1935, Muhammad al-Mahdi al-Hajwi described al-Hasan al-Wazzan as a captive, who had been constrained in his conversion, had always remained attached to his people and his religion, and had himself influenced the pope. Forty-five years later, in 1980, the first Arabic translation of al-Wazzan's Africa book was published in Rabat. Its translator, Muhammad Hajji, had defended his thesis at the Sorbonne on the intellectual life of Morocco in the sixteenth and seventeenth centuries not long before and was now professor of history at the University of Rabat. Introducing his translation from

Épaulard's French, Hajji reclaimed al-Wazzan by insisting that he had feigned conversion to Christianity and that certain features of the *Description*, such as his use of the word "we," showed his continuing devotion to Islam.[11]

Such questions were recast at a Paris conference on "Léon l'Africain" in 2003, which brought together scholars from the Maghreb, Europe, and North America interested in this enigmatic figure. The task of reclaiming him for Morocco had become less sensitive by then. In part, the way had been cleared not by a scholarly text but by a widely read and lively novel, *Léon l'Africain* (1986), written by Amin Maalouf. Born in Lebanon into a family of mixed religious loyalties and much geographical outreach, Maalouf worked as a journalist for the Arab press and then, as the civil wars tore apart his native land, moved to France. There he completed his studies in economics and sociology, wrote for and edited *Jeune Afrique*, a periodical of African independence movements and newly formed states, and in 1983 brought out a book of readings—in French and Arabic editions—on the Crusades as viewed by the Arabs.

Three years later Maalouf found his voice as a historical novelist, writing in French about the Arab and Islamic past, and he created in Leo Africanus/al-Hasan a figure who perfectly represented his own way of rising above constrictive and exclusive identities of language, religion, and nation. "I come from no country, no city, no tribe," his hero says at the opening of the novel. "I am the son of the highway, my country is a caravan . . . all languages, all prayers belong to me." Of himself, Maalouf has said, "I claim all the cultural dimensions of my country of origin and those of my adopted country"; and again, "I come from a tribe which has been nomadic forever in a desert of worldwide dimensions. Our countries are oases that we leave when the water dries up . . . We rely only on each other, across the generations, across the seas, across the Babel of languages." Routes, not roots: in Léon l'Africain, Maalouf saw a figure from his Mediterranean past who combined its "multiple cultures."[12]

Historians might find Maalouf's portrait of al-Wazzan somewhat free-floating in its facile accretion of tastes, stances, and sensibilities, but it opened the door to new questions. At the 2003 colloquium, colleagues from the Maghreb had varied views on al-Wazzan's cultural placement, but all thought it an issue to confront. The philosopher Ali Benmakhlouf gave a strictly European context to al-Wazzan's art of describing; the historical anthropologist Houari Touati saw his treatment of African animals as connected with earlier Arabic constructions; for Ahmed Boucharb, al-Wazzan's treatment of the battles between the Portuguese and the Moroccans was an extension of certain forms of Arabic historical writing, but his impartiality showed that he had dropped all feeling for the world of his origins; meanwhile Abdelmajid Kaddouri interpreted al-Wazzan's *Description* in terms of both Arabic and European genres.[13]

THE INTEREST IN cultural placement and movement of these Maghrebi colleagues is closest to my own concerns. I first came upon al-Hasan al-Wazzan's *Description of Africa* more than forty years ago, when I had just completed my doctoral dissertation on Protestantism and the printing workers of sixteenth-century Lyon. One of those Lyon Protestants was the merchant-publisher Jean Temporal, who was translating the *Description* into French and having it printed in the mid-1550s. I marveled at Temporal's breadth of interests and at the illustrations of an imagined Africa engraved by his brother-in-law.[14] But my attention then was on something else: on the confrontation of worker with employer and of layman with cleric within the dense life of a French city, subjects little attended to by the history-writing of the 1950s. The encounter between Europe and Africa embedded in the *Description* seemed far away and less urgent. The conversions I was trying to fathom were from Catholic to Protestant, perhaps especially interesting because they were taking place in the hearts and minds of *menu peuple*, little people. The sustained interplay between Islam and Christianity that I might have detected in the life and writing of "Jean Léon l'Africain" would have seemed too middling a religious stance to invite analysis.

In the mid-1990s the relation between European and non-European populations was at the center of things, and polar ways of thinking were being challenged. Scholars like Homi Bhabha were configuring cultural relations between colonized and colonizer in India in terms of "hybridity" rather than clear "difference" and "otherness." Domination and resistance were still essential to understand the past, but the American historian Richard White could then go from there to map a "middle ground" in which diplomacy, trade, and other forms of exchange took place between Native Americans and the English who settled in their ancestral lands. Paul Gilroy was charting his *Black Atlantic*, "mov[ing] discussion of black political culture beyond the binary opposition between national and diaspora perspectives . . . locat[ing] the black Atlantic world in a webbed network, between the local and the global." I, too, was rethinking that Atlantic as I wrote about European women "on the margins," in contact with Iroquoian and Algonquian women in Québec and with Carib and African women in Suriname.[15]

It seemed a fine moment to return to Jean Léon l'Africain, whom I began to think of as al-Hasan al-Wazzan, the name he had for most of his life. I now also had family connections with his part of the world, in Morocco and Tunisia. Through his example, I could explore how a man moved between different polities, made use of different cultural and social resources, and entangled or separated them so as to survive, discover, write, make relationships, and think about society and himself. I could try to see whether these processes were easy or a struggle, whether they brought delight or disappointment. Like some others I have written about, al-Hasan al-Wazzan is an extreme case—most North African Muslims were not captured by Christian pirates or, if they were, were not handed over to the pope—but an extreme case can often reveal patterns available for more everyday experience and writing.[16]

A more serious danger was brought sharply to my attention when I was lecturing in Lyon, by an immigrant to France of non-European origin. He would have had me talk about the harsh policies of governments toward strangers and the economic and sexual exploitation of immigrants, not about cultural exchanges and newcomers' strategies of accommodation, some of them surreptitious. I have taken his warning seriously—relations of domination and relations of exchange always interact in some way—and my picture of al-Hasan al-Wazzan notes when he was under the thumb of a master or a captor or ruler of some sort.

The years in which al-Wazzan lived, the last decades of the fifteenth century and the opening decades of the sixteenth, were packed with political and religious change and conflict. In the eastern Muslim world, the Ottoman Turks were on the move, conquering not only their Shi'ite neighbors in Persia but also their fellow Sunni rulers in Syria and Egypt. In the Maghreb (as the Islamic west was called) and especially in Morocco, Sufi religious movements and allied tribal leaders were threatening to shift the authority on which political rule was based. In Christian Europe, the Habsburg rulers were on the rise, expanding their domination of the Holy Roman Empire through shrewd marriage to control of Spain. The French monarchs challenged them at every turn, if not in their growing overseas empire, then for power in Europe and especially in Italy. As a vigorous Catholicism was giving new force to dynastic rule in Spain, the Lutheran movement was sprouting in Germany and challenging papal government in the church. While Muslims and Christians fought among themselves, the two religious groups were also confronting each other, the Spanish and Portuguese chalking up victories in the Iberian peninsula itself and the western Mediterranean, the Ottomans in the Balkans and the eastern Mediterranean. Yet, in a paradox found often in history, these decades were also full of exchange across the same borders—trade, travel, and the movement of ideas, books, and manuscripts—and of shifting alliances that turned enemies into temporary collaborators. Such were the worlds, as we shall see in more detail, in which the hero of this book played his part.

I have tried to locate al-Hasan al-Wazzan as fully as possible in the sixteenth-century society of North Africa, peopled by Berbers, Andalusians, Arabs, Jews, and Blacks, and with Europeans eating away at its borders; to spell out the diplomatic, scholarly, religious, literary, and sexual perspectives he would have brought with him to Italy; to show him reacting to that Christian European society—what he learned, what interested and troubled him, what he did, how he changed, and especially how he wrote while there. My portrait is of a man with a double vision, sustaining two cultural worlds, sometimes imagining two audiences, and using techniques taken from the Arabic and Islamic repertoire while folding in European elements in his own fashion.

As I have pursued al-Hasan al-Wazzan, the silences in the contemporary record and the occasional contradictions or mysteries in his texts have haunted me. Reading the letters, say, of a patron for whom al-Wazzan prepared a manuscript, I would hold my breath for mention of his name, and close the folder disappointed not to find it. Noting contradictions or implausibilities in, say, his travel times or biographical reports, I fussed to see if I could resolve them, and failed as often as I succeeded. Noting his own silence in regard to subjects that I thought would have been close to his heart, I clucked my tongue in disapproval. Finally, I realized that silences and occasional contradictions and mysteries were characteristic of al-Wazzan, and that I should accept them as clues to understanding him and his position. What kind of a person invites silence in his own societies and times? What kind of an author leaves a text with mysteries, contradictions, and inventions?

My strategy is to start with the persons, places, and texts that good evidence affirms or suggests he knew, and build from additional sources about them what he would have been likely to see or hear or read or do. Throughout I have had to make use of the conditional—"would have," "may have," "was likely to have"—and the speculative "perhaps," "maybe." These are my invitations to the reader to follow a plausible life story from materials of the time. Al-Wazzan's writings carry the main body of my tale, not just their content, but their author's strategies and mentality as they can be deduced from his manuscripts and their language. Changes in the later printed texts of his Africa book suggest what kind of man the Europeans preferred him to be.

Having traveled with al-Hasan al-Wazzan this far, I have tried to figure out how his story ended when he recrossed the Mediterranean to North Africa. What was the upshot of his life and his legacy? Did the Mediterranean waters not only divide north from south, believer from infidel, but also link them through similar strategies of dissimulation, performance, translation, and the quest for peaceful enlightenment?

CHAPTER ONE

Living in the Land of Islam

SITTING IN A ROMAN PRISON in 925/1519, a Muslim captive decided to write his three-part name in Arabic on a manuscript he had borrowed from the Vatican Library: al-Hasan ibn Muhammad ibn Ahmad al-Wazzan (figure 1). So we learn that his father was Muhammad and his grandfather Ahmad al-Wazzan. "Al-Fasi," he continued, showing his origins in the Arabic fashion, "from Fez," though elsewhere he inserted "al-Gharnati" to make clear he had been born in Granada and then brought up in Fez.[1]

Would that al-Hasan al-Wazzan had been as forthcoming about his date of birth. He gave only hints in his great manuscript on Africa, where he wrote that he had first visited the Moroccan town of Safi on the Atlantic coast "as a youth, twelve years old," and then again "about fourteen years later" (or has the scribe written "about four years later"?). Giovanni Battista Ramusio, who prepared the first printed edition of al-Wazzan's book, read the crucial number, either from context or from another copy of the manuscript, as "fourteen." On the second trip, al-Wazzan had carried an official message from two sultans to an important Berber from Safi, himself an officer of the king of Portugal.[2]

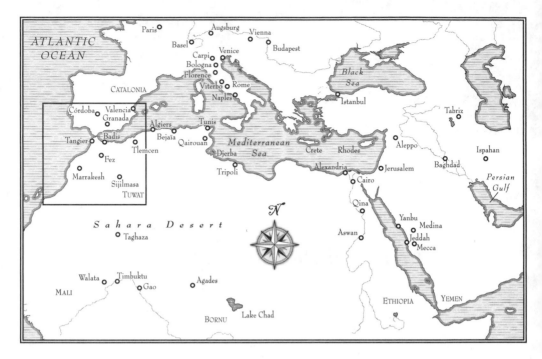

ATLANTIC
OCEAN

CATALONIA

Paris
Augsburg
Vienna
Basel
Budapest
Carpi
Venice
Bologna
Florence
Viterbo
Rome
Naples

Black
Sea

Istanbul

Tabriz

Ispahan

Baghdad

Córdoba
Valencia
Granada
Tangier
Badis
Fez
Tlemcen
Algiers
Bejaïa
Qairouan
Tunis
Djerba
Tripoli

Mediterranean
Sea

Crete
Rhodes

Alexandria

Aleppo

Jerusalem

Persian
Gulf

Marrakesh
Sijilmasa
TUWAT

Cairo

Qina

Aswan

Yanbu
Medina
Jeddah
Mecca

Sahara   Desert
Taghaza

Walata
Timbuktu
Gao
MALI

Agades

ETHIOPIA

YEMEN

BORNU
Lake Chad

ATLANTIC

OCEAN

Valencia
Córdoba
Seville
Granada
Málaga
Ceuta
Tangier
Asila
Tetouan
al-Ma'mura
Melilla
Rif Mts.
Badis
Tlemcen
Rabat
Meknes
Fez
Debdou
Azemmour
Taghya
Middle Atlas Mts.
Safi
Marrakesh
Figuig
HAHA
High Atlas Mts.
Sijilmasa
SUS
Anti-Atlas Mts.
DRA'A
Sahara   Desert
TUWAT

Mediterranean Sea

Al-Wazzan described the Berber's military actions and his tribute-collecting, which took place, according to the Portuguese authorities watching the Berber's every move, within the years 918–21/1512–14, most likely in the early summer of 918/1512.[3] This puts our hero's birth to the wife of Muhammad ibn Ahmad al-Wazzan in Granada about 891–93/1486–88, which fits well with other stories he told about himself.[4]

Al-Hasan ibn Muhammad had just a few years to take in the sights and sounds of Granada. The region of Granada fell within the ancient Roman province of Baetica, but the town itself—Gharnata in Arabic—became significant only after the Arab and Berber Muslims had crossed the Strait of Gibraltar to conquer Christian Spain in the early seventh century. In the eleventh century, Granada was the center of a little Berber principality; in the thirteenth century, as the Christians began to advance in the reconquest of Spain and overall political authority foundered in Islamic al-Andalus, Granada became the capital of a kingdom under the Nasrid sultans, a last vigorous expression of Muslim culture on the Iberian peninsula. Two decades before al-Wazzan's birth, an Egyptian visitor had found "Granada, with its Alhambra, among the greatest and most beautiful cities of Islam," with splendid buildings and gardens, and a galaxy of illustrious poets, scholars, jurists, and artists. He bemoaned the infidels lurking nearby, who had seized so much of al-Andalus.[5]

When al-Hasan ibn Muhammad was born, Granada was a city of about fifty thousand people—mostly Muslims, but also Jews and Christians—its winding streets increasingly thronged with Muslim refugees who had fled Málaga and other Granadan towns when they were reconquered by the Christian Castilian forces in the 1480s. His family seems to have been well established, not so elevated as the entourage of Boabdil, the Nasrid sultan of Granada, but nonetheless with some property and standing. They would have lived in one of the busy quarters on either side of the Darro River, packed with the shops of artisans and traders and interspersed with mosques, including the beautiful

Great Mosque, and shrines. From there they could look up the rocky hill to the imposing buildings of the Alhambra, with its palaces, fort, mosque, fine shops, and gardens, where the sultan and his family and high officials lived in splendor.

Al-Wazzan—that is, the weigher—seems to have part of the surname of both al-Hasan's father and grandfather. They may well have been aides to the *muhtasib*, the important magistrate who supervised everything from morals to markets in Granadan towns; if so, they would have stood at his side at the Al-Caicería market, ascertaining the weight of bread and other necessities.[6]

As a little boy, al-Hasan learned his mother tongue of Arabic, and his father may have started him off already on some Spanish. Colloquial Arabic of the Granadan streets and countryside was peppered with words and phonemes of Spanish origin, reflecting interchange between Arabic and Spanish. Notables, the learned, and people of high station also spoke and read classical Arabic and often knew enough Spanish to deal with Christian traders, captives, and political agents, writing that Romance tongue in Arabic characters.[7] Meanwhile al-Hasan would have overheard whiffs of conversation among his parents and relatives: about the advancing Castilian armies and Granadan resistance, about the violent struggle going on at the same time between the sultan Boabdil and his relatives, about conversions to Christianity of a few prominent Muslims, and about the increasing number of Granadans leaving for North Africa.

Perhaps Muhammad ibn Ahmad packed up his family for departure even before the capitulation of Granada; or perhaps he stayed through the terrible early winter of 897/late 1491, when hungry beggars filled the city streets, and through January 1492, when victorious Castilians replaced the crescent on the Alhambra with a cross and instituted ceremonies of Christian purification in the mosque of al-Taʾibin. Whatever the date, Muhammad ibn Ahmad wanted to raise his family in a land where governance was firmly in Muslim hands. As it turned out, the freedom of religious practice promised to Granada Muslims by the

Christian monarchs was already in serious jeopardy within a few years. The family property was sold, and the al-Wazzans joined the flow of émigrés from Granada, many of them headed toward Fez.[8]

Al-Hasan al-Wazzan took with him some images—glazed tiles, which he recalled when he saw the like later in a mosque school in Marrakesh; the distinctive knee-length white veil that his mother would have wrapped herself in when she walked with him in the streets and that she probably continued to wear in Fez (figure 15)—and some memories. The account of his circumcision and the feast and dancing that went with it, he must have heard from his parents, for it was the usual custom in Granada and the Maghreb to perform it on the seventh day after the boy's birth.[9] The rest—the past of Muslim al-Andalus, its celebrated men and women, its poets and religious scholars, its mosques and monuments—he learned about from stories, readings, and reminiscences in another land.

Some of the Andalusian émigrés complained bitterly about their new situation: they could find no way to make a living in Morocco and wished they were back in Granada. So vociferous were they that the learned Fez jurist Ahmad al-Wansharisi rebuked them for their weakness of faith. Other emigrés thrived. The religious scholars—the ʿulamaʾ—of Granada had long had close connection with those of Fez, and distinguished emigrés in Fez became preachers not only at the mosque of the Andalusians, but also at the city's great mosque of al-Qarawiyyin.[10]

Al-Hasan ibn Muhammad's family was among those that did well. His uncle, presumably part of an earlier emigration, served as diplomat for Sultan Muhammad al-Shaykh, founder of the new Wattasid dynasty at Fez that had ended two centuries of Marinid rule. This highly placed relative must have eased the transition of the al-Wazzans to their new life. Perhaps Muhammad al-Wazzan became an aide to the officer of weights and measures at Fez; perhaps he went into the sale of European woolen cloth or silk, trades dominated in Fez by the Granadan refugees. Al-Hasan's father was able to purchase vineyards up north in the Rif

Mountains and rent a castle and property in a mountain above Fez, but the family's base remained in the city.[11]

With a population of about one hundred thousand inside its walls, Fez was twice the size of Granada, its streets frequented by Arabs, Berbers, Andalusians, Jews, Turks, and slaves of European and sub-Saharan origin. Stretching out on either side of the Fez River, the city welcomed to its markets traders from a large surrounding region, bringing textiles, metals, and foodstuffs. The call to prayer issued from hundreds of mosques throughout Fez, the centuries-old mosque of al-Qarawiyyin on the west side of the river being the most celebrated. To its lectures and library flocked students and scholars from towns and villages throughout the Maghreb. To the west of the old city was New Fez, created as a center of government two centuries earlier, with palaces, stables, and bazaars. The al-Wazzan family presumably settled on the streets rising above the east bank of the river, in the Andalusian quarter, where emigrants and refugees from across the Strait of Gibraltar had been installing themselves for centuries. There the youth al-Hasan grew up all eyes and ears for the hills, buildings, gardens, and intense life of Fez.[12]

His studies began at one of the many neighborhood schools, where boys were taught to recite the Qur'an from start to finish and read and write. Al-Hasan ibn Muhammad later recalled the banquet that fathers put on in Fez when their sons had learned the entire holy book by heart: the lad and his fellow pupils arrived on splendid horses, singing hymns to the glory of God and the Prophet.[13]

Then he went on to more advanced studies at a Fez *madrasa*, a mosque school. Al-Wazzan seems to have attended lectures and discussions at al-Qarawiyyin mosque and at the elaborate Bu ʿInaniya madrasa nearby (figure 16). Grammar, rhetoric, religious doctrine, and *fiqh* (Sunni law and jurisprudence) were the heart of his curriculum, the last interpreted by the Malikite school of law, which prevailed in the Maghreb.[14]

Two major scholars were enthralling their listeners during al-Wazzan's student years: the polymath Ibn Ghazi and the jurist Ahmad al-Wansharisi. The latter was then completing his multivolumed compilation of the decisions of all the jurists of al-Andalus and the Maghreb. The former was writing and lecturing on topics ranging from the Qur'an, hadith (traditions relating to the saying and deeds of the Prophet), and fiqh to history, biography, and poetic meters. From his teachers, al-Wazzan would have been introduced to major concerns of Islamic scholars in the Maghreb of his day, questions that would be of import in the twists and turns of his later life. What attitude should one take toward sects within Islam, toward Jews, toward renegades? What was one to think of the innovations—the *bid'a*—that could not be justified by the Qur'an and the Law? The celebrated Moroccan Sufi Zarruq (d. 899/1493) had condemned as bid'a both ascetic excess and ecstatic utterance, on the one hand, and obsessive insistence on prayer rugs and decorated rosaries, on the other; none of this had to do with *shari'a* (religious law) or Sunna, that is, the example of the Prophet. But were there innovations that could be accepted? What about laxities in regard to the law such as the wine-drinking in the Rif Mountains and the unseemly relation of men and women in dancing and other matters? Some of these excesses were going on in the expanding Sufi lodges and instruction centers.

Especially, how was one to define the responsibility of *jihad*, holy war, at a time when the Portuguese were seizing Islamic coastal towns along the Mediterranean and the Atlantic? Al-Wazzan would have heard Ibn Ghazi lecture on this, and then years later seen him, septuagenarian though he was, in the entourage of the sultan of Fez in 919/1513, when the Muslims were trying in vain to retake the Atlantic town of Asila, south of Tangier, from the Christians.[15]

His student years brought other experiences to al-Hasan ibn Muhammad. No longer could a student count on full financial support from his madrasa for seven years as had been the case in the past. Pious donors had set up foundations (*ahbas, awqaf*) to subsidize education, but these gift-properties had been ravaged by the wars among the Marinid and Wattasid rivals for supremacy in Morocco in the late fifteenth century and were now being nibbled away by the Wattasid sultan hungry for funds. Al-Wazzan supplemented his scholarship money by working for two years as a notary at the Fez hospital for sick travelers and the insane. This was a responsible post, to which he would have been named by a judge (*qadi*) and which required him to assess the reliability of witnesses who came before him. Years later al-Wazzan could remember the crazy inmates in chains, beaten when they were rowdy, harrassing visitors and complaining of their lot.[16]

But al-Wazzan still had time for student friendships, as with the brother of a holy man from Marrakesh with whom he had listened to lectures on the Muslim creed.[17] And there was also time for poetry, a form of expression dear to scholars learned in the law, holy men, young men in love, merchants, warriors, and desert nomads alike. Al-Wazzan had learned poetic forms at the madrasa—important religious teachings might well be in verse—and would also have had his uncle, a skilled poet, as a model. Recitations were often held in public, a high point of the year in Fez being the poetry contest on the Mawlid an-Nabi, the Prophet's birthday. All the local poets met in the courtyard of the head qadi and from his chair recited a poem of their own composition in praise of the Messenger. He who was judged the best became Prince of Poets for the year ahead. Al-Wazzan did not say whether he ever won.[18]

AL-HASAN IBN MUHAMMAD STARTED traveling young. Beyond the periodic trips north to the family vineyards in the Rif Mountains and summer stays in the family's rented castle above Fez, his father took him as a boy on the annual post-Ramadan procession from Fez to a saint's tomb in the Middle Atlas, the mountain range south of the city that housed many a holy shrine. At the age of twelve, in the train of his father or his uncle, he visited Safi on the Atlantic coast, a port town buzzing with trade among regional merchants—Muslims and Jews alike—and those from Portugal, Spain, and Italy. Apart from the grains and cereals waiting to go off to Iberia, he would see the leather goods dyed in Safi shops and the bales of cloth, woven by Safi women, with the colored stripes on them prized by sub-Saharan women. Here he got his first dose of rivalry between Muslim factions under the scheming eyes and agents of the Portuguese.[19]

Al-Wazzan also claimed to have traveled much farther "at the beginning of his youth"—to Persia, Babylonia, Armenia, and the central Asian lands of the Tatars. Perhaps he went with his uncle on such a distant voyage to all these places, but if so, there is little sign of it in his existing writing. Could he have wanted to exaggerate his youthful adventures so as to compete, for instance, with the range of travel of the celebrated geographer-historian al-Mas'udi centuries before?[20]

More circumstantial is his picture of himself scouring cemeteries in the kingdom of Fez for verse inscriptions on the tombs of sultans and other dignitaries, and then in 910/1504, when he was about sixteen, presenting his collection to Mulay al-Nasir, brother of the new Wattasid sultan Muhammad al-Burtughali. The old sultan, their father Muhammad al-Shaykh, had just died, and al-Wazzan thought the epitaphs would be consoling.[21] Such a gift would, of course, call him to the attention of the dynasty.

About the same time, al-Wazzan's political connections and diplomatic training were much advanced as he accompanied his uncle on an embassy for Muhammad al-Burtughali to the great ruler of Timbuktu and Gao on behalf of the new sultan of Fez. Muhammad al-Burtughali presumably wanted to assess the commercial, political, and religious situation in the important Songhay empire below the Sahara Desert. As they passed south through the High Atlas, a local chieftain, learning of the ambassador's eloquence, invited him to visit. Pressed for time, the uncle sent his nephew and two companions, bearing gifts and a newly composed poem in honor of the chieftain. Al-Wazzan presented everything with grace, read a poem he had written himself, and maneuvered successfully between his own Arabic and the Atlas Berber of his host. What admiration he received, for "[he] was then only sixteen years old." Laden with return gifts, he rejoined his uncle for the arduous and exciting trip on camel across the desert. Now he could see a procession of ostriches, going single file and looking from a distance like men riding horses on their way to attack them. Now he would have to heed his uncle's warnings to look out for poisonous desert snakes. Now he could be thankful for the wells, lined with camel hide and spaced at intervals of five to seven days' travel. Along his route were the bones of merchants who had died of thirst after their caravans had been caught in sirocco sandstorms that had covered these precious sources of water.[22]

A few years after his return, al-Hasan al-Wazzan embarked on traveling missions in his own right. Commerce may sometimes have been a goal: over the years he crossed the Saharan deserts and journeyed along the North African coast with merchant caravans of Muslims and Jews, and he had a keen eye everywhere he went for markets, fairs, goods, and prices. In a salt mine center in the Sahara, he once stayed three days, "the time it took to load the salt" to be sold in Timbuktu. Perhaps he was one of the sellers.[23] There was also a narrow escape while he was on a trip that seems to have been for trade. A snowstorm threatened his caravan of merchants as they crossed the Atlas Mountains with their cargo of dates, returning from the desert to Fez just before winter was setting in. Several Arab horsemen invited him, or pressured him, and a Jewish trader to go off with them. Suspecting that they might rob and kill him, al-Wazzan said he had to piss and sneaked off to bury his coins. He then survived one peril after another—their stripping him in the cold for his money (he said he had left it with a relative on the caravan), two days of snowstorm closeted with his dubious escort in a shepherds' hut—and emerged to discover that most of the caravan had perished in the snow and that his money was safe where he had hidden it.[24]

Especially he traveled as the emissary, servant, soldier, informant, and ambassador of the sultan of Fez. Muhammad al-Burtughali, so called because he had spent his boyhood as a captive in Portugal, faced the same uphill battle as his father had to extend his power effectively beyond the region around Fez in northern Morocco. Tribal and military chieftains, Berber and Arab—a long-term presence throughout North Africa—continued their domination of many towns, mountain settlements, and nomadic communities through alliance and force. As is evident from al-Wazzan's own writing, the sultan's governors and agents in these areas could be sure neither of substantial tribute and taxes nor of the supply of horsemen for the royal army. Sometimes gunpowder and marriage alliances tipped the balance for the Wattasids. Facing serious revolt in the eastern Middle Atlas town of Debdou in 904/1498–99, Muhammad al-Shaykh had finally triumphed by marshaling eight hundred harquebusiers against the crossbowmen of the rebels. After their capitulation, the sultan married his two daughters to the sons of the repentant Zanata Berber chieftain. When al-Wazzan visited Debdou in 921/1515, the old leader was still loyal to Fez.[25]

Meanwhile the Portuguese were making inroads along the Mediterranean and Atlantic coasts, as they had been for decades. They usually started with a treaty in which a town made itself a vassal under the protection of the Portuguese king. Fortified Portuguese trade enclaves and Catholic priests followed. When the townsfolk became uncooperative and/or divided by factions, the Portuguese sent in their military force, as in Safi in 913/1507–8 and Azemmour in 919/1513. Henceforth the Portuguese planned to rule and trade under their own governors, collect tribute, seize Berbers and Arabs more easily to be slaves back home, and, as King Manuel I wrote in triumph to the newly elected Pope Leo X, win the entire kingdoms of Fez and Marrakesh for Christianity.[26]

The Wattasid defense against the Portuguese was sporadic and often unsuccessful. Berber and Arab tribesmen were resistant to domination from Fez in any venture. Further, every Portuguese conquest was made with support from some parties among the local Muslims and Jews, who saw at least a provisional economic or political benefit from collaboration with the Christians. Muhammad al-Shaykh himself had consolidated the Wattasid hold on Fez by virtue of a peace treaty with the Portuguese, though his son Muhammad al-Burtughali now wanted, in al-Wazzan's words, "nothing but vengeance" against the Portuguese.[27]

A striking example of this complicated politics is the Berber Yahyau-Ta'fuft, a figure well known to al-Hasan al-Wazzan. In 912/late 1506, he was the accomplice of an ambitious friend in assassinating the Muslim mayor of Safi. He then prevented his co-conspirator from sharing power in the town, gave support to the Portuguese even while intriguing with their opponents, and took refuge in Lisbon when his life was in danger. Several years later he was back as lieutenant to the Portuguese governor, having been appointed because the inhabitants of Safi had requested "a Muslim to serve as an intermediary between the Muslims and the Christians" (or as al-Hasan al-Wazzan put it, because "the governor did not know the customs of the people"). Yahya-u-Taʿfuft proceeded, on the one hand, to delight King Manuel I by his military victories over Mulay al-Nasir, brother of the Wattasid sultan, and over the sultan of Marrakesh and, on the other hand, to anger the Portuguese governor by collecting taxes and issuing ordinances in his own name rather than in those of the Christian authorities. To Muslim leaders, Yahya claimed to be secretly supporting their cause and biding his time till he could attack the Portuguese; to King Manuel I, he proclaimed his loyalty. Meanwhile he built a base for himself among villages, towns, and tribesmen in the region east and south of Safi. Indeed, he issued ordinances with penalties for wrongdoing as if he were superior to the Malikite judges at Fez.[28]

To this powerful intriguer, al-Hasan al-Wazzan brought a message, probably in the early summer of 918/1512, from Sultan Muhammad al-Burtughali, who may well have been trying to discover Yahya's actual position in regard to the Portuguese.[29] In delivering the message, al-Wazzan was also acting as spokesman for a man he called "the sharif, amir of Sus and Haha." This was Muhammad al-Qaʾim, founder of the Saʿdiyan dynasty and known as *sharif*, that is, a descendant of the Prophet. In southern Morocco—in the deserts and valleys of the Draʿa region below the Anti-Atlas, where the Saʿdiyan family had got its start; in the agricultural Sus plain between the Anti-Atlas and the High Atlas; and in the neighboring Haha region along the Atlantic coast with its merchants and herders—Muhammad al-Qaʾim was winning support around this privileged genealogy, which transcended the tribal networks at the basis of the shaky Wattasid power. The Wattasid sultans sought legitimation from learned Malikite jurists like Ibn Ghazi, Ahmad al-Wansharisi, and their pupils, whose religious force came through their power to imprecate and condemn. In contrast, the Saʿdiyans sought legitimation from holy men of extravagant mystical practice, who predicted the coming of the Mahdi, or "guided one," to bring righteousness to the world.

The supreme example was the Sufi mystic al-Jazuli (d. 869/1465), much revered by disciples and rural lodges in southern Morocco. His remains had been carried around by one of his followers in the course of rebellion against late Marinid and early Wattasid sultans and finally buried in Afughal, a settlement in Haha. To associate himself with al-Jazuli and his spiritual and political tradition, Muhammad al-Qaʾim moved his court to Afughal in 919/1513 and, when he died in 923/1517, had himself buried right next to the saint.[30]

Holy war against the Christians was a priority for the Saʿdiyan sharif, and he was summoned to it by the local marabouts (*murabitun*, holy men) and the Sufi lodges, rural and, in some cases by now, urban. Trade with Spanish, Genoese, and Portuguese merchants was acceptable, but not the occupation of Dar al-Islam, the Land or Abode of Peace, by Christians. In the midst of Wattasid losses at Safi and elsewhere, Muhammad al-Qaʾim could report victories against the Portuguese farther south. For this reason, the Wattasid sultan began to seek alliance with him, sending al-Hasan al-Wazzan in 918/1512 and 920/1514 with messages to facilitate joint military action. In the spring of 921/1515 al-Wazzan was part of a delegation from Fez to organize resistance with the Saʿdiyan sharif against the Portuguese, then threatening the town of Marrakesh and its sultan. The troops fought together against the Christians and won.[31]

The Saʿdiyan sharif's aspiration went beyond the ousting of the Christians, however. "Al-Qaʾim," which he had added to his name in 915/1509, was part of a title: He Who Has Arisen by the Command of God. Supposedly he was hearkening to a prophecy of the great destiny awaiting his sons. Indeed, by the middle of the sixteenth century, the Saʿdiyans would unseat the Wattasids in bloody battle and would become the ruling family of the whole geographical region that came to be known as "Morocco." The seizure of Marrakesh in 931/1525 by al-Qaʾim's son and successor was a dramatic step forward in that venture. But in al-Hasan al-Wazzan's day as diplomat, there was intermittent collaboration between the two dynasties; in 918/1512 Muhammad al-Burtughali bestowed on Muhammad al-Qaʾim's sons, former students at a Fez madrasa, the white flag and drum of the high military leader.[32]

Al-Wazzan not only went on missions from the sultan of Fez to Muhammad al-Qaʾim but once or twice conducted negotiations for both of them together, spent time in the sharif's court, and traveled in his entourage in southern Morocco. He even did errands for him, accompanying one of his chancellors to a market in the Sus region to buy slave women from below the Sahara for his service.

Like many others in the Wattasid circle, al-Wazzan had reservations about the Saʿdiyan sharif's religious style, especially his linking himself to the tradition of al-Jazuli. Al-Jazuli's disciple al-Sayyaf had rebelled against the early Wattasids and was, in al-Wazzan's eyes, a heretic who spoke against shariʿa. Al-Wazzan would surely have been troubled, too, by another follower of al-Jazuli, the radiant al-Ghazwani, who spent some years in Fez around 919/1513: hearing a woman ululate in honor of Sultan al-Burtughali, al-Ghazwani reproached her shouting, "I am the sultan of this world and the next." Ultimately, al-Ghazwani would leave Fez and throw all his holy power and followers behind the Saʿdiyan sharif.[33] While al-Wazzan was in the entourage of Muhammad al-Qaʾim, however, he would have had to keep any critical views to himself.

Most of al-Wazzan's missions and errands over the years were for the sultan of Fez.[34] In two different rounds, he went throughout northern and central Morocco, visiting towns, villages, and settlements, traveling on horseback from coastline to high mountain. When he journeyed in the well-watered north, in the Rif Mountains near the Mediterranean and along the plain and northern slopes of the Middle Atlas, he could enjoy the crops of grapes, figs, and other fruit and the olives ripening over the summer. If he were caught in the late spring rains in that region, he could rejoice with the inhabitants who called it "*nusu* water" (water of growth), blessed by God, and saved little bottles of it in their houses. Ascending the Middle Atlas was more worrisome, for lions and leopards lurked in the mountain forests. Then there were the ravines to cross by a distant pass or bridge. Al-Wazzan especially recalled the "miraculous bridge" over the Sebou River constructed by a clever Berber community in the Middle Atlas: a sturdy basket, large enough for ten people, that was transported across the ravine by pulleys. He had enjoyed his ride until he heard about the time the basket was overloaded and passengers plunged into the river far below; "it made his flesh creep in terror."[35]

In some of al-Wazzan's movements he was part of a military expedition: more than once at Asila, which Muhammad al-Burtughali failed to recapture from the Portuguese; in 915/1509 at the town of Tefza, on the northern slope of the High Atlas, where al-Wazzan proposed the negotiating strategy that brought the rebellious inhabitants back to obedience to the sultan of Fez; and in 921/1515 at the Atlantic coastal town of al-Maʿmura, where the Portuguese tried to set up a fortress and were sorely defeated by the troops of Muhammad al-Burtughali and his brother. Al-Wazzan long remembered the sights and sounds of that battle, stressing the destructive force of the Wattasid cannons on the Portuguese ships. "For three days," he said, "the sea was spouting waves of blood."[36]

At other times he was in the entourage of Muhammad al-Burtughali or else with a delegation or on his own, bearing the sultan's letters of recommendation and instructions to see and establish relations with a certain *shaykh* (chieftain), town official, or local ruler.[37]

In the midst of his Moroccan rounds—sometime in 918/1512, after his early summer meeting with Yahya-u-Taʿfuft at Safi on behalf of the sultan—al-Hasan al-Wazzan left for the long two-month crossing of the Sahara to Timbuktu. From Safi he went down to Marrakesh, then southeast over the High Atlas and Anti-Atlas mountains to Sijilmasa, an oasis on the edge of the desert. Once a beautiful walled city and a political and economic center of earlier Berber dynasties, Sijilmasa was in the early sixteenth century a cluster of fortified settlements, each with its own chieftain, where Berbers, Jewish traders and artisans, and merchants from North Africa and elsewhere busied themselves with the trans-Saharan trade. Al-Wazzan listened to the gossip about prices and custom duties, examined the coins from local mints, and watched the Arab horsemen trying to collect tribute, until finally the weather turned right for departure of the desert caravans.[38]

On his first such trip with his uncle about eight years before, he had been learning the ropes of diplomacy; this time he was on a full mission of his own to the Songhay empire. Since the mid-fifteenth century, the Songhay rulers had replaced those of Mali as the dominant power in the area called Bilad al-Sudan (from *sudan*, blacks), the Land of the Blacks. The Mali empire, established by one of the Mande peoples, had extended from the city of Gao in the Middle Niger area all the way to the Atlantic Ocean. As the Malian power weakened and Gao slipped from its grasp, the Songhay Sunni ʿAli—"a man of great strength, colossal energy, and a butcher," in the words of a local historian—began his conquest of the Middle Niger. Now under Askia Muhammad, with his Islamic ardor and military enterprise, the multiethnic empire was centered at Gao and Timbuktu and extended west beyond the Niger River, if not to the Atlantic, and hundreds of miles east to the sultanate of Aïr (in present-day Niger), bordering on the Hausa kingdoms. Eventually Askia Muhammad's conquests went as far north in the Sahara as the lucrative salt mines of Taghaza—a twenty-day trek from Timbuktu—though during al-Hasan al-Wazzan's second visit the price of salt was still very high in Timbuktu.[39]

Al-Hasan al-Wazzan knew Askia Muhammad's story well: how, while a trusted governor for the Songhay ruler Sunni ʿAli, he had revolted against Sunni ʿAli's son and successor in 898/1493 and made himself king; and how a few years later, moved by devotion and the hope to legitimize his usurpation, he had made a pilgrimage to Mecca with an enormous entourage of soldiers and scholars and a copious treasure for gifts. This pious act and the debts it had incurred were still being talked about when al-Hasan ibn Muhammad made his first trip to the Land of the Blacks with his uncle in 910/1504.[40]

He and his uncle must also have been all ears for what the religious scholars of Timbuktu were saying about the recent visit to Gao of the stern Maghrebian scholar al-Maghili. Al-Maghili preached the strictest rejection of infidels, especially Jews, of apostates from Islam, and of supporters of *takhlit* (from *khalata*, "to mix"), here the mixing of acts and rites of unbelief with those of Islam. Having incited the Muslims of the oasis of Tuwat in the northern Sahara not only to break trade ties with Jews but also to destroy their synagogues, seize their property, and kill them, he was viewed with alarm by less purist North African rulers like the Wattasid sultan of Fez. Shortly after the desert massacres, al-Maghili went to Fez to expound his views, but he angered both the jurists and the sultan and was expelled from the city.

Undaunted, al-Maghili went south to the Land of the Blacks, where in about 903/1498 he met in Gao with Askia Muhammad, who was freshly returned from his pilgrimage to Mecca and infused with its *baraka*, its spiritual blessing sent from God. In a set of questions and answers, al-Maghili advised the fervent ruler on the rightful actions to take against "unbelievers" and "wrongdoers." These categories he defined very broadly: he would sanction Askia Muhammad's confiscation of the properties of Sunni ʿAli on the grounds that the former Songhay ruler had not been an authentic Muslim and had allowed polytheism to flourish; he would prescribe that Askia Muhammad free any of Sunni ʿAli's slaves who had been truly Muslim at the time of capture; and he would sanction Askia Muhammad's future conquest of lands under rulers, even Muslim rulers, who wrongly seized the property of their people.[41]

On his first and second trips to the Land of the Blacks, the consequences of these righteous convictions were evident to al-Hasan al-Wazzan. He could see the many captives brought back from Askia Muhammad's wars, some enslaved as unbelievers who had never been Muslims, some enslaved as the wives of men who were not true Muslims. He noted the policies of heavy tax and/or tribute that Askia Muhammad had in his conquered lands. And he observed of Askia Muhammad:

The sultan of Timbuktu is a mortal enemy of the Jews, so much so that no Jew is found in the region. And beyond that, if the sultan learns that anyone among the merchants from Barbary trades with Jews, or is in partnership with or an agent of Jews, . . . he confiscates all his goods and puts them in the royal treasury, leaving him scarcely enough money to get back home.[42]

A major task of our diplomat was surely to report on all such matters to Muhammad al-Burtughali back in Fez. Commercial ties with the Songhay empire were of central importance: textiles—some of them from Europe—copper goods, manuscripts, dates, horses, and harnesses flowed south from Fez, Marrakesh, and their regions through Sijilmasa down to Taghaza or the oasis of Tuwat to Timbuktu and Gao; gold, slaves, leather products, pepper, and other spices from the whole region below the Sahara flowed north from Timbuktu and Gao via the same routes. The sultan of Fez had to be told of anything disruptive of this trade along with information about goods and prices at the markets. The sultan also needed on-the-spot observation of political and religious life in the Bilad al-Sudan: what kingdoms had come under the sway of Askia Muhammad and how were they ruled? what was the state of the scholars and jurists? Connections between Berber dynasties and the region had been sustained for centuries, and in al-Wazzan's time there was much movement of learned men and books between Fez and Timbuktu.[43]

Al-Hasan al-Wazzan did not leave us his exact itinerary in the Land of the Blacks, but he did give detail on some of his stops during his second mission. At Timbuktu he seems to have had his first audience with Askia Muhammad in a palace, so al-Wazzan learned, that had been designed by an Andalusian architect two hundred years before. The main royal palace was at Gao, but like European monarchs, Askia Muhammad traveled with a large entourage of courtiers and conducted affairs of state as he went. Al-Wazzan had to kneel before him and sprinkle dust on his head and shoulders, the required ceremony of abasement "even for the Ambassador of a great prince." A century and a half earlier the celebrated traveler and writer Ibn Battuta had witnessed similar acts of reverence by subjects of the emperor of Mali and had wondered how they managed not to blind themselves with the dirt.[44]

All communication with the Askia, whether delivered in Songhay or in Arabic, passed through an intermediary. When al-Wazzan went to the nearby river port of Kabara, he at last enjoyed direct conversation with its top official, himself a relative of the ruler and a man whom al-Wazzan called "just," a rare compliment. While in Timbuktu and Kabara, al-Wazzan evidently met traders from the towns and settlements of Mali up the Niger and from the proud city of Jenne and its hinterland, located two hundred miles southwest off a branch of the Niger. Both areas had been captured for the Songhay by Sunni ʿAli decades before, and al-Wazzan heard much about them as he watched the Timbuktu merchants loading their small boats for their own voyages up the river. Possibly al-Wazzan had been taken to these regions with his uncle on his first visit to the Land of the Blacks, but this time he seems rather to have turned east toward the populous city of Gao, the center of Songhay rule with its rich traders and many markets. At the splendid palace, he was impressed by the great courtyard and its galleries where Askia Muhammad received visitors; perhaps the ambassador from Fez had a second audience with the emperor.[45]

From Gao, al-Wazzan seems to have gone northeast by caravan to Agades, the town from which the Tuareg sultans ruled their kingdom of Aïr (within present-day Niger). There al-Wazzan observed that in the wake of the Songhay military incursion eleven years before, the sultans were paying a large tribute to Askia Muhammad, but that nonetheless the royal revenues from their lands and customs duties were substantial. Al-Wazzan noted the mixture in the population: Agades was dominated by Berbers—the Tuareg elite, descendants of immigrants from the Sahara—while the countryfolk, who supplied soldiers to the royal army and raised goats and cows in the southern Aïr, were Blacks, as were the slaves.[46]

He must have heard, too, about the takhlit, the mixture of religious belief and practice in the kingdom of Aïr. Among the non-Tuareg were many non-Muslims, and even among the followers of the Prophet, people were continuing "to worship idols and offer them sacrifice." Interestingly enough, the Agades sultans were getting advice from the learned Egyptian al-Suyuti, a scholar much more flexible in this regard than al-Maghili. Al-Suyuti urged the sultans to rule with justice in the spirit of the Prophet and shari'a, but when asked about the making and use of amulets and charms, he commented that it was not forbidden "so long as they contained nothing reprehensible."[47]

Al-Hasan al-Wazzan's next major stop took him on a long trek south to the Kanuri-speaking kingdom of Bornu, and specifically to Ngazargamu, its capital city located a few miles west of Lake Chad.[48] Bornu was beyond the Songhay reach. Its *mai*, or sultan, at the time was Idris Katakarmabi, a man remembered by al-Wazzan as well as in Bornu chronicle and epic as a successful warrior against the neighboring Bulala of Kanem, longtime aggressors. In the rhetoric of the contemporary jurist who wrote of his deeds, Mai Idris was "just, god-fearing, devout, brave [and] dauntless," a ruler who had made pilgrimage to Mecca. Al-Wazzan noted rather his cagey practices of payment and his love of display. Bornu was at the southern end of one of the least strenuous desert crossings, and Mai Idris had merchants bring him horses across it from the Maghreb. Then he made them wait for months, sometimes a whole year, until he had rounded up enough slaves from his military adventures to pay them. The traders complained to al-Wazzan about their lot, especially frustrating since at the same time gold was everywhere in Idris Katakarmabi's court: on the bowls and basins, on the harnesses of horses and the spurs of riders, even on the leashes for the dogs.[49]

After a month in Bornu, al-Wazzan traveled through the kingdom of "Gaoga," a mysterious region whose center historians have associated with one or another section of the present-day state of Sudan. As al-Wazzan described him, the Muslim ruler Homara ('Umar or 'Amara) lived up to his reputation for generosity, recompensing each gift made to him with one double in value. His court was much frequented by merchants from Egypt, eager for exchange, and it was in all likelihood with one of their caravans that al-Wazzan crossed the Nubian lands for one of his three visits, perhaps the first, to the country along the Nile. The trip was a dangerous one—their guide lost his way to an oasis and the party had to make five days' worth of water in their bags last for ten— but the wonders at the end of the trip were worth it.[50]

AL-WAZZAN EXPLORED every corner of "the great and populous city" of Cairo, but as a diplomat, he was required to discover the political moods and currents at the court of the elderly Mamluk sultan, Qansuh al-Ghawri. Qansuh had a long and remarkable tradition behind him: he was twenty-second in a succession of rulers mostly of Circassian origin, all of them Turkish-speaking, all of them starting as military slaves (*mamluk* in Arabic means "owned by someone"), and all of them having to renounce the Christianity into which they had been born; each one coming to power not in principle by inheritance but through maneuvers, connections, and military force. Their empire included Egypt and the Levant, the latter area being known as al-Sham (Syria) and including the Holy Land. They also claimed suzerainty over the Hijaz, as west central Arabia was called, and set up garrisons and fortresses there to protect Mecca, Medina, and other towns. Among the moneys flowing into the Mamluk treasury were profits from their control of the spice and fine wood trade with India.[51]

Qansuh al-Ghawri had begun as the Circassian slave of the great sultan Qaytbay and had emulated his former master in extensive building projects. Al-Wazzan was especially impressed by the marble madrasa and mosque that the sultan had constructed in 908/1502 in the hat market, with his future mausoleum nearby. The people of Cairo admired its rich decoration but also made ironic jokes about the confiscations, seizures of marble, and deflection of funds from existing gift-properties that had gone to finance it. As for the celebrated citadel of Cairo, al-Wazzan found its palaces "marvelous." There the sultan mounted sumptuous feasts and received his officials, governors, and ambassadors.[52]

Interestingly enough, the diplomat from Fez seems not to have been formally received by Qansuh al-Ghawri during his months in Cairo. The chronicler of the sultan's reign, Muhammad ibn Ahmad ibn Iyas, who gave loving detail to all such events in his journal, never mentioned an ambassador from Fez. In part, 919/1513 was a bad year for receptions. The plague had struck Cairo in Muharram/March, and many had died of it in the next three or four months. Then the sultan came down with an eye malady and did not resume his full public duties until Sha'ban/October.[53] In part, it would have been difficult for al-Hasan al-Wazzan to prepare for an expensive appearance before the Mamluk ruler. When the ambassador from the sultan of Tunis was received the year before, he offered Qansuh al-Ghawri costly fabrics, fine Maghreb horses, weapons, and other precious items, worth—so the gossip went—ten thousand dinars.[54] Presentation of this magnitude was required of any ambassador to the august "ruler of two lands and two seas." After his demanding year of travel through the Land of the Blacks, could the diplomat from Fez have arranged such an affair?

In any case, the Maghreb did not loom large for Qansuh al-Ghawri. Persons from the Maghreb lived in both Cairo and Alexandria—sailors, soldiers, and especially traders and their families—and in 913/1507 the sultan even had his official translator ransom some of those whom Christian pirates had seized and imprisoned in Rhodes and elsewhere. In his early years as sultan, emissaries had come to Qansuh al-Ghawri from rulers in the Maghreb with complaints about the Spanish persecution of the Muslims in Granada, and the Mamluk sultan threatened reprisals against Christians in the Holy Land if the situation did not improve. Subsequently, in 916–17/1510–11, Qansuh al-Ghawri rejoiced at Muslim gains against the Christians at Tlemcen and Djerba and mourned Muslim losses at Tripoli, but on the whole news from these regions rarely preoccupied him. Indeed, the ambassador from Tunis in 918/1512 was the only other envoy from the Maghreb he formally received during the fifteen years of his reign.[55] Much more important were the Portuguese boats in the Red Sea and Indian Ocean, interfering with Egyptian and Syrian commerce there, and especially the political and religious ambitions of two rulers in the East: the charismatic Shiʿite shah Ismaʿil Safawi in Persia and the new Ottoman sultan, Selim.[56]

Though al-Hasan al-Wazzan did not have an audience with the sultan, he did become informed about his high officers and administrative staff and was able to frequent the Citadel. He may well have been received by the sultan's *dawadar*, or secretary of state, whom he described as second in command, or by one of his subordinates. From such encounters, al-Wazzan would have learned that Qansuh al-Ghawri had sent envoys to Istanbul to congratulate Selim on his succession and negotiate a treaty of friendship, even while he welcomed in Cairo the sons of the brother whom Selim had slain to secure his office. Ibn Iyas wrote in his journal what al-Wazzan probably heard in the palace corridors: "After having done away with all his relatives, the Ottoman Sultan could now turn to the defense of his country against the Europeans." Perhaps, too, the diplomat from Fez tried to interest the Mamluk sultan's officers in the attacks being mounted against the Christians at the other end of the Mediterranean.[57]

BUT NOW it was time to return to his master. As he recalled his movements later, al-Wazzan must have got back to Fez sometime in Shawwal 919/December 1513. He would have much to tell Sultan Muhammad al-Burtughali about his months away. On policy matters to the south, he could certainly recommend cultivating relations with the ever-more-powerful Songhay ruler Askia Muhammad and, to the east, appealing to the Ottoman sultan Selim rather than to the aging and indecisive Qansuh al-Ghawri for help against the Christians.[58]

It also must have been time to return to Fez to get married or, if he already had a wife—a strong likelihood by now—to return to her and his household. High points of Amin Maalouf's novel *Léon l'Africain* are the women he imagines in the life of al-Hasan al-Wazzan, including a wife in Fez, already kin to him as a cousin. The writings of al-Wazzan himself give little direct help on this matter to either historian or novelist, but that our North African had a wife is a certainty. Marriage was

the path for the vast majority of Muslim men and women. Very few
were tempted by the high renunciation that had been favored by one coterie of early Sufis centuries before. Leading holy men of the Maghreb,
like al-Jazuli, had wives and children, as had, of course, the Prophet
himself. Scholars of the law, theology, and literature were eager for sons
who would follow in their footsteps. The jurist Ibn Ibrahim, who listened to Ibn Ghazi's lectures in Fez at the same time as al-Wazzan, already had his first son born when he was twenty-one.[59]

Al-Wazzan, now about twenty-five and a *faqih* (scholar trained in
law), would have expected to have a wife and children of his own. A
young woman from a family of other Granadan refugees would have
been a likely choice. His later hour-by-hour account of the making of
marriage at Fez surely drew from his own experience not just from what
he had seen: the notarized contract that spelled out the dowry (*mahr* or
sadaq) promised by the husband to the wife, which included money, a
black slave woman, silken textiles, fine slippers, beautiful scarves, combs,
and perfumes; the garments, rugs, bedclothes, and wall-hangings that
made up the wife's trousseau from her father; the bridal procession with
pipes, trumpets, and drums to the groom's house; their first sexual
intercourse and the display of the wife's bloody undergarment; the banquets and the dancing, the men and women each celebrating in their
separate space. Maybe al-Wazzan had already had a son in these years
and had basked in the festivities of the boy's circumcision on the seventh day, which he described later in detail: the coins put by the father's
friends on the face of the barber's assistant, who shouted their names
till the money was all collected and the baby circumcised; the separate
dances of the men and women afterward. Maybe he had had to settle
for a daughter, "when there was less merriment."[60]

We can imagine al-Wazzan approving the cooking, sewing, and spinning that he wrote was expected from a good Fez wife. We can imagine
him listening to her tell what she had seen from the decorated terrace on
the roof of their house, the female space to which she and other women
in the household repaired from time to time. We can imagine him on hot
days bathing in the pools around the interior fountains in their house,

as did his wife and children—a memory he carried with him years later. We can imagine him watching his wife garb herself for going out to the streets as he himself described the custom at Fez—her golden bejeweled earrings and bracelets well hidden under a veil and her face covered with a cloth with space only for her eyes.[61]

Having a wife and family did not, however, prevent a man from traveling for extended periods of time, though he had to provide for her maintenance while he was away. The celebrated Ibn Khaldun had married in his native Tunis for the first time by the age of twenty; his activities as political adviser, judge, diplomat, and scholar took him to Tunis, Fez, Granada, Biskra, and Cairo among other places. Sometimes his wife and children joined him; other times he sent them to live with her brothers in Constantine. In his autobiography, he recorded his "extreme affliction" when she and some of his children drowned in a shipwreck on the way to live with him in Egypt.[62] Ibn Battuta left his native Tangier in 725/1325 at the age of twenty-one for twenty-four years of travel variously as pilgrim, student, judge, political adviser, diplomat, and curious observer. His strategy was to marry women along the way, starting with the daughter of a fellow pilgrim as they crossed Libya. In Damascus, he married the daughter of a Maghreb scholar, and repudiated her three weeks later. In the Maldive islands, he took four wives, the number permitted him as a Muslim, but they too were shed not long after.[63]

Did al-Wazzan ever acquire a wife for a time on his travels? One wonders when one reads his report of the Saharan town of Touggourt, some four hundred miles southwest of Tunis. Its prosperous artisans and notables were hospitable to foreigners, as was its young and generous shaykh ʿAbdulla, with whom he lodged. The inhabitants would "more willingly give their daughters to strangers than to local men, and as dowries, they give properties to the husbands of their daughters, as is the custom in many places in Europe." Perhaps, attracted by the welcoming atmosphere and the possibility of having a date grove for a time (this in contrast to Fez and the usual Islamic practice, where the dowries went from husband to wife), al-Wazzan married and, when he was ready to leave, used the thrice-said formula of repudiation (the *talaq*) and went on his way.[64] Such a liaison is amusing to think of but is much more conjectural than a marriage at Fez, the ordinary step for a young Muslim faqih like him.

Apart from domestic activities after his return from Cairo, al-Wazzan also resumed his diplomatic and military rounds in Morocco, including the missions to bring about collaboration with Sharif Muhammad al-Qa'im against the Portuguese. Al-Wazzan's tales of the energetic new Sultan Selim would have fallen on willing ears, and presumably they led to al-Wazzan's next mission. Muhammad al-Burtughali, rejoicing in his summer victory over the Portuguese at al-Ma'mura in 921/1515, sent al-Wazzan out of the kingdom once again, now as his envoy to other rulers of the Maghreb and then to the Ottoman court at Istanbul.[65]

THE BERBER DYNASTIES of the central Maghreb—the one based at Tlemcen and the other at Tunis—had even more trouble than the Wattasids in maintaining control over the tribes and towns within their kingdoms at this time. Algiers had a ruler of its own, currently an Arab tribal chieftain, and various towns along the Mediterranean coast simply tried to govern themselves. But two new actors were changing the balance of power in the region and were surely the occasion for al-Hasan al-Wazzan's embassy. The Spanish, hoping both to defend Christianity and to get a slice of the lucrative trade with the Sahara, were capturing towns along the Mediterranean shore, collecting tribute from their occupants and building fortresses in which to install their powerful artillery. Already in 903/1497 they had seized Melilla from the territory of the sultan of Fez. By 916/1510 the pirate-trained Pedro Navarro and other captains had delivered to King Ferdinand a string of places on the coast: all the way from Peñon de Velez on the west (a rock-island across from Badis, which the Spanish fortified and which is still contested today between Spain and Morocco) to Bejaïa in the middle to Tripoli in the east. Facing this, the ruler of Algiers agreed to pay tribute to Ferdinand and surrendered an island across from the city to be used as a Spanish fortress. The next year the Zayyanid sultan at Tlemcen acknowledged Ferdinand as his suzerain.

Resistance to the Spanish was led by ʿAruj Barbarossa and his brothers, Muslim pirates from Mytilene. With the support of Sultan Muhammad ibn al-Hasan of Tunis, ʿAruj conducted profitable attacks on merchant vessels from his bases at La Goulette, above Tunis, and the island of Djerba—sharing the take with the sultan—and fought the Spaniards at every turn. At Djerba in 917/1511 he repelled a Spanish assault, with much loss of life on the Christian side, a victory that we have seen Qansuh al-Ghawri celebrating in Cairo. It was surely this situation—the continuing advance of the Spanish, the capitulation of his fellow princes, and the success of ʿAruj—that led the sultan of Tunis to send his ambassador to Cairo, though he seems to have returned empty-handed.[66]

By the time the sultan of Fez dispatched al-Hasan al-Wazzan to these parts, ʿAruj and his brother Khayr al-Din had tried and failed to recapture Bejaïa from the Spaniards, ʿAruj losing an arm in the process, and were planning further attacks. Muhammad al-Burtughali evidently instructed his envoy to touch all bases. The Zayyanid court at Tlemcen was an essential stop. There al-Wazzan was received by Sultan Abu ʿAbdulla Muhammad, who gave audience only to "the most important courtiers and officials." But the diplomat from Fez also noted how angry the local merchants were at the customs duties their sultan had introduced in the wake of his submission to the Spanish. These and the tribute they had to pay the Christians were soon to lead to a revolt against the sultan's successor and the seizure of the town by the pirate ʿAruj.[67]

Algiers was another essential stop. There al-Wazzan could hear all the details of the capitulation of the local prince to King Ferdinand, for he lodged with the man who had been ambassador to Spain for the negotiation. Here, too, he heard much grumbling about the tribute paid to the Christians, especially among the Andalusian refugee community. Several months later, after King Ferdinand's death in 1516, the townsfolk invited ʿAruj Barbarossa into Algiers to end their subjection to

Spain: ʿAruj killed their Arab ruler, declared himself amir, and had coins minted in his name. "And that was the start of the rule and kingdom of Barbarossa," commented al-Wazzan.[68]

Actually, as al-Hasan al-Wazzan told his story, he met ʿAruj several months before this triumph at Algiers. Aided by troops from the sultan of Tunis, ʿAruj was making a second try to recapture Bejaïa, and al-Wazzan visited him as he besieged the Spanish fortress. The attack failed, and ʿAruj set up a new camp in the nearby settlement of Jijel, where, said al-Wazzan, "the inhabitants gave themselves to Barbarossa of their own will." During the siege, the ambassador from Fez seems to have come to some kind of understanding with ʿAruj, because within two years, once he and his brother had established their political bases, the pirate-prince sought an alliance with the Wattasid sultan for a common front against the Spanish. The seeds for this agreement must have been sown in the meeting with al-Wazzan at Bejaïa in 921/1515. Al-Wazzan left with a mixed assessment of ʿAruj: he was "arrogant and brutal" in murdering the local Maghreb rulers, but his military force against the Spanish was impressive and his moderate tax policy toward his new subjects praiseworthy.[69]

The last diplomatic stop was the "great city" of Tunis. As he had at Cairo, al-Wazzan visited madrasas, mosques, markets, and baths, but his duty was at the court, whose elaborate official staff he got to know well. For two centuries the Hafsid sultans of Tunis had been celebrated for their patronage: they allied themselves with Malikite jurists; they encouraged the study of hadith in mosque and madrasa; they welcomed scholars and artists to their court. As for al-Hasan al-Wazzan, he admitted that the present sultan, Muhammad ibn al-Hasan, bestowed "many benefits" upon him, but he found the ruler too sensual and self-indulgent, surrounding himself with his slaves, his women, and his musicians and singers. That their melodies showed a strong influence from al-Andalus seems to have made no difference to the Granada-born diplomat.[70]

On the political front, al-Wazzan may have left the court with another uncertainty. The sultan of Tunis had authorized piracy against

Spanish ships and sponsored the anti-Spanish campaigns of ʿAruj Barbarossa, but as ʿAruj extended his own political kingdom, the pirate began to look worrisome. One Hafsid prince turned for help to the Spanish. Might the Hafsid sultan himself follow suit?[71]

Sometime in 922/1516 al-Wazzan took a boat to Istanbul. Presumably the sultan of Fez was hoping to establish relations with "the Great Turk Selim" and count on better support against the Christians.

THE BALANCE OF POWER in the eastern Mediterranean had shifted since Qansuh al-Ghawri had sent an envoy in friendship to Selim during al-Hasan al-Wazzan's earlier visit to Cairo. Selim had not, after all, "turned to the defense of his country against the Europeans," as Ibn Iyas had predicted. Rather he had sent military forces against Shah Ismaʿil of Persia, whom he accused of threatening to "abolish Islam and exterminate the Muslims," a greater danger than the Christians. Qansuh al-Ghawri, Sunni though he was, had refused to take sides in this quarrel between the Sunni in Istanbul and the Shiʿite in Tabriz; he hoped the war would bring disaster for Selim and Ismaʿil both. When news came at Ramadan 920/October 1514 of the Ottoman's stunning victory over Shah Ismaʿil, Qansuh al-Ghawri rightly feared that Selim's next move would be against his own lands. In 921/1515 the Ottoman sultan did indeed invade the Mamluk's vassal state in southeastern Anatolia, sending Qansuh al-Ghawri, as proof of his success, the heads of the appointed ruler and his vizier. "What are these heads being sent me?" Qansuh al-Ghawri asked Selim's envoy indignantly. "Are these the heads of European princes?"[72]

By the time al-Hasan al-Wazzan arrived in Istanbul, Selim and his armies had moved into Syria, turning their superior artillery against the Mamluk troops of Sultan Qansuh al-Ghawri himself. In Istanbul al-Wazzan could hear that Selim's spies had intercepted secret messengers from Qansuh al-Ghawri to the "heretic" Ismaʿil. In Istanbul he could hear of the disarray of Qansuh al-Ghawri's troops and the treachery of one of his lieutenants during the battle at Marj Dabiq north of

Aleppo in Rajab 922/August 1516, and of Qansuh al-Ghawri's heart attack and death on the field once he realized all was lost. And in Istanbul al-Wazzan could hear of Selim's sweep through Damascus down to Gaza and of his entrance into Cairo in triumphal procession in Muharram 923/January 1517. The 267 years of rule of the slave-sultans had come to an end.[73]

During Selim's absence from Istanbul, the ambassador from Fez would have been received by one of the viziers whom the sultan left behind and/or another palace official. Al-Wazzan did not gave details of these conversations and ceremonies, but they surely must have prepared the way for the overtures toward the Wattasids that the Ottoman sultan began not long afterward.[74]

Al-Wazzan then decided to observe the transformation of Egypt firsthand and left by boat for Cairo. He may not have arrived early enough to see the four-day slaughter of inhabitants and Mamluks that started on 8 Muharram 923/31 January 1517. But he witnessed the Ottoman janissaries (elite military slaves) pillaging the treasure of popular sanctuaries, such as the tomb of Saint Nafisa, and looting many private dwellings, despite Selim's prohibitions. He would have learned about the summary trial, imprisonment, and execution of Mamluk officials. In the mosques he would have heard Selim's name replacing Qansuh al-Ghawri's, as the preachers called for the blessing of the ruler during the Friday sermon. In the streets, he would have heard the women ululating from their windows when Selim processed through Cairo. He would have noted the marble being dismantled from the palaces at the Citadel so that Selim could take it back to Istanbul and use it for a madrasa to be built exactly like that of Qansuh al-Ghawri, which al-Wazzan had much admired in his earlier visit. He would have heard about the many important people to be deported to Istanbul: religious judges and government officials, great merchants, including traders from the Maghreb community, leading Jews, shopkeepers, and carpenters and masons to construct the new madrasa. Selim had just come from overseeing arrangements for their departures from Alexandria in Jumada-l-Ula/June, when al-Wazzan encountered him at Rashid

(Rosetta). Al-Wazzan said he and the sultan were both admiring the beautiful baths there.[75]

The diplomat from Fez seems to have regarded all these events with mixed feelings. He was to say later to his Italian captors that he had been "celebrating the [sultan's] victories in Syria and Egypt," but his brief references to the Ottoman takeover of Cairo in his Africa manuscript were somber.[76] Perhaps he had a formal meeting with Selim or one of his officials at Rashid. In any case, the Ottoman-Wattasid connection had been established.

Selim returned to Istanbul in Sha'ban/September, leaving a governor of Egypt behind him. Around this time, al-Hasan al-Wazzan seems to have embarked on a boat trip up the Nile to Aswan, stopping at many places along the route. On the return trip, he disembarked at Qina, a prosperous town located on the Nile at its closest point to the Red Sea. From there, as al-Wazzan pointed out, merchants and pilgrims crossed the desert to the port of al-Qusayr and then took boats south on the Red Sea to the ports nearest Mecca and Medina.[77]

And this is just what he did himself. Qina was an especially appealing stop for Muslims from the Maghreb on pilgrimage to Mecca: buried there was the ascetic ʿAbd al-Raim, who had been born near Ceuta in Morocco in the late twelfth century and, after years in Mecca, had become one of the most venerated saints of Egypt. Ibn Battuta visited his tomb during his stay at Qina, and al-Wazzan surely did the same, curious about the cures claimed to be accomplished by those who prayed and walked around it.[78]

From Qina, al-Wazzan wrote, "the author went through the desert to the Red Sea, which he crossed to arrive on the shore of Arabia at the ports of Yanbu and Jeddah." From Yanbu, al-Wazzan would have gone on to the holy town of Medina, where he could visit and marvel at the Prophet's tomb, his mosque, and the cemetery with the remains of the heroes of early Islam. To get from there to Mecca, he apparently went back to Yanbu and then by sea to Jeddah, only a few miles from Muhammad's birthplace. If he was hoping to perform the Hajj, that is, the greater pilgrimage with its fixed date, he would have arranged his arrival so as to make his seven circumambulations of the Ka'ba, the sanctuary of the Black Stone, on 8 Dhu-l-Hijja 923/23 December 1517. During the next five days he would have followed the prescribed movements, prayers, and rituals appropriate to this center of the divine presence in the world. Possibly he thought of the diplomatic possibilities of his stay and tried to arrange an audience with the sharif Barakat, whom Sultan Selim had approved as ruler of Mecca not long before.

Surely he would have seen the hundreds, if not thousands, of pilgrims who came on the annual caravan from Cairo down the east coast of the Red Sea. The celebrated Egyptian pavilion, or *mahmal*, carried by a camel was at its head, representing now the Ottoman victors. Groups from the Maghreb and the Land of the Blacks were often part of the Egyptian caravan, and al-Wazzan may have greeted some of his fellow countrymen (and countrywomen) among them even in this turbulent year.[79]

Perhaps al-Hasan al-Wazzan joined their caravan for the return to Cairo: the pilgrims who arrived there on 28 Muharram 924/10 February 1518 complained that hunger, illness, death of camels, heavy rain, and attacks from the Bedouins had troubled their passage.[80] Perhaps al-Wazzan took another route entirely, crossing the Red Sea again or traveling in Felix Arabia. He may even have gone to Istanbul once again. He has left us no clues. All we know for sure is that in the summer of 924/1518, he left Cairo and boarded a boat to return to his master in Fez.

AL-HASAN IBN MUHAMMAD AL-WAZZAN'S diplomatic activities and court service required him to speak, listen, and write well and to know the gestures for courteous deference, banqueting, and gift exchange (figure 21). He would have had to keep a keen eye for shifts in rules and tastes as he traveled across Africa and the Near East and improvise his behavior accordingly. Many of the forms of diplomacy resemble those described in the autobiography of the Maghreb jurist, diplomat, and historian Ibn Khaldun, written more than a hundred years before. Others, such as the increased importance of papers of identification, may have emerged more recently. Al-Wazzan himself failed to have adequate papers on him in crossing an Arab toll-station south of Sijilmasa, where all Jews had to pay a special fee: to distinguish himself from the many Jews in his caravan, he recited Muslim prayers. Ordinarily he had a letter of safe conduct or other identification drawn up by the chancellor of Sultan Muhammad al-Burtughali.[81]

Al-Wazzan sometimes traveled with an entourage—there were nine people plus servants on his delegation to Marrakesh in 921/1515—and sometimes only with a servant or two. The Wattasid sultan could pretend to little more, in contrast, say, to the king of France, who sent his ambassador to Sultan Qansuh al-Ghawri in Cairo in 918/1512 with an entourage of fifty persons. The ambassador from Tunis was received at the Mamluk court the same year, with no entourage worth mentioning in Ibn Iyas's journal.[82]

On his travels, al-Wazzan might stay with a local notable, imam (prayer leader), faqih, or holy man, or simply at a hotel for strangers, if there was one. In a town on the slopes of the High Atlas, a prosperous émigré from Granada insisted on lodging him as a fellow Andalusian, along with his eight companions and their servants; on the land route from Tlemcen to Tunis, al-Wazzan sometimes had his servants put up tents for the night. Once arrived in a location where he hoped for a formal meeting with the ruler or an important officer, al-Wazzan would usually be lodged by his host, either at his own residence, as in his youthful visit to the chieftain in the High Atlas and in his later meeting with Yahya-u-Ta'fuft, or at a place arranged by the ruler, as in Algiers, where we have seen him staying at the home of the former ambassador to Spain.[83]

Then the diplomat had to to seek audience with the ruler. Every court had its special officer of etiquette. "The sultan [of Fez] has a master of ceremonies," wrote al-Wazzan, "who, when the sultan is holding council or an audience, sits at his feet and arranges the placement and speaking order of the visitors according to their rank and dignity." He encountered similar figures at Tlemcen, Tunis, and Cairo; at the court of Askia Muhammad in Gao and Timbuktu, the *koray-farma*—"the one in charge of the whites"—specialized in relations with Arabs and Berbers and envoys from the Maghreb.[84] From such a person, the ambassador would learn, if he did not already know it, the gestures of deference required before the ruler: a mere kiss of the hand for an Atlas chieftain, a kiss on the ground underneath the feet of the sultan of Fez, three deep bows and kissing the ground in front of the rug of the Mamluk sultan at Cairo, kneeling and sprinkling dust on one's head before the Songhay emperor in the Land of the Blacks.[85] Of course, the dress of the ambassador and his entourage at the audience was of the utmost importance, attesting to the dignity of his own ruler and to the respect shown to the ruler approached. Ibn Iyas noted in his diary the garb of diplomats received by the Mamluk sultan when it was especially splendid, and an elegant robe was a frequent return gift to a departing diplomat.[86]

Gift exchange might begin even before the audience, as the ruler sent food to the ambassadors. Ibn Battuta was disappointed with the paltry food brought to him as a "hospitality gift" from the sultan of Mali back in 753/1352; the French ambassador and his party in Cairo in 918/1512 were immediately sent several sheep by Sultan Qansuh al-Ghawri, to which they responded by return gifts of goslings, chickens, butter, sugar, honey, and fruit.[87] Al-Wazzan remembered long afterward the exchange that took place when his uncle sent him to the chieftain of a mountain in the High Atlas. From his uncle al-Wazzan gave his host a pair of stirrups, ornamented in the Moorish style; some handsomely fashioned spurs; two silk cords, one peacock blue, the other sky blue, worked with gold thread; and a beautifully calligraphed manuscript, freshly bound, of the lives of the saints and holy men of the Maghreb, a genre much appreciated in the region.[88] He also presented his uncle's poem extolling the chieftain and read aloud his own poem as "a little gift in words." The chieftain reciprocated with eight hundred gold coins, three slaves, and a horse for the uncle; fifty gold coins and a horse for al-Wazzan; ten gold coins for each of his two servants; and a promise for more gifts to the uncle on his way back from Timbuktu.[89] Presumably this encounter built up good will also between the sultan of Fez and the mountain chieftain.

Gift exchange established a frame of courtesy and amiability for the conveyance of messages that were not always as welcome as these poems of praise. In Cairo in 920/1514, the Ottoman ambassador was giving Qansuh al-Ghawri furs, velvets, silver vases, and male slaves, while his official letter brought disturbing news about Sultan Selim's military adventures.[90] Al-Hasan al-Wazzan may well have carried unpleasant messages along with gifts when he was visiting certain of al-Burtughali's subject chieftains or rival rulers in Morocco.

Whatever the content of the diplomatic message, it had to be expressed and written in an elegant language and presented with gracious style. Formal letters were drawn up by the chancellor's office in Fez, often on paper colored in the reddish or pinkish hue so appreciated in the Maghreb. Using the elevated phrases customary in addressing persons of importance, the letters were also punctuated with religious invocations from start to finish. Once the message had been penned in the best Maghrebi script, the "faithful chancellor" (as al-Wazzan called him) authenticated the letter with a formula inherited by the Wattasids from earlier dynasties, and the sultan himself signed with his distinctive monogram (*tughra*) of overlapping or interlaced letters. The letter was then sealed by the chancellor and folded tightly so as to conceal its contents.[91]

Al-Hasan al-Wazzan was not himself associated with the chancellor's office, but he had spent several years as notary for the hospital for the insane and was expected to write letters frequently during his diplomatic missions. Indeed, at Tefza in the High Atlas in 915/1509, al-Wazzan—with the approval of the sultan's captain—forged a letter in the name of the sultan of Fez in order to persuade rebellious townsfolk to cease their disobedience to the sultan's commands.[92] Thus, he was familiar with the conventions of epistolary and diplomatic language and calligraphy in all their complex beauty.

Formal correspondence and dispatches were almost always couched in the highly prized, centuries-old "rhymed prose" (*sadj*ᶜ), a rhythmic language without fixed meter, but with assonances, alliterations, and occasional rhyme. Ibn Khaldun gave examples of such diplomatic correspondence in his autobiography and wrote it himself; in answering one letter from Granada, he said that he did not dare resort to sadjᶜ this time because he could never equal its author in the art.[93] Al-Wazzan undoubtedly wrote his diplomatic letters in rhymed prose (indeed, he was still using sadjᶜ in writing important letters in Arabic in Italy), while the metered verse he composed and declaimed to rulers in the course of his visits took the form of *al-madh*, that is, the Arabic panegyric.[94]

Throughout his travels, his language of oral address was Arabic, known to some rulers and to all faqihs like himself wherever he went. Though spoken Arabic varied somewhat from town to countryside and from one region to another, al-Wazzan seems to have managed without a translator. The repeated exchanges of travel, trade, and diplomacy seem to have given men like him the flexibility to adapt their idiom. Only when he was in the Rif Mountains could he have used the local Berber tongue, which he would have picked up during stays at his father's vineyards.[95] For towns or courts where the authorities knew only other Berber languages (these varied considerably among themselves and in the extent to which they included Arabic words) or sub-Saharan tongues, al-Wazzan communicated through a translator. Men who could function as interpreters were surprisingly widespread: a secretary translated al-Wazzan's panegyric for the High Atlas chieftain while he listened to the young man recite; an interpreter traveled with the tribal leader of the nomadic Sanhaja in the Sahara and translated for al-Wazzan and his companions when they were treated to a desert banquet.[96]

Al-Hasan al-Wazzan was proud of his skills of expression, savored good poetry whenever he heard it, and made fun of envoys he found incompetent. He recalled the day when a ruling chieftain of a populous mountain region in the Anti-Atlas sent the sultan of Fez, his "great friend," one hundred black slaves, ten eunuchs, twelve camels, a giraffe, ten ostriches, sixteen civet cats, ambergris, musk, six hundred oryx skins, dates, Ethiopian pepper, and more. Accompanying these ample gifts was an ambassador who was "short, fat, very black, and barbarous in his language." The letter from the chieftain was awkwardly expressed "in the style of the ancient orators," and even worse was the ambassador himself delivering his speech. Everyone present did his best not to laugh, though the sultan still thanked the ambassador graciously and received him and his large train with courtesy.[97]

The life of an ambassador was not merely one of ceremony, oratory, and astute observation. It could involve intrigue, danger, and disloyalty. Ibn Khaldun recounted that his services as counselor, secretary, ambassador, and judge had been solicited in flattering invitations from competing rulers from al-Andalus to Syria, and that he had sometimes switched sides, a risky business that at least once led to imprisonment. Matters could be worse in al-Wazzan's day. In 921/1515 ambassadors from the Mamluk court in Cairo were afraid to take an unpleasant message to Sultan Selim lest he kill them. The next year, as Selim prepared for his invasion of the Mamluk lands, he put Qansuh al-Ghawri's envoy in irons, then sent him back clad in humiliating garments and riding an old nag.[98]

Al-Wazzan certainly heard about such episodes and also observed abrupt switches of allegiance within the Islamic political world, including turns for help to a Christian ruler. Whether tempting offers came his own way he does not say. At the very least he performed services for Muslim rulers other than the sultan of Fez. We have already seen him buying slave women for the Saʿdiyan sharif back in Morocco, but here is a service of greater moment that he rendered for the Zayyanid sultan of Tlemcen.

A holy man had set himself up as a shaykh in a plain about a two-day ride from Tlemcen. Surrounded by his wives, concubines, and progeny, he taught his many disciples special names by which to address Allah in daily prayer. (Evidently he was following the practice of certain Sufi masters, who through grammatical or etymological wordplay made additions to the Ninety-nine Divine Names revealed in the Qurʾan or accepted in Islamic tradition.) In return, his followers tilled his lands, herded his animals, and showered him with alms. None of this money ever found its way to the tax coffers of the Zayyanids, however, and furthermore the saint's growing reputation, said al-Wazzan, "was making the sultan of Tlemcen tremble." This was the kind of religious leader who would favor the anti-Christian struggle and political pretensions of the pirate ʿAruj against the compromising sultan. Al-Wazzan went to visit the holy man for three days and concluded reassuringly that he was nothing but a "magician" with very little to teach.[99]

NORTH AFRICAN AMBASSADORS WERE NOT always strictly scheduled, and al-Wazzan sometimes interrupted his missions for other activities. On at least two occasions, he acted as ad hoc judge, or qadi, in communities lacking an arbiter, deciding cases by the Malikite school of law favored throughout the Maghreb. Though not formally named a judge by the sultan, al-Wazzan would have been traveling with a certificate, or *ijaza*, from his law professor, affirming that he had studied certain books with him and authorizing him to teach them to others. This document or his evident quality as a faqih was good enough for the villagers in a remote settlement in the High Atlas Mountains. They would not let him leave until he arbitrated their disputes and recorded their acts; after nine days sleeping on the bare ground, he was rewarded with onions, garlic, chickens, and an old goat, which he had to leave behind. In a town in the kingdom of Tlemcen, where neither the sultan nor the warring Barbarossa had provided an officer, he spent two months judging cases, enjoying both the honor with which he was received by the inhabitants and their generous payments. Then, remembering his loyalty to his Fez master, he went on to Tunis.[100]

Al-Wazzan's travels opened up paths of discovery in every direction. On an early trip during his "unbridled youth"—presumably on his way to Timbuktu with his uncle—he tried to ride a desert ram from one of the herds of the Sanhaja Berbers and managed to stay on for a quarter of a mile.[101] More soberly, he continued his youthful quest for epitaphs in the kingdom of Fez itself, marveling at and recording those of the Marinid sultans and their spouses at their mausoleum in Chella close to

Rabat (figure 17). He scrutinized Latin inscriptions on ruins in the hills near Tunis, deciphering them with the aid of a local Sicilian convert to Islam. He was sorry no one could help him make sense of the inscriptions and pictures on some ancient medallions found near cemeteries farther south.[102]

Then there were libraries to enjoy, owned by his hosts along the route: in a Berber hill town in the Haha region west of Marrakesh, the many chronicles of African history belonging to a wealthy notable; in Algiers, the hundreds of Arabic manuscripts purchased recently in Valencia by the town's envoy to King Ferdinand. The prayer leader in another Haha town, himself an Arab, kept al-Wazzan in his house for almost a month reading aloud an Arabic manuscript on rhetoric.[103] And we can only imagine what riches he may have seen among the manuscript collections at Timbuktu and the great madrasa libraries of Cairo.

Everywhere al-Wazzan took part in discussions, asked questions, and listened to answers. Years afterward he recalled a conversation in Aït Daoud, a mountain town at the western end of the High Atlas. Descendants of Jews who had converted to Islam, the townsmen were immensely learned in the law and debated questions late into the night, such as the one he witnessed: was it licit to sell *ahbas* (as *awqaf* were called in the Maghreb), charitable trusts funded in perpetuity, for the needs of the people? Al-Wazzan, who already regretted the Wattasids' seizure of these endowments from the Fez madrasas for their military needs, followed this High Atlas argument with interest.[104]

For information about political and local events of the past, al-Wazzan was insatiable. From ex-disciples of al-Sayyaf in Haha, he sought details on the teachings and scandalous life of that fifteenth-century rebel against the Wattasids: al-Sayyaf had become a tyrant and was slain by one of his wives when she found him sleeping with his stepdaughter. From participants in political strife in Safi, al-Wazzan learned that their quarrel had begun when the daughter of the *qaʾid* (mayor, governor) became enamored of her father's opponent, and it ended when the Portuguese took complete authority over the divided population. The story would go into one of his later writings "to show how party spirit and a woman can bring ruin to the land, the people, and the religion of Haha."[105]

Al-Wazzan was also curious about matters of every day. In a town on the Atlantic, he learned from an elderly Jew that the reason there were so many dead whales on the beach was not because the biblical Jonah had been vomited up at that spot, the local explanation, but because there were sharp reefs two miles out to sea. In the Atlas Mountains he heard tales of the marvelous Sarmak plant, which when eaten enhanced men's prowess at sexual intercourse. Indeed, men had an erection and young women lost their virginity just by passing over the plant. (Al-Wazzan had his doubts, saying that the story was made up to conceal the penetration of a real penis.) In the desert of Dra'a he discussed the price of different kinds of dates; in Timbuktu, the brisk trade in manuscripts from the Maghreb; in the market at Gao, the price of slaves; in a town on the Nile, the tax paid to the sultan for the right to have a sugar manufactory, with its many wage-workers. From a busker in Cairo, he found out how he had taught his camel to dance to the sound of a tambourine.[106]

Whether on a mountain horse-trail, a desert caravan, or a vessel crossing the Mediterranean, al-Hasan al-Wazzan always had books and writing materials in his pouches. Indeed, studying and recording while on a *rihla*, a voyage, was an old and important Islamic tradition. Late at night on a boat going up the Nile to Qina, al-Wazzan was in his cabin "studying by candlelight" long after everyone else was asleep.[107]

All this ended in the summer of 924/1518, when the boat on which he was returning from Cairo to Fez was attacked by Christian pirates and he became their prisoner. His life of travel and voracious curiosity was to go in a new direction.

CHAPTER TWO

Living in the Land of War

AL HASAN IBN MUHAMMAD AL-WAZZAN had long been fearful of Christian pirates on the Mediterranean. On an earlier voyage between Cairo and Tunis, he suspected attack from Sicilians or the Hospitallers of Rhodes, those religious knights sustaining Christian power in the eastern Mediterranean. He also knew that Berbers fishing west of the Moroccan port of Badis were so apprehensive of Spanish pirates that the minute they saw a mast, they rowed to shore and hid in the Rif Mountains. As it turned out, his captor was a Spaniard well known in Mediterranean waters, Don Pedro de Cabrera y Bobadilla.[1] People gave different stories about where al-Wazzan's boat was seized. His editor Ramusio and Orientalist scholars later said that it had been off the Tunisian island of Djerba, a reasonable stop in an itinerary from Cairo to Fez; a papal secretary said it had been hundreds of miles farther east near Rhodes. Venetian observers reported that Bobadilla had taken over a Ragusan ship with "60 Turks" on board in June 1518, and perhaps al-Wazzan was one of the "Turks."[2]

Whatever the case, the pirate's course was leisurely, with a stop at Tripoli, now in the hands of the Spanish Christians, who had seized it several years before; al-Wazzan saw the castle they had newly fortified there and was probably imprisoned in it for a time. The boat docked also at Rhodes and other islands. Meanwhile, Bobadilla followed the usual pirate practice of questioning his captives and deciding which ones to try to ransom and which ones to sell into slavery. What a pleasant surprise for him to discover the identity of al-Hasan al-Wazzan! The pirate could easily recognize the importance of a North African ambassador with Ottoman connections; after all his own brother was the bishop of Salamanca, who resided in Rome and was close to the pope.[3] Word about the diplomat surely got also to the militant Hospitallers of Rhodes, collectors of intelligence about "the perfidious enemies of the Christian faith" in the Mediterranean and themselves pirates for the papal cause; they, too, would have urged he be put to good use. Bobadilla decided to make a gift of al-Wazzan and the writings in his pouches to Pope Leo X—a "votive offering," as one observer called it, that won the pirate absolution for some of his excesses. A few of the other kidnapped Muslims were presented to important cardinals.[4]

By late October 1518, the capture of a Muslim diplomat was stirring up talk in Rome, although not always with much clarity about which sultan he had been serving. (Perhaps al-Wazzan himself was contributing to the confusion.) A French cleric in Rome wrote of the seizure of "a Turkish ambassador, sent by the Great Turk to the king of Tunis." The Venetian envoy to Rome reported back home about the "orator [the usual word for "ambassador" in Italy] of the king of Tlemcen," who, when questioned by the pope, said he had been at the court of the Turkish sultan "celebrating his victory in Syria and Egypt." In late November, the Vatican librarian got it right, saying that he had lent a manuscript to "*assem facchi, oratoris regis fezze,*" "to Hasan faqih— Hasan, man of Muslim learning, orator of the king of Fez, prisoner in the Castel Sant'Angelo."[5]

The Castel Sant'Angelo was an ancient building that had been a fortress for the Vatican for centuries; its walls and towers had recently been strengthened, and its dungeons had long been the abode of various enemies of the papacy and the faith (figure 23). Al-Wazzan must have shuddered at news of the terrible pit, called "Sammaraco" or "Sammalò," into which the most targeted prisoners were lowered and left, and of the dank cells without light down below. Moldering in one of them only a year or so earlier was Fra Bonaventura, who prophesied the death of Leo X and the invasion of Italy by the Turks, announced himself "Angelic Pope" and "savior of the world," and proclaimed the king of France as God's agent to convert the Turks to Christianity.[6]

Al-Wazzan may have got word of Bonaventura's prophecies and also of the five cardinals accused in 1517 of conspiring to poison the pope. Two of them and their associates had been imprisoned, tried, and tortured at the Castel Sant'Angelo; the heads of those executed were still perched on the castle wall. The alleged ringleader, Cardinal Petrucci, had been ordered to be strangled in his cell with a silken cord by a black Muslim slave—"a giant with tremendous force"—a public death at the hands of a Christian being considered too shameful for a prince of the church.[7]

The Castel Sant'Angelo also had sumptuous apartments, chapels, and treasure rooms for the pope, and Leo X dined and lodged there from time to time, especially during the hot summer months, when he preferred it to the Vatican Palace. From its windows the pope watched important processions; in its chambers he offered plays with music on a stage designed by Raphael; in its drained moat and under its battlements he arranged games, races, and tournaments, including at carnival 1519 a tournament of people throwing oranges.[8] Al-Wazzan, as prisoner, could not have observed these affairs, but he may well have heard gossip about them.

In any case, he was not being held in the Sammaraco pit or in a lightless dungeon. The former diplomat may have had some of the freedom of movement enjoyed for a time by the goldsmith Benvenuto Cellini during his later imprisonment at the Castel Sant'Angelo: "[The castellan] let me go about the place freely," Cellini wrote, having conversations with guards and other prisoners and setting up a workshop.[9] Al-Wazzan was treated well enough to be loaned manuscripts in Arabic from the Vatican Library within a month of his arrival in 1518. The

Arabic collection at the Vatican, originating in the religious and scholarly interests of Pope Nicholas V in the mid-fifteenth century and now
encouraged by Leo X, was not extensive, but there was enough to keep
al-Wazzan busy. In November came the life of the austere Syrian "pillar-
hermit" saint Simeon Stylites; in December, the life of the Egyptian
saint Pachomius, once a devotee of the god Serapis, then a founder of
eastern monasticism; a manuscript on the Trinity and other doctrines;
and a refutation of Jewish objections to Christian teaching. By the
spring of 1519 he had read on the faith of the eastern Christians (Mar-
onites, Jacobites, and Nestorians); on the errors of the Jews and the
Muslims; and on *The Intentions of Philosophers* (*Maqasid al-falasifa*).
The last was an early work by the great philosopher-theologian al-
Ghazali describing Arabic Neoplatonism. Known to Christian scholars since the twelfth century in a truncated Latin version, it was here a
complete text, originating in Egypt, and one of the few Islamic books
in Arabic in the Vatican. Leo X evidently thought it was now safe for
the faqih to read one of his own kind.[10]

At the same time al-Wazzan must have been improving whatever
skills he had brought with him in the Italian and Latin languages
through conversations with his jailers, the Castel soldiers, and other
prisoners (a bankrupt Roman financier was clapped into a cell not long
after al-Wazzan's arrival[11]); with the Vatican librarian and other churchmen; and with Leo X himself. He would have known a version of Spanish from his boyhood, as we have seen, though he would have written it
more likely in Arabic (*aljamiado*) than in the Latin alphabet. He may
well have known some Portuguese, learned from Sultan Muhammad
al-Burtughali; and he may have had a smattering of Italian, acquired
in conversations with Genoese and other Italian merchants at Fez and
Tunis. Even more likely, with them, with Italian diplomats he could
have met in Cairo, and with sailors and passengers on his Mediterranean boat trips, he would have picked up the lingua franca of Arabic
and Italian words spoken on the Mediterranean and in its port cities.[12]

We can visualize him, then, advancing his Italian with the elderly
castellan of Sant'Angelo, Giuliano Tornabuoni, bishop of Saluzzo and

part of the domestic staff of his fellow Florentine Leo X. Among other matters, Tornabuoni had much to tell about the imprisoned cardinals whose jailer he had been the year before. Then there was the learned Dominican Zenobi Acciaiuoli, now librarian of the Vatican, who sometimes sent manuscripts via the castellan and other times furnished them himself. Here was a chance for al-Wazzan to improve his Latin, and for Acciaiuoli, who was interested in the prophetic renewal of Christendom, to talk to a Muslim up close. Evidently the librarian did not mind that the faqih inscribed his name in Arabic on the manuscripts before returning them: "Praise to God. Al-Hasan ibn Muhammad al-Fasi, the servant of God, has read this book."[13]

His most important interlocutor for a time was Leo X. Their meetings must have been impressive and fearsome occasions for al-Wazzan; he who had once stood in the presence of Sultan Selim was now before the spiritual ruler of Christendom. Presumably he knew that the pope was the son of the rich and powerful Lorenzo de' Medici and had some inkling of Leo's generous patronage of artists, scholars, and favorites, which was putting a strain on the papal treasury. The Muslim prisoner would probably not have heard that in the fall of 1518 one of Leo's cardinals was up north in Augsburg trying in vain to persuade a certain Martin Luther to abandon his heretical ideas.[14] (Indeed, at that date Luther's disobedience was still thought of as a local German matter.)

But al-Wazzan was surely aware of the pope's attitude toward Islam. Since the beginning of his reign in 1513, Leo had been committed to a crusade against the Turks and the conversion of all Muslims to Christianity. January 1514 saw him celebrating special masses in honor of the victories of King Manuel of Portugal "over the infidels in the parts of Africa called Morocco (Marochius)." Two months later a magnificent procession arrived in Rome from Portugal, bringing the pope gifts and trophies from Manuel's conquests. Birds and beasts from "Libya, Mauretania, Ethiopia, Arabia, Persia, and India" moved through the streets with the bejeweled Portuguese emissaries, but the prize for spectators, cardinals, and pope was the white elephant from India with a silver tower on its back, saluting the crowd with its trunk at the commands of its two Muslim attendants, a black "Moor" and the "Saracen" al-Farab. Al-Farab stayed on as one of the elephant's keepers in a building near the papal palace and the Castel Sant'Angelo, but the elephant died in June 1516, his demise having been foretold by the imprisoned prophet Bonaventura. The pope composed the epitaph for his tomb: "Under this great hill I lie buried / Mighty elephant which the King Manuel / Having conquered the Orient / Sent as captive to Pope Leo X."[15]

The captive from Fez undoubtedly heard about the captive white elephant from old-timers at the Castel Sant'Angelo when he arrived there two years later. By then Leo X had advanced in his efforts against Islam. The mood in Rome was fearful in the wake of news of Sultan Selim's conquest of Egypt: during the winter of 1517–18, so the papal master of ceremonies reported, lightning flashes and other omens at Rome and elsewhere presaged an invasion by the Turks. Not to be daunted, the pope had Raphael paint his portrait with his hand resting on the opening verses of the Gospel of John: he, baptized Giovanni de' Medici, would follow his namesake John the Baptist and bear witness to a new age of light and union of all people in belief. More practically, in March 1518 Leo dispatched four cardinals to the kings of England, France, and Spain and to the Holy Roman emperor to get them to agree to a five-year truce among themselves and to win their support for a crusade against the Turks. (At the same time, this could divert them from wars and conquests in Italy.) The same month he proclaimed a general procession to that end. For three days the streets of Rome were full of laypeople, priests, and religious, praying for union among the Christian princes and for a holy expedition, as Leo X put it in his printed call, to "defeat the diabolic Mohammedan rage . . . against the Holy Catholic Faith."[16]

The ambassador of Muhammad al-Burtughali, sultan of Fez, thus fell into the pope's hands at an opportune moment. Intelligence about the Ottomans and Muslim rulers was coming into Rome and especially to Venice all the time. The Venetians, who both resisted Ottoman encroachments on their Mediterranean empire and sustained trade with the Levant, had "orators" in Cairo, Istanbul, and elsewhere in the

Muslim world; in 1518 one of them reported back that Selim was reading the life of Alexander the Great and hoped to imitate him, bringing Africa, Asia, and Europe under his control. The Turks had a diplomat in Venice in 1518, a Latin-speaking janissary, a slave to the sultan; and every once in a while Sultan Selim himself sent letters to the Signory of Venice. Still, the Venetians were currently more interested in a truce with the Turks, safeguarding commerce, than a crusade against them, even while they did not openly oppose Leo's project. Though Selim once addressed a letter to the pope, on the whole Leo's information about him and other Muslim princes came less directly.[17]

The papers in al-Hasan al-Wazzan's bags were promptly translated from Arabic by someone in the pope's service and may have brought useful inside information on, say, contacts between Fez and the pirate-rulers Barbarossa ('Aruj had been killed in battle about the time al-Hasan was kidnapped, and his brother Khayr al-Din had succeeded him) and between Fez and Sultan Selim in Istanbul. Al-Wazzan must have been repeatedly interrogated about his own activities and his views on rulers and policies throughout Islam. What did he think, for instance, of the appearance of an ambassador from the sultan of Tunis in Venice in the spring and early summer of 1519, seeking (as the sultan said in his letter to the Signory) "to renew peace between you and us"?[18]

Al-Wazzan would have surely pondered the fate that might await him if he showed no sign of cooperation: languishing in prison, or perhaps enslavement like any common Muslim captive, working as a domestic if he were lucky, or in stables or farming or in the galleys. What answers he gave remain unknown. Might he have suggested that Sultan Muhammad ibn al-Hasan of Tunis was seeking association with Christian Venice since they both currently feared the expanding power of the Muslim Khayr al-Din? Might he have wondered whether the Venetians had asked the Tunisian ambassador about himself, since his imprisonment at the Castel Sant'Angelo had been reported months before to them? If such questions were put, might he have hoped that word of his situation would get back to his sultan and his family in Fez?[19]

Reading accounts of Leo X's reactions to Selim, "il Signor Turco,"

during 1519, we can look to see where he might have been influenced
by information from al-Hasan al-Wazzan. In February the pope was a
little calmer, assuring people that a Turkish attack was not to be feared
during the coming year; the worry was over whether Sultan Selim would
invade Hungary.

Whatever the consequence of al-Wazzan's political revelations, there
was one thing about him that could be of use to the pope: his soul. In
April 1519 an inspired prophetess foretold at St. Peter's that the Turk
would indeed come to Rome and, victorious, lead his horse to eat fod-
der on the altar of the cathedral; whereupon, the horse refusing, by a
miracle the Turk would turn Christian. That drama did not come to
pass, but a smaller one did in the baptism of al-Hasan al-Wazzan in
front of the same altar where the visionary horse would refuse to eat.[20]

THE POPE CHARGED his master of ceremonies, Paride Grassi, and
two other bishops with the task of examining and catechizing al-Hasan
ibn Muhammad al-Wazzan over the months of his imprisonment.
Grassi was bishop of Pesaro, but his life centered on the public events,
liturgies, celebrations, and quarrels at the papal court, recording all
these in his journal. Grassi would have been an excellent source for
al-Wazzan on the ceremonial life of the church. Of the other two,
Giovanni Battista Bonciani, bishop of Caserta, was a Florentine and
former tutor to Leo X and now busy with the papal choir; Gabriel
Fosco, archbishop of Durazzo and bishop of Castro, was an Augustinian friar and papal sacristan, just back from a mission to Spain to raise
money for the crusade against the Turks.[21]

Al-Hasan al-Wazzan presented himself to these gentlemen as an
extraordinary polymath. "Truly learned," recorded Grassi in his journal, "for in his language he is said to be most expert in philosophy and
medicine, on which count many philosophers and physicians came to
dispute with him. And to universal praise, he corrected manuscripts in
the Arabic language, which in many places were falsely, foolishly, and

badly interpreted."[22] All evidence we have from and about al-Hasan al-Wazzan suggests that he merited the title faqih, learned in law and religion, appropriately bestowed on him by the papal librarian, and that he was a lover of poetry besides. But his achievements in philosophy and medicine seem inflated. One of a kind in the Rome of those years, he had no one there to unmask him.

His catechizers undoubtedly knew that he was reading Christian manuscripts in Arabic from the Vatican Library, especially on thorny subjects like the Trinity. Discussion with al-Wazzan was wide-ranging, however, including comparison of Islamic shari'a and canon law. What effect did such conversations have? Al-Wazzan's eventual decision to say that he believed the articles of the Christian faith was in part coerced: continued imprisonment and/or enslavement would have been his destiny otherwise. Yet it also involved more complicated thoughts, feelings, and attractions, to be explored in later chapters when we shall consider his subjectivity, beliefs, and comportment as a Muslim.

On January 6, 1520, the Feast of the Epiphany, Leo X, assisted by Grassi, baptized al-Hasan ibn Muhammad ibn Ahmad al-Wazzan at an ornate ceremony at St. Peter's, not yet the reconstructed and magnificent building it would be later in the century, but still luminous with beautiful candles and silver candelabra.[23] Al-Wazzan would have compared it to the ceremony held when an important Christian male voluntarily converted to Islam—"submitted" or "surrendered" to Allah, to use the preferred Arabic wording. In that situation, the convert was dressed in North African or "Turkish" garb and turban, led on a horseback parade through the streets to the shrine of a holy man, where, with his right index finger raised, he recited the confession of faith (the *shahada*) three times before witnesses: "I bear witness that there is no god but Allah, and I bear witness that Muhammad is the Messenger of God." Feasting followed, after which he was circumcised and usually took a Muslim name.[24]

Present at al-Hasan al-Wazzan's baptism as a Christian was the castellan of Sant'Angelo, who would now see his prisoner go free, and

three godfathers, chosen by the pope for their connection to the struggle against Islam (figure 2). One was the Spaniard Bernardino López de
Carvajal, cardinal of Santa Croce, Latin patriarch of Jerusalem, and
long a supporter of church reform. (He had inspired a schismatic reform council against Julius II in 1511, been removed from his cardinal-
ship by that angry pope, and then been restored by Leo X.) Already in
1508 Carvajal had been preaching that the ruin of Islam in its falsity
and error was at hand. The reconquest of Granada was the start, and
prophetic signs pointed to the conversion of the Muslims and the apocalyptic rejoicing of the church. At the time of al-Wazzan's capture, his
future godfather was part of a papal commission on the means of uniting Christians against the Turks.[25]

Also on that papal commission was al-Wazzan's second godfather,
Lorenzo Pucci, cardinal of Santi Quattro. As Leo X's grand peneten-
tiary, Pucci managed the revenue from the sale of papal indulgences,
acquiring a reputation for dishonesty and theft. He was the kind of
churchman who added fuel to Martin Luther's attack on the theology
of indulgences ("Papal indulgences do not remove guilt," the German
monk insisted in 1517), but Catholics could be shocked as well. A satir-
ical poem in the voice of Leo X's deceased elephant bequeathed the animal's jawbones to "the Most Reverend Cardinal di Santi Quattro so
that he can devour all the money of the entire republic of Christ." Still,
the pope had a fondness for Pucci, both as his fellow Florentine and as
an able canon lawyer. Among other charges connected with the reforms
proposed by the Fifth Lateran Council (1512–17), he had Pucci checking
on Jews and Marranos feigning to be good Christian converts.[26] Presumably the pope thought Pucci would keep an eye on this new convert
from Islam.

The most important of the godfathers for al-Wazzan's future was
Cardinal Egidio da Viterbo. Longtime general of the Augustinian order
and since 1517 cardinal of Santo Bartolomeo in Isola, Egidio was a celebrated orator before pope, church council, king, emperor, and signory.
He preached a new golden age, as in his manuscript *Historia XX Saecu-
lorum* (History of Twenty Centuries), completed in 1518 and dedicated

to Leo X: he foresaw a rebirth of the arts, a deepening of biblical studies, and a world united in Christianity under the pope—the Turks crushed, and Jews, Muslims, and the Indians of the New World converted to the true faith. He had spent 1518–19 in Spain as the pope's legate, rousing the Habsburg king, Charles, to war against the Turks.[27]

Those surrounding al-Hasan ibn Muhammad at the baptismal font were thus all eager to efface the religion into which he had been born. He was given the new name of Joannes Leo after the pope who sprinkled water on him, so the two men were henceforth linked by the spiritual kinship that canon law establishes between the baptizing priest and the baptized person. The ex-Muslim needed a surname, too, and by Grassi's record (figure 2), the pope gave him that of his own house: "de Medicis." In no sense was this naming a legal adoption: formal adoption had been virtually unknown among Florentine families for the last three centuries. Rather, it resembled the practice, known both in Florence and in Venice, of giving converted Muslim slaves the surname of their master, who served as godfather at the baptism. Al-Wazzan had been a prisoner, not a slave, but the Medici surname linked him to a great household in a dependent status, just as did the livery worn by servants and retainers.

Interestingly enough, the convert never used "de' Medici" as a surname in his future references to himself, once calling himself merely "*servus Medecis* [he spelled the name wrong!]" "servant to the Medici" (figure 4). No one else used the name either. For the Christians of his day, he was now just Joannes Leo, Giovanni Leone, from Africa.[28] As for me, I shall more often call him by the name he gave himself in Arabic after his conversion: Yuhanna al-Asad—Yuhanna the Lion. It suggests the entanglement of values, perspectives, and personae in his life in Italy in the next seven years.[29]

Once baptized, Yuhanna al-Asad was free to leave the Castel Sant'Angelo. As he crossed over the Tiber River and walked along its banks, he would have compared Rome to other cities he had seen and especially to the Fez he knew so well. Rome was a little more than half the size of Fez in population, but it was the center of a celibate

European religious institution that drew men from many nations to the Vatican; Yuhanna al-Asad would have heard numerous languages beyond Latin and Italian in its streets, squares, and courtyards. Rather than a concentration of governmental palaces in one part of town, as in the sultan's New Fez, he would have noted the distance between the Vatican and the Capitoline Hill, where the ancient offices of the communal government were found, the Senate of the Roman People. There he would have seen monuments dating from centuries long before Fez's foundation, but they were in a sorry state; stones were being carted away from the Colosseum. In Fez the Wattasids seem not to have initiated much grand building or made additions to the beautiful mosques from the past; the main urban challenge was to find space for Muslim and Jewish refugees from Spain. In Renaissance Rome, Yuhanna al-Asad could see signs of the process that was to transform the city some decades later into one of the most magnificent in Europe. Julius II and Leo X had opened new streets, including the Via Leonina, passing not far from Egidio da Viterbo's convent. New palaces were planned. But the process was uneven: the reconstruction of St. Peter's, in which Raphael had a hand, slowed down in the 1520s, and wolves still prowled at night up to the Vatican walls.[30]

Leo X was going to provide the new Giovanni Leone with some kind of office or income, or so the Venetian ambassador in Rome heard after the baptismal ceremony.[31] It is difficult to imagine Yuhanna al-Asad in a secretarial or scribal post in the papal household or Curia, where skill in writing the Latin alphabet and mastery of European tongues were essential. Rather it was his knowledge of Arabic and of the manuscripts and mentalities of the Islamic world that were of value to the pope—as to cardinals and aristocrats. Thus, he might have translated documents from the Arabic for Cardinal Giulio de' Medici's papal chancery and for other papal secretaries.[32] He might have served for a time as adviser to the Vatican librarian, now the humanist Girolamo Aleandro. Aleandro knew Hebrew and Greek and, assisted by a scholar from Greece, immediately set about making an inventory of the Greek manuscripts in the Vatican collection. He also had a burgeoning interest in Arabic. Before he left for a papal mission against Luther in the summer of 1520, Aleandro could have suggested that Giovanni Leone advise his two curators about the Arabic codices: they had been described only partially in an inventory of 1511–12 and in 1518–19 were simply lumped together in an inventory with unspecified "books in diverse languages."[33]

Leo X himself was deeply interested in the use of Oriental languages to disseminate Latin Christianity to the eastern churches and bring about their union with the West, and to help win Muslim converts. Already in 1514 he had sponsored the publication of a Roman breviary in Arabic, thought to be the first book printed in Europe entirely in that tongue. In 1516 the Genoese Dominican Agostino Giustiniani dedicated to him an edition of the Psalter with parallel texts in Latin, Greek, Hebrew, Aramaic, and Arabic. Its missionary fervor embraced the West as well as the East: to the verse in Psalm 19, "their line is gone out through all the earth, and their words to the end of the world," Giustiniani appended a footnote giving the life of Christopher Columbus, "chosen by God to fulfill this prophecy" and add another world to Christendom. If Leo X, with his "sublime authority," approved, Giustiniani would prepare a multilingual edition of the whole Bible.[34]

Conversations on these editions may well have taken place between the pope and his faqih from Fez. A lover of Tuscan poetry, Leo could also have talked of verses with his namesake, who was always ready, in the fashion of a man of Arabic letters, to mix his everyday prose with poetry. Perhaps, too, Leo would have recalled to Yuhanna al-Asad an earlier Muslim captive-guest of the papacy: the Ottoman prince Djem, who in 1481 had lost out to his older brother Bajazet in the struggle to be sultan of the Turks. An honored prisoner in France for several years, Djem had been transferred to Rome and received by Pope Innocent VIII in 1489. Unlike the simple diplomat al-Wazzan, Prince Djem had entered the city on a splendid horse, a gift of the pope, in a procession of Roman dignitaries, and was installed for the six years of his captivity in fine papal chambers. Leo himself had seen him in Rome in 1492, when as the youthful Giovanni de' Medici he made his own entry as a newly appointed cardinal. As he surely remembered, this "Muslim with a proud soul" had refused to convert to Christianity; Leo would have congratulated Yuhanna al-Asad on his greater wisdom.[35]

In the summer of 1521, Leo X may also have turned to Giovanni Leone for information about Ethiopia. A letter had arrived from King Manuel of Portugal with the triumphant news that the Christian kingdom of the wondrous Prester John, which Europeans had sought for centuries in the East, had been found by Portuguese captains in Ethiopia. Manuel had made a pact with the kingdom's ruler, who was prepared to place his people under the obedience of the Roman Church and to collaborate, as some medieval tales had promised, in the destruction of the infidel Muslims. Leo had a mass sung in celebration and had Manuel's letter published, but his cardinals expressed doubts about the whole venture. Yuhanna al-Asad would have fed such doubts, if we can judge by what he wrote a few years later. Yes, there was a Christian kingdom in the region the Europeans called "Ethiopia," though he had not visited it. Yes, it was ruled by a "patriarch," that is, a man with both religious and political powers, but it was the Europeans who had given him the name "Prester John." And, he went on accurately, a Muslim ruler dominated a considerable part of the area known to Europeans as Ethiopia.[36]

In addition to such conversations, the pope might well have found the convert from Islam an ornamental addition to the poets, prelates, and jesters gathered at his numerous court festivities. Playing lute songs for the pope was another convert, a German Jew from Florence with the baptismal name of Giovan Maria; he was a favorite servant of Leo X and had also been given the surname "de Medicis."[37]

Leo X died suddenly in December 1521. Yuhanna al-Asad might have then expected a call from his godfather, Bernardino de Carvajal. Carvajal had the Maronite Christian Elias bar Abraham transcribing the Gospels for him in Syriac with the Latin Vulgate alongside it;[38] might he ask his godson Giovanni Leone to undertake similar holy work in Arabic? The Spanish cardinal was as dedicated as ever to the destruction of Islam: in the summer of 1521, when he had written to congratulate the recently elected emperor Charles V on his condemnation of the heretical Augustinian monk Martin Luther at the Diet of Worms, he had asked the emperor to turn to the more important task of ending the Turkish peril. Carvajal tried desperately to get himself elected pope and bring about renewal in the church and the world, but he lost out to Adrian of Utrecht. He died in 1523 with none of his prophecies fulfilled.[39]

APART FROM THE POPE, we can trace Yuhanna al-Asad most surely in the service of two other great figures, to whom he purveyed his knowledge of Arabic for their Christian and scholarly ends. One was Alberto Pio, prince of Carpi, a diplomat as al-Wazzan himself had once been, though on a grander scale (figure 25). After a stint as ambassador for Mantua and for King Louis XII of France, Pio became the representative of the Emperor Maximilian to the pope. With the death of Maximilian in 1519 and the election of his son Charles as emperor, Pio switched once again to become ambassador to the pope for François I, the new king of France and Charles's rival. If ever Yuhanna al-Asad wanted an example of how Christian and European politics was marked by the same realignments and shifting loyalties that he had observed in the politics of Islam, in North Africa and the Levant, he could find it in the career and diplomatic duties of the prince of Carpi.[40]

Alberto Pio was also a humanist, a student of Aristotelian thought, and collector of religious, medical, and astronomical writings in Hebrew, Arabic, and Syriac. For him, Yuhanna al-Asad transcribed an Arabic translation of Saint Paul's Epistles, copying the manuscript borrowed by Pio from the Vatican Library. As Yuhanna al-Asad put it in a Safar 927/January 1521 Arabic colophon, in language only approximating the fulsome praise that was customary in the Islamic world, the copy was done "for the library of the most high, most powerful, most exalted, and most elevated prince, Count Alberto di Carpi." The prince may also have asked him to translate or make summaries of the other Arabic works in his possession, such as treatises by Averroës, Avicenna, and al-Ghazali.[41]

In Alberto Pio's Roman household on the Campo di Fiori, Yuhanna al-Asad also had the chance to meet other foreigners and outsiders like himself. The Jew Abraham ben Meir de Balmes was busy making translations of the prince's Hebrew manuscripts. The Maronite Christian Elias bar Abraham had transcribed Syriac texts for Pio as he had for Carvajal, including the Gospels, and now he took time to add a decorative border to the title page of Yuhanna al-Asad's transcription of the Epistles of Saint Paul. The convert and the Maronite could have compared their different forms of arrival in Italy, Elias as a member of the Maronite delegation invited to Rome by Leo X in 1515, Yuhanna al-Asad on Bobadilla's boat. They could have reminisced about Elias's Lebanon and Syria, where Yuhanna al-Asad had traveled through while a Muslim only a few years before. They could have reflected on ideas about divinity: the trinitarian belief preached in Rome; the single divine nature of Jesus Christ taught to Elias in Antioch; the exalted prophetic and messianic role of Jesus in Islam.[42]

And if Yuhanna al-Asad was still connected with Alberto Pio's household in 1522, he might have met there the Andalusian Juan de Sepúlveda, whose fresh translations of Aristotle were just then attracting the prince's patronage. Several years later Sepúlveda was to use his Aristotelian learning to call for war against the barbarous and uncivilized Turks in defense of the "liberty and salvation of the Christian republic."[43]

Yuhanna al-Asad prepared his transcription of Saint Paul's Epistles while he was living in the Campo Marzio in Rome, in or near the Church of St. Augustine and the Augustinian convent there (figure 24). Here dwelled his godfather Egidio da Viterbo, a more important and enduring influence on his life than Alberto Pio. Along with his activities as reformer of the Augustinian order, orator, and papal legate, Cardinal Egidio was a poet and a humanist, deeply immersed in Plato and the Neoplatonists, a philosophical choice quite different from Alberto Pio's Aristotelianism. Over the years he had also become convinced of the hidden wisdom of the Jewish Cabala, whose true interpretation he believed had passed from the stubborn Israelites to learned Christians like himself. Egidio sought counsel and translations from Jewish scholars, and in 1515 he invited the talented Jewish grammarian Elijah ben Asher Halevi, as hc was known in Hebrew—Elia Levita, as he called himself in Latin; Elijah Levita, as we call him—to copy cabalistic texts for him. Two years later he brought Levita, his Jewish wife, and his children into his own household in Rome. There Levita remained until 1527, producing books on Hebrew grammar and lexicography, the Aramaic language, and the long textual tradition of the Hebrew Bible, and explaining scriptural words and meanings to the cardinal.[44]

As for Islam, Egidio thought that Muslim books, though filled with impieties, could in Christian hands inspire to pious study and the understanding of divine prophesy. Especially such texts were useful for the holy tasks of conversion and the conquest of the Turkish enemy. While in Spain in 1518, he had found a certain Joannes Gabriel of Teruel to copy the Qur'an for him in Arabic and make a Latin translation. Several months later he asked a certain friar Francesco from Tuscany to compile introductory notes on the Arabic language and began himself to practice writing the alphabet (figure 26). What good fortune, then, upon his return to Rome in the summer of 1519 to meet the catechumen al-Hasan al-Wazzan, and how suitable that he should serve as one of the Moroccan's three godfathers at the Epiphany baptism. Yuhanna al-Asad became Egidio's tutor in Arabic, which quickly became known to the little band of scholars in Europe concerned, as one of them wrote, to further "the dignity of Arabic letters among Christians."[45]

The relation between godfather and convert continued over the next years. In 1525, now at the cardinal's residence in Viterbo, Yuhanna al-Asad revised and commented on the Arabic transcription and Latin translation of the Qur'an that Egidio had brought back from Spain, clarifying obscure passages "for [his] reverend lord" and correcting mistakes in translation.[46]

Egidio da Viterbo was also an active participant in the humanist sodalities of Renaissance Rome, and at least three men in these circles would have found it useful to talk to the cardinal's North African tutor in Arabic.[47] Angelo Colocci presided over one of these sodalities at his

villa. Polymath and papal secretary, Colocci would have been curious to
meet an insider who could tell him about Arabic number practices in
both calculating and symbolizing, and Arabic weights and measures.
Hoping one day to write a vast volume on ancient and modern weights
and measures as a key to God's organization of the world, Colocci
would have listened raptly to Giovanni Leone describing (as he would
later in his writing) how one estimated distances between one place and
another in Africa and how numbers were used in Arabic occult sciences.
The ounce weighed the same in Italy and in the Maghreb, the North
African was to note, but while the Italian *libbra* was sixteen ounces, the
Moroccan *ratl* (*rethl*) weighed eighteen ounces. A link between the two
world-measurers is suggested by a manuscript in Colocci's library, *Vite
de arabi*, in all likelihood a copy of Giovanni Leone's biographical
dictionary, which we shall hear about later.[48]

Pierio Valeriano, poet and mythographer, would have enjoyed discussing animal symbolism with Giovanni Leone, for Valeriano was then
composing his Latin *Hieroglyphica*, with its many references to ancient
Egyptian lore. The men had a number of things in common: Valeriano
too was a "servant" to the Medici family, as secretary to Cardinal Giulio
de' Medici, notary to Leo X, and then tutor to the pope's nephews
Ippolito and Alessandro de' Medici; Valeriano, too, had received public
encouragement from Egidio da Viterbo for his early studies. In gratitude
for his patronage, Valeriano dedicated his chapter on the stork to Cardinal Egidio. Responding to Valeriano in a letter of April 1525, Egidio
contrasted the mythographer's reconstruction of the ancient wisdom
and holy mysteries of the Egyptians with the recent "demonic" destruction of the monuments and ancient buildings of Egypt by Selim, "prince
of the Turks."[49] Here Egidio may well have been drawing upon scenes
reported by the eyewitness Giovanni Leone.

Valeriano especially sought allegorical meanings drawn from animals and often cited Pliny the Elder in support of his interpretations; in
most of his writing the North African faqih described rather the behavior of animals, ways of catching them, and how they tasted, and found
that Pliny, who was known in the Arabic tradition, had many small

errors when it came to Africa. Despite these differences, there are echoes of conversation between the two men. Reflecting on impudence, Valeriano compared male monkeys displaying their shameful organs with men who do the same thing "today among the Egyptians, around the Nile, and among the Moors and Turks, where . . . they are much revered, believed to be endowed with a singular innocence and simplicity, and where it is thought to be an act of piety to collect money for them." His source here was surely Giovanni Leone, whose writings reported that he had seen "swindlers" in the streets of Fez, Tunis, and Cairo, who went around nude, "showing their shame," and even having sex with women in public, and yet were believed to be holy men by the deluded spectators.[50]

The historian Paolo Giovio had different burning questions for Giovanni Leone. Currently physician to Giulio de' Medici and remaining in his household after the cardinal became Pope Clement VII in 1523, Giovio had already begun drafting his *Histories of His Time*. Like his *Commentaries on the Affairs of the Turks*, his *Life of Leo X*, and his biographical *Eulogies* of illustrious men, the *Histories* appeared in print only years later. But he was busy collecting evidence, including on Sultan Selim's recent war against Shah Isma'il of Persia and his conquest of Mamluk Egypt. The Turks were the enemy of the Christians; all the more important for the historian to write about them knowledgeably. Giovio put questions to merchants and travelers and extracted what he could from Alvisi Mocenigo, Venetian ambassador on an "amity and peace" mission to Selim during his stay in Cairo in 1517.[51]

When the former diplomat from Fez appeared on the Roman scene in the service of Egidio da Viterbo, Giovio must have jumped at the chance to interview him. We can imagine him peppering the North African with questions about people: the defeated Mamluk Qansuh al-Ghawri, the triumphant Selim, the pirate 'Aruj Barbarossa, to name only a few with whom Yuhanna al-Asad had had direct contact and who were to figure in Giovio's writing.[52]

In such conversation with Giovio, the convert would have had to watch his words more carefully than with the mythographer Valeriano.

Sultan Selim had died of the plague in September 1520 and been succeeded by his son Suleyman; Christian rulers rejoiced for a moment, believing, as Giovio put it, that "a furious lion had left a gentle lamb as his
successor." But the fall of Belgrade to the Turkish army in 1521 and of
Rhodes to the Turkish fleet and land forces in 1522 quickly disabused
them. Yuhanna al-Asad would have greeted this news with feelings
rather different from Giovio's—among other things, he had been a captive when taken to Rhodes on the voyage that brought him to Rome—
and he would have had to be cagey in responding to Giovio's questions.
Giovio's later portraits of Selim stressed his ferocity and cruelty—"he
shed more blood in his eight years of rule than Suleyman has in
thirty"—but also acknowledged reports of his grandeur, his military
skill, and his efforts at just rule. As for the Mamluk sultans, Giovio was
curious about the intrigue from the harem surrounding their succession—their election system, he decided, resembled that of the pope by
the college of cardinals. He wanted to hear not only about Qansuh al-
Ghawri but about his predecessor and former master, the great Qaytbay.
Was Giovanni Leone aware of Qaytbay's gifts of a giraffe to Lorenzo de'
Medici and a ferocious tiger to Giangaleazzo Sforza? He could see a fine
painting of the latter in the castle at Milan.[53]

If such conversations took place—and I believe they did—we must
nonetheless note that neither Valeriano nor Giovio made direct mention
of "Giovanni Leone" in his poems, letters, or texts. Valeriano talked
about the pope's elephant Hanno in his entry on the elephant, but did
not mention the North African godson in his dedicatory letter to Cardinal Egidio. Giovio attributed some of his information about Sultan
Selim to the Venetian ambassador to the "Grand Turk" but not to the
former ambassador from Fez.[54]

What does such silence mean? It means that Yuhanna al-Asad was
on the margins of these elite humanist circles. He had useful information and good stories to tell, but he was not important enough to be
taken into the heart of the sodalities or at this date, well before he had
become an author on his own, to be publicly cited for anything other
than his initial capture and his conversion. His mastery of Italian and

Latin speech was still imperfect; how did he sound to these men of re-
fined literary taste? (They had even turned against a Belgian humanist
trying to make his way in the papal Curia for being too "barbarian.")
The North African's baptism was a Christian victory, but how reliable
was a convert? Yuhanna al-Asad's style was slippery.[55]

YUHANNA AL-ASAD WAS most at home, as he had been in Alberto
Pio's household, with the other foreigners and outsiders in Cardinal
Egidio's entourage and service. The Maronite Elias bar Abraham was
here as well, transcribing Syriac texts for Egidio as for Alberto Pio and
Carvajal; his last signed text is 1521, however, and he may have returned
to his monastery in Antioch.[56] Especially there was Egidio's Hebrew
teacher Elijah Levita. Speaking in their shared Italian, Elijah could have
recalled for Yuhanna al-Asad his boyhood in Germany and his years
with his wife and children teaching, writing, and publishing in Padua
and Venice from 1496 to 1515. Yuhanna al-Asad could have told him of
his own boyhood in Granada and Fez and of the many Jews he had seen
and talked to in North Africa. They might have discussed Elijah's copying of the Hebrew translation of al-Ghazali's book on Aristotelian
logic, *Mi'yar al-'Ilm* (The Standard of Knowledge). Surely Yuhanna
al-Asad knew this work by the great Muslim theologian and philosopher; was he not amused to learn that its medieval translator, Jacob ben
Makhir, was descended from a Jewish family of Granada? And what
did Yuhanna al-Asad think of this Arabic manuscript by al-Buni, *Sharh
al-Asma al-Husna*, a divinatory and talismanic study of the Ninety-
nine Divine Names? Yuhanna al-Asad recorded later that it had been
shown to him in Rome by "a Jew from Venice," presumably Elijah Levita
himself.[57]

In a literary vein, Levita could have described his Yiddish epic poem,
adapted from the Italian, recounting the chivalric and romantic exploits
of Duke Buovo. (Among other events, a Muslim princess saves him from
execution by her father, the sultan of Babylon.) He could have explained his study of the fine points of Hebrew grammar, lexicography,

and verse. All these were subjects dear to the heart of Yuhanna al-Asad, who could have responded with accounts of his own poetry and of Arabic rhymed prose and poetic meters.

Were there not crossovers between their languages? In a later work on unusual Hebrew and Aramaic words, Levita gave some examples similar to the Arabic: about the origin of the Hebrew word for cursive handwriting, transcribed here as "*maschket*," he commented, "many years ago it was indicated to me that this was an Arabic word and meant thin and stretched out." In all likelihood, it was Yuhanna al-Asad who gave him the Arabic adjectives *mamshuqana*, *mashiq*, with just those meanings.[58]

In February 1524 another foreigner arrived at Cardinal Egidio's door, dressed in silk garments like an Arab and riding a white horse, accompanied by a crowd of Jews: "a small dark man" calling himself David, son of Solomon, brother of King Joseph, who ruled over two and a half of the Lost Tribes of Israel in the biblical desert of Habor in Arabia.[59] (Later Jewish chronicles would add Reuveni, the Reubenite, to his name.) As his brother's messenger, David promised a large army of Jewish warriors to collaborate with Christian armies in a final battle against the Turks. The eschatological sparks in this project won over Cardinal Egidio, who presented the Jewish prince to Pope Clement VII. Prince David offered his services as peacemaker between Emperor Charles and the French king and asked for ships and arms. The pope prudently responded that this matter should best be handled by King John III, the new ruler of Portugal.

While waiting several months for the pope's letter to the Portuguese monarch, David saw much of Cardinal Egidio, and since he claimed to speak only Hebrew and some Arabic, Elijah Levita and Yuhanna al-Asad must have often served as translators for these discussions with their master. If David repeated to Egidio any of the things he had written in his diary, Yuhanna al-Asad surely raised numerous questions about him. David had crossed the Red Sea from Arabia to the "Land of Kush" somewhere in east Africa. Even if he had not been in the "Land of Kush," Yuhanna al-Asad would still have wondered about the Jew's description of the queen and concubines of the Muslim King "Amarah" ('Umar?) as being naked except for gold armlets, bracelets, anklets and a gold chain around their loins. Or his stories of the two lion cubs, presented to him by youths from the Lost Tribes of Israel living in the Land of Kush. He had taken the cubs down the Nile to Cairo in 1523 and given them as "gifts" to the customs officials, who then sent them on to Sultan Suleyman in Istanbul.[60]

Meanwhile David's machinations in 1525–26 involved correspondence with the sultan of Fez and the young Sa'diyan amir sharif al-A'raj, whose late father, the Amir Sharif Muhammad al-Qa'im, al-Wazzan had known well during his days as diplomat. Conversations with the onetime ambassador from Fez may have fed David's grandiose hopes to be in touch with Jews from Meknes and Fez and the Land of the Blacks.[61]

The prince of Habor was finally unmasked in 1530, when he was caught in Mantua forging letters from "his brother King Joseph."[62] But to Yuhanna al-Asad in 1524, he would have seemed another in the succession of African holy men and political saviors, whose uncertain merits he had been critically assessing throughout his travels.

Such are the circles in Rome in which we can document the presence of Yuhanna al-Asad. We can speculate on a few other possibilities. Perhaps Francisco de Cabrera y Bobadilla, bishop of Salamanca, wondered what had become of the man his pirate brother had captured. The prisoner had initially been held at the bishop's palace in Rome before his incarceration in the Castel Sant'Angelo, and now, as Giovanni Leone, he might have been summoned there once again. If so, he might have heard about and even met the high-spirited young goldsmith Benvenuto Cellini. Bobadilla loved Cellini's work, even while quarreling with him about payment, and ordered candlesticks and a silver vase from him in 1523–25, much admired by the pope, cardinals, and visiting Spaniards.[63]

A more exciting and more dangerous possibility for Yuhanna al-Asad was to connect himself with other Muslims or converts from Islam living in or passing through Rome. He would have learned about some of them quite soon, such as the black Muslim slave ordered to

strangle Cardinal Petrucci in his cell at the Castel Sant'Angelo in 1517.
Great households in Rome were filled with slaves and servants, all the
former and some of the latter from non-Christian lands: "a true
seraglio," wrote Paolo Giovio of the household of the newly appointed
Cardinal Ippolito de' Medici, "Numidians, Tartars, Ethiopians, Indians,
Turks, who all together speak more than twenty languages." Owners
had their will with their slaves, and the child resulting from heterosexual encounters was sometimes accorded high birth. Yuhanna al-Asad
would surely have heard the gossip about Ippolito's brother, Alessandro
de' Medici, whose mother was a "*schiava mora*" in the Medici household and whose face and hair suggested an African origin. His father, so
everyone said, was not really Lorenzo II de' Medici but Pope Clement
VII himself.[64]

In contrast to the publicly owned galley slaves, domestic slaves in
Italy were often urged by their owners to convert to Christianity. Baptism did not bring automatic manumission, however. The question
whether it was legitimate to keep a converted Christian as a slave was
just beginning to be raised in the 1520s—and then in regard to conquered Native Americans in the New World rather than to captured
Muslims in Italy. Masters taking their slaves to the baptismal fonts in
Rome were not obliged to give up their property.[65] (Pondering such a
matter, Yuhanna al-Asad would recall that conversion to Islam by no
means brought manumission to the slave of a Muslim master. Belief
was critical exclusively at the moment of enslavement: only a person
who was a non-Muslim at the time he or she was captured or seized
could become rightfully the property of a Muslim. Yuhanna al-Asad
would have remembered how the North African zealot al-Maghili
stretched that right for the Songhay emperor to include the capture and
enslavement of inauthentic Muslims.)[66]

Italian baptism ceremonies for slaves were far more modest than Giovanni Leone's exceptional baptism at St. Peter's. (Similarly, Christian
slaves who converted to Islam in North Africa usually just said the shahada, the confession of faith, and raised the index finger before witnesses
at their master's house. Circumcision for men followed, of course.) The

domestic slaves and manumitted converts living in Rome in the 1520s rarely had the learning of Yuhanna al-Asad or his previous status. They would have been unlikely to have read esoteric texts by al-Ghazali. In the Campo Marzio district where Yuhanna al-Asad dwelled for a time, five of the 939 households were headed by Christian women of color, who probably had once been slaves. The intriguing exception in another part of town was the "Fillia del Gran Turcho," the daughter of the Great Turk.[67] Yuhanna al-Asad may not have approached such women soon after his release from prison, but at least he knew they were there.

During the short reign of the austere Dutchman Pope Adrian VI, Yuhanna al-Asad, like other Medici dependents, presumably had little to do with the papal court. But once Cardinal Giulio de' Medici had been chosen pope in a highly contested election in late 1523, Yuhanna al-Asad's services may have been used once again. Pope Clement VII immediately set up two commissions of cardinals, one to find ways to stop the Lutherans, the other to unite the Christian princes against the Turks. The latter proved an even more difficult task than it had been during the reign of Clement's cousin Leo: the conflict between France and the Holy Roman Empire was once again making a battleground of Italy (François I even gave secret notice to Sultan Suleyman about when it would be opportune for him to attack their current mutual enemy Charles V); the Grand Turk was winning spectacular victories in Hungary; and Tunisian and other Muslim pirates were seizing the pope's galleons at the very mouth of the Tiber. Yuhanna al-Asad's familiarity with the Maghreb political scene may have been drawn upon, say, in regard to expected attacks by the pirate prince Khayr al-Din Barbarossa against Sicily.[68] He may have once again translated Arabic letters for the papal chancellery. At least one of the new curators at the Vatican Library was interested in Muslim doctrine and may have sought counsel from Yuhanna al-Asad, but no fresh inventory of manuscripts was started until several years later.[69]

But the Vatican librarian Girolamo Aleandro was back in Rome in 1525–26 and was linked to Yuhanna al-Asad in an account of a conversation that circulated among Orientalist scholars. In one version, the exchange took place between Egidio da Viterbo and a Jewish Cabalist from Africa.[70] In the other version, the exchange was between Girolamo Aleandro and a converted Arab faqih resembling Yuhanna al-Asad. The latter story comes from a good source: Girolamo's cousin Pietro Aleandro, a young churchman then living in Rome and acting as Girolamo's agent there. Talking of the fish promised to the just at their banquet in Paradise, the learned Arab asked Aleandro why Christ so preferred this food. Aleandro replied at length, referring evidently to the fish also given by Christ to his apostles after his resurrection (John 21: 9–13). Whereupon the Arab said "as a joke," "I see that the Messiah did not want to disappoint his disciples in their expectation of this banquet." Even if Yuhanna al-Asad never said these words, the story shows the kinds of conversations in which contemporaries found it plausible to place him.[71]

BY THE MID-1520S, Yuhanna al-Asad was able to combine his Arabic teaching, transcribing, translating, and writing with travel beyond Rome and its environs. Leaving Rome, he saw aqueducts that made him think of those built three hundred years before by the great Almohad caliph al-Mansur to bring fresh water to the town of Rabat. He went as far north as Venice, whose waterways reminded him of Cairo when the Nile was at flood ("on such days, Cairo becomes a Venice"). In Florence the black paving stones recalled those he had seen at Gafsa in the kingdom of Tunis. In Naples, stranger though he was, he found himself conversing with men who in 1520 had witnessed the Muslim retaking from the Spanish of the island of Peñon de Velez on the Rif coast: the Christian commander had been murdered by one of his own Spanish soldiers, whose wife he had seduced, and then the army sent by the sultan of Fez had done the rest. Throughout, Yuhanna al-Asad kept his foreigner's ear tuned for many local words—those for textiles or tools or fish or agricultural products.[72]

His most important stays outside of Rome were at Viterbo and Bologna. Viterbo, which is not far from Rome, was Cardinal Egidio's hometown, where he had first joined the Augustinian order and begun his studies. Egidio went back there often over the years, with especially important duties after December 1523, when Clement VII appointed him bishop.[73] On one such visit, his godson was with him, for it was in Viterbo in 1525 that Yuhanna al-Asad finished correcting Joannes Gabriel's translation of the Qur'an into Latin.

That same year Egidio gave sermons throughout his diocese. If Yuhanna al-Asad heard his godfather deliver them or read his drafts, he must have been, on the one hand, dazzled by the powerful and accessible oratory, evident even to a foreigner's ear or eye, and, on the other hand, disturbed by the bishop's treatment of Islam. Egidio told worshipers at Bagnaia that Ishmael and his Muslim descendants were the terrible instrument of retribution against Hebrews and Christians because of Abraham's sin in casting out Ishmael's mother, Hagar.[74] Yuhanna al-Asad knew the very different Islamic tradition: that Isma'il was most likely the son that Abraham took to be sacrificed, that Isaac was then Abraham's reward for his obedience to God, and that Abraham later visited Isma'il in the land that was to become Mecca, where they built the Ka'ba together. ("House," wrote Yuhanna al-Asad on this verse in Egidio's copy of the Qur'an, correcting Joannes Gabriel's "temple" with the proper Muslim term for the Ka'ba.)[75]

The Qur'an links Isma'il and his brother Isaac (2:136):

> Say you: "We believe in God, and
> in that which has been sent down on us
> and sent down on Abraham, Ishmael,
> Isaac and Jacob, and the Tribes,
> and that which was given to Moses and Jesus
> and the Prophets, of their Lord; we
> make no division between any of them, and
> to Him we surrender."[76]

Egidio, in contrast, stressed division when he asked his listeners at Bagnaia: "Who holds Asia? Muslims! Who occupies Africa? Muslims!

Who has conquered a fine and notable part of Europe? Muslims! . . .
How long Hagar and Ishmael have reigned far and wide."[77] Yuhanna al-
Asad would have shaken his head at these indignant words. Could his
interpretation of the Qur'an ever change the way Egidio looked at the
legacy of Isma'il?

Yuhanna al-Asad's visit to Bologna a year and half earlier must have
been easier. Now part of the Papal States, Bologna was flourishing in
1523. He may have taken a look at its shops for silk manufacture, a craft
that had particularly interested him in Morocco, where it was introduced by refugees from Granada. Even more he would have been impressed by the university, with its celebrated faculties in medicine and
law. He went to see the college for the students from Spain, some of
them probably from his native Granada, and perhaps heard some lectures.[78] Teaching philosophy at Bologna till his death in 1524 was the
Aristotelian Pietro Pomponazzi, who had shaken up the scholarly world
in 1516 by arguing that by natural reason one could not prove the immortality of the soul. In the ensuing controversy, Pomponazzi published
two more tracts stoutly defending his view by reason, while affirming
his wholehearted commitment by faith to the teachings of the church on
resurrection and grace that made immortality possible. Years before
Pomponazzi had taught Aristotle to Alberto Pio and had continued to
receive the prince's patronage and attention. Yuhanna al-Asad may well
have learned of Pomponazzi while working on Alberto Pio's manuscripts in Rome. At the same time he may have heard Cardinal Egidio
attack Pomponazzi's impieties in regard to the soul and his "effrontery"
in claiming that one could not establish by reason that God punished sin
and rewarded virtue in the next world.[79] Whatever positive reaction he
had to Pomponazzi, Yuhanna al-Asad would have had to keep secret
from his godfather.

His most important associate in Bologna was the Jewish physician
and learned translator Jacob Mantino. The family of Jacob ben Samuel
had fled from Catalonia to Italy about the same time that the al-Wazzan
family had left Granada for Fez. After medical studies at Padua (Jewish
men could attend lectures in medicine at Italian universities), Mantino

set up a practice in Bologna, which had a substantial community of Jews: bankers, traders, scholars, silk weavers, physicians, and their families. He also began to make Latin translations of commentaries on Aristotle drawn from Hebrew texts, especially Hebrew translations of the celebrated Muslim philosopher and jurist Averroës (Ibn Rushd) of Córdoba. As he said in a 1521 dedication to Pope Leo X, many of Averroës's writings existed only in Hebrew translations or in unintelligible and "barbaric" Latin translations from the Arabic. Without good Latin translations of Averroës, one could not understand the "divine genius" of Aristotle.[80] Yuhanna al-Asad would have agreed, believing himself that Averroës's commentaries on Aristotle were "most excellent, most distinguished" (*praestantissimus, notissimus*), and telling Jacob ben Samuel excitedly that he had visited Averroës's first burial place (595/1198) at Marrakesh.[81]

The Jewish scholar was probably the one who initiated the connection with the faqih in Rome. Mantino long had a dream to learn to read Arabic, expressed in the early 1520s in an unusual project for an Arabic-Hebrew-Latin dictionary and many years later in a voyage to Damascus. His path to Yuhanna al-Asad was short: not only did Leo X know the two men—and Mantino visited Rome for the publication and presentation of his 1521 book to the pope—but Alberto Pio was to use one of Mantino's translations and Egidio da Viterbo, while disagreeing with the Jewish scholar about the value of Averroës, considered him among "the most learned in Hebrew" in Italy.[82]

Yuhanna al-Asad must have welcomed the invitation to produce an Arabic-Hebrew-Latin dictionary with Jacob ben Samuel. The practical matter of translation had long been one of his activities as a diplomat and was part of his daily life in Italy. A dictionary would also link him to the traditions of scholarly translation into Arabic: from the Greek during the ʿAbbasid caliphate in ninth-century Baghdad, which he wrote about with approval; and, he claimed, from the Latin during the caliphate in tenth-century Córdoba. He recalled "with amazement how many works he had seen [in Arabic] drawn from the Latin, works no longer found anywhere [in Europe] in Latin."[83]

Doing his share of an interlinguistic vocabulary would have been an adventure for him. A few Arabic-Latin dictionaries and Arabic-Spanish dictionaries had been composed by Christians in medieval Spain, and presumably by Jews in Arabic-Hebrew as well, but Mantino would have told his Arabic-speaker how rare such manuscripts were in Italy at the time.[84] Yuhanna al-Asad was well aware of the centuries-old production in Arabic lexicography in Islamic lands—indeed, he was just then introducing Mantino to al-Khalil ibn Ahmad al-Farahidi, the eighth-century creator of the genre. His reading and travels may also have brought an Arabic-Persian or Arabic-Turkish dictionary or word list before his eyes. But he may never have seen a written vocabulary in Arabic-Latin or Arabic-Hebrew-Latin.[85]

The resulting manuscript is of great interest, even though it is not complete (figure 5). The Arabic columns written by Yuhanna al-Asad are all there: some 5,500 words, a small number compared to the 60,000 entries in the *Qamus*, an often-copied Arabic dictionary of a hundred years before, but still requiring from its unpracticed compiler much thought about what to include. The semantic range is considerable: everyday objects, institutions, roles, verbs of action, concepts, kinship terms, animals, and more. The letters were carefully written for easy recognition, arranged alphabetically by the first letter of the Arabic word (not always the root) and then by the order of the subsequent letters. This was not the only system found in Arabic dictionaries—the words in the *Qamus* were arranged by rhyme, that is, by the final sound—but Yuhanna al-Asad chose the one most familiar to Europeans while following the distinctive alphabetical order used in the Maghreb of his day.[86]

Yuhanna al-Asad ended the manuscript with an Arabic colophon signed with both his Christian and his Muslim-Arabic names. The Hebrew and Latin columns peter out early, however: there are only 170 Hebrew entries by Mantino and 438 Latin entries, roughly half of them by Mantino and the rest in a later hand.[87] My guess is that Yuhanna al-Asad was called back to Rome abruptly—he signed the colophon in late January 1524, and Prince David the Reubenite arrived in Rome in February—and then Mantino lost heart or had insufficient knowledge of Arabic to continue.

Still, the courteous colophon attests to the good spirit with which Yuhanna al-Asad did his share for "the teacher and skillful physician Yaʿqub ibn Shamʿun [*sic* for Samuel], the trustworthy Israelite, may God maintain him in his grace." Their dictionary contrasts with the printed Spanish-Arabic dictionary, all in Latin script, composed by Pedro de Alcala in 1505 and dedicated to the first archbishop of Granada. Pedro's dictionary, together with his book on Arabic grammar, would help to convert those who believed in the "devilish errors and heresies" of the "cursed 'Mahoma'."[88] The "trustworthy Israelite" would be using Yuhanna al-Asad's dictionary to other ends—say, to try to decipher an Arabic manuscript when one came into his hands.

There are further signs of exchange between the two men. Both were interested in the great Persian physician and philosopher Avicenna/Ibn Sina. Yuhanna al-Asad would write of him as *raʾis*, "chief" or "leader" of all physicians, and complain about his Latin translators who, "ignorant of Arabic grammar, did not understand its common nouns." Mantino would speak of him similarly a few years later as "first in renown among the Arabs in the art of medicine" and comment on "his idiomatic Arabic usage, not so easy for men of Latin origin to understand." The Latin translations of Avicenna were full of errors; he would help correct them by his translation of part of Avicenna's medical *Canon* from the Hebrew.[89]

Mantino was already working on a Latin translation of the *Eight Chapters on Ethics* by Moses ben Maimon (Maimonides), an ethical treatise drawing on Aristotle and Arabic philosophers such as al-Farabi as well as on rabbinic teachings.[90] Soon Yuhanna al-Asad was to depict Moses ben Maimon as a great Jewish physician, philosopher, and theologian and make up a story—or more likely draw it from some mix of Arabic and Jewish traditions—about Maimonides as student and then friend of Averroës. Accused of heresy late in his career, so Yuhanna al-Asad told it, Averroës was ordered by the Almohad caliph al-Mansur to go and live with the Jews of Córdoba. After being stoned by the boys of Córdoba while preaching at the mosque, Averroës escaped to Fez, the current place of refuge of his disciple Maimonides. Maimonides, fearing that because of their association he would be questioned and forced to reveal Averroës's presence, preferred to flee with his family, eventually finding his way to Egypt.[91]

Now, modern scholars have found no personal association between Maimonides and Averroës. The former's first mention of the latter is not until a 586/1190 letter from Cairo: Maimonides had recently received all of Averroës's books on Aristotle and found them "extraordinarily correct." Both men suffered from Almohad persecution, but Maimonides's father had taken his family to Fez and Maimonides had left that city for Cairo decades before 590/1194, when Averroës was banished for a time from Caliph al-Mansur's favor. Still, there are so many parallels and common sources in the thought of these two philosophers, born thirteen years apart in Córdoba, that it is not surprising that medieval readers imagined that the Jew had studied directly with the Muslim. Moreover, the house in Fez in which Maimonides had spent a few years of his youth and had written his early work had become something of a shrine; around such a site a legend crossing disparate lives could readily arise—especially if one was hazy about chronology.[92] In the easy atmosphere of Mantino's household, where conversions and crusades were not being plotted, Yuhanna al-Asad could cheerfully offer his host this Muslim-Jewish link.

Mantino was also to do a translation of Averroës's commentary on Aristotle's *Poetics*, a text of ever greater interest to Italian rhetoricians (figure 27). Here, too, Yuhanna al-Asad had something to offer him: Averroës had written many poems in his youth, some of them filled with moral examples, some of them love poems, and then in his old age had ordered them burned. Fortunately, two of them had been saved, and he, Yuhanna al-Asad, could recite some lines by heart: "For as a youth, I was disobedient to my will, and when time vexed me with baldness and old age, I was obedient to my will. Would that I had been born old!"[93]

Though Averroës is known in modern scholarship for writing about poetry rather than composing it, Yuhanna al-Asad's account is plausible, especially when one remembers how readily speakers of Arabic slipped from prose into poetry in those centuries. In any case, such a story would have amused Mantino as he worked over Averroës's evaluation of the diverse genres of Arabic poetry: the young should be warned against love poems that inclined people to sinful and prohibited actions and should hear those that exhort through imitation to courage and renown.[94]

Such conversations also helped inspire a book by Yuhanna al-Asad: a treatise on Arabic grammar and on Arabic poetic metrics. Leaving Bologna for Rome, he either gave a copy of this manuscript to Jacob Mantino or promised to send it to him one day, surely useful for all the subsequent scholarship of "the trustworthy Israelite."[95] The book also represented something new for Yuhanna al-Asad, once known as al-Hasan ibn Muhammad al-Wazzan. His stay with the Jewish physician confirmed for the North African faqih the creative move of his Italian years: beyond transcription, beyond commentary, beyond translation, to become an author of his own.

CHAPTER THREE

Writing in Italy

Two years after promising Jacob Mantino a copy of his treatise on Arabic grammar and prosody, Yuhanna al-Asad could describe himself as the author of four other works as well. He was just finishing a big book on the geography and cosmography of Africa, and in its pages he found frequent excuse to refer his readers to his other compositions. There was his history book *The Epitome of Muslim Chronicles*. There was *The Faith and Law of Muhammad according to the Malikite School of Law*. And there was his book of collective biographies, *The Lives of Arab Scholars*.[1]

Each of these writings is an expression of Yuhanna al-Asad's life on both sides of the Mediterranean. On the one hand, they were each representative of a well-established genre in Arabic literature, including the abridgment (*mukhtasar*) of earlier history books,[2] and al-Hasan al-Wazzan may have had notes on some of their subjects in his bags when the pirates picked him up. He was a poet and a critical listener to poetry wherever he went; why would he not have jotted down comments on poetic meter along the way? He was twice solicited to be a qadi on his travels; why would he not have carried with him some reminders of Malikite jurisprudence?

On the other hand, these books were to serve readers in Europe as introductions to the world of Islam. Consider the treatise on Arabic metrics, which has come down to us copied "from the original" in 1527 by a scribe with a standard Italian humanist hand.[3] It is in Latin, though a Latin with some mistakes, which show that its author had still not fully mastered that tongue. (Scribes copied texts closely, mistakes and all.) The book opens with the "god-fearing and devout" al-Khalil al-Farahidi, the inventor of the art of Arabic metrics as well as of Arabic lexicography. Yuhanna al-Asad tells the familiar Arabic tale about al-Khalil that one day his brother came upon him in their house reciting nonsense syllables; he rushed into the streets to announce that al-Khalil had gone mad. In fact, these were the rhythmic words by which al-Khalil defined his metric patterns, and Yuhanna al-Asad goes on to use them throughout his text.[4]

Yuhanna al-Asad translates a few of al-Khalil's verses into Latin for his readers. "I am content with the small stock of my patrimony," the scholar had written in refusing to leave his native Basra to serve an important ruler in Arabia. "If you pursue fortune, you will not get near it; if you turn your back to it, fortune will pursue you."[5] Yuhanna al-Asad may have thought of his own very different choices as he recollected al-Khalil's words.

Yuhanna al-Asad then defines the nine kinds of Arabic metric feet, comparing them when relevant to Latin spondees and dactyls and pointing to contrasts in vocalizing syllables. Clearly he has made strides in his knowledge of European forms. Next come the seven metric patterns that different types of poems may have, starting off with one of his favorites, the long meter of *al-tawil*. He gives Arabic metric examples in transcribed Latin characters and includes a verse from a certain Kaʿb ibn Zuhayr: he is "our Arab poet," Yuhanna al-Asad explains, keeping to himself that Kaʿb was a pre-Islamic poet, who after writing against the Prophet signaled his surrender by a celebrated poem from

which a cited line—"only as the seive holds on to the water"—is taken
(figure 7). The scribe left space in the manuscript for an occasional
word in Arabic to be inserted, but in this copy Yuhanna al-Asad filled
in only two.[6]

The manuscript could certainly get a European reader started on the
principles of Arabic prosody, a subject on which only scanty information had been available to medieval scholars. But it is more compressed
than what its author would have written for Arab readers alone, for
whom he might have discussed alternative approaches to prosody from
that of al-Khalil, some of them quite important. And he might have
given many more examples and expanded his subject of metrics into
connections with metaphor and genre, as in the ninth-century Arabic
treatise on poetry by Tha'lab that he had borrowed from the Vatican
Library sometime after his baptism.[7]

CONSIDER ALSO his biographies of illustrious scholars. Here, too, we
have a Latin manuscript, also copied by a scribe "from the original" in
1527, with the title *De Viris quibusdam Illustribus apud Arabes* (On
Some Illustrious Men among the Arabs) and an additional section, *De
quibusdam Viris Illustribus apud Hebraeos* (On Some Illustrious Men
among the Jews). According to the title, the author is making a translation from his own Arabic text—"*ex ea lingua maternam traductis*"—
which belongs to the genre of the *tabaqat*, biographical compendiums
beloved by Arabic and Islamic scholars for centuries. These collections
grouped people by some criterion—say, occupation or place of origin—
and assessed their reliability and trustworthiness as transmitters of
knowledge from the past and as contributors to it. As such, each entry
should best include the subject's full name, with all it conveyed about ancestors and geographical origins; the names of the persons he had studied with or been trained by; and information about travel, contacts, and
publications, as well as the sources for the biographer's claims. (Some
compendia also included women noted for their holiness or learning.)[8]

Yuhanna al-Asad's *Illustrious Men* has several of the qualities of the tabaqat (figure 8). The collection is small compared to the dictionaries of hundreds and even thousands of people composed in Dar al-Islam: here only twenty-eight men are depicted among the Arabs, including three Nestorian or Jacobite Christians, and five men among the Jews.[9] But the lives, arranged chronologically, cover some of the customary ground: geographical and family origins, occupations, publications, personal anecdotes, and quotations; and they often include the names and views of previous biographers. Most of the men are physicians and philosophers, some branching into theology, astronomy, geography, or law, and many of them write poetry, as was expected among persons cultivated in the Arabic tongue. Thus from the philosopher al-Farabi, Yuhanna al-Asad recalls two lines of verse, which appear in the manuscript in his own Arabic hand and in Latin translation:

> Base bread, well water, and woollen garment in peace
> Are better than excessive delight ending in penitence.[10]

About the Jacobite Christian Masawayh al-Maridini, practicing medicine in eleventh-century Cairo and author of books on remedies and syrups, he tells the story of a farmer who came complaining to him about his sore penis. The farmer confessed that he had been giving his male member extra use penetrating the anus of his donkey. Al-Maridini pounded the man's penis roughly, got him to ejaculate some strange fluid, and sent him back to his farm hurting less and with the warning, "Don't direct your member into the aperture of your ass."[11]

The inclusion of such an immodest tale in a biographical compendium was not exceptional. The celebrated thirteenth-century biographer Ibn Khallikan recorded the joking exchange in verse between a Baghdad physician and learned translator and his vizier the night the former had to take a laxative.[12]

At the same time, *De Viris Illustribus* shows the marks of Yuhanna al-Asad's Italian years and his anticipated European audience. The teachers or students of his Arab luminaries are mentioned in only a few cases, and a full list is given only for Ibn Rushd (Averroës). Now, to Muslims this information was believed essential to authenticate a person's reliablity in transmitting a theological, legal, or philosophical tradition. In North Africa, the writer would have done his best to acquire or recall a scholar's *isnad*, that is, to place him wherever possible in the chain of transmission. In Europe, he scarcely bothered to make up such a chain: for European readers he could simply announce that a scholar was a *"maximus Philosophus,"* or *"singularissimus"* in medicine and philosophy and theology, or *"doctus*—learned in all sciences."[13]

Second, amid much valuable and enduring detail about Yuhanna al-Asad's subjects are mistakes in dates (always given in the Muslim form), places, events, and titles, or we should better say, these are departures from what he would have known from texts and traditions in North Africa. In part, his lapses are an understandable failure of memory in a situation where he lacked the manuscripts to help him: the Arabic biographical dictionaries he would have consulted at a madrasa library could not be found in the Vatican Library or the collections of Alberto Pio or Egidio da Viterbo.[14]

But in part, these departures are the fruits of unacknowledged invention, a practice resorted to more than once by our man between worlds. Take, for example, what he writes about the great physician and philosopher Abu Bakr al-Razi. Some of al-Razi's medical and alchemical manuscripts were already available in Europe in Latin translation, but very little was known there about his life. Yuhanna al-Asad starts off with al-Razi's birth in Persia in the ninth century and his training and practice in Baghdad, as was depicted in the standard earlier biographies by Ibn Khallikan and others. From Baghdad, Yuhanna al-Asad has al-Razi going to Cairo, where suddenly his fame wins him an invitation from one al-Mansur, the chamberlain and effective ruler of the Umayyad caliphate of Córdoba, and al-Razi moves west to a position of prominence and reward in this center of Muslim al-Andalus. There he writes his wide-ranging medical treatise *Kitab al-Mansuri* (The Book of al-Mansur) and spends the rest of his life. Citing the eleventh-century chronicler Ibn Hayyan, Yuhanna al-Asad reports a fascinating conversation between al-Mansur and al-Razi, where the former believes the physician has resurrected a man from the dead, and al-Razi explains that only God can do that, his cures come from his medical practice.[15]

A scholar in the Islamic world would have been surprised to read this account, as existing biographies of al-Razi never got him much farther west than Baghdad, had him dedicating his famous book to the *Persian* Mansur al-Samani, and had him dying in his native town of Ray. Furthermore, the real al-Mansur of Córdoba held sway some fifty years after the physician al-Razi was in his grave; and there was a western "al-Razi," but he was a local historian, one 'Isa al-Razi, whose job was to celebrate the Cordovan ruler by his writing and who was referred to by Ibn Hayyan in this connection. To be sure, Ibn Khallikan had raised the question about which Mansur was the dedicatee of *The Book of al-Mansur*, but he had two Persian potentates in mind. (Al-Mansur, which means "rendered victorious [by God]," was a name adopted by quite a few rulers.) Ibn Khallikan concluded with a standard Islamic formula when the evidence is uncertain: "God knows best which of these statements is true."[16]

Yuhanna al-Asad never uses such a phrase in his biographies, which come to his European readers without controversies about their truth. Here, where his memory is full of holes or his information skimpy, he simply puts together two men into an interesting life story and attributes it to a real historian. At a time when Jacob Mantino would have told him of the numerous editions of the *Liber Almansoris* recently published in Venice, Bologna, and Pavia, Yuhanna al-Asad could have some of al-Razi's medical glory rub off on the Muslim al-Andalus of his ancestors.[17]

Yuhanna al-Asad created vivid portraits of learned men, sometimes well substantiated by memory and whatever notes he had brought with him to Italy, sometimes improvised, approximate, or simply made up. Even with their mixture of what he believed as fact and what he knew was fabulation, they opened a world of scholarship for Europeans, adding to their meager knowledge of, say, the philosopher-theologian al-Ghazali and introducing them to unknown figures. They could learn of al-Tughra'i, described in the *Illustrious Men* as an alchemist, poet,

and historian of Persia (d. ca. 515/1121). They could learn of the remarkable Lisan al-Din ibn al-Khatib (d. 776/1374), described as historian, poet, physician, philosopher, and high political officer in the
kingdom of Granada. Ibn al-Khatib's letters, couched in rhymed prose,
were celebrated for their style and were found in many legal libraries in
Fez and elsewhere.[18]

Further, since *Illustrious Men* was presenting European readers with
an Islamic and Arabic genre unfamiliar to them, the tabaqat, and with
some if not all of its literary conventions, they could see how Muslim
scholars used citation and learn the names of the biographers: "Ibn
Juljul, chronicler, said in the Lives of Philosophers that many princes of
Asia sent for [al-Farabi], inviting him to come to their courts, promising
money and stipends"; "Ibn al-Abbar . . . historian of Spain . . . said
that Averroës was asked how he felt during the period of his persecution. He answered that he felt both pleased and despised." Some of the
citations are spurious, to be sure. A story attributed to Ibn Khallikan,
about how Avicenna (Ibn Sina) justified harnessing his mule with silver
rather than iron, is not to be found in Ibn Khallikan's pages.[19] But the
forms of the tabaqat are respected, and European readers could discover how Muslim scholars recorded conversation and wit. And as with
the Arabic-Hebrew-Latin dictionary, the lives were described without
religious polemic, and with Muslims of different theological schools,
Christians, and Jews coexisting within the same learned frame. A copy
of the manuscript seems to have been in Egidio da Viterbo's hands, and
one wonders what the cardinal thought.[20]

WHATEVER JOY or frustration came to Yuhanna al-Asad in composing these minor works pales in comparison with what he must have felt
as he wrote the great book of his Italian years: *Libro de la Cosmographia et Geographia de Affrica*. He finished its last lines on March 10,
1526. We know the book best and most accurately from the sole surviving copy: a 936-page manuscript in an early sixteenth-century Italian
hand, now at the Biblioteca Nazionale Centrale in Rome.[21] It is written

in a clear and often lively Italian but with a simplified syntax and a word use sometimes lacking in precision and nuance; its style is different from the turns of phrase, extended vocabulary, and alliterative prose that the orator-poet would have used in Arabic.

Its spelling yields clues as well. There was much diversity in orthography in early sixteenth-century Italy, but the spelling choices in this manuscript, while within the range of practice, are less those of a regional speaker than those of a speaker accustomed to the vowel sounds of Arabic and for whom the boundaries between Italian, Spanish, and Latin were not always sharp. Such was Yuhanna al-Asad. For instance, he prefers *"el Re"* to *il Re,* *"el patre"* to *il padre,* *"el populo"* to *il populo,* *"el templo"* to *il tempio,* *"el thesaurero"* to *il thesoriere,* and *"la abundantia"* to *l'abbondanza.* In oasis towns, he always mentions *"dattoli"* for dates, a word used for that fruit in Venice, but also closer to the Spanish *dátils* or the Latin *dactyli* than to the common Italian *datteri.* Latin-like phrases—*"dicto"* and *"prefato"* (for "aforesaid")—crop up now and again.[22] All of this was to be changed, along with many other modifications, by the Venetian Giovanni Battista Ramusio, when he first published the book as *La Descrittione dell'Africa* in Venice in 1550: the syntax became more complex, the vocabulary more varied, the style more flowery and elevated, and the spelling more in line with that urged by reformers.

How did Yuhanna al-Asad prepare his manuscript? In its closing phrase, just before the colophon, he uses language that recalls the ancient tradition of oral delivery: "the author cannot recall more because of the frailty of his memory . . . so he falls silent and ends his speaking." The reference to "speaking" here is figurative, a significant literary convention like Yuhanna al-Asad's use of the verb *dicere,* "to say," every time he cites an author in his *Illustrious Men*: it evokes direct transmission even though the message is carried by a valued written book.[23]

For centuries in Islamic societies the practice of oral delivery to copyists had been supplemented by the practice of writing one's own manuscript and then making copies oneself or having them made by scribes or students or others in one's circle. Sometimes oral delivery itself was coupled with writing, the author reciting not from memory alone but from a draft. To be sure, in 757/1356 at Fez, Ibn Battuta had dictated his long travel narrative to a talented writer and jurist, Ibn Juzayy, who edited it and added some observations of his own. Sultans dictated their letters to secretaries, and the lecture notes of students were used as a version of some books. More frequently in al-Wazzan's day, authors prepared their own manuscripts for copyists. An early draft of al-Maqrizi's topography of Cairo, written in the fifteenth century, shows how much crossing out and rewriting went on as an author readied his book for the scribe. Al-Wazzan's teacher al-Wansharisi had a pupil compile a book by copying the marginalia he had written on a legal text.[24]

This is the practice that al-Hasan al-Wazzan, himself a notary during his youth, would have followed if he had completed his books in North Africa. His Italian experience reinforced that choice, where authors like Boccaccio and Petrarch had written their own manuscripts themselves. Important figures like Alberto Pio dictated their diplomatic correspondence, of course. The busy Cardinal Egidio dictated some of his compositions and sermons to a secretary, but he also wrote certain major texts out first, covering many pages fully in his fine hand.[25] Less highly placed learned men wrote their own compositions, fitting this in with their hours of teaching, or preparing ecclesiastical correspondence, or treating patients, and then took their manuscripts to scribes for further copies unless they went straight to the printer.[26]

Since the character of the Italian in the *Cosmography and Geography* matches so closely the linguistic experience of Yuhanna al-Asad, it is evident that he wrote his own final draft, taking as long a time as needed to maneuver his pen from left to right in the Latin alphabet. Then he gave his manuscript to a scribe, who copied it, distinctive spelling and all, in an italic hand with some ornamental flourish to its letters.[27] Tiny corrections are found in the first quarter of the manuscript, most in the hand of the scribe, the rest possibly but not surely in the author's hand.[28] But Yuhanna al-Asad did not give a thorough scrutiny to this copy. If he had, he would have corrected two spectacular scribal errors later in the manuscript (each in the midst of pages, thus not a binder's mistake): an account of the end of al-Wazzan's visit to the Algerian town of Médéa, where he served as a qadi for a while, is tacked on inconsequently to a description of another little town nearby; and a few pages on, as events in Algiers are described, the text abruptly shifts to two other towns and then back to Algiers again in midsentence.[29] The author would never have let these go by.

Ramusio's publication of the Africa book corrected the order of these passages, and though he might have straightened them out himself simply by what made sense, he was almost certainly guided by another copy of the manuscript of the man he called Giovanni Leone Africano. Yuhanna al-Asad must have had at least two copies of his text made in 1526.[30] As I interpret the evidence, these two manuscripts closely resembled each other, with one major exception: the story of a seduced wife and a gullible husband appears in Ramusio's printed edition and not in the manuscript at the Biblioteca Nazionale Centrale in Rome. (We shall look at the story more closely in a later chapter.)

Apart from this, the many changes in the printed book—using a more complex and literary Italian, making brief omissions and additions, substituting words—are virtually all the work of Ramusio. Often these revised wordings convey the author's meaning, but some of them change his content and self-presentation in ways consistent neither with the Arabo-Islamic views that he would have brought with him from North Africa, nor with the attitudes and sensibilities he developed during his Italian years.[31]

A Venetian of high birth, Giovanni Battista Ramusio had in earlier years been an ambassador to France and elsewhere in Europe and had served as secretary to the Venetian Senate and Council. (Ramusio was in charge of interviewing David Reuveni, when he arrived in Venice in 1530 still claiming to be the Jewish prince of Habor and hoping to "lead the dispersed Hebrew people back to the promised land." Ramusio accepted David at his word, finding him "very learned in the Jewish law and the science called Cabala." He must have been taken aback to discover later that the prince was an impostor.[32]) Among Ramusio's humanist interests, geography and maps were his passion, and when in his last years he turned to publishing the travel accounts he had collected, the Africa manuscript of Giovanni Leone came first.[33] Having failed to unmask the exotic Jew from Arabia, Ramusio was certainly not going to let this prize African appear unpersuasive for his European readers. He edited and revised the text accordingly.

The *Libro de la Cosmographia et Geographia de Affrica* is thus a precious guide. Occasionally, changes made by Ramusio or translators of the book as he printed it will show us the pressures under which Yuhanna al-Asad lived in Italy and the ways in which his European interpreters wanted to reshape him.

THE *Cosmography and Geography of Africa* is disposed in nine "parts": a general introduction on geography, weather, customs, economy, and culture; seven parts each devoted to a description of towns, villages, mountains, and deserts of a region of Africa and the people dwelling there; and a conclusion on rivers, minerals, plants, birds, and animals. Interestingly, it mixes several genres valued for centuries in the cultures of Islam.

Geography had long been a central strand, pursued with different goals and approaches.[34] The influential al-Masʿudi (d. 346/957), a historian and geographer of encyclopedic interests, had gone well beyond Dar al-Islam in his description and brought into his ken many features of the earth's surface, its peoples, and their past. Along with a critical use of information and traditional stories, he insisted on travel as essential for the geographer and reproached scholars who had never seen the places they wrote about. As for him, he had journeyed from his native Baghdad as far as India, al-Andalus, and Zanzibar. "One can apply to me," he wrote, "the poet's verse: 'He has traveled the world in every direction . . . to countries so remote that no caravan has ever entered.'"[35]

A few decades later al-Muqaddasi had traveled almost as widely from his native Jerusalem, trading, consulting libraries, and meeting everyone from scholars and Sufis to storytellers: "I researched the taxes . . . I tasted the air, I evaluated the water." His *Best Divisions for Knowledge of the Regions* had a narrower range in space and time than al-Mas'udi's work: it was limited to the peoples, languages, and places of Islam, from al-Andalus to the lower Indus Valley, and it concentrated on the state of affairs in al-Muqaddasi's own time period. But his observations were richly detailed and fresh, and his organization as clear as his title promised.[36]

Al-Muqaddasi did not have much good to say about the Fez of his day ("crude and ignorant people, scholars are few, disturbances frequent"[37]), but the next two centuries were to see important geographers native to western Islam itself. Al-Bakri (d. 487/1094), a poet and diplomat for the amir of Seville, wrote a broad description of all kingdoms known to his Muslim contemporaries. His substantial section on North Africa covers some of the same ground as Yuhanna al-Asad's *Cosmography and Geography*, but does so following the old tradition of consulting, evaluating, and citing books and documents. Al-Bakri never left al-Andalus, yet his transition from section to section of his book is not based on some system of regions, but on routes—on how many days, for instance, it took to get from Fez to Sijilmasa.[38]

In the middle of the twelfth century, the renowned al-Idrisi entitled his geography *The Recreation of Him Who Yearns to Travel across the World*. Some scholars say he voyaged from his native al-Andalus as far west as Asia Minor and as far east and north as England; others, that he may have traveled little more than in the western Mediterranean to the then Norman Christian kingdom of Sicily and in North Africa, where his medical training gave him a good eye for plants and their pharmaceutical uses. The rest of his ample information came from geographical texts and royal archives.

Al-Idrisi dedicated his book to Roger II, son of the Norman conqueror of Muslim Spain, patron of Arabic culture, and in al-Idrisi's eyes, a philosopher king. His geography had something to say about all parts of the world known to the writer, sometimes with considerable detail about towns and their monuments. Days required for travel and routes were regularly given, but the geography was organized according to the traditional seven climatic zones that united all regions from east to west. These *aqalim*, called *klimata* in Greek, were latitudinal zones that Ptolemy had defined according to the height of the noonday sun at the solstice. One school of Arabic geographers in the east pursued this astronomical approach, reevaluating Ptolemy's figures and assigning improved latitudinal and longitudinal values to places on the earth's surface.[39] This was not al-Idrisi's way: he explained in his prologue that although the climatic zones were drawn from astronomical observation, he identified them by natural features and settlements—"the first climate begins at the west, with the western sea called Shadowy Ocean [the Atlantic]." He added to his written text a world map (figure 11) and many sectional maps by which these spatial relations and the climates could be visualized.[40]

Maps were an important tool for many Arabic geographers, whether or not they coupled them with astronomical calculation. Al-Muqaddasi had developed a color code for the regional maps in his *Best Divisions*: red for routes, yellow for sand, green for the sea, blue for rivers, and brown for mountains. Later maps for al-Idrisi's geography followed this or a similar prescription.[41]

Yuhanna al-Asad cited three of these authors—al-Mas'udi, al-Bakri, and al-Idrisi. (He devoted an appreciative entry to the last in his *Illustrious Men among the Arabs*.)[42] He probably knew al-Muqaddasi's great book as well. In his own book, he could place himself in the line of those who saw travel as essential to geographical description, along with oral inquiry and the consultation of texts. His geography was confined to one spatial unit, albeit a very large one, rather than covering all the countries of Islam or the known world, but perhaps with these other geographers in mind, he said he hoped one day to write about Asia and Europe as well.

Though Yuhanna al-Asad called his book both a *cosmography* and a *geography*—words found in titles of recent Latin editions of Ptolemy[43]—he did not use Ptolemy's latitudes and longitudes to give locations or even refer to astronomical means of determining place. (Indeed, *Geography* can serve me henceforth as a better short title for his book.) Nor did he locate places by days of travel between them, as had al-Bakri and al-Idrisi. Rather, he based his estimates of distance between places in miles (*mil, amyal* in Arabic): "Aït Daoud is an ancient settlement built by the Africans on a high mountain . . . It has about 700 households and is almost fifteen miles south of Tagtessa," he writes of a town in the Haha region of Morocco; "Asyut is a very ancient city built by the Egyptians on the Nile about 250 miles from Cairo."[44]

No maps accompanied Yuhanna al-Asad's manuscript. These he might have included if he had been preparing his book in North Africa— not a world map like the one in Ibn Khaldun's *Muqaddima*, nor a map of Mediterranean harbors, shoals, and inlets like the ones being drawn by Admiral Piri Reis in 931/1525 to accompany his *Book of Navigation* for Sultan Suleyman (figure 13), but sectional maps, helpful for travelers and rulers that showed the relation between places like those in al-Muqaddasi's *Best Divisions*.[45] In Italy, he must have wondered how readers would use such maps: European traders stayed close to their city compounds in North Africa; European captives were in chains or otherwise limited. As for European soldiers, why facilitate their movements in Dar al-Islam?

Further, having maps made in Italy, in the European style unfamiliar to him, would have been difficult. Even an accomplished geographer, the German Jacob Ziegler, who was in Rome in the early 1520s, had an artist traveling with him to draft his maps. Yuhanna al-Asad would have had to find a cartographer like the Venetian Giacomo Gastaldi, who forty years later drew a remarkable map of Africa that appeared in Ramusio's *Voyages* (figure 14). But how was Yuhanna al-Asad to get to such a person, and who would pay him? For all their breadth of learning, neither Alberto Pio nor Egidio da Viterbo had maps as a central interest. The historian Paolo Giovio drafted maps himself and knew others who did, but he was a busy man and not a patron of our convert. Clement VII asked Giovio to get information about Russia, including geographical information, but he seems not to have turned to Giovanni Leone for visual images of Africa.[46] Yuhanna al-Asad thus settled for verbal descriptions in a foreign tongue.

Travel figures in the *Geography* not only as a form of proof but as a form of life for its author. Since the ninth century travel had become a path to discovery for the Muslim scholar—discovery not of something considered foreign and exotic but of the character and meaning of Islam itself. Travel was also a test, hardships being welcomed as an ascetic challenge: the mountain and the desert were places where encounters with the sacred might be expected. Eventually, scholars began to write about their travels; a full recital of them was called a rihla.[47] A highly appreciated one was by the Andalusian Ibn Jubayr (d. 614/1217), whose pilgrimage to Mecca took him from Granada to Egypt, Syria, and Iraq, with a return across the Latin kingdom of Jerusalem and the Norman kingdom of Sicily. Even while describing the latter two in arresting detail, he exclaimed,

> There can be no excuse in the eyes of God for a Muslim to stay in any infidel country, save when passing through it, while the way lies clear in Muslim lands . . . The heart will be distressed by the reviling of him [Muhammad] whose memory God has sanctified . . . There is also the absence of cleanliness, the mixing with the pigs, and all the other prohibited matters.[48]

We have already heard something of the rihla of Ibn Battuta, who went from his native Tangier as far east as China and as far south as Mogadishu. He sought Muslim worthies wherever he could, and though he did not hasten away from infidel lands, he did say of one of them:

> China was beautiful, but it did not please me. On the contrary, I was greatly troubled thinking about the way paganism dominated this country. Whenever I went out of my lodging, I saw many blameworthy things. That disturbed me so much that I stayed indoors most of the time and only went out when necessary. During my stay in China, whenever I saw any Muslims I always felt as though I were meeting my own family and close kinsmen.[49]

Yuhanna al-Asad's adventures as recounted in his *Geography* are not consecutive, as in a rihla. They weave in and out of his narrative; sometimes the reader is following his actual path, sometimes not. But the spirit of Islamic voyage and the literary potential of the rihla helped him interpret and write about his own travels, so strangely interrupted and redirected to an infidel land.

Yuhanna al-Asad's Africa book also included history, as did the geographies of al-Masʿudi and al-Bakri. His description of Marrakesh, for instance, calls forth a review of its Almoravid and Almohad rulers of centuries before; the description of Tunis opens with a précis of its history since the fall of Carthage. Local and recent history in Moroccan lands he often gleaned from interviews during his travels, as we have seen. Among his written sources, the most influential was the great *Kitab al-ʿIbar* (The Book of Examples) of Ibn Khaldun, that universal history ranging from a broad science of civilization to a circumstantial account of the Berbers and the Arabs to autobiography; its many volumes had been available at the mosque of al-Qarawiyyin in Fez, a signed gift from the author. (The *Kitab al-ʿIbar* was surely one of the history books summarized in Yuhanna al-Asad's lost *Epitome of Muslim Chronicles*.) The *Geography* echoes Ibn Khaldun's social vision in certain ways, especially in its appreciation of urban patterns of living.[50]

Beyond this mixture of geography, travel account, and history, other topics weave in and out of Yuhanna al-Asad's text. There are autobiographical nuggets spread throughout. There are asides on Sufism, on the Four Schools of Law among the Sunnis, and on the various Muslim sects. A stop at an inhospitable town in the kingdom of Tunisia triggers the quotation of a vituperative verse about the place by al-Dabbag, a "marvelous" poet from Málaga, who, like him, had been rebuffed there. Yuhanna al-Asad goes on to explain some of the conventions of such poetry of invective (*hijaʾ*), comparing al-Dabbag's verses with the laudatory verses of the Granadan Ibn al-Khatib on the same towns. He regrets that his Italian translation cannot convey the "elegance" of the verse in Arabic.[51]

Anecdotes like these are found throughout the *Geography*, and we

have already heard a few from the *Lives of Illustrious Men*. Here
Yuhanna al-Asad was drawing upon the long-established criteria of
adab: rules both for decorous, seemly, and humane conduct—appropriate
at court; and for cultivated, witty, and knowledgeable expression—
appropriate for "profane literature." Except for his book about Muslim
faith and Malikite law, most of Yuhanna al-Asad's compositions fell
into this broad category. Writing in his still somewhat simple Italian, he
could not hope for elegant style, but at least he could incorporate one
element essential to adab literature, the entertaining and instructive anecdote. Whatever else, one must not be boring. Cultivated Italians,
reading or soon to be reading Baldassare Castiglione's *Courtier*, would
nod assent.[52]

Yuhanna al-Asad said several times that he was "telling the truth" in
his book. He was recounting what he had observed with his own eyes,
so he assured his readers often, or had heard about from some local person. As he puts it in regard to towns along the Nile, for example, "the
writer says he has seen these towns, in some cases entering them and
in others passing next to them, but he always informed himself fully
by talking to their inhabitants and to the boatmen who took him
from Cairo to Aswan." He goes on to express his doubts about al-
Mas'udi's claims concerning the mountains around the headwaters of
the Nile: though it was credible that emeralds were found there, al-
Mas'udi's report of wild folk running like goats was probably one of
his "lies."[53]

In making these comments, Yuhanna al-Asad was associating his
book with the truth status claimed for historical writing, geography,
and travel accounts. Ibn Khaldun opened his *Prolegomena* acknowledging the unavoidability of some "untruth" in historical information, gave
many examples of erroneous and baseless stories that had bounced
down the centuries (including some "absurdities" found in al-Mas'udi),
and then recommended methods of social and political analysis by
which historians could "find the path of truth and correctness." Ibn
Battuta explained that however much the recital of travel delighted the

mind and ears with anecdote, it was supposed to give true and useful knowledge at the same time.[54]

Along with his claims to speak true, Yuhanna al-Asad's imagination was touched by the fictional tales entitled *Maqamat* (Assemblies). The most celebrated were by the Persian al-Hamadhani (d. 398-399/1008), creator of the genre, and the Iraqi al-Hariri (d. 516/1122). Their *Maqamat* were copied many times over and had their imitators in al-Andalus. In these stories, expressed in rhymed prose (sadj') interspersed with metered verse, a learned and literary voyager tells his fellow scholars and merchants about his adventures and especially about an amazing man who appears in different disguises in the far-flung cities of Dar al-Islam. This man begs, he argues, he preaches, he pleads, always breaking into poetry, which the narrator quotes, and he always ends up on his feet and usually with fresh gifts and alms, bestowed upon him by his trusting listeners. Whatever his imposture, he is finally recognized by the storyteller as the same man: the shaykh Abu-l-Fath from Alexandria in al-Hamadhani's *Maqamat*, Abu Zayd from Saruj in al-Hariri's. As he told his own story, Yuhanna al-Asad put himself in the position of the traveling narrator and the trickster vagabond both.[55]

OF ALL OUR VOYAGER'S WRITINGS, a book on Africa is the one al-Wazzan would have been most likely to compose even if he had never left the world of Islam. He was keeping notes throughout his travels and consulting manuscripts whenever he could; he may have had an initial plan for a book and partial drafts of some sections in Arabic on his person when he was kidnapped.[56] However that may be, it was in Italy that he became an author, and the final version of the *Libro de la Cosmographia et Geographia de Affrica* bears the stamp of his stay there, quite apart from the choice of language. With so few Arabic manuscripts available in Rome and Bologna, he was cut off from sources in which to verify his citations and his facts of history and geography. Whereas in his book of biographies, he concealed his vulnerability, in the *Geogra-*

phy he confesses to it—"I haven't seen a history book for ten years"—and explains that he must rely on his "weak memory" for, say, a picture of the origins and genealogy of "Berberized Arabs," rather than being able to look it up "in the History of the Arabs by Ibn Khaldun."[57]

And indeed, his memory sometimes failed him: some facts are wrong, some citations lead nowhere. Scholars in North Africa made similar mistakes, of course; even Ibn Khaldun's *Muqaddima*, the book of introduction that opens his great history, has some unreliable references.[58] Apart from slips in memory, a scholarly system depending so heavily for authority on citation invited some play with the practices of transmission. The temptation may have been all the stronger for a faqih far from home writing in Italian.

In a sense, though, Yuhanna al-Asad wrote his book with two audiences in mind. His primary audience was in Italy. For his Italian readers, he searched for equivalents in weights, measures, coinages, foods, and material objects. For them, he sought Italian translations for words for which there was no perfect equivalent, such as *shaykh, qadi, Ramadan, khalifa, imam, qabila,* and *waqf.* For instance, *qabila,* or "tribe," came out "*populo*" (people) or "*sterpe*" (race); *khalifa,* or "caliph," came out "*Pontefece,*" that is, pope. (Surely his work with Mantino on the dictionary helped him here.) For them, he struggled valiantly to transcribe Arabic words, names, and place-names. So Ibn Khaldun, as we transcribe it today, becomes Ibnu Calden and Ibnu Chaldun; al-Buni (d. 622/1225) and his encyclopedic book on secret knowledge of divine things, *Sams al-ma'arif,* become El Boni, *Semsul meharif.* For Italian readers, too, he included only those animals "not found in Europe or that were in some ways different from those in Europe."[59]

Yet Yuhanna al-Asad also had African or at least North African readers and listeners in part of his mind as he composed. He must have imagined at least a few of them as possible readers of this Italian manuscript, and many of them as potential readers of a much-revised Arabic version. Would not a new book that included information on Mamluk Egypt on the eve of the Ottoman occupation, or the Land of the Blacks under the Songhay emperor, be of interest to educated people and rulers in the Maghreb? Much of the local detail and anecdote on religious conflict and political intrigue in the Maghreb may also have been included for their eventual benefit. (Occasionally Ramusio shortened it for the later printed edition, so as not to tire a European audience.)[60]

What were the dangers and difficulties of imagining a double audience? From the Muslim point of view, Yuhanna al-Asad was living in Dar al-Harb, the Land of War, the abode of infidels. Venice, which sustained diplomatic and commercial ties with the Ottoman empire, might be defined as Dar al-ʿAhd, the abode of treaty or covenant. Yuhanna al-Asad would have recalled the treaty that the Wattasid amir of Badis had made with the Venetians back in 913/1508 before the Spanish had seized that coastal town: the two sides affirmed a state of peace between them and promised they would not enslave each other's inhabitants or seize a compatriot for the crimes or debts of another.[61]

But Rome, Bologna, and Viterbo were certainly not in that peaceful category. Yuhanna al-Asad was living in Italy as a Christian convert, not himself at war with Italy but not wholly at peace either. Writing the *Geography*, he had to think carefully about what he should say and especially what he should *not* say, lest he offend those on whose favor he depended so long as he remained in Italy. Perhaps Yuhanna al-Asad thought back to the sharif al-Idrisi, composing his geography in Norman Sicily for the Christian king Roger, but had to admit how much easier his predecessor's situation was than his: al-Idrisi had been allowed to practice the Five Pillars of his faith and had been praised by King Roger as another Ptolemy (so Yuhanna al-Asad said in his biography).[62]

For possible North African or Muslim readers, too, Yuhanna al-Asad would have had to take precautions. At the end of part eight of the *Geography*, he announces that he wants very much to write a book about the parts of Asia and Europe he has visited, and that he has resolved that "once, with the grace of God, he had returned safe and sound from his voyage in Europe, he would arrange such a book . . . and put it together with the present work."[63] Yuhanna al-Asad had to write an Africa book that, if it fell into the hands of a Muslim dignitary who could read Italian or have it translated—say, the Ottoman ambassador to Venice—would not be too offensive. He had to write a book about Africa that would allow him one day to go back and write another.

His "voyage in Europe," "*viagio de la Europa*"—his sole reference to a trip that began with his kidnapping and more than a year in prison— is an example of Yuhanna al-Asad's strategic caution. To please Christian readers, he would have had to express his thankfulness for his seizure by pirates, which opened the path leading to his baptism; to please possible Muslim readers, he would have had to condemn that violence. Better not to mention the pirate Bobadilla at all and savor the irony of sly reference to other pirates at other times. ʿIsa ibn Hisham, the traveling narrator in al-Hamadhani's *Maqamat*, opens one of his stories of the trickster vagabond, "I was suspected on account of some property I had gotten and so I fled . . . until I came to a desert." That is all that ʿIsa ibn Hisham reveals about the occasion for his flight.[64] Yuhanna al-Asad had even more reason for circumspection.

CHAPTER FOUR

Between Africa and Europe

THE *Cosmography and Geography of Africa* is a book of description and commentary, in which its author consciously moves back and forth between Europe and Africa, between the different cultures and polities of Africa, and between Islam and Christianity. Yuhanna al-Asad offers us a few clues to interpret his double vision.

The first is early in the book. After an overview of the peoples and customs of Africa, he concludes with an account of the "virtues" and "vices" of the Africans, those living along the Mediterranean coast, those living in the nomadic communities of the deserts, and those living in the Land of the Blacks. This pro-and-con weighing is found in other Arabic geographies, but Yuhanna al-Asad goes on with an unusual reflection: "The author admits to not a little shame and confusion in . . . disclosing the vices and disgraceful qualities of Africa, having been nourished and raised there, and known as a man of purity. But it is necessary for anyone who wants to write to tell things as they are."[1]

He, Yuhanna al-Asad, must be "similar in his act of composition" to the executioner found in a story in *The Book of the Hundred Tales (nel*

libro del cento novelle). He then tells a story about taking responsibility. A man is sentenced to be whipped, and the executioner is his good
friend, who, he hopes, will have compassion for him. Instead the executioner beats him especially hard and cruelly. The beaten man cries out,
"Oh my friend, you are treating your friend very badly." The executioner answers, "My friend, have patience. I must do my duty as it ought
to be done."[2]

But having done his duty, will Yuhanna al-Asad then be thought by
readers to have the vices of the Africans and to lack their virtues? Antici-
pating such a suspicion, he tells a story that reframes the question of responsibility; it, too, he had found in the *Hundred Tales.* Once there was
a bird that could live either on land or under the water. He lived in the air
with the other birds until the king of the birds came demanding his
taxes. Immediately the bird flew to the sea and said to the fish, "You know
me. I'm always with you. That idle king of the birds has been asking me
for taxes." The fish welcomed him and he stayed with them, "comforted
and consoled," until the king of the fish came around asking for taxes.
Whereupon the bird shot out of the water, flew back to the birds, and told
them the same story. So he continued without ever paying any taxes.

> The author concludes from this that whenever a man sees his advan-
> tage, he always follows it . . . I will do like the bird . . . If the Africans
> are being vituperated, [this writer] will use as a clear excuse that he was
> not born in Africa, but in Granada. And if the Granadans are being
> railed against, he will find the excuse that he was not brought up in
> Granada.[3]

Through the sequence of the executioner's tale and the bird story,
Yuhanna al-Asad provides his readers with a key to interpret his writings: he will tell the truth about "things as they are," but in doing it, he
will not pin himself down in a fixed location. Rather as author, he will
be free to move strategically between different cultural positions.

The bird story not only is about ruse and invention but was created by ruse and invention. In the early sixteenth century, there was no

Arabic collection with the precise title of the *Hundred Tales*.[4] Yuhanna al-Asad seems to have been trying to associate his stories with Arabic translations of the famous old Persian collections of Shahrazad's stories, circulating in variant forms entitled either *A Thousand Nights* (*Alf layla*) or *A Thousand and One Nights* (*Alf layla wa-layla*). In none of these manuscripts appear tales resembling in content or tale-type either the bird story or the story of the dutiful executioner. But no matter— Europeans of Yuhanna al-Asad's day would not have known the exact title or the whole contents of the *Thousand and One Nights*, only some individual tales or motifs that, for instance, had passed from the Arabic into Latin at the hands of the remarkable Petrus Alfonsi in the early twelfth century, and then into Spanish and other European languages.[5] Yuhanna al-Asad could evoke an Arabic origin without establishing it.

At the same time the *Hundred Tales* also evoked two Italian collections. One was the hundred stories of Boccaccio's *Decamerone*, copies of which had been pouring from Italy's presses since the 1470s. Then there was a celebrated collection of Italian tales, going back in different manuscript traditions to the thirteenth century and appearing in print in Bologna in 1525, with the title *Le Ciento Novelle Antike* (The Hundred Ancient Tales). Yuhanna al-Asad would easily have heard of this book: it was drawn from a copy prepared in 1523 for Cardinal Pietro Bembo, who was in the circle of his most important patron, Cardinal Egidio da Viterbo. But neither the *Decamerone*, filled with tricksters and ruses, nor the *Ciento Novelle Antike* (or its earlier manuscript variants) has stories or tale-types similar to those of the executioner or the amphibian bird.[6]

Thus, Yuhanna al-Asad invented a source for these self-revelatory tales that, he might hope, would evoke for his readers both an Arabic origin and a popular Italian collection of stories. Then he went on to craft his own tales.

For the story of the dutiful executioner, I have not found Yuhanna al-Asad's source. In contrast to his rigorous executioner, the Arabic and the European traditions are replete with stories of a "compassionate executioner" who for one reason or another lets off the sentenced person;

and of the sentenced person who escapes punishment by disguise, shamming, or substitution.[7]

For the bird story, Yuhanna al-Asad was recasting a traditional Arabic tale. Birds who talk, rule, advise, seek, and quarrel have a strong presence in Persian and Arabic literature. They are found in the classic *Kalila and Dimna*, tales going back to India, which were translated from Persian into Arabic in the eighth century; in *The Conference of the Birds* by the early thirteenth-century Sufi poet ʿAttar, where birds seeking their king under the leadership of a hoopoe are allegories for the spiritual quest of human souls; and in some beautiful stanzas of the *Mathnawi* by Rumi, the great thirteenth-century Sufi. Perhaps there was an amphibious bird using stratagems in a thirteenth-century book called *Subtle Ruses*, but its chapter on "the ruses of animals" has been lost.[8] Perhaps, too, there was such a crafty bird flying about in stories current in the Maghreb of al-Wazzan's youth.[9]

As best I can see, Yuhanna al-Asad's source was a much-told tale recorded in the celebrated *Book of the Animals* (*Kitab al-Hayawan*) of the ninth-century Iraqi polymath al-Jahiz. There, an ostrich excuses himself from carrying a load because "I am a bird," and from flying because "I am a camel." Al-Jahiz commented, "People use this story in a proverbial manner for a person who always finds an excuse to evade an assignment."[10] The saying was passed down over the generations, and Rumi put it in one of his poems:

> Like the ostrich: when they say "Fly!" you say:
> "I am a camel, and how could a camel fly, oh Arab of Tayy?"
> When the time of burden comes, you say: "No, I am a bird.
> How could a bird carry the burden?"[11]

From such motifs, Yuhanna al-Asad composed his own tale of a creature who escapes obligation and blame by claiming different identities. He must then have been delighted to find in Italy a similar tale in a Latin translation of Aesop. Aesop was known in the Arabic tradition only as a name, some of his fables (though not the one we are about to look at) being attributed to the legendary wise man Luqman.[12] But in Italy Aesop's *Fables* were available both in a printed edition dedicated to Lorenzo de' Medici and in an illustrated manuscript owned by the Medici—that is, circulating in the network in which Yuhanna al-Asad sometimes served in the 1520s. In Aesop the tricking figure is a bat, which escapes being eaten by a weasel who hates birds by saying he is not a bird but a flying mouse; not long after, the bat escapes another weasel who hates mice, saying he is not a mouse but a bird.[13]

Through his bird story, Yuhanna al-Asad was linking himself to a wide Arabo-Islamic cluster of ideas and narratives about *hila*, that is, ruse, artifice, stratagem, "ingenious means to get oneself out of a difficult situation." Such practices were multivalent, approved in some circumstances and decried in others. *Subtle Ruses* tells of the stratagems of angels, the devil, prophets, sultans, and judges. The beloved trickster figures of the Maghreb—the clever fool Djiha and the old woman Laʿaba—use everything from good-natured guile to "satanic stratagems" to get what they want or unmask some abuse or falsity around them.[14]

The Qurʾan itself used hila-like terms—*makra* (ruse, artifice, trick), *khadaʿa* (to deceive, dupe), *kaid* (ruse, stratagem)—to refer to both the actions of unbelievers and the actions of God: "And they devised, and God / devised, and God is / the best of devisers" (3:54); "The hypocrites seek to trick God, but God / is tricking them" (4:142); "They are devising guile, / and I am devising guile" (86:15–16).[15] Yuhanna al-Asad had been considering such phrases when he worked over Egidio's Latin Qurʾan not long before he wrote down his bird story. The Latin verb that was settled on there to translate the Arabic "devising" and "tricking" was *decipere*, "to deceive, snare, beguile." When Joannes Gabriel, the initial translator, used it for these verses, Yuhanna al-Asad let the translations stand; when he turned to a milder verb, like "to arrange," Yuhanna al-Asad corrected it to "*decipere.*"[16]

In Italy, Yuhanna al-Asad had also met a cluster of ideas and tales associated with disguise, ruse, stratagem, and tricks, sometimes reproved, often applauded. Apart from Aesop and Boccaccio, he might have noticed, as he was copying the Arab translation of Saint Paul's Epistles for Alberto Pio, how that apostle referred to "guile" and craft when he wrote to the Corinthians. On the one hand (2 Cor. 11:3), Paul did not want them to be "corrupted" by bad preachers "as the serpent beguiled Eve through his subtilty": Yuhanna wrote "*makr*" for "subtilty." On the other hand (12:16), Paul claimed to have won over the Corinthians to his own view by "being crafty"—"I caught you with guile." Paul's "being crafy" was "*makir*," too, as Yuhannah al-Asad wrote it, and "with guile" was "*bi-l-hila*."[17]

Perhaps, too, Yuhanna al-Asad got a whiff of how deception was being written about in Rome in the early 1520s and by people connected to Leo X and Clement VII. Baldassare Castiglione was just then asking in his *Cortegiano* whether "a certain circumspect dissimulation" was not needed for the perfect courtier. Niccolò Machiavelli and Francesco Guicciardini were reflecting on the role of disguise, guile, and openness in political life: Machiavelli had advised the prince that depending on "the variations of fortune," he might have to break faith and go against the dictates of religion, while always seeming openly to follow them; Guicciardini was noting that deception was useful only "in rare and important cases," but that a citizen should use "as much diligence to hide [his] secret thoughts [from a tyrant] as [the tyrant] uses to discover them."[18]

Thus, the invented source of Yuhanna al-Asad's introductory stories— the *Hundred Tales*—and the ruse of his ingenious bird had resonance on both sides of the Mediterranean. With them, he was building a bridge for himself, one that he could cross in either direction. With the stories of the executioner and the amphibian, he was also advising his Italian readers that the condition for his truth-telling was that he be not too tightly classified.

Yuhanna al-Asad's second clue to his double vision comes in the midst of a long and often critical account of North African diviners and magicians and various Muslim sects. Certain men, he tells us, practice a rule called *za'iraja*, which means "cabala," a cabala residing not in writings but in nature, by which the diviners find out the secrets and future events they are asked about. The rule is very difficult, and in order not to be baffled by it, one must become a most perfect arithmetician and astrologer.

He himself had read commentaries on the rule by Jamal ad-din al-Marjani and by Ibn Khaldun. Especially he had seen za'irajat performed: one by three masters at Fez, at the Bu 'Inaniya mosque (figure 16), and another at Tunis, conducted by "a most excellent master," descendant of the famous al-Marjani himself. At Fez, concentric circles and diameters were drawn on the marble floor, and at specified places were recorded the points of the compass, the planets, the signs of the zodiac, the phases of the moon, the days and months of the year, the letters of the Arabic alphabet, Arabic numerals, and other such information. A question was asked. By a long and elaborate procedure—at Fez it lasted a whole summer's day—letters from the words in the question were separated, recombined, and replaced by specified numbers, which were matched up with certain sites on the za'iraja design. After extensive calculations, connected with the angle of the ecliptic at the moment, they were turned into letters again. The answer finally came in the distinctive Arabic metric form, al-tawil, which Yuhanna al-Asad had described in his poetry book. "And in the verse, generated in such a way, is found the true response to the question asked . . . And the divination never fails. A wondrous thing! The writer says he has never seen the like in nature."[19]

Suddenly, after expressing so much admiration for za'iraja, Yuhanna al-Asad switches his tone and backs away from it:

The author has to say it is out of laziness that he has refused to learn the said rule since he had the time and a master willing to teach him free of charge. But even more he refused because according to Muslim theologians, such a rule and science are forbidden as dishonest and almost a heresy. Their scripture says any divination of texts is vain. No one knows the future and its secrets but God alone. Sometimes their inquisitors imprison and persecute those who get mixed up with such a science.[20]

Surely Yuhanna al-Asad knew he had a good topic when he broached za'iraja. Would not Egidio da Viterbo, master of the Hebrew Cabala, and other scholars like him be interested to hear of this hermetic procedure of learned Muslims? It was one of the most complex of the Arabic occult sciences and had inspired treatises for five hundred years, including many pages in Ibn Khaldun's *Muqaddima*. Ibn Khaldun claimed to know the "secret" of the surprising poetic outcome of za'iraja: from the beginning, a verse in al-tawil meter was the model. Moreover, Ibn Khaldun went on, nothing supernatural was discovered from it: "things of the future belong to the supernatural," knowledge of which belonged to God alone. Yet Ibn Khaldun still said za'iraja was "a remarkable operation and a wondrous procedure" for finding a relation between sets of words, between question and answer. Al-Marjani recalled that when he had first taught the procedure to Ibn Khaldun, and the answer to his question—"is za'iraja an ancient or a recent science?"—came through, Ibn Khaldun had danced and twirled with delight.[21]

Yuhanna al-Asad's za'iraja story crosses the Mediterranean well and communicates something important about its author. In the bird story, Yuhanna al-Asad moves freely and strategically between different cultural polities, using ruse when needed. In the za'iraja story, he is deeply curious about difficult and surprising cultural operations; he wants to observe them and try them out, but then retires from their danger. These tales can guide us as we see how Yuhanna al-Asad—former diplomat and traveler in Dar al-Islam—describes his movement between Europe and Africa, between Christianity and Islam, and through the different regions of Africa itself.

ON NONTHEOLOGICAL MATTERS, Yuhanna al-Asad flew back and forth between Europe and North Africa with ease. Sometimes he assigned equal quality to each, finding similarities in beauty and splendor and in dirt and disorder. "Most of the Arabs [of the deserts] of Numidia are poets," he said, "ever composing lengthy songs about their battles and hunts and also about matters of love with great elegance and sweetness. Their verses are rhymed in the manner of the vernacular verses of Europe."[22]

Closer to the Mediterranean were the poems about one Hellul, a celebrated warrior from the mountainous region just north of the Rif, which had often sent its men across the Strait of Gibraltar to fight for the Granadans against the Spanish. "Hellul," says Yuhanna al-Asad, fought and died in the battle led by the Almohad caliph al-Nasir against the Spanish at the Fort of the Eagle (al-ʿUqab) in al-Andalus in 609/ 1212, where the Moors lost sixty thousand men. For the Christians, it was the start of the victories that culminated in the seizure of Granada by King Ferdinand 285 years later. Despite this disaster, insists Yuhanna al-Asad, Hellul had a permanent legacy: "in Africa and in Baetica [the old Roman name for southeastern Spain], the people have stories of his battles written in prose and verse, just as the deeds of Roland are found in the Latin vernacular."[23]

Despite a dramatic shift in the Christian/Muslim balance of power, a shift that ultimately had so influenced his life, Yuhanna al-Asad was insisting on a symmetry in European and North African poetry and popular memory. Some invention seems to have gone into the symmetry. Who was this Hellul? Hellul is Yuhanna al-Asad's transcription for the Arabic name Hilal. In his extensive history of the Berbers and Arabs of the Maghreb, Ibn Khaldun tells of Shaykh Hilal ibn Hamidan, who came from a region "distinguished by the bravery of its warriors," but his territory was located far from the Rif, and Hilal ibn Hamidan was very much alive in the years after the disaster at the Fort of the Eagle, leading his tribesmen in revolt against the caliph's brother. Other historians closer to that battle say nothing of a heroic warrior named Hilal and attribute the catastrophe to the bitterness of unpaid troops and the evil conduct and advice of the caliph's vizier.[24]

"Hilal" is, however, the name given to an epic cycle of poems associated with the invasion-migration into the Maghreb by the nomadic Arab tribe of Banu Hilal in the eleventh century: *Sirat Bani Hilal*, The Song of the Banu Hilal. Ibn Khaldun included some of the verses in his *Muqaddima*, and the poems have been recited over the centuries in the

Maghreb. ("That's Hilalian!" the reciters will exclaim today as they tell
of an action showing sure intelligence.)[25] Yuhanna al-Asad seems to
have taken a name with epic resonance in North Africa and invented a
culture hero in the war of Granada against Spain.[26]

And what of the Christian Roland, slain at Roncesvalles in 161/778
and transformed through legend and poetry into the hero of a world-
shaking battle between his uncle Charlemagne and the Saracens? "Charlemagne" was a name that Yuhanna al-Asad would have encountered
early on in al-Mas'udi's geography-history, a book he referred to in his
Geography, but he would not have seen "Roland" until he got to Italy.
There, amid calls for a new crusade against the Turks, Lodovico Ariosto's acclaimed *Orlando Furioso* had had its first two editions in 1516
and 1521, and though Ariosto's love-mad Orlando differs from the warrior Roland of the medieval romance, heroic action against the Saracens
is central to the poem. Yuhanna al-Asad could have heard about this
book and the stories behind Orlando from several people he met in
Italy—including Alberto Pio and Jacob Mantino—but perhaps most
easily from Elijah Levita, author, we recall, of his own epic poem in Yiddish of a medieval romance.[27] Out of such conversations, Yuhanna al-
Asad could conceive the dual symmetry of "Hilal" and Roland.

Pairing occurs in other connections. The hotels in Fez, Yuhanna
al-Asad reports, were very large, especially those in the vicinity of the
al-Qarawiyyin mosque, with fountains and sewage systems sufficient
for 120 rooms and more. "The like does not exist in Italy except at the
College of the Spaniards in Bologna and the Palace of St. George in
Rome." (Indeed, Rome's water problem was severe for its growing population in the 1520s; it did not become a city of fountains until after papal action in 1561 and later.)[28] Yuhanna al-Asad had to admit that some
of the Fez hostelries were the haunts of men involved in sexual mischief:

> They go about dressed as women and adorn their persons like women,
> they shave their beards and talk like women, and they spin. Each of
> these accursed hotel-dwellers takes another man as a husband, and it is

said they also use each other in the fashion of the women prostitutes in the brothels of Europe.

Sexual disorder took place on both sides of the Mediterranean.[29]

Even in narrating warfare between the Portuguese Christians and the Muslims of the Maghreb, some of it witnessed with his own eyes, Yuhanna al-Asad is relatively balanced. A boastful note does slip into his account of his fellow Granadan refugee the valiant ʿAli al-Manzari. Celebrated for his military prowess against the Spanish just before the reconquest of Granada, al-Manzari rebuilt the fortress and town of Tatouan, previously destroyed by the Portuguese, and used it as a base of operation against them around Ceuta and Tangier:

> With about 300 horsemen from Granada, highly skilled in arms and practiced in war, he scoured the countryside, taking many Christians captive. He put the Christians to work on the fortifications and treated them badly. This writer saw there more than 3000 Christian slaves, all dressed in wool sacks and sleeping in chains in the ditches. But [al-Manzari] was extremely generous to any stranger who passed through his lands.[30]

Describing the battle between the Portuguese and the troops of the sultan of Fez at al-Maʿmura, however, Yuhanna al-Asad expresses virtually no partisanship, though he must have been cheering for the Muslims at the time he fought there in 921/1515. He analyzes the military situation with the candor of Machiavelli, who was writing *The Art of War* and his *History of Florence* during Yuhanna al-Asad's years in Italy, a candor found as well in some of the best Islamic military historiography. The Portuguese lost because they were sorely outnumbered, comments Yuhanna al-Asad; this was a hard fact they should have taken more seriously. They also tried to join with Castilian troops, leading inevitably to disagreement about tactics. Here in victory, the Muslims were cruel ("the Moors are brutal people") and killed the Portuguese or let them drown rather than taking them prisoner. When the Christians won, they showed little mercy as well, enslaving, for instance, much of the population of Asila after its initial capture in the late fifteenth century.[31]

In other evaluations of North Africa and Italy, one region might come out better than the other, but the approval did not always go in the same direction. On the one hand, Yuhanna al-Asad expresses strong reservations about the table manners in the land where he grew up. Having contrasted the simple couscous meals of the people with the sumptuous repasts of the wealthy, he remarks:

> But in comparison with the nobles of Europe, the life of Africa seems vile and miserable, not because of the small quantity of food, but because of the disorderly customs. In eating, everyone sits around a low table without table linen. No one has a napkin in hand. When they have couscous or some other food, they take it together out of one pot, eating with their hands without a spoon. Soup and meat are all in one pot, and each person takes a piece of meat and, without a knife, breaks it apart with hand and teeth. They all eat at a furious pace, and have nothing to drink until their hunger is sated. Then everyone drinks a cup or bottle of water. Such is the common practice, though men of learning and quality live more politely. In short, a simple Italian gentleman lives with more refinement than any great chief or notable in Africa.[32]

Yuhanna al-Asad was describing a society that had codes about eating and drinking, both local codes and those drawn from Malikite law and ritual. Eat and drink with the right hand only, went the legal teaching. Reach for food only from the nearest part of the platter, and do not breathe on the food while doing so. Chew your food thoroughly before swallowing it. Drink in moderate sips, moving the cup away from your lips in between sips so as not to breathe on the beverage, then pass the cup to the person on your right. Do not lean on your elbow while eating. Do not enter a mosque right after eating leek, garlic, or raw onion.

Beyond these rules, there was also a literature of manners for dining together going back to al-Jahiz's mockery of gluttony and selfishness around the common pot.[33]

Even before he was kidnapped, Yuhanna al-Asad seems to have believed that these codes were not being lived up to, and that the local rules did not go far enough: his talk of the greater delicacy of North African men of letters and quality suggests as much. But his years in Italy strengthened his distaste for the Maghrebian common pot. European elites were themselves just moving away from the habits of the common pot, with the Italians especially insistent on the fork as an implement that made dining a "politer" affair. Erasmus's *On Good Manners for Boys* appeared only in 1530, but its precepts—"it is boorish to plunge your hands into sauced dishes, you should take what you want with a knife and fork"; "it is impolite to lick greasy fingers, you should wipe them with a napkin"—were already being uttered in great Italian households in earlier years. Yuhanna al-Asad had adopted the standards that he had observed at the tables of prince and cardinal.[34]

On the other hand, his account of the hospitality extended by Muslim notables, even in remote mountain settlements, suggests that in this virtue, so highly valued in Arabic lands, they surpassed Europeans. An example was the chief of a Berber community in the High Atlas, a man "of great liberality" (*grandissimo liberale*). It was to his court that the sixteen-year-old al-Hasan ibn Muhammad had repaired years before, bearing a poem and gifts from his ambassador uncle and a panegyric of his own. The meal offered the young envoy he could still remember with pleasure: the many kinds of roasted meat wrapped in a pasta resembling firm lasagne, the couscous, and other foods. Gratified by the poetry in his praise, the chief had bestowed on al-Hasan ibn Muhammad—we recall the gifts once again—eight hundred ducats, a horse, and three slaves for his uncle; fifty ducats and a horse for himself; ten ducats for each of his companions; and a promise of more. "This story is meant to show readers of the present work that in Africa there are such nobles as the chief of this mountain."[35]

Yuhanna al-Asad also describes city life in Fez, Tunis, and Cairo as dazzling: their endless markets, where (as he says of Cairo) one can find anything from rose water and cooked meat to gorgeous textiles, spices, jewels, and golden objects of great cost (*grande richezza*); their skilled artisans; their mosques and madrasas; their baths; their street fairs and entertainments; their beautiful women and well-dressed men; their learned scholars; their courts. In Fez "the fifty great mosques are well constructed and decorated with colored marble and other ornaments, each one with a beautiful fountain, made of the most beautiful marble and other stones unknown in Italy"; the gorgeous gardens of Fez, with their fountains, pavilions, and fragrant flowers and fruit trees, are like "a terrestrial paradise" (*paradiso terrestro*: his image evokes both biblical Eden and the Qurʾanic al-Janna, or garden). Never had he seen a market, "neither in Africa, nor Asia nor Italy," with so many people and things as the one on the outskirts of Fez. As for Cairo—"Cairo's fame flies everywhere, a very great and wondrous city" (*una cipta grandissima et mirabile*).[36] These towns more than matched anything he had seen in Italy.

THERE WAS ONE European wonder that Yuhanna al-Asad did not mention: the printing press. He must have heard its fruits extolled by Alberto Pio, patron of the great humanist publisher Aldo Manuzio in Venice and founder of a press in his own estates at Carpi. Surely Pope Leo X had put into the hands of his namesake Giovanni Leone some of the printed works dedicated to him: for instance, that 1516 Psalter in Latin, Greek, Hebrew, Aramaic, and Arabic; or the 1519 Latin translation of the *Theology or Mystical Philosophy according to the Egyptians*, found by its editor in an Arabic manuscript in Damascus and attributed (fancifully) to Aristotle.

Yuhanna al-Asad must also have visited printing shops: in Rome, taken, say, by Elijah Levita to see the Hebrew press of his printer not far from Egidio da Viterbo's dwelling; in Bologna, invited by Jacob Mantino to watch the reprinting of one of his translations of Averroës.

He might even have been consulted by persons hoping to develop printing in Arabic.[37]

Yet the *Book of the Cosmography and Geography of Africa* makes no mention of printing as an alternative to the scribal copying and highly wrought calligraphy so important to the Islamic world its author describes. Presumably Yuhanna al-Asad shared the religious concerns, both philosophical and visual, of other Muslim scholars and authorities that made printing in Arabic an unwelcome art in Dar al-Islam. A fault in a text loomed much larger here than in the Christian or Jewish tradition. The account of how the Qur'an had been received by the Prophet from Allah and ultimately recorded, the weight assigned to a trustworthy chain of sources for reports of the sayings and acts of the Prophet (hadith)—these traditions encouraged strong loyalty to and controversy about the authenticity and accuracy of a text. Stories bounced down the centuries about scholars who burned or poured water over their manuscripts, even manuscripts on nonreligious subjects, lest they be copied with mistakes and mislead future readers. Most scholars had their manuscripts copied, of course, but the author or someone else was supposed to read and approve each copy for accuracy before publication.

When block printing emerged centuries earlier in Muslim lands, it was never used for anything except popular amulets, talismans, and pilgrimage certificates. When printing with movable type appeared, it was rejected for Arabic: Sultan Selim confirmed its prohibition in the Ottoman empire in 921/1515, not long before al-Hasan al-Wazzan's embassy to his court, and presumably there was similar opposition in the Maghreb. The ʿulamaʾ, the religious scholars, and the myriad copyists spread through Islamic lands approved. The Jews living in Dar al-Islam were permitted to print: refugees from Spain had already set up presses in Istanbul by the opening of the sixteenth century; and in 922–28/1516–21, one Samuel and his son Isaac were printing Talmudic tractates in Fez with type brought from Lisbon. But Jews were forbidden to print in Arabic or Turkish. What was the fear? That the damage done by the spread of a faulty printed edition of a religious text would be much greater than that by a single text made by an aberrant scribe. Indeed, when a Venetian printing house brought out an Arabic Qur'an around

1537, with the dubious hope of exporting copies to the Ottoman lands, it was so riddled with errors that almost all the copies were destroyed (figure 30).[38]

Yuhanna al-Asad certainly could have heard about printing errors from Elijah Levita, who fumed about the "numerous faults" in the Istanbul edition of his Hebrew grammar book—"and no one to correct a single error." Further, he would have asked himself whether the beauty and intricacy of Arabic calligraphy—styles seeking to give visual expression to the sacred text of the Qur'an (figure 29)—could ever be reproduced on the printed page. The Jews insisted that the scrolls of the Torah must always be handwritten, but in printing other books, the printer could be thought "the performer of a holy work." As Elijah Levita pointed out, Jews used the same Hebrew word, *daphos*, for God stamping out man in his own image and the printer stamping out a book. The Muslims assigned that holy task only to the wielder of the pen.[39]

The crucial distinction for the author of the *Geography*, as we shall see, was between communities that had letters and those that had none. Books counted wherever he had come upon them. In a mountain region of the Middle Atlas, the inhabitants wrote "a beautiful script," transcribing many books, which were then sold in the bookshops at Fez. And how welcome a sight were the many manuscripts from the Maghreb being sold in the market at Timbuktu.[40]

Yuhanna al-Asad esteemed the long-established book culture of North Africa and simply stayed away from the sensitive topic of the printing press. But he surely would have asked himself whether one day the manuscripts he was going to leave behind in Italy might be printed. In that case, as he was composing the *Geography*, the Europeans whom he imagined among his readers would be unknown and anonymous, more numerous than the coterie of scholars and patrons whom he had met. And would printing increase the chances that his book might come before the eyes of Muslims? His strategies of flying back and forth would be challenged by these Mediterranean uncertainties.

CHAPTER FIVE

Conceiving Africa

"AFFRICA in the Arabic language is called Ifrichia [*Ifriqiya*]," Yuhanna al-Asad says in opening his *Geography*, and then gives two explanations of the name. The first is very unusual in the geographical and historical writing of Islam. "Affrica" (as he always spells it) comes from the Arabic *faraqa*, "to separate," "and this part of the earth is separated from Europe and from a part of Asia by the Mediterranean." The second is his version of a theory familiar in the Islamic world: Ifriqiya comes from "Ifricos, a king of Yemen," who, chased from his realm by the Assyrians, crossed the Nile with his people and settled in the region of Carthage. "That is why the Arabs consider as Africa only the region around Carthage, and the rest of Africa they call the western part [that is, Maghreb, *magrib* in Arabic means west]."[1]

Indeed, both in Arabic geographical and historical literature and in common parlance, Ifriqiya was limited to the region around Tunis and the nearby towns of Carthage, Qairouan, and Mahdia. Every once in a while scholars used the word "ʿAfariqa" to refer not to a place but to a people who lived in this area: "Gabes is the town of the ʿAfariqa," said al-Idrisi; or more fancifully, in the account of a ninth-century historian

of Egypt, "the ʿAfariqa received this name because they were the children of Fariq, son of Bayssar, who took over the land between Barqa
and Ifriqiya."[2]

The land mass that for centuries in Europe was called Africa, in expansion of the ancient Roman province by that name, was rarely identified
by a single place-name in the Arabic tradition. Consider their differing
adaptation of Ptolemy. In his *Geography*, the ancient astronomer-
cartographer (like Strabo and Pliny the Elder before him) had used the
word "Libye" to refer to what he knew of the land mass of Africa apart
from Egypt. Ptolemy's second-century Greek text was finally translated
into Latin in the early fifteenth century, and by the time it appeared in
print in the late fifteenth century, "Africa" had replaced "Libye" as the
general term: "Exposition of all of Africa," "the four maps of Africa."
So Yuhanna al-Asad would have seen it in the editions of Ptolemy published in Rome in 1508, say, or Venice in 1511 (figure 12).[3]

But he had known an Arabic version as well and refers to Ptolemy
three times in his own *Geography of Africa*. Arabic translations of
Ptolemy's *Geography* had been made already in the ninth century, and
formed the basis, for example, of *The Book of the Picture of the World*
by the mathematician al-Khwarizmi. Al-Khwarizmi's pages on Africa
gave the latitude and longitude of towns, mountains, rivers, and islands
but never referred to an inclusive land mass called "Ifriqiya" or "Lubiya" (as Libya was called in Arabic).[4]

Nor was Europe called "Europe" in most Arabic geographies. The
word "Awrufa" existed, but in the ninth century a Persian geographer
used it to include Spain, the Franks, the Slavs, the Byzantine empire, and
all of Mediterranean Africa but Egypt! More often, Europe was the
"land of the Rum," or "the Franks," or "the Christians," and described
simply by its particular kingdoms, regions, and towns. "By land from
Rome to Pisa . . . forty miles," said al-Idrisi. "Rome is one of the
columns of Christianity, the seat of a patriarchate . . . [Its] perimeter is
immense."[5]

Medieval maps show nicely the difference between the European and the Arabic ways of naming and characterizing "continents." (The word took on its geographical meaning in English and French only in the sixteenth century.) The European world maps or *mappaemundi* in their symbolic tripartite form labeled their sections Asia, Europa, and Africa; when zones and many other geographical features were added (as in a fifteenth-century map drawn in Venice), Asia, Europa, and Africa were still likely to be marked on them in large letters. Of course, Christian geographers also cared deeply about the spatial distribution of the true faith: "the red spots are cities of the Christians," wrote one mapmaker, "the black ones in truth are the cities of the infidels." But this and other descriptive divisions did not dislodge their habit of thinking of the world in terms of distinct land masses. The discoveries of the New World and then, with Magellan's circumnavigation of the globe in 1519–21, of a fourth "continent" strengthened Europe's continental imagination.[6]

Arabic world maps stressed other divisions and connections. The world map of the tenth-century Iraqi traveler Ibn Hawqal was organized around south-north and west-east axes, and prepared the way for his description of the domain of Islam: it stretched, he reminded his readers, from the Jaxartes River in the east to the Maghreb and al-Andalus in the west, about three hundred days of travel. Al-Idrisi's world map, and Ibn Khaldun's following it (figure 11), illustrated the division of the world into the seven climatic zones of the Ptolemaic tradition, which cut latitudinally across all land masses. Tangier is located on the map, as is Bornu; Venice, as is Brittany; but there are no continental labels.[7]

During his Italian years, Yuhanna al-Asad picked up the terms "Africa" and "Europe" and wedded them to Arabic geographical narratives. Here his double vision was brought into play. Writing for Italian readers, he had to take on their categories. But this adoption had implications for his thinking about and describing the lands he had visited earlier. Could he envision a unity, however tenuous, in that vast expanse of difference and even strangeness? Imagining a book he might someday revise in Arabic, would he prepare for these other readers an "Africa" with new meaning?

"ACCORDING TO our scholars and cosmographers," wrote Yuhanna al-Asad, "Africa is divided into four parts, that is, Barbary, Numidia, Libya, and the Land of the Blacks."[8] These "parts" were first of all the latitudinal climatic zones, or aqalim, used by al-Idrisi and Ibn Khaldun to organize their description, except that al-Idrisi went beyond the Mediterranean all the way north to England and Norway in the seventh *iqlim*; and Ibn Khaldun took the third *iqlim* from the Atlas Mountains beyond the Red Sea to China. Aqalim could also just mean "regions," that is, political-geographical units like "the region of Misr [Egypt]," which is what al-Muqaddasi used to depict the empire of Islam.[9] Yuhanna al-Asad organized his book both ways.

"Africa" sometimes slips or narrows under Yuhanna al-Asad's pen, as when "the Africans" become merely the ancient inhabitants—that is, the Berbers—of northwest Africa. But in a general section on "the Faith of the ancient Africans," he speaks inclusively of "*li Affricani de la Barbaria*," "*li Affricani di Numidia et Libia*," and "*li Affricani nigri*."[10]

Barbary went from the kingdom of Tunis in the east across North Africa through the Atlas Mountains to the ocean. This "is the most noble part of Africa": there are several kingdoms, existence of a kingdom being a mark of distinction in Arabic geographical writing, and many towns, and the people are "white and reasoning" (*li Homini bianchi et rationabili*). Numidia, the zone south of Barbary, extended from the oasis of Al Wahat in Egypt west to the Atlantic; it was a place of less quality (*de mino conditione*), a palm-growing region without kingdoms and with only widely dispersed towns. Libya, the next zone south, was a desert area with nomadic people and occasional settlements. The Land of the Blacks, the Bilad al-Sudan, in contrast, had three principal kingdoms and other smaller ones, some with "rich and skillful inhabitants and good governance," others living "worse than beasts." He knew from the merchants of Timbuktu something of the lands beyond the Niger River over to the Atlantic Ocean but had never seen them.[11] (He did not mention that Portuguese navigators had discovered the sea passage between the Atlantic and Indian Oceans in 893/1488, and that the next year a navigator from Arabia had independently described the Cape of Good Hope in his *First Principles and Rules of Navigation*.[12] We shall return to his silence later.)

To these four divisions of Africa, Yuhanna al-Asad adds a fifth, "the very celebrated [*famosissima*] province of Egypt." Here he is taking a position in a controversy among geographers—once he even specifies among "African scholars"—who disagreed about how much of Egypt "belonged to Africa" and about whether the Nile was the boundary between Africa and Asia. Who were these scholars? None of the major Muslim geographers show much concern about this schematic division; they see Egypt as a link to, rather than a boundary between, different parts of Dar al-Islam, and they describe the Nile as it fits into the latitudinal climates. The status of civilized Egypt had long been a question among Europeans, however, and for makers of Christian *mappaemundi* the boundary between Africa and Asia was a hot issue: was it the Nile or the Red Sea? Yuhanna al-Asad seems to be responding primarily to a European concern. He has decided to concede to Asia the east bank of the Nile over to the Red Sea. Similarly, Ethiopia belongs to Asia. On the west side of the Nile, Egypt was "of Africa."[13]

In addition to describing Africa by its regions, Yuhanna al-Asad characterizes it by its peoples. The oldest inhabitants, he writes, were the Blacks. North of the Bilad al-Sudan, the lands were uninhabited for centuries. About the Blacks' origins and ethnic structures, he admits he knows little. But their languages were diverse, as he could testify from having heard Songhay and Gobi, among others.[14]

The Berber peoples were the original "white Africans." The historians were not in agreement about where they came from: perhaps their ancestors were the Philistines of Palestine, perhaps Sabaeans of Yemen, perhaps people from farther east who had come through Greece. (Ibn Khaldun reviewed even more theories, and ended up classing most Berber tribes as descendants of the Philistines, and two of them, in-

cluding the Zanata, as originating in Yemen.) Dispersed through North
Africa and divided into "*populi*," that is, tribes and lineages, the Berbers
differed in their way of life from region to region. They had built many
of the towns of North Africa and had supplied some of its great ruling
dynasties: from the Lamtuna branch of the Sanhaja had come the Almoravids; from a branch of the Zanata, the Marinids.[15]

As for the various Berber tongues, Yuhanna al-Asad notes differences among them in pronunciation and vocabulary but still conceives
them as a common language: "the native language of Africa," called by
those who spoke it "*awwal amazig*," "the noble or foremost language,"
and by the Arabs simply "Berber" (*la lengua Barbaresca*). The Arabic
verb *barbara* meant "to babble," like the cries of animals, Yuhanna
al-Asad points out, but he does not make that judgment himself (in
contrast to earlier writers like al-Muqaddasi, who had exclaimed "in-
comprehensible"). Rather he is interested in the extent to which different Berber communities kept a "pure" speech and whether in ancient
times it had ever had a written form.[16]

Next, for Yuhanna al-Asad, were the Arab peoples, who had come
to North Africa in waves of conquest and migration from the seventh to
eleventh centuries. Divided into three important tribes and many lineages, they were scattered throughout northern Africa, their customs
differing from desert to desert, from tent to town to mountain. Most
at home as nomads ("Arabs out of the desert are like fish out of water"),
some had prosperous communities with many horses and camels, splendid tents, and bejeweled women. Those living in the regions between the
Atlas Mountains and the Mediterranean practiced agriculture; others
farther south were nomads crossing the desert to Timbuktu each year;
others yet were so poor they lived off theft and marauding. Some paid
tribute to the sultan of Fez or did military service for the sultan of Tlemcen; others refused all ties of dependence, collecting tribute from or prey-
ing upon Berber or other Arab communities. But whatever their way of
life, Yuhanna al-Asad observes, "the Arabs who dwell in Africa are called
'*Arabi Mustehgeme*' [*aʿrab mustaʿjam*], which means 'barbarizing Arabs'
[*Arabi inbarbarati*], because they came to live with a foreign people."[17]

In addition to these peoples, there were the Egyptians, or at least the Copts, descendants of the original inhabitants of the land of Misr. Discussing Egypt in a separate section of his book, Yuhanna al-Asad does not compare the antiquity of the Coptic presence in Africa to that of the Blacks, but he probably considered them contemporaries. Most Egyptians were brown in color, he says, with white-skinned people seen sometimes in the towns. Back in the tenth century, al-Muqaddasi could write that "the majority of the people of the countryside are Copts," many of them still Christian and speaking Coptic. By al-Wazzan's day, that picture had changed: much of the population had converted to Islam and "mixed with the Arabs and Africans."[18]

Finally, Yuhanna al-Asad mentions Jews in towns, villages, mountain settlements, and desert oases throughout northern Africa. Here they were merchants and traders; there goldsmiths, ironworkers, dyers, and leatherworkers; here they produced fine wines; and in a few parts of the Atlas Mountains, the men were well-armed and valiant horsemen and followed with their families the nonrabbinic, biblically based Judaism of the Karaites. In only one instance does he refer to a group of Jews of Africa as having its own distinct ethnic origin: the town of Aït Daoud, in the foothills of the High Atlas, still had many Jewish artisanal families, but "it is said that the people of this region had all been Jews of the stock of David [*de la stirpe de David*] until the Muslims acquired the area and the inhabitants passed to Islam." Elsewhere he describes the Jews of Africa rather as descendants of Berber and Black communities, even kingdoms, that had converted to the Jewish religion many centuries before. To their numbers were added Jewish immigrants, as in his own day when Jewish refugees from Spain joined the long-established community in New Fez (*Fas Jadid*). There they lived with the *dhimmi* status accorded "People of the Book" in Dar al-Islam, required to wear distinctive clothes and headdress, behave in a deferential manner, and pay a tribute or poll tax to the sultan.[19]

Amid all this diversity, Yuhanna al-Asad affirms unity: the various populations of Africa—black, white, and brown—were descended from Noah, most from his son Ham, some from his son Shem. The Blacks were descendants of Cush, son of Ham; the Copts were descendants of Mizraim, son of Cush, son of Ham; the Berbers were descendants of either Mizraim, son of Cush (the Philistine origin), or Saba, son of Raamah, son of Cush (the Yemenite origin). The ancient Jewish settlers "of the stock of David" descended from Isaac and thus back through Abraham to Shem. As for the Arabs who migrated to North Africa, he gives only a partial genealogy: two major tribes descended from Ishmael, son of Abraham, and thus ultimately from Shem, son of Noah; one tribe descended from Saba, son of Raamah, son of Cush, son of Ham. The full tree, he says to his readers, could be found in the "big volume" of Ibn Khaldun, whose details he has forgotten. And indeed, Ibn Khaldun's complex genealogy for the Arabs all led back to one or another of the sons of Ham, except for the Ishmaelite branch, which went back to Shem.[20]

Yuhanna al-Asad's quest for origins was a characteristic enterprise in the Islamic world. The Islamic genealogy did not always accord with that of the Bible—for instance, Mizraim, the son of Cush for Yuhanna al-Asad, is the brother of Cush in Genesis 10:6. Islamic scholars disagreed at least as much if not more than Christian ones in medieval Europe about which son of Noah got which lands around the world and fathered which peoples. The medieval *mappaemundi*, the simplest expression of the Christian vision, placed Shem in the frame for Asia, Ham in the frame for Africa, and Japhet in the frame for Europe. They did not clutter space with the double progenitors—Ham and Shem—of the Africa of Ibn Khaldun and Yuhanna al-Asad.

Italian readers of Yuhanna al-Asad's account would also have been struck by his silence about the curse of Noah on Canaan, son of Ham, and Noah's blessing of Shem: "Cursed be Canaan; a servant of servants shall he be unto his brethren . . . Blessed be the Lord God of Shem; and Canaan shall be his servant" (Gen. 9:25–26). Extended in Christian writing to all the offspring of Ham and eventually incorporating blackness of skin as well as servitude, this curse was more varied and also less prominent in Islamic traditions. The Qur'an does not mention it at all: the only son of Noah who goes wrong there is an unnamed unbeliever, who refuses to join his father on the arc and is drowned in the flood (11:42–43). According to the late ninth-century historian al-Tabari, Noah's curse fell on Ham and involved blackness and enslavement, but "Noah took a milder attitude toward Ham afterwards and prayed that he should be granted compassion by his brothers." Decades later the Persian abridger of al-Tabari's chronicle extended the curse to Japhet as well as Ham, both of them guilty of laughing at their father's nakedness; the people and the fruit in the lands of Ham were to be black (the origin of the dark grape), but enslavement was not part of the story. In the twelfth century, the learned al-Jawzi dismissed the malediction of blackness as "not proven and not correct." Ibn Khaldun did mention the biblical curse of enslavement falling on the descendants of Ham but drew no conclusions from it for the future of servitude. As an explanation of blackness, he found the curse ridiculous and wholly ungrounded in the Pentateuch. Color of skin, said Ibn Khaldun, was determined solely by the climate, the ʿiqlim, in which one lived.[21]

Yuhanna al-Asad was familiar with these arguments, and during his own youth the influential Egyptian scholar al-Suyuti added a hadith to them: the Prophet said that God had created Adam from earth taken from all parts of the world, and his descendants simply turned out different colors. Well into the seventeenth century and afterward, when sub-Saharan Africa became the last reservoir for Maghreb slavery, religious scholars rebuked slave-traders and owners who cited the Hamitic myth in their defense. People could be enslaved only because they were unbelievers persisting in unbelief, or as the ʿulamaʾ put it, "any unbeliever among the children of Ham or anyone else may be possessed [as a slave] if he remains attached to his original unbelief."[22]

The text of Yuhanna al-Asad gave the peoples of Africa entangled ancestry without necessary implications for matters of servitude or color.

THE AFRICAN PEOPLES DIFFERED among themselves, however,
and discussing their relations, Yuhanna al-Asad talks of social and cultural "mixture." The barbarizing Arabs had "corrupted their language
and altered their customs," he says, and it is especially language that at-
tracts his attention. Indeed, the word *a'jam*, which he uses to describe
them, means in the first instance "people speaking incorrect Arabic"
and only secondarily "barbarians" or "non-Arabs." Both Berbers and
Arabs had changed the way they talked. Those Berbers living near Arab
communities and having frequent business with them incorporated
many Arabic words into their vocabulary; some Berber tribes simply
spoke "corrupt Arabic." Meanwhile, in the centuries after the conquest,
some Arabs had settled in Berber towns,

> and they became mixed with the Africans . . . so that the Arabic tongue
> was corrupted . . . From the port towns on the Mediterranean to the
> Atlas mountains, everyone speaks corrupt Arabic, except in the king-
> dom of Marrakesh, where a true Berber language is spoken.

Farther east, in the kingdom of Nubia, the mixture (*mischia*) was of
Arabic; "Chaldean," that is Ethiopic; and "Egyptian," that is, Coptic;
while up the Nile beyond Aswan, the *"lengua misculata"* was Arabic,
Coptic, and Ethiopian.[23]

Yuhanna al-Asad's use of the word "corrupt" here was informed by
the great esteem accorded the Arabic of the Qur'an, as a sacred language and a standard for pure Arabic throughout the world of Islam.
The mathematician and historian al-Biruni (d. 442/1050)—himself born
in central Asia and a learner of Arabic rather than a native speaker—
had put it this way:

> As long as . . . the Qur'an in lucid Arabic is recited among the wor-
> shipers standing in rows behind the imam, and its refreshing message is
> preached in the mosques . . . the bond of Islam will not be broken . . .
> Branches of knowledge from all countries in the world have been trans-
> lated into the tongue of the Arabs, embellished and made seductive, and

the beauties of the language have infused the veins and arteries of the peoples of those countries . . . I am a guest in both the [Arabic and Persian] tongues . . . but I would rather be reproved in Arabic than complimented in Persian.[24]

The initial Arabic of the Hijaz (west central Arabia, where Islam got its start) had changed for those Arabs who came into contact with non-Arabs, as Yuhanna al-Asad observes. Al-Muqaddasi had long since found the Arabic spoken in Egypt "incorrect and lax." Ibn Khaldun had discussed this "corruption" at length in his *Muqaddima* and described the various sciences—grammar, lexicography, syntax, literary criticism—developed to sustain the best criteria for the language.[25] If we had Yuhanna al-Asad's lost manuscript on Arabic grammar, we would surely hear him saying more on this same theme.

Still, a mixture in language was not necessarily a literary disaster. "Vowel endings have nothing to do with eloquence," Ibn Khaldun maintained, and went on to give eloquent examples from the Arabic poetry of the Maghreb and other Bedouin communities. Of the prosperous nomadic Arabs in the deserts below Tlemcen and Tunis, Yuhanna al-Asad affirms: "They are most elegant in their verse and in their common speech, even if their language is at present corrupted . . . Some of their poets are rewarded by their leaders beyond what they would ever ask because of the grace and purity of their verse."[26] As he wrote of "corrupt" Arabic, Yuhanna al-Asad must have thought ironically of himself, mixing with foreigners and writing his own book in a "corrupt" Italian.

The other kind of mixture that Yuhanna al-Asad singles out was sexual, both across lines of religion and across lines of color. Here was a subject with an extensive history of legal commentary and, at least in regions like Spain and al-Andalus, of transgressive sexual practice and community conflict. By Islamic law, sexual intercourse outside the permitted ties of marriage or rightful slave dominion was the sin and crime of *zina'* (adultery, fornication). But Muslim men could include free Jewish women and Christian women among their permitted four

wives—that is, women who belonged to "Peoples of the Book"—and
they could have intercourse with Jewish and Christian women they
owned as slaves, though their children in all cases must be raised as
Muslims. Muslim women were required to marry within the faith, and
free Muslim women could not have sex with their slaves.[27] In contrast,
in Jewish and Christian law the sexual border was firmly closed for
everyone. Rabbinic law forbade all intercourse with or marriage to non-
Jews. Canon law and Christian authorities forbade all intercourse with
or marriage to non-Christians.[28]

These borders were frequently crossed in practice. In the medieval
crown of Aragon, Muslims were in the minority under Christian rule,
so Muslim men were unlikely to include Jewish and Christian women
among their wives, whatever the rights granted them by shari‘a. But
there were many cases of cross-religious sex, most often involving Muslim women (slaves, prostitutes, free women) with Christian or Jewish
men. Every once in a while a free Christian or Jewish woman had a
Muslim lover. These patterns of behavior persisted despite punitive actions by the authorities of all three groups, directed with special harsh-
ness against transgressive women.[29]

In the Muslim Granada of Yuhanna al-Asad's forebears and in
the Fez of his boyhood, the Muslim husband with a Jew or Christian
among his wives was a real possibility. And prohibited though it was by
both Muslim and Jewish law, Jewish men at Fez may sometimes have
visited Muslim prostitutes.[30] Interestingly enough, Yuhanna al-Asad's
one affirmation about sex across the prohibited religious boundary concerns the unusual case: Jewish women and Muslim men. He describes
the introduction and spread of syphilis in North Africa, called "the
French disease" in the Maghreb just as it was in Italy. He could be sure
of interest in the subject among his Italian readers, for the dreadful pus-
tules and excruciating pains of syphilis had first appeared in connection
with the French king's military campaign to conquer Naples in 1495–96.
By the time he was writing, the disease had touched every rank of Italian society, including the cardinals; papal physicians and other Italians
had composed treatises arguing about the origin and character of the

"*Morbus Gallicus*," and Leo X had refounded the hospital of San Gia-como in Rome in 1515 especially for those suffering from syphilis.[31]

As for North Africa, Yuhanna al-Asad remarks, there was no sign of the "French disease" until

> Don Fernando, King of Spain, chased the Jews from Spain. Many of the Jews who came to Barbary . . . carried the disease from Spain. Some un-happy Moors mixed with the Jewish women, and so little by little, within ten years, one could not find a family untouched by the disease. At first, the disease was judged to be leprosy, and those infected were chased [from their houses] and forced to live with the lepers. Then, as the number of infected increased every day, it was discovered that many people in Spain had the ailment. So the people who had been chased from their houses returned to them.

Barbary had been much affected, Yuhanna al-Asad goes on, especially in the cities and along the coast; and much damage had been done in the kingdoms of Tunis and Egypt. The countryside and the Atlas Moun-tains had not suffered, however; neither had the nomadic Arabs or the peoples of the deserts and the Land of the Blacks. Indeed, to be cured, it was enough for an infected person to go and breathe the air in Nu-midia or the Land of the Blacks.[32]

An account of the expulsion from Spain written by a Jewish scholar, Abraham Adrutiel, who was eleven in 1493 when his family took refuge in Fez, suggests that Yuhanna al-Asad's "mixture" of Moorish men and Jewish women was in fact rape: rape by Portuguese Christians and by Arabs as the suffering refugees were on their way to Fez. The disease Rab Abraham recalled was "plague," surfacing only after the Jews were installed in difficult circumstances in the Jewish quarter of New Fez. A contemporary Castilian account, based on reports from Jews so badly treated on arriving in North Africa that they had returned to Spain and asked for baptism, tells a similar story.[33] Yuhanna al-Asad was perhaps reworking these events, but more likely he was remembering a separate episode a few years later.

Whatever the case, scholars today see both refugee Muslims and refugee Jews as bringing epidemic and syphilis from the Iberian peninsula into Morocco in the late fifteenth century and early sixteenth century.[34] Yuhanna al-Asad makes only the Jews the initial carriers of syphilis. This takes the onus off his fellow Granadans, but more important, his story is marked by troubling inversions. Muslim men are having intercourse with Jewish women; civilized cities are more dangerous than mountains and deserts; the lands of the "noble whites" are less healthy than the Land of the Blacks. People with the new disease are forced into a suburb of Fez, crowded with lepers and people with other incurable diseases. But then, as the story ends, the tension is released. It turns out that it is a Spanish disease, not just a Jewish disease.

Here Yuhanna al-Asad's account diverges from that of Sigismondo de' Conti, historian and poet in the papal service of Alexander VI and Julius II, who had claimed that syphilis—which he identified with leprosy—had been introduced into Naples not by the French but exclusively by Jews driven out of Spain. Leprosy, he said, was an ancient sign of Jewish incontinence.[35] For Yuhanna al-Asad, syphilis is a new disease, not a form of leprosy; everyone can go home from quarantine and live with the damage.

Sex across the color line Yuhanna al-Asad describes without censure or signs of anxiety. Miscegenation in one case was due simply to geographical proximity: "the inhabitants [of the town of Aswan] are almost all brown because they mixed [sonno mesculati] with those of Nubia and Ethiopia."[36]

In a few instances, slaves of color are central to his story. As we have seen, the male Muslim slave owner was entitled to have sexual intercourse with any of his slave women; children born from that intimacy were to be fully under his control. If the slave owner formally recognized himself as father of the children, they would become free and be included among his heirs; the slave mother would then have a special legal status and must be manumitted at the owner's death. In addition, slaves themselves—both men and women—could marry with permission of their owner; indeed, owners could marry their slaves off at their own initiative.[37]

These features of Islamic law provide a frame for the progeny of color that Yuhanna al-Asad reports from his travels. South of the Atlas Mountains, in the desert region bordering the Draʿa River,

> the women are beautiful and fat and agreeable, and there are a large number of prostitutes. The people there have many black slaves, men and women, whom they marry to each other. The owners keep the fathers and the children in their service. Because of such mixture [*misculatione*], most of the people are either black or brown, and few are white.[38]

Of the oasis town of Warjala, well supplied with artisans and merchants plying the trade between Barbary and the Land of the Blacks, he says:

> The inhabitants are for the most part black, not because of the climate of the place [referring to the old theory, supported by Ibn Khaldun, that skin color derived from the climate], but because they have many black slaves and make children with them. About a fifth of the people are white, and all the rest are black and brown. The people are generous and agreeable and give a good welcome to strangers.[39]

Evidently, the sexual mixture did not ruin their temperament and conduct.

 For Yuhanna al-Asad the important thing about how people looked was not the long-term action of climate but current social practices and customs. As he used his various renderings of the Italian *mescolanza* or *mescolata*, he seems to have been seeking an equivalent of the positive Arabic word *mizaj*, "mixture, blend, medley, disposition," rather than of the stronger and sometimes pejorative *khalit*, where mixing could slip into promiscuity, confusion, disorderly muddle, and madness.[40] (*Takhlit*, we recall, was the word used by the zealous al-Maghili in denouncing as impure the persistence of pre-Islamic rites with those of Islam.) For Yuhanna al-Asad, even when mixing brought "corrupt"

speech or painful disease, it did not destroy good poetry or the possibility of people sometimes managing to live in peace in their adjacent
neighborhoods.

HOW THEN does Yuhanna al-Asad judge the different regions of Africa?
He opens his book calling Barbary, his own region, the "most noble part
of Africa . . . the people white and reasoning," and this makes us anticipate a highly partisan tale. Yet he promises his readers "to tell things as
they are," and this means describing both virtues and vices everywhere,
including close to home.

Such balance was found in earlier Islamic literature of geography
and travel. Al-Muqaddasi told how one day in Basra a gathering of
learned men was debating which town in their world was "the most sublime." "My own native town," he said, and went on to describe the
beauty, abundance, and excellence of his Jerusalem. But after delighting
the company, who "agreed to the truth of it," al-Muqaddasi went on to
list for his readers the "disadvantages" of Jerusalem—its filthy baths,
high-priced food, and disregard of men of letters.[41]

Through his bird story Yuhanna al-Asad claims that his double origin should make it easier for him to be detached and frank. In fact, he
has a hierarchy of values, but traits that he approves or dislikes win
praise or blame wherever he notices them across Africa. Like Ibn Khaldun, he prefers great cities, as in the marvels of Fez, Tunis, and Cairo.
But cities also had their "vices," sexual excess calling forth especially
strong denunciation. In Tunis, the inhabitants took hashish (el hasis),
an ounce of which led to sudden cheerfulness, enormous appetite, and
miraculous coupling.[42] In Cairo excess in language and conduct took
place within families: the father asked the son how many times he had
had intercourse with his wife the past night; the son asked his mother
the same question about his father; the mother lamented to the son
about the lack of sexual stamina in her husband and took her com-
plaint before the judges.[43] By Sunni schools of law prevalent in North
Africa (Malikite in the Maghreb and the Malikite and Ḥanabalite in

Cairo), wives were allowed to demand adequate sexual intercourse with their husbands. Such cases may well have come before the courts—and sex was always a subject of delicious gossip in Cairo, promptly reported in the journal of Ibn Iyas, along with the political and ceremonial events that we heard about earlier. Al-Wazzan, educated in the law and with some practical experience as a judge, may have talked to a qadi in Cairo or even witnessed a judgment. Perhaps, too, he was reminded of the scene in al-Hamadhani's *Maqamat* where the vagabond trickster-poet Abu-l-Fath, for once on the defensive, has been called before a judge by his two wives, one of whom accuses him of inadequate sexual performance.[44]

Throughout all the regions of Africa were places, even quite small ones, that Yuhanna al-Asad praises. The little town of Tagodast, high in the Atlas Mountains, had busy farmers growing fruits, grapes, and olives; numerous artisans; traders selling their wool, leather, and other products in Fez, Meknes, and desert towns; beautiful women bedecked with silver jewelry; and prayer leaders and judges providing good governance. Aït Daoud, another mountain town a little farther south, was filled not just with Jewish artisans—shoemakers, metalworkers, dyers, and goldsmiths—but also with Muslim men learned in the law. Yuhanna al-Asad recalls discussing points of the law with these faqihs late into the night.[45] At Figuig, an oasis settlement with date groves in the Numidian desert, the women wove woolen cloth so fine that it looked like silk, bringing a high price at markets throughout the Maghreb; the men were "very clever" (*de grande inguenio*), some of them merchants trading with the Land of the Blacks, others studying in Fez and returning to the desert as prayer leaders and preachers.[46] In the Land of the Blacks, the large rural town of Mali was a royal center, with some six thousand households and many preachers and learned men teaching in the temples. Its grains, meats, and cotton were abundant; its merchants respected; its inhabitants rich from trade with Jenne and Timbuktu.[47]

Yuhanna al-Asad applauds a cluster of traits: economic energy and prosperity; pleasant appearance; some literate culture; order and rule brought by judges, prayer leaders, and preachers. Places with not even one of these qualities he disdains. "Without reason, without rule," he sometimes writes, meaning without connection with books, without preachers, formal prayer leaders, and judges. The hamlets on Dadès Mountain in the High Atlas please him least of any place he saw in all of Africa. The people were badly dressed, the women were ugly and worked like donkeys; their dwellings were filthy and stank of goats; the men were indolent, violent, treacherous, and quarrelsome, setting on travelers and holding up merchants; there were, of course, no judges or religious leaders. Other mountain settlements in the Maghreb and in Gaoga in the Land of the Blacks called forth such sentiments as well.[48]

One of the traits that Yuhanna al-Asad finds hardest to forgive is lack of hospitality. Avaricious, disagreeable, and suspicious inhabitants broke essential rules of communication and trust among people from different parts of Africa. Thus, the town of Tebessa, an ancient Roman settlement in the kingdom of Tunisia, had been rightly scorned by the traveling poet al-Dabbag: only its walnut trees, walls, and clear river water were of any interest; the town dwellers had no more virtue than pigs.[49]

In contrast, the presence of hospitality could make up somewhat for other shortcomings. A description of Berber nomads in the Sahara, rather ill dressed and ill fed and "without reason," shifts mood when the tribal chief of the Sanhaja insists that al-Wazzan and members of his caravan come to his encampment and be his guests for two days of banqueting and courteous honor. Plentiful meats, well seasoned with spices from the Land of the Blacks, and delicious bread and dates were offered round. The chief explains agreeably through his interpreter that no grain grew in the region but that he imported it just so that he could offer bread to strangers and eat bread at Ramadan and the Feast of the Sacrifice.[50]

Similarly, the presence of poetry could compensate in part for the lack of book learning in a community, even if it could not guarantee peacefulness among its warriors.[51]

WHAT ROLE DID color play in these judgments about "Africa"? Islamic traditions offered three different ways of conceptualizing that matter. The first drew on the seven aqalim. "Climates" could be used not only to define latitudinal regions on a map and to account for skin color, as we have seen, but also, with much influence from Greek humoral thought, to explain physical appearance, temperament, customs, and government. The temperate zones, which included the Maghreb, Syria, and Spain among other places, were the best. The kinky-haired Blacks in the hot first zone and the pasty white Slavs and Germanic peoples in the cold seventh zone were the worst. Ibn Khaldun had summed up the position in regard to the first zone:

> Negroes are in general characterized by levity, excitability, and great emotionalism. They are found eager to dance whenever they hear a melody. The real reason for these [opinions] is that . . . joy and gladness are due to expansion and diffusion of the animal spirit . . . Heat expands and rarefies air and vapors and increases their quantity . . . Now, Negroes live in the hot zone. . . . As a result, they are more quickly moved to joy and gladness, and they are merrier. Excitability is the direct consequence.

Variation could occur within zones, especially as the peoples lived closer to the temperate range; and change was possible, too, as shown in the emergence of, say, the Mali dynasty. But farther south, "there is no civilization in the proper sense." Using standard images going back centuries in Arabic literature, Ibn Khaldun described these peoples as living more like animals than humans, dwelling unsocially in caves and thickets, eating uncooked food, and even eating each other.[52]

A second tradition either discounted all differences of appearance or status among peoples in the name of the supreme value of piety, or else gave positive appreciation to traits found among the Blacks. The Qur'an told of God's welcome to all "tongues and hues" (30:22). Allah was concerned not about attributes of belonging but about devotion:

O mankind, We have created you
male and female, and appointed you
races and tribes, that you may know
one another. Surely the noblest
among you in the sight of God is
the most godfearing of you. (49:13)[53]

"God enjoins you to look after the people with black skin and with kinky hair," the Prophet had said to Muslims in an oft-cited hadith, "for among them are your parents and relatives"—"parents," that is, because Hagar, mother of Isma'il and ancestor of the Prophet, was among them, and "relatives" because the Messenger of God had an Egyptian concubine. Another version concluded, "for among them are three lords of the people of Paradise," that is, the black sage Luqman and two notable Ethiopians who had given early assent to Islam. A tenth-century Andalusian scholar extended the inversion of status much farther: "God has decreed that the most devout is the noblest even if he be the bastard of a Negro woman."[54]

Meanwhile even earlier al-Jahiz, whose writings on animals and table manners we have already heard about, had turned the world upside down against the pretensions of some Persians in his witty *Boasts of the Blacks over the Whites*. Of the Zanj people of eastern Africa, the stereotypical ugly and uncivilized Blacks in al-Mas'udi and others, al-Jahiz said, "There is no people on earth in whom generosity is so universally well developed." He praised their talent for dancing and added singing and especially eloquent language to their achievements. They were strong and courageous, and their good temper was not a consequence of hot lightness but "a sign of noble character."[55]

The third tradition available emerged from first-hand reports given to geographers and historians by Muslim visitors to the sub-Saharan regions and from travelers, like Ibn Battuta, who wrote their own accounts. Though this literature presented the Sudan in part through the filters of low/high, it also gave varied details on appearances, behaviors, institutions, and activities, which were often indifferent to or at variance with these hierarchical categories. For example, Ibn Khaldun's historical description of the kingdom of Mali under the just rule of Mansa Musa, "an upright man and a great king," was totally at odds with the light-headed excitability of the Blacks of the first climate alleged in his *Muqaddima*. His fresh and detailed picture was taken from conversations with people who had been on the spot—a faqih, a qadi, a warrior—whom he named.[56]

Yuhanna al-Asad uses all three approaches in his *Geography*.[57] Negative images of the Blacks appear early in the book—though without seeking explicit support from the climate theory—as he lists the "vices" of all the peoples of Africa:

> The inhabitants of the Land of the Blacks . . . lack reason . . . and are without wits and practical sense. They are ill-informed about everything, and live like animals without law or rule. There are many prostitutes and cuckolded husbands among them. [Yuhanna al-Asad gives similar vices to rural and mountainous people of Barbary and to the inhabitants of Numidia and Libya, calling them "bestial" and "ignorant."] The exception is in the great cities, where there is a little more rationality and human sentiment.[58]

Similarly, in his brief reconstitution of the early history of the Bilad al-Sudan at the opening of part seven, he uses the old commonplaces. "According to African cosmographers," the peoples in the Land of the Blacks once "had lived like beasts, having no king or rulers or republic and no civility. They had scarcely known how to sow grain." They had no individual wives, but rather, after working the soil and herding their animals all day, had slept together on animal skins in a hut in groups of ten or twelve. Some of these peoples had worshiped the sun and bowed before it every morning. Others, such as the people of Walata, had worshiped fire. In the eastern end of the Land of the Blacks had been Christians, like those of Ethiopia.[59]

In editing these words for publication years later, Ramusio much intensified the uncivilized qualities of the Blacks by putting this paragraph in the present tense, and the French and Latin translators then did the same.[60] Only in one instance in his manuscript does Yuhanna al-Asad claim that a specific community of Blacks was living in such a fashion in his own day—the dreadful mountain-dwellers of Bornu—and these were people he had not seen himself:

> They go about naked in the summer except for a leather cloth over their shameful parts; in winter they cover themselves with sheepskin, which they also sleep on. They are people with no Faith, neither Christian, Jewish, nor Muslim, and in this way are like animals. They have wives in common, the women work like the men, and they live all together as if they were a single family . . . From what the present writer has heard from a merchant who knew the language of these mountain people and conversed with them, they do not even give people a personal name . . . but just call them by some quality . . . like Tall . . . or Short.[61]

Along with this image of uncivilized living are Yuhanna al-Asad's expressions of disdain for the features of some inhabitants of sub-Saharan lands: "the people of Zamfara are tall, but are very black, with broad faces like brutes"; in Katsina, "the population is very black, the people have noses and lips much too large."[62] Here he is following old expressions of color prejudice found among Berbers and Arabs, though by the time he was writing those words a more appreciative view of Black appearance had long since emerged in the travel literature and elsewhere. It was still associated with inversion of status, for the beauty praised was often that of enslaved women or eunuchs. Thus, Ibn Battuta described the slave women of Takkada (Azelik), far to the east of Gao in present-day Niger, as "beautiful" and tried to buy one for himself. But he also found "handsome" a well-dressed youth in the royal town of Mali: the chain on his foot was a sign not of enslavement but of his determination to learn the Qur'an by heart.[63]

Yuhanna al-Asad regularly comments on the appearance of Berber and Arab women in different locations, their beauty or ugliness. We have also just heard him saying that the women of the Dra'a region, where there was much "mixture" between Berber and Black, were "beautiful and fat and agreeable." About the look of the women in the Land of the Blacks itself, however, he says little. He notes that in Timbuktu free women veiled their faces while slave women went uncovered, but that was a rare observation. Nor does he comment on the appearance of the Black slave women whom he had bought at a market for the Sa'diyan sharif years before, though beauty was always a consideration in the purchase of females available for their owner's pleasure and perhaps for carrying his children and winning a special status.[64]

Whatever the sources of his reserve, color is not the determining factor in Yuhanna al-Asad's final assessment of the Sudan. Remembering Abu Bakr, a judge serving the Songhay emperor, Yuhanna al-Asad remarks, "He was very black, but a man of great worth, wise and just."[65] As he gave the vices of all the regions of Africa early in his manuscript, so he gave their virtues:

> The inhabitants of the Land of the Blacks are people of integrity and good faith. They treat strangers with great kindness, and they please themselves all the time with merry dancing and feasting. They are without any malice, and they do great honor to all learned men and all religious men. They have the best time of any of the Africans and peoples whom the present writer has seen in the world.[66]

Here, as in al-Jahiz's *Boasts of the Blacks*, Yuhanna al-Asad either insists on certain favorable qualities or else puts a positive twist on traits, like the pleasure of dancing, that Ibn Khaldun took as evidence of excitability.

He reports other things he liked in his travels in the Land of the Blacks, especially from the towns or courts where he spent time and was able to communicate in Arabic or through a translator. We have already heard him celebrate the wealth, trade, and learning of the town of Mali. The "big village" of Jenne had abundant produce for trade from the surrounding countryside and well-dressed and well-mannered (*civili*) inhabitants, including merchants, preachers, and scholars. Timbuktu was possessed of a fine mosque and palace rich in gold, busy artisans and merchants selling goods from all over the world, prosperous citizens enjoying musical instruments and dance, and a sultan with a finely ordered court. Scholars, preachers, and judges were numerous and honored. Manuscript-sellers earned more than any other trader in Timbuktu. Even while describing the inhabitants of the poor Songhay villages northwest of Timbuktu as "very black and dirty [vili]," Yuhanna adds, "but they are quite agreeable, especially to strangers."[67]

Blackness, then, did not stand in the way of creating and sustaining great towns, a vigorous economy, religious and legal learning, and hospitality. Nor did Yuhanna al-Asad visualize slavery as a state for which only Blacks were suitable. Shariʿa taught him, as we have seen, that any nonbeliever captured in legitimate circumstances could be enslaved. Christians and Jews—Peoples of the Book—living in Dar al-Islam and paying special taxes there as "protected people" could not be enslaved, but seized outside its borders, they could.[68] Yuhanna al-Asad described white Christian slaves in considerable number in Maghreb towns, including men serving as bodyguards and soldiers and women serving in the harem, along with slaves of color, at the courts of Fez, Tlemcen, and Tunis.[69] And, of course, he knew of the light-skinned military-political slaves (the janissaries) in Mamluk Egypt and in the Ottoman empire, non-Muslim at the time of their enslavement and then converted afterward. As he says of Egypt to his Italian readers:

> The Mamluks are Christians from the province of Circassia above the Black Sea. There the Tartars are accustomed to sail and steal little boys and men, take them to Cafa, and sell them to merchants, who then bring them to Cairo. The sultan buys them and immediately makes them repudiate [their faith]. They learn to read and write Arabic and to speak Turkish, and little by little they rise in grade and dignity.[70]

Religion is the element that Yuhanna al-Asad thinks necessary, if not sufficient, for a society to live with "reason," "rule," and "civility."

Preferably the religion would be Islam, but if not, at least a religion that Islam recognized as having a divinely revealed scripture and prophet. The worst thing about the mountain people in Bornu was that they had "no faith, neither Christian, Jewish, nor Muslim." And the Blacks were transformed from their early condition of "living like beasts" by conversion. The process began, he says, with trade and exchange between desert Berbers and Blacks. After the veil-wearing, ascetic Almoravids consolidated political power and religious reform in the Maghreb in the eleventh century, they turned their attention to the Land of the Blacks. (Yuhanna al-Asad assigns the initiative to the remarkable ruler Yusuf ibn Tashfin, while al-Bakri, writing during Yusuf's lifetime, dated the start of conversion somewhat earlier and with other leaders.) Preachers came down, Yuhanna al-Asad goes on, and "a large part of the Blacks became Muslims and began to learn the laws and civility and the necessary arts." Traders from Barbary followed, and commerce developed between the Maghreb and the Land of the Blacks. Having said of the people of Mali, "they are the most civilized and clever [*civili e ingeniosi*] in all the regions of the Blacks," Yuhanna al-Asad adds, "they were the first to become Muslims."[71] Civilization and Islam went together.

YUHANNA AL-ASAD TOOK the term "Africa" from his European conversations and reading and used it to conceive a geographical unit differently from his Islamic and Arabic forebears. Al-Bakri's description of the Maghreb and the Land of the Blacks was part of a much wider *Book of Routes and Realms*; that of Ibn Khaldun, part of a multivolumed *Book of Examples*. In a manuscript limited expressly to the land mass of Africa, Yuhanna al-Asad had to think about what gave his subject coherence. He did use the aqalim to help organize his literary exposition, but these zones did not cut up his Africa with strong doses of climatic humoral theory. The "vices" and "virtues" of his introductory section were distributed through all the regions he knew; flourishing communities and those "without reason" were found everywhere, from the north of the Whites to the south of the Blacks.

In its variety of languages and peoples, his Africa was held together by trade relations; political relations, including warfare, domination, and the exaction of tribute; and the movement and mixture, including linguistic and sexual mixture, of peoples. Perhaps as a son in an émigré family that seems to have had weak connections with any Berber or Arab tribe, he found it easier to seek these cross-regional ties. In any case, al-Hasan ibn Muhammad al-Wazzan had traveled through several of the different worlds of this Africa, and Yuhanna al-Asad united them in his imagination and writing by several means: by his activities, skills, and eloquence as diplomat and occasional trader; by his entering into the institutions and patterns of hospitality found almost everywhere; by his love of poetry, which could be indulged in the diverse Arabic-speaking regions; and perhaps, too, by sexual encounters.

Most important in providing unity was the embrace of Islam, which was found in almost every region that he visited in Africa, even if sometimes ill practiced by his lights. In this sense, his *Book of the Cosmography and Geography of Africa* fulfilled for him a classic goal of the Muslim vocation of travel: the understanding of the meaning of Islam. Writing in his Christian clothes from Dar al-Harb, he may have found it easier to get this broad perspective.

The Africa that he presented to Europeans in his manuscript of 1526 was different from the one they had inherited from ancient and medieval writing. For them, it had long been "the third part of the world." The areas known were especially Egypt, Ethiopia, and the North African towns as they had been described centuries before by Strabo and Pliny the Elder. Christian traders, soldiers, and ex-captives could now add detail about North Africa, and Portuguese seamen about the coastal regions of west Africa, but Joannes Boemus in 1520 was still citing Herodotus in the Africa chapter of his book on the customs of all peoples; his Egyptians were worshiping cats, crocodiles, and other animals, and west of Egypt lived Troglodytes and Amazons. Apart from Egypt, Africa was a continent of extremes in the European imagination: arid and sterile on the one hand, fecund and teeming on the other. The diversity of its animals was "marvelous," its human populations animal-like in their languages, and in their ways of life violent, nomadic, and uncivilized. As the old saying went, already an adage among the ancient Greeks and still alive in Europe, "Africa always brings us something new, never before seen." And the new things might well be beyond nature, troubling surprises, like the bizarre hybrids born, according to Pliny, because the female animals in Africa coupled with males of all species.[72]

This marvelous, monstruous, unceasingly novel Africa was brought down to earth by Yuhanna al-Asad's towns, villages, mountains, and sands, his dynasties and tribes, his violent wars, and the clicking looms and pounding hammers of his everyday lives.

ONE PIECE OF NEWS about Africa Yuhanna al-Asad might have found important, yet it is strangely absent from his *Geography*: the existence of the cape at the south of the African land mass, which was rounded by the Portuguese in 1488 and independently described by the Indian Ocean navigator Ibn Majid in a manuscript of 895/1489–90. Al-Wazzan knew and mentioned the Portuguese presence off the Guinea Coast and could easily have heard of their further discovery in diplomatic circles, especially in Cairo, where Portuguese navigation in the Indian Ocean was a hot issue. The map presented by the seasoned Turkish admiral Piri Reis to Sultan Selim in Cairo in 923/1517—when al-Wazzan was in the city—showed Portuguese ships sailing toward the Cape; Piri Reis had learned much about their voyages from Portuguese seamen themselves. Once in Italy, al-Wazzan would have found that the Cape of Good Hope was well known. A 1525 edition of Ptolemy's *Geography*, published in Strasbourg, still had the traditional headless humans drawn on the maps of Africa, but one map had added the Cape of Good Hope and various towns around the coast.[73]

Yuhanna al-Asad may have been silent here because he was relatively indifferent to coastlines except insofar as they might harbor pirates: he was not thinking as a navigator who needed a chart with every cove and headland. His geographic eye fell on interior land spaces and their inhabitants and on distances by land.[74] But as with the printing press, his silence also may have been strategic. The Portuguese seizures along the Moroccan coast, fraught with Christian hopes, were central to his story—and we have seen the prudent balance he used in describing them and the Moroccan resistance to them. But the faraway tip of Africa could be left in the shadows, giving credit neither to Portuguese Christian nor to Arab Muslim navigators. Silence was a way of keeping Africa and its expanses his, belonging to Muslims and African populations rather than to the Christians of Europe.

CHAPTER SIX

Between Islam and Christianity

THERE IS a difficult displacement in Yuhanna al-Asad's *Book of the Cosmography and Geography of Africa*, a back and forth between his identity as a Muslim and his identity as a Christian convert. Here we can see the tension within himself and with his imagined readers, Christian and Muslim, at its strongest. His literary device of hila, his use of "ingenious means to get himself out of a difficult situation," was a complex one. He wrote about the two religions in a relatively impartial way, itself an unusual move at the time. He also created a text that had some Muslim markings and showed appreciation for Islam but did not give full expression to Islamic belief and rhetoric and left space for other perspectives.

"They have no faith, neither Christian, Jewish, nor Muslim," Yuhanna al-Asad writes in condemning the mountain people of Bornu. In extending respect to the three scriptural religions, he could draw support from verses of the Qur'an: "Surely they that believe, and those of Jewry, / and the Sabaeans, and those Christians, / whosoever believes in God and the Last Day, and works righteousness— / no fear shall be on them"(5:69). His later Italian editor and French and English translators did not tamper with this passage, for he was contrasting these religions with paganism, not with each other.[1]

But Yuhanna al-Asad also takes a nonpartisan tone in his general account of Jews, Christians, and Muslims in the early religious history of Africa. First there was a period in which the peoples of Barbary, Numidia, Libya, and the Land of the Blacks were idolaters, "following their fantasy and without guidance from a Prophet." After a time,

> some of them became Jews and remained so for a long period, while certain kingdoms among the Blacks became Christian [and stayed so] until the coming of the sect of Muhammad. In the year 268 of the Hijra, the people of Libya became Muslim by means of certain preachers. This led the people of Libya to fighting many battles with the Blacks, with the result that the kingdoms of the Blacks bordering Libya became Muslim. At present there are still some kingdoms where there are Christians, but the [kingdoms] of the Jews were destroyed by the Christians and the Muslims . . .
>
> As for the people of Barbary, they remained idolaters for a long time, until 250 years before the birth of Muhammad. Then all of the people of the Barbary coast became Christian. The region of Tunis and Tripoli was dominated by certain lords from Apulia and Sicily, while the coast of Caesaria and Mauritania was dominated by Goths. Many Christian lords from Italy fled from the Goths, came to Carthage, and established dominion there. The Barbary Christians did not hold to the observances or order of the Roman Christians, but to the rule and faith of the Arians. Among them was Saint Augustine.
>
> When the Arabs arrived to take over Barbary, they found the Christian lords there. They fought many wars, the Arabs were the victors, the Arians returned to Italy and Spain. About 10 years [a scribal error for what must have been 200] after the death of Muhammad, almost all of Barbary became Muslim.[2]

Yuhanna al-Asad goes on to mention Berber rebellions against the Arab caliphs and the warriors sent by the latter to suppress them.

"Schismatic" Muslims arrived from the east (the Kharijites, who were opponents of the caliphate), but, he seems to suggest, they actually helped spread the knowledge of Islam. (His hint here fits with what present-day scholars say about the Kharijites not only as leaders of Berber revolts in the eighth century but also as educators of Berber tribes beyond the reach of Sunni scholars.) "Then the faith of Muhammad became firm in Barbary, though many heresies and differences lay ahead."[3]

If Yuhanna al-Asad's brief account of the spread of Islam roughly follows that of his fellow Africans, his story of the coming of Christianity to North Africa is not what he would have heard from, say, Egidio da Viterbo: his godfather would have assured him that the true faith spread among the inhabitants of Roman Africa well before the fourth century and before the arrival of Gothic mercenaries and Vandals.[4] But no matter. Our interest here is in the tone of his story, not in the fullness of his knowledge. Yuhanna al-Asad was evenhanded when it came to the religions of Peoples of the Book.

Some of his Christian translators found this balance intolerable, and in their versions put extragavant anti-Islamic words into his mouth. Interestingly enough, Ramusio changed the substance and tone of the text here rather little, preferring only to add the more theologically demanding phrase "faith of Christ" where Yuhanna al-Asad had used only the descriptive "Christian."[5] But this was not strong enough for the French translator of Ramusio's edition, Jean Temporal, a Lyon publisher with a burgeoning interest in Protestant reform. For Temporal, the Black kingdoms remained Christian

> until the damnable Mohammedan sect began to spread in the year 268 of the Hijra. Then disciples of Muhammad came to preach in these parts and by deceptive words and false exhortations drew the hearts of the Africans to their false and Satanic law.

Finally, the Barbary coast became "infected."[6] The Latin translation by John Florian in 1556 and the English translation by John Pory in 1600 followed the same practice: "certain of Mahomet's disciples so be-witched [the Africans]," wrote Pory, "that they allowed their weake minds to consent."[7]

Christian audiences, reading about Islam, would not have taken eas-ily to Yuhanna al-Asad's balance. More acceptable was the virulence ex-pressed by a convert from the kingdom of Valencia, son of the learned legist 'Abdallah and himself a faqih. Baptized a Christian as Juan An-drés in 892/1487, he went on "with the help of God, [to] convert many souls among the infidel Moors," including in Granada: he was probably preaching there just as the al-Wazzan family departed. Now that he was no longer "a slave of Lucifer," he wrote a book published in 1515 to ex-pose the "fabulous fictions, frauds, deceits, bestialities, madness . . . lies and contradictions . . . of the Mohammedan sect."[8]

Yuhanna al-Asad relieved himself of the awkwardness of evaluating his own conversion by simply not mentioning it directly in his *Geogra-phy*, just as he had not mentioned his seizure by Christian pirates. The only explicit sign of its occurrence is the name he gave himself in the colophons at the very end: "Joan Lione Granatino," "Joannes Leo."[9]

This relative detachment also contrasts with the vehemence of French travel accounts in talking of Islam. The visionary and learned Oriental-ist Guillaume Postel, in his *Republic of the Turks*, was appreciative of much that he had seen in his travels throughout the lands of the Sublime Porte in 1535–37 and 1549–51—the abundant alms and charitable gifts, for example, and the low number of "usurers and bloodsuckers." And he was in the 1550s an enthusiastic reader of the Arabic grammar of "Joannes Leo Africanus." But when it came to the Qur'an, Postel spoke of its "follies," "bestialities and dreams," and of the hypocrisy and voluptuousness taught by Islam. True, the Qur'an contained quotations and stories from the Bible, "but for one word of truth there are a hun-dred fables." Similar language of condemnation could be found in other Christian travel accounts.[10]

Muslim writing about Christianity in the war-filled sixteenth cen-tury could also lack restraint. Of the capture of Constantinople, the Ottoman historian and mufti Hoca Saduddin Efendi declaimed:

For the evil-voiced clash of the bells of the shameless misbelievers was substituted the Muslim call to prayer, the sweet chant of the Faith of glorious rites, repeated five times ... Churches ... were emptied of their vile idols, and cleansed of their filthy impurities ... The temples of the misbelievers were turned into the mosques of the pious, and the rays of the light of Islam drove away the hosts of darkness from that place so long the abode of the despicable infidels.[11]

Recalling the loss of Granada to the Spaniards, a later Ottoman geographical-historical text, *Fresh News*, spoke of the "many thousands of Muslims and pious ones ... in the hands of despicable nonbelievers ... They raise prayerful hands to God [asking] that ... he may spread the seeds of jihad and war ... and with the hell-fire of wrath brand their malice-filled breasts." What a pity that this good land of the Maghreb now bordered a region "filled with the wrongs of disbelief and error."[12] Whatever our Granadan thought, he refrained from expressing such judgment.

YUHANNA AL-ASAD WROTE extensively of Islam in the *Cosmography and Geography of Africa*. Almost all the events in the book he dates by the year from the Hijra: "the year 24 of the Hijra," "the year 918 of the Muslim era." Only here and there does he give a date in both calendars, as in the celebrated battle where Spanish Christians began to reconquer Moorish towns, and not always accurately: "the year 609 of the Hijra, which must be by the reckoning of the Christians the year 1160 [*sic* for 1212]." His stop at Tripoli, when he was in the hands of his Spanish captors, took place, he writes, in "the year 1518 from the nativity of Christ," his only use of this exact phrase in the manuscript.[13]

Muhammad's name he always spells "*Mucametto*," an idiosyncratic spelling copied by his scribe and at odds with the current Italian practice of *Macometto* (as in the 1547 *L'Alcorano di Macometto*) or *Maumetto* (Ramusio's preferred spelling, sometimes *Mahumetto*) or the Spanish *Mahoma*.[14] This orthography placed his vowel sounds a little closer to those heard in Arabic, while retaining some difference—a difference that, as we shall see, he could put to good use.

But how to write "Muslim" and "Muslims" in Italian? How to refer properly to "those who have surrendered to God"? *Musulmano,* derived from the Arabic word meaning "belonging to Islam," was first used in Italian in 1557 and spread only in the seventeenth century.[15] All that was available to Yuhanna al-Asad were the Italian *Macomettani* or *Maumettani,* words that, like "Mohammedan" in English, denoted a religion based on the claimed deification of its founder. To be sure, Sufi mystics did talk of the "Muhammadan Image" and the "Muhammadan way," but these phrases referred not to divinity but to the spirit of a Perfect Human Being, breathed by God into each person, and realized by saints who lived in full imitation of the Prophet.[16] Yuhanna al-Asad settled for the idiosyncratic *"Mucamettani,"* a fabricated spelling that perhaps was a device to ease his own discomfort at the suggestion of deification.[17]

Whatever the spelling, Yuhanna al-Asad ordinarily refers to Muhammad only by that name. He uses the Islamic title Prophet—at the schoolboys' banquet in Fez, they "sing many songs in praise of God and his Prophet Muhammad"—but only a few times and does not employ honorific names like "Lawgiver" or "Messenger of God" or "The Banner of Guidance."[18] The invocation that in Islamic expression should rightly follow Muhammad's name, such as "May God bless him and grant him peace," is omitted.

Indeed, prayer and religious invocation, found in all genres of Arabic literature, including geographies, travel accounts, and histories, are uttered sparingly in the Italian pages of Yuhanna al-Asad. Al-Idrisi opened his geography with a long prayer and ended every description of a latitudinal clime: "Praised be God—the [next] clime will follow, if God wills it." Al-Muqaddasi began the *Best Divisions:* "In the name of God the most Benignant, the Merciful. Facilitate my task . . . Praise be to God who created the world . . . May God abundantly put his blessing on the best of creation and the most noble of men, Muhammad." Speaking of the "empire of Islam," he exclaimed, "May God the exalted watch over it." The reader is regularly reminded of the limits of human knowledge: "I have used reasoning by analogy when it seemed good and fitting, but by God is all success granted." The same pattern is to be found throughout Ibn Khaldun's *Muqaddima*, which opens with a long prayer and every section of which ends with a reference to Allah such as "God is the best heir," sometimes through a quotation from the Qur'an: "'God leads astray whom he wants to lead astray, and He guides whomever He wants to guide.'"[19]

Yuhanna al-Asad's *Geography* has no such references. Early in his book he remarks that back in Africa, "in the flower of his youth, he had traveled in great hunger and danger and had investigated things in the name of God" (*col nome de Dio*, surely a translation of part of the *basmala*, the Arabic formula "In the name of God, the merciful, the compassionate"). Late in his book he writes that he hoped to return to Africa from his trip to Europe "safe and sound, with the grace of God" (*con la Dei gratia*, perhaps closer to the Christian formula than to the Arabic "God willing"). When an old man on his boat on the Nile reached into the river for what he thought was a board, only to be snapped up by a crococile, Yuhanna al-Asad "thanked God" that it had not been he. Only at the very end, after the table of contents, is there a fuller invocation as one might find in an Islamic composition, though still in words that could pass among either Muslims or Christians: "Here ends in felicity the table of this work by the foresaid Joannes Leo, ever in praise, glory, and honor of God all-mighty for all eternity, Amen."[20]

The only partisan prayer in the book—the one that could not travel across the religious border—he puts in the mouth of his sultan Muhammad al-Burtughali, addressing Allah before his counselors and religious advisers:

O God, may you know that my intention in coming to this wild country is only to be of help and to free the people of Duccala from the grasp of impious and rebellious Arabs and from the hands of Christian enemies. If you know and see the contrary, punish me in my person.[21]

Only twice in his book does Yuhanna al-Asad use words inexcusable from an Islamic point of view, both of them in the late section on Egypt. Following a neutral account of religious change in the land of Misraim, he gives a second version of that story:

> After the nativity of Christ, the Egyptians became Christian and re-mained within the Roman Empire. With the demise of the Roman Empire, the emperors at Constantinople took care to maintain the kingdom . . . After the coming of the pestilence [*pestilencia*] of Muham-mad, the [Egyptian] king was seized by the Muslims by a captain named ʿAmr son of al-ʿAs. [ʿAmr] was captain of a large Arab army authorized by ʿUmar, the second caliph. Having conquered the kingdom, the cap-tain left the people in their own faith, so long as they paid tribute . . . When the armies of the Muslims came, they established themselves in the middle of the kingdom; they considered that there they could keep peace between the two groups [Christians and Muslims], while if they stayed in the maritime region, they feared assaults from the Christians.

The unacceptable word in this account of a relatively tolerant and pacifying Arab conquest is, of course, "pestilence." At that, it was not pe-jorative enough for the French translator Temporal, who enlarged the con-demnation: "with the pernicious coming of Mahomet, the sectaries of this damnable and reproved heresy took over the Kingdom [of Egypt]."[22]

A few pages on, Yuhanna al-Asad turns to describing Alexandria: "In the middle of the city, amid ruins, is a little house like a shrine . . . It is said that this is the tomb of Alexander the Great, who was called Prophet and King according to the folly [*pazia*] of Muhammad in the Qurʾan."[23] This "folly" is shocking: nothing like it is found in any other reference to the Qurʾan in Yuhanna al-Asad's writing. We shall try to figure out what possessed him to use these terms.

Most of the time in Yuhanna al-Asad's corpus, he speaks apprecia-tively of Islam, its religious figures, and its sensibility. His *Illustrious Men* includes religious philosophers, as we have already seen. In his

Geography, he explains that Islam held Africa together in law and learning. A one-eyed holy man in the Anti-Atlas Mountains was "a good man, wise, and generous," a pacifier of local conflict "who truly deserved all praise for his justice." The scholars of the Qurʾan, hadiths, and Islamic law were "doctors of great intelligence," "doctors held in great credit." Islam was a religion that should embrace "the whole world" (*lo universo mundo*) of the Muslims, a religion long rent and ravaged by the heresy and apostasy of Shiʿites in the east, now harmed by the dominance of the Shiʿite Shah Ismaʿil in Persia, and at its best as practiced in Egypt.[24]

There along the Nile Muslims could choose to follow one or the other of the four Sunni schools or rites of law (*madhahib*)—the Malikite, Hanafite, Hanbalite, and Shafiʿite. They differed in ceremony, prayer, and law, Yuhanna al-Asad explains, but their learned founders had all drawn their particulars from the "universals" of the Qurʾan and been guided by the "prince of theology" al-Ashʿari. Each of the four schools had a head qadi leading a body of lesser judges and advisers. The Shafiʿite qadi, favored by the Mamluks, was supreme chief over them all, but Muslims were judged by men of their own *madhhab*. Yuhanna al-Asad especially approved of the efforts made to keep ordinary believers of the different schools from expressing hostility toward each other. The Cairo scholars debated interpretations of the law but were not allowed to speak evil of the four founding fathers. "Regarding faith, they are all equal."[25]

This was a somewhat prettified picture of the relations between the four legal schools: about the time Yuhanna al-Asad was leaving Cairo in 919/1513, a judge assisting the chief Shafiʿite qadi had been caught in adultery with the wife of a judge assisting the chief Hanafite qadi, and the ferocious conflict between the two schools about their punishment had led the impatient Mamluk sultan to replace all four chief qadis and their staffs. By the time Yuhanna al-Asad was writing the *Geography*, the new Ottoman rulers were appointing a supreme qadi from their preferred Hanafite school.[26]

Still, the principle of a symmetrical broad practice of Islam in Cairo is what he remembered and presented to European readers. One wonders what he had come to think of his Maghreb, where only the Malikite school was permitted to instruct and judge the faithful. The faqihs there knew legal opinions from other schools—al-Wazzan would have read some in his madrasa days—but since the Marinid dynasty of the thirteenth century, the Malikite prescriptions and commentaries held sway in the schools, courts, and mosques of Fez.[27] Was his praise of tolerance within a universal frame in part a reaction to his experiences, negative and positive, in Italy, as a Muslim and then as a Christian convert?

YUHANNA AL-ASAD promised his readers more substantive information about Islamic doctrine, law, and ceremony in his book on *The Faith and Law of Muhammad according to the Malikite Rite*, a manuscript that is unfortunately lost. But in the pages of *Illustrious Men* and *Geography of Africa*, his Islamic sensibility emerges—in part as he remembered himself as a Muslim and in part as he still was even after his baptism.

The author of these books had ordinarily turned, for guidance on Muslim worship and ethical conduct, to Muslim law and its scholars rather than to the forms of highly charged internal devotion, esoteric knowledge, and mystical union taught by the Sufi masters. He respected, as we have just seen, the Sufi hermit whom he had met in the Anti-Atlas, "holy" in his closeness to God and using his spiritual power (*baraka*) for peacemaking. Surely he had known, too, of the line of moderate Sufis in Morocco, who had trained in the law; one of them, Zarruq, had taught his followers, "Be a specialist in the law first and a Sufi second."

But Zarruq himself had criticized the excesses of some Sufi holy men in the late fifteenth century, apostles of the luminous al-Jazuli:

They started gathering the ignorant and vulgar, male and female, whose hearts are blank and whose minds are immature. They instilled into them . . . the belief that repentance is to be had by shaving the head, gobbling up food, gathering for banquets, invoking by turn utterances and cries, using the mantles and beads, making a show of themselves, and holding that so-and-so is their master and there is no other master save him . . . They persuade the vulgar to believe that the ʿulamaʾ are obstructing the way to God . . . So they became enemies of the learned and learning.[28]

Quite apart from his political concerns about Sufi Jazulite rebels against the Wattasids, Yuhanna al-Asad had found this spiritual style troubling. "There exist at Fez certain people called Sufis," he explains to his Italian readers. "Their scholars and moral teachers observe certain rules beyond those of the law of Muhammad . . . and make some things licit that are prohibited in the law of Muhammad. For some theologians they are orthodox, for others they have little credit, but the people hold them to be saints."

His own description of the Sufi excesses in Fez begins like that of Zarruq:

About a hundred years ago, ignorant and uneducated people became part of the sect and maintained that [Sufis] did not need doctrine and learning, but the holy spirit directed those with a pure heart through their good will . . . The superfluous commands of their Rule they left behind . . . and took pleasure in those that were licit.[29]

Yuhanna al-Asad then elaborates on one of the activities that the Sufis claimed were "licit," the banquet: "They sing beautiful songs and hymns of Love, and all dance together. Some of them tear their clothing, as it fits with the verses being sung and dissolute touches . . . Many of them fall to the floor while dancing." They claim that their cries and the rending of their garments are under the impulse of Divine Love. But Yuhanna al-Asad believes that it all came from eating too much: "each one eats enough for three people." (Ibn Khaldun had also opined that excesses of the belly led to excess in sex.) He concludes with a descrip-

tion of the sexual licentiousness among Sufi men when a Sufi master
and his disciples were invited to wedding banquets by the scholars and
honest citizens of Fez.[30]

This behavior was the more disturbing to our author because in earlier centuries the Sufi movement attracted persons of holiness, eloquence, and learning. As his uncle's messenger, had he not years before
presented a book on the Maghreb's Sufi saints to a chieftain in the High
Atlas? Now, in the *Geography*, he speaks of the founders and leading
Sufis of earlier centuries as men of "great worth," such as al-Harith ibn
Asad al-Muhasubu (early ninth century), who wrote "a beautiful work."
Ibn Khaldun had devoted many pages in his *Muqaddima* to describing
and assessing Sufi teachings and mysticism, but Yuhanna al-Asad centers his brief account on the relation of the Sufi masters to specialists in
the law. He tells a story—perhaps just a generic saint's tale—of an unnamed Sufi who with his many disciples was denounced to the caliph by
men of the law. The judges sentenced them to death as heretics, whereupon the Sufi asked the caliph for a public debate with the lawmen. So
well did the Sufi pray and reason from the Qur'an that the caliph wept
and was converted. The men were freed and the caliph supported the
holy work of the Sufi in founding communities (*ribats*) for prayer and
spiritual exercise.[31]

The great peacemaker between the Sufis and the lawmen was al-
Ghazali (d. 505/1111), "a man of the highest ability in all the sciences."
In both his *Geography* and his *Illustrious Men*, Yuhanna al-Asad tells
al-Ghazali's dramatic story: how he taught law to a rapt audience of
hundreds at the great madrasa at Baghdad, newly founded by the Persian vizier Nizam al-Mulk; how he changed, gave up his professorship,
put on the habit of a hermit, and lived as a Sufi, in pilgrimage and study.
Through it all al-Ghazali wrote and wrote: books on law, theology,
philosophy, prayer, spirituality, and poetry. As a young man Yuhanna
al-Asad had recited many of his poems from memory, "composed in the
most elegant Arabic." The most powerful volumes were those in which
al-Ghazali, assisted by Aristotelian logic, reconciled the Prophet's law
and reasoned theology with the mystical sensibility of Sufism. Yuhanna

al-Asad ends with a tale—perhaps fictive—of a good banquet. The vizier had al-Ghazali's books on reconciliation read publicly before the lawyers, who could find nothing to reproach. A feast was then held of lawmen and Sufis; they dined together, a sermon was preached on peace, and "everyone was content."[32]

Yuhanna al-Asad also shows al-Ghazali supporting and even strengthening the theology of the great al-Ash'ari (d. 324/935). The achievement of both scholars was their resolution of deep disputes between different schools and sects in Sunni Islam, finding a middle ground between the extremes beyond which was heresy. "At his time," Yuhanna al-Asad writes in his *Illustrious Men*, "the discord among Muslims on matters of faith, divine reasons, and the Qur'an was extreme." For instance, the rationalist Mu'tazilites claimed the Qur'an was the created Divine Word and could be reasoned about; their opponents claimed, on the contrary, that the Qur'an was uncreated and eternal and should be understood literally and through faith. Al-Ash'ari knew this conflict from his own experience, for he started off as a Mu'tazilite, then "separated himself from them and declared the [Qur'an] more divine, giving natural reasons and arguments."

Al-Ash'ari affirmed that the Word was eternal, existing in full, uncreated, in God's speech, while its expression in human words took place in history. As to how the Qur'an could be both created and uncreated, al-Ash'ari answered characteristically, "have faith without asking how." This was a reconciliation of opposing views that Yuhanna al-Asad had always liked: though God's will is finally inscrutable, the Qur'an and Tradition (Sunna) can still be explored and interpreted by human reason. Writing about al-Ash'ari at his Italian desk, Yuhanna al-Asad recalls the many Ash'arite books he read at school and the prose and poetry he memorized (figure 8).[33]

Yuhanna al-Asad had also followed a middle way in regard to the paths of the body. At one extreme were the ascetic followers of the "rule of *suuach*," that is, *saum*, or abstinence: they fasted and refused foods well beyond the requirements of Ramadan and the prescriptions of *halal*, which prohibited only pig and meat that had not been ritually slaughtered. Some hermits lived in the woods and mountains of Morocco, he says, shunning all human contact and eating only wild plants and fruits.[34]

More interesting were those who put fasting to use for a higher end, spelled out centuries before by the "most worthy and eloquent" Persian al-Suhrawardi. As Yuhanna al-Asad explains it—not, alas, doing justice to the blend of Plato and Zoroaster in the illuminism of al-Suhrawardi's *Oriental Theosophy*—these people believed that by "abstinence, bizarre fasts, and good works" they could purify heart and mind and rise up a gradient of dimensions to perfection. Then God would forgive all their sins and they could please themselves. Some judges and theologians found this heretical, Yuhanna al-Asad comments to his Italian readers, but he does not add that al-Suhrawardi had died in an Aleppo prison, condemned as a heretic.[35]

He has no taste for this heroic asceticism. His *Geography* is full of the meats, especially mutton and lamb, sold at markets and roasted for dinners and celebrations in different places in Africa. His mouth waters as he remembers the delicious flavor and color of the meat roasted at the Fez market; the "most wonderful white bread" made of semolina in Tunis; the sweets, some made of sugar, some of honey, at the Cairo market, so different from those found in Europe.[36]

But he has reservations about excessive indulgence and not only at the Sufi banquets at Fez. Wine was forbidden by Muslim law, he reports in the *Geography*. If some medieval physicians mixed wine with herbs for an anesthetic, in Malikite law it was prohibited even for healing. Yet according to the fatwas collected by al-Wazzan's teacher al-Wansharisi, the sale of wine and "Muslim wine-drinkers" were constant presences in the Maghreb.[37] Writing for Christian wine-drinkers in Italy, Yuhanna al-Asad recalls these wine-drinkers in different ways. On the one hand, he locates public wine sales in houses on the low-life outskirts of Fez, where there were prostitutes, dice games, and dancing to all hours of the night. Notables who drank too much wine and ate too much chicken ended up with gout. On the other hand, he describes wine production and consumption in many places in the kingdom of Fez, including one

Rif mountain town where everyone drank wine, including the faqihs, who did so in secret even while saying it was forbidden. In Badis, people took wine out on little boats on the Mediterranean and enjoyed themselves drinking and singing; in Taza, the wines made by the Jews and drunk by Muslim and Jew alike were "the best in the region." It sounds as though he knew the taste.[38]

The Qur'an prohibits wine in this world (2:219, 5:90–91), but in Paradise it promises rivers of water, milk, wine—"a delight to the drinkers"—and honey (47:15, 56:18–19, 83:22–25). Wine on earth makes humans hate each other and forget God, but not in the garden of Paradise, where it is part of the banquet of immortality. "Pure," adds Yuhanna al-Asad to the description of that celestial liquid, when he corrects the Latin translation of the Qur'an.[39] Among Sufis, wine symbolized the rapture in knowing Allah and invoking his name, the love flowing between God and those believing in him, as in the mystic Wine Ode of Ibn al-Farid. Yuhanna al-Asad writes of the grace and extraordinary beauty of Ibn al-Farid's allegorical poems, recited for three hundred years at the gatherings of the sectaries. The Wine Ode, composed in one of his favorite meters, cannot have been far from his mind when he lived in Italy, observing the centrality of wine in the Christian mass and drinking it as an everyday beverage.[40]

Yuhanna al-Asad was similarly ambivalent toward two other cultural practices that a learned faqih might think threatening to Islamic orthodoxy: divination and miracles. There is a continuum in Islamic thought between true prophecy and the long-enduring Arabic practice of divination. The Prophet's revelation was believed to come directly from God and was always true: Muhammad was God-filled in his inspiration. Diviners (*kahins*) had recourse to angels at best, to djinns or spirits who were sometimes reliable and sometimes not, and to demons with their false counsel at worst. Other seekers (*'arraf*) scrutinized natural, celestial, or human shapes for information. Their inspiration came not from God but from some special capacity or endowment and from self-manipulation. Their predictions were unreliable: as the Prophet remarked, in a hadith going back to his wife 'A'isha, "The true part in what they say comes from the djinn who cackles it in their ear, like a chicken; they mix it with a hundred lies."

Yet the Qurʾan and Sunna did not absolutely prohibit divination, so long as its claims were kept within limits. Not surprisingly, these were difficult to determine, and al-Masʿudi had long ago remarked that faqihs and religious scholars could not agree upon the value of the divinatory arts. "One of the qualities of the human soul is the desire to learn the outcome of affairs," Ibn Khaldun had observed, "and to know what is going to happen . . . life or death, good or evil." That desire was very unequally fulfilled by the various types of diviners and soothsayers he reviewed, some of them "reprehensible," others uttering "truth and falsehood" mixed together. When people did acquire supernatural knowledge, it came not through human mechanics but because God had revealed it to them in their sleep or during spiritual exercises, like those of the Sufis.[41]

As he looked back on North African divinatory practices from Italy, Yuhanna al-Asad had the same reaction as Ibn Khaldun. Some diviners were ridiculous, such as those who dropped oil into water, watched through a mirror the arrival of demons in the fluid, and asked them questions that were answered by a movement of the demon's hand or eye. Only crude people believed in this and wasted their money on such diviners. Some diviners were bad, such as the women in Fez who claimed they had special connections with demons of different colors—red, white, black—whom they summoned to possess them by special perfumes, ventriloquizing the demons' voices and answering questions put to them reverently by simple folk, who then left a gift. Rumors had it that they snared their women clients into demonic sexual pleasures.[42]

When divining was allied with learning, however, it aroused our author's curiosity and even esteem. There were people who knew the science of letters and words—ʿilm al-huruf, onomancy—rather like "cabalists," he explains. They fasted, prayed at special intervals, and wore amulets with talismanic letters and numbers on them, which enabled "good spirits [to] appear to them and speak with them and give them news of the world universally." Their greatest master was al-Buni

(d. 622/1225), several of whose books Yuhanna al-Asad had read and whose celebrated manuscript on the Nintey-nine Divine Names had been shown him by "a Jew from Venice."[43] He also admired za'iraja, that most "wondrous" and elaborately learned form of divination, which fascinated him even as he acknowledged that it threatened to impinge on Allah's supreme knowledge of the future.[44]

About miracles, Muslim theologians sometimes had their differences, as Ibn Khaldun had observed: divine action was always essential to the working of wonders, but did the prophet or saint play any productive role as well? For Yuhanna al-Asad, who had traveled about Africa with a sharp eye for popular religious practice, the question was a little different: were reported miracles authentic or fraudulent? When fraudulent, he blamed the credulity of the people and sometimes their rulers. Thus in Tunis, it was not just the common folk who foolishly believed in the holiness of crazy men who went nude through the streets throwing stones and shouting; the sultan had also constructed a beautiful oratory for one of them.[45]

In Cairo the tomb of Saint Nafisa, a descendant of the Prophet's cousin, was the site of miracles. Yuhanna al-Asad had seen its silver candlesticks and silken rugs and noted its many visitors from near and far. The women of Cairo flocked to the shrine, hoping for the miraculous cures Nafisa's body would bring; merchants did not return to their boats or caravans without stopping to pay respect to Nafisa. All of them left offerings, which were then divided between the poor descendants of the Prophet and the supervisors of the shrine. Nafisa had been "virtuous and chaste," Yuhanna al-Asad admits, but the miracles around her burial place had been "invented by the simple folk and the caretakers of her tomb."[46]

But here again his condemnation of popular piety was not absolute, for at least one devotion won his assent. Abu Ya'za, a Berber saint of the twelfth century, was buried in the little town of Taghya in the Middle Atlas (today Moulay Bouazza). He had been reputed to perform miracles to calm the ferocious lions swarming in the forests nearby, and his tomb had become the site of an annual pilgrimage of men, women, and

children from Fez. Yuhanna al-Asad, who had been taken there as a boy
by his father, later read about the miracles in al-Tadili's respected biographies of holy men and decided to view them seriously as at least "the
result of some magic art or some secret [the holy man] possessed
against lions." Twice in his travels he escaped being devoured by lions,
and so he went to visit the tomb several times, perhaps now with a son
of his own.[47]

IN WRITING of different sects and practices within Islam, Yuhanna al-
Asad was sometimes critical and even scornful, but he never called for
violence against them. His strongest denunciation was of the Shi'ites,
whom he found "destructive" of Muslim unity, the Shi'ah shah of Persia
trying to impose his sect on others "by force of arms." Possibly in
920/1514, as ambassador of Fez, he had applauded Sultan Selim's attack
on Shah Isma'il, but he did not acknowledge this in his *Geography*.
Rather, he said he would explain the Shi'ite "heresy" of the Imamate (a
line of preeminent spiritual leaders succeeding the Prophet) in a separate book on *Muslim Faith and Law*.[48]

His first impulse in regard to the diverse sects and heresies within
Islam was to describe and classify them. "Seventy-two major sects have
emerged from the faith of Muhammad," writes Yuhanna al-Asad,
slightly misquoting a saying of the Prophet that gave the number as
seventy-three, "and each thinks it is the good and true one that will lead
to salvation." By such citations had certain Muslim historians over the
centuries justified their histories of sects and innovators in Islam. Al-
Shahrastani (d. 548/1153), one of the most important of them, had
added the rest of the Prophet's saying: "and of the seventy-three, only
one has assurance of salvation." He went on:

> I impose upon myself the obligation of giving the views of each sect as
> I find them in their works without favor or prejudice, without declaring
> which are correct and which are incorrect, which are true and which are

false; though indeed, the glimpses of the truth and the odor of lies will not remain undetected by minds versed in intellectual matters. And God will be our help.[49]

Al-Shahrastani did in fact use the word "heresy" now and again, but his *Muslim Sects and Divisions* was not written in a spirit of violence. Yuhanna al-Asad recommended a similar book by the fourteenth-century encyclopedist Ibn al-Akfani.[50]

We can see, then, that at the time he composed his *Cosmography and Geography of Africa*, Yuhanna al-Asad was not inflamed by the passion of jihad or holy war and that this attitude was not new. Already back in Fez, he seems not to have espoused a sweeping and eschatalogical version of that obligation to "struggle" and "strive" (the core meanings of the verb *jahada*).

As servant to sultans in Africa, al-Wazzan had known several forms of jihad. Most evident was the call to fight against the Portuguese Christians, who were seizing towns along Morocco's Atlantic and Mediterranean rim. "It is preferable not to start hostilities against an enemy," went the Malikite commentary, "without first having summoned them to embrace Islam, unless the enemy takes the offensive." The most powerful voice for such jihad in the Fez madrasas in al-Wazzan's youth was the Sufi jurist and poet al-Tazi (d. 920/1514). In the wake of Muhammad al-Shaykh's shameful peace treaty with the Portuguese in 876/1471, made so he could capture Fez for the Wattasids, al-Tazi cried out:

> Worshipers of God, what is this great heedlessness that has fixed itself in your hearts? . . . Are you not aware that your enemies . . . are employing every stratagem to get at you? . . . You are divided against your Muslim brethren and care nothing that the religion of the Lord of Messengers is being debased and that believing worshipers of God are being taken captive . . . [The people of this land] will be shackled with chains . . . They will be robbed of their possessions, their women will

be taken from them . . . and [the unbelievers] will seduce them away
from their religion . . . What is this heedlessness about your brethren,
oh Muslims?

The Maghreb needed "a just leader" who would "arrange [the Mus-
lims] in the ranks of battle . . . The herald has announced: 'Heaven is
under the shade of [drawn] swords.'"[51]

Sultan Muhammad al-Burtughali had responded to that call, and as
we have seen, al-Wazzan supported and served him in the endeavor. But
the "just leader" whom al-Tazi had in mind was someone with a wider
program of moral transformation than that of the down-to-earth Wattasids. Al-Wazzan had seen a prince aspiring to such charisma in the
Saʿdiyan sharif Muhammad al-Qaʾim: through his unrelenting jihad
against the Portuguese, this descendant of the Prophet could follow the
Straight Path of al-Jazuli and Sufi holy men, while at the same time
achieving the dynastic rule prophesied for his sons. As a diplomat, al-
Wazzan had helped forge the collaboration between the prince sharif
and Muhammad al-Burtughali in the holy war against the Christians,
but he and his sultan would have been uneasy about the expansionist
possibilities in the Saʿdiyan understanding of jihad. In 931/1525 one of
the sharif's sons seized Marrakesh from its tribal prince, and the Wattasid sultan was forced to acknowledge the Saʿdiyan rule in the southern
region of Morocco. If word of this got to Yuhanna al-Asad in Rome, he
would have felt his suspicions confirmed.[52]

Al-Wazzan had known about sweeping uses of jihad in other instances, and especially about the zealous Maghreb scholar al-Maghili,
who had proclaimed holy war against Jews in the Sahara and beyond.
He would also have known that some important Maghreb judges, including the muftis of Tlemcen, Tunis, and Fez, had disagreed with
al-Maghili, saying that the Jews of the oasis towns of Tuwat were living
humbly in their own neighborhoods, and that their local synagogues
could stand, since they were built on land properly acquired by *dhimmis*, that is, by a tribute-paying, protected People of the Book. Al-
Maghili had responded that "such a fatwa could come only from an

impostor" and had sought more scholarly opinion until he got the decisions he wanted: that the Jews were conducting themselves in an impudent fashion, violating the rules of dress and more and their synagogues were unlawfully constructed in "a territory of Islam." Whereupon al-Maghili organized an attack on the oasis synagogues and on the Jews themselves, offering a bounty for each person slain. Paradise was promised to those who destroyed buildings that were an insult to the Messenger of God, and the Fire to those who opposed demolition. "Rise up and kill the Jews," went his summons in verse. "They are indeed the bitterest of enemies who reject Muhammad."

Not long after in Fez, al-Maghili was rebuffed by the jurists and expelled from the city. Though a few of the judges, including al-Wazzan's later teacher al-Wansharisi, had supported the demolition of synagogues on the grounds that they could not be built in towns founded by Muslims, they were troubled by the ensuing bloodshed and by al-Maghili's claim that any Muslim who disagreed with him or even traded with Jews was an "unbeliever." Against al-Maghili's expanded jihad, men of the law could cite Qur'an verse and Malikite text that one made war on a People of the Book only if, having refused conversion, they refused to pay the special dhimmi tax. Warring against the oasis Jews thus violated shari'a.[53]

What of other targets for jihad? "Scholars agree that all polytheists should be fought," Ibn Rushd (Averroës) had said centuries earlier in his legal handbook, but even there, he went on, at least the Malikite school was willing to offer them the status of poll-tax tributaries if they refused conversion. As for accusing a Muslim ruler of being an unbeliever (*kafir*) before attacking him, this was an old story in the Abode of Peace. We have already seen that a few years after his war against the Jews, al-Maghili gave the receptive Songhay ruler Askia Muhammad approval for attacking Muslim rulers who had been accused of "mixing," or permitting their subjects to mix, acts and rites of unbelief with those of Islam. But here, too, there was disagreement. The condemned amulets and charms were thought acceptable by the celebrated Egyptian scholar al-Suyuti "so long as they contained nothing reprehensible."

"There is nothing wrong," said a Malikite handbook, "in protecting oneself by charms against the evil eye and other such things, nor in pronouncing protective formulas . . . It is all right to hang amulets around the neck containing verses from the Qur'an."[54]

ALTHOUGH YUHANNA AL-ASAD had harsh words for Muslim communities generally ignorant of the true practice of Islam, what they needed, in his view, was prayer leaders and judges—imams and qadis— not holy warriors.[55] As for Jewish communities, he writes of Jews both good and bad in the *Geography* but always as belonging to Africa and as a group with whom he himself had connection. He had gone on merchant caravans with Jews and conversed with Jewish men whom he met on his travels. He had admired the warrior Karaite Jews whom he had observed in the Atlas Mountains, even though their horseback riding was strictly forbidden by the dhimmi laws. (To be sure, the Karaites were considered heretics by the other Jews of Africa, since they rejected the authority of rabbis and followed their own interpretation of the Pentateuch.) "The Jews are much deprecated at Fez," he comments, mentioning the requirement that their footwear be cane slippers, not shoes, but he also had seen Muhammad al-Burtughali welcome rich Jewish refugees from Portugal to his court, and one of them was sent on an embassy to the Portuguese king in 914/1508. Were Jewish refugees believed to have brought syphilis from Spain? Muslim refugees from Granada had brought the disease as well. Were the Jews of Azemmour accused of delivering their town to the Portuguese? In nearby Safi, the collaborators were Muslims.[56]

And to his *Lives of Illustrious Men among the Arabs*, Yuhanna al-Asad appended *Some Illustrious Men among the Jews*: the five men, including Maimonides and the poet Ibrahim ibn Sahl, were identified as physicians and philosophers, traditional markers for Jews included in Arabic biographical dictionaries, and all had some link to North Africa and/or al-Andalus.[57]

His *Illustrious Men* concludes with a biography of Harun ben Shem

Tov, the Jewish vizier of the last Marinid sultan, ʿAbd al-Haqq (d. 869/1465). "Born into the highest of Jewish families of Fez," Harun was an astrologer, says Yuhanna al-Asad, assigning him a skill that Muslim rulers often drew upon in deciding on future plans. ʿAbd al-Haqq had been unable to rule, so dominated had he been since boyhood by a Muslim vizier. Harun advised the sultan to kill the vizier, which was done, whereupon the sultan named the Jew vizier, partly, explains Yuhanna al-Asad, as an angry gesture to keep the people of Fez in their place. After six years of Harun's administration, one day when the sultan was out of town, "the people of Fez rebelled and killed the Jews. When word of this got to the [sultan's] camp, the captains and notables rose up against the sultan and killed Harun." ʿAbd al-Haqq was deserted by his soldiers, paraded back to Fez on a mule, and his throat cut.[58]

Yuhanna al-Asad gives no details on the power struggles and grievances that had led to this revolt: for instance, that the line of viziers dominating ʿAbd al-Haqq were all Wattasids, whose descendants he and his uncle had served as diplomats, or that the sharifs of Fez were angry about his decision to end tax exemption for them and their families.[59] I stress only that with his characteristic strategy of neutrality, he does not speak explicitly against the killing nor refer to the great Sufi Zarruq, who strongly opposed the assault on the Jews of Fez at the time. But he does not speak for the murders either.

Moreover, linking the murder of a Jewish vizier with the assassination of a legitimate sultan does raise questions about the rightfulness of the violence. Here, for contrast, are the words of an Egyptian jurist traveling in the Maghreb just as the revolt took place: "This Jew ended up with the right to command and forbid in the kingdom of Fez . . . This accursed man gave free rein to all faults, depravities, and abuses. Through his doing, the domination of the Jews over the Muslims of Fez increased." When one of Harun's relatives insulted and attacked a sharif's wife refusing to pay her tax, the Egyptian went on, the preacher at al-Qarawiyyin mosque, already declaiming every Friday against the Jews, rushed into the streets shouting: "Whoever does not rise up for the cause of God has neither virtue or religion. Holy war! Holy war!"[60]

The passion that al-Maghili stirred up in the oasis towns of Tuwat and nearby Gurara some twenty-eight years later, Yuhanna al-Asad describes in the *Geography* in few words: "In the area [of Gurara] and Tuwat . . . arrived a preacher from Tlemcen, who began to preach against the Jews. The people rose up, pillaged the Jews, and killed many of them, and most of their wealth fell to the preacher." Mindful of his European audience, Yuhanna al-Asad recalls their own violence: "This event happened the same year [that the Jews] were chased out of Spain and Sicily."[61]

Yuhanna al-Asad's reservations about holy war against Jews, shared with jurists in Fez and elsewhere, were evidently strengthened by his experiences in Italy, including his relations with Elijah Levita and Jacob Mantino. Let us recall his praise of the latter in the colophon of their Arabic-Hebrew-Latin dictionary: "the teacher, the skillful physician . . . the trustworthy Israelite. May God maintain him in his grace." "Trustworthy," *wafaʾ*, is a compliment in Arabic use: it is applied to someone who can be counted on to live up to a promise and to transmit a tradition correctly and faithfully, as Mantino was doing with his editions of Averroës. Surely Yuhanna al-Asad would have wanted Mantino to be among the readers of his *Illustrious Men* and his *Geography*, even though we can imagine his sometimes approving, sometimes taking umbrage at their pages.

AL-WAZZAN HAD ALSO come in contact with the most visionary and encompassing ideal of holy war, one associated with the Last Age. Then a divinely chosen World Conqueror would come, establish universal empire, and prepare for the arrival of the Mahdi, the "guided one," a man descended from the family of the Prophet, who would destroy false religion and restore righteousness and the Islamic faith throughout the world, a universal caliphate. Sometimes it was believed that the two roles—Conqueror and Mahdi—could be played by one figure; sometimes it was believed that the Mahdi would be accompanied by Jesus, who had not died on the cross but been taken to heaven with God.[62]

The years when al-Wazzan grew up were of immense importance in this scheme, for it had been prophesied that the tenth century after the Hijra would usher in the Last Age. In 898/1493 al-Suyuti reported from Cairo on the excited exchange of hadiths among the learned and the populace alike as the year 900 neared; he proposed himself as the *mujaddid*, the supremely learned scholar who appears at the end of each century to restore religion. But he also predicted that the Last Age would begin only in 1450/2028. For those who expected it sooner, signs of the coming multiplied: the conquest of Constantinople, the second Rome, in 857/1453 foreshadowed the Muslim taking of Rome itself; the fall of Granada two decades later was another sign of the Last Age. The learned al-Bistami (d. 858/1454), specialist in the science of letters and names, left a treatise with prophecies about the coming savior: the savior's name had been foretold long ago by the reformer Ibn Tumart: "the Sound One"—that is, "Salim"—"of the lineage of ʿUthman." He would be a ruler from the north who would conquer Egypt. Then the Mahdi would take Rome.[63]

When al-Wazzan was in Cairo and Istanbul, such prophecies were being applied to Sultan Selim's victories against Shah Ismaʿil in Persia and against the Mamluks, and to his uniting all of Anatolia, Syria, and Egypt under his rule (figure 20). In 923/1517, the year when al-Wazzan saw Selim at the baths in Rashid, the sultan was acclaimed in a Persian text as "succored by God" and "Master of the Conjunction," who would have rightful dominion everywhere. Letters sent to Selim on the occasion of his victories hailed him as Mahdi and World Conqueror.[64]

How did al-Wazzan react to this eschatological excitement at the time? When he was captured, he told his Italian questioners that he had been "celebrating the [sultan's] victories in Syria and in Egypt."[65] After all, Wattasid diplomacy had looked toward Ottoman support against the Christians. But his memories of destruction and dismantlement in Cairo seem to have troubled him, and he cannot have welcomed the possibility—foretold in the World Conquering scenario—of Selim taking over all of North Africa.

Of course, when al-Wazzan arrived in Rome, eschatological prophecies filled the air, but concerning precisely the opposite holy war—against the Turks and Islam. In the popular Italian press, any "monstrous" birth or unusual conjunction in the heavens was taken as a sign of needed repentance, the cleansing of the church, and coming war against the infidels. Prognostication swirled around the imperial election of 1519 from which might come the ruler who would "make all the world obedient, reform the church, and make a new order." Bernardino de Carvajal, godfather to the newly Christian Yuhanna al-Asad, had been preaching the Last Days since the Christian conquest of Granada; Egidio da Viterbo was naming the Turks as the Beast of the Apocalypse and calling for their defeat and the conversion of all peoples to Christianity under Pope Leo X. (Later Egidio would cast Pope Clement VII in that universal role.) Yuhanna al-Asad would have also gotten a whiff of Jewish apocalyptic excitement from his likely encounter with the self-styled Prince David from the desert of Habor. Egidio da Viterbo had taken him seriously as another sign of the coming Golden Age, though Yuhanna al-Asad would have heard doubts from Jacob Mantino.[66]

By the time he came to write his *Cosmography and Geography of Africa*, the earlier reservations Yuhanna al-Asad had about the eschatological version of jihad were strengthened. He refers to the general belief in the eventual advent of the Mahdi: such a man would be "the just Caliph prophesied by Muhammad in the scriptures."[67] But the Mahdi's coming was in some indeterminate future. Those living in constant expectation of his arrival, Yuhanna al-Asad found foolish. He describes a mosque outside the Berber town of Massa along Morocco's Atlantic coast as a center of "great devotion," because it was believed that the Mahdi would emerge from its chambers. Already Ibn Khaldun, in deriding various false Mahdis in the Maghreb, had recalled this Sufi lodge (ribat) in Massa and the "weak-minded people" who traveled to it in hopes of greeting the Guided One. A holy man had "taken advantage" of their belief and proclaimed himself al-Mahdi there in the early fourteenth century, winning many followers among the Berbers until he was killed by tribal chiefs.[68] Yuhanna al-Asad exposes further the credulity of the local people, for Massa was the place where they believed that Jonah had been cast out of the whale, and they believed that through divine intervention any whale passing near the holy building was beached. (Whale bones had been used for joists in the mosque.)[69]

In the *Geography*, Yuhanna al-Asad did not confront directly the dangers in eschatological impulse in contemporary world conflicts, but he did so indirectly by casting doubt on two alleged Mahdis of the past. Both were major political figures viewed with mistrust in the historical memory of the Marinid and Wattasid dynasties. One was Muhammad ibn Tumart (d. 524/1130), born in the Anti-Atlas. After scholarly travels, Ibn Tumart brought back to the Maghreb an intensely unitarian concept of God, devoid of the anthropomorphic qualities that Almoravid theologians had assigned him. He declared the Qur'an and the ways of the Prophet and his Companions as the sole source of true law, purified of Malikite accretions and juridical misreadings. The mores of his day did not escape his notice: his sermons denounced wine drinking, unveiled women mixing with men in the streets of Marrakesh, and musical instruments. Before long Ibn Tumart claimed to be a descendant of the Prophet and had his followers recognize him as the divinely guided Mahdi of all Muslims. As leader of a political-religious movement centered in the High Atlas Mountains, al-Mahdi sent out his fellow Masmuda tribesmen as the Party of God to war against the Almoravids. After his death, a close disciple, 'Abd al-Mu'min, finished the struggle and became the founding caliph of the Almohad dynasty. The Mahdi's name rang out at Friday services and adorned Almohad coins for many decades.[70]

Yuhanna al-Asad writes nothing of al-Mahdi's teachings: these he would have treated separately in his lost books on history and Muslim theology, surely decrying there Ibn Tumart's hostility to Malikite law. In the *Geography*, he identifies al-Mahdi simply as a Masuda Berber, a preacher, and a mountain warrior with loyal disciples and makes no mention of a possible descent from the Prophet. That Ibn Tumart had drawn on a tribal institution to elect the first Almohad caliph was "a new usage in the law of Muhammad," a phrase that suggests a bad innovation, or *bidʿa*, which the jurists condemned.

In his description of the High Atlas town of Tinmallal, the Mahdi's center and his holy burial place, Yuhanna al-Asad dissociates himself openly from Ibn Tumart's pretensions. The mosque was beautiful, but the inhabitants fancied themselves learned in Ibn Tumart's theology and argued it arrogantly with any stranger who came their way, he writes; their doctrine was "heretical and malignant." Yuhanna al-Asad was surely thinking here of Ibn Tumart's claim to be "the infallible Imam," a formulation of his role as the Mahdi that, as Ibn Khaldun had noted, smacked of Shiʿism and heterodoxy.[71]

The other messianic warrior described by Yuhanna al-Asad was ʿUbayd Allah Saʿid (d. 322/934), leader of the dualistic Ismaʿili sect of Islam, itself a spinoff from the Shiʿites. They had taken their name from Ismaʿil, who had died before he could be the seventh imam, and for almost two hundred years the sect had been waiting for one of his descendants, hidden imams, to come forth publicly as the divinely guided Caliph. ʿUbayd Allah had claimed to be that figure, pointing to his descent from the Prophet's daughter Fatima. He came from Syria to the Maghreb to join a fellow sectary who had successfully proselytized among the Kutama Berbers and conquered territory from Sunni Muslim rulers. Declaring himself the Mahdi, ʿUbayd Allah made himself head of the movement, built as his center the new town of Mahdia in Tunisia, and established a kingdom where Shiʿite doctrines held sway and Malikite teaching was forbidden. At the time of his death, Fatimid efforts to control the western Maghreb had failed, though his successors were to conquer Egypt.[72]

Describing the fortress at Mahdia, Yuhanna al-Asad calls ʿUbayd Allah the "heretical Caliph" and like others before him questions his genealogy.[73] ʿUbayd Allah had come to Qairouan in Tunisia disguised as a pilgrim, he writes, and had led the people there to believe that he was a descendant of Muhammad. To win credit among them, he had declared himself "the Mahdi, the rightly guided Caliph," and they rebelled against their governor and made him their ruler. Yuhanna al-Asad's account

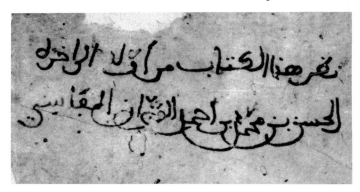

FIGURE 1: Al-Wazzan signs a Vatican Library manuscript in 1519, nine months before his baptism: "Al-Hasan ibn Muhammad ibn Ahmad al-Wazzan al-Fasi has examined this book from beginning to end."

FIGURE 2: The pope's master of ceremonies records al-Wazzan's baptism, the names of his three godfathers and his past jailer, and his Christian name, Joannes Leo de Medicis.

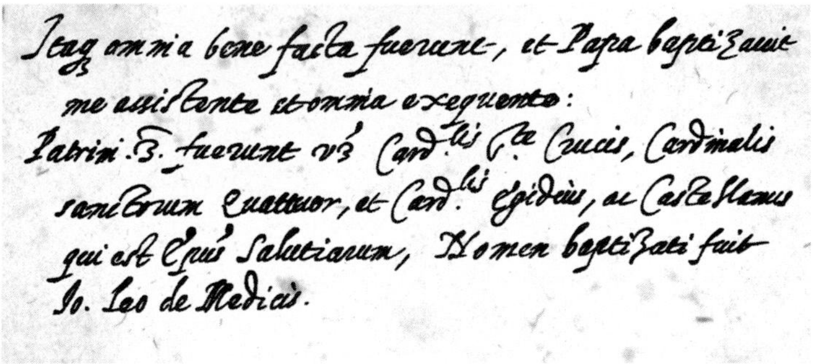

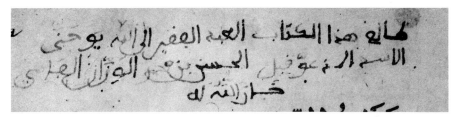

FIGURE 3: Yuhanna al-Asad signs a Vatican Library manuscript in 1520, after his baptism: "The poor servant of God, Yuhanna al-Asad, formerly named al-Hasan ibn Muhammad al-Wazzan al-Fasi, has studied this book. May God give him good."

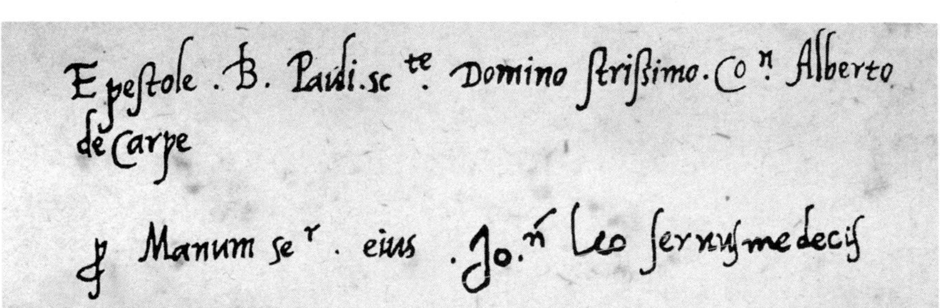

FIGURE 4: Elias the Maronite writes the Latin title for the Arabic transcription of Saint Paul's Epistles, 1521, and Yuhanna al-Asad adds his name as transcriber: "Joannes Leo, servant of the Medici."

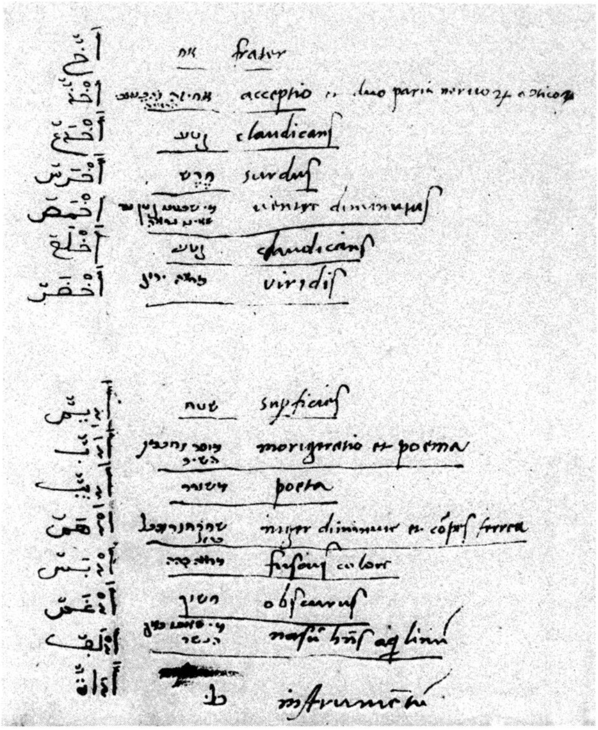

FIGURE 5: A page from the first letter of the alphabet (*alif*) in the dictionary of 1524, with Yuhanna al-Asad's column in Arabic and Jacob Mantino's columns in Hebrew and Latin.

FIGURE 6: Yuhanna al-Asad corrects Joannes Gabriel's Latin translation of the Qur'an (an early-seventeenth-century copy of their manuscript). In verses 24–25 in the Sura of the Pilgrimage (today 22:26–27), he corrects "do not blaspheme me" to "do not associate [anyone] with me" and adds that seventy thousand people come to Mecca every year.

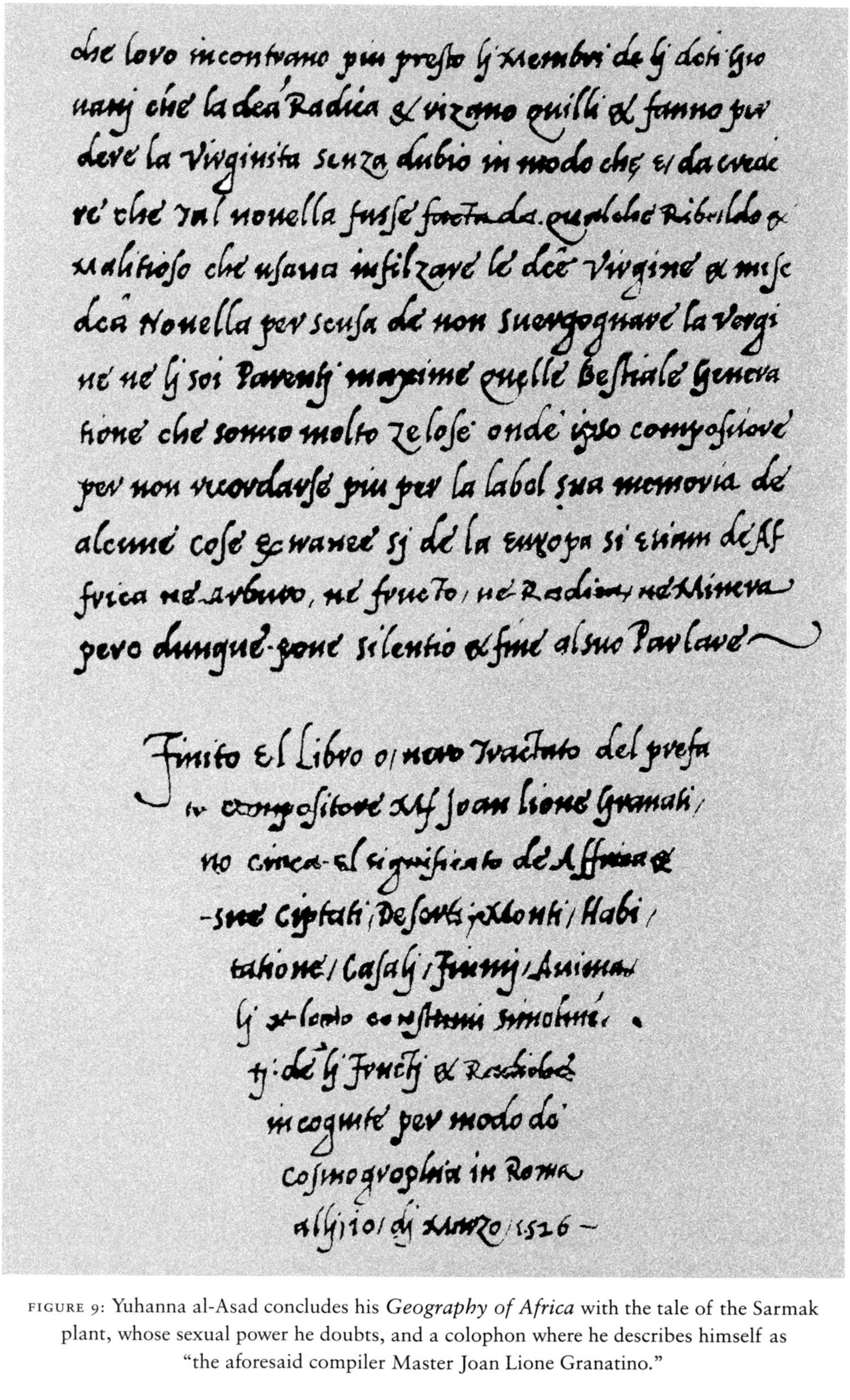
che loro incontrano piu presto li membri de li doti gio
uani che la dea Radica & vizano quilli & fanno per
dere la Virginita senza dubio in modo che e/ da crede
re che tal nouella fusse facta da qualche Ribaldo &
malitioso che usaua infilzare le dcẽ Virgine & mise
dcã Nouella per scusa de non suergognare la Vergi
ne ne li soi Parenti maxime quelle Bestiale Genera
tione che sonno molto zelose onde ipso compositore
per non ricordarse piu per la labol sua memoria de
alcune cose ex wanee sj de la europa si etiam de Af
frica ne arbuxo, ne fructo, ne Radice, ne Minera
pero dunque pone silentio & fine al suo Parlare

Finito el Libro o/ uero tractato del prefa
to compositore M. Joan Lione Granati/
no circa el significato de Affrica &
sue Ciptati, Desorti, Monti, Habi
tatione, Casali, Fiumi, Anima
li & secondo consttuni similmente
sj de li fructi & Radice
incognite per modo de
Cosmographia in Roma
alli 10 di Marzo 1526

FIGURE 9: Yuhanna al-Asad concludes his *Geography of Africa* with the tale of the Sarmak plant, whose sexual power he doubts, and a colophon where he describes himself as "the aforesaid compiler Master Joan Lione Granatino."

Della radi- | Quest'altra è similmente vna radice, che nasce nel monte Atlante, ma nelle parti di ponente, la ce Surnag | qual, come dicono quelle genti, ha virtu di confortare il membro dell'huomo, & moltiplicare il rabil, ppric | coito a chi la mangia in qualche lattouaro. Anchora affermano che se vno per auentura s'incō ta di far riz | tra ad orinar sopra la detta radice, che subito il detto membro se gli rizza. nè voglio tacer ancho zar il mem | ra quello che dicono tutti gli habitatori del monte Atlante, che si hanno truouate molte gioue- bro all'huo | ni di quelle, che vanno pascendo gli animali per questo monte, che hanno perso la loro virgini- mo. | tà, non per altro accidente, se non per hauer orinato sopra detta radice. alliquali per giuoco io re- spōdeua, creder esser vero ciò che diceuan di detta radice & appresso che se ne trouauan di tanto auuelenate, che non solamente faceuan perder la virginità, ma anchora enfiarli tutto il corpo.

Questo è in soma quāto di bello & memorabile ho veduto Io Giouan Lioni in tutta l'Afri ca, laqual è stata da me circondata di parte in parte, & quelle cose che mi parsero degne di memoria si come io le viddi, cosi con diligenza di giorno, in giorno le andai scriuendo. & quelle che non viddi, me ne feci dar vera & piena infor - matione da persone degne di fede, che l'hauean vedute. & dapoi con mia cōmodita questa mia fatica messi insieme, & fecine vn corpo trouandomi in Roma, L'anno di CHRISTO, MDXXVI. alli. X. di. Marzo.

Finisce il Libro di Giouan Lion nasciuto in Granata & alleuato in Barberia.

FIGURE 10: Ramusio concludes his edition of *The Description of Africa* with changes in Giovanni Leone's response to the Sarmak plant and especially in the colophon, where he adds "in the year of CHRIST" to the date.

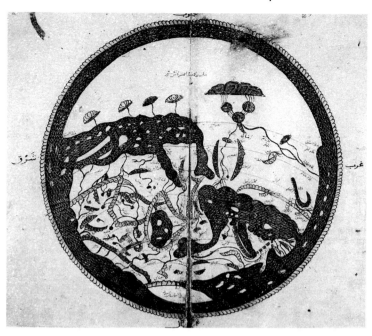

FIGURE 11: Al-Idrisi's influential world map, as reproduced in Ibn Khaldun's *Muqaddima*, copied in 804/1402. South is up, and the upper right quadrant shows Africa, with the Nile and the Niger having a common source.

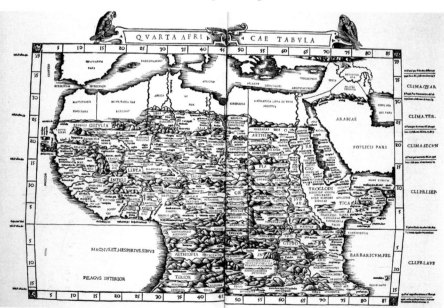

FIGURE 12: The fourth map of Africa in the edition of Ptolemy's *Geography* published in Venice in 1511. The editor corrected the traditional map to take into account recent information from Portuguese navigators about the western coast. "Cannibals" (*ant[h]ropophagi*) are still present in the southeast.

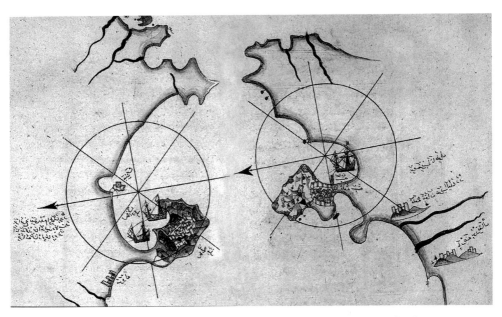

FIGURE 13: The Strait of Gibraltar and towns on either side, from the *Book of Navigation*
(932/1526) of Piri Reis, Ottoman admiral and cartographer. Reis depicted in
great detail the entire Mediterranean coast.

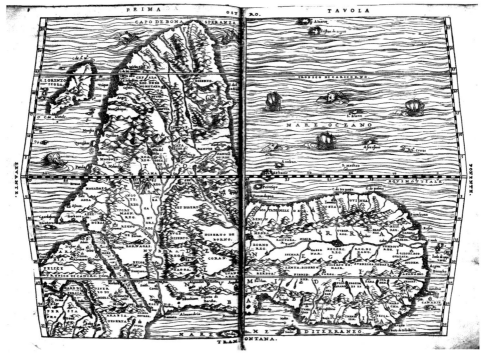

FIGURE 14: Map of Africa by the cartographer-engineer Giacomo Gastaldi, which
first appeared in a woodcut for the 1554 edition of Ramusio's
Navigationi et Viaggi and then was engraved for the
1563 edition. Again, south is up.

FIGURE 15: Woman of Granada with her veil, as pictured by a German traveler in 1529. Such was the street garb that al-Wazzan's mother would have brought with her to the Andalusian quarter of Fez.

FIGURE 16: The courtyard of the Bu ʿInaniya madrasa at Fez, where al-Wazzan heard lectures and watched learned diviners perform a *zaʾiraja*.

FIGURE 17: The portal to the necropolis of Chella near Rabat, where al-Wazzan copied epitaphs from the tombs of the Marinid sultans.

FIGURE 18: A sultan seeking advice from his viziers as represented by a sixteenth-century artist, probably a Morisco refugee from Granada in the Maghreb.

FIGURE 19: Two slave favorites at a sultan's court, as depicted by the same artist.

FIGURE 20: Sultan Selim as victor over the Shi'ite shah Isma'il Safawi in 920/1514, a few years before al-Wazzan met Selim at Rachid. Selim is dressed in the green mantle of the Prophet as a sign that he defends Islam.

FIGURE 21: An ambassador presents his gifts to the Ottoman sultan, a ceremony that al-Wazzan knew well from his days as diplomat.

FIGURE 22 *(left and middle)*: Scenes from tale 28 of al-Hariri's *Maqamat*. In a Samarkand mosque, the traveling storyteller hears a moving sermon and discovers the speaker is the vagabond poet Abu Zayd. Later, over wine, Abu Zayd swears the storyteller to secrecy and tells him in a poem to "take people as they come . . . and the whole earth as a single house."

FIGURE 23 *(below)*: The Castel Sant'Angelo in Rome, where al-Wazzan was imprisoned in 1518–19. Pope Leo X put on festivities in its upper chambers, and Pope Clement VII and many churchmen took refuge there during the sack of Rome in 1527.

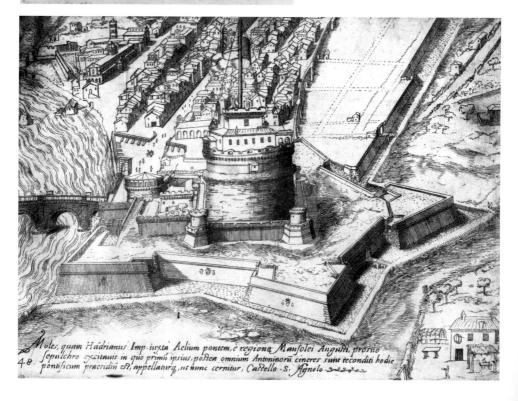

48

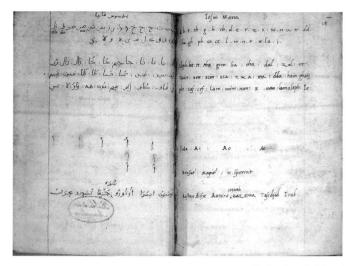

FIGURE 26: Cardinal Egidio da Viterbo practices writing the Arabic alphabet and vowel sounds in a grammar book acquired not long before he began lessons with Yuhanna al-Asad. The Arabic phrase at the top of the page is an exact transliteration of "Iesus Maria" rather than the Arabic 'Isa Maryam.

AVEROIS
CORDVBENSIS
PARAPHRASIS IN LIBRVM
POETICÆ ARISTOTELIS,
Iacob Mantino Hispano Hebræo,
Medico interprete.

10

Vius libelli propositum est expo-
nere id, quod in libro Poeticæ Aristotelis de regulis vniuersalibus,
atq; cõmunibus, omnibus vel plu-
ribus nationibus continetur: cùm
tamen multa in eo contineant, quæ
non sunt regulæ propriæ Arabum
Poesis, neq; eorum consuetudini, et
id septem capitulis complectemur.

20

Caput Primũ. Quot, & quæ sint Imitationis genera:
ac ex quibus sermonibus imitatio ordinetur.

Nquit Aristoteles. Propositũ nostrum nunc est de
Poeticæ arte, de eiusq; generibus tractare. Opor-
tet autem, vt si quis velit rectè tradere eius regu-
las, vt primo dicat, quæ nã sit actio (seu facultas) vniul'
cuiusq; generis poematum: & ex quibus ipsæ fabulæ
poeticæ, ac ex quot rebus constent: nec non, quæ nam
sint earum partes tum cõmunes, tum propriæ, quibus
etiam consistent ipsæ: quot ue sint g era rationum, quę
in fabulis confy derantur: initio scilicet sumpto ab ipsis
principiis, quæ nobis natura isunt circa hoc. Inquit.
Omnis Poesis, omnisq; fabula poetica in vituperandi,
vel laudandi genere consistit, quod quidem inductio-
ne probari potest de ipsis poematibus, præsertim de
Græcorum poematibus, quę de rebus voluntariis age-
bant: nempe ex honestis & inhonestis. ita quoq; res le
habet in artibus imitatibus ipsam Poeticam, quæ quidem ad pulsationem cichararum, ac tibiarum accom-
modantur, eas scilicet hęc duo proposita confy derare.
Fabulæ autem poeticæ sunt sermones imitatorij: quæ
ra vero imitationis & similitudinis sunt tria: duo sim-
plicia, & tertium compositum ex illis. Ex duobus autem illis simplicibus vnũ consistit in imitatione alicuius rei, ac eius similitudine alicui alteri rei. hoc autem
prout est vnicuiq; idiomati familiare per dictiones fi-
bi proprias, quæ apud Arabes literæ similitudinis vo

40

cantur. Alterum vero consistit in acceptione alicuius
similis, vice alterius similis: quod quidem in hac arte
permutatio appellat. Nec te latere debet sub hac parte includi ea genera, quæ hac nostra ętate Metaphora,
ac Cognominatio nuncupantur. Verum cognomina-
tiones vt plurimum sunt permutationes ex affectibus
affectuũ rei: sed metaphora est cõmutatio rerũ illi pro-
portionariũ, hoc est, cũ vnius rei proportio ad secun-
dam sit proporto tertię ad quartã, & permutetur nomen tertię in primã, vel ecõtra. in libro autẽ Rhe-
toricæ explicatur est quot modis fiãt cõmutationes.

50

Tertium vero genus poeticarum orationum ex duobus nunc dictis constat. Inquit. in natura quidem
homines imitantur æmulanturq; plęraq; inter se se in
actionibus, ita vt aliqui coloribus, & figuris, nonnul-
li vocibus imitentur: & hoc vel arte & habitu, qui imi
tatoribus inest, vel ob consuetudinem, quam prius de
hoc habuerũt: ita quoq; in orationibus sunt natura imi
ratores. Imitatio autem in sermonibus poeticis, atq;

æmulatio

FIGURE 27 (left): Jacob Mantino's Latin translation from the Hebrew of Averroës's commentaries on Aristotle's Poetics, a text he surely discussed with Yuhanna al-Asad.

באן דער אוברש טין אובט אאט וט

Bittel	Lictor	קלקטר	בוטיו
Zoller	Telonarius	מוכס	צואישטור
Trumeter	Tubicen	שופרן	טרומיטיר
Vogt	Præfectus	פקיד	בוקט
Iud	Iudæus	יהודי	יד
Christ	Christianus	נוצרי	קרישט
Türck	Turca	תוגרמי	טורק
Araber	Arabs	ערבי	האייד
Mor	Aethiops	כושי	אור
Griech	Græcus	יוני	קריך
Frantzoß	Gallus	צרפתי	פרנצות
Hispanier	Hispanus	ספרדי	שפאניו
walch	Italus	לועז	וואליך
Teutscher	Germanus	אשכנזי	טיוטשר
Vnger	Vngarus	הזרי	אונגר
Tarter	Tartarus	קדרי	טארטור
Zegeiner	Paganus	כותי	צייגנר
Haid	Ethnicus	גוי	האייד

באן דער בוט ורויבט

| Vatter | Pater | אב | פאטר |
| Müter | Mater | אם | מוטר |

D 2

FIGURE 28 (above): A page from Elijah Levita's Yiddish-Hebrew-Latin-German dictionary, a project similar to the Arabic-Hebrew-Latin dictionary of Yuhanna al-Asad and Jacob Mantino.

بسم الله الرحمن الرحيم
الحمد لله رب العلمين الرحمن
الرحيم ملك يوم الدين
اياك نعبد واياك نستعين
اهدنا الصراط المستقيم
صراط الذين انعمت عليهم
غير المغضوب عليهم ولا الضالين

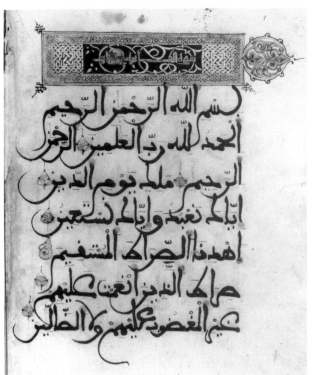

FIGURE 29: Opening Sura of the Qur'an, copied on paper in the Maghreb in the late fifteenth century. The verses are separated by rosettes. This manuscript was seized by Emperor Charles V during his military expedition to Tunis in 1535.

سورة البقرة مايتان
بسم الله الرحمن الرحيم
الم ذلك الكتاب لا ريب فيه هدي للمتقين
الذين يومنون بالغيب ويقيمون الصلوة ومما
رزقناهم ينفقون والذين يومنون بما انزل
اليك وما انزل من قبلك وبالاخرة هم يوقنون
وثمانون وست ايات

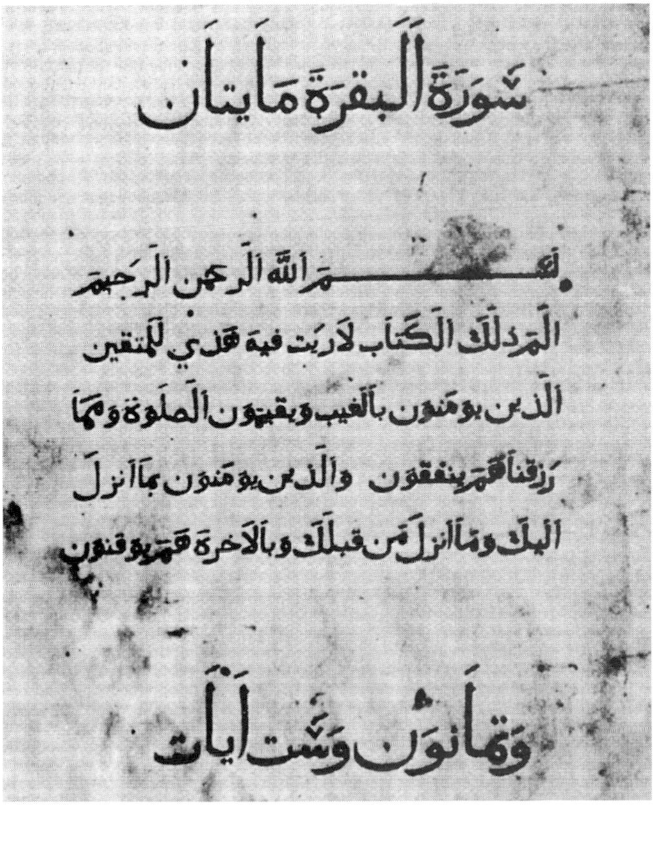

FIGURE 30: Opening of the Sura of the Cow in the Qur'an published in Venice in 1537–38, the first Qur'an printed in Arabic in Europe. The Arabic text has frequent errors; on this page, there is a spelling mistake in the phrase describing the number of verses in the Sura.

FIGURE 31: Sultan al-Hasan of Tunis with his entourage in 941–42/1535, as portrayed by Jan Cornelisz Vermeyen, artist with Charles V's military expedition to Tunis. The sultan, the figure in the foreground with a splint on his hand, was the ruler of Tunis when al-Wazzan came there after his years in Rome.

FIGURE 32: Ahmad, son of Sultan al-Hasan, in 1535, as portrayed by Vermeyen. He would later unseat and blind his father.

undermines his "rightly guided" character. The Mahdi had been thrown into prison by the rulers of Sijilmasa and been rescued by the warrior by whose favor he had been acknowledged as Caliph (the initial Isma'ili proselytizer); but once back safely in Qairouan, he had had his benefactor killed. The Mahdi was a "malignant man," the government he set up "tyrannical and unjust."[74]

Yuhanna al-Asad's suspicions of messianic figures may account in part for the startling statement in the *Geography of Africa* about Alexander the Great: "Alexander the Great was Prophet and King, according to a folly of Muhammad in the Qur'an."[75] Alexander was a major figure in Islamic traditions, as he was in Christian and Jewish ones. Among Muslims, Iskandar was the World Conqueror who had prepared the way for the revelation of Islam. For some though not all religious scholars and in the popular imagination, he was also identified with the figure of Dhu-l-Qarnayn, "he of the two horns" or "he of the two Ages" in the Qur'anic Sura of the Cave (18:83–101). Ordained by God, Dhu-l-Qarnayn follows a path to different peoples in the far West and then in the far East until he reaches "a people barely able to understand speech." They beg him to protect them from the destructive forces of Gog and Magog. He erects a rampart of iron and brass to guard them until the Last Days, when the trumpet shall be blown and Gehenna will be set before the unbelievers.[76]

Muslim geographers located this wall or barrier in central Asia. Religious scholars interpreted it as a metaphor for the Law or shari'a. Either way, Dhu-l-Qarnayn gave protection against the powers of chaos to vulnerable human societies. Thus, for those who identified Iskandar with Dhu-l-Qarnayn, the Greek ruler could be seen not only as a World Conqueror but perhaps also as a prophet, and surely as one of the personages, along with the Mahdi and the returning Jesus, who was central to the eschatological drama at the End of Time.[77]

We shall consider in a later chapter the debates among the 'ulama' about Iskandar's powers and roles, but here let me stress only this point: Yuhanna al-Asad's doubts were partly fueled by his reservations about the sweeping eschatological version of holy war, and they were reinforced by what he saw and heard in Italy. Charles V, after his election as Holy Roman emperor, was named the second Charlemagne and called to fulfill the prophecy of universal Christendom; he promised to "go against the infidels" and regain one day the holy sepulchre in Jerusalem. Sultan Selim, after his victory in Egypt, was named an Alexandrine Conqueror and called to fulfill the prophecy of universal Islam. In 924/1518 Selim was reading the life of Alexander the Great, the Venetian ambassador reported, and hoped to follow in his footsteps.[78] Who knew how this would all end?

While Yuhanna al-Asad does not infuse his recitals of wars between Christians and Muslims and among Muslims with the spirit of jihad, there is a wistful note in his mention of the "power and pomp" of the empire of the twelfth-century Almohad caliph Abu Yusuf Ya'qub al-Mansur, stretching from al-Andalus across North Africa, and then the losses of these lands to the Christians under his son al-Nasir. But he said nothing of rights and wrongs. And as we have seen, his account of the recent battles between Christians and Muslims in the Maghreb was also relatively detached. He describes them simply as military-political events; religious commentary would have been imprudent if he wished to please the audiences he was writing for. In these struggles, however, he had been a strongly partisan participant, and knew that the Muslim law of holy war firmly approved of defense against aggression. His father and he had surely hoped that the Muslims would one day retake Granada. This position appears in muted form in his praise for the "prowess" of a Granadan captain in the war against Spain, and his blame of the "sinfulness" of the Marinid sultan Abu Sa'id 'Uthman, who, told of the Portuguese seizure of Ceuta in 818/1415, refused to interrupt his feast, with its dancing and music, to go to the aid of the city.[79]

Yuhanna al-Asad's characteristic tone toward religious violence and destruction over the centuries, however, is elegiac. There is always a note of regret in his mentions of the buildings, walls, and dwellings ruined and populations slaughtered in war, whether during the Arab conquest of Christian Carthage, the Kharijite Berbers' revolts in the name of Islam against the caliphs, the struggles between declining Almohad sultans and upcoming Marinids, or the Portuguese seizure of Morocco's coastal towns. Ruins and depopulated towns, as he remembered them from his travels, evoke loss, nostalgia, and the memory of tears.[80]

In the one passage where Yuhanna al-Asad expands on religious iconoclasm, he sets it in a context. All conquerors erase culture. Of an early written Berber language that had been used for inscriptions and was effaced by the Romans when they took over Barbary, he writes:

> The Romans, their enemies, were now their masters. They removed the letters and memorable events recorded on the buildings and replaced them with their own, so that no memory would last but theirs. The Goths did likewise to the buildings of the Romans, and the Arabs to the buildings of the Persians. So the Turks do the same to the memorials of the Christians, damaging the fine figures painted in their churches. And in our own time, we see a pope who spends thousands of ducats to construct a grand edifice and then dies leaving it unfinished. Whereupon the next pope finishes it up at minimal cost, while effacing the arms and all other signs of his predecessor, who had been responsible for most of the building.[81]

Writing in Rome in 932/1526, the losses of war rather than its triumphal purifications haunt Yuhanna al-Asad, once known as al-Hasan ibn Muhammad al-Wazzan.

THE *Cosmography and Geography of Africa* and *Lives of Illustrious Men among the Arabs* give us some idea of Yuhanna al-Asad's Muslim past and present but not much of him as a Christian. He refers to the early Christian sect of Arians in Africa as those who "did not hold to the observances or order of the Roman Christians," but he explains nothing of their doctrine. This is an interesting silence: the Arian belief that Christ was the highest of created mortals but not of divine substance was closer to the Muslim view of Jesus than to that in the Nicene

Creed of the church. He opens his *Illustrious Men* with the the ninth-century Nestorian Christian Yuhanna ibn Masawayh, physician and esteemed translator from the Greek at the court of al-Ma'mun in Baghdad, but does not comment on Nestorian teaching in regard to the duality of Jesus, human and divine. Rather he stresses al-Ma'mun's tolerance: when the caliph was asked why he confided the translation of Aristotle to a Christian, he answered, "If I entrust to him the governance of my body, where dwells my spirit and soul, why would I not confide to him the words of others, which pertain neither to his faith nor to ours?" Likewise, Yuhanna al-Asad notes many Jacobite Christians in Alexandria but says nothing of their belief, shared for centuries with their brethren in Syria, that Christ had a single divine nature. Jacobite monasteries in Egyptian towns he praises only for their hospitality to all strangers and their alms for the Christian poor.[82]

Yuhanna al-Asad names a specific Christian prayer only once, saying that a poison sold in the kingdom of Nubia was so strong it could kill a man "in the time it would take to say a Pater Noster." (Ramusio replaced this in his printed version of the text with "a quarter of an hour.") The Last Supper of Christ he mentions only in connection with the Muslim seizure of the gold and bejeweled table on which it was believed to have been held, a treasure in the cathedral at Toledo until the armies from North Africa conquered the Visigothic kingdom of Spain. And he notes few Christian practices, and then only as he believes they were sources for popular customs still carried on at Fez, such as masked children singing and begging for food on the first day of the Julian year, which was associated with the birth of Jesus, and burning fires on Saint John the Baptist's Day.[83]

Yuhanna al-Asad's intriguing treatment of Saint Augustine seems to place him among the Arians: "The Barbary Christians did not hold to the observances or order of the Roman Christians, but to the rule and faith of the Arians. Among them was Saint Augustine." As godson of the former general of the Augustinian order, how could Yuhanna al-Asad have been unaware of Augustine's spiritual voyage—of his dualist Manichean years, his conversion to Roman Christianity, his tracts and bishop's actions against Manicheans, Pelagians, and Donatists? Augustine had spoken against the Arian heresy in his *Confessions*, and in the years before his death in 430, he had defended the Trinity against the Arian beliefs of Gothic mercenaries and Vandals then conquering the Roman provinces of Africa: "the Son [is] begotten from the nature of the Father." Yuhanna al-Asad's patron Alberto Pio knew these polemics and used them in arguing with Erasmus about the Trinity; the prince of Carpi would never have given his servant the impression that the bishop of Hippo was an Arian.[84]

Was this a confusion or a ruse? Perhaps Yuhanna al-Asad was trying to reclaim the saint for the Africa that had persisted after the fall of the Roman provinces. An anti-Trinitarian Augustine was a better antecedent for Islam than a Trinitarian one. And then there was a legend, which al-Wazzan would have known from his youth, that Augustine had been born in Morocco. Some said his birthplace was Tagaoust, in the Sus (a name resembling faraway Thagaste, Augustine's actual hometown). Some said it was farther north in the Duccala region: so the Portuguese captors of Azemmour asked King Manuel I in 920/1514 to build a convent to Saint Augustine in a local mosque, since the people there had a "mystery" about him, believing him "native to this land." Others said Marrakesh. Indeed, a surprising tradition identified Augustine with Abu-l-ʿAbbas Sabti (d. 601/1204), a great Sufi saint, ascetic, teacher, and caretaker of the poor, who had drawn people to him in Marrakesh for decades during Almohad days. After his death his powers of protection extended widely, including to those captured by Christian pirates. Even Christians and Jews could turn to him without subsequent conversion. Al-Wazzan had visited his tomb in Marrakesh.[85]

Out of this welter of associations, I suggest, Yuhanna al-Asad fashioned an Arian Augustine bridging the gap between Islam and Christianity. Virtually all European readers of his Africa book would miss this connection; future Muslim readers of a revised manuscript might get it.

The most expressive religious texts from the pen of Yuhanna al-Asad are the opening and the colophon to his transcription in Arabic of

the Epistles of Paul. Expressing himself in his native tongue one year after his baptism, he wrote a series of invocatory prayers that have the
rhythm and rhymed prose (sadjᶜ) of an Arabic composition. With two
exceptions he used no doctrinaire words and skated the border between
religious sensibilities. He begins: "In the name of God, the kindly, the
compassionate, these are the letters of the holy apostle Paul, the messenger of the Son of God, Jesus the Messiah, may his blessings be with
us. Amen." And he closes the manuscript:

> The Epistles of Paul end here, praise be God. These letters have been
> transcribed for the library of the most illustrious, most powerful, most
> high, most exalted, and most elevated prince, the brave commander and
> lord, Count Alberto di Carpi, may God prolong his power and honor!
> The poor servant of God, praised be his Name, and the servant of the
> aforementioned excellency, Yuhanna al-Asad al-Gharnati al-Fasi—may
> God protect him from the malice of his own soul and make his today
> better than his yesterday—has written this with his own mortal hand
> in the Campo Marzio inside the city of Rome, protected by God, on
> Thursday the last day of January 1521 according to the Christian date
> of the Incarnation, which corresponds to the 24th of Safar, the year 927
> according to the Arab date. Praise be God from the beginning of time
> to the end. May God have mercy on the reader and the writer and the
> one for whom it has been written and on the one who looks into it and
> the one who hears it and the one who studies it. I beseech you by God
> that you pray for the enlightenment of the writer's heart and for his re-
> pentance and that he may be guided so as to please the Lord in this life
> and join the circle of saints in the upper regions of Paradise after his
> death.[86]

Several phrases are standard in Islamic exhortation but transfer ac-
ceptably into Christian prayer. The formula "In the name of God, the
kindly, the compassionate"—"Allah ar-Raʾuf ar-Rahim"—give two of
the most important Divine Names and is a slight variation on the basmala, the repeated Arabic salutation used throughout the Qurʾan and

also used by Ibn Hawqal, Ibn Jubayr, al-Idrisi, and Ibn Battuta at the opening of their geographies and travel books.[87] "The poor servant of God" and "may God protect him from the malice of his own soul and make his today better than his yesterday" are expressions al-Hasan ibn Muhammad al-Wazzan brought with him from Fez: he wrote them along with his Arabic name on Vatican manuscripts during his first months as a prisoner in the Castel Sant'Angelo.[88] Both Islam and Christianity have saints, though the "upper regions of Paradise" is a more Christian celestial image, Islam imagining Paradise more readily as a garden.

Two words do not cross the Islam-Christianity border. One is "Incarnation": belief in incarnation of the divine is inadmissible in Islam, where there can be no compromising the absoluteness of God. Likewise "Son," in the phrase "the Son of God, Jesus the Messiah." While "Messiah" is one of Jesus' titles in Islam, along with "Prophet" and "Messenger of God"—the Qur'an calls him "Spirit" from God and "Word" from God (4:171)—Jesus cannot be the "Son of God." He is the son of Mary.[89]

Here, then, Yuhanna al-Asad gives an outward sign of adherence to a purely Christian doctrine, but it is a single sign and not repeated in his later writings. How do we account for this reticence in regard to Christianity? For several years, Giovanni Leone had been presumably attending Latin mass, his body turned to the altar, fasting at Lent, confessing his sins to a priest, and taking communion at least twice a year. No longer was he openly performing ablutions and praying five times a day in Arabic, his body turned to the *Qibla* (in the direction of the Ka'ba in Mecca), fasting at Ramadan, sacrificing a sheep at 'Id al-Adha (a commemoration of Abraham's sacrifice of the ram), and paying *zakat*, the annual tax for the poor required of all Muslims. He had been hearing church bells ring throughout the day rather than the periodic intonation of the muezzin's call; he had been contemplating religious paintings and statues—for example, at the Church of Saint Augustine, Raphael's recent fresco of the prophet Isaiah and the marble tomb of Augustine's Berber mother Monica[90]—rather than the calligraphic and geometric

ornaments on the pillars and walls of the Bu 'Inaniya mosque at Fez (figures 16, 24). He had been catechized by men in the pope's own circle,
and had studied at the very least the Gospels and Epistles of Saint Paul
as well as Arabic manuscripts on the Trinity and on Nestorian, Maronite, and Jacobite Christianity, not to mention the conversations he
had had with Christian scholars.

It is possible that Yuhanna al-Asad's state of mind was like that of a
Jewish Marrano or a Morisco *converso*: persons forced to convert or
conform to one religion while inwardly holding to and even clandes-
tinely practicing their old faith. (As the Catholic Inquisitors of Granada
said in 1560, "all Moriscos are secretly Muslim.") Taking this point of
view, we could see the Christianity of al-Hasan ibn Muhammad al-
Wazzan's Italian years as a cover that he had to assume in order to be
freed from prison.[91] And indeed, both Sunni and Shi'ite Islam allow
the practice of *taqiyya*, that is, precautionary dissimulation of one's
faith and religious practices under circumstances of coercion. As the
Qur'anic verse puts it (16:106):

> Whoso disbelieves in God, after
> he has believed—excepting him
> who has been compelled, and his heart
> is still at rest in his belief—
> but whosoever's breast is expanded
> in unbelief, upon him shall rest
> anger from God, and there awaits them
> a mighty chastisement.[92]

In al-Wazzan's own Maghreb, a jurist in Oran had issued a fatwa in
910/1504 specifically permitting Muslims of Granada to resort to *taqiyya*
under the increasing Christian pressure to convert. Their inward loyalty
to Islam was the important thing, he said. If forced to pray at Christian
altars at the time for Muslim prayer facing toward Mecca, their prayer
could count so long as they directed it from within to Islam. If ordered

to revile the Prophet, they should pronounce his name as the Christians did, but have the intention of reviling the devil. If compelled to say that Jesus was the son of God, they could do so by changing the words appropriately within their minds, saying inwardly, for instance, "Jesus is the son of Mary who worships God." If required to drink wine and eat pork, they could do so as long as they intended their bodies not to benefit from such intake and continued to believe that pork was unclean. Meanwhile they should try to find some covert means to perform their required Muslim prayers if only in simplified form. Granadan Moriscos welcomed the fatwa. They had already sent a poem to the Ottoman emperor saying they had been forced to convert, "yet under the Prophet Muhammad's religion we used to oppose the governors of the Cross with our inner intentions." A century later the historian al-Maqqari was to say, "Such of the Muslims as still remained in Andalus, although Christians in appearance, were not so in their hearts."[93]

Precautionary dissimulation is surely part of the story of our protagonist's conversion, and it could account for his reserved, limited Christian references. It could also account for his writing "the pestilence of Mucametto," a lone phrase that would have reassured his godfather and master, Cardinal Egidio, and could be excused through taqiyya as the use of an idiosyncratic, incorrect version of the Prophet's name. Forced dissimulation and inner rewording would also be essential excuses for "Incarnation" and "Son of God" were he to return to North Africa and seek pardon from Muslim judges.

Taqiyya sets up a very simple model for Yuhanna al-Asad's behavior and mentality in Italy: outside—a false Christian performance; inside— a sincere Muslim. But this stark dichotomy does not help us understand why he extended an open appreciation to Islamic culture and Muslim figures in his writings in Italy, or why he suddenly used gratuitously harsh language about the prophetic role attributed to Alexander the Great—"a folly of Mucametto in the Qur'an." And why did he not make a getaway sooner from "the abode of war," Dar al-Harb, if coercion-dissimulation was the only issue? Once out of prison in early 1520, and especially after the death of Pope Leo X at the end of the next year, what held him in Italy? Could he not have found a way to sneak off to a boat bound for North Africa?

The amphibian creature in Yuhanna al-Asad's bird story shifts identities each year according to his interest. The vagabond poets of the *Maqamat* came in and out of their disguises, roles, and tricks, admitting who they were to the traveling narrator at the end of each adventure and appearing in a new disguise and place for the next. Yuhanna al-Asad, this crafty and curious bird, had more in play than taqiyya alone.

CHAPTER SEVEN

Curiosity and Connections

LET US ASK what might have attracted Yuhanna al-Asad to his life in Rome. What features of Christianity might have appealed to him or aroused his curiosity, at least for a time? What rewards might he have found, at least for a time, in the people whom he met, the circles he frequented, the friendships—perhaps intimacies—he formed, the sights that he saw in Renaissance Italy? What might he have wanted to explore about people in the world outside Islam and Africa and, indeed, about himself?

Let us listen to al-Hasan ibn Muhammad al-Wazzan al-Fasi being examined in 1519 by his catechizer, Paride Grassi. The bishop reported that the "infidel" was troubled by "variety" and "confusion" in the Muslim faith, with its multiple sects, and especially by the "many confusions of its law." When he "understood some of the rubrics of our Christian law, they accorded with each other so well that he altogether wished to master it." He still had doubts on some matters, Grassi went on, but "after instruction by our doctors," he was finally "questioned on the articles of the faith and responded that he believed them all."[1]

Such concerns about diversity and confusion accord with Yuhanna al-Asad's later comments in the *Geography* about divisiveness in Islam, especially the "destructive" rupture of the Shi'ite "heresy." In 1519, imprisoned in the Castel Sant'Angelo, this Malikite faqih might well have been curious about and attracted to the structures of the Roman Catholic canon law. As he would have heard from his catechizers, the body of canon law was composed of several fundamental texts, from Gratian's *Decretum* on, and the work of commentators was to harmonize or reconcile them. For al-Wazzan, this would be an interesting contrast to the four schools of Sunni law, which sought rather to maintain their borders.

Then there was the papacy. Along with an Arabic manuscript on the Trinity, a Vatican librarian had brought the prisoner a printed edition of Juan de Torquemada's book *On the of Power of the Pope*. This tome was surely a challenge to al-Wazzan's Latin, and perhaps the Sant'Angelo castellan, Tornabuoni, helped him look into it. Torquemada made strong claims about the supreme power of the papacy over church councils and any other rival jurisdictions.[2] We can imagine al-Wazzan weighing the advantages of a centralized Roman structure against the weak and rival caliphs of Sunni Islam. The claims of the Nasrid sultans in al-Andalus had evaporated with the Christian conquest of Granada. The symbolic 'Abbasid caliphate in Mamluk Egypt ended with the Ottoman conquest of Egypt: al-Wazzan would have seen the last 'Abbasid caliph forced to leave Cairo for Istanbul in the early summer of 923/1517.[3]

Several years later in his *Geography*, Yuhanna al-Asad simply said wistfully that the caliphs had "passed away."[4] By 1526 he was evoking a universal ideal of Islam and creating an idealized image of respectful debate among the Sunni schools of law in Cairo. By then, too, he would see that Martin Luther was turning Germany and the Roman Church upside down. In 1519, enclosed in the Castel Sant'Angelo, this "confusion" in the church would not yet have been apparent to him. Instead, lawman that he was, he could contemplate the principle of a reconciled body of religious law and a centralized religious institution.

Was his heart in it when he told Grassi that he believed the articles of the Christian faith? All the writings of Yuhanna al-Asad suggest that he must have been dissimulating when he said he accepted the doctrine of the Trinity and the Incarnation. But Grassi may have offered something else to whet the appetite of his convert: the ceremonies of the church, about which he, Grassi, was an expert. In *Geography of Africa* Yuhanna al-Asad recalls in sharp detail the ceremonies of his own past: those marking the schoolboy's memorizing the Qur'an; those around circumcision, marriage, and death; those at different courts he had visited as a diplomat. The myriad candles in the great mosque of al-Qarawiyyan burned brightly in his memory: the central section of the mosque alone had 150 bronze candelabra, each with enough oil for five hundred candles.[5] Perhaps Catholic ceremony offered Yuhanna al-Asad a dangerous but exciting performance.

Compare the account of the geographer al-Muqaddasi, who said he had gone to every length in his travels to become familiar with the ideas, practices, languages, stories, and "complexions" of peoples "so that [he] could classify them." When he got to al-Sus, in western Iran just north of the Persian gulf, he acquired local garments and went to the mosque:

I made my way to the Sufi meeting. When I approached them, they did not doubt that I was a Sufi, and received me with welcome and greeting, sat me down amongst them, and began questioning me. They then sent a man who brought some food, but I refrained from eating as I had not associated with this sect before that time. So they began to wonder at my abstention, and my refraining from their practices. I wished then that I had associated with this creed, and thus would have known their rituals and learned their truths. But I said to myself, "This is your opportunity, for this is a place in which you are unknown." Thereupon I opened up to them, and put off the mask of diffidence from my face. Then sometimes I would converse with them, other times I would scream with them, then again I would read them poems. And I used to go out with them to the cells, and attend their convocations, until, by God, they began to trust

me, as did the people of the town to the extent that I had never intended. I became famous there, visitors sought me out; clothing and
purse were brought to me, and I took them and paid for them completely
on the spot, because I was rich; around my middle [in a money belt]
I had a lot of money. I attended a convocation every day—and what a
convocation!—and they used to think that I was becoming an ascetic. So
people began to stroke my clothes [for a blessing], and proclaim an account of me, saying, "We have never, never, seen a *faqir* [Sufi mendicant]
more deserving than this man." The result was that when I had learned
their secrets and found out what I wanted to from them, I fled them in
the calm of night. By morning I had put a long distance between us.[6]

Al-Muqaddasi's performance was within the bounds of Islam and
did not cross the border of apostasy. But it certainly was contrary to his
hope "always to deal honestly with Muslims so as to please God."[7]
Especially it cannot be interpreted as simple taqiyya, for to satisfy his
curiosity and broaden his experience, al-Muqaddasi had been completely caught up in Sufi actions and feelings.

This kind of mood seems to be behind the more transgressive
act of our Christian convert. Passing from al-Hasan ibn Muhammad
al-Wazzan to Yuhanna al-Asad, he could play the Christian for a time
as he had once longed to play the suspect za'iraja back in Fez and Tunis.
And he could for a time become part of a fascinating, cosmopolitan
world of learning and get a glimpse of the high circles of European
power and wealth. He had certainly loved comparable experiences in
Africa, eagerly presenting himself in his *Geography* as a habitué at the
court of the sultan of Fez; as welcome in the entourage of the Saʿdiyan
sharif in southern Morocco; as received and favored by the sultans of
Tlemcen and Tunis; and as visitor to the Songhay palace at Gao and the
Mamluk palaces in Cairo.

Think then of Yuhanna al-Asad's associations in Italy. The masters whom we know he served: Leo X, Cardinal Egidio da Viterbo,
Prince Alberto Pio of Carpi. Great figures whom he may have served:
the Vatican librarian Girolamo Aleandro, the papal chancellor Giulio

de' Medici, a cardinal who then became pope. Italian humanists who conversed with him, if only briefly, and whose interests and activities would have been known to him: Angelo Colocci, Paolo Giovio, Pierio Valeriano. The savant foreigners or partial outsiders, with whom he had his easiest and friendliest relations: the Maronite Christian Elias bar Abraham and the Jews Elijah Levita and Jacob Mantino. He heard many languages in these privileged circles—Latin, Arabic, Syriac, Hebrew, Yiddish, Italian, and Spanish—and translation of words, phrases, ideas, and motifs was a constant theme.

To be sure, the Jews and the Muslim convert were included in such a network on terms set by the Christian patrons and masters: Jewish and Islamic learning was always to be bent to Christian purpose. The evidence for this struck Yuhanna al-Asad repeatedly: calls for crusades against and condemnation of Islam; visions of a Christian golden age. Still, his curious eyes and ears saw and heard much else in Rome and in his travels in Italy. The faqih, who had not yet made his mark in North Africa as a man of authority, became in Italy a sought-after scholar and finally a writer with expert status. Here he was distinctive. And though power was centered in the hands of the Christian elite, this multilinguistic world still had space left in the 1520s for non-Christian agendas.

Elijah Levita gives us an idea of this space, continuing to live as a Jew with his wife and children (presumably keeping the laws of *kashrut*) in some corner of Cardinal Egidio's household, praising his Christian patron in biblical phrases such as "wise as Solomon, . . . learned and seeking God, a just man among the just." His case was easier than that of Yuhanna al-Asad, in that he was not forced to convert, but he had been living in Venice in 1496 when the yellow hat was introduced for Jews, and he was in Padua in 1509, when all the Jewish houses were sacked and he lost everything.[8]

Levita had also been reproached by Jewish rabbis who cited Psalm 147:20 ("and as for his [the Lord's] judgments, they [the Gentiles] have not known them") and "pronounced woe to my soul because I taught the Law [Torah] to a Gentile." In fact, his writings were intended for both Jews and Gentiles, and he was glad they were read by both.

Yes, I have been a teacher to the *goyim*. I am a Jew, thanks be to God, and revere the Lord. I have not sinned, for the Sages prohibit only the communication to a Gentile of the import of the Law and . . . subjects that contain esoteric doctrines . . . They have not ruled that whosoever teaches a Gentile commits a sin. Rather the Sages permit teaching the Noachide precepts to the Gentiles. This argues most powerfully for me. How can the Gentiles fully understand the seven precepts [commanded by God to Noah for all humankind] unless they first know the Hebrew language?

Thus, he, Elijah ben Asher, was advancing knowledge of Jewish moral precepts by his teaching. His Gentile pupils were "good and upright men, who with all their power have acted kindly toward the people of Israel. The very knowledge of our language among the *goyim* has actually been to our advantage."[9]

Yuhanna al-Asad undoubtedly had comparable hopes for his own teaching. Whatever guilt he may have felt about his conversion and whatever conflict about his years of involvement in Italian life, he left several manuscripts behind him that gave a view of Muslim societies and their past, of Arab scholars and Arabic poetry, and of an Islam that differed from the stereotypes prevailing in Christian Europe. His annotations on Egidio da Viterbo's Qur'an brought clarification to Islam's sacred book, a text little understood in Italy. He would not have expected Christian "kindliness" toward Muslims as a consequence of his writings, but he may have hoped they would facilitate more reasoned diplomatic encounters.

YUHANNA AL-ASAD MAY ALSO have discovered aspects of Italy through intimate liaisons. Erotic connections are a well-known channel for cultural crossings.

As I have argued earlier, Yuhanna al-Asad would have made a marriage at Fez. By the time he left prison and converted, that marriage would, by Muslim law, have been either dissolved or in great jeopardy.

As a legal scholar, he would have known this. "In case of the apostasy of one of the spouses," the Malikite doctrine taught, "the marriage is dissolved by divorce and by one view dissolved in full law." If our convert hoped to get around this dissolution one day by claiming taqiyya, he still had another hurdle to face. When a husband disappeared, the wife notified the authorities; if there was no word from him over a specified time—it could vary from, say, two to four years according to different judges—the marriage was ended as if he were dead, and she was free to remarry.[10] By 928/1522 four years had passed since Yuhanna al-Asad had been kidnapped, and he had no assurance that his family knew his whereabouts. It was a good year to try to escape, for Medici retainers like himself were not especially welcome at the newly austere court of Pope Adrian VI. But he stayed in Italy.

This unusual situation helps us understand the absolute silence in Yuhanna al-Asad's writing about his marriage. To be sure, a personal reference was not expected in Arabic geographies and travel books: Ibn Jubayr and al-Muqaddasi, for instance, said nothing about their wives, and Ibn Battuta mentioned his only as he made marriages en route. Yet Arabic autobiographical writing sometimes stretched to talk of spouses, and autobiographical strains run through Yuhanna al-Asad's *Geography*.[11] Yuhanna al-Asad wrote of his father, uncle, and other male relatives, but a Muslim wife back in Fez would have been an embarrassment before his Christian readers in Italy and a reproach before imagined Muslim readers. He omitted her as he omitted his capture and conversion.

Still, Yuhanna al-Asad left many clues to his attitudes toward women and erotic experience. He never repeated conversations he may have had with women he met during his travels, as he did with men, but he made observations and told stories. He even drew two scenes from North African marriages. One was a pleasant one, learned from the husbands among the prosperous Arab nomads who frequented the deserts south of Tlemcen and Tunis and in whose spacious, well-appointed tents Yuhanna al-Asad had lodged. He, an outsider, could see only the women's eyes through their veils, but for their husbands'

viewing, the wives had painted their faces, chests, and arms from shoulder to fingertips—a sight of beauty, according to their poets, and a
stimulus to desire. The other scene he found improper and disruptive of
marriage: wives in Cairo hauling their spouses before the qadi with
complaints that the husbands had had intercourse with them only once
during the night. This led to more divorce.[12]

Yuhanna al-Asad also used women's work as a marker for cultural
difference and cultural similarity. In the Haha region he had seen
women grinding grain; in the Hascora region, going out to the fields
with their slaves; in parts of the Anti-Atlas, carrying water from wells
and wood from the forests; in the Rif Mountains, tending their goats. In
place after place he noted slave women, many of them Black: attendants
at the bath houses in Fez; on errands in the streets of Timbuktu, their
faces unveiled; domestic servants at royal courts. In the oasis town of
Tichit was an unusual reversal: the women had studied and taught the
girls and boys until the latter were twelve and had to leave school and go
to work with their fathers.[13]

Most frequently he remarks on women in two trades. First were
those employed in the Maghreb's textile manufacture, especially those
responsible for high-quality work: in some places, women spun and
wove woolen cloth so beautifully that it looked like silk. In Tunis, he
could get a look at the women spinning their fine linen thread: they let
their spindles down from their windows to give the strands more tension. In Fez, the women sold their linen thread in the market.[14]

Second was prostitution, reproved in the Qur'an (24:33) but widespread since the days when the Prophet's wife, 'A'isha, had raised her
voice against "the turpitudes" of the women of Egypt. Yuhanna al-Asad
remarks on women prostitutes throughout Africa—in the Land of the
Blacks, in oasis towns, in towns along the Nile, in Tunis, in Fez. In his
home city, he describes where it went on: in hotels; in institutionalized
bordellos supervised by governmental officers who collected revenue
from them; and in a suburb of Fez full of muleteers and tough guys,
with shops for wine, prostitution, and gambling, a place of "liberty
and harmful good times." In the desert region near the Dra'a Valley, he

admits to having been close enough to them that he could report that "the women are beautiful and . . . pleasant, and many of them are prostitutes [*meretrice*]."[15]

Yuhanna al-Asad had also seen something of the richly garbed slave-courtesans, the talented singers and dancers who were found in the sultans' courts and the households of great men and who were privileged figures in Arabic love stories (figure 19). Especially he remembered them from the Hafsid court at Tunis, where they delighted the sensuous ear of Sultan Muhammad ibn al-Hasan. In Cairo, he would have heard the names of the most celebrated singers of his day, Hifa the Delicious, Khadidja, Badriya bint Djuraiʾa.[16]

But the appearance and dress of women and their sexual accessibility beyond the trade of prostitution won his attention even more. Other Arab travelers and geographers made note of this, Ibn Battuta enthusing, for instance, about the beauty and elegance of form of the women in a town in Yemen, and al-Bakri claiming—from books and hearsay, not from experience—that male travelers among the Berber Ghomara near the Mediterranean town of Badis could expect their host to offer them a widow or other celibate female relative for the night.[17]

Yuhanna al-Asad gives details about the women he saw: in the High Atlas Berber town of Aït Attab, they have "very white skin and go about in good order wearing many ornaments of silver; their hair is oiled and they all have black eyes." He seems to have preferred his women plump, for more than once he combined this quality with beauty: in a town in the Haha, the women are "very beautiful creatures, very white, fat and very polite and pleasant." Here, as in other rural and mountainous regions of Morocco, he could easily make such an assessment, since the women ordinarily left their faces uncovered. The "natural whiteness" of the Berber women pleased him, though he also found "very beautiful and graceful" the mulatto women he came across south of the Anti-Atlas and in the Sahara.[18]

He describes veiling especially for women in the major cities. In Tunis as in Fez, women went out with their faces covered except for their eyes, but a man passing by could still catch the delicious scent of their perfume.

In Meknes, the women from good families scarcely left their dwellings, except when it was dark, and then with their faces covered. In Cairo, in contrast, wealthy women were seen in the streets all day long, gorgeously appareled and bejeweled from head to toe and wearing diaphanous black veils that kept men from seeing their faces but allowed them to see out.[19]

He hints at more direct contact in Berber areas, if nothing like that allowed by al-Bakri's Ghomara hosts. Especially welcoming were the women among the Berber nomads in the Sahara (we would call them Tuareg today): they were "friendly in conversation, touched hands, and sometimes let themselves be kissed. But one must not press things further, because the men kill each other in such a cause." Yuhanna al-Asad makes this pairing of "pleasant" women and "jealous" husbands in many Berber settlements, but only once does he suggest to his Italian readers how far he went in testing the men's hot anger. He and his party spent three days at the home of a fellow refugee from Granada in El Medina, on the slopes of the High Atlas, where "the very beautiful women [bellissime] took their pleasure with strangers in secret."[20]

Muslim teaching absolutely forbade as the grave sin of zina' any sexual intercourse outside of marriage or the legitimate congress of a male slave owner with his female slave. Adultery was especially serious. In his Neckring of the Dove on Lovers and Love, the Andalusian philosopher and poet Ibn Hazm (d. 456/1064) told understanding stories of love and desire, licit and illicit, including some about himself; but he added a chapter on sinful acts and the power of temptation: "no one is sheltered from the seduction of the devil."[21]

Yuhanna al-Asad expresses mild disapproval of the sleazy rowdiness connected with female prostitution in Fez and thinks that it was "great poverty" that turned so many women to prostitution in Tunis.[22] Adultery had troubling, even momentous consequences when it overflowed into political life. But in describing dalliance and male efforts to approach wives and daughters, he raises not the sin of zina' but only the question of honor, when jealous husbands and fathers were the danger.

What most drew his expressions of ire—as in the condemnations in the Qur'an, hadith, and Islamic religious commentary[23]—were erotic relations between men and between women. Female diviners of Fez who, claiming to be possessed by djinns or demons, foretold the future or served as healers, were in fact *suhaqiyat* (*sahacat*, as he transliterated into Italian the current Arabic word for "tribades," lesbians), women who had the "evil custom" of "rubbing" (*fregare*) each other in sexual delight. Assuming the voices of demons, they lured beautiful women into their lascivious company, singing, dancing, and having sex with them, enticing them to trick their husbands along the way.[24]

Even more dangerous in his eyes, and deserving of much more serious punishment in Islamic law, was *liwat* (from the biblical Lot)—that is, sexual practice between men.[25] The people of Azemmour had been conquered in 919/1513 by the Portuguese Christians partly as punishment for their "great sodomy," with a father seeking "a friend" for his own son. In Fez lived that "breed who call themselves *el cheva*" (perhaps we should read *el chena*; here Yuhanna al-Asad was transliterating either *al-hiwa*, an Andalusian word for "sodomites," or *al-khanith, mukhannath*, "effeminate men"). In their special hostelries, these men shaved their beards, dressed, talked, acted like women, and "kept a man like a Husband." They were "accursed," writes Yuhanna al-Asad; they were forbidden to enter the mosques and were scorned by all literary men, merchants, and right-thinking artisans. Only "idlers" went to their quarters, where wine could be had and men could find female whores as well. But, he has to admit, these "wretched" cross-dressers served as cooks for the sultan's army and as lamenters at the death of the city folk in Fez, beating drums and singing verses in praise of the deceased.[26]

And what of the Sufi masters and their disciples at wedding banquets and other festivities in Fez? They began to dance, weep, and rend their garments, and though they said it was out of divine love, Yuhanna al-Asad thinks it was rather out of love for the "beardless youths" among their disciples. The younger men lifted the older Sufis from the floor when they fell, wiped their faces, and kissed them. "As the Fez proverb puts it, 'After the holy men's banquet, twenty will be changed to ten,' that is, during the night after the dancing, when it is time to sleep, each of the disciples will be touched."[27]

Yuhanna al-Asad could attest to these practices because "many times he had found himself at their banquets." This phrase (omitted by Ramusio in his printed edition) suggests a more complicated, even contradictory relation to homoerotic behavior than mere rejection and distance. What was he doing at those banquets? About his visits to Tunis, he notes that the "ill-fated boys" (*li putti di mala sorte*) were more importunate, "behaved even worse" than the female prostitutes.[28] It sounds as though he knew from experience.

Yuhanna al-Asad had also read about homoerotic desire in literature. The sources here were abundant—from the celebrated ribaldry (*mujun*) poetry of Abu Nuwas (d. 194–95/810), with its earthly paradise of golden wine and male sex with boys and men, to al-Jahiz's *The Mutual Rivalry of Maidens and Young Men*, an unabashed, comic debate between a male lover of women and a male lover of men. In *The Neckring of the Dove* Ibn Hazm told of men who fell passionately in love with other men, whom he reproached only when their affection was translated into sexual action.[29]

Yuhanna al-Asad mentions the appearance of such themes in different genres. Ending his Sufi banquet story, he refers enigmatically to similar unseemly happenings in one of the rhymed prose tales of the *Maqamat* of al-Hariri. The vagabond-poet Abu Zayd extracts money from the governor of Al-Rahba by playing on the latter's well-known love of young men. Using his own beautiful son as bait, Abu Zayd claims that the lad is a stranger who has killed his son. In an agreed-upon scenario, Abu Zayd requires the lad to swear that if he lies in saying he has not killed the son, may his eyes become sticky with mucus, his teeth turn green, and other disgusting damage be done to his charms. The lad refuses to swear such an oath, and the enamored governor offers money to Abu Zayd so long as he drops the case and lets him pass the night with the accused. Abu Zayd takes the money, and he and his son get away before the governor has had the chance to satisfy his passion.[30]

Such desires were also expressed in poetry. The poets of Fez wrote love poems not only to women, says Yuhanna al-Asad, but also to "young men, publicly, without shame." In his own biographies of *Some*

Learned Men among the Jews, he describes such a poet: "Abraham ibnu Sahal," that is, Ibrahim ibn Sahl (d. ca. 648/1251) from Seville. Whatever symbolic or mystical meanings inhered in Ibn Sahl's verses, Yuhanna al-Asad writes of their literal meaning. Ibn Sahl's Arabic love poetry was directed to a man, real or imagined, a Jew named Moses (Musa in Arabic), and Yuhanna al-Asad quotes from it, "I have received the Torah or the Law of my love from Moses." Along with other inventions, Yuhanna al-Asad makes up an end for Ibn Sahl, or he perhaps takes it from some garbled North African tradition: the poet was given poison by the relatives of a youth whom he had sodomized. Still, Yuhanna al-Asad describes his love verses as "most elegant and most sweet."[31]

Yuhanna al-Asad had brought with him from North Africa a complex set of attitudes and desires about intimate life and sexuality—or so it would seem from what we can glean from his writings a few years later, and from customs and expressions in the Maghreb and the Islamic world. Though he valued women's work and the institution of marriage, he concerned himself as a writer more often with women's appearance and their availability to men, within or without marriage. In regard to sexual relations and passionate feelings between men, he expressed ambivalence. He singled them out for condemnation as shameless and "accursed," but he had known something of these networks and was appreciative of beautiful poetry whatever its inspiration.

Two examples show Yuhanna al-Asad's range in feelings. He praised the love poetry of the Egyptian Sufi Ibn al-Farid and saw it as "allegorical" of the higher teaching of Muslims seeking union with God through ascetic and mystic paths. Ibn al-Farid used both males and females as metaphors for divine things, which was a troubling evocation for some orthodox or puritanical Muslims but acceptable to Yuhanna al-Asad, despite the uncertain effect of the poetry.[32]

More down to earth was the North African story about lions. Yuhanna al-Asad had "understood from many men and women that when [a lion] encountered a woman alone in a remote place, if she uncovered her genitalia, the animal would roar loudly, lower his eyes, and go away without doing the woman any harm." We recall not only that

Yuhanna al-Asad had an enduring fear of lions, but that he had become a "lion," *al-asad*, at the time he wrote that story down. Such may have been the power of female sexuality for him.[33]

THE SEXUAL ECONOMY and gender relations that Yuhanna al-Asad witnessed during his years in Italy were both similar to and different from what he knew from North Africa and the world of Islam. In Rome perhaps sixty percent of the 54,000 city dwellers were men, an asymmetry due in part to the high number of churchmen in its convents and palaces; the pilgrims, diplomats, and others who swelled its population during the year were more often men as well.[34] During his sixteen months in the Castel Sant'Angelo, al-Wazzan would have scarcely seen a woman—perhaps a glimpse of a servant or a female prisoner, or of a woman in the street if he was taken out for questioning or to catechism.

Once released as Yuhanna al-Asad, the circles he first frequented were made up mostly of Christian men, celibate in principle if not always in practice: men of the papal court, the Vatican Library, and the papal chancellery, or in the entourage of Cardinal Egidio and his other godfathers. When he was transcribing Saint Paul's Epistles at Alberto Pio's Roman residence, his Christian companions once again were mostly celibate men. He would have learned much about celibacy as a holy state, obligatory for the clergy's high and sacramental tasks. This was a contrast to the major sweep of Islamic teaching, where only a little-followed strain of Sufism taught that "clearing a desire of lust in man's heart" was necessary to move up the ladder toward God's love. Nowhere in his writing did Yuhanna al-Asad give assent to such a view. His single description of an Islamic sect using "abstinence" among other ascetic techniques to rise to the grade of angels and the love of God ended up with the self-deniers "taking on all the pleasures of the world."[35]

Doubts about the holiness of celibacy would have been reinforced by the conduct of the clergy in Italy. Cardinal Egidio may have remained true to his Augustinian vows, but Giovanni Francesco Pico della Mirandola reproached his audience of pope and cardinals at the 1517 Lateran

Council for their "concubines," whom they adorned with jewels. The "honest courtesans" (*cortigiane oneste*) of Rome and other cities had eminent laymen and clerics among their lovers and protectors. In North Africa such women were the talented and beautiful slaves in a sultan's court or in the dwellings of great families, but here in Rome the most successful of them had sumptuously appointed households of their own and were known for their fine dress and sometimes for their learning. The celebrated Imperia had once received high Roman churchmen and the great banker Agostino Chigi; and Faustina Morosina was maintained by the literary critic Pietro Bembo, himself in minor orders in the 1520s and secretary to Pope Leo X.[36]

Men of more modest status sought sexual pleasure from prostitutes, the *meretrice*. Once he was free to walk through the streets of Rome, Yuhanna al-Asad would have been quick to see and hear of them as part of the city's public face. As in North Africa, their trade was considered sinful and dishonorable, but it was tolerated and to some extent regulated. In Venice and Florence, *meretrice* were confined to certain neighborhoods; in Rome, in Yuhanna al-Asad's day, they lived everywhere. Egidio da Viterbo had preached an emotional sermon to the city's prostitutes in 1508, but only a few were inspired to repentance. In 1521 an especially large number of them dwelled in the Campo Marzio quarter, Yuhanna al-Asad's neighborhood and not far from Egidio's Augustinian convent. These hardworking and lively women came from every part of Italy and from France, Germany, Greece, and Spain. They stood in their windows and at their doors, marking their houses with special linens or rugs, and went about the streets attracting attention through their clothes and manner.[37]

Two works composed in Rome during Yuhanna al-Asad's years there capture the sexual sensibilities of the city, the proximity of the sacred and the profane, the celibate and the erotic. One was *I Modi* (The Positions), a set of sixteen pictures of heterosexual intercourse—not between antique gods but between present-day ordinary mortals in their bedchambers. Giulio Romano, Raphael's pupil and heir, had taken time away from finishing the frescoes in the Sala di Costantino in the Vatican

to draw them and then pass them on to the engraver Marcantonio Raimondi. By late 1524 *The Positions* was in print, and the engraver had
been clapped into the Castel Sant'Angelo. Pope Clement VII had not
objected to the drawings when circulated to a small group, but their dis-
semination in print was a scandal. Still, protests at the imprisonment
came in from a cardinal and from the poet, playwright, and irreverent
satirist Pietro Aretino, one of the pope's familiars, and the engraver was
released. "Touched by the spirit that moved Giulio Romano to design
them," Aretino then decided to write *Sonetti Lussuriosi* (Lustful Son-
nets) to go with the pictures. "What harm is there in seeing a man
mount a woman?" Aretino asked. "It is the conduit from which gushes
the stream of life."[38]

Aretino's lines were published only in Venice in November 1527, after Yuhanna al-Asad had almost certainly left Italy for North Africa.
But if he had heard about the prints in 1524, he would have been curious and perhaps shocked: surely the latter if the subject came up while
he was transcribing the Qur'an for the worthy Egidio da Viterbo in
1525. Pictures of people were uncommon in Arabic books in the
Maghreb, but they had been added to manuscripts in the East for centuries. Presumably he had seen illustrated manuscripts in libraries at Fez
or Tunis or in his visits to Cairo and Istanbul, but he probably had never
come upon anything like the explicit erotica of *The Positions*.[39]

Another work produced in Rome during those years was the *Retrato
de la Lozana Andaluza* (Portrait of Lozana, the Andalusian Woman) by
Francisco Delicado. Delicado was born in Córdoba, probably to a family of converted Jews, in the same decade as al-Wazzan was born in
Granada to a family of staunch Muslims. Even before the reign of Pope
Leo X, Delicado was established in Rome as priest and physician, and
by 1524 he had completed a draft of his *Lozana*. A native of Córdoba
like her creator, Lozana comes from a family of Jewish *conversos*,
spends part of her youth in conquered Granada and elsewhere in Spain,
and has numerous adventures in Turkey and the Levant before arriving
in Rome in time to witness the installation of Leo X. Settling in the
Eternal City, she becomes an accomplished beautician (eyebrows and

clear skin are her specialty), skilled Mediterranean cook, healer of sexual ills and disorders, and prostitute—at first a simple whore charming men by her beauty and witty conversation, then a courtesan, and finally manager of and go-between for other courtesans. Her clients are men high and low, including ambassadors, friars, and a canon. Her loyalty remains to her servant, partner, and lover Rampín: he too is the son of Jews or Jewish *conversos*, and he vomits when he eats ham. Lozana says or does whatever is required to get what she wants and prides herself on her independence: "I eat at my own expense, which makes for a tastier meal, and I have no envy, not even of the Pope." One of her observers, a man attracted to her beauty but critical of her antics, sounds a somber note about the excessive freedom in Rome: "Why else do you think Rome is given the name Babylon . . . ? Why else would they call Rome a strumpet?"[40]

Delicado's *Lozana Andaluza* was not published until 1528 in Venice (with ominous references to the coming sack of Rome by imperial troops added to his 1524 dialogues). Once again Yuhanna al-Asad could not have read the printed book, and unless the two men crossed paths earlier in Rome —a possibility, as we shall see—he would not have known of Delicado's creation. But *Lozana Andaluza* opens up a social and sexual world that was swirling around Yuhanna al-Asad and contains ways of talking about it that he could have heard from others and used for himself.

Both Aretino and Delicado mentioned in passing homosexual desire, Aretino recalling as inspiration an ancient marble statue in the garden of the banker Chigi: a satyr is attempting to penetrate a youth. Homoerotic practices were harshly condemned in Christian Italy as in Islamic societies, being considered sinful and now even diabolic, but they were carried on in various circles, with some caution and with more likelihood of actual surveillance and prosecution than in North Africa. During the very months al-Hasan al-Wazzan was being delivered to the Castel Sant'Angelo, one papal court fined five men for "sodomy" in Rome, including a Spanish immigrant, a Jew, and a priest, and rewarded a sixth for providing information.[41]

Once released from prison, Yuhanna al-Asad would have readily discovered that the "beautiful boy," the beardless youth, was an important
figure in the male imagination in Italy as in North Africa. Among the
humanist-clerical network in Rome, men were accused of homosexual
acts, including the bishop-historian Paolo Giovio, claimed in one
learned poem to maintain a *cynaedus*, that is, a youth who was the passive partner. Castiglione, who redrafted his *Courtier* in Rome in the
early 1520s, gave a playful exchange between two gentlemen visiting the
city during Lent: one, seeing some beautiful Roman women, quoted
Ovid, "Your Rome has as many maidens [*puellas*] as the heaven has
stars," whereupon the other, seeing a group of young men, responded,
"Your Rome has as many *cinaedos* as the meadows have lambs." In
1524–25 Benvenuto Cellini took on such a lad as his assistant while he
was working on a vase for the bishop of Salamanca; so beautiful was
this Paulino that Cellini was taken with love for him, played music for
him just to see his beautiful and honest smile, and was "not at all surprised by those stories the Greeks wrote about their gods."[42]

Meanwhile in Venice and Florence, whole groups of male adoles-
cents had relations with older men as an expected initiation into sexuality. Some became young prostitutes, some sustained relations with
men, many married women once they moved into adulthood. A web of
language, jokes, customs, and meeting places had sprung up around
these practices, surviving despite surveillance, prosecution, and punishment by the authorities and, in the case of Florence, despite Savonarola's
sweeping attack on "the abominable vice" during the republic of
1494–98. Not long after the Medici returned to rule Florence in 1512
and then again in 1520, the severe penalties for sodomy imposed during
Savonarola's years were softened, especially in regard to the young.[43]

Linked as he was to Medici circles in Rome, Yuhanna al-Asad must
have heard about this world. By the time he came to write his *Lives* and
his *Geography*, he had picked up local words and turns of phrase associated with homoerotic activities, the same words and phrases uttered
to the Florentine Officers of the Night by participant-informers and

found also in popular texts. For example, as Yuhanna al-Asad tells it, the youthful son of the current sultan of Tunis, sent by his father to administer the town of Constantine, was rebelled against by the townsfolk not only because he was unjust but also because he was *"un cinedo et grande imbriaco"*—that is, a youthful passive partner and coupler with men. Cross-dressing men in the Fez hostels "keep a man like a husband," as the older men in Florence talked of "keep[ing] a boy like a woman." The Fez populace wished death to such *"giottoni,"* Yuhanna al-Asad's spelling for *ghiotti*, or gluttons, a word used in popular poetry and slang to refer to sodomists.[44] And in mentioning the *"fregatrice"* of Fez, he seems to have had a good ear for the popular words used at the time in Italy for erotic acts between women.[45]

Besides learning about sexual networks and intimate relations in Italy, did Yuhanna al-Asad take part in them? A vigorous man in his thirties, he would have recalled that masturbation was forbidden by Malikite law, even if allowed by some other Muslim jurists when done "to ease desire." Christian teaching also included masturbation among the prohibited "sins against nature," to be reported to one's priest in confession.[46] In any case, onanism was a lonely consolation for a man who presented himself as gregarious.

Yuhanna al-Asad probably carried with him the same complicated attitudes about homoerotic relations with men as he expressed in his writings on Islamic societies—condemning them, yet immensely curious about them and close enough at least to report on them. Did he go to neighborhoods in Venice and Florence where the *bardassi*, the boy prostitutes, might pursue him, as such lads had pursued foreign men during his visits to Tunis?

But his eyes and sensibility in the *Geography* were primarily directed toward women, and we can expect the same in his life in Italy. Yuhanna al-Asad had ample opportunity to see them: women, slave and free, serving in Christian households, women going about their business in the streets and markets of Rome and other Italian towns he visited, women praying in church. Some aristocratic husbands in Venice tried to keep their wives indoors much of the time, but most women went about in public at least as much as they did in Cairo. A keen observer of women's appearance, he would have noted headdresses everywhere, face-covering much less often than in Muslim towns—light veils perhaps for wealthy women, more substantial covering sometimes for the faces of well-bred young women.[47]

In his many references to Europe in his *Geography of Africa*, Yuhanna al-Asad mentioned one sexual institution explicitly: the brothel.[48] Away from the disapproving regard of his godfather Egidio da Viterbo, he may well have had contact with the prostitutes in Rome. In their society, as described by Francisco Delicado, he would have found a welcome as a onetime Muslim and foreigner at least as easy as that extended to him in the cosmopolitan circles of learned celibates. Jews, converted Jews, Moors, Moriscos, and Christians all frequent Lozana's world, not worrying about converting each other but exchanging foods, spices, information, gossip, sex, textiles, remedies, money, jewels, and garments. The language heard was not a "perfect Castilian," Delicado explained, but a mixed speech—popular Spanish phrases, Catalan, Portuguese, Italian, even an Arab word once in a while: "I tailored my speech to the sound of my ears."[49] (One thinks of the lingua franca spoken on the Mediterranean boats and in its port towns.) Along with her Spanish and Jewish origins, Lozana has connections with Arab ways and Muslim lands. With her first lover, a merchant from whom she has been cruelly separated, she has traveled to Turkey, the Levant, North Africa, and even the Barbary Coast. Some of her best beauty secrets come from the Levant, while the dishes she prepares are taken from both Jewish and Arabic cuisine. Delicado was writing of Lozana's pride in her couscous with chickpeas (*alcuzcuzu con garbanzos*) at the same time Yuhanna al-Asad was describing in his *Geography* how to make *el cuscusu* (*al-kuskusu*) Fasi style.[50]

Lozana's lover, go-between, and servant in Rome, named Rampín, has been brought up in a house where his mother receives both "Moors and Jews." Though a Jew or converso, Rampín is referred to by one sarcastic house servant as "Abenamar," that is, Ibn al-Ahmar, founder of the Nasrid dynasty in al-Andalus; while a jealous gallant calls him "*al-faqui*"—surely the only other faqih in Rome besides Yuhanna al-Asad. When one of Lozana's gentlemen needs a special gift, Rampín can quickly put his hands on a Tunisian headdress.[51]

Among the whores around Lozana are a mother and daughter from Granada, the former so elderly that she could have been living in that city before it fell to the Christians. Giving some hard-boiled advice to her, Lozana says, "Do you think by chance you are still in Granada, where things are done for love? Dear lady, here it's a matter of money and give and take."[52]

The Rome/Granada comparison suggests, as do the image of *Roma putana* (Rome the whore) and the forebodings of the sack of Rome, that Delicado had moral and critical goals in writing his book. But the *Lozana* is simultaneously a comic and a ludic work, closely attentive to what its author had seen and heard in Rome. That Delicado had met the converted faqih from Granada in the course of his "field work" seems plausible. The streets of the Campo Marzio quarter, where Yuhanna al-Asad lodged in 1521, as described in a census a few years later, were peopled with women like those in Delicado's pages: the Spanish courtesan Jeronima and the Italian courtesan Francisca, living next door to Maria the Moor and Beatrix from Spain, to give only a few examples.[53] Especially in the first years after his release from Sant'Angelo, Yuhanna al-Asad was most likely to have had contact with such women and the common languages of their world, with as much or perhaps more ease than he had had back in Africa.

BY 1526, a further change seems to have come into his life. One "Io. Leo"—Joannes Leo—is listed on the January 1527 Roman census as heading a household of three persons in the Regula quarter. The chances are very good that this was Yuhanna al-Asad. The combination of his two baptismal names—Giovanni Leone, Joannes Leo—was rare in Rome in his day, and in the entire census list there is only one Joannes Leo. In countless notarial documents, criminal fines, papal payments, and reports of consistorial meetings of the 1520s, I found only "Jo. Leo venetus," "Giovanni Leone Venetian," sentenced in November 1522 to pay three ducats for preventing someone from going out the door of his house and other provocations. On the 1527 census, people are ordinarily listed with their place of origin, and no Venetian Joannes Leo is found there.[54]

It would have made things easier if the census-takers had qualified "Ioannes Leo" as "africanus" (an adjective used nowhere on the list) or as "morus" (which follows a number of other names). But Yuhanna al-Asad, with his in-between status, was hard to characterize; the census-takers might well have thought that a North African convert was sufficiently identifiable by his distinctive name. I think it reasonable to assume that "Ioannes Leo," head of a household with two other people, is our man.

What of the gender and age of the people? The census does not give such information, but it seems unlikely that Joannes Leo was directing a household of men. For that kind of life, he could just as well have remained in the Campo Marzio quarter, near Cardinal Egidio. And if he wanted simple independence, he could have set himself up alone: a number of single men were living thus in the Regula quarter.[55]

I speculate, then, that the household included a woman and a young child. The novelist Amin Maalouf has imagined as much, having Cardinal Giulio de' Medici himself give Giovanni Leone a Jewish conversa for a bride in 1521.[56] Rather than the busy and distant cardinal, one of Yuhanna al-Asad's godfathers—probably Egidio da Viterbo, to whom he was most closely linked—would have discussed such a delicate matter with him. The question of spouses from prior Muslim marriages came up from time to time in sixteenth-century Italy, where converted slaves and converted freed slaves were permitted to marry. Canon law was complicated on this point, generally insisting that a prior marriage was not dissolved when a person was baptized as a Christian, but allowing remarriage if the unconverted spouse would not live with the new Christian or put obstacles in the way of his or her religious observance. If he wanted to marry, the faqih Yuhanna al-Asad knew how to convince his godfather that he fit through this loophole: my marriage was dissolved by Muslim law the minute I converted to Christianity, he would have said, and I have been so long and so far away from my wife that she has surely remarried.[57]

If his argument failed and he still wanted to live with a woman in Rome at least for a time, concubinage was the solution. It was by no means unheard of, though by resorting to it, Yuhanna al-Asad would surely have risked Cardinal Egidio's displeasure. In any case, late 1525 or 1526 would have been a good moment for a change: his years of Arabic transcription, of work on the Qur'an, and of Italian travel were behind him, and he could set up a household in Rome.

Yuhanna al-Asad would have learned of Italian family life mostly through Jewish households. Alberto Pio was married, but the prince's wife lived in his estates in Carpi, and a mere scholarly servant and transcriber would have had no connection with her. Elijah Levita and his family in Rome and Jacob Mantino and his family in Bologna were different. Elijah ben Asher had taken a young Ashkenazic wife in Venice in 1494, and by the time Yuhanna al-Asad met him at Egidio da Viterbo's household, he had several children: a grown-up son, Judah; a daughter, Hannah, soon ready to marry; and younger sons and daughters. Jacob ben Samuel, a man closer to Yuhanna al-Asad's age, had married Gentilesca Cohen (likely, with that first name, to have come from an Italian family rather than to have been of Catalan origin like himself); they had at least one son, Samuel, whom his devoted father was training to be a scholar.[58]

As among the Muslims, these Jewish families expected their children to wed: Rabbi Leon Modena of Venice was later to say, "Every Jew is bound by the Law to marry." Back in North Africa, Yuhanna al-Asad had associated with Jewish men but not with Jewish women. Now he could observe Jewish family life with the women included, and the household as the setting for Jewish religious practices.[59] (Socializing between Jews and Christians went on in some circles in Italy in those years, despite ordinances intending to prevent it.)[60] As we can imagine Yuhanna al-Asad talking cosmopolitan street lingo with the Roman prostitutes, so we can imagine him conversing politely with these Jewish women, that is, nonkin unveiled women, though in the presence of the husband. With Elijah Levita's wife or daughter, who probably spoke Yiddish among themselves, Yuhanna al-Asad would have spoken his foreigner's Italian.[61] In Jacob Mantino's household, they may have talked in some version of Spanish as well.

The later autobiography of Ahmad al-Hajari gives us an inkling of how Yuhanna al-Asad might have felt when he first had such genteel conversations. An Andalusian Morisco returned to Islam, al-Hajari left his wife and children in Marrakesh in 1020/1611 for a two-year diplomatic mission to France for the sultan of Morocco. Along the way, he instructed himself and his companions "against the incitations of the soul and those of Satan in relation to forbidden women, because Satan is used to instill evil in us often, [especially] by means of unveiled women." Nonetheless, in the Vendée town of Olonne, he was quite taken with the beautiful, still unmarried daughter of a royal officer and she with him (or so he reported): he conversed with her and agonized over whether he could "stretch out his hand to young women and amuse them," as was the custom in France. Finally, after a talk with her alone in a concealed part of the family garden, they separated; "I ask God forgiveness for the words I expressed to her and for having looked at her."[62]

From Jacob Mantino, versed enough in Jewish law to serve later as arbitrator for marriage and other disputes among Jews in Rome, Yuhanna al-Asad could have learned about Jewish and Christian dowry practices.[63] Twice in his *Geography*, he compared those he knew from the Maghreb with the European dowry brought by the bride to the groom. "In Italy people say that among the Muslims, the husband gives the dowry to the wife." That is true, he went on, but they do not realize that the bride's father gives much more through the trousseau to his daughter. Any father would be "ashamed" not to do so. "Thus, the daughter is the ruin of the father in every country."[64]

Yuhanna al-Asad perhaps received a European dowry during his Italian years, but I doubt that our converted Moor had found someone of the high station of Othello's Desdemona. His crowded quarter running along the Tiber had only one palatial household, that of the Cardinal Farnese, and only a few others with more than twenty members. Yuhanna al-Asad's near neighbors were shoemakers, tailors, washerwomen, water-carriers, bakers, masons, and other artisans, with an occasional physician or painter. As elsewhere in Rome, the people came from all over: from many parts of Italy, some from Spain, and a good number from Germany. Several streets away from Yuhanna al-Asad, the houses were packed with Jews. Yuhanna al-Asad's companion was in all likelihood a foreigner in Rome, perhaps a *mora*, a converted Moor from his former neighborhood in the Campo Marzio, where many of them lived. If he had made a marriage with her, it would have been a simple affair, without the kin alliances constructed for more settled households in Rome, and with a very small dowry, jotted down by a notary, a nuptial ring for the wife, and a blessing from the priest in church.[65] Such a marriage would also be easier to defend when he returned to North Africa. According to the 910/1504 fatwa on taqiyya, Morisco men, like Muslim men, were permitted to marry Christian women; so much the better if both of them had been forced to convert.[66]

OF ONE THING we can be sure: from the start of his time in Rome, Yuhanna al-Asad was plied with questions about Muslim women, men, marriage, and sexual practices. He himself reported conversations about the Muslim dowry, and surely he heard queries like those put to al-Hajari in France decades later: "Do you marry more than one wife?" "Are your women veiled?" "How can the girls express their love?"[67]

The sources for answers to such questions about North and sub-Saharan Africa were skimpy in the Europe of the 1520s. The Saracens in the reworked medieval romances were generic types: the women, such as the vehement and single-minded Floripas in the medieval romance of *Fierabras* and the Babylonian princess Margrete in Elijah ben Asher's *Bovo*, were at their best when saving Christian heroes whom they loved;

the men, like Ruggiero in Ariosto's *Orlando Furioso*, were at their best
when they converted to Christianity and purged themselves of violence
and extravagance. Ariosto's Rodomante of Algiers, who stays loyal to
Islam, is completely lacking in courtesy and destroys the town of Paris
with ferocious hatred.[68]

Details about women's garb, the seclusion of well-born women, and
multiple wives in North Africa might be passed on by Europeans who
had visited those regions, virtually all men: soldiers and priests in the
Maghrebi enclaves that Portuguese and Spaniards captured; Genoese
traders in Tunis, Fez, or Cairo; Venetian envoys to Mamluk Egypt;
European Christians ransomed from slavery in North Africa; Christian
pilgrims to Jerusalem going through Alexandria and Cairo. The most
important recent account of Muslim lands to appear in print concerned
Turkey, not Africa: *The Genealogy of the Grand Turk*, written by the
Greek Theodore Spandugino, who spent several years in Istanbul as
well as living in Venice and France. First published in a French translation in 1519, the book was known in Rome, where Spandugino had
presented Italian manuscripts to Leo X and Gianmatteo Giberti, later
to be one of Pope Clement VII's most important officials. Spandugino
devoted a chapter to Turkish dowry customs and wedding festivities,
but his text is infused with the mysteries of Turkish sexual practices:
the sultan's harem of around three hundred beauteous women, who
are guarded by one hundred eunuchs and honored when they become
pregnant; Turkish women, wondrously clean from going often to their
scented baths and "strongly attracted to the sin of lust"; similarly lustful
Turkish men, whose desire and fertility are fed by the sweets they
eat; their land of Turkey also "infected with sodomy," forbidden by
Muhammad, but practiced openly. Even Spandugino's account of
dowry and gift exchange weaves sex into it: the Turkish husband tries to
unveil and undress his new wife, but she fights him off until he promises
to add more money to the dowry.[69]

Yuhanna al-Asad's *Geography of Africa* unsettled these sexual images, if not so profoundly as he did other stereotypes current in European beliefs about Africa (fertility, sterility; monstrosity, etc.). As an

indigenous informant, he could demystify or normalize domestic and intimate events. Some women go about veiled, but some go unveiled, he explained. Large harems exist, with black eunuch guards, but they are a routine part of court life and ceremonial, administered by the sultan's bureaucracy. If Yuhanna al-Asad found Sultan Muhammad al-Hasan of Tunis immersed in sensuality with his slave dancers and musicians, he made clear this was not the inevitable court scene, but a shameful contrast with his Hafsid predecessors.[70]

Baths he described as pleasant places to get scrubbed clean, steamed, and refreshed, men and women at separate times or locations. The young men went about naked without embarrassment; the older men put towels around themselves. Both women and men ate and sang at the baths—"and amuse themselves in various ways," Ramusio added to his printed edition, but Yuhanna al-Asad had suggested no untoward goings-on in his manuscript. Nor did he describe the women's removal of their bodily hair, which Spandugino had made an essential part of the wedding preparations.[71]

While aware of and responding to European curiosity about the subject of sexuality, Yuhanna al-Asad wrote of it in his own terms, with the assumptions and tones of a North African man, an Arab, and a Muslim. As he presented himself, he was neither Ariosto's wild discourteous Rodomante nor a fully converted Ruggiero; neither a man dreaming deliciously of the virgins he will enjoy in Paradise, as in Spandugino's pages, nor scheming to take "as many wives as he can feed."[72] The narrator-observer of the *Geography* assessed women's beauty and reported on the accessibility of Berber and Arab women, but he was reserved about his own possible successes.

Female sexuality had a powerful appeal—witness the lion story—but Yuhanna al-Asad's women and men are not saturated with lust, as in the Spandugino stereotype, and female sexual appetite is not linked to demonic witchcraft, as in some current European writing. He portrays sex as central in marriage, sometimes as a rightful delight (the painted wives of the Arab nomads south of Tlemcen and Tunis), sometimes as disruptive excess (the quarreling families of Cairo). Prostitution is widespread and same-sex relations are present, but these are produced not by some general Muslim miasma or "infection" but by special institutions and places (certain hotels, wine houses, and government-taxed bordellos); by special religious practices (Sufi dancing, banquets; divining by women claiming access to djinns); and by religious metaphors and literary convention. If human concupiscence was to blame, so in some circumstances, like those at Tunis, was extreme poverty.

And as Yuhanna al-Asad makes clear to his readers in his reference to European brothels and his use of Italian slang for same-sex intimacy, the western Christian world had its share of such institutions and behavior. Ramusio replaced the slang with more genteel terms, but readers of the printed edition may still have made the analogies.[73]

The printed edition also contains a sexual tale that is absent from the sole surviving manuscript of the *Geography*, although it seems to have been written by the North African author, perhaps embroidered a little by his Italian editor. A comic story of seduction, adultery, and ruse, it would be at home on both sides of the Mediterranean. Its source was said to be the chancellor of the ruler of Debdou, an old Berber chief with whom al-Wazzan had lodged during a diplomatic visit to the Middle Atlas. The chancellor told al-Wazzan about an officer sent on a mission to one of the ruler's villages. Smitten with the wife of a villager, the officer followed the couple one day as they went to collect wood in the forest, and when they were out of sight, he detached their donkey from the tree where it had been hitched. When the couple came back to the tree with their wood and found the donkey gone, the husband left to look for it. The officer emerged from his hiding place, promptly won over the wife to his amorous enterprise, and then made his getaway just as the husband returned with the donkey. Tired from his search, the husband stretched out with his wife and began to fondle her playfully as he liked to do. Finding her all soft and wet in her private parts, he said,

"Wife, what does this mean? Why are you all wet?" Whereupon the mischievous wife responded, "I wept seeing you not come back and thinking that our donkey was lost. Feeling this, my sister [*sirocchia*] began to weep, out of pity for me." The foolish husband believed her and told her to be consoled and not to cry any longer.[74]

Though I have not found this exact story in any Arabic or Italian collection, its motifs are common in both traditions: the paramour (here would-be paramour) sending the husband off on a "fool's errand"; the paramour escaping just in time; the unfaithful wife put to the test and finding a clever deception; the gullible husband. Al-Hawrani's *Unveiling of the Ruses Woven by Women*, a fourteenth-century collection, includes a wife caught by her husband in a tryst at a wine parlor; she turns the tables on him and humiliates him as an adulterer. Boccaccio, in his *Decameron*, filled its seventh day with clever paramours, cooperative wives, and successful ruses.[75]

Even the detail about the wet genitalia and their transformation into a "weeping sister" had resonance on both sides of the Mediterranean. Among Arabic tales, semen, real or sham, is used to deceive or win an argument, and the genitalia are sometimes personified: in a dialogue in al-Jahiz's *Book of the Animals*, the vagina is dubbed an "unbeliever" because, in contrast to the penis, it faces away from the Qibla (the direction of Mecca) when the woman kneels in prayer; by an old tradition, Maghreb women refer to their periods as a visit from their (maternal) aunt.[76] And in Italian stories, bodily fluids are also revealing, and especially we find the vulva called "sister" in an amusing recital by the writer Pietro Fortini (ca. 1500–62). A lascivious abbot is summoned upon to choose among three nuns for the next abbess of a convent. Each proclaims her practical skills and also raises her gown to show her bodily charms. Suor Cecilia wins when she holds together the lips of her "sister" (*sorella*), leaving only a little space through which she urinates into the eye of an embroidery needle held by a young priest, without spilling a drop. In another tale, Fortini also called the penis "brother."[77]

Like al-Wazzan's bird story, then, the Debdou story was a bridge across the Mediterranean. The criteria for adab literature included delightful anecdotes as part of good writing, and what better place to insert one than in a description of the region in the Middle Atlas where he had been so warmly welcomed? Perhaps the chancellor had in fact given al-Wazzan a version of this story, and then, once in Italy, he changed the wording, picking up "sister" for vulva the way he had picked up sodomitic slang. The important point is that in the Debdou story, the mix of sexual play, comic transgression, and ruse is not distinctively African and does not represent Berber Muslims as saturated with lust.

Yuhanna al-Asad also undermined European stereotypes about Muslim women—or simply repaired European ignorance—by mentioning the women's work that he observed throughout his travels. To be sure, his Arabo-Islamic sources might have yielded more. He reported women selling linen thread at the Fez market, but he would have known from al-Wansharisi's fatwas and his other legal studies that women were also active in larger-scale commerce, lending money from their dowries, buying and selling grain and other properties, and founding and managing charitable endowments. Along with the women who healed through divination, he might have mentioned the midwives, whose skill in bringing babies into the world and in treating their ills had been praised by Ibn Khaldun in the *Muqaddima*.

Along with the unusual female schoolteachers he recalled seeing in the Tichit oasis, he might have included a learned woman teacher or two in his *Illustrious Arabs*. Ibn Hazm had said of his upbringing in Córdoba: "[Women] taught me the Qur'an and recited many poems to me and drilled me in calligraphy," while the big biographical dictionary of al-Sakhawi (d. 902/1497) included entries for almost four hundred women who had studied and received licenses to teach. Yuhanna al-Asad did mention in his work on prosody one Jumeima bint Abi-l-Aswad, but he passed over the verses of the most celebrated women poets of al-Andalus, Wallada and Hafsa bint al-Hajj.[78]

Women appear in the political narratives of Yuhanna al-Asad's *Geography* as the fomenters or subjects of love intrigue, with "ruinous" outcomes as in the violence and conquest of Safi. (He could portray Christian adultery with positive consequences at least for the Muslims, as when the murder of the Christian commander of Peñon de Velez by a cuckolded Spanish soldier led the way to the sultan of Fez retaking that island.) In a town on a slope of the High Atlas, Muslim women donated bracelets and rings for their husbands' ransom from the sultan's soldiers, although they did so "by a trick" (*per malitia*), concealing the fact that they had more money at home. More grandly, Yuhanna al-Asad writes of the wife of the Almohad ruler Abu Yusuf Yaʿqub al-Mansur, who sold her jewels and gold and silver ornaments from their wedding exchange to pay for golden balls atop the minaret of the Kutubiya mosque in Marrakesh. They had become prized objects in the popular imagination of the townsfolk, planets imbued with guardian spirits, never to be removed even when later rulers needed the gold to pay for defense against the Christians.

Yet in recounting the rise of the Almoravid ruler Yusuf ibn Tashfin, Yuhanna al-Asad did not mention his wife and counselor Zaynab, a female figure especially remembered in the Maghreb for her effect on policy: it was she, said Ibn Khaldun in his *History of the Berbers*, who had urged her husband to independence, "a woman distinguished by her beauty and her political skill."[79]

Perhaps Yuhanna al-Asad said more about women's political, economic, and religious roles in his lost books on Malikite law and Muslim history. But it is certain he was not writing as a champion of women's qualities and possibilities. There was no exact Arabic analogue to the European genre in which strong claims were made for women's similarity or superiority to men—as in Christine de Pizan's *City of Ladies* (1405), Cornelius Agrippa von Nettesheim's *On the Nobility and Excellence of Womankind* (1509), and *Apology for Women* (1529) by Cardinal Pompeo Colonna, dedicated to his cousin, the poet Vittoria Colonna. Instead, women's achievements were exemplified in biographical dictionaries or demonstrated through figures like the clever Shahrazad, who survives and ultimately wins the Persian sultan Shahriyar as her husband by her many nights of gripping storytelling.[80]

In Castiglione's *Courtier*, the gentlemen debate women's defects, virtues, and achievements in front of the court ladies. A somewhat different debate takes place in a fourteenth-century tale by al-Hawrani. The Yemeni woman Hurra (her name means "free") is repudiated by her suddenly ascetic husband; becomes the manager of a group of beautiful, talented, and articulate slave women; travels with them to Cairo and elsewhere, amazing rulers by her education and advice; and ends up married to the son of the sultan of Baghdad. Before her new court, she commands two lawyers to argue, one to the honor of women, the other to the honor of men. They talk of marriage and lovemaking, but when their debate is unresolved, Hurra concludes with a story about human beings, cruel and kind, in which through the help of djinns and clever women, the right man and woman end up married.[81]

Yuhanna al-Asad did not portray any talented Shahrazads or Hurras in his *Africa* book. His women are more restricted in their maneuvers; the only master trickster in the *Geography* is the amphibian author himself. Yuhanna al-Asad may have heard echoes of the Italians' "debate about women" including, on the negative side, Giovanni Francesco Pico della Mirandola's dialogue on Witchcraft, *Strix*, published in Bologna a few months before Yuhanna al-Asad's visit there; he may have got word from Jacob Mantino about the influential duchesses at the courts of Mantua and Ferrara; he may have gleaned scraps of information about learned women in Italy.[82] But such information had little effect on his account of African women. What *did* affect him were his observations and experience of sexual, intimate, and family life in Italy—in the families of Jews, in the popular quarters of Rome with prostitutes, and in his own household. Here, at the dining table that he said he preferred to the floor and common pot, as in Morocco, he could get his strongest sense of how to compare the two social worlds, assess their similarities, and hold on to their differences.

CHAPTER EIGHT

Translation, Transmission, and Distance

"YOU KNOW ME, I am one of you," says Yuhanna al-Asad's amphibian bird when he arrives among the fish. He must remain with the fish, resemble them, for a year, and yet be distant enough to be ready for quick departure when the tax-collector comes around. So with Yuhanna al-Asad in Italy over the seven years after his conversion. He found ways to be close and to be distant to both his old world and his new one. His curiosity and artfulness allowed him to flourish as a writer, scholarly companion, and perhaps lover without being overwhelmed by guilty conflict and anxiety. And his experiences turned him in unexpected directions.

The most accessible mode for sustaining a double identity was to find equivalents, to locate places where worlds seemed to converge. Yuhanna al-Asad had already developed the habit of comparison and translation during his years as diplomat and traveler in Africa and the Levant. He had noted customs that varied sharply (female excision was "ordered by Muhammad," but practiced only in Syria and Egypt by "old women, who were like master barbers and who cut the tip of the crest of Nature"), but despite these differences within Dar al-Islam, everything was held together by a common religion.[1]

Describing North Africa to Italians was harder, and Yuhanna al-Asad had to reach for likenesses to make things clear: for example, pastoral Berbers in the High Atlas had light bark houses, easily moved, their "roof beams arranged in circles like those on the tops of baskets that go with women riding mules, as is the custom for travel in Italy."[2] And he frequently found equivalents for measures and money. To readers of his Latin book on Arabic prosody, he showed where Arabic feet were like Latin feet and where they were different. The Arabic word for verse or strophe—*bait*—also meant "house" and "tent," hardly the same as the grid of words around the Latin *carmen*; still there were Arabic equivalents to the Latin spondee and dactyl.[3]

His first systematic training in translation was the 1524 Arab-Hebrew-Latin dictionary, especially enlightening for him because his collaborator was Jewish. Translation, as Umberto Eco has pointed out, is a movement between languages and also between cultures, as the translator seeks words that will bring about the same effect as those in the source language.[4] The dictionary planned by Yuhanna al-Asad and Jacob ben Samuel gave single words without contexts; the task was to find the best linguistic equivalent each time. For the first 170 entries, which Mantino filled in with the Hebrew and the Latin, while presumably consulting with Yuhanna al-Asad, cultural likenesses and differences surely surfaced often. For instance, *khitan*, or circumcision, had a similar technical meaning in the various languages, but it carried a different emotional freight for these two circumcised men than it did for the Christians around them, for whom it was a reproved mark of difference. *Imam* (prayer leader, spiritual leader) called forth the Latin *sacerdos* (priest) from the Christian owner who inherited the manuscript from Mantino and subsequently annotated it. Yuhanna al-Asad in his *Geography* settled for *sacerdote*, which in Italian has ritual and sacramental connotations quite inappropriate for the praying and preaching activities of the Muslim figure.[5] Still, the assumption was that equivalent words could be found, and this despite Arabic's privileged standing for Yuhanna al-Asad—it was the language in which God had uttered the Qur'an—and Hebrew's for Mantino.

Some important words invited convergence even while leaving room for variation—*Allah* first of all. Here Mantino left a blank after Yuhanna al-Asad's Arabic. The Hebrew four-letter name of God and its variations carried awe, sanctity, and power. The Name would have been inscribed on the back of the mezuzah on Mantino's door, but he did not write it in its place in this mundane dictionary. (The subsequent Christian owner later added a wrongly spelled Hebrew "name": *Heh, Lamed*, instead of the correct *Aleph, Lamed*.)[6]

Yuhanna al-Asad and Mantino would have talked about *Iblis* and *Shaitan*, Arabic names for the devil and both entered at the appropriate letter. As they considered the Hebrew choices, they would have compared the devil's many forms: the adversary, the deceiver, the disobedient arch-rebel to God, and so on. *Shaitan* came late in the dictionary, in a part of the alphabet where Mantino had stopped his columns, but he would have planned to write *Satan* in Hebrew, perhaps telling Yuhanna al-Asad about Maimonides's etymology for that name: *satah*, "to turn away," "to go astray." He may even have planned to add "Samaël," for had not Maimonides said in his *Guide for the Perplexed* that "Samaël is the name generally applied by our Sages to Satan"?[7]

Iblis came early in the dictionary. What other names could Mantino use for Iblis besides Satan and Samaël? Apart from Hebrew terms for "evil spirit," "the adversary," and the like, the other name most recited in his day was probably "Lilith," the powerful she-demon, identified in some cabalistic sources as Samaël's wife. Mantino, a physician, would have known how often Lilith's name appeared on Hebrew charms intended to protect newborn children against harm. But could he and Yuhanna al-Asad find this a suitable translation of *Iblis*?[8]

Instead, Mantino wrote the word "Lucifer" in Latin characters in the Hebrew column, a name stressing the devil's origin as the fallen angel, "the shining one," of Isaiah 14:12. Ancient and medieval rabbis had not used the name "Lucifer," but some of them told of a fallen angel named Shemhazai, who, tricked by ʿAsterah/Ishtar, inadvertently made possible her rise to the heavens and her placement as the morning star. From such traditions, it seems—probably discussed with Yuhanna al-Asad—Mantino settled on "Lucifer," which at least had connection with the Qurʾanic accounts of Iblis as a fallen angel.[9]

By the time Yuhanna al-Asad came to set down words related to the Five Pillars of Islam, the five requirements that all Muslims must fulfill, he could perceive deep similarities along with detailed differences. His various Arabic terms for "service to God, blessing, supplication, prayer"—ʿubudiya, baraka, daʿwa, salah—could be given their Hebrew and Latin equivalents. Likewise when he wrote "abstinence" (imtinaʿ), he could think not only of the Hebrew and Latin words to be penned next to his but of the fasts of Yom Kippur and Lent. And his hajj to Mecca would lead him to anticipate the Hebrew and Latin pilgrimages to Jerusalem.[10]

The dictionary was in part a spiritual exercise for Yuhanna al-Asad. Zakat and sadaqa are equivalent to "alms," ihsan to "generosity": when Yuhanna al-Asad gave money to a beggar or made another charitable donation, instead of intending it only internally as his annual obligatory zakat (as urged upon Moriscos in the 910/1504 fatwa on taqiyya), he could also acknowledge it as a beneficent action shared by Islam and Christianity.[11]

Let us take a much more sensitive example, one found not in Yuhanna al-Asad's dictionary but in the 1521 opening to his Arabic transcription of Saint Paul's Epistles: his calling Jesus "the Son of God." There he could say to himself, as the fatwa recommended, that while needing outwardly to please his patron, Alberto Pio, he had inwardly intended the phrase to be "Jesus is the son of Mary who worships God."[12]

But he could also understand the phrase as incorporating an idea found in some strains of Islam, including that developed by the philosoper and mystic Ibn ʿArabi, born in al-Wazzan's al-Andalus three centuries before. Ibn ʿArabi linked Creator and Creature in an eternal duo, not through shared substance—unacceptable in Islam—but through waves of revelation. Thus, he enhanced the divine aura of the prophets who brought revelation, including Jesus, precursors to the perfect Muhammad. Muslims should follow the path of those whom God has blessed, said Ibn ʿArabi, that is, the Path of Muhammad, which embraces all revealed religions that went before it. But God had engendered *all* beings and disclosed something of himself to *all* believers. "The path of God is the general path upon which all things walk, and it takes them to God. It includes every divinely revealed religion and every construction of the rational faculty." In a mystical state, Ibn ʿArabi saw the unity of different religions:

> My heart is open to all forms;
> it is a pasturage for gazelles
> and a monastery for Christian monks,
> a temple for idols and the
> Kaʿba of the pilgrim,
> the tables of the Torah and
> the book of the Qurʾan.[13]

Yuhanna al-Asad displayed little mystical sensibility in his writings that have come down to us, but he held dear the tradition of al-Ghazali with its mystic strains, and he recited his poems and rhymed prose by heart during his years in a Christian clime. In Arabic and in Latin translation, he recalled for his Christian readers a celebrated line from al-Ghazali: "The ways are many, truly the way is single, travelers on it are the elect." The ways, the way—*tariq*—were favorite themes of al-Ghazali, and here Yuhanna al-Asad was probably remembering the moment in al-Ghazali's autobiographical *Deliverance from Error* when he put aside the ways of the philosophers and scholastic theologians for the way of the mystic Sufis.[14] Mystic teachings helped to ease Yuhanna al-Asad's life between two worlds.

THE PRACTICE OF translation led Yuhanna al-Asad to forms of convergence and inclusiveness, but other experiences led to forms of difference and maintaining distance. His years in Italy—as teacher, author, partial convert, go-between—and his various social and intimate relations there seem to have affected his self-definition, unmooring him in painful ways but also expanding his sense of intellectual possibility.

His scholarly self-presentation in his writings broke with what would have ordinarily been expected in Islamic texts. In Islamic learning, the critical act legitimating all knowledge was the chain of transmission supporting it, the *isnad*. The core chain was that giving credence to a hadith, a sequence of trustworthy Muslims testifying, one person to the next, to an act or a saying of the Prophet. Of course, such a policy also left the door open to lively debates about the accuracy and reliability of the reports, and the creation of apocryphal sayings and chains.

Lines of transmission were also sought for other forms of learning and art: any legal opinion, or literary form, or information about the past had to be placed on a chain. The individual author or scholar was expected to locate himself (sometimes herself) so as to appear a trustworthy recipient and passer-on.

Certain authorities or scholars shortened or provisionally rose above these chains: those jurists (muftis) who reasoned independently beyond the precedents in their school of law; and those innovating historians from the eleventh century on, who cut or pruned the chains or wrote contemporary history, while making their own assessments of reliability. But they still had to establish themselves as believable scholars. Ibn Khaldun did not use transmission chains to support his "new discipline" but instead, using analogies from other sciences like law, reasoned about historical plausibility, social organization, and the nature of civilization; he cited sources as they satisfied these criteria for truth. Nonetheless, he wrote the biographies of his teachers and his teachers' teachers right into his autobiography, which formed the last part of his multivolume history, *The Book of Examples*.[15]

Yuhanna al-Asad named other geographers and historians in his *Geography*, sometimes adding a critical judgment about their works. Once he showed how a chain would operate: "[he] had heard from many of his teachers [*maestri*] how they had heard from their teachers" that the

Marinid sultan Abu ʿInan, seeing how costly had been the construction of his Bu ʿInaniya madrasa, threw the account books into the stream and recited the verse:

> An expensive thing that is beautiful is not expensive,
> A thing that pleases the soul has no price.[16]

But who were these teachers? Yuhanna al-Asad does not say. He reports nothing about those who taught him grammar, theology, and Malikite jurisprudence at the madrasas of Fez, though he had occasion to do so. He mentions a potential teacher without giving his name—the man willing to show him the rules for zaʾiraja—a path he decided not to take. The author is present in his Africa book exclusively as observer, collector of information from other contemporaries, reader of Arabic manuscripts, and describer of important figures, scholars, and poets of the Islamic past. That past—"our learned men and cosmographers"[17]—belongs to him, but he does not put himself fully in an Islamic chain of transmission, with its prestige and possible constraints.

Yuhanna al-Asad's *Illustrious Men* offered an even better opportunity for detailed self-placement. Historical biography was a preferred way to establish transmission in all fields and to claim the quality and trustworthiness of scholars. In his much-read *Obituaries* (as he called his biographical dictionary), Ibn Khallikan provided teaching links for many of his 865 figures and, when appropriate, connected himself to them. For example, as a youth he had studied under Sharaf al-Din al-Irbili, a jurist of the Shafiʿite School "and one of the most distinguished and talented men of his age." "I never yet heard anyone who lectured so well . . . He was the best of men and when I think of him, the world is of little value in my eyes." Ibn Khallikan was proud that he had lent his teacher a manuscript with useful notes.[18]

In contrast, Yuhanna al-Asad cites Ibn Khallikan and other biographers as his sources, but he does not name the scholars who taught him, say, al-Ghazali. He reveals only that he had memorized the great poem on the Qurʾan by the Persian polymath al-Tughraʾi, "when he studied in

Fez as a boy." As in the *Geography*, he was busy in *Illustrious Men* collecting information from earlier texts and, when possible, observing on his own. He himself had seen a manuscript of the *Disputations* of al-Baqillani, a follower of the great al-Ash'ari. He himself had access to a copy of the remarkable political correspondence of Ibn al-Khatib, polymath and diplomat for the sultans of Granada and Fez; he had always kept it at hand and used it until his departure from Fez.[19]

His reason for uprooting himself—and also freeing himself?—from a direct line of transmission was not just prudent concealment of religious ties. Yuhanna al-Asad's appreciation for Muslim scholars was evident to Christian readers with or without their names. Was he trying to obscure the precise North African identity of "Joan Lione Granatino" (the name in the colophon to the *Geography*), lest word of this manuscript come to the ears of suspicious Muslims? Why then did he leave so many other signs there of his Fez past? I would suggest that the silence about his chains of transmission was an effort to claim a different basis for his authority as a commentator on the world at a time of new and mixed identity.

Yuhanna al-Asad's reshaping involved two moves, and they diverged from both a strict European model and a North African model. First, he presents himself simply as an independent polymath, widely read and traveled, experienced, and able to write on many subjects. Lacking a legitimating sequence of teachers, he might lose some of his credibility in Muslim eyes, but this polymathic persona also carried insufficient scholarly weight for his European editor in 1550. In the printed edition of the *Description of Africa*, Ramusio twice gave Giovanni Leone the Renaissance title of "historian" and had him following the historian's "rules," where Yuhanna al-Asad had written merely that he was obliged to tell the truth simply as "every person" must (on the first occasion, listing the general vices of the Africans, on the second, describing the cross-dressed *mukhannath* of Fez).[20]

In this he was following other Arabo-Islamic writers on events and people of the past, who preferred to apply the word "historical" to their books rather than to themselves, since many of them were trained in the law and wrote in several genres. Yuhanna al-Asad used the words

"*Historiographus*," "*Historiografo*," "*Chronista*," and "*Cronechista*"—translations for *akhbari* and *mu'arrikh*—to characterize his sources in the *Illustrious Men* and the *Geography*. And he knew that the matter of truth-telling was discussed in historical works, as in Ibn Khaldun's *Muqaddima*. But in his own manuscripts he did not identify himself primarily as historian; he simply said he composed an *Epitome of Muslim Chronicles*.[21]

Yuhanna al-Asad did, however, use two other terms to describe himself, both evoking the role of "author." In the *Cosmography and Geography of Africa*, he appears regularly as "*el Compositore*," "the composer" or "the collector" or "the compiler." He knew the Italian word *autore* and used it occasionally, but for himself he chose an apt Italian equivalent for the Arabic *mu'aliff*, meaning "compiler"; many Arabic prose works presented themselves with conventional modesty as mere compilations.[22] Similarly, in the numerous self-references in the *Illustrious Men*, Yuhanna al-Asad called himself "*Interpres*"—"interpreter," "translator"—rather than the Latin *auctor*. Here again, he was importing an Arabic usage, for *tarjama*, the word for "biographical notice," also means "translation" or "interpretation." An *interpres* was a *mutarjim*, a translator, interpreter, biographer.[23]

The Interpres and Compositore take on their own life in Yuhanna al-Asad's books. "The biographer says," "the biographer memorized," "the author lodged there," "the writer heard," "the writer himself has seen"—and the sentences continue in the third person, as "he" visits or escapes or does not remember or thanks God. In the more than nine hundred pages of the *Geography*, Yuhanna al-Asad wrote "I" and used the first-person verb only in rare instances. Introducing the bird story, the Compositore, wondering whether he is in danger of being accused of all the vices he has attributed to the Africans and none of the virtues, suddenly exclaims, "I will do like the bird" (*io faro como uno ucello*), who lives on both the land and the sea.[24]

Use of the third person and indirect self-reference had not been a standard convention in Arabic writing for several centuries. In autobiographical literature, including that by al-Ghazali and Ibn Khaldun, the self was usually "I." When the author of a biographical dictionary wanted to place a self-portrait in his collection, then he might well say "he" rather than "I" for that single entry, but other self-reference was ordinarily in the first person, as we have just seen in the excerpt from Ibn Khallikan's *Obituaries*. Al-Muqaddasi inserted his adventures into his geographical *Best Divisions* with an "I"; and even a dictated text, such as Ibn Battuta's travel account, was filled with "I departed from," "I visited," "I saw this amir," and the like. One hadith attributed hubris to the Arabic "I," *ana*, but writers used it much of the time anyway.[25]

Nor was third-person self-reference a custom Yuhanna al-Asad would have picked up in Italy. Spandugino's account of Turkey (1519) and Hernando Cortés's second and third letters from Mexico, published in Italian translation in 1522–24, all had an "I" at their center. "Utterative markings" in the first person, as scholars call them— "I saw," "I heard"—were deemed guarantees of the real in sixteenth-century travel literature.[26] When Ramusio came to publish Giovanni Leone's *Africa* at the opening of his *Navigations and Voyages*, he simply removed "*el Compositore*" from most of its pages and replaced him with "I" and with first-person verbs. The French, Latin, and English translators followed Ramusio's text.[27]

Why did Yuhanna al-Asad create "*el Compositore*"? I think he gained distance through it: distance from Italian life and from his life as a Muslim in the Maghreb; a provisional distance, allowing him to play the Christian for time, to reflect on his Muslim identity, and then, when ready, return safe and sound to North Africa.

DOES THIS reshaped identity as the writer-compiler-translator-interpreter, cut off from immediate ties of direct Islamic transmission, help us to understand these shocking words in the *Geography*: "Alexander the Great was Prophet and King, according to the folly of Mucametto in the Qur'an"? Even allowing for hedge that he was not using Muhammad's proper name but "Mucametto," as taqiyya permitted him to do to avoid insult, it is still scandalous. Yuhanna al-Asad may have recognized it as such and cut it from one of the manuscripts, for "folly of Mucametto" does not appear in Ramusio's printed version.[28] But even if he used it only temporarily, we still must try to account for it.

Perhaps it was an audacious experiment of a man still loyal to the ideal of Islam as a religion to encompass "the whole world" of Muslims but, in his mixed and expanded religious state, suddenly free to strike a critical note about Iskandar's status as prophet. The "folly" phrase occurs in the description of Alexandria, where foreigners had returned after the Arabs had captured the city from the Byzantine Greeks, and where "a shrewd caliph of the Muslims made up a big lie [*una bona bogia*] in the form of a prophecy said to be that of Mucametto, granting a large recompense to those who would come to live in Alexandria . . . and to those who would leave alms for the city's protection."[29] Here Yuhanna al-Asad exposes a ruse used to exploit people's piety, and also makes the legitimate Muslim move of claiming that a hadith is apocryphal.

Continuing his account, he writes:

> In the center of the city, amid ruins, is a little house serving as a shrine [*una Ecclesiola*] in which there is a tomb much venerated and honored by the Muslims, with candles burning in it day and night, and it is said that this is the tomb of Alexander the Great, who was Prophet and King according to the folly of Mucametto in the Qur'an. And all the strangers who come to Alexandria go visit the tomb as a pious action and leave alms for those who take care of it.[30]

The popular devotional practices that were associated with Iskandar's status aroused Yuhanna al-Asad's suspicion. Who stood to gain from such piety? The location of Iskandar's tomb was in fact uncertain: al-Mas'udi had said in 332/943 that it was inside the city on a pedestal of white and colored marble; al-Harawi heard during his visit two centuries later that Iskandar and Aristotle were buried together in the famous Lighthouse; "but God alone knows what is true in this affirmation." Several travelers to Alexandria gave no notice of the tomb, while al-Suyuti, writing of the city a few decades before al-Wazzan's visit, mentioned a mosque to Dhu-l-Qarnayn. From his own observation, al-Wazzan evidently questioned the claims about the tomb, endowed as a *waqf* to benefit its caretakers.[31]

In a third instance of skepticism, Yuhanna al-Asad comments on a saying attributed to the Prophet. A little mountain settlement west of Fez known as Pharaoh's Palace, "*el Palazo de Pharaon*" (Qasr Far'un), was believed by local people and even some historians to have been established by "Pharaoh, king of Egypt at the time of Moses and ruler of all the world." Other historians said this was "nonsense" (*una baia*), since the Egyptians had never ruled in these parts.

> This nonsense was derived from a manuscript of Muslim Sayings, the work of an author named al-Kalbi, who stated that Muhammad had said that two faithful kings and two unfaithful kings had ruled all the world. The faithful ones were Alexander the Great and Solomon, son of David; the unfaithful, Nimrod and the Pharaoh of Moses. [The people of Qasr Far'un] used the words of their Prophet to give reason to their error.

But they were wrong. Romans had founded the place; the writing on its walls was in Latin script.[32]

With the "shrewd caliph," Yuhanna al-Asad doubted the hadith. With the people of Qasr Far'un, he scoffed at their misapplication of a saying attributed to the Prophet, and he also challenged the validity of Ibn al-Kalbi's citation. The Iraqi Ibn al-Kalbi (d. 206/821) had a mixed reputation, praised by some, accused by many of lies and false attribution. Reporting the same tradition a century later, the historian al-Tabari named the Babylonian Nebuchadnezzar as the second impious universal ruler, not the Pharoah of Moses. When Yuhanna al-Asad came to talk of the Pharaohs, he claimed that they were "very powerful, very great," but not that they "ruled the world."[33] In neither case was he stepping beyond the legitimate bounds of Islamic questioning.

Iskandar as prophet drew Yuhanna al-Asad's language across that line. For centuries, Jews, Christians, and Muslims had woven stories around Alexander the Great as World Conqueror, universal ruler, traveler to the ends of the earth, founder of cities, and consulter of wise men. Islamic romances added their own motifs: Iskandar was sometimes cast as half-Persian, the son not of Philip of Macedon but of Philip's daughter and a Persian prince; and he always became a Muslim, instructed by his supremely wise counselor, al-Khadir, of the coming of Islam and Muhammad.[34] But was Iskandar a prophet?

Prophets in Islam were either "Messengers" founding a new religion, such as Abraham, Moses, Jesus, and Muhammad, the greatest and final prophet; or "bringers of glad tidings" and "warners," such as Hud, Isma'il, Isaac, Elijah, John the Baptist, and Mary. In Iskandar's case, his status as prophet was in part dependent on his being identified with Dhu-l-Qarnayn—"he of the two horns," "he of the two ages"—in the Sura of the Cave (18:82–100). Many Muslim scholars, including Ibn Khaldun, made that identification; Dhu-l-Qarnayn's visits to peoples in the West and in the East and his building of the wall against Gog and Magog were also motifs in the Alexander/Iskandar romances.

Other scholars disagreed. Some assigned the name Dhu-l-Qarnayn to two men: Abraham was the messenger in the Sura of the Cave; Iskandar was the other. Ibn Hisham (d. 220/835), himself a biographer of the Prophet, quoted traditional authorities to show that Iskandar was called the "Two-Horned One" only because he had built two lighthouses, not because he was the two-horned messenger in the Qur'an. The geographer al-Idrisi went on to claim that "everyone who reaches the two ends of the earth is in fact called by this name."[35]

Stories circling around Iskandar's ascension above earth brought him down a peg, even for those calling him Dhu-l-Qarnayn. In Christian versions, Alexander rises in a carriage powered by griffons or eagles, who reach for meat perched just above them. In the Islamic tradition, this means of elevation is reserved for impious world-rulers like Nimrod, whose arrogance leads him to build the tower of Babel. The Muslim Iskandar, after founding Alexandria, is lifted by an angel, who gives him a vision of the earth that he will rule in a godly manner. But he sees only the earth, nothing of the celestial or higher spiritual world revealed to Muhammad the Messenger. So limited, as one commentator has recently said, Iskandar "remains this side of the threshold of prophecy," "at the juncture between . . . kingship and prophecy."[36]

Al-Hasan ibn Muhammad al-Wazzan had clearly been among these doubters. As a prophet, Iskandar would be entitled to the popular devotion that had troubled him when he had seen it in Alexandria. As a prophet, Iskandar would have all the more force as World Conqueror and savior, a role that Yuhanna al-Asad now wanted to mute and put off, along with other eschatological efforts, to distant Last Days. And in Italy, where he could claim more authority than he had won for himself in North Africa, he expressed himself less equivocally.

Yet Yuhanna al-Asad could have said of Dhu-l-Qarnayn, as al-Suyuti had a few decades before, "His name was Iskandar, and he was never prophet."[37] To add the phrase "according to the folly of Mucametto in the Qur'an" was to question the reliablity of that text and of the Prophet himself.

By Islamic teaching, the Qur'an was a revelation from God to the Prophet in the Arabic tongue. It was not a created book, brought into being only when God enunciated it to Muhammad, as the heretical Mu'tazilites had once maintained. In his *Illustrious Men*, Yuhanna al-Asad referred to al-Ash'ari's answer to that claim: the Qur'an existed as an eternal archetype in God, independent of its revelation in words by the Angel Gabriel to the Prophet.[38]

Yuhanna al-Asad also knew the oft-told tale of the Qur'an's redaction: how followers of the Prophet took to recording bits and pieces of his revelation right at the time, using parchment scraps, palm leaves, shoulder bones, leather hide, and stones; how some collation began during the Prophet's life, but that at his death the whole Qur'an was known in memory only by four of his Companions; how after some earlier efforts, the caliph 'Uthman set up a committee under the Messenger's own secretary to prepare a definitive text and then ordered all other versions destroyed.

But variations remained in pronouncing and reading 'Uthman's codex, for it included no vowel or diacritical marks. In the words of Ibn

Khaldun, "eventually, seven specific ways of reading the Qur'an became established . . . with their particular pronunciation . . . They came to be ascribed to certain men . . . who had become famous as their transmitters." Some put the seven ways of reading back to the time of Muhammad, quoting the Messenger as saying, "Gabriel taught me to recite in one mode, and when I replied to him and kept asking him to give me more, he did so till he reached seven modes." By the tenth century, vocalization for the approved seven ways was systematized and any further modes rejected. Ibn Khaldun applauded the various sciences that grew up around Qur'anic reading, pronunciation, and spelling.[39]

This history, with its allowed variant readings, left much space for exegesis and interpretation of the sanctified Arabic text. The Qur'an itself affirmed its own difficulty (3:7):

> It is He who sent down upon thee the Book,
> wherein are verses clear that are the Essence
> of the Book, and others ambiguous.
> As for those in whose hearts is swerving,
> they follow the ambiguous part, desiring
> dissension, and desiring its interpretation;
> and none knows its interpretation, save
> only God. And those firmly rooted in
> knowledge say, "We believe in it; all
> is from our Lord."

This famous verse was much debated: which were the "ambiguous" verses, and how should this verse be punctuated? Should a pause follow "save only God" (the majority view), or should the sentence run on so that "those firmly rooted in knowledge" share with God the right interpretation? (Yuhanna al-Asad, in working over the Qur'an translation, stuck with the majority view.)[40]

But did this exegesis leave room for debate about the text itself? Would al-Wazzan ever have heard anyone question whether the words in the Qur'an were what the angel Gabriel had actually said to the

Prophet? Certainly Muslim theologians accused the Jews, especially
Ezra, of tampering with the text of the Torah, revealed to them by God
(the head rabbi of Cairo in al-Wazzan's day complained of these recur-
ring Muslim charges); they also pointed to contradictions in the Gospels
as evidence for the careless errors, bad memories, and even "lies" of
their authors about the life and sayings of the Prophet Jesus. Some
Shiʿite commentators claimed that the revelation to the Messenger had
included references to the fourth caliph Ali and his progeny and that
they had been omitted in the final redaction of the Qurʾan. This would
not carry weight for al-Wazzan, who considered the Shiʿite doctrine of
the Imamate heretical.[41]

The commentators whom he had read during his studies at Fez were
ordinarily respectful of the words and the purity of the language in the
revered Arabic text. Every once in a while, an individual word was
thought to be in error, the fault blamed perhaps on an ancient tired
scribe or an ink spill. By tradition, Caliph ʿUthman himself noticed a
few mistakes when he read the final redaction but remarked, "Don't correct them, for the Bedouin Arabs will correct them with their tongues."
Such observations did not lead to revising the text but remained part
of the eddy of discussion around the Qurʾan. In al-Wazzan's youth,
al-Suyuti had followed earlier commentators in compiling a list of foreign words in the Qurʾan. This might seem a daring enterprise since
Arabic was so intrinsic to the revelation that the Book had no liturgical
value if recited in translation, but al-Suyuti's goal was to solve problems
of meaning.[42]

At the time that al-Hasan al-Wazzan was kidnapped by Christian
pirates, he would have thought of the Qurʾan that he had memorized as
a boy with knowledge of the divergent streams of interpretation it had
inspired, but with certainty that its Arabic text was fixed, carrying perhaps a few tiny mistakes, but pure enough to last unchanged.

IN ITALY, Yuhanna al-Asad would have been confirmed in his view
that Iskandar was not a prophet but shaken in his conception of the

Qur'an as an untouchable text. As for Alexander, as he would now be called, Yuhanna al-Asad might have heard of how he figured in medieval Christian romances and in elaborations on the prophecies of Daniel and the biblical Gog and Magog. Though ordinarily represented as a pagan, he was sometimes endowed with Christian virtue, presented as an exemplar of generosity and sexual restraint and as a source of proverbial wisdom. Moreover, Alexander as World Conqueror was still part of Egidio da Viterbo's long historical vision and Pierio Valeriano's uncoding of symbols in his Renaissance *Hieroglyphica*.[43]

Alexander also cropped up in newer settings. Yuhanna al-Asad surely knew of the 1521 burlesque poem of Domenico Falugi on the *Great Triumph and Famous Wars of Alexander*; its carnival humor so pleased Pope Leo X that he awarded Falugi the poet's crown. That same year Machiavelli published in Florence his *Art of War*, in which Alexander is a model for how the commander can arouse his troops with trumpets and speeches and other good military practices. Meanwhile Castiglione was writing Alexander into his *Courtier* as exemplifying the admirable ambition and political achievements of the great prince, as well as the qualities, like love of music and Homer's poetry, suitable for everyone at the prince's court. In Christian Europe, Yuhanna al-Asad would have heard Alexander the Great depicted as one of the Nine Heroes—three pagans, three Jews, three Christians—but not as one of the prophets.[44]

Yuhanna al-Asad's conversations with Elijah Levita and Jacob Mantino could have added other images from the ancient, still vital Jewish tradition. Especially important was Josephus's story of Alexander's visit to Jerusalem on his way to war against Darius, as retold in the popular Jewish book called *Josippon*. Advised by an angel, Alexander prostrated himself before the high priest of the Temple, exclaimed, "Blessed is the Lord God of Israel, God of this House," and offered gold to craftsmen to make a statue of himself as a memorial "in the House of the Great God." The high priest explained that Jews did not place statues in the Temple but promised that all the sons born to priests in Judah that year would be named Alexander. Bringing forth the Book of Daniel, the high priest identified Alexander as the he-goat that would destroy the ram of Darius. "So the priest strengthened the king's heart, and Alexander departed from Jerusalem rejoicing and cheerful."[45] This story, which caused discomfort to Christian theologians, was easier for Muslims to accept. But it, too, did not qualify Alexander as a prophet.

During these same years, Yuhanna al-Asad was close to and himself busy with processes needed to interpret sacred texts and assess their traditional language. His godfather Egidio da Viterbo was studying Hebrew and Aramaic with Elijah Levita not only to use Jewish Cabala for interpreting the Bible but also to read the Old Testament in the earliest form then believed available: the Masoretic text with its essential commentaries (sixth to tenth centuries C.E.) on vocalization, controversial words and variations, and "emendations of the Scribes." Yuhanna al-Asad would have learned from both men how diverse the manuscripts of the Jewish scriptures had been since the ancient claim that not a word of what Moses had written had been touched. Even the Masoretic scholars at Tiberias had broken into two factions, and, complained Levita, scribes had spoiled the meaning of their commentaries, preferring fancy ornamentation to accurate copy. (Levita's own edition of the *Massoret ha-Massoret* was intended to resolve such problems.)[46]

Perhaps, too, Egidio had told his godson about recent efforts to revise Jerome's Latin translation of the New Testament. Egidio had met Erasmus in Rome in 1509, a few years after the Dutch humanist had called for such a move: Saint Jerome had improved on the earlier translations, and now his Vulgate Bible needed the same treatment. By 1516 Erasmus had published an edition of the New Testament in Greek together with his own Latin translation. Shock waves went through the scholarly world, for it seemed that the new Latin text changed important doctrine. How dared he touch the Vulgate, so long honored and approved by the church? Meanwhile a polyglot edition of the Bible, including the New Testament in Greek, was already under way in Spain, sponsored by Cardinal Ximénes de Cisneros. Even if Egidio did not agree with Erasmus's translation, this ferment was probably a source for his hopeful comment in 1518 that biblical criticism was one of the great signs of the time.[47]

Revising the Vulgate, itself a mere translation, would not for Yuhanna al-Asad carry the same unsettling force as revising the Qur'an: God had not revealed the New Testament to the apostles in Latin. Still, in 1525 he was himself involved in improving a translation of the Qur'an from its holy Arabic into Latin. Here was a high point in Yuhanna al-Asad's quest for religious equivalents in the midst of difference, and also an occasion for him to look at the Qur'an with a foreigner's eye—simultaneously an insider and an outsider, close to and distant from both his religious worlds.

During his 1518 stint in Spain as papal legate, we recall, Egidio da Viterbo had commissioned a copy of the Qur'an from one Joannes Gabriel from the town of Teruel in the kingdom of Aragon. This unknown figure, with a name unusual among the Old Christians in his region, seems to have been a convert from Islam, for in 1504 we find "Joan Gabriel," formerly called "Ali Alayzar" (al-ʿAzar), among the newly baptized Christians in Teruel.[48] Joannes Gabriel copied the Qur'an for the cardinal in a Maghrebi hand, transcribed it in the Latin alphabet, translated it into Latin, and provided annotations—all of this in adjacent columns, a recent innovation in European translations of the Qur'an.[49] Good humanist that he was, Egidio must have insisted on this mode, which had been used two years before in Giustiniani's Latin-Greek-Hebrew-Aramaic-Arabic edition of the Psalms. How else could one take comparison seriously?

Fresh from his contribution to the Arabic-Hebrew-Latin dictionary, Yuhanna al-Asad was ready when the cardinal proposed that he review the translation of the Qur'an. Medieval Christian translators of the Qur'an had already displayed knowledge of Muslim commentary,[50] and if Joannes Gabriel was a convert from Islam, he would have had such familiarity from his youth. Whatever the case, Yuhanna al-Asad claimed that his learning went deeper. He spoke proudly, after finishing his work, of how, "with God's help," he had clarifed "obscurities" in the Qur'an, retranslating individual words or explaining the meaning of a verse. He advised the cardinal "to delete the marginal annotations, which, because of the ignorance of the initial translator, did not fit with the text."[51]

Yuhanna al-Asad may have also been amused at the Arabic numerals with which Joannes Gabriel had marked the Latin verses for the
cardinal—this was a recent addition to Qur'an translations in Europe.
(It was not to be applied to biblical verses until Protestant New Testa-
ments in Greek and French in 1551–52.) In an Arabic Qur'an, verses
or groups of verses were separated for recitation by colored rosettes,
circles, or other marks (figure 29), but any faqih who had memorized
the Qur'an in boyhood knew where verses were in a Sura (Qur'an chapter) without numbers.[52]

So Yuhanna al-Asad went about adding words in the interlinear
spaces, struggling for the best expression in a language that he had not
completely mastered. Sometimes he paraphrased or amplified the text.
Above Joannes Gabriel's "God is praised, Lord of all being" in the
opening Sura (1:2), Yuhanna al-Asad added "Praise to God, Lord of the
universe, that is, of angels, men, and animals." Sometimes he made a
correction: instead of Joannes Gabriel's "Guide us in the path of the
blessed" in Sura 1, he insisted properly on "the straight path."[53]

Some of these comments and corrections derived from his preferred
Islamic glosses on the verse. So in Sura 2:22, where the translator had
God enjoining humans "not to set up enemies for God," Yuhanna
al-Asad followed the respected al-Tabari when he added, "do not establish other equal gods," as do polytheists. Underscoring the centrality of
monotheism—making clear that God did not have "helpers"—was one
of Yuhanna al-Asad's most consistent tasks of correction. Where Joannes
Gabriel wrote "blasphemers" or "they blaspheme," Yuhanna al-Asad
corrected this to the more precise "idolaters" or used a verb suggesting
a false belief that God had other gods who "associated with" or "assisted" or "participated" with him.[54]

Yuhanna al-Asad had his chance when it came to Dhu-l-Qarnayn in
the Sura of the Cave. Following earlier Latin translations of the Qur'an,
Joannes Gabriel had started the verse: "They will ask you about
Alexander." Annotating and correcting this name, Yuhanna al-Asad
wrote, "Combining two horns . . . which in Arabic means 'one [he] of

two horns.'" Then he seems to say that it is "wholly crazy" to assign this title to Alexander and refers to the claim that Alexander was the son of the god Ammon. According to this story, found in both Christian and Muslim legends, Alexander/Iskandar's mother Olympias was visited in the absence of her husband Philip by Ammon in the guise of an Egyptian king; later Alexander discovers his divine birth from Ammon's oracle. Yuhanna al-Asad seems to be suggesting that Iskandar as Dhu-l-Qarnayn is no more likely than Iskandar as the son of Ammon.[55] And he ascribes blame for the error not to the Qur'an but rather to a tradition about Iskandar.

Still, he knew well that Egidio da Viterbo wanted to understand Islam's holy book so as better to convert Muslims, and he had been named titular patriarch of Constantinople only the year before. And Joannes Gabriel's glosses often addressed the relation of a verse to some Christian theme; for instance, where the Qur'an says [3:59] "Truly, the likeness of Jesus, in God's sight, is as Adam's likeness; He created him of dust, then said He unto him,'Be,' and he was," Joannes Gabriel comments, "As the creation of Adam was miraculous, so was the creation of Jesus miraculous." At least, the glosses had a scholarly tone, expanding on the text and occasionally referring to "the glossators."[56] This Qur'an was not strewn with marginal exclamations— "superstition," "lies," "fable"—as was the important Protestant edition of the Qur'an, published in Basel in 1543. "Nonsense is told about how Alexander of Macedon enclosed some peoples in the mountains," the Basel margin reads, "how the Jews recount fables [*fabulantur*] to the common folk about Gog and Magog." About the verse promising absolution to "those who are forced to recant while their hearts remain loyal to the Faith" (16:106), Yuhanna al-Asad simply added a word about belief, but the Basel margin summed up the point and went on: "This [view] is held commonly by certain heretics."[57]

The contrast between Yuhanna al-Asad and Juan Andrés of Valencia, another faqih-convert from Islam who had addressed himself to the Qur'an, is especially interesting. In addition to his *Confusion of the*

Mohammedan Sect of 1515, Andrés had published a Spanish translation of the Qur'an, now lost. Andrés's *Confusion* suggests the tone
of the translation, as he mounts evidence for the "brutish" language
and "falseness" of the Qur'anic text.[58] In contrast, Yuhanna al-Asad's
searching comments and corrections have no missionary goal. He is
playing with fire, but he does not intend to stoke the flames. Could he
have even hoped that his corrections might dampen his godfather's zeal?

Why, then, did he write of "the folly of Mucametto in the Qur'an,"
the year after his work on the Qur'an translation, even if eventually he
may have removed the phrase? I think that its rash vigor grew out of his
complicated life in Italy. There was his temporary experience of inner
independence, cut off from networks of Islamic transmission and criticism, while concealing some of his views from Christian masters—and
all the while summoned to an authority beyond any that he had known
in North Africa. Second was his growing knowledge of the vulnerability of holy texts and the complications of language. And thirdly, the pe-
jorative language was a deferential sign to Egidio da Viterbo of his
Christian conversion. All his other references to the Prophet are respectful, if restrained; and though his distaste for the violence and destruction accompanying the Arab expansion into Africa was clear, he
describes the spread of Islam as a civilizing process, even if it engendered conflicts and heresies.

Thus, the words "folly" and "pestilence" should be taken finally as
Yuhanna al-Asad's concession to his godfather Egidio and to his other
masters. In North Africa, he would hope to be forgiven, if anyone
should learn of them, as a necessary dissimulation, that is, taqiyya. Several pages on, he wrote that he was "determined, with God's grace to return safe and sound from his European voyage" to Africa.[59] However
much he had enlarged his view of Islam, Yuhanna al-Asad still wanted
to go back to it.

CHAPTER NINE

The Return

IN 1526, Yuhanna al-Asad announced in his *Geography* what he planned to write when he returned to North Africa. He would describe the lands he had seen in "Asia," including all of Arabia as well as the parts of Babylonia and Persia he claimed he had been taken to in his youth. He would describe the Mediterranean islands and sections of Europe he had visited. He would order his book so that Europe came first, he assured the Italian readers, "as the worthiest and noblest part," followed by Asia, and then by his Africa. He must have thought of that return with growing impatience. How long would he, a lover of Arabic poetry and the beautiful rhythms of the Arabic language, want to keep writing in his simplified Italian and only for audiences that could not read his mother tongue? How long would he want to stay away from the shores and cities he had first known and appreciated? He wrote in the *Geography*, "Africa was his wet nurse and had given him suck."[1] And if I am right that Yuhanna al-Asad and the Joannes Leo living in the Regula quarter in January 1527 were one and the same person, then he might well be eager to get his recently established family back to the abode of Islam.

In any case, the events of the year 1527 shook his world and all his connections in Italy. News of Turkish victories in Hungary had reached Rome the year before, and the rivalry between the Christian monarchs François I and the emperor Charles V for dominance in Italy loomed large. Pope Clement VII kept changing his policy toward the emperor and was rewarded for his vacillation by an uprising in September 1526, led by Cardinal Pompeo Colonna, scion of a powerful Roman family and a supporter of the imperial cause. The looting of the Vatican and St. Peter's was a harbinger of what the Medici pope had ahead of him.

In the next months imperial troops—German Lutherans and Spanish Catholics both—moved down the Italian peninsula, sacking towns as they went. On May 6, 1527, they breached the walls of Rome, losing their commander, the visionary French renegade Charles de Bourbon, to Italian gunpowder during the assault. (The goldsmith Benvenuto Cellini boasted that the shot had come from his harquebus.) Unrestrained, the soldiers embarked on ten days of killing, torturing, raping, kidnapping for ransom, and looting on a scale that must have gone beyond what Yuhanna al-Asad had witnessed in the Ottoman seizure of Mamluk Cairo ten years before. Indeed, some Christian observers made the comparison. As one humanist put it, "we have seen practiced upon priests tortures from which a victorious Carthaginian or Turk indisputably would have abstained."[2]

Clement VII watched this devastation from the balconies of the Castel Sant'Angelo, where he, thirteen cardinals, Paolo Giovio and other humanist scholars, and hundreds of others had fled for refuge. (Giovanni Leone's godfather Cardinal Pucci was passed bleeding through an unbarred window.) Alberto Pio was among those crowded into the fortress: as ambassador for the French king, the prince was a special target for Charles V, and his estates in Carpi were occupied by imperial troops and were lost forever. Egidio da Viterbo was out of the city on a papal mission elsewhere in Italy. Churchman though he was, he tried to raise troops to come to Rome's aid, but too late. The cardinal's treasured library, in which Yuhanna al-Asad had spent many hours, was looted.[3]

Elijah Levita suffered as well: "I was despoiled of my goods and all my books were stolen. I had finished more than half of my new manuscript, but all that was left was some notebooks and some pages I found filthy and torn in the middle of the street. I collected them, put them in a box, and carried them with me into exile."[4] In the weeks of depredation, fires, plague, and famine that followed the sack of Rome, Levita packed up his family and after some wandering found his way to Venice. Egidio da Viterbo also sought refuge there for a time and began to ponder the prophetic meaning of the sack. Soon he would compose his cabalisic *Scechina*, where the Hebrew holy spirit proclaims that the sack and all its horrors had been prophesied. Charles de Bourbon was perhaps an instrument of God, punishing the church for its sins before the golden age of universal Christianity could be ushered in.[5]

In September 1527 Alberto Pio left the Castel Sant'Angelo for Paris and the French court. There he advised King François I on foreign policy, including relations with the Ottoman Turks. He also began to publish attacks on the religious philosophy of Erasmus, together with Erasmus's response, a debate that was concluded in a posthumous edition shortly after Alberto Pio's death in France in 1531. Back in Italy, some commentators recalled his political career as one of "lies," "duplicity," and "the fraud of simulated friendship."[6]

Yuhanna al-Asad, too, seems to have left Rome right after the sack. As so often with our trickster bird, the evidence is ambiguous. A printed annotation in the 1547 Italian translation of the Qur'an tells of an Arab faqih (*Rabi Arabo*) who was seized in Africa, presented to the pope and baptized by him, and, at the time of the sack, "took flight and made himself Turk again." The faqih's name is Zematto (the name of a Jew in Egidio da Viterbo's circle), not Wazzan; the pope is Clement VII, not Leo X; but no such Arab figure is known from Clement's early papal years. I take this as a reference to Yuhanna al-Asad getting to his boat in 1527.[7]

Five years later his godfather Cardinal Egidio, if he had not forgiven him, at least thought well enough of him to direct the young Orientalist scholar Johann Widmanstadt to his whereabouts in North Africa.[8] And

a comment by Pierio Valeriano in his *Hieroglyphica*, written not long after 1529, suggests the disappointment and anger Yuhanna al-Asad may
have left in his wake. Valeriano put the ostrich and the bat—the two
creatures analogous to Yuhanna al-Asad's amphibious bird—together
as "monstrous," that is, not fitting clearly into a single category of nature. The mixed nature of the ostrich, with wings but unable to fly, and
legs almost like a steer's, was in some ways an allegory of the human
position in the universe, "a constitution on the border between the
elements [of earth] and heaven." But the ostrich also symbolized
hypocrisy, folly, and the person who aimed high but was distracted by
worldly matters.[9]

The mixed nature of the bat, soaring by means of a membrane
rather than of wings, emblematized the rapid social ascension of a person without the required qualities. ("Rome is full of such people," Valeriano added.) He then recounted how the bat escaped death by tricking
the two weasels, as in Aesop's fable, and, in another version, by telling
a cock he was a mouse and telling a cat he was a bird. This evasion was
not a success story for Valeriano, as it had been to some extent in
Yuhanna al-Asad's tale of the bird. It was the sign of a person with "an
impure or profane soul":

> There are men who fly hither and thither. Having received only the wa-
> ter of Baptism, among the Catholics, they avow that Jesus Christ has
> built his Church on Saint Peter. Among the heretics, they ridicule and
> laugh at [Saint Peter, that is, the pope]. Among the Jews, they mock
> Our Lord. Among the Muslims, they speak badly of both the Chris-
> tians and the Jews . . . They are similar not only to bats, but also to
> those nicknamed Marranos, certainly abominable.[10]

Valeriano here could be referring not only to Nicodemites among the
Christians and Marranos among the Jews, but very possibly to the Muslim convert whom he had once known as Giovanni Leone and who had
now flown back to North Africa.

✑

THE RETURN CANNOT have been easy for the man who would resume the name of al-Hasan ibn Muhammad ibn Ahmad al-Wazzan and
the dress of a North African. Would people in the Maghreb have heard
of his doings for the past nine years? The most sustained flow of information from Christian Italy to Islam was through Venice, with Venetian
ambassadors regularly placed in Istanbul and other Ottoman towns,
and the Venetian Signory occasionally receiving ambassadors from Sultan Suleyman. Al-Wazzan's initial capture in 1518 had been reported to
the Signory, and news of his conversion had also reached Venice. Moreover, a manuscript of his Africa book was circulating in Venice in 1529,
not long after Levita's arrival there and Egidio da Viterbo's visit: Jacob
Ziegler, the German geographer who read it, referred to its author not
by his baptismal name of Giovanni Leone or as the "Joan Lione Granatino" that appears on our copy of the manuscript, but as "Hussan,
Arab from Granada."[11]

The story of al-Hasan al-Wazzan's activities in Italy was partly out,
then. Word about him might also have got back to the Maghreb through
the visionary letters sent by the self-styled Jewish prince David Reuveni
to the sultan of Fez and the Saʿdiyan prince sharif during the months he
was close to Egidio da Viterbo's household in Rome; or through traders
or sailors who had met Yuhanna al-Asad during his travels in Italy.

Whatever the case, al-Wazzan could not expect a favorable reception
in Fez. In his family life, he would return to disgrace and divorce; it
would be difficult to settle in Fez and make amends. In political life, as
former ambassador for Sultan Muhammad al-Burtughali, he would be
suspected of collaborating with enemies of Islam during his sojourn in
Italy in circles close to the pope. He would have heard that in 930/1524
the sultan, advised by local faqihs, had burned alive a captured Muslim
who had converted to Christianity and served the Portuguese in the Atlantic town of Asila. Hardly a promising portent.

Muhammad al-Burtughali had died not long after, and al-Wazzan

had few ties with his son Ahmad, who eventually succeeded him. Former habitué of the Wattasid court, al-Wazzan would have looked with
wistfulness and envy at Ahmad's vizier, Ibrahim ibn 'Ali ibn Rashid,
known as Mulay Ibrahim. A man of his own age, son of a Castilian
mother converted to Islam and a father claiming descent from the
Prophet, Mulay Ibrahim had risen from a chieftainship in the Rif
Mountains to become a flamboyant military and political figure in the
kingdom of Fez and husband of Sultan Ahmad's sister. Al-Wazzan had
written briefly of Mulay Ibrahim's father in his *Geography* as a rebel
against the Wattasids and a fighter against the Portuguese Christians.
Now the son had far surpassed the father in a career that al-Wazzan
could never hope to emulate.[12]

Thus, al-Wazzan was not at the side of Sultan Ahmad and Mulay
Ibrahim in 938/1531–32 when an Italian Franciscan, Andrea da Spoleto,
arrived in Fez and began to preach publicly the truth of the Trinity. To
deflect him, the vizier sent him to preach in the synagogues; even the
Christian captives in Fez begged him not to stir up trouble. Undaunted,
the Franciscan offered to perform miracles in support of the Christian
faith, including the trial by fire that Saint Francis had undertaken before
the Mamluk sultan at Cairo centuries before. Mulay Ibrahim finally
permitted this and, according to the Christian account, the friar survived the flames unscathed, after which the Muslim crowd, enraged at
what he had said about "the cursed Mahomet," stoned him to death. A
martyrology of the Franciscan was rushed into print in France; one
would love to know how al-Hasan al-Wazzan, with his doubts about
miracles, would have recounted this episode.[13]

Al-Wazzan could not expect much from the Sa'diyan sharifs either.
During his absence, the sons of Muhammad al-Qa'im had consolidated
their power in the south, seizing Marrakesh in 931/1525 to the dismay of
the Wattasids. Their association with the Jazulite Sufi tradition had
grown all the stronger since their father had had himself buried in
923/1517 right next to al-Jazuli's tomb. Al-Ghazwani, called by some
the "pole" (*qutb*) or spiritual center of his time, was now living in
Marrakesh and putting his miraculous power behind the program of

these descendants of the Prophet: they would free the abode of Islam from Christian conquest and establish a saintly kingdom.[14]

Al-Wazzan had already mistrusted Jazulite extravagance in his days as diplomat, and his last years in Italy had distanced him even further from political eschatology. Being in the orbit of the Sa'diyan brothers, one of whom came to be called "al-Mahdi," would have been difficult. Of course, a repentant apostate would be unacceptable to the zealous Muhammad al-Shaykh and his brother. What secrets might al-Wazzan have leaked to the pope about his days in the entourage of their father? His past link with Fez was also a drawback, for the Wattasid sultan kept sending out soldiers to get Marrakesh back.

The convert from Europe turned his steps elsewhere. He might have considered living in Ottoman Cairo, whose urban marvels and conventions of religious debate under Mamluk rule he had praised, but it seems he made no connections there. Tunis was a better idea. Not long before his death in 1532, Egidio da Viterbo told Widmanstadt that Giovanni Leone had settled in Tunis; eager for lessons in Arabic, Widmanstadt set off to visit him there, but his boat was turned back by tempestuous weather on the Mediterranean.[15]

Al-Wazzan had written of Tunis at length in his *Geography*, praising it as "the most singular city in all Africa in regard to its civility." He stressed its cosmopolitan quality, with its mix of Muslims, Jews, and Christian slaves and its quarter for foreign merchants from Italy and Spain. Its great mosque of the Qasba was beautiful, it had well-endowed madrasas, its judges and scholars were celebrated in his own Malikite school of law, and its weavers were renowned for their skill. In Tunis he had seen a za'iraja performed, and in Tunis he had "received many benefits" from the Hafsid sultan, Muhammad ibn al-Hasan. He had also written in his *Geography* of the sultan's vices of and fondness for bodily pleasure, and of the misdeeds of his sons in Constantine, but presumably he hoped that his manuscript would not reach Tunis.[16]

One of those sons, al-Hasan, had succeeded his father, who had died in 932/1526. Contemporaries described al-Hasan as a voluptuary given to perfumes and also as a fine horseman, skilled at the lance, an imperious and arbitrary ruler, a lover of the illuminated manuscripts in the magnificent Hafsid library, and well versed in Arabic philosophy and astronomy. Politically, his situation was precarious. To the south, a great tribal family had taken control of the religious center of Qairouan. To the west, Khayr al-Din Barbarossa had seized Algiers, submitted his loyalty to the Ottoman sultan, and been named by Suleyman as "bey of beys" over a principality going as far east as Jijel and Constantine. From his imposing port in Algiers, constructed by the labor of Christian captives, Khayr al-Din was offering help to Morisco rebels in Spain and sending out his ships to prey on Christian vessels, but he was also casting his eyes on the Ifriqiya of Sultan al-Hasan.[17]

Al-Hasan al-Wazzan may have thought, given his previous ties to the Hafsid court and to Barbarossa's late brother ʿAruj, that Tunis would be a safe city to live in or even that he might find some diplomatic function to perform there. But wherever he alighted, resuming his place as a Muslim was his most urgent and difficult task. Like any ransomed or liberated slave who had converted to Christianity during his captivity, he would have had to go before a qadi to establish his story of coercion and inner sincerity. If he had brought an apostate wife with him, she would have had to do the same.

A fatwa in al-Wansharisi's influential collection gave grounds for hope: a Muslim had converted to Christianity in enemy lands, married a Christian there, and then returned to Dar al-Islam and his faith; his wife converted as well. Acknowledging divergent opinions among the jurists, the judge said the marriage should be annulled but that after the wife had passed three menstrual periods, the husband could remarry her. Neither would be punished.[18] The Malikite judges in Tunis must have had to deal with a number of such cases since the Oran jurist had issued his fatwa on taqiyya to the Muslims of Granada in 910/1504. Tunis had for years been a haven for Muslims and Moriscos fleeing persecution in Spain, as well as for slaves escaping from Italy, some of them Christian converts.[19]

A French traveler has left us the account of a prominent convert who returned to Islam in Tunis a century later. Muhammad, the youthful son of one of the Ottoman deys (governors) of Tunis, had fled to Sicily rather than marry the daughter of the pasha of Tripoli, had been baptized in Palermo with the name of Philippo, and had taken a Christian wife. He was then kidnapped and brought back to Tunis, where he decided to convince people he had always been inwardly Muslim by taking a pilgrimage to Mecca. A few years later he was still using the name Dom Philippo, at least when conversing with the French traveler. "If he had not had well-placed friends," the traveler commented, "he would have had his head cut off."[20]

The stakes would be high for al-Hasan ibn Muhammad al-Wazzan, especially if people learned he had been teaching Arabic and interpreting the Qur'an to a Christian cardinal. As there was a school of rabbis critical of teaching Hebrew to learned Christians, so there was a school of faqihs critical of teaching Arabic to Christian theologians "lest they stir up trouble," in the words of Nicolas Clenardus, a Flemish humanist trying to study Arabic and buy manuscripts in Fez in 1540. To reassure Muslims who asked him why he wanted to learn Arabic, Clenardus replied that he was interested in grammar and in making a better translation of Avicenna and Averroës, but he concealed his real goal: to learn about and refute effectively the heresies of Islam.[21]

Evidently al-Wazzan was successful in his plea of taqiyya, and/or found some important person to vouch for him, for he was said to be living in Tunis in 1532. Perhaps like the later "Dom Philippo," he established his sincerity by another Hajj to Mecca and Medina.

APART FROM the 1532 reference, we have no further word of al-Hasan ibn Muhammad ibn Ahmad al-Wazzan in North Africa. We can only imagine how he might have been involved in political events of the time. During Charles V's military expedition to Tunis in 1535, a letter was found that was supposedly written by Alberto Pio sometime before his death in Paris in 1531 and sent to Khayr al-Din in the name of François I: in it the French king proposed an alliance with Khayr al-Din and Sultan Suleyman against Charles V.[22] Had conversations with his former Arabic transcriber Giovanni Leone helped to orient Alberto Pio when he counseled the French king about these Turkish and North African ties? Could al-Wazzan have served as a go-between at any point?

In 941/1534, emboldened by military victories and diplomatic alliance, Sultan Suleyman encouraged Khayr al-Din, now named admiral of the Ottoman fleet, to conquer Ifriqiya. In an easy campaign, Khayr al-Din won the support of anti-Hafsid factions, took Tunis and other towns, and deposed the sultan. As with the pillaging of St. Peter's during the 1526 Colonna uprising in Rome, the ravaging of Tunis by Barbarossa's troops anticipated further violence. The deposed al-Hasan turned to the Christian emperor for aid against his Muslim brethren. Charles V was delighted with the possibility not only of countering Ottoman power in the Mediterranean but of taking on the mantle of leader of a great crusade, a new Scipio Africanus, a new Saint Louis.[23]

Preparations in Spain and Italy called forth a flurry of maps and topographies. Paolo Giovio gathered information to make maps and pictures of Tunis, seeking out merchants, captives, and slaves for details. Among them were "Iosuf," a Turk, former pirate, and now slave of Cardinal Ippolito de' Medici, and "Giovanni," a Moor born and raised in Tunis and now a slave in one of the households of the great Orsini family. But also floating around Italy was the manuscript of the *Cosmography and Geography of Africa*, with its many pages on Tunis, its harbor, and Carthage. Giovio surely had heard of this book and may have consulted it as well. Thus Giovio's comment about the "penury of water" in Tunis may echo al-Wazzan's *Geography*: "there is within the city no spring, no river, no well."[24]

Charles V entered the port of Tunis the first days of Muharram 942/July 1535 with several hundred ships and thirty thousand men, and within a week the city was taken, with many Muslims slain and Christian captives freed. Sultan al-Hasan was restored as ruler, his subjects adding the cost in bloodshed to the grievances they already had against him. Mounds of booty were seized and packed to be taken to Italy and Spain: garments, jewelry, weapons (Charles V took Khayr al-Din's steel helmet, but Giovio got the admiral's ring and washbasin), and magnificent manuscripts, including copies of the Qur'an. There was human booty as well: Tunisian Muslims were shipped to Spain and Italy as slaves.[25]

During the battle, the sacking of the city, and the drawing up of the treaty of alliance, al-Hasan and the Spanish officers conversed on the philosophy of Averroës in the emperor's tent and the sultan's palace. One of the Spanish officers was Diego Hurtado de Mendoza, born in the Alhambra at Granada, which his father had conquered and taken from the Muslims decades before.[26] Could al-Wazzan have been a translator when Hurtado de Mendoza talked to the Hafsid sultan? or as the treaty of agreement between emperor and sultan was prepared in Latin, Spanish, and Arabic?[27] His Italian years would at least not discredit him as a servant in the eyes of Sultan al-Hasan, himself so entangled in complicity with Spain. If al-Wazzan then won a place at the sultan's court (figure 31), he would not have found the going easy. Al-Hasan retained his power only with the support of a Spanish garrison, and in 949/1542 his son Ahmad began to plot against him. (One of the co-conspirators was a skilled gun maker from Granada.) Al-Hasan was dethroned and blinded by Ahmad (figure 32). In later exile in Italy, he was heard to boast of his descent from the Caliph 'Umar and to moan "[I]'d give up a city for [my] books."[28]

If al-Wazzan lived through the events of 942–49/1535–42, he could put Tunis next to Rome and Cairo as places where he had witnessed horrendous violence across shifting religious lines. Such sights would have confirmed the elegiac and skeptical tone that he had taken toward political and religious war in his *Geography*.

About al-Wazzan's personal life, we have no clues. Did he establish a Muslim family and a line of children? Did he finally learn how to perform a za'iraja from, say, a pupil of that "most excellent master" whom he had observed in Tunis years before? Did he resume the travel he so enjoyed and perhaps return to the little town south of Algiers—now part of an Ottoman regency—where he had been informal qadi years before? Or instead did he have a conversion experience, like that which he had described for al-Ghazali in his *Lives of Illustrious Men,* and live in pious retirement? Indeed, how long did he live?

If on all these matters this trickster bird eludes our grasp, one silence allows us relative certainty. The books he promised about Europe and Asia and an Arabic edition of the *Cosmography and Geography of Africa* were evidently never written. Or if they were, they were unnoticed by his contemporaries and uncopied: no manuscripts on these subjects have been found that we can attribute to him. Even if he had lived no later than 939/1532, these five years of little or no composition in North Africa contrast with the remarkable productivity of his years in Italy.

I attribute this silence to the sweeping nature of his break with *isnad,* that is, with chains of transmission and networks of communication. In Arabo-Islamic cultures that habitually talked about teachers and pupils and memorialized scholars and their writings, al-Hasan ibn Muham-mad al-Wazzan al-Fasi is not found in the stream of biographical dic-tionaries of the Maghreb until the twentieth century—and then only for the book on Africa that he wrote in Italy. During Nicolas Clenardus's eighteen months in Fez in 1540–41, conversing with learned Jews and Muslims, including faqihs and a scholar of rhetoric from Egypt, his name never came up. Indeed, good Catholic priest though he was, Cle-nardus had not heard of al-Wazzan's Italian past as Giovanni Leone, teacher of Arabic to Cardinal Egidio: "up till now to the best of my knowledge, no one has taught Arabic among the Christians."[29] This si-lence must mean that al-Wazzan could not insert himself into the all-important group of listeners and readers, students and teachers, to whom he could tell his stories.[30]

What was wrong with the stories he had to tell? Travel accounts (rih-las) and geographies were still being produced in his day, some about voyages within the Maghreb, some across North Africa to Istanbul. Piri Reis's *Book of Navigation,* covering the islands and coastal towns of the entire Mediterranean and describing voyages to the Indian Ocean and across the Atlantic to the new world, was presented to Sultan Su-leyman in 932/1526 and inspired at least twenty-four copies (figure 13). Turkish geographies of the next decades included Seydi Ali Reis's manuscript on the Red Sea, Persian Gulf, and Indian Ocean and the anonymous *Fresh News: A History of the India of the West*, a world geography followed by an account of Spanish discoveries in America.[31]

Al-Wazzan could not, however, have written about his trip to Europe using the classic Arabo-Islamic mode of travel as ascetic test and holy learning. Nor could he offer observations on Italy as being incidental to a pilgrimage or diplomatic mission. An example of the first mode is found in the late sixteenth-century biographical dictionary of the Sufi qadi Ibn ʿAskar. Native of a Rif town that al-Wazzan had described in his *Geography*, Ibn ʿAskar gave portraits of Maghreb scholars who had some odor of sanctity. One of them was "a great voyager": al-Shutaybi, born in Morocco of an Andalusian family and a few years younger than al-Wazzan. He spent long years in the East, visiting learned men in different places, and wrote on many subjects, including divination by words and alchemy. Ibn ʿAskar stressed his ascetic simplicity and his dream visions, in which a saint and even the Prophet appeared and ordered him to return to the Maghreb.[32]

Clearly al-Wazzan's "great voyages" did not fit this mold. His account would have to be a captivity narrative along with a story of voluntary adventure that strayed beyond Dar al-Islam, an anomalous and disturbing combination for Muslim listeners and readers of his time. (It may have emerged only in the nineteenth century with Arabic autobiographies written by Muslim Africans who had been slaves in the United States or the Caribbean.)[33]

It would also be a troubling combination for the author. Al-Wazzan's intellectual experiments during his Italian years both connected disparate worlds through equivalencies and distanced and detached its author from them. The distancing may have gone so far that it was difficult for him to know how to resume as a writer in Arabic. The vagabond poets of the *Maqamat*—al-Hamadhani's Abu-l-Fath from Alexandria and al-Hariri's Abu Zayd from Saruj—changed disguises and roles, but however widely they traveled and however transgressive their actions, they always remained within the abode of Islam.

For the returned apostate al-Wazzan, repentant mysticism or con-

tinued dissimulation were choices he could make, but without a network to sustain him, neither would help move his pen.

THE SCHOLARLY LEGACY of al-Hasan al-Wazzan remained, then, in
the writings he left in Europe. Possibly some printed editions of the
Description of Africa found their way to a few Muslim readers. The
Turkish author of *Fresh News: A History of the India of the West* had
read some parts of Ramusio's *Navigationi et Viaggi*, but if they included the book by "Giovanni Leone Africano," it seems not to have influenced his geographical vision: "Africa" is still the Tunisian region of
"Ifriqiya" and the world is still organized by the climes of Ptolemy and
al-Mas'udi.[34]

In Europe, traces of the man Giovanni Leone surfaced when Johann
Widmanstadt talked of him with the dying Egidio da Viterbo in 1532
and surely in 1539 when Widmanstadt visited Jacob Mantino to exam-
ine and borrow Hebrew manuscripts. The person lived again in Mantino's conversations with Hurtado de Mendoza, who was serving the
emperor in Venice in the 1540s and collecting books for his own library. Mantino was his physician there and passed on to his patron the
Arabic-Hebrew-Latin dictionary. Signed "Yuhanna al-Asad al-Gharnati,
previously named al-Hasan ibn Muhammad al-Wazan al-Fasi," the
manuscript could remind the Spanish nobleman that he and its author
had been born in the same town. Memory of Giovanni Leone must have
been bright for Elijah Levita in 1541, when he prepared the columns
of his own Yiddish-Hebrew-Latin-German dictionary (figure 28). He,
too, corresponded with Johann Widmanstadt.[35]

Al-Wazzan's writings carried his legacy to different parts of Europe,
both Protestant and Catholic. The Arabic-Hebrew-Latin dictionary
ended up in the Escorial, offered with the rest of Hurtado de Mendoza's
celebrated library to Philip II in 1575. By the last years of the century,
the transcription and translation of the Qur'an with al-Wazzan's corrections had passed through the hands of Filippo Archinto, a papal
vicar interested in Oriental languages, and found their way also to the

Escorial; another copy was inscribed in Arabic with the name of the early English Protestant William Tyndale (d. 1536).[36] By the early 1550s the Arabic grammar was delighting the eyes of the French Orientalist Guillaume Postel, probably seen during his stay in Venice; he dreamed of the harmony of the many languages and polities of the world through a single language and a Christian universal monarch. To that end, he borrowed the Qur'an manuscript from the papal vicar and, neglecting its original translator, called it "the distinguished volume of Joannes Leo Africanus." Postel also read the Africa book before its publication, and he quoted its sections on learned divination, cabalism, and perfectionist ascesticism when he made comparisons, as his search for commonalities led him to do, between Muslim sects and Christian friars.[37]

One copy of the *Lives of Illustrious Men among the Arabs and among the Hebrews*, with al-Wazzan's *Metric Art* inserted into it, may have been in Egidio da Viterbo's hands and was surely acquired by the Florentine churchman, poet, and book lover Antonio Petrei. A century later the Zurich pastor Johann Heinrich Hottinger, a church historian and scholar of Arabic, got word of the manuscript from his Florentine friends. He published the *Lives* in 1664 as part of an encyclopedic project of comparing world religions. The good pastor omitted al-Wazzan's shocking sexual details: gone was the farmer's penis sore from bestiality and cured by one of the illustrious Arabs, a Jacobite Christian no less; gone was the alleged sodomy that led to the murder of one of the illustrious Jews.[38]

The main legacy was, of course, the Africa manuscript, revised, edited, and published as the *Descrittione dell'Africa* by the Venetian political figure and editor Giovanni Battista Ramusio. If al-Hasan ibn Muhammad al-Wazzan could have known of the many editions and translations his book would go through and of the "Giovanni Leone Africano" emerging from them, he might well have had mixed reactions. The writer still finding his way in Italian has become a master of the language. The author of a relatively neutral religious text has become a convinced Christian convert, with anti-Islamic sentiment put into his mouth in especially the French, Latin, and English translations. The distanced Compositore has been replaced by a first-person narrator chatting with Europeans. The polymathic observer of societies and scholars has turned into a "historian" following Renaissance rules. Al-Wazzan's belief in the unity of Africa through Islam has been weakened by the recasting of his clichés about the ancient mores in the Land of the Blacks as present-day description.

But the trickster bird is still there, even if the invented *Cento Novelle* has been omitted, and much of the story that al-Wazzan had wanted to tell remains. By the seventeenth century, an indignant Spanish inquisitor was writing "Prohibited in full" on the title page of the 1556 Latin translation; he went through the entire text crossing out objectionable sentences and putting a big star in the margin next to the bird story.[39] Al-Wazzan's book was used for many purposes, but for the myriad educated readers it reached over the centuries, it bore witness to the possibility of communication and curiosity in a world divided by violence.

Epilogue: Affinities

IN THE SUMMER of 1535 François Rabelais was in Rome once again. For the moment he need not keep track of how his publications were doing in his native land: his French translations of Greek medical texts and his popular almanacs; his *Pantagruel*, which went through eight editions after its first printing in 1532, whatever hackles it raised among traditional theologians at the Sorbonne; his *Gargantua*, fresh off the Lyon presses a few months earlier. Now he could savor the sights of what he had called with some irony "the capital of the world," explore once again the streets and lanes he had discovered during his first visit to Rome in 1534, enjoy the conversation of its learned men, and familiarize himself with the papal archives, courts, and officers required for his business and that of his protector, the bishop of Maillezais back in France. He had made fun of this bureaucracy in *Pantagruel*, but if he wanted to be forgiven for moving from one Benedictine house to another and studying medicine without papal permission, he would have to resort to "the salvo of farts of bullists, copyists, and dataries."[1]

Opening doors for Rabelais in Rome was his patron, Jean du Bellay, bishop of Paris, newly named cardinal by Pope Paul III and charged by François I with an important mission to the Papal See. In 1534 Rabelais had praised Du Bellay's marvelous eloquence in urging the late Clement VII toward concilation with the rebellious Henry VIII; in 1535–36 Du Bellay had several other issues to discuss with the recently elected Paul III, including Sultan Suleyman, with whom the French king, ever competing with Charles V, had an alliance.[2]

All of this provided food for Rabelais's ever-hungry eyes, ears, and mind, and also it led him to paths and persons linked to Yuhanna al-Asad. Jacob Mantino was serving as physician to Pope Paul III; previously he had won Clement VII's gratitude by supporting the pope's opposition to Henry VIII's plan to divorce Catherine of Aragon and marry Anne Boleyn. In 1530 the English king sent agents to consult learned Jews in Italy: did not Leviticus 18:16 say "Thou shalt not uncover the nakedness of thy brother's wife" and had not Catherine once been married to Henry's brother? Mantino maintained that the relevant verse was Deuteronomy 25:5—if a widow is childless, "her husband's brother shall go in unto her, and take her to him to wife"—and his view carried the day. By 1535 Henry had married Anne Boleyn, had had himself declared supreme head of the English church, and was under threat of excommunication. Still, Henry hoped the new pope would compromise, as did the French king, who instructed Jean du Bellay to try to prevent the excommunication. Rabelais, physician to the sciatic Du Bellay, was following closely the cardinal's interventions on this English matter; he may well have met Mantino and heard about the Arabic-Hebrew-Latin dictionary.[3]

Certainly among Du Bellay's Roman connections Rabelais knew Bishop Rodolfo Pio da Carpi, nephew of Alberto Pio and heir to his uncle's books and manuscripts—including the Arabic epistles of Saint Paul that Yuhanna al-Asad had transcribed for the prince. Soon to become a cardinal, Rodolfo Pio had acquired a splendid palace at the Campo Marzio, where Du Bellay and his entourage, including Rabelais, had been housed during 1534.[4]

Then there was the historian Paolo Giovio. During Du Bellay's 1535–36 visit, Giovio did his best to cultivate the new cardinal, hoping that he would recommend him to the French king for a pension. Among other gestures, Giovio gave Du Bellay two of the Arabic manuscripts seized during the Tunis expedition in July 1535: a Qur'an and an Islamic theology text. Rabelais was in touch with Giovio and surely saw these manuscripts. Eager for news of events in North Africa and the movements of Sultan Suleyman, Rabelais also acquired and sent back to France the plan of Tunis made under Giovio's supervision and Agostino Veneziano's famous engraving of Admiral Khayr al-Din Barbarossa, based on a drawing in Giovio's possession.[5] Perhaps Giovio told him stories of Giovanni Leone, former teacher of Arabic and writer in Rome who had returned to North Africa.

Rabelais picked up other signs of the non-Christian world as he prowled the market stalls of Rome, buying "marvelous little items" not only from Cyprus and Crete but also from Constantinople.[6] In his wanderings and exchanges, did he ever come across the manuscript on the *Cosmography and Geography of Africa* by one "Joan Lione Granatino"? During his last visit to Rome with du Bellay, in 1548–49, did he get word of Giovanni Battista Ramusio's forthcoming edition of the *Description of Africa* by "Giovanni Leone Africano"? Might Jean du Bellay, on a mission to Rome in 1550, have acquired a newly printed copy to bring back to him in Paris?

We can imagine with what pleasure Rabelais might have read al-Wazzan's Africa book, but his later publications and revisions and emendations of his text show no sure sign that he did so. In 1552 appeared the final version of the *Quart Livre*, his great account of the travels of Pantagruel, Panurge, and their companions. In its glossary of unusual terms, Rabelais defined "Cannibals" somewhat jokingly as "monstrous people in Africa, having faces like dogs and barking instead of laughing." He could see references to "Anthropophagi"—"flesh-eaters"— in the maps of Africa in recent editions of Ptolemy's *Geography*, placed either in "Aethopia" or in southeastern "parts unknown" (figure 12), but he would not find them in al-Wazzan's Africa.[7] (In the *Muqaddima* Ibn Khaldun had tucked flesh-eaters into the first zone, south of the Land of the Blacks, where "humans are closer to dumb animals than to rational beings," but his text was unknown in Europe, and al-Wazzan had not followed it. The worst al-Wazzan said of the uncivilized southerners was that "like animals," they had no religious faith and held their wives in common.)[8]

To give another example, Rabelais defined the "Cataracts of the Nile" as "the place in Ethiopia where the Nile falls from high mountains with such a horrible noise that the neighbors are almost deaf, as Claude Galen writes. The Bishop of Caramit, who was my teacher of the Arabic language in Rome, told me that one hears this noise more than three days' travel away. That's as far as Paris to Tours." Rabelais gave references to Ptolemy, Strabo, and other classical writers but not to al-Wazzan. Arabic geographies did describe two cataracts on the Nile: one just south of Aswan and another—"terrifying," "thundering"—several days upstream toward Dongola. Al-Wazzan had mentioned neither, speaking only of a possible falls at a distant Mountain of the Moon, al-Qamar, believed by some to be the origin of the Nile; but all this was "guesswork, because no one has been there or seen it."[9]

In Rabelais's Bishop of Caramit, we hear, perhaps, an echo of Giovanni Leone's Arabic lessons. But this, too, may be a joking reference, since a Monophysite Christian from Greater Armenia, where Caramit is located, is an unlikely source for Arabic, and Rabelais's knowledge of the language seems to have been limited to a few words.[10]

LET US, then, consider al-Hasan al-Wazzan and François Rabelais not in terms of whether the first served as source or inspired a story for the second, but rather as lives and ways of thinking and writing in their time in which we can detect striking similarities across a divide of difference. Of course, there are disagreements between the two men. Al-Wazzan would have deplored the irreverent remark that Rabelais put in Panurge's mouth: that Muhammad boasted of his sexual prowess in the

Qur'an, but that he, Panurge, could surpass him as he could Hercules, or any other hero in that department. Al-Wazzan would have winced at Pantagruel's quotation of the adage "Africa always produces things new and monstrous," a view that his *Geography of Africa* was intended to counter.[11]

Still the lives of the two men had common elements in them, to which they responded in analogous ways. On both sides of the Mediterranean, syphilis and plague were taking their toll; religious movements were prompting conversions, reconversions, conflicts, and persecution within and across the borders of Christianity, Islam, and Judaism; and wars, local and large, were sometimes converging with and sometimes cutting through other loyalties. Al-Wazzan and Rabelais illustrate not only the flow of information, objects, and persons across the Mediterranean, but also the availability of similar cultural repertories.

The two men were roughly the same age, Rabelais just a few years older. Their relations to women and family were different, Rabelais in religious orders fathering his children in Paris out of wedlock, al-Wazzan following the Islamic path of marriage.[12] Rabelais's special training was in medicine, al-Wazzan's in law. Rabelais's learning ran much deeper than al-Wazzan's and would have done so even if al-Wazzan had had continuous access to an Arabic library, but both men had wide intellectual interests, loved poetry, and started writing it early; both composed in several prose genres as well.

Both men knew something of diplomacy; both valued travel and wrote travel accounts—their own or that of fictitious characters—though Rabelais wandered only within the kingdom of France and to the Piedmont, Italy, and once to Metz, still outside France's borders. Both were multilingual, did translations, and wrote in languages other than their mother tongue: Rabelais in his major work stretching his native Touraine speech into a vernacular of astonishing originality and range, al-Wazzan in his major work resorting to lively storytelling in the simplified Italian of a stranger. Both men were sharp observers of popular devotional and healing practices, the efficacy of which the North African discounted while the Frenchman used them merely to enrich his stories and speech, not worrying whether he would ever use them as a physician. Both were fascinated by and ambivalent about divination, al-Wazzan describing the learned za'iraja, which culminated in an answer in poetic form, Rabelais ending his saga with the oracle of the Bottle and with Panurge, having drunk the priestess Bacbuc's wine, chanting his answer in verse.[13]

Both men suffered religious pressure and harassment for their beliefs and the expression of them. Rabelais's tales of Gargantua, Pantagruel, and Panurge were placed on the Sorbonne's list of condemned books; he left his medical post in Lyon abruptly in early 1535 during a crackdown on heretics; and he was briefly imprisoned toward the end of his life—tamer matters, to be sure, than al-Wazzan's kidnapping and incarceration. But for all the differences, Rabelais was in his way as consciously "between worlds" as al-Wazzan. Both men had to write with sustained awareness of their audiences, al-Wazzan taking care to placate the Christians while not defaming Islam, Rabelais trying to create or revise a text so that it could squeak by the Sorbonne—or when condemned, not lead to prosecution—and still invite his readers "to interpret it in a higher sense."[14] Both of them knew the languages of secrecy and dissimulation.

Al-Wazzan's executioner's tale spoke to the historian's responsibility to tell the truth and his bird story to the importance of ruse. Rabelais stressed the need for historical truth-telling by laughing at careless or mendacious practice: the pages from medieval chronicles, wrapped in warm linen, were a fine remedy for toothache; his report of the giant Pantagruel drowning a whole camp of enemy soldiers when he pissed was "histoire tant veridicque," "very truthful history."[15] And in Panurge, he created one of the great tricksters of all time, connecting him with Hermes or Mercury, silver-tongued crosser of boundaries, god of merchants and thieves, bearer like Ulysses of "cunning intelligence," what the Greeks call *mètis*. *Mètis* draws on craft, skill, eloquence, and resourceful cleverness; it can be used for good or ill. Panurge, well-favored, fluent of speech, low in funds but "with sixty-three ways to find it when in need," put cunning intelligence to use as a follower of Pantagruel.

Silently miming his gestures, he answers questions on Cabala and occult sciences for a learned scholar from England who seeks Pantagruel's guidance; pulling a medicinal ointment from his pocket, he sews the head back on of Pantagruel's beloved teacher, cut down in battle.[16]

Especially important here is Panurge's story of capture by and escape from the Turks. He was taken prisoner at Mytilene, he explains (a reference to the ill-fated French army that had fought the Turks at Lesbos in a crusade inspired by Pope Alexander VI in 1502). The Turks plan to roast and eat him, but when already larded and on the spit, Panurge manages to get a brand in his teeth while his captor dozes and he starts a fire. He then kills his despairing pasha—at the Muslim's request, Panurge insists—takes his jewels, and escapes through the streets. The city-dwellers, running to put out the flames, throw water on Panurge's burns and give him food. The fire spreads to thousands of houses, and as he leaves town, Panurge is pursued by more than thirteen hundred dogs attracted by the smell of his partly roasted flesh. He diverts them with morsels of lard and gets away, cheerful and happy.[17]

Reading Panurge's tale with al-Wazzan's life and writings in mind gives us food for thought. Scholars have connected Panurge's lies with the falsehoods of the clever Ulysses, to whom Panurge compared himself. But the exaggeration in his insults—Turkish cannibals and Turkish dogs—is all the more outrageous when we compare them to contemporary events. Al-Wazzan's Turks were cruel, as in his report of Selim's troops sacking Cairo, but the fate of a Christian captive was enslavement, not to be eaten garnished with (forbidden) pig fat. Rabelais exposes Panurge as a fabricator and ingrate, of course, unappreciative of the help the kind Turks give him when they offer him food and water ("these devilish Turks . . . don't drink a drop of wine") and indifferent to the losses in the city he has set aflame.[18] The Islamic and Arabic traditions of ruse underscore the constructive and destructive possibilities in all these trickster figures of cunning intelligence, whether Mercury or Panurge, Shaykh Abu-l-Fath or an amphibious bird.

Rabelais and al-Wazzan have similarities in their overall view of world saviors and war. The French author had no rosy view of Muslim polities: the Goliath-like giants of Dipsodie, wrongful invaders of their neighbors, swear by "Mahon" (Muhammad) when they threaten Pantagruel and his men and finally give up the ghost. But when Rabelais created Picrochole, a king possessed by grandiose ideas of world rule, he modeled him not after Sultan Suleyman but after the Christian emperor Charles V. The stubborn and angry Picrochole will not resolve a quarrel among his subjects and those of Grandgousier (Gargantua's father) by diplomacy and arbitration but instead allows his advisers to convince him he can be another Alexander of Macedon. They visualize his future kingdom for him, encompassing all of Christian Europe, North Africa, and the Muslim world to the Euphrates. Barbarossa will become his slave and turn Christian; when he enters Libya, he will be given 200,000 camels and 1,600 elephants taken on the hunt at Sijilmasa.[19]

In al-Wazzan's critical portraits of tyrannical, cruel, or heretical Mahdi figures of the past, he had taken issue with the eschatological hope for world rulers; Rabelais did this through humor. Al-Wazzan did not spell out his alternative but seems to have preferred multiple empires, diplomacy and alliance, and local wars. Rabelais described good kings, like Grandgousier, Gargantua, and Pantagruel, who "administered their own lands, did not invade the land of others in hostility," and treated those they had defeated fairly and generously. He praised a village arbitrator, Perrin Dendin, for taking on the most difficult cases, waiting until his parties were exhausted and penniless from conflict and then reconciling them over drink at some festivity. With his techniques, Perrin Dendin could even make peace between the pope and his enemies in Italy, or between the Ottoman sultan and the Persian shah.[20] There is, to be sure, a utopian strain in Rabelais's thought: Gargantua builds the Abbey of Thélème, where men and women live beautifully in natural virtue. But this ideal model is a local affair, not a millenarian world plan.

Neither al-Wazzan nor Rabelais, at odds with the eschatological call for world conquerors uttered in their day, was a voice crying in the wilderness. Both could draw on practices of diplomacy. Al-Wazzan could look to the historical and legal views of the world of Ibn Khaldun and Ahmad al-Wansharisi, Rabelais to the pleas for peace and institutional arbitration of the humanist Erasmus.

The two men resemble each other in the bridges they built between different cultures and their perception of elements common among them. Al-Wazzan spoke of common ancestors, the traditional sons of Noah, but also of peoples and their languages mixing through sex, marriage, movement, and settlement. Rabelais gave his hero Pantagruel a genealogy of mythic and legendary giants, among whom were the Hebrew Hurtaly and several Saracens. Briefly, he even thought of marrying Pantagruel to "the daughter of the king of India, Prester John." The few references Rabelais made to the Qur'an were flippant, but Arabic had a venerable status, like that of early Ionian Greek, and Gargantua instructs Pantagruel to learn Arabic, along with Hebrew. Meanwhile Panurge does not speak in Arabic during his multilingual entreaty to Pantagruel when they first meet, but he later claims he could talk to his Turkish captors in their own tongue.[21]

Exuberant inclusiveness was Rabelais's most characteristic form of movement between cultures, in contrast to al-Wazzan's more measured details of languages, objects, and customs. In the always difficult effort to understand, translation was a key for both men—tested most thoroughly for al-Wazzan as he composed his major work in a foreign tongue and prepared his part of a multilingual dictionary. Rabelais reminded readers of the costly breakdowns and failures in communication when speakers insisted on a language or jargon or lingo that listeners could not hope to understand. Panurge's listeners cannot respond to his desperate plea for food when he puts it in thirteen different languages they do not know, and Pantagruel cannot make sense of a student's ornate, ridiculous Latinisms—the student is a Limousin trying to pass himself off as a Parisian—and threatens to skin him if he does not speak naturally.[22] Later in their travels, Pantagruel, Panurge, and their companions arrive at a glacial sea where words, frozen from a battle there the year before, are beginning to defrost. But they cannot understand them for they are in *"languaige Barbare,"* the language of barbarian peoples. As they listen, they hear horrifying sounds of

fighting, the beat of drums, the call of trumpets, and two words—
"Gog, Magog"—common to the Bible and Qur'an.[23]

Translation was part of al-Wazzan's everyday life in Italy. I have suggested this led him to the idea of cultural and religious equivalencies. It
was only one possible mode for him—ruse and strategies for maintaining distance were at least as important—but it was a sustaining one.

Rabelais often sought equivalencies, suggesting that his figures represented other figures and carried multiple associations. Pantagruel in
his strength has Hercules as a prototype and, as a wise and charitable
prince, is a figure for Christ—not only Christ, according to recent scholarship, but also for certain popular Christian saints and the Jewish
prophet Elijah.[24]

Such plentiful associations were facilitated in Rabelais's day by the
old Christian love of allegory and by the newer humanist taste for low-
ering the bar between classical virtue and Christian virtue. Ancient
Egypt was important here, since it was believed to be the source of
Hermetic texts carrying a hidden classical *and* Mosaic theology of
monotheism. Rabelais knew Egypt from translating the second book
of Herodotus, which gives a vivid picture of the Egyptians' worship of
multiple gods, and from studies of Egyptian hieroglyphics that per-
suaded him that these letters encoded ancient wisdom.[25] Though always tempted to make fun of excess in occult mysteries, Rabelais still
drew on these old and new forms of interpretation to support ecumeni-
cal or universalistic ideas. There were limits to them, however: Jews and
Jewish learning were included (the priestess of the Bottle at the end of
Panurge's quest is the Jewish Bacbuc) but no Muslim prophets, theologians, or holy figures.

Al-Wazzan's Arabic and Islamic world provided several paths to
equivalencies or at least the means to open the border between Muslims
and non-Muslims. The important pre-Islamic figures outside the communities of Jews or Christians could be considered virtual Muslims in
advance of the Prophet Muhammad—the sage Luqman, for example—
and they could be construed as prophets, bringing warnings or divine

messages to their Arab tribes, as the Qur'an said of Hud and Salih. Aristotle, respected as a great philosopher—indeed, a "divine" thinker, according to al-Farabi—could be drawn upon in support of Islam and "human philosophy" without regard to his precise religious status.[26] Of course, it would have been scandalous to see the false gods worshiped by pre-Islamic pagans as anticipations of the one God. Their idols were smashed and should be smashed. Still, their prognosticators persisted— their kahins and kahinas—with their oracular divination in rhymed and rhythmic Arabic prose, which was to have a long history.[27]

The Jews and Christians were Peoples of the Book, with their prophets. As the Qur'an said in Sura 2:87:

> And We gave to Moses the Book, and after him
> sent succeeding Messengers; and We gave Jesus
> son of Mary the clear signs, and confirmed him
> with the Holy Spirit.[28]

With their errors, however, their communities were not equivalent to the community of Islam. Al-Wazzan knew this passage well from his own commentary on the Qur'an and from his study of Malikite law.[29] For a wider embrace, he would have to turn to the Sufi thought of Ibn al-'Arabi: "Each revealed religion is a path that takes to God, and these paths are diverse. Hence the self-disclosures must be diverse, just as divine gifts are diverse . . . But He is He, none other than He."[30]

IF ONLY François Rabelais had got to Italy a decade earlier and conversed with al-Hasan al-Wazzan, during his days as Yuhanna al-Asad, and with Jacob Mantino sitting in as well. A conversation over the ample wine to which Rabelais summoned all good drinkers—a miraculous fluid like that from Bacbuc's fountain, which could be water or wine as the drinker imagined it, a pure fluid for the spirit, like that pictured by Ibn Farid—would have made for an exchange of frank stories, like those

at al-Hamadhani's *Assemblies* and like those al-Wazzan had enjoyed
on his travels across Africa. When he came to write of Pantagruel and
Panurge, Rabelais might then have added a Muslim traveling companion for them. And al-Wazzan might then have realized how powerful a
stratagem humor could be. Before taking flight, the trickster bird could
make people laugh at the foibles of the great.

Notes

ABBREVIATIONS

AM Al-Hasan al-Wazzan, *De Arte Metrica Liber*. MS Plut. 36.35, 54r–61v. Biblioteca Medicea Laurenziana, Florence.

AMC Angela Codazzi, "Il Trattato dell'Arte Metrica di Giovanni Leone Africano." In *Studi orientalistici in onore di Giorgio Levi Della Vida*, 1:180–98. Rome Instituto per l'Oriente, 1956.

Arberry *The Koran Interpreted*. Translated by Arthur J. Arberry. 2 vols. New York: Macmillan, 1955.

ASR Archivio di Stato di Roma.

ASV Archivio Segreto Vaticano, Vatican City.

BNF Bibliothèque Nationale de France.

CEI Cyril Glassé, *The Concise Encyclopaedia of Islam*. London, 1989.

CGA Al-Hasan al-Wazzan, *Libro de la Cosmogrophia [sic for Cosmographia] et Geographia de Affrica*. MS V. E. 953. Biblioteca Nazionale Centrale, Rome.

DAR Al-Hasan al-Wazzan, *La Descrittione dell'Africa*. In Giovanni Battista Ramusio, ed., *Primo volume, et Terza editione delle Navigationi et Viaggi*. Venice, 1563, 1r–95v.

Dict Al-Hasan al-Wazzan, Jacob Mantino, et al., Arabic-Hebrew-Latin, Spanish dictionary. MS 598, Manuscritos árabes. Real Biblioteca del Escorial, Spain.

EAL *Encyclopedia of Arabic Literature*, ed. Julie Scott Meisami and Paul Starkey. 2 vols. London and New York, 1998.

EI1 *The Encyclopaedia of Islam*. Leiden, 1913–34; supplement 1938.

EI2   *The Encyclopaedia of Islam.* New Edition. Leiden, 1954–2001.

Ép   Jean-Léon l'Africain, Description de l'Afrique. Translated by Alexis Épaulard. New ed. Paris, 1980–81.

EpiP   The Epistles of Saint Paul in Arabic. Transcribed by al-Hasan al-Wazzan. MS Orientale 16-alfa.J.6.3. Biblioteca Estense Universitaria, Modena.

QAn   *Al-Qurʾan* in Arabic and Latin. Translated and annotated by Joannes Gabriel of Teruel; corrected by al-Hasan al-Wazzan; transcribed by David Colville. MS D100 inf. Biblioteca Ambrosiana, Milan.

Ram   *La descrizione dell'Africa di Giovan Lioni Africano.* In Giovanni Battista Ramusio, *Navigazioni e Viaggi*, vol. 1, 19–460. Edited by Marica Milanesi. Turin, 1978.

Rauch   Dietrich Rauchenberger, *Johannes Leo der Afrikaner. Seine Beschreibung des Raumes zwischen Nil und Niger nach dem Urtext.* Wiesbaden, 1999.

SIHME   Henry de Castries, ed., *Les sources inédites de l'histoire du Maroc. Archives et bibliothèques d'Espagne.* 1st series. 3 vols. Paris and Madrid, 1921–61.

SIHMF   Henry de Castries, ed., *Les sources inédites de l'histoire du Maroc de 1530 à 1845. Archives et bibliothèques de France.* 1st series. 4 vols. Paris, 1905–26.

SIHMP   Pierre de Cenival and Robert Ricard, eds., *Les sources inédites de l'histoire du Maroc. Archives et bibliothèques de Portugal.* 1st series. 5 vols. Paris, 1934–53.

VIA   Al-Hasan al-Wazzan, *De Viris quibusdam Illustribus apud Arabes.* MS Plut. 36.35, 31r–53v, 62r–65r. Biblioteca Medicea Laurenziana, Florence.

VIAHott   *De Viris quibusdam Illustribus apud Arabes, per Johannem Leonem Affricanum [sic]*, in Johann Heinrich Hottinger, *Bibliothecarius Quadripartitus*, 246–86. Zurich, 1664.

VIH   Al-Hasan al-Wazzan, *De quibusdam Viris Illustribus apud Hebraeos.* MS Plut. 36.35, 65v–69v. Biblioteca Medicea Laurenziana, Florence.

VIHHott   *De quibusdam Viris Illustribus apud Hebraeos per Joannem Leonem Africanum*, in Johann Heinrich Hottinger, *Bibliothecarius Quadripartitus*, 286–91. Zurich, 1664.

Wehr   Hans Wehr, *A Dictionary of Modern Written Arabic*, 4th ed. Edited by J. Milton Cowan. Ithaca, N.Y., 1994.

NOTE REGARDING THE QURʾAN

All references to verses from the Qurʾan in the text and in the endnotes follow the current Egyptian verse-numbering system. Since the verse-numbering system used by Arthur J. Arberry for his translation has been superseded, the endnotes will provide only the volume and page number when quotations are used from his translation; the current numbering of these quoted verses is given in the text in parentheses. The Latin translation of the Qur'an made for Egidio da Viterbo, corrected by al-Hasan al-Wazzan and referred to in the endnotes as QAn, has a slightly different numbering for the Suras and for the verses than that followed today. In referring to QAn in the endnotes, I shall use the Latin name of the Sura given by the translator and his verse numbering, but shall indicate in brackets the numbering used today.

INTRODUCTION · CROSSINGS

1. Silvio A. Bedini, *The Pope's Elephant* (London: Carcanet, 1997), especially chaps. 2, 4, 6–7.

2. *Johann Leo's des Africaners Beschreibung von Africa*, trans. Georg Wilhelm Lorsbach (Herborn, 1805), discussed in Rauch, 165–71.

3. Miguel Casiri, *Bibliotheca Arabico-Hispana Escurialensis*, 2 vols. (Madrid: Antonius Perez de Soto, 1760–70), 1:172–74; *Description de l'Afrique tierce partie du monde escrite par Jean Léon African*, ed. Charles Schefer, 3 vols. (Paris: Ernest Leroux, 1896–98). Schefer (1820–98) founded the École des langues orientales, edited a number of texts about Persia and travel to Muslim lands, and built up a great collection of Arabic manuscripts, subsequently purchased by the Bibliothèque Nationale. *The History and Description of Africa... written by Al-Hassan Ibn-Mohammed Al-Wezaz Al-Fasi, a Moor, baptized as Giovanni Leone, but better known as Leo Africanus*, ed. Robert Brown, 3 vols. (London: Hakluyt Society, 1896). The Lorsbach German translation also referred to an Arabic name in its introduction (Rauch, 31 n.118).

4. Louis Massignon, *Le Maroc dans les premières années du 16e siècle. Tableau géographique d'après Léon l'Africain* (Algiers: Typographie Adolphe Jourdan, 1906), 43–45. Massignon thanked both his thesis director, the colonial geographer Augustin Bernard, and the folklorist René Basset, a specialist on the folktales of the Berbers and North Africa (ix–x). Daniel Nordman has presented an excellent paper on Massignon's book at the Colloque "Léon l'Africain," held at the École des Hautes Études en Sciences Sociales, Paris, 22–24 May 2003: "Le Maroc dans les premières années du XVIe siècle. Tableau géographique d'après Louis Massignon," to be published in François Pouillon and Oumelbanine Zhiri, eds., *Léon l'Africain*, forthcoming at the Institut d'Étude de l'Islam et des Sociétés du Monde Musulman (EHESS), Paris. On the French "colonial sciences," see Li-Chuan Tai, "L'ethnologie française entre colonialisme et décolonisation (1920–1960)," doctoral thesis, EHESS, 2001.

5. Angela Codazzi, "Leone Africano," *Enciclopedia italiana* (Rome, 1933), 20:899. Angela Codazzi, "Dell'unico manoscritto conosciuto della *Cos-*

mografia dell'Africa di Giovanni Leone l'Africano," *Comptes rendus du Congrès international de géographie. Lisbonne 1949* (Lisbon, 1952), 4:225–26. Angela Codazzi, "Il Trattato dell'Arte Metrica di Giovanni Leone Africano," in *Studi orientalistici in onore di Giorgio Levi Della Vida*, 2 vols. (Rome: Istituto per l'Oriente, 1956), 1:180–98 (henceforth AMC). Giorgio Levi Della Vida, *Ricerche sulla formazione del più antico fondo dei manoscritti orientali della Biblioteca Vaticana* (Vatican City: Biblioteca Apostolica Vaticana, 1939), viii (dedication dated Rome, August 1939), 99–110.

6. Jean-Léon l'Africain, *Description de l'Afrique*, trans. Alexis Épaulard, annotated by Alexis Épaulard, Théodore Monod, Henri Lhote, and Raymond Mauny, Publications de l'Institut des Hautes Études Marocaines, no. 61 (Paris: Librairie d'Amérique et d'Orient, 1956), v–xvi (This edition was reprinted in 1980–81 and will henceforth be referred to as Ép.). Use of manuscript V.E. 953 at the Biblioteca Nazionale Centrale, Rome, by Alexis Épaulard, 6–20 June 1939, recorded on the list inserted into manuscript. Épaulard (1878–1949) trained as a physician at the University of Lyon, with a thesis on *Vampirisme, nécrophilie, nécrosadisme, nécrophagie* (Lyon, 1901). Monod, a professor at the Museum of Natural History in Paris, was one of the two founders of the Institut Français d'Afrique Noire in 1938. By the time the *Description* was published, Monod had become one of the supporters of the new review founded by African intellectuals, *Présence africaine*, published in Dakar and Paris (Tai, "Ethnologie," 195, 253–55).

7. For instance, Pierre Kalck, "Pour une localisation du royaume de Gaoga," *Journal of African History* 13 (1972): 520–40; R. S. O'Fahey and J. L. Spaulding, "Comment: The Geographic Location of Gaoga," and Pierre Kalck, "Response," *Journal of African History* 14 (1973): 505–8. Humphrey J. Fisher, "Leo Africanus and the Songhay Conquest of Hausaland," *International Journal of African Historical Studies* 11 (1978):86–112. Djibo Mallal Hamani, *Au carrefour du Soudan et de la Berberie: Le sultanat touareg de l'Ayar* (Niamey: Institut de Recherches en Sciences Humaines, 1989), 177–78, 181, 184. John O. Hunwick, *Timbuktu and the Songhay Empire: Al-Saʿdi's Taʾrikh al-Sudan down to 1613 and other Contemporary Documents* (Leiden: Brill, 1999), 113, 285 n.74. Pekka Masonen, *The Negroland Revisited: Discovery and Invention of the Sudanese Middle Ages* (Helsinki: Finnish Academy of Science and Letters, 2000), chap. 4 (Masonen doubts that al-Wazzan saw anything of sub-Saharan Africa beyond a first visit to Timbuktu, 188–89). Hunwick concludes that al-Wazzan visited at least some of the sub-Saharan areas he described; his use of al-Wazzan's text is judicious and persuasive and is informed by his extraordinary mastery of the sources for the history of sub-Saharan Africa. Kalck is unusual in explaining seeming error or omission in the *Description* by something other than weak memory or passing on rumor:

he asks, given the situation of "Léon l'Africain" at the time he was writing, what he would have wanted to say and what withhold. Kalck, "Pour une localisation," 546–47.

8. Oumelbanine Zhiri, *L'Afrique au miroir de l'Europe: Fortunes de Jean Léon l'Africain à la Renaissance* (Geneva: Librairie Droz, 1991); *Les sillages de Jean Léon l'Africain: XVIe au XXe siècle* (Casablanca: Wallada, 1995); "'Il compositore' ou l'autobiographie éclatée de Jean Léon l'Africain," in Ali Benmakhlouf, ed., *Le voyage des théories* (Casablanca: Éditions Le Fennec, 2000), 63–80. In the wake of Zhiri's *Afrique*, a younger generation of literary scholars have been using al-Wazzan's text to rethink how issues of race, non-European sexuality, and colonization have acted on the European imagination. See especially Kim F. Hall, *Things of Darkness: Economies of Race and Gender in Early Modern England* (Ithaca and London: Cornell University Press, 1995), 28–40, and Bernadette Andrea, "The Ghost of Leo Africanus from the English to the Irish Renaissance," in Patricia Clare Ingham and Michelle R. Warren, eds., *Postcolonial Moves: Medieval Through Modern* (New York: Palgrave Macmillan 2003), 195–215. See also the informative Web site of Cristel de Rouvray, www.leoafricanus.com.

9. Rauch, 237 (quoting Raymond Mauny). Rauchenberger also transcribes the pages of al-Wazzan's manuscript on sub-Saharan Africa.

10. Juan León Africano, *Descripción general del África*, ed. and trans. Serafín Fanjul with the assistance of Nadia Consolani (Barcelona and Madrid: Lunwerg Editores, 1995), introduction, 11, 47. Like Massignon in the early years of the century, Fanjul characterized the work as "Arabic in its subject if Italian in its form and immediate inspiration" (43). An earlier Spanish translation of the Ramusio edition appeared in 1940, published by the Instituto General Franco de Estudios e Investigación Hispano-Arabe.

11. Muhammad al-Mahdi al-Hajwi, *Hayat al-Wazzan al-Fasi wa-atharuh* (Rabat, 1935). Al-Hasan al-Wazzan, *Wasf Ifriqiya*, trans. Muhammad Hajji (Rabat, 1980); Hajji, *L'activité intellectuelle au Maroc à l'époque Sa'dide*, 2 vols. (Rabat: Dar El-Maghrib, 1976–77). Important papers were given on al-Hajwi's study and on Hajji's translation at the Colloque "Léon l'Africain" (EHESS, Paris, 22–24 May 2003): on the former by Alain Roussillon, "Une lecture réformiste de Leo Africanus: Patrimonialisation d'un renégat," on the latter by Driss Mansouri, both to be published in Pouillon and Zhiri, eds., *Léon l'Africain*.

12. Amin Maalouf, *Léon l'Africain* (Paris: J.-C. Lattès, 1986), 7, 9. Amin Maalouf, *Les croisades vues par les Arabes* (Paris: J.-C. Lattès, 1983). "Amin Maalouf," in Marcos Ancelovici and Francis Dupuis-Déri, *L'archipel identitaire. Recueil d'entretiens sur l'identité culturelle* (Montréal: Boréal, 1997), 169–72. Amin Maalouf, *Origines* (Paris: Bernard Grasset, 2004), 9–10. Amin Maalouf, interview by author, Paris, 17 October 1997.

13. Ali Benmakhlouf, "Cosmologie et cosmographie au XVIe siècle: Le statut épistémique de la description"; Houari Touati, "La girafe de Léon l'Africain"; Ahmed Boucharb, "La conquête ibérique du littoral marocain d'après la *Description de l'Afrique*: Vision d'une entreprise guerrière en terre d'Islam"; Abdelmajid Kaddouri, "Al-Wazzan de part et d'autre de la Méditerranée: Lire Léon dans une perspective de regards croisés," all papers presented at the Colloque "Léon l'Africain" (EHESS, Paris, 22–24 May 2003), to be published in Pouillon and Zhiri, eds., *Léon l'Africain.* Two other Moroccan scholars have also written about al-Wazzan in a book that has come into my hands as my own goes to press: Hamid Triki and Amina Aouchar, who contribute introductory essays to a handsomely illustrated edition of Épaulard's translation of al-Wazzan's pages on Fez (*Fez dans la Cosmographie d'Al-Hassan ben Mohammed al-Wazzan az-Zayyat, dit Léon l'Africain* [Mohammedia, Morocco: Senso Unico Editions, 2004]).

14. *Historiale Description de l'Afrique, tierce partie du monde . . . Escrite de nôtre tems* [sic] *par Iean Leon, African*, trans. Jean Temporal (Lyon: Jean Temporal, 1556/1557). The title page gives 1556 as the date of publication, but Henri II's privilège to Jean Temporal indicates that the printing was concluded on 4 January 1556, old style, that is 4 January 1557, new style.

15. Homi Bhabha, *The Location of Culture* (New York and London: Routledge, 1994), chaps. 1, 6, 10. Richard White, *The Middle Ground: Indians, Empires and Republics in the Great Lakes Region, 1650–1815* (Cambridge: Cambridge University Press, 1991). Paul Gilroy, *The Black Atlantic. Modernity and Double Consciousness* (Cambridge, Mass.: Harvard University Press, 1993), 29. Natalie Zemon Davis, *Women on the Margins: Three Seventeenth-Century Lives* (Cambridge, Mass.: Harvard University Press, 1995).

16. For some examples of this approach, see Leo Spitzer, *Lives in Between: Assimilation and Marginality in Austria, Brazil, West Africa 1780–1945* (Cambridge: Cambridge University Press, 1989) and Mercedes García-Arenal and Gerard Wiegers, *A Man of Three Worlds: Samuel Pallache, a Moroccan Jew in Catholic and Protestant Europe*, trans. Martin Beagles (Baltimore: Johns Hopkins University Press, 2003).

CHAPTER ONE · LIVING IN THE LAND OF ISLAM

1. MS Vat. Ar. 115, 295v, Biblioteca Vaticana. Levi Della Vida, *Ricerche*, 102, 155; Rauch, 69, 463. EpiP, 68. On the parts of the Arabic name, see Jacqueline Sublet, *Le voile du nom. Essai sur le nom propre arabe* (Paris: Presses universitaires de France, 1991), introduction.

2. *CGA*, 66v–67r, 85v–86r. The scribe often put slant marks on either side of his numbers—/4/—but in this case the first line is much firmer than the

second and the second very light. Ram, 92, 110–11; Ép, 99, 120–21 (follows Ramusio). On the strong likelihood that Ramusio had available another manuscript of the Africa book, see chapter 3 below. Throughout these notes, following each citation of pages from al-Wazzan's Africa manuscript (*CGA*), I shall cite the relevant pages in a 1978 edition of Ramusio's *Navigationi e Viaggi* (Ram) and in the French translation of Épaulard (Ép). Among the many differences between the manuscript and the printed versions, I shall indicate in the notes only those especially relevant to my overall argument. In these cases I shall also cite the folio number from the Venice 1563 edition of the *Navigationi et Viaggi* (henceforth *DAR*), the one on which the 1978 edition is based. Since the 1978 edition has modernized the spelling of certain Italian words, all direct quotations from Ramusio's edition of al-Wazzan's Africa book will be taken directly from the Venice 1563 edition.

3. The fullest collection of sources for the Portuguese expansion into Safi and its region is found in *SIHMP*, vol. 1 (July 1486–April 1516). The name of the Berber to whom al-Wazzan delivered a message was Yahya-u-Taᶜfuft; on him see 151–61, 177–78, 191, 197, 271–80, 316–29, 335–53, 381, 545–58, 596–637, 642–63. He was made a captain for the Portuguese governor of Safi, Nuno Fernandes de Ataíde. The governor arrived in Safi from Lisbon by the summer of 916/1510. Yahya, who had been in Lisbon since the summer of 1507, might possibly have come with him in 1510, but his name is not given in the detailed report of the Portuguese siege of Safi in December 1510, and the first sure mention of him in action in Morocco is in October 1511. Yahya's role as tribute collector, lawgiver to communities around Safi, and military leader is found in documents from 918/1512 to 921/1514. Al-Wazzan says the crucial meeting with Yahya-u-Taᶜfuft took place when the latter was near Marrakesh with five hundred Portuguese horsemen and two thousand Arab horsemen. Independent evidence places this military event in early summer 918/1512: *SIHMP*, 1:335–36; Damião de Góis, *Crónica do Felicissimo Rei D. Manuel*, ed. J. M. Teixeira de Carvalho and David Lopes, 4 vols. (Coimbra: Universidade de Coimbra, 1926) 3:125–28, chap. 35; Matthew T. Racine, "Service and Honor in Sixteenth-Century Portuguese North Africa: Yahya-u-Taᶜfuft and Portuguese Noble Culture," *Sixteenth-Century Journal* 32 (2001): 71–80. *CGA*, 86r.

4. Rauchenberger assumes that the "4" in *CGA* is what al-Wazzan intended rather than a scribe's aberration (Rauch, 33–36). He then gives al-Wazzan a birth date late in the year 900/1494. But this requires Rauchenberger making assertions difficult to square with the evidence, including his giving an impossibly early date—917/1511—for al-Wazzan's meeting with Yahya-u-Taᶜfuft. Even then, by Rauchenberger's chronology, al-Wazzan would be collecting epitaphs from royal graves and presenting them at the court of Fez at the age of ten; having an important conversation with a

major conspirator in Safi in the midst of political bloodshed at the age of twelve; and emerging as a full-fledged diplomat on an important mission at the age of sixteen, whereas al-Wazzan described himself as just learning the ropes under the tutelage of his uncle at that age.

5. Rachel Arié, *L'Espagne musulmane au temps des Nasrides (1232–1492)* (Paris: Éditions de Boccard, 1973), 52–62, 302. Al-Idrisi, *La Première Géographie de l'Occident*, ed. Henri Bresc and Annliese Nef, trans. Jaubert and Annliese Nef (Paris: Flammarion, 1999), 289. ʿAbd al-Basit ibn Halil, "El Reino de Granada en 1465–66," in J. Garcia Mercadal, trans., *Viajes de estranjeros por España y Portugal*, 3 vols. (Madrid: Aguilar, 1952), 1:255–56.

6. Miguel Ángel Ladero Quesada, *Granada después la conquista: Repobladores y mudéjares* (Granada: Diputación Provincial de Granada, 1988), 235–43. Catherine Gaignard, *Maures et chrétiens à Grenade, 1492–1570* (Paris: Éditions L'Harmattan, 1997), 59–65. Arié, *Espagne*, 293–95. I found no reference to anyone with the family name al-Wazzan in the summaries of fifteenth-century Granadan notarial documents in the collection of the Biblioteca Universitaria of the University of Granada (BHR/caja C, printed summaries in Luis Sece de Lucena Paredes, "Escrituras árabes de la universidad de Granada," *Al-Andalus* 35 [1970]: 315–53); Maya Shatzmiller, who has worked closely with these materials, also does not recall seeing the name. Of course, these are only a fraction of the contracts passed at Granada during those years.

7. Rachel Arié, *Aspects de l'Espagne musulmane. Histoire et culture* (Paris: De Boccard, 1997), 11–13. Gaignard, *Maures*, 93, 193–94. Federico Corriente, *A Grammatical Sketch of the Spanish Arabic Dialect Bundle* (Madrid: Instituto Hispano-Arabe de Cultura, 1977), 6–8, and *Árabe andalusí y lenguas romances* (Madrid: Editorial Mapfre, 1992), 33–35. Mark Meyerson, *The Muslims of Valencia in the Age of Fernando and Isabel: Between Coexistence and Crusade* (Berkeley and Los Angeles: University of California Press, 1991), 227–30. Reinhold Kontzi, "La transcription de textes aljamiados," in Abdejelil Temimi, ed., *Las practicas musulmanas de los moriscos andaluces (1492–1609). Actas del III Simposio Internacional de Estudios Moriscos* (Zaghouan, 1989), 99.

8. Arié, *Espagne*, 164–78. Fernando de Zafra to Ferdinand and Isabella, October 1493, in Miguel Salvá and Pedro Sainz de Baranda, eds., *Colección de Documentos Inéditos para la Historia de España*, 112 vols. (Madrid, 1842–95), 11:552–55. Ángel Galán Sánchez, *Los mudéjares del reino de Granada* (Granada: Universidad de Granada, 1991), 39–62. Gaignard, *Maures*, 23–37, 67, 121–29, 210–23, 251–52. José Enrique López de Coca Castañer, "Granada y el Magreb: La emigracion andalusi (1485–1516)," in Mercedes García-Arenal and María J. Viguera, eds., *Relaciones de la península Ibérica con el Magreb siglos XIII–XVI. Actas del Coloquio (Madrid, 17–18 diciembre 1987)* (Madrid: CSIC, 1988), 409–51.

9. *CGA*, 71r–v, 169v. Ram, 97, 187–88; Ép, 105, 202. Hieronymus Münzer, *Viaje por España y Portugal (1494–1495)*, trans. José López Toro (Madrid: Ediciones Polifemo, 1991), 129–31. Christoph Weiditz, *Authentic Every day Dress of the Renaissance: All 154 Plates from the "Trachtenbuch,"* ed. Theodor Hampe (New York: Dover Publications, 1994), plates 79–88; Gaignard, *Maures*, 201–6; Fathia Harzallah, "Survie grenadine à travers le costume féminin et les recettes culinaires, en Tunisie, au XVIIe siècle," in Fatma Haddad-Chamakh and Alia Baccar-Bournaz, eds., *L'écho de la prise de Grenade dans la culture européene aux XVIe et XVIIe siècles. Actes du Colloque de Tunis 18–21 novembre 1992* (Tunis: Cérès, 1994), 85–86. A. J. Wensinck, "*Khitan,*" *EI2*, 5:20–22.

10. Galán Sánchez, *Mudéjares*, 63. Vincent Lagardère, *Histoire et société en Occident musulman au Moyen Âge: Analyse du "Miʿyar" d'al-Wansharisi* (Madrid: Casa de Velázquez, 1995), 48, no. 182. Jamil M. Abun-Nasr, *A History of the Maghrib in the Islamic Period* (Cambridge: Cambridge University Press, 1987), 142. Mercedes García-Arenal, "Sainteté et pouvoir dynastique au Maroc: La résistance de Fès aux Saʿdiens," *Annales.ESC* 45 (1990): 1029–30.

11. *CGA*, 99v, 155r, 163v, 203r, 240r–v. Ram, 123, 176, 183, 214, 251; Ép, 136, 198, 207, 241–42, 287–88.

12. Jean Brignon, Abdelaziz Amine, Brahim Boutaleb, et al., *Histoire du Maroc* (Casablanca: Librairie Nationale, 1994), 185–89. *Le Maroc andalou: À la découverte d'un art de vivre* (Casablanca: EDDIF and Aix-en-Provence: Édisud, 2000), 86–130. *CGA*, 137v–140r, 159r–v, 192v–195r. Ram, 160–64, 179–80, 206–8; Ép, 182–85, 202–3, 232–35.

13. *CGA*, 173r–v. Ram, 191; Ép, 215–16.

14. *CGA*, 140r–142r. Ram, 162–64; Ép, 184–86. Muhammad B. A. Benchekroun, *La vie intellectuelle marocaine sous les Mérinides et les Wattasides* (Rabat, 1974), 56–75; Hajji, *Activité*, 95–132; Fernando Rodriguez Mediano, *Familias de Fez (SS. XV–XVII)* (Madrid: Consejo Superior de Investigaciones Científicas, 1995), 32–53.

15. Benchekroun, *Vie*, 385–401, 486–88; Hajji, *Activité*, 233–334, 399–400; Mediano, *Familias*, 43–50. David S. Powers, *Law, Society, and Culture in the Maghrib, 1300–1500* (Cambridge: Cambridge University Press, 2002), 407. E. Lévi-Provençal, *Les historiens des Chorfa: Essai sur la littérature historique et biographique au Maroc du XVIe au XXe siècle* (Paris: É. Larose, 1922), 226–29. Ali Fahmi Khushaim, *Zarruq the Sufi* (Tripoli: General Company for Publication, 1976), 189–202; García-Arenal, "Sainteté," 1034; Muhammad Kahly, *Société, pouvoir et religion au Maroc à la fin du Moyen-Âge (XIVe–XVe siècle)* (Paris: Maisonneuve and Larose, 1986), 317–18. *CGA*, 219r–v. Ram, 231; Ép, 262.

16. *CGA*, 142v–144r. Ram, 165–66; Ép, 187–88. Hajji, *Activité*, 141, 151–52.

17. *CGA*, 75v, 78v (another reference to friends from student days at Fez, scholars of law later living in the High Atlas in the region of Marrakesh). Ram, 101, 104; Ép, 109, 112.

18. *CGA*, 172r–v. Ram, 190; Ép, 214–15. Hajji, *Activité*, 107. Al-Wazzan described the more splendid ceremony for the Mawlid under the Marinid sultans, which included large prizes to the winning poet from the sultan himself. Under the Wattasids, "since about the thirty years or so," the sultans had stopped their formal celebration of the Mawlid (172v; Ramusio says "one hundred thirty years," but *CGA*'s "thirty" seems more plausible in terms of the political chronology). Roger Le Tourneau, *Fez in the Age of the Marinides*, trans. Besse Albert Clement (Norman: University of Oklahoma Press, 1961), 142–43; Kably, *Société*, 285–88.

19. *CGA*, 85v, 125r–126r. Ram, 110, 148–49; Ép, 120, 168. For detail on the annual pilgrimage to Taghya (now Moulay Bouazza), see chapter 6, pp. 169–70. On Safi in these years, see *SIHMP*, 1:152–53, and Vincent J. Cornell, "Socioeconomic Dimensions of Reconquista and Jihad in Morocco: Portuguese Dukkala and the Saʿdid Sus, 1450–1557," *International Journal of Middle East Studies* 22 (1990): 383–92; this study also includes valuable material drawn from Ahmed Boucharb's book *Dukkala waʾl-istiʿmar al-Burtughali ila sanat ikhlaʾ Asafi wa Azammur* (Casablanca, 1984).

20. *CGA*, 433r. Ram, 429; Ép, 537–38. Ramusio added to his printed edition a passing reference to a market for medicinal drugs and spices in the town of "Tauris city in Persia" (Ram, 177; followed by Ép, 200), but this is not found in the *CGA* manuscript. Al-Wazzan simply says he has not seen anything similar to the Fez spice and drug market anywhere (*CGA*, 157r). Though most of the voyages described by al-Masʿudi he actually made, a few were fictitious, his observations drawn from earlier writers (Houari Touati, *Islam et voyage au Moyen Âge* [Paris: Éditions du Seuil, 2000], 151–52).

21. *CGA*, 191r–v. Ram, 204–5; Ép, 230–31.

22. *CGA*, 33r–v, 99v–101v, 459r. Ram, 55–56, 123–25, 454; Ép, 53, 136–38, 571–72.

23. Trips with merchant caravans, *CGA*, 21r, 31r, 359v–360r. Ram, 38–39, 53, 357; Ép, 38, 51, 431. The salt-loading episode at Taghaza (today Terhazza) in the Sahara, *CGA*, 374r–v. Ram, 371; Ép, 455–56.

24. *CGA*, 31r–32v. Ram, 53–55; Ép, 51–52. Al-Wazzan never applied the word "merchant" to himself, but Ramusio added it in opening this episode (*DAR*, 8v): "partiti insieme molti mercatanti da Fez," "many merchants of Fez left together."

25. Levi Della Vida, *Ricerche*, 101: "orator Regis fezze." *CGA*, 236v–238v, 250r–253r, 254v–255r, 266v–267R. Ram, 247–49, 250–61, 263, 274; Ép,

283–85, 300–304, 316. E. Fagnan, ed. and trans., *Extraits inédits relatifs au Maghreb (Géographie et histoire)* (Algiers: Jules Carbonel, 1924), 335. Abun-Nasr, *Maghrib*, 206–8; Brignon et al., *Maroc*, 171–79. Weston F. Cook, Jr., *The Hundred Years War for Morocco: Gunpowder and the Military Revolution in the Early Modern Muslim World* (Boulder, Colo.: Westview Press, 1994), 30–39, 109–15. Al-Nasir, brother of Sultan Muhammad al-Burtughali, took as two of his wives the daughters of the shaykh of the influential Berber tribe of Chawiya (*SIHMP*, 1:438–39, 555). For a general approach, see Philip S. Khoury and Joseph Kostiner, eds., *Tribes and State Formation in the Middle East* (Berkeley and Los Angeles: University of California Press, 1990), pt. 1.

26. *SIHMP*, 1:17–35, 151–61, 394–402, 434–45. Abun-Nasr, *Maghrib*, 207–9; Brignon et al., *Maroc*, 174–77; Cornell, "Socioeconomic Dimensions," 387–89, 393–94; Cook, *Hundred Years War*, chaps. 3–5. Robert Ricard, *Études sur l'histoire des portuguais au Maroc* (Coimbra: Universidade da Coimbra, 1955), chaps. 1–3, 7, 9. Bernardo Rodrigues, *Anais de Arzila*, ed. David Lopes, 2 vols. (Lisbon: Academia des Ciências de Lisboa, 1915). *Chronique de Santa-Cruz du Cap de Gué (Agadir)*, ed. and trans. Pierre de Cenival (Paris: Paul Geuthner, 1934), 20–39. Góis, *Crónica*, 3:45–57, 160–85, 230–46.

27. *CGA*, 218v–219r. Ram, 230; Ép, 262. Abun-Nasr, *Maghrib*, 207; Cook, *Hundred Years War*, 111–12, 126–27, 150.

28. *SIHMP*, 1:151–61, 177–78, 191, 197, 316–25, 335–53, 373, 381–84, 545–58, 596–97, 601–2, 619–29, 630–37, 642–48, 658–63; Pierre Gros, "Deux Kanouns marocains de début du XVIe siècle," *Hespéris* 18 (1934): 64–75. *CGA*, 83r–85v. Ram, 108–10; Ép, 118–20. See also the insightful study of Yahya-u-Ta'fuft by Racine, "Service."

29. *CGA*, 85v–86r. Ram, 110–11; Ép, 120–21. In addition to the military detail that allows us to date this message to Yahya-u-Ta'fuft in early summer 918/1512, there is political evidence. Though Yahya had won a victory against the sultan of Marrakesh, he was immediately accused by the suspicious Portuguese governor and others of giving presents to the defeated sultan and trying to make a deal with him (*SIHMP*, 1:337–53; Racine, "Service," 74–77). This would have been an opportune moment for the sultan of Fez and the amir of Sus to approach him.

30. Abun-Nasr, *Maghrib*, 206–11; Brignon et al., *Maroc*, 206–8; Hajji, *Activité*, 45–48. Kably, *Société*, 252, 317–19, 329–30, 334–35, 332. García-Arenal, "Sainteté," 1029–36. Dahiru Yahya, *Morocco in the Sixteenth Century: Problems and Patterns in African Foreign Policy* (London: Longman, 1981), 2–7. Cornell, "Socioeconomic Dimensions," 395–99; Vincent J. Cornell, *Realm of the Saint: Power and Authority in Moroccan Sufism* (Austin: University of Texas Press, 1998), chap. 6.

31. Abun-Nasr, *Maghrib*, 209–11; Hajji, *Activité*, 48–49; Cornell, *Realm*,

chap. 8. *CGA*, 86r, 89v–90r, 93r. Ram, 110, 114, 117; Ép, 120, 125, 130. *SIHMP*, 1:687–92.

32. Fagnan, ed., *Extraits*, 361. Cornell, *Realm*, 258–60; Cornell, "Socioeconomic Dimensions," 398. *SIHMP*, 1:256, 256 n.3.

33. *CGA*, 49v–50v, 52r, 54r–v ("ragione contra la lege publica"), 55v, 56v, 57v, 59v, 62v, 63v–64r, 82v, 86r, 89v–90r. Ram, 75, 77, 79, 81–83, 85, 87, 89, 107–8, 110, 114; Ép, 78, 80, 82, 84–86, 89, 92, 94, 117, 120, 125. García-Arenal, "Sainteté," 1024–26; Cornell, *Realm*, 247–63.

34. Bernard Rosenberger has followed his movements in "Jean Léon l'Africain: Une carrière politique au service du sultan Wattasside de Fès," Colloque "Léon l'Africain" (EHESS, Paris, 22–24 May 2003), forthcoming in Pouillon and Zhiri, eds., *Léon l'Africain.*

35. Abun-Nasr, *Maghrib*, 6–9. *CGA*, 34v–35v (35v: "Acqua di Nuisan"), 258v–259r, 449r–451r. Ram, 57–59, 267–68, 445–46; Ép, 54–56, 308–9, 561–62. Wehr, 1131 ("*nusu*").

36. *CGA*, 104r–110r, 130r–132r, 219r–v. Ram, 127–33, 152–54 ([*DAR*, 30v] increases al-Wazzan's figures on the number of Wattasid horsemen from 5,000 to 50,000 and other modifications to make the Portuguese loss less humiliating), 231; Ép, 142–47, 172–75, 262. *SIHMP*, 1:695–702, 728–31; Góis, *Crónica*, 3:243–46, chap. 76; Cook, *Hundred Years War*, 154. Al-Maʿmura is now known as Mehdiya.

37. *CGA*, 93r, 109v–110r, 131v–132r, 219r–v, 253r. Ram, 117, 132, 154, 231, 261; Ép, 130, 147, 174–75, 262, 302. *SIHMP*, 1:695–702, 728–31.

38. *CGA*, 33v, 115v, 354r–v, 356v–359r. Ram, 55, 138, 352–53, 354–56; Ép, 53, 153, 424–25, 428–30. Abun-Nasr, *Maghrib*, 49–50, 107, 112. The region of Sijilmasa is today known as the oasis of Tafilalt, with the trading town of Rissani as its center. Ibn Battuta began his trip south across the Sahara from Sijilmasa to Timbuktu in Muharram 753/February 1352 and began his return trip from Takadda in Aïr to Sijilmasa in Shaʿban 754/September 1353 (Ibn Battuta, *Ibn Battuta in Black Africa*, trans. Said Hamdun and Noël King [Princeton, N.J.: Markus Wiener Publishers, 1994], 30, 73). Al-Wazzan said that it was dangerous for caravans to make the crossing before the cold season began in the desert in mid-September because of the possibility of sandstorms covering the wells. Rauchenberg stresses the importance of the rainy season before December for leaving on such a trip and accordingly locates al-Wazzan's departure in September–November 1512 (Rauch, 52 n.224, 53).

39. On the Mali and Songhay empires and Askia Muhammad, see Hunwick, *Timbuktu*, especially xxxvi–liv, 13–16, 91–117. John O. Hunwick, *Shariʿa in Songhay: The Replies of al-Maghili to the Questions of Askia al-Hajj Muhammad* (Oxford: Oxford University Press, 1985); Edward William

Bovill, *The Golden Trade of the Moors*, 2nd ed. (Princeton, N.J.: Markus Wiener Publishers, 1995), chaps. 9, 15. Mahmud Kati, *Tarikh el-Fettach ou Chronique du chercheur pour servir à l'histoire des villes, des armées et des principaux personnages du Tekrour*, trans. O. Houdas and M. Delafosse (Paris: Librairie d'Amérique et d'Orient, 1964), especially chap. 6. Sékéné Mody Cissoko, *Tombouctou et l'Empire Songhay* (Paris and Montréal: L'Harmattan, 1996). CGA, 374v, 381r. Rauch, 276; Ram, 371, 378; Ép, 455, 468.

40. CGA, 377v. Rauch, 262 (Rauchenberg gives an exact transcription of al-Wazzan's manuscript section on the Land of the Blacks, and I include the page references here); Ram, 374; Ép, 462–63.

41. Hunwick, *Shariʿa*, chaps. 2, 4, 5, especially 118–31 on the issues of *takfir* (declaring another to be an unbeliever) and jihad. J. O. Hunwick, "Notes on Slavery in the Songhay Empire," in John Ralph Willis, ed., *Slaves and Slavery in Muslim Africa*, 2 vols. (London: Frank Cass, 1985), 2:16–20. For further detail on al-Maghili's attack on the Jews and the legal argument about their status in the oasis towns, see below, chapter 6.

42. CGA, 382r, 385r. Rauch, 280, 292; Ram, 379, 382; Ép, 468, 473.

43. Hunwick, *Timbuktu*, 55, 67, 74, 80, 97. Hajji, *Activité*, 84. Elias Saad, *Social History of Timbuktu: The Role of Muslim Scholars and Notables, 1400–1900* (Cambridge: Cambridge University Press, 1983), 39, 66–67. CGA, 382r. Rauch, 280; Ram, 379; Ép, 468–69.

44. CGA, 380v–382v. Rauch, 274–82; Ram, 377–79; Ép, 467–69. Ibn Battuta, *Black Africa*, 49. Hunwick, *Timbuktu*, xxxviii, xlviii.

45. CGA, 378v–380v, 382v–384v. Rauch, 266–72, 282–90; Ram, 376–77, 379–81; Ép, 464–66, 469–72. Hunwick, *Timbuktu*, xlvii-xlviii. Cissoko, *Tombouctou*, 101–6. Al-Wazzan wrote early in his Africa book, "We navigated [the Niger], from the kingdom of Timbuktu in the east, descending with the water toward the kingdom of Jenne or the kingdom of Mali, which are in the west" (CGA, 3r; Ram, 21; Ép, 5). Since the Niger flows east, this statement has led scholars to say that al-Wazzan never visited Jenne and Mali at all. Perhaps this is one of al-Wazzan's exaggerations, but it is noteworthy that his statement comes as part of his discussion of geographical controversy about whether the Niger and the Nile were a single river, with a common origin in the east—the prevailing scholarly view—or whether it was a separate river with an origin of its own, presumably the view of local boatmen and traders. Al-Wazzan's use of the term "we," rather than his more usual "he" for self-reference (see below, chapter 8), suggests a boat trip with his uncle. Scholarly preconceptions and the passage of time since a youthful visit may account for al-Wazzan's observation about the flow of the Niger. In any case, it is very unlikely that he had time for such a long trip west during his 918/1512 visit, when he was on a formal mission of his own.

46. *CGA*, 385r–386r. Rauch, 292–98; Ram, 382–83; Ép, 473–75. Hunwick,
    Timbuktu, xli; Hamani, *Au carrefour*, 171–73, 181–83. *The Chronicle of
    the Sultanate of Aïr* says that two brothers—Muhammad Al-Adil and
    Muhammad Ahmad—co-ruled as sultans for ten years from 907–8/1502;
    al-Wazzan mentioned only one sultan, so presumably Muhammad Ah-
    mad had died by the time of al-Wazzan's visit in 919/1513 (Hunwick,
    Timbuktu, 71; H. R. Palmer, *Sudanese Memoirs. Being mainly transla-
    tions of a number of Arabic Manuscripts relating to the Central and
    Western Sudan*, 3 vols. [London: Frank Cass, 1967], 3:48; Hamani, *Au
    carrefour*, 173). Hamani notes inaccuracies in al-Wazzan's geographical
    description of the northern Aïr and the desert north of it but stresses the
    accuracy of his description of Agades and the region south of the town.
    He concludes that al-Wazzan never visited Agades and indeed "never set
    foot in the regions east of Timbuktu." Instead, he obtained information
    about Agades from conversations in Timbuktu (177–78, 181, 184; also on
    the geographical inaccuracy, Ép, 449 n.160, 451 n.162). The inaccuracy in
    regard to the "desert where the Targa people live" is better understood by
    the fact that al-Hasan al-Wazzan had never crossed it (he came south on
    both trips by Sijilmasa and Taghaza and came to Agades from Gao also
    by a southerly route) and that he was composing his book from incom-
    plete notes many years later in Italy with no access to any texts or persons
    who could assist his description (see below, chapter 4). His accuracy in re-
    gard to precise details in Agades is much more reasonably understood as
    drawn from an actual visit.

47. Hamani, *Au carrefour*, 162–63, 168–69, 192. E. M. Sartain, *Jalal al-din
    al-Suyuti. Biography and background*, 2 vols. (Cambridge: Cambridge
    University Press, 1975), 1:50–52.

48. Al-Wazzan seems to have gone to Bornu by passing through the Hausa-
    lands of Gobir, Katsina, and Kano, regions that Askia Muhammad would
    soon attack though never successfully control. Songhay occupation of
    Gobir is described by the scholar Boubou Hama on the basis of a text by
    the holy man Malaam Issak written sometime in the period 912–919/
    1506–1513 (Boubou Hama, *Histoire du Gobir et de Sokoto* [Paris, 1967],
    25–37). According to al-Saʿdi's *Taʾrikh al-Sudan* and Kati's *Taʾrikh al-
    fattash*, Askia Muhammad first attacked Katsina late in the year 919/1514
    (Hunwick, *Timbuktu*, 113; Kati, *Tarikh*, 147), thus a few months after
    al-Wazzan's departure from the Land of the Blacks. Al-Wazzan describes
    the Hausalands of Gobir, Katsina, Kano, Zamfara, and Zaria as under
    Songhay domination, though he does *not* date their conquest (*CGA*,
    386r–387v; Rauch, 296–304; Ram, 383–84; Ép, 476–78). He could have
    been reporting rumors he heard after his return to Fez from the Land of
    the Blacks, or writing his account years later in Italy, he could have been
    confused or misremembered. H. J. Fisher argues that the Songhay inter-
    vention in the Hausaland was minimal, confined only to Askia Muham-

mad's attack on Katsina. He is unconvinced of further conquest without seeing the manuscript mentioned by Boubou Hama. He doubts that al-Wazzan was ever in the region at all (Fisher, "Leo Africanus," 86–112). Hunwick suggests that al-Wazzan may have confused Songhay domination over these Hausa regions with what he had heard of Kebbi control over them (*Timbuktu*, 285 n.74). Cissoko simply accepts al-Wazzan's account (*Tombouctou*, 79). On the whole, Hunwick's judgment seems especially well grounded and reliable in regard to the area and al-Wazzan's reports of it. In any case, al-Wazzan did not state that he had spent any significant period of time in Gobir, Kano, and Katsina.

49. *CGA*, 388r–390r. Rauch, 306–14; Ram, 385–87; Ép, 479–81. Ahmad Furtu, *A Sudanic Chronicle: The Borno Expeditions of Idris Alauma (1564–1576) according to the Account of Ahmad B. Furtu*, trans. Dierk Lange (Stuttgart: Franz Steiner Verlag, 1987), 20, 34, 114–17, 158–59. Augustin F. C. Holl, *The Diwan Revisited: Literacy, State Formation and the Rise of Kanuri Domination (AD 1200–1600)* (London and New York: Kegan Paul International, 2000), preface, 15. Palmer, *Sudanese Memoirs*, 3:24–25. Hunwick notes that the *mai*'s method of payment in slaves still to be captured is found in the region in the early nineteenth century (*Timbuktu*, 291 n.94). Al-Wazzan remembered the *mai*'s name years later as Habraam, that is, Ibrahim (*CGA*, 388r), his version of Katakarmabi, one of the two names given the *mai* (Furtu, *Sudanic Chronicle*, 20).

50. *CGA*, 390r–393r. Rauch, 314–26; Ram, 387–89; Ép, 481–85. Kalck, "Pour une localisation," 529–48; O'Fahey and Spaulding, "Comment," 505–8.

51. Linda S. Northrup, "The Babri Mamluk Sultanate, 1250–1390," in Carl F. Petry, ed., *The Cambridge History of Egypt*, 2 vols. (Cambridge: Cambridge University Press, 1998), vol. 1, chap. 10; Jean-Claude Garcin, "The Regime of the Circassian Mamluks," ibid., vol. 1, chap. 11.

52. *CGA*, 405r, 406r, 414r–v ("bellissime mura," "li mirabili Palazi," "bellissime Finestre," etc.). Ram, 403, 411; Ép, 503–4, 513–14. Dietrich Brandenburg, *Islamische Baukunst in Ägypten* (Berlin: Bruno Hessling, 1966), 197–200. Muhammad ibn Ahmad ibn Iyas, *Journal d'un bourgeois du Caire: Chronique d'Ibn Iyas*, ed. and trans. Gaston Wiet, 2 vols. (Paris: Librairie Armand Colin and SEVPEN, 1955–1960), 1:48–50, 252; 2:90–92. On Qansuh al-Ghawri's reign, see Carl F. Petry, *Protectors or Praetorians? The Last Mamluk Sultans and Egypt's Waning as a Great Power* (Albany: SUNY Press, 1994).

53. Ibn Iyas, *Journal*, 1:277–91, 304, 309–13.

54. Ibid., 1:152. On other gift presentations, see 1:240, 242, 249.

55. Ibid., 1:80, 184, 195–96, 211, 251, 423–24; 2:167, 220, 335. The emissaries from the Maghreb ("oratores . . . numidas et mauritanos") who came to protest to al-Ghawri the treatment of the Muslims of Granada are men-

tioned by Pietro Martire d'Anghiera, who was dispatched to Cairo by Ferdinand and Isabella in 1501 to justify the Spanish actions. Pietro Martire d'Anghiera, *Una Embajada de los Reyes Católicos a Egipto según la "Legatio Babylonica" y el "Opus Epistolarum de Pedro Mártir de Anglería,"* Latin ed. and trans. Luis García y García (Valladolid: Consejo Superior de Investigaciones Científicas, 1947), 84–87, 109–10; James T. Monroe, trans., "A Curious Morisco Appeal to the Ottoman Empire," *Al-Andalus* 31 (1966): 281–83.

56. Ibn Iyas, *Journal*, 1:106, 248–49, 254, 268, 287, 292, 309–10; Petry, *Protectors*, 49–60.

57. *CGA*, 422v–427v. Ram, 418–22; Ép, 523–28. Ibn Iyas, *Journal*, 1:271–73, 287. Petry, *Protectors*, 15. Ahmet Ugr, *The Reign of Sultan Selim in the Light of the Selim-Name Literature* (Berlin: Klaus Schwarz Verlag, 1985), 222, 225.

58. *CGA*, 52v, 63v. Ram, 77, 89; Ép, 80, 94. Rauchenberger dates al-Wazzan's return early 920/spring 1514 (Rauch, 54), but that means ignoring al-Wazzan's specific references to a visit to Haha and Sus in 919, which ended at the last day of Dhu-l-Hijja, 25 February 1514. Of course, it is always possible that our traveler misremembered his exact dates.

59. Maalouf, *Léon l'Africain*, 247–53. Wiebke Walther, *Women in Islam from Medieval to Modern Times*, trans. C.S.V. Salt (Princeton, N.J.: Markus Wiener Publishers, 1999), 54–55; Abdelwahab Bouhdiba, *La sexualité en Islam* (Paris: Quadrige/Presses Universitaires de France, 1998), 16–24. J. C. Bürgel, "Love, Lust, and Longing: Eroticism in Early Islam as Reflected in Literary Sources," in Afaf Lutfi al-Sayyid-Marsot, ed., *Society and the Sexes in Medieval Islam* (Malibu, Calif.: Undena Publications, 1979), 86–91, 105–17. Annemarie Schimmel, "Eros—Heavenly and Not So Heavenly," ibid., 121–28. Cornell, *Realm*, 193; Mediano, *Familias*, 123–268 for many scholarly dynasties; examples of the father having his first son at age twenty-one are found at 148–58, 176–77 ('Abd al-Rahman ibn Muhammad ibn Ibrahim, b. 889/1484, d. 962/1554–55; son born 910/1504–5).

60. *CGA*, 165v–179r. Ram, 185–88 (185: Ramusio changes the flow of the Muslim dowry from husband to wife, to the European pattern of the dowry going from the bride's father to the husband); Ép, 209–12 (follows Ramusio's modification of dowry flow). The departures of Ramusio and Épaulard from *CGA*, 165v–169v, have also been analyzed by Dietrich Rauchenberger in "Jean-Léon l'Africain et son manuscrit de 1526 vus à travers sa description des cérémonies de mariage à Fez," Colloque Léon l'Africain (EHESS, Paris, 22–24 May 2003), forthcoming in Pouillon and Zhiri, eds., *Léon l'Africain*. On dowry and trousseau in the Maghreb, see the cases drawn from al-Wansharisi's *Mi'yar* in Lagardère, *Histoire*, 91–110, and Maya Shatzmiller, "Women and Property Rights in al-

Andalus and the Maghrib: Social Patterns and Legal Discourse," *Islamic Law and Society* 2 (1995): 231–36.

61. *CGA*, 139r–v, 164r–v. Ram, 161–62, 183–84; Ép, 183–84, 208.

62. On the requirement to maintain the wife during the husband's absence, see Émile Amar, ed. and trans., *Consultations juridiques des faqihs du Maghreb*, in *Archives marocaines* 12 (1908): 428–29. Ibn Khaldun, *Le voyage d'Occident et d'Orient. Autobiographie*, trans. Abdesselam Cheddadi, 2nd ed. (Paris: Sindbad and Arles: Actes Sud, 1995), 87, 158. The autobiographical text translated here is the *Taʿrif*, which made up the last section of the last book of Ibn Khaldun's monumental history, the *Kitab al-ʿIbar* (27–28).

63. Ross Dunn, *The Adventures of Ibn Battuta, a Muslim Traveler of the 14th Century* (Berkeley and Los Angeles: University of California Press, 1986), 39, 62, 207, 233–35, 237. Ibn Battuta, *Voyages*, ed. Stéphane Yerasimos, trans. C. Defremery and B. R. Sanguinette, 3 vols. (Paris: Librairie François Maspero and Éditions La Découverte, 1982–97), 1:89–90.

64. *CGA*, 364r–365r. Ram, 361–62 ([*DAR*, 75r] has al-Wazzan frequenting rather than lodging with ʿAbdulla); Ép, 437–38 (follows Ram in omission). Walther, *Women*, 65, 172; Ibn Abi Zayd al-Qayrawani, *La Risâla, Ou Epître sur les éléments du dogme et de la loi de l'Islam selon le rite Mâlikite*, trans. Léon Bercher (Paris: Éditions IQRA, 1996), chap. 32, 143–45.

65. *CGA*, 96r, 132r. Ram, 120, 154; Ép, 133, 175 and 175 n.81 on some of the problems in the dating of al-Wazzan's departure.

66. Abun-Nasr, *Maghrib*, 147–50, 168–69; Charles-André Julien, *Histoire de l'Afrique du Nord (Tunisie, Algérie, Maroc) de la conquête arabe à 1830*, 2nd ed., 2 vols. (Paris: Payot, 1964), 2:250–57. Ibn Iyas, *Journal*, 1:211, 252. *CGA*, 230v, 242r–v, 271v–272r, 282v–283r, 288r–288v, 292v–293r, 339v, 343r. Ram, 241, 252–53, 278, 292, 295–96, 337, 340; Ép, 275, 290, 324–25, 336, 341–42, 346, 401, 406. Muradi, *La vida, y historia de Hayradin, llamado Barbarroja: Gazavat-I Hayreddin Paşa*, ed. Miguel A. de Bunes and Emilio Sola and trans. Juan Luis Alzamora (Granada: Servicio de Publicaciones de la Universidad de Granada, 1997), 40–48.

67. *CGA*, 281v–283r. Ram, 287–88; Ép, 335–36. Abun-Nasr, *Maghrib*, 149. Muradi, *Vida*, 52–56.

68. *CGA*, 296r–297r. Ram, 297–98; Ép, 348–49. Abun-Nasr, *Maghrib*, 149; Julien, *Histoire*, 2:255. Muradi, *Vida*, 50–51.

69. *CGA*, 296r–297r, 302r–303r. Ram, 297–98, 306; Ép, 348–49, 361–62. Abun-Nasr, *Maghrib*, 149–50; Julien, *Histoire*, 2:255–56.

70. *CGA*, 317r–328r. Ram, 319–27; Ép, 378–88. Julien, *Histoire*, 2:250; Robert Brunschvig, *La Berbérie orientale sous les Hafsides des origines à*

la fin du XVe siècle, 2 vols. (Paris: Librairie d'Amérique et d'Orient, 1940–47), 1:280, 366 n.5; 2:288–316, 364; Ahmad ʿAbd al-Salam, *Les historiens tunisiens des XVIIe, XVIIIe et XIXe siècles* (Paris: C. Klincksieck, 1973), 24–25. Jelloul Azzouna, "Apport maghrébin à la musique andalouse: Le cas de la Tunisie," in Haddad-Chamakh and Baccar-Bournaz, eds., *Écho*, 383–90.

71. Abun-Nasr, *Maghrib*, 149.

72. Ibn Iyas, *Journal*, 1:347, 350, 364, 369, 411, 423, 427. Ugr, *Selim*, 232. Petry, *Protectors*, 24, 49–51.

73. Ibn Iyas, *Journal*, 2:65–67, 139–43. Petry, *Protectors*, 25–26. H. Jansky, "Die Eroberung Syriens durch Sultan Selim," *Mitteilungen zur osmanischen Geschichte* 2 (1923–26): 173–241.

74. Leslie Peirce, *The Imperial Harem: Women and Sovereignty in the Ottoman Empire* (New York and Oxford: Oxford University Press, 1993), 65. Abun-Nasr, *Maghrib*, 155–56: "The Ottomans seem to have viewed the Wattasids of Fez as potential allies against the Spaniards from the time when ʿAruj invaded Tilimsan [Tlemcen] in 1517."

75. CGA, 402v, 411v, 420r. Ram, 399, 409, 416; Ép, 499, 510, 520. Ibn Iyas, *Journal*, 2:139–98.

76. Marino Sanuto, *I Diarii di Marino Sanuto*, 58 vols. (Bologna: Forni Editore, 1969, reprint of the Venice 1879–92 edition), 26:195.

77. Ibn Iyas, *Journal*, 2:196–98. CGA, 431r–432v. Ram, 427–29; Ép, 535–37.

78. G. Wiet, "*Kuna*," EI2, 5:385–86. Ibn Battuta, *Voyages*, 1:147, 2:135.

79. CGA, 432v ("li barcharoli che menorono ipso compositore dal Chairo fine alla ciptade Asuan et con quelli essare tornato fine da Chana [Qina] et de indi andato per el deserto allo Mare rosero lo quale ha trapassato alla banda de la Arabia deserta al Porto del Iambuh [Yanbu] et de Gedda [Jeddah]"). Ram, 429; Ép, 537. Ibn Battuta, *Voyages*, 1:259–350. CEI, 214–16, 313–16. Jacques Jomier, *Le mahmal et la caravane égyptienne des pèlerins de La Mecque, XIIIe–XXe siècles* (Cairo: Institut Français d'Archéologie Orientale, 1953), chaps. 1–2, 4, 6. Ibn Iyas, *Journal*, 1:85, 163, 321, 324; 2:188, 208. Le Tourneau, *Fez*, 137–38.

80. Ibn Iyas, *Journal*, 2:217, 228.

81. Ibn Khaldun, *Voyage*. W. Björkman, "Diplomatic," EI2, 2:303. CGA, 198r, 253r ("lettere de Favore del Re"), 269r ("salvo conducto"), 359v. Ram, 210, 261, 275, 357; Ép, 237, 302, 318, 431. Jean Thenaud, *Le voyage d'outremer (Égypte, Mont Sinay, Palestine) de Jean Thenaud, suivi de la Relation de l'ambassade de Domenico Trevisan auprès du Soudan d'Égypte, 1512*, ed. Charles Schefer (Paris: Ernest Leroux, 1884), 28.

82. CGA, 93r, 94v, 97r, 285r. Ram, 117, 119, 121, 289–90 ([DAR, 60v] omits reference to servant); Ép, 130–31, 134, 338. Ibn Iyas, *Journal*, 1:238, 252.

83. *CGA*, 55v, 67r, 77r, 93r, 94r–v, 97r, 100r, 285r, 297r. Ram, 81, 92, 103, 117, 119, 121, 124, 289–90 ([*DAR*, 60v] omits reference to purchase of tent cords for his trip to Tunis); Ép, 84, 99, 111, 130–31, 134, 137, 338–39, 349. For the arrangement of lodging for ambassadors in Cairo, see Ibn Iyas, *Journal*, 1:238, 248, 252; Thenaud, *Voyage*, 22–23, 36.

84. *CGA*, 199r, 281v, 325r, 327v, 422v. Ram, 211, 287, 325–26, 418; Ép, 238, 335, 386–87, 523–24. Ibn Iyas, *Journal*, 1:213 ("l'introducteur des ambassadeurs"), 249, 251, 356. Hunwick, *Timbuktu*, 145 and 145 n.2; Cissoko, *Tombouctou*, 106.

85. *CGA*, 99v, 381v. Ram, 123–24; Ép, 137, 468. *SIHME*, 1:652. Thenaud, *Voyage*, 45; Ibn Iyas, *Journal*, 1:238.

86. Ibn Iyas, *Journal*, 1:238, 242; 2:9–10.

87. Ibn Battuta, *Black Africa*, 45. Thenaud, *Voyage*, 43.

88. *CGA*, 100r. Ram, 123–24; Ép, 137. Al-Wazzan entitled the manuscript given to the chieftain "La Vita de li sancti Affricani" (The Life of African Holy Men), but as we will see in chapter 5, the word "African" would not be used in North Africa at that date, except as "Ifriqiya," to refer to the region around Tunis and Carthage. It is unlikely that al-Wazzan's uncle would have been carrying a book on the holy men of the Tunisian region on his way to see Askia Muhammad in Timbuktu. But several books existed on the holy men and saints of the different regions of Morocco, including biographies of the saints of southern Morocco by al-Tadili (early thirteenth century); of Fez and its region by al-Tamimi (early thirteenth century); of the Rif Mountains by al-Badisi (early fourteenth century); and of forty holy men of Fez, Meknes, and Sala by al-Hadrami (mid-fourteenth century) (Cornell, *Realm*, 98–100, 143; Benchekroun, *Vie*, 309–18, 440–42; Halima Ferhat and Hamid Triki, "Hagiographie et religion au Maroc médiéval," *Hespéris Tamuda* 24 [1986]: 17–51).

89. *CGA*, 100v–101r. Ram, 124–25; Ép, 137–38. Al-Wazzan described an exchange between a merchant from the Egyptian port town of Dumyat and the ruler of "Gaoga," who reciprocated each gift with at least double its value: the merchant offered a horse, a Turkish saber, a chain-stitched shirt, a small firearm, and some beautiful mirrors, combs, coral rosaries, and knives, worth in all about fifty Egyptian ducats. The sultan responded with five slaves, five camels, five hundred golden coins, and 150 pieces of elephant tusk (*CGA*, 391v; Rauch, 316; Ram, 388; Ép, 483).

90. Ibn Iyas, *Journal*, 1:347, 356–57, 366–69.

91. G. S. Colin, "Diplomatic: Maghrib," *EI2*, 2:307–8. *CGA*, 198r. Ram, 210; Ép, 237. *SIHMF*, 1:170–77; *SIHME*, 1:92–94, 142–43. Abdelkebir Khatibi and Muhammad Sijelmassi, *The Splendor of Islamic Calligraphy* (London and New York: Thames and Hudson, 2001), 152. Jonathan

Bloom, *Paper Before Print: The History and Impact of Paper in the Islamic World* (New Haven and London: Yale University Press, 2001), 85–89.

92. *CGA*, 108r–110r ("Alhora el compositore ymaginata la suo opinione disse signore capitano fingete domatina havere recepute lettere del re," "In quella matina scrivemo una lettera incontra mano de lo Re," 108r). Ram, 131–32 ([*DAR*, 25v] attributes the plan to forge the letter to "un suo consigliere" rather than to al-Wazzan); Ép, 145–47.

93. Ibn Khaldun, *Voyage*, 104–8, 262 n.89. F. Krenkow, "*Sadjʿ*," *EI2*, 8:732–38. Benchekroun, *Vie*, 472–75.

94. *CGA*, 100r–101r. Ram, 124; Ép, 137–38. Colophons in *sadjʿ*: EpiP, 68; Dict, 117b–118a. On the Arabic panegyric, see Régis Blachère, *Histoire de la littérature arabe des origines à la fin du XVe siècle*, 3 vols. (Paris: Librairie d'Amérique et d'Orient, 1964–66), 3:580–89; Amjad Trabulsi, *La critique poétique des Arabes jusqu'au Ve siècle de l'Hégire (XIe siècle de J. C.)* (Damascus: Institut Français de Damas, 1955), 220–25.

95. *CGA*, 6v–7r, 240r–v. Ram 25, 251; Ép, 12–13, 287–88.

96. *CGA*, 21r–22r, 100v–101r. Ram, 42–43, 124; Ép, 38–39, 137–38. On the range in Berber "dialects" and in Arabo-Berber speech within the Moroccan region alone, see David Montgomery Hart, "Tribal Place Names among the Arabo-Berbers of Northwestern Morocco," *Hespéris Tamuda* 1 (1960): 457–511.

97. *CGA*, 101v–103r. Ram, 125–26; Ép, 138–40.

98. Ibn Khaldun, *Voyage*, 75, 82–84, 91–93, 150. Ibn Iyas, *Journal*, 1:431–32, 435; 2:60, 64.

99. *CGA*, 286r–287r. Ram, 290–91; Ép, 340–41. On the Divine Names and additions to them, see *CEI*, 37, 99–100, and Khushaim, *Zarruq*, 151.

100. *CGA*, 77r. Ram, 103; Ép, 111–12. There is a scribal error in *CGA* from 294r–295v: the section on al-Hasan al-Wazzan's role as judge in a town in the kingdom of Tlemcen is appended to the end of the town of Mazouna, but it clearly makes sense only at the end of Médéa, which is where Ramusio has placed it (Ram, 299; Ép, 351–52). Ramusio may well have been working from another copy of the manuscript (see below, chapter 3). On the appointment of a qadi and the delivery of *ijaza*, see Benchekroun, *Vie*, 74–76; Hajji, *Activité*, 121–27, 139–40; Mediano, *Familias*, 52.

101. *CGA*, 371v–372r, 448r–v. Ram, 368, 445; Ép, 447, 560–61.

102. *CGA*, 124r, 346r (ruins in the mountains near Tunis: "Molti epitafii scripti in lengua latina como ipso compositore dice havere visto et alcuni de quillo serono lecti et interpretati da uno ciciliano renegato"), 367v–368r. Ram, 147, 343 ([*DAR*, 71v] omits reference to the Sicilian convert), 365; Ép, 166, 409, 442.

103. *CGA*, 48v–49r, 297r. Ram, 73–74, 298; Ép, 76–77, 349. On libraries and collections in the world of Islam, see Houari Touati, *L'armoire à sagesse: Bibliothèques et collections en Islam* (Paris: Aubier, 2003).

104. *CGA*, 53r, 142v. Ram, 78 ([*DAR*, 14r] wrongly turns al-Wazzan's "li beneficii"—clearly the Arabic "awqaf" or "ahbas" of the Maghreb—into "quello, che alcuno possedeva," "something possessed by an individual"), 165; Ép, 81 (follows Ramusio), 187.

105. *CGA*, 54r–v ("grandissimo tiranno"), 82v–86r, 97r. Ram, 79–80, 108–10, 121; Ép, 82, 118–20, 133–34. Cornell, *Realm*, 191–94.

106. *CGA*, 59r–v, 352v, 382r, 383v, 404v, 445v–446r, 464r–v. Ram, 84–85, 351, 379–80, 401–2, 442, 460 (modifies al-Wazzan's response to the story of the Sarmak plant); Ép, 88–89, 423, 468–69, 471, 502, 557, 579 (modifies the story of the Sarmak plant).

107. *CGA*, 454v. Ram, 450; Ép, 567. Hajji, *Activité*, 133. Touati, *Islam et voyage*, chaps. 2, 4.

CHAPTER TWO • LIVING IN THE LAND OF WAR

1. Sanuto, *Diarii*, 25:195. *CGA*, 25v, 231v. Ram, 47, 242; Ép, 43, 276. Don Pedro was the son of Don Andrès Cabrera, in military service to Ferdinand and Isabella, and Doña Beatriz de Bobadilla (Bernardo Dorado, *Compendio Historico de la Ciudad de Salamanca* [Salamanca: Juan Antonio de Lasanta, 1776], 351). On pirates in the Mediterranean, see Fernand Braudel, *La Méditerranée et le monde méditerranéen*, 2 vols. (Paris: Armand Colin, 1966), 2:190–211; Salvatore Bono, *Corsari nel Mediterraneo: Cristiani e Musulmani fra guerra, schiavitù e commercio* (Milan: Arnoldo Mondadori, 1993), especially pt. 2; Salvatore Bono, *Schiavi musulmani nell'Italia moderna* (Naples: Edizioni Scientifiche Italiane, 1999), chaps. 1–2; and Wolfgang Kaiser, "Kaufleute, Makler und Korsaren: Karrieren zwischen Marseille und Nordafrika im 16. und 17. Jahrhundert," *Berliner Historische Studien* 25 (1997): 11–31.

2. Giovanni Battista Ramusio, ed., *Primo volume, et Seconda editione delle Navigationi et Viaggi . . . nella quale si contengono La Descrittione dell' Africa* (Venice: Giunta, 1554), *iii r. Ram, 6. Johann Albrecht Widmanstadt, *Liber Sacrosancti Evangelii de Iesu Christo Domino et Deo nostro . . . characteribus et lingua Syra* (Vienna: Michael Zymmerman, 1562), a***4a–b (dated June 1555): "propè Lotophagiten insulam à classe nostra cum caeteris vectoribus caperetur"; the Homeric island of the Lotus Eaters was identified as Djerba by sixteenth-century scholars, and the name is given to Djerba on maps of Africa in editions of Ptolemy's *Geography*; for example, *Liber Geographiae* (Venice, 1511), tabula 2 of Africa "lothophagitis insula" on the island of Djerba. As we shall see,

Widmanstadt had been in touch with three people close to al-Hasan al-Wazzan during his Italian years. The report of the seizure at Rhodes comes from the papal secretary Biagio de Martinelli, who witnessed al-Wazzan's baptism in 1520 (Rauch, 457). Sanuto, *Diarii*, 25:571–72. Rauchenberger accepts the seizure near Crete (65), though mysteries remain about the matter.

3. Francisco de Cabrera y Bobadilla was bishop of Salamanca from 1511 to 1529 but resided in Rome on diocesan and church business for much of his office (Dorado, *Salamanca*, 351–74; José Luis Fuertes Heireros, ed., *Estatutos de la Universidad de Salamanca, 1529* [Salamanca: Ediciones Universidad de Salamanca, 1984], 48–49).

4. *CGA*, 343r, 432v. Ram, 340, 429; Ép, 406, 538. Sanuto, *Diarii*, 25:571, 26:195, 28:178. Widmanstadt, *Liber Sacrosancti*, a***4a. Michel Fontenay, "Les missions des galères de Malte, 1530–1798," in Michel Vergé-Franceschi, ed., *Guerre et commerce en Méditerranée* (Paris: Éditions Veyrier, 1991), 103–22.

5. Rauch, 60 n. 268. Louis Madelin, ed., "Le journal d'un habitant français de Rome au XVIe siècle," *Mélanges d'archéologie et d'histoire* 22 (1902): 255–56. Sanuto, *Diarii*, 26:195. As late as January 1520 the pope's secretary Martinelli misidentified him as "orator for the king of Syria" (Vat. Lat. 12276, from notes in the papers of Angela Codazzi, Rauch, 457). Vat. Lat. 3966, 119, cited in Levi Della Vida, *Ricerche*, 101.

6. Cesare D'Onofrio, *Castel S. Angelo* (Rome: Cassa di Risparmio di Roma, 1971), 206–9. Benvenuto Cellini, *La vita*, ed. Lorenzo Bellotto (Parma: Ugo Guanda, 1996), 431–32, 431 n.22; *Autobiography*, trans. George Bull (London: Penguin, 1998), 218–19. Ottavia Niccoli, "High and Low Prophetic Culture in Rome at the Beginning of the Sixteenth Century," in Marjorie Reeves, ed., *Prophetic Rome in the High Renaissance* (Oxford: Clarendon Press, 1992), 207–10. Bedini, *Pope's Elephant*, 138–42.

7. Paolo Giovio, *Le Vite di Leon Decimo et d'Adriano Sesto Sommi Pontefici*, trans. Lodovico Domenichi (Venice: Giovanni de' Rossi, 1557), 83r–86v. Fabrizio Winspeare, *La congiura dei cardinali contro Leone X* (Florence: Leo S. Olschki, 1957), 114, 156–58. Ingrid Rowland, *The Culture of the High Renaissance. Ancients and Moderns in Sixteenth-Century Rome* (Cambridge: Cambridge University Press, 1998), 240. Maurizio Gattoni, *Leone X e la Geo-Politica dello Stato Pontificio (1513–1521)* (Vatican City: Archivio Segreto Vaticano, 2000), chap. 6 (from an observer of the murder: "entrò lo schiavo nero nella camera che era . . . un gigante di aspetto tremendo e di una forza incredibile," 204 n.66).

8. D'Onofrio, *Castel S. Angelo*, 213–19, 275ff. Bedini, *Pope's Elephant*, 23, 51–53, 89–90, 208.

9. Cellini, *Autobiography*, 190–92; *Vita*, 377–81.

10. Levi Della Vida, *Ricerche*, 29, 50–61, 83, 101–3; *Elenco dei manoscritti arabi islamici della Biblioteca Vaticana* (Vatican City: Biblioteca Apostolica Vaticana, 1935), 36, no. 357; Rauch, 461–63. Al-Ghazali's *Maqasid al-falasifa* had been translated into Latin under the title *Logica et philosophia Algazelis Arabis* and criticized by Christian scholars over the centuries along with the works of other "Arab philosophers." Omitted from the Latin text was al-Ghazali's opening and conclusion, in which he said that he had expounded the philosophy of al-Farabi and Ibn Sina (Avicenna) with the intention of next writing about the inconsistencies of their doctrines with Sunni Islam (Henry Corbin, *Histoire de la philosophie islamique* [Paris: Gallimard, 1986], 254; W. Montgomery Watt, "Al-Ghazali," *EI2*, 2:1040). An edition of the *Logica et philosophia* was published in Venice in 1506.

11. Sanuto, *Diarii*, 26:216–17, 244, 251, 285 (December 1518, imprisonment in the Castel Sant'Angelo of the failed banker Lorenzo di Tassi).

12. CGA, 128v–129r, 218v, 320v. Ram, 151, 230, 321; Ép, 171, 262, 382. Gaignard, *Maures*, 193–94. On the "mixture of language" in Italian port cities, see Paolo Trovato, *Storia della lingua italiana: Il primo Cinquecento* (Bologna: Il Mulino, 1994), 32–35, 61–64; and on the development of a Mediterranean lingua franca from business and diplomatic contact, see John E. Wansbrough, *Lingua Franca in the Mediterranean* (Richmond, Surrey: Curzon Press, 1996).

13. Alessandro Ferrajoli, *Il ruolo della corte di Leone X*, ed. Vincenzo de Caprio (Rome: Bulzoni, 1984), 136 n.3, 160–69. Levi Della Vida, *Ricerche*, 100–102 (Acciaiuoli was director of the Vatican Library from September 1518 until his death in June 1519). Josephine Jungić, "Joachimist Prophecies in Sebastiano del Piombo's Borgherini Chapel and Raphael's *Transfiguration*," in Reeves, ed., *Prophetic Rome*, 336. Vat. Ar. 80, f. 2, Biblioteca Apostolica Vaticana. On the possibility of a prisoner conversing while in the Castel Sant'Angelo, see Cellini, *Autobiography*, 190–92; *Vita*, 378–80.

14. Heiko A. Oberman, *Luther: Man between God and the Devil*, trans. Eileen Walliser-Schwarzbart (New Haven: Yale University Press, 1989), 14–16. Cardinal Cajetan's main responsibility was to gain support within Germany for a crusade against the Turks; the interrogation of Luther was thought a relatively minor affair.

15. Paride Grassi, *Diarium An. 1513 ad 1521*. MS E53, vol. 2, 46v–48r, 73r, Department of Special Collections, Spencer Research Library, University of Kansas. Bedini, *Pope's Elephant*, 28–29, 46–49, 79, 86, 139–41, 145. For full details on Leo X's politics in regard to the Turks and his hopes for a crusade, see Kenneth M. Setton, *The Papacy and the Levant (1204–1571)*, 4 vols. (Philadelphia: American Philosophical Society, 1976–84), 3:142–97.

16. Setton, *Papacy*, 3:172–83. Grassi, *Diarium*, vol. 2, 217r–v, 219v–230r. Nelson Minnich, "Raphael's *Portrait of Leo X with Cardinals Giulio de' Medici and Luigi de' Rossi*: A Religious Interpretation," *Renaissance Quarterly* 56 (2003): 1005–46; Minnich suggests that the addition of the cardinals, both of them Medici cousins, to what was initially a portrait of the pope alone reflects Leo's hope that they would carry on his mission of renewal. Antonio Pucci (papal legate to the Swiss), *Sanctissimi Domini nostri Papae Leonis Decimi, una cum coetu cardinalium, Christianissimorum que regum, et principum oratorum consultationes, pro expeditionem contra Thurcum*, n.p. [Basel?], n.d. [1518]. Leo X, *Bando de le Processioni per la unione de Principi Christiani contra Turchi* (Rome, 1518).

17. Sanuto, *Diarii*, 25:439, 26:166, 247, 458, 265–67, 476, 502; 27:475. Setton, *Papacy*, 3:155–57.

18. Ibid., 26:195; 27:60–63, 301, 402–3, 406–7. CGA, 297r. Ram, 298; Ép, 349.

19. Steven Epstein, *Speaking of Slavery: Color, Ethnicity and Human Bondage in Italy* (Ithaca, N.Y.: Cornell University Press, 2001), 132–39; Bono, *Schiavi*, chaps. 4, 7. CGA, 327v–328r. Ram, 326–27; Ép, 388. Sanuto, *Diarii*, 26:195.

20. Ibid., 26:458, 469, 502; 27:224, 283, 541. Cardinal Giulio de' Medici, chancellor to his cousin Leo X, was writing letters in late 1518 and early 1519 to Cardinal Egidio da Viterbo, papal legate to the king of Spain, but he makes no mention of al-Hasan al-Wazzan or of information clearly obtained from him (*I manoscritti torrigiani donati al R. Archivio di Stato di Firenze: Descrizione e saggio* [Florence: M. Cellini, 1878], 280–88, 324–25, 330–32, 340–41, 355–56, 363).

21. Grassi, *Diarium*, vol. 2, 309v. Pius Bonifacius Gams, ed., *Series episcoporum ecclesiae catholicae* (Leipzig: Karl Hiersemann, 1931), 407, 716, 870. Ferrajoli, *Ruolo*, 9, 39–42, 107–10. Sanuto, *Diarii*, 27:365–67. Bedini, *Pope's Elephant*, 8–9, 46, 68, 75. Rowland, *High Renaissance*, 243. Rauchenberger gives a transcription of Grassi's entry from the Vatican Library copy of the *Diarium* (Vat. Lat. 5636) as "sic sacrista palatinus ep(iscopu)s casertanus et ego," and goes on to identify the "palace sacristan" with the bishop of Caserta (73, 455–56). However, the Grassi manuscript (MS E53) at the Department of Special Collections, Spencer Research Library, University of Kansas clearly reads "sic sacrista palatinus *et* [emphasis added] ep(iscop)us Casertanus et ego." In any case, Giovanni Battista Bonciani, bishop of Caserta, was not the papal or palace sacristan.

22. Grassi, *Diarium*, vol. 2, 309v.

23. Ibid., 310r–v.

24. CEI, 88. John L. Esposito, ed., *The Oxford Encyclopedia of the Modern*

Islamic World, 4 vols. (New York and Oxford: Oxford University Press, 1995), 1:318–21; Bartolomé Bennassar and Lucile Bennassar, *Les Chrétiens d'Allah: L'histoire extraordinaire des renégats, XVIe–XVIIe siècles* (Paris: Perrin, 1987), 314–18, 325–28, 339. Mayte Penelas, "Some Remarks on Conversion to Islam in al-Andalus," *Al-Qantra* 23 (2002): 194–98.

25. Nelson H. Minnich, "The Role of Prophecy in the Career of the Enigmatic Bernardino López de Carvajal," in Reeves, ed., *Prophetic Rome*, 111–20, and Jungić, "Joachimist Prophecies," ibid., 323–26. Nelson Minnich, *The Catholic Reformation: Council, Churchmen, Controversies* (Aldershot: Variorum, 1993), 2:364–65. Bernardino López de Carvajal, *La Conquista de Baza*, trans. Carlos de Miguel Mora (Granada: Universidad de Granada, 1995), especially 120–21. Sanuto, *Diarii*, 25:76.

26. Ibid., 25:76. Guilelmus van Gulik and Conrad Eubel, *Hierarchia catholica medii aevi*, 6 vols. (Regensburg, 1913–58), 3:13. Melissa Meriam Bullard, *Filippo Strozzi and the Medici: Favor and Finance in Sixteenth-Century Florence and Rome* (Cambridge: Cambridge University Press, 1980), 103, 108 n.61, 116. Bedini, *Pope's Elephant*, 159. Minnich, *Catholic Reformation*, 1:454, 4:134–36. Roland Bainton, *Here I Stand: A Life of Martin Luther* (New York: New American Library, 1959), 61.

27. On Egidio da Viterbo, see Giuseppe Signorelli, *Il Card. Egidio da Viterbo: Agostiniano, umanista e riformatore, 1464–1532* (Florence· Libreria Editrice Fiorentina, 1924), John W. O'Malley, *Giles of Viterbo on Church and Reform: A Study in Renaissance Thought* (Leiden: E. J. Brill, 1968); *Egidio da Viterbo, O.S.A. e il suo tempo. Atti del V convegno dell'Istituto Storico Agostiniano, Roma-Viterbo, 20–23 ottobre 1982* (Rome: Ed. "Analecta Augustiniana," 1983); Marjorie Reeves, "Cardinal Egidio of Viterbo: A Prophetic Interpretation of History," in Reeves, ed., *Prophetic Rome*, 91–109; Francis X. Martin, *Friar, Reformer, and Renaissance Scholar: Life and Work of Giles of Viterbo, 1469–1532* (Villanova, Pa.: Augustinian Press, 1992).

28. Grassi, *Diarium*, vol. 2, 310v: "Jo. Leo de Medicis." The ceremonial diary of Biagio de Martinelli also suggests the informal character of the naming "de Medicis": The pope "eum . . . imposuit nomen Joannes et inde inita missa me instante donavit illi coognomen de domo sua de Medicis" (Vat. Lat. 12276, cited from the papers of A. Codazzi, Rauch, 456–57). EpiP, 1r-v. Jean Benedicti, *La Somme des Pechez* (Paris: Denis Binet, 1595), bk. 4, chap. 6, 464–65, on the forms of spiritual parentage contracted among persons at the sacrament of baptism. Christiane Klapisch-Zuber, "L'adoption impossible dans l'Italie de la fin du Moyen-Âge," in Mireille Corbier, ed., *Adoption et fosterage* (Paris: De Boccard, 1999), 321–37; Thomas Kuehn, "L'adoption à Florence à la fin du Moyen-Âge," *Médiévales* 35 (Autumn 1998): 69–81; Bono, *Schiavi*, 287; Christiane Klapisch-Zuber, letter to author, 5 March 2003. Rauchenberger describes Giovanni

Leone as "adopted" by Leo and refers to the pope as his "Adoptivvater," Giovanni Leone as the pope's "Adoptivsohn" (Rauch, 74, 88, 90). His text was written, however, before he had the chance to read these recent studies on legal adoption and informal fosterage in Florentine families.

29. EpiP, 68; Dict, 117b; Vat. Ar. 357, 1a, Biblioteca Apostolica Vaticana.

30. Jean Delumeau, *Rome au XVIe siècle* (Paris: Hachette, 1975), 60–81; Peter Partner, *Renaissance Rome. 1500–1559* (Berkeley and Los Angeles: University of California Press, 1976), chap. 6.

31. Sanuto, *Diarii*, 28:178.

32. On posts at the Roman court, see Ferrajoli, *Ruolo*; John F. D'Amico, *Renaissance Humanism in Papal Rome: Humanists and Churchmen on the Eve of the Reformation* (Baltimore and London: Johns Hopkins University Press, 1983), chap. 2; and Peter Partner, *The Pope's Men: The Papal Civil Service in the Renaissance* (Oxford: Clarendon Press, 1990).

33. Girolamo Aleandro was made secretary to Giulio de' Medici in 1517 and was in touch with people who came to know Giovanni Leone, including Egidio da Viterbo. Aleandro was appointed Vatican librarian in July 1519, immediately after Zanobi Acciaiuoli's death, and he had the catalogue of Greek volumes prepared before December 1521 (Jules Pasquier, *Jérôme Aléandre de sa naissance à la fin de son séjour à Brindes* [Paris: E. Leroux, 1900], 113–24; Jeanne Bignami Odier, *La Bibliothèque Vaticane de Sixte IV à Pie XI* (Vatican City: Biblioteca Apostolica Vaticana, 1973), 29–30, 42 n.98). Josée Balagna Coustou, *Arabe et humanisme dans la France des derniers Valois* (Paris: Éditions Maisonneuve et Larose, 1989), 21–24. On the 1511–12 inventory by Fabio Vigile and the 1518–19 catalogue by curator Lorenzo Parmenio, see Levi Della Vida, *Ricerche*, 34–47, 111–12. Levi Della Vida points out that until the mid-sixteenth century, each inventory was based on examining the books themselves, not on prior catalogues, and stresses the problems posed to the Vatican librarians and custodians unable to read the languages of the codices. Parmenio, who had been at such a loss in dealing with the Arabic manuscripts, might well have welcomed assistance from the new convert Yuhanna al-Asad. Parmenio died around 1522 without producing formal additions to the inventory, however, and he and his fellow curator Romolo Mammacini, alias Bernardo, were replaced not long after (Odier, *Bibliothèque*, 112; ASV, Camera Apostolica, Introitus et Exitus, no. 559, 214v; no. 560, 226r; no. 561, 153v, 158r, 174v, 180r, 197v).

34. Alastair Hamilton, "Eastern Churches and Western Scholarship," in Anthony Grafton, ed., *Rome Reborn: The Vatican Library and Renaissance Culture* (Washington D.C.: Library of Congress; New Haven: Yale University Press; Vatican City: Biblioteca Apostolica Vaticana, 1993), 233–40. The 1514 breviary in Arabic was printed in Fano. *Psalterium Hebraeum, Graecum, Arabicum, Chaldeum cum tribus latinis interpretationibus et glossis*, ed. Agostino Giustiniani (Genoa: Petrus Paulus Porrus, 1516), 2r,

25r–27r. Geoffrey Roper, "Early Arabic Printing in Europe," in Eva Hanebutt-Benz, Dagmar Glass, Geoffrey Roper, and Theo Smets, eds., *Middle Eastern Languages and the Print Revolution. A Cross-Cultural Encounter* (Westhofen: WVA-Verlag Skulima, 2002), 131–32.

35. Nicolas Vatin, ed., *Sultan Djem. Un prince ottoman dans l'Europe du 15e siècle d'après deux sources contemporaines: "Vaki'at-I Sultan Cem," "Oeuvres" de Guillaume Caoursin* (Ankara: Imprimerie de la Société Turque d'Histoire, 1997), 50, 55–56, 196–208, 342–46, 343 n.9.

36. Manuel I, *Epistola Invictissimi Regis Portugalliae ad Leonem X.P.M. Super foedore inito cum Presbytero Joanne Aethiopiae Rege* (N.p. [Strasbourg], n.d. [1521]). Grassi, *Diarium*, vol. 1, 340r–341r. CGA, 3r. Ram, 21; Ép, 6. Robert Silverberg, *The Realm of Prester John* (Athens: Ohio University Press, 1972), 210–64.

37. Bedini, *Pope's Elephant*, 89–90. H. Colin Slim, "Gian and Gian Maria, Some Fifteenth- and Sixteenth-Century Namesakes," *Musical Quarterly* 57, no. 4 (1971): 562–74; Hermann Vogelstein and Paul Rieger, *Geschichte der Juden in Rom*, 2 vols. (Berlin: Mayer and Müller, 1895), 2:119–20; Rauch, 102–7.

38. BNF, MS Syriaque 44: *Liber quatuor Evangelistarum Caldaice Scriptus Anno incar. 1521*; text in parallel columns, Syriac and Latin. Colophon, dated May 1521, dedicatory poem and prayers from Elias bar Abraham in honor of Bernardino de Carvajal, patriarch of Palestine, cardinal of Santa Croce, in parallel columns of Syriac, Latin, and Arabic (178r–186v). In 1517 Elias did a transcription of the Psalter in Syriac and Latin for Carvajal (Levi Della Vida, *Ricerche*, 134 n.2).

39. Bernardino López de Carvajal, *Epistola ad invictissimum Carolum in Imperio E. super declaratione M. Suae contra Lutherum facta* (N.p., n.d. [June 1521]), 3r–4v. Minnich, "Role of Prophecy," in Reeves, ed., *Prophetic Rome*, 117–20.

40. On the diplomatic career of Alberto Pio, prince of Carpi, see Sanuto, *Diarii*, vols. 20–46 passim; Setton, *Papacy*, 3:88, 134, 136, 172–73, 226; Bedini, *Pope's Elephant*, 46, 57. Odoardo Rombaldi, "Profilo biografico di Alberto Pio III, Conte di Carpi," in *Alberto Pio III, Signore di Carpi (1475–1975)* (Modena: Aedes Muratoriana, 1977), 7–40; Alberto Sabattini, *Alberto III Pio: Politica, diplomazia e guerra del conte di Carpi* (Carpi: Danae, 1994); Nelson Minnich, "The 'Protestatio' of Alberto Pio (1513)," in *Società, politica e cultura a Carpi ai tempi di Alberto III Pio. Atti del Convegno Internazionale (Carpi, 19–21 Maggio 1978)*, 2 vols. (Padua: Editrice Antenore, 1981), 1:261–89; Elena Svalduz, *Da Castella a "città": Carpi e Alberto Pio (1472–1530)* (Rome: Officina Edizioni, 2001), 100–44. Diplomatic correspondence of Alberto Pio during his years as ambassador for Maximilian I, MS Lea 414, nos. 1–56, Special Collections, University of Pennsylvania Library.

41. Levi Della Vida, *Ricerche*, 103–7. EpiP, 68. Pietro Puliati, "Profilo storico del fondo dei Manoscritti Orientali della Biblioteca Estense," in Carlo Bernheimer, *Catalogo dei Manoscritti Orientali della Biblioteca Estense* (Modena: Libreria dello Stato, 1960), vii–x: Alberto Pio had a copy of the same work by al-Ghazali that al-Wazzan had read from the Vatican Library. Cesare Vasoli, "Alberto Pio e la cultura del suo tempo," in *Società*, 3–42; and Charles Schmitt, "Alberto Pio and the Aristotelian Studies of His Time," ibid., 43–64.

42. Schmitt, "Alberto Pio," in *Società*, 60–61; Ernesto Sestan, "Politica, società, economia nel principato di Carpi fra quattro e cinquecento," ibid., 685. EpiP, 1r. Prayer by Elias bar Abraham for Alberto Pio, "a just man, lover of Christ, lover of strangers, with pity for the poor," MS Syriaque 44, 184v, BNF. Levi Della Vida, *Ricerche*, 106–7, 133–36, plate 6, no. 3.

43. Schmitt, "Alberto Pio," in *Società*, 61–63; Angel Losada, *Jean Ginés de Sepúlveda a través de su "Epistolario" y nuevos documentos* (Madrid: Consejo Superior de Investigaciones Científicas, 1973), 37–46. Anthony Pagden, *Lords of All the World: Ideologies of Empire in Spain, Britain and France c.1500–c.1800* (New Haven and London: Yale University Press, 1995), 99–101. Juan Ginés de Sepúlveda, *Ad Carolum V. Imperatorem ut bellum suscipiat in Turcas cohortatio* (Bologna: Giovanni Battista di Phaelli, 1529).

44. On Egidio da Viterbo, in addition to the references in note 27 above, see F. Secret, *Les Kabbalistes chrétiens de la Renaissance* (Paris: Dunod, 1964), 106–23; John W. O'Malley, "Egidio da Viterbo and Renaissance Rome," John Monfasani, "Sermons of Giles of Viterbo as Bishop," and Francis X. Martin, "Giles of Viterbo as Scripture Scholar," in *Egidio da Viterbo*, 67–84, 137–89, 191–222; Rowland, *High Renaissance*, chap. 6. On Elijah Levita, see Gérard E. Weil, *Élie Lévita, humaniste et massorète (1469–1549)* (Leiden: E. J. Brill, 1963), especially chaps. 4, 9–10, and on his multiple names, pp. 3–8. Among the other Jews assisting Egidio da Viterbo with his studies were Baruch de Benevent, who translated some texts of the cabalistic *Zohar* for him (Secret, *Kabbalistes*, 109), but Elijah Levita was his closest and most enduring teacher.

45. O'Malley, *Giles*, 72, n. 1. Martin, *Friar*, 173, 178 n.45; Martin, "Giles," in *Egidio da Viterbo*, 218 n. 79. *Al-Qur'an*, in Arabic with Latin translation and annotations copied in 1621 by David Colville from a codex in El Escorial, commissioned by Egidio da Viterbo, Biblioteca Ambrosiana, Milan, MS D100 inf., 1a–2b [henceforth QAn]. Oscar Löfgren and Renato Traini, *Catalogue of the Arabic Manuscripts in the Biblioteca Ambrosiana*, 2 vols. (Milan: Neri Pozza Editore, 1975), no. 43, 1:41–43. "Rudimenta Linguae Arabicae, excerpta per me Fratrem Franciscum Gambassiensem, anno 1519, sic volente ac iubente Reverendissimo D. Egidio Cardinali meo patrono," MS SS. 11/4, Biblioteca Angelica, Rome. Widmanstadt, *Liber Sacrosancti Evangelii*, a***4a–b.

46. Quotation from "Ioannes Leo," copied from the 1518–25 Qur'an, QAn, 1a–2b; Löfgren and Traini, *Arabic Manuscripts*, 1:43. Al-Wazzan's work on the translation of the Qur'an is discussed in chapter 8 below.

47. On these circles see Julia Haig Gaisser, "The Rise and Fall of Goritz's Feasts," *Renaissance Quarterly* 48 (1995): 41–57; Bedini, *Pope's Elephant*, 80, 154, 161, 207; Kenneth Gouwens, *Remembering the Renaissance: Humanist Narratives of the Sack of Rome* (Leiden, Boston, and Cologne: E. J. Brill, 1998), 7, 14–19.

48. Ibid., 14, 105. *CGA*, 60v (*rethl*), Ram, 85–86; Ép, 90. On Angelo Colocci's interest in calculation, numerology, and world measurement, see Rowland, *High Renaissance*, chap. 5. I am grateful to Ingrid Rowland for showing me the entry, *Vite de arabi*, in Colocci's library collection; Rowland is preparing an edition of this collection. Though the one manuscript we have of Yuhanna al-Asad's biographical dictionary is entitled *De Viris quibusdam Illustribus apud Arabes*, he himself referred to it as *Le Vite de li Philosophi arabi* (*CGA*, 418v, slightly different in Ram, 201); Colocci thus owned another copy. Colocci also compiled a manuscript of "Notes on the Ottoman Empire," which might have included material provided by our convert (Vat. 4820, cited by S. Lattès, "Recherches sur la bibliothèque d'Angelo Colocci," *Mélanges d'archéologie et d'histoire de l'École française de Rome* 48 [1931]: 343).

49. Gouwens, *Remembering the Renaissance*, chap. 5. Pierio Valeriano, *Hieroglyphica seu De Sacris Aegyptiorum aliarumque Genium Literis Commentarii* (Lyon: Paul Frellon, 1602), bk. 17, 167–68. Pierio Valeriano, *Les Hieroglyphiques*, trans. Jean de Montlyart (Lyon: Paul Frellon, 1615), bk. 17, 209–11. The manuscript of the *Hieroglyphica* was first printed in Basel in 1556. Pierio Valeriano, *Amorum Libri V* (Venice: G. Giolito, 1549), 81r–82v: "Ad Aegidium Viterbien. Hermitarum Antistitem De Vero Amore"; *Hexametri, Odae et Epigrammata* (Venice: G. Giolito, 1550), many poems to Leo X and 21v–23r, a poem dedicated to Alberto Pio, prince of Carpi.

50. Valeriano, *Hieroglyphica*, bk. 6, 62; *Hieroglyphiques*, bk. 6, 77. *CGA*, 183r–v, 441v–442r. Ram. 198–99, 439; Ép, 223–24, 554.

51. T. C. Price Zimmerman, *Paolo Giovio: The Historian and the Crisis of Sixteenth-Century Italy* (Princeton, N.J.: Princeton University Press, 1995), 14–59. On Giovio's attitude toward historical writing and biography and the timing of the composition and publication of his works, see 24–27, 221–22, 268–74, 287–90. Paolo Giovio, *Commentario de le cose de' Turchi* (Rome: Antonio Blado, 1532), 25v–26r; *Turcarum rerum commentarius*, trans. Francesco Negri (Paris: Robert Estienne, 1539), 60–61. Sanuto, *Diarii*, 24:290–91 (instructions to Alvisi Mocenigo and Bartolomeo Contarini, "monstrando la vera amicitia e paxe è tra soa excelentia et nui"); 25:142–58, 626–32 (142: letter from Sultan Selim to the Doge of Venice on the successful outcome of the embassy, 24 Sha'ban 923/10 September 1517).

52. For instance, Giovio wrote of Selim's wars against Shah Isma'il and Mamluk Qansuh al-Ghawri in *Turcarum commentarius*, 41–61, and in *La Prima Parte delle Historie del suo tempo*, trans. Lodovico Domenichi (Venice: Domenico de' Farri, 1555), bks. 17–18, 477r–540r (pages written by 1524, Zimmerman, *Giovio*, 287). In his *Eulogies* of celebrated military and political figures, Giovio included portraits of Qansuh al-Ghawri, Selim, Suleyman, 'Aruj Barbarossa and his brother Khayr al-Din, as well as of several other Mamluk and Ottoman sultans, a recent sultan of Tunis, and the Sa'diyan sharif of Morocco (*Elogia virorum bellica virtute illustrium veris imaginibus supposita* [Florence: Lorenzo Torrentino, 1551]; *Gli Elogi Vite Brevemente Scritti d'Huomini Illustri de Guerra, Antichi et Moderni*, trans. Lodovico Domenichi [Florence: Lorenzo Torrentino, 1554]).

53. Setton, *Papacy*, vol. 3, chap. 6. Giovio, *Commentario Turchi*, 18r–26r; *Turcarum commentarius*, 41–61; *Elogia virorum bellica virtute*, 153–56, 218–19, 325–26; *Elogi Huomini de Guerra*, 197–201, 272–79, 419–21.

54. Valeriano, *Hieroglyphica*, bk. 2, 20, bk. 17, 167–68; *Hieroglyphiques*, bk. 2, 24–25, bk. 17, 209–11. Giovio, *Commentario Turchi*, 25v–26r; *Turcarum commentarius*, 60–61.

55. Rowland, *High Renaissance*, 250–53. Dietrich Rauchenberger has suggested (Rauch, 79–80) that Joannes Leo is the figure in a ca. 1519–20 portrait by the Venetian painter Sebastiano del Piombo: "Portrait of a Humanist," National Gallery of Art, Washington, D.C. (Samuel H. Kress Collection, 1961.9.38). This is highly unlikely. First, Michael Hirst, specialist in the paintings of Sebastiano, has argued convincingly that the figure here is the humanist scholar and poet Marcantonio Flaminio. Flaminio had many connections to Sebastiano; he was in Rome at this time and, born in 1498, was of the right age for the youthful portrait in Sebastiano's painting. The face, hair, and beard of the figure in the National Gallery portrait strongly resemble those in a medallion of Flaminio, identified as such. Michael Hirst, *Sebastiano del Piombo* (Oxford: Clarendon Press, 1981), 101–2. Second, there is nothing in the visage of the man, in his scholarly black gown or his gloves, or in the book, globe, and writing materials on the shelf next to him that suggests a faqih from North Africa or a former ambassador for the sultan of Fez to the court of the Grand Turk. The book at the scholar's arm is not written in Arabic. The globe, like the map, is a frequent object in a painting of a scholar in Italy—and this one seems not to be displaying Africa. There are none of the conventional indications found in early sixteenth-century Italian painting that the man has a non-European origin and Muslim origin: no distinctive headdress, no cloak or mustache. There is not even an Ottoman carpet covering the table at the scholar's elbow, a motif introduced earlier by Sebastiano in Italian portraiture; nor are there the accoutrements of an ambassador from the Muslim world. On

such pictures, see Lisa Jardine and Jerry Brotton, *Global Interests: Renaissance Art between East and West* (Ithaca, N.Y.: Cornell University Press, 2000), 40–44.

56. Martin, "Giles," in *Egidio da Viterbo*, 216–17: "Giles of Viterbo was one of the patrons [of the Maronite Christian Elias bar Abraham], as the Innsbruck [Syriac Psalter] manuscript shows and was probably also one of his pupils." On his unknown whereabouts after 1521, Levi Della Vida, *Ricerche*, 134 n.1.

57. Weil, *Lévita*, 37–38; Arthur Z. Schwarz, *Die hebräischen Handschriften der Nationalbibliothek in Wien* (Vienna: Verlag Ed. Struche, 1925), no. 152 C8, pp. 162–63; *Encyclopaedia Judaica*, 15:1323. The translator was Jacob ben Makhir, physician of Montpellier and descendant of the scholar and translator Judah ibn Tibbon of Granada. *VIA*, 42v; *VIAHott*, 263. *CGA*, 184v. Ram, 199; Ép, 225. On al-Buni (d. 622/1225) and his writing on the Names of God and other secret sciences, see Toufic Fahd, *La divination arabe. Études religieuses, sociologiques et folkloriques sur le milieu natif de l'Islam* (Paris: Sindbad, 1987), 230–38.

58. Weil, *Lévita*, 39–43, 95–104, 175–83, 254–85. Elijah Levita, *Sefer ha-Bahur* and *Sefer ha-Harkabah*, both printed in Rome in 1518 by Giovanni Giacomo Facciotti and Isaac, Yom-tov, and Jacob, sons of Abigdor Levi. Levita, *Sefer Ha-Buohur . . . Liber Electus complectens in Grammatica quatuor orationes* (Basel: J. Froben, 1525). Levita, *Opusculum Recens Hebraicum . . . cui titulum fecit . . . Thisbites, in quo 712 vocum quae sunt partim Hebraicae, Chaldaicae, Arabicae, Grecae et Latinae, quaeque in Dictionariis non facilè inveniuntur* (in Hebrew and Latin), trans. Paul Fagius (Isny: Paul Fagius, 1541), 2–4, 63–64, 131–32, 105–8 [*sic* for 205–8]. Wehr, 1068. Levita's sixteenth-century Hebrew word for cursive writing, משקיט, differs slightly from contemporary Hebrew, משיט (R. Alcaly, *The Complete English Hebrew Dictionary*, 3 vols. [Massada: Chemed Books, 1990], 1:896.)

59. Miriam Eliav-Feldon, "Invented Identities: Credulity in the Age of Prophecy and Exploration," *Journal of Early Modern History* 3 (1999): 203–32. Secret, *Kabbalistes*, 115–18.

60. S. Hillelson, "David Reubeni, an Early Visitor to Sennar," *Sudan Notes and Records* 16, pt. 1 (1933): 56–65. Eliav-Feldon, "Identities," 213, 216. Weil also thinks that Elijah Levita, on meeting David Reuveni, would have suspected an impostor (*Lévita*, 210).

61. David Reuveni, *The Story of David Hareuveni* (in Hebrew), ed. Aaron Zeev Aescoly (Jerusalem: Bialik Institute, 1993), 74–79: David describes the letter he has received while at the court of Portugal (thus during October 1525–June 1526) from "a king of the Maghreb, farther away than Fez . . . a Muslim, a descendant of their prophet, and his title is Sharif,"

and his answer to it. Eliav-Feldon, "Identities," 210, 216; Abun-Nasr, *Maghrib*, 211.

62. Eliav-Feldon, "Identities," 227.

63. Rauch, 60. Cellini, *Vita*, bk. 1, chaps. 19, 22–25; *Autobiography*, 32–33, 35–38. The bishop was also building up a large book collection, which he planned to donate to the University of Salamanca when he returned to his see in Spain in 1529. Clement VII had the books seized at the port of Naples and placed instead in the Vatican Library (Heireros, ed., *Estatutos*, 48–49). The collection would also have been interesting for Yuhanna al-Asad to visit.

64. Bono, *Schiavi*, 305–6, 334–39. Cellini, *Vita*, bk. 1, chap. 88; *Autobiography*, 158.

65. Bono, *Schiavi*, 252–95.

66. John Hunwick, "Islamic Law and Polemics over Race and Slavery in North and West Africa (16th–19th Century)," in Shaun Marmon, ed., *Slavery in the Islamic Middle East* (Princeton, N.J.: Markus Wiener Publishers, 1999), 46–50. Hunwick, *Shariʿa*, 77–79: al-Maghili to Askia Muhammad: "As for the people you described [men and women who have pronounced the Muslim profession of faith, but continue to have idols, sacrifice to trees, etc.], they are polytheists without doubt . . . so make jihad against them, killing their men and enslaving their women and children . . . Every one of them whom you release because he claims to be a free Muslim, then it becomes plain to you that he is an unbeliever, reduce him to slavery again and seize his property, unless he repents and becomes a good Muslim."

67. Bennassar and Bennassar, *Chrétiens d'Allah*, 309–14. D. Gnoli, ed., "Descriptio urbis o censimento della popolazione di Roma avanti il Sacco Borbonica," *Archivio della R. Società Romana di Storia Patria* 17 (1894): 395, 420–22, 425.

68. Setton, *Papacy*, 3:221–55.

69. The new curators were Fausto Sabeo and Niccolò Maggiorani. Sabeo had read a manuscript of the *Doctrina Machumet* (Theology of Muhammad), a reworked Christian medieval translation of an Arabic text (Hartmut Bobzin, *Der Koran im Zeitalter der Reformation* [Beirut and Stuttgart: Franz Steiner Verlag, 1995], 50, 217, 326, 332). Sabeo and Maggiorani started an inventory of the Vatican manuscripts sometime after the sack of Rome in 1527 and thus after al-Wazzan's departure from Italy. Finished in 1533, it included the Arabic manuscripts but without the added expertise Yuhanna al-Asad would have given. Levi Della Vida, *Ricerche*, 113–19.

70. The story was first told in print in 1543 by Johann Albrecht Widmanstadt as part of his Latin annotations on the *Doctrina Machumet*, or *Theologia*

Mahometis, as he called it (see note 69 above). Commenting on the enormous fish (its head in the east, its tail in the west) to be served at arrival in the Muslim Paradise, Widmanstadt remarked that the Talmudists and Cabalists had much to say about such a fish and then went on to give the exchange between Egidio da Viterbo and "his teacher M. Zemato." The latter has been identified elsewhere as a "learned Jew originating in Africa." Johann Albrecht Widmanstadt, ed., *Mahometis Abdallae Filii Theologia Dialogo explicata, Hermanno Nellingaunense interprete. Alcorani Epitome Roberto Ketense Anglo interprete* (n.p. [Nuremberg], 1543), n4v–o1r. Secret, *Kabbalistes*, 109; Joseph Perles, *Beiträge zur Geschichte der hebräischen und aramäischen Studien* (Munich: Theodor Ackermann, 1884), 186 n.1; Bobzin, *Koran*, 298 n.139, 331–32, 360 n.444.

71. This version of the story appeared in print in 1547 in an Italian translation of *Theologia Mahometis*, which, together with other writings on Islam, was included in the first Italian translation of the Qurʾan, published by Andrea Arrivabene in Venice. The translator included Widmanstadt's marginal annotations to "La Dottrina di Macometto," but he changed those at the fish story to say that the conversation took place between Cardinal Aleandro (Girolamo had been made a cardinal in 1538) and "M. Zematto Rabi Arabo preso in Africa," "a learned Arab seized in Africa." He then gave details about Zematto, which had been told to him by "my own uncle Pietro Aleandro": that the Arab had been presented to Pope Clement VII, baptized, lived in Rome for three years, and then at the sack of Rome fled and "made himself a Turk once again." As François Secret has also suggested, this is surely a version of al-Hasan al-Wazzan's story, crossed with the name of the Jewish Zematus and with confusion about the pope involved. There is no report of a learned Arab seized in Africa and baptized by Clement VII. *L'Alcorano di Macometto, Nel qual si contiene la Dottrina, la Vita, I Costumi, et le Leggi sue. Tradotto nuovamente dall'Arabi in lingua Italiana* (n.p. [Venice]: Andrea Arrivabene, 1547), 22v–23r; Bobzin, *Koran*, 263–64; Secret, *Kabbalistes*, 126 n.89; Carlo de Frede, *La prima traduzione italiana del Corano* (Naples: Istituo Universitario Orientale, 1967), 31–48, 63–73. Pietro Aleandro was a canon in the church of Aquileia and the son of Girolamo's cousin Luigi, and did various tasks for Girolamo in Rome (Pasquier, *Aléandre*, 10 n.2, 225 n.7, 352 n.5; Giammaria Mazzuchelli, *Gli Scrittori d'Italia*, 3 vols. [Brescia, 1753], 425, 431). Thus one of Pietro Aleandro's nephews may be the unknown editor/translator of the edition.

72. CGA, 123r, 146v, 152r–v, 231r, 353v, 369v, 414r. Ram, 146, 168, 173, 241, 352, 366, 411; Ép, 165, 190, 196, 275–76, 424, 444, 513. Brignon et al., *Maroc*, 174. Also, he notes the similarity between tiles seen in Assisi and Fabriano to the thin black tiles seen in mountain villages in the Atlas (CGA, 115r; Ram, 137; Ép, 153). He compares tiles on a college in Marrakesh with those currently used in Spain (CGA, 71r–v; Ram, 97; Ép,

105); this may be a memory of Granada from his childhood confirmed by comments from his parents, for there is no evidence that al-Hasan al-Wazzan ever returned to Spain.

73. Martin, *Friar*, 13–28, 183.

74. Monfasani, "Sermons," in *Egidio da Viterbo*, 184–85 (Latin text of Egidio da Viterbo's sermon from Vat. Lat. 6320). "A Sermon Delivered by the Most Revered Giles of Viterbo, O.S.A. at Bagnaia (Balnearia) on 15 October of the Year of Salvation 1525," trans. Joseph C. Schnaubelt, in Martin, *Friar*, 331–32.

75. *CEI*, 193: the majority of Muslim commentators identify Isma'il as the son offered for sacrifice, though the Qur'an does not give the name of the son in the critical verse (37:102–3). Yuhanna al-Asad did not add a name in reviewing those verses in Joannes Gabriel's Latin translation, just changing the translator's "Oh, my son," to "Oh, my little son" (QAn, 444b, Sura "De Ordinibus," verses 93–94). Qur'an 2:122–33; QAn, 18b, 21a–21b, Sura "Vacca," verses 120–34.

76. Arberry, 1:45.

77. Monfasani, "Sermons," in *Egidio da Viterbo*, 185. Egidio da Viterbo, "Sermon," in Martin, *Friar*, 332.

78. *CGA*, 146v ("el collegio di spagna che e in Bologna"); Ram, 168; Ép, 190. Carlo Malagola, *Monografie storiche sullo studio bolognese* (Bologna: Zanichelli, 1888), 182, 184, 190, 191: lists several Spanish rectors at the university, all of whom had been students at the Collegio di Spagna in the first three decades of the sixteenth century.

79. John Herman Randall, Jr., "Introduction," and Pietro Pomponazzi, "On the Immortality of the Soul," trans. William Henry Hay II, in Ernst Cassirer, Paul Oskar Kristeller, and John Herman Randall, Jr., *The Renaissance Philosophy of Man* (Chicago: University of Chicago Press, 1948), 257–381. Schmitt, "Alberto Pio," in *Società*, 47–52, 59. O'Malley, *Giles*, 41–48; David Ruderman, *The World of a Renaissance Jew: The Life and Thought of Abraham ben Mordecai Farissol* (Cincinnati: Hebrew Union College, 1981), chap. 9. Jacob Mantino praised Pomponazzi in a 1523 dedication of his Latin translation of a commentary of Averroës, and would have been another source for Yuhanna al-Asad to learn about the philosopher (David Kaufmann, "Jacob Mantino. Une page de l'histoire de la Renaissance," *Revue des études juives* 27 [1893]: 223).

80. On the Jews in Bologna, see David Ruderman, "Introduction," in David Ruderman, ed., *Essential Papers on Jewish Culture in Renaissance and Baroque Italy* (New York and London: New York University Press, 1992), 7, 8, 30; Maria Giuseppina Muzarelli, ed., *Banci ebraici a Bologna nel XV secolo* (Bologna: Società Editice il Mulino, 1994). Kaufmann, "Mantino," 30–60, 207–38. On pp. 220–23: Mantino's dedications to the early editions

of his Latin translations of Averroës from the Hebrew, that is, Averroës's commentary on Aristotle's *De Partibus et generatione animalium*, dedicated to Leo X (Rome, 1521); and Averroës's commentary on and summary of Aristotle's *Metaphysics*, dedicated to Ercole Gonzaga, Bishop of Mantua (Bologna, 1523). On the role of Jewish scholars more generally in perpetuating the thought of Averroës, see Alfred L. Ivry, "Remnants of Jewish Averroism in the Renaissance," in Bernard Dov Cooperman, ed., *Jewish Thought in the Sixteenth Century* (Cambridge, Mass.: Harvard University Press, 1983), 243–65, and on Mantino's importance, see Charles Burnett, "The Second Revelation of Arabic Philosophy and Science: 1492–1562," in Charles Burnett and Anna Contadini, eds., *Islam and the Italian Renaissance* (London: Warburg Institute, 1999), 192–98. On Mantino's origins in Catalonia, see Kenneth Stow, *The Jews in Rome*, 2 vols. (Leiden: E. J. Brill, 1997), 1:161, no. 415 and 1:162, no. 417: Giacobbe Mantino speaks for the Scola Catalana Aragonese.

81. *VIA*, 52v; *VIAHott*, 279. On Ibn Rushd's burial in Marrakesh and later reburial in Córdoba, see Miguel Cruz Hernández, *Abu-l-Walid ibn Rushd (Averroes): Vida, obra, pensamiento, influencia* (Córdoba, 1986), 37.

82. Kaufmann, "Mantino," 32–33, 56–57; O'Malley, *Giles*, 46–47. Schmitt, "Alberto Pio," in *Società*, 62 n.66.

83. *HIA*, 31r–33r; *HIAHott*, 246–49. *CGA*, 36v. Ram, 59; Ép, 57. On translation in the Arab world, see Philip K. Hitti, *History of the Arabs from the Earliest Times to the Present*, 10th ed. (New York: St. Martin's Press, 1996), 310–15, and Dimitri Gutas, *Greek Thought, Arabic Culture: The Graeco-Arabic Translation Movement in Baghdad and Early Abbasid Society (2nd–4th/8th–10th Centuries)* (London: Routledge, 1998). Translation from the Latin into Arabic has been much less studied, but scholars have been finding increasing evidence of it during the caliphate at Córdoba and later: translations of Roman chronicles, the writings of Orosius and Isidore of Seville, Roman agricultural texts (Columella, Varro), and the Bible and texts of canon law, these last translated by Mozarabs, or Christian Arabs. Janina M. Safran, *The Second Umayyad Caliphate. The Articulation of Caliphal Legitimacy in al-Andalus* (Cambridge, Mass.: Harvard University Press, 2000), 164–66; Joaquín Valvé Bermejo, "Fuentes latinas de los geógrafos arabes," *Al-Andalus* 32 (1967): 241–60; Lucie Bolens, *Agronomes andalous du Moyen-Âge* (Geneva: Librairie Droz, 1981), 34, 44–49; Hanna E. Kassis, "The Mozarabs," in María Rosa Menocal, Raymond P. Scheindlin, and Michael Sells, eds., *The Literature of al-Andalus* (Cambridge: Cambridge University Press, 2000), 423–25. Yuhanna al-Asad said he had read an agricultural text, *The Treasure of Agriculture*, translated from the Latin in the late tenth century (*CGA*, 36v).

84. John A. Haywood, *Arabic Lexicography. Its History, and its Place in the General History of Lexicography* (Leiden: E. J. Brill, 1960), 128–29. A Latin-Arabic glossary prepared by Christian Arabs in Spain in the late

twelfth or early thirteenth century was acquired in the sixteenth century by the French Orientalist Guillaume Postel. See P. Van Koningsveld, *The Latin-Arabic Glossary of the Leiden University Library* (Leiden: New Rhine Publishers, 1977), 1–6. The only Arabic-Latin dictionary I have come across in an Italian collection is a late twelfth–early thirteenth-century manuscript in the library of the Dominican convent in Florence: two-thirds Latin-Arabic, one-third Arabic-Latin (C. Schiaparelli, ed., *Vocabulista in Arabico* [Florence: Le Monnier, 1871], xii–xxi). There was evidently none at the Vatican Library in Mantino's time.

85. *AM*, 54r–55v: "El Chalil filius Hacmede el Farahidi"; *AMC*, 185–86. On al-Khalil, see Haywood, *Arabic Lexicography*, chaps. 3–4; on Arabic-Persian and Arabic-Turkish dictionaries, ibid., 107, 118–19. The best known was the Arabic-Persian dictionary by al-Zamakhshari (d. 538/1144).

86. Haywood, *Arabic Lexicography*, chaps. 6–8. Al-Zamakhshari gave alphabetical order to his Arabic dictionary but arranged his Arabic-Persian dictionary by topic (105–6, 118–19). Yuhanna al-Asad's dictionary begins with "alif" and ends with "ya," but between "zay" and "ha," there is an order followed in the Maghreb until the twentieth century and different from that in Islamic societies in the East. (I am grateful to Houari Touati for his guidance on this matter.)

87. The entries in Hebrew end on fol. 6a. The Latin entries are in two early sixteenth-century hands and end on 13a. From 12b to the end at 117b, there are many Spanish entries in several later hands, probably from the seventeenth century. For the fate of the manuscript in the 1540s and afterward, see chapter 9 below.

88 *Dict*, 117b–118a. Pedro de Alcala, *Arte para ligeramente saber la lengua araviga* and *Vocabulista aravigo en letra castellana* (Granada: Juan Varela, 1505), a 2r: "Prologo dirigido al reverendissimo senor don fray Bernardo de Talavera primero arcobispo de Granada." The judgment of the linguist Corriente on this text: "the bulk of the material is dialectal, though flawed by frequent misprints and the author's poor knowledge of the language" (Federico Corriente, *A Dictionary of Andalusi Arabic* [Leiden: E. J. Brill, 1997], xiii).

89. *VIA*, 37v; *VIAHott*, 256–57. *Avicennae Arabis Medicorum . . . principis. Quarta fen, primi. De universali ratione medendi nunc primum M. Iacob. Mantini, medici hebraei, latinitate donata* (Ettlingen: Valentinus Kobian, 1531 [first ed. Venice, 1530]), A 1r. Mantino acknowledged the improved translation by Andrea Alpago, published in 1527, but said there were still errors.

90. Kaufmann, "Mantino," 39, 223: *Praefatio Rabi Moysis Maimonidis Cordubensis Hebraeorum doctissimi in aeditionem moralem seniorum massecheth Avot apud Hebraeos nuncupatam octoque amplectens capita eximio artium et medicinae doctore M. Jakob Mantino medico hebraeo interprete* (1526). Raymond L. Weiss and Charles Butterworth, eds., *Eth-*

ical Writings of Maimonides (New York: New York University Press, 1975), 11–16, 59–104.

91. This story is put together both from Yuhanna al-Asad's portrait of Averroës/Ibn Rushd (*VIA*, 50r–51r, *VIAHott*, 276–77) and from his portrait of Maimonides (*VIH*, 66v–67r, *VIHHott*, 288). He cited two sources for his biography of Ibn Rushd: ʿAbd al-Wahid al-Marrakushi of Marrakesh, and Ibn al-ʿAbbar (thirteenth century) of Valencia, but does not indicate where precisely he got this inaccurate report of the Ibn Rushd–Maimonides connection.

92. Maimonides, "Letter to Joseph," in *Ethical Writings*, 123 and 127 n.71. Salomon Munk, *Mélanges de philosophie juive et arabe* (Paris: J. Vrin, 1927), 425, 487. Cruz Hernández, *Ibn Rushd*, 251. Majid Fakhry, *Averroës (Ibn Rushd). His Life, Works and Influence* (Oxford: One World, 2001), 132. Mohamed Mezzine, "Journée d'un Juif à Fes," in *Maroc andalou*, 136–37.

93. *VIA*, 51v–52r; *VIAHott*, 278–79. *Averois Cordubensis Paraphrasis in Librum Poeticae Aristotelis, Iacob Mantino Hispano Hebraeo, Medico interprete* in Aristotle, *Omnia quae extant Opera*, 11 vols. (Venice: Giunta, 1550–52), 2:89r–94r. On the new interest in the *Poetics* among Italian scholars, see Eric Cochrane, *Italy*, ed. Julius Kirshner (London and New York: Longman, 1988), 210–11.

94. Averroës, *Paraphrasis in Librum Poeticae*, chap. 2 in Aristotle, *Omnia Opera*, 89v. In 1539 Mantino was to publish his Latin translation of Averroës's paraphrase of and commentary on Plato's *Republic*, drawn as always from a good Hebrew translation. Here, too, Averroës talks of the value of poetry in instructing the young but warns against "expressions provoking voluptuousness . . . which are frequent in Arab poems" (*Averois Paraphrasis Super libros de Republica Platonis, nunc primum latinitate donata, Iacob Mantino Medico Hebraeo Interprete* [Rome: Valerio and Luigi Dorici, 1539], B5r, B8v).

95. Yuhanna al-Asad mentions the text on the Arabic metric art as part of his text on Arab grammar ("la Arte metrica arabica," "la grammatica arabica") in *CGA*, 178r (Ram, 194; Ép, 219). Ramusio says in his dedication to the Italian edition that the manuscript had been in Mantino's possession: *Navigationi et Viaggi* (1554), *iiir; Ram, 6. Levi Della Vida, *Ricerche*, 311, 313, 321. On the "trustworthiness" of some Jews and Christians, see the Qur'an, 3:75.

CHAPTER THREE • WRITING IN ITALY

1. "La brevita de le croniche mucamettani," cited in *CGA*, 49r, 54v, 62v, 70v, 74v, 335r (Ram, 73, 80, 87, 96, 100, 333; Ép, 76, 82, 92, 103, 108, 396). "Operino in la fede et lege di Mucametto secundo la Religion di Malichi,"

cited in *CGA*, 27v, 418v (Ram, 50, 415; Ép, 47, 518). "Le Vite de li Philosophi arabi," cited in *CGA*, 186r (Ram, 201; Ép, 226). Yuhanna al-Asad also seems to have thought of appending the treatises on grammar and metrics, the abridgment of Muslim chronicles, and the lives of illustrious men to his manuscript on Africa, but this is not the case in the existing manuscript 953.

2. Chase F. Robinson, *Islamic Historiography* (Cambridge: Cambridge University Press, 2003), xii, 7, 178.

3. The fourteen pages of *De Arte Metrica Liber* are bound into the manuscript Plut. 36.35, Biblioteca Medicea Laurenziana, Florence, where they suddenly interrupt the manuscript of *De Viris quibusdam Illustribus*. The colophon with the date 1527 is at the end of *VIH*, but since *AM*, *VIA*, and *VIH* are in the same hand, it is a reasonable assumption that they were copied at the same date.

4. *AM*, 54r–v; *AMC*, 185–86. Yuhanna al-Asad was recalling the pages devoted to al-Khalil in the well-known biographical dictionary of grammarians by al-Zubaydi (d. 378–79/989). Al-Zubaydi and other sources say it was al-Khalil's son who came upon him reciting nonsense syllables metrically, but Yuhanna al-Asad remembered it as his brother (Haywood, *Arabic Lexicography*, 21; *AMC*, 186 n.1).

5. *AM*, 55r; *AMC*, 187.

6. *AM*, 58r, 60r; *AMC*, 191, 195. Ka'b ibn Zuhayr, "The Mantle Ode," in *Selections from Akhbar Majnun Banu 'Amr and Ka'b ibn Zuhair*, trans. Arthur Wormhoudt (Oskaloosa, Ia.: William Penn University, 1975), li. 10. The Prophet was so moved by Ibn Zuhayr's poem that he threw his mantle over the poet's shoulders; hence the name of the ode. Yuhanna al-Asad also cites the pre-Islamic poet al-Nabigh al-Dhubyani, but those lines, too, are in fact by Ibn Zuhayr. *AM*, 60r; *AMC*, 195 n.1.

7. On late medieval knowledge of Arabic poetry and prosody, see Charles Burnett, "Learned Knowledge of Arabic Poetry, Rhymed Prose and Didactic Verse, from Petrus Alfonsi to Petrarch," in John Marenbon, ed., *In the Middle Ages: A Festschrift for Peter Dronke* (Leiden: E. J. Brill, 2001), 29–62. Levi Della Vida, *Richerche*, 102. Trabulsi, *Critique poétique*, chaps. 3–4, especially 171–77 on prosody. Though *AM* is not a complete text, it reads as though Yuhanna al-Asad was limiting himself to metric questions and not going on to genres.

8. *VIA*, 31r, *VIAHott*, 246; *VIH*, 65v, *VIHHott*, 291. On the genre of biographical compendiums or "tabaqat," see Wadad al-Qadi, "Biographical Dictionaries: Inner Structures and Cultural Significance," in George N. Atiyeh, ed., *The Book in the Islamic World: The Written Word and Communication in the Middle East* (Albany: SUNY Press, 1995), 93–122; Robinson, *Islamic Historiography*, 66–74; and Dwight F. Reynolds, ed., *Interpreting the Self: Autobiography in the Arabic Literary Tradition*

(Berkeley and Los Angeles: University of California Press, 2001), 40–43, 64–66. On the inclusion of women in some biographical compendia: Reynolds, ed., *Interpreting the Self*, 40; Ruth Roded, ed., *Women in Islam and the Middle East. A Reader* (London and New York: I. B. Tauris, 1999), 132–33.

9. I say twenty-eight men among the Arabs, even though there are only twenty-five entries written in the manuscript. This is because the end of one life and the beginning of another were cut off just at the point where *AM* was bound into *VIA* (53v, 62r) and, further, the pages for two lives were lost entirely during the binding. On 53r, Yuhanna al-Asad begins a biography of "Ibnu El Chathib Rasi," that is, the critical philosopher Fakhr al-Din al-Razi, also known as Ibn al-Khatib and Khatib al-Rayy (544/1149–606/1210). After the interruption in the manuscript, the text picks up (62r) in the last part of the life and writings of Lisan al-Din ibn al-Khatib (d. 776/1374), an extraordinary polymath and political figure in al-Andalus and the Maghreb. We know the two missing biographies from the names in the table at the end (69r–v): Ibn al-Banna, a thirteenth-century mathematician born in Marrakesh, and Ibn Hudayl, a fourteenth-century figure at the court of the Nasrid sultans in Granada and author of treatises on military matters, holy war, and horseback riding (Arié, *Espagne*, 229, 245–52, 430, 437).

10. *VIA*, 35v (includes Arabic); *VIAHott*, 253 (Arabic omitted). Cf. Abu Nasr al-Farabi, *Aphorismes choisis*, trans. Soumaya Mestiri and Guillaume Dye (Paris: Fayard, 2003), 53–54. The Arabic hand in these verses resembles closely Yuhanna al-Asad's hand in the Arabic-Hebrew-Latin dictionary.

11. *VIA*, 40v–41v. Yuhanna al-Asad gives him his Latin name Mesua; Masawayh al-Maridini was known as Mesua the Younger. Yuhanna al-Asad recalled correctly that he practiced at the court of the Fatimid caliph al-Hakim, but he has him dying in 496/1102–3 rather than 406/1015 (Hitti, *Arabs*, 311 n.7). The penis story was omitted from *VIAHott*, 262.

12. Ibn Khallikan, *Biographical Dictionary*, trans. Mac Guckin de Slane, 4 vols. (1842–72; repr., New York and London: Johnson Reprint, 1961), 1:187–89: Ishaq ibn Hunayn (ninth century). In his entry on Ibn Sina (Avicenna), Ibn Khallikan was frank about his "extreme addiction to sexual pleasure," indulged in even when he was very ill with dysentery (1:440–46).

13. *VIA*, 33r–33v, 35v, 41v, 47r, 48r–v; *VIAHott*, 249, 251, 254, 262, 271–73. On "isnad," see Reynolds, ed., *Interpreting the Self*, 3–4, 37–38, 41–43; Robinson, *Islamic Historiography*, 15–16; and the more extended discussion in chapter 8 below.

14. Among many examples, the geographer al-Idrisi is placed in the court of Roger I of Sicily more than fifty years before Roger II actually asked him

to prepare a description of the locations and qualities of the known world (548/1154); al-Idrisi gave his dates in the prologue to his geography, a book much admired and described accurately by Yuhanna al-Asad. *VIA*, 45r–v; *VIAHott*, 267–68. Al-Idrisi, *Première géographie*, 14–19, 62. Only one Arabic biographical dictionary is mentioned in the Vatican Library; it concerned Sufis of Tunisia and became part of the Vatican collection only after 1569 (Levi Della Vida, *Ricerche*, 279). Bernheimer does not list an Arabic biographical dictionary in Alberto Pio's collection, *Catalogo*, and there is no sign of one in what we know of Egidio da Viterbo's library.

15. *VIA*, 35v–36v; *VIAHott*, 253–55.

16. Ibn Khallikan, *Biographical Dictionary*, 3:311–14; al-Nadim, *The Fihrist of al-Nadim: A Tenth-Century Survey of Muslim Culture*, trans. Bayard Dodge, 2 vols. (New York and London: Columbia University Press, 1970), 701–9, 704 n.169. Robinson, *Islamic Historiography*, 144. On Muhammad ibn Abi ʿAmir al-Mansur (d. 392/1002), the Cordovan chamberlain who ruled the Umayyad Caliphate, and the Cordovan historians ʿIsa ibn Ahmad al-Razi (d. 379/989) and Ibn Hayyan (d. 469/1076), see Safran, *Second Umayyad Caliphate*, chaps. 3, 5. Ibn Hayyan drew much of his *al-Muqtabis* from ʿIsa al-Razi's chronicle, and this association of names must be a source for Yuhanna al-Asad's fantastic association of persons.

17. The Short Title Catalogue of the British Library lists nine editions of all or parts of the *Liber Almansoris*, published in Venice from 1476 through 1508; the catalogue of the National Library of Medicine lists twelve other editions, either separate works or those included in larger medical collections, published in Italy from 1508 to 1524, nine in Venice, two in Pavia, and one in Jacob Mantino's Bologna (Richard Durling, ed., *A Catalogue of Sixteenth Century Printed Books in the National Library of Medicine* [Bethesda, Md.: National Library of Medicine, 1967], 422–30).

18. *VIA*, 43v–44v, 62r–63v; *VIAHott*, 265–67, 281–84. Ibn al-Khatib had spent two years in Fez and in the Atlantic town of Salé during his exile from the Nasrid court in Granada; he took refuge in Fez at the end of his life, accused of heresy and with many enemies in Granada. He was strangled to death by assassins in a Fez prison in 776/1375 (Alexander Knysh, "Ibn al-Khatib," in Menocal et al., eds., *Literature*, 358–71). Given all of Ibn al-Khatib's connections to Morocco, it is not surprising that al-Wazzan reported his letters in Fez libraries. Ibn Khaldun was also an admirer of Ibn al-Khatib's rhymed prose and poetry (*Voyage*, 87, 90–97, 104–11, 120–31), and for the later historian of Muslim Spain Ahmad al-Maqqari, Ibn al-Khatib was "the prince of poets and historians of his time and the model of viziers" (*The History of the Mohammedan Dynasties in Spain*, trans. Pascual de Gayangos, 2 vols. [London: W. H. Allen, 1840–1843], 2:367).

19. *VIA*, 35r, 39v, 48r, 51v; *VIAHott*, 253, 259–60, 272, 278. *VIA* contains citations from at least twelve different authorities. Cf. Ibn Khallikan,

Biographical Dictionary, 1:440–46. Yuhanna al-Asad also cites *The Book of Physicians and Philosophers* of Ibn Juljul (d. ca. 384/994) as a source for figures who lived long after the date of Ibn Juljul's death (*VIA*, 38r, 39r, 46v; *VIAHott*, 257–59, 270).

20. The manuscripts of *AM*, *VIA*, and *VIH* became the possession eventually of the scholar and bibliophile Antonio Petrei (1498–1570). Petrei had been close to Cardinal Niccolò Ridolfi, who acquired what was left of Egidio da Viterbo's library at the latter's death in 1532. Thus, one could assume a passage of these manuscripts from Egidio to Ridolfi to Petrei (Codazzi in *AMC*, 181–82).

21. Title given *CGA*, 465r; *Cosmographia* is here spelled *Cosmogrophia*. The manuscript, discovered by Angela Codazzi some seventy-five years ago, may soon be available in printed form: Oumelbanine Zhiri plans a straight transcription for readers, and Dietrich Rauchenberger is preparing a critical edition.

22. *CGA*, 44r: "el prefato compositore"; *DAR*, 11v (Ram, 67): phrase omitted. *CGA*, 44r: "ecco el Re de li Pesci"; *DAR*, 11v (Ram, 67): "In capo del quale il re de' pesci." *CGA*, 74r: "tal che fu causa che intro el Populo di Marin . . . et levosi el populo di Abduluad"; *DAR*, 18v (Ram, 100): "che appresso il popolo di Marin entrasse . . . si solleva etiando il popolo di Habduluad." *CGA*, 140r: "uno se chiama el templo del Carauiien el quale e un templo grandissimo"; *DAR*, 32v (Ram, 162): "il quale è chiamato il tempio del Caruven, il qual è un grandissimo tempio." *CGA*, 173r: "alhora el Patre e obligato de dare al Maestro . . . alhora el Patre fami convito a tutti le scolari"; *DAR*, 39r (Ram, 191): "è tenuto il padre di fargli . . . allora fa il suo padre a tutti gli scolari un molto solenne convito." *CGA*, 212r: "per la abundantia del Paese"; *DAR*, 46v (Ram, 224): "per la molta abbondanza del paese." *CGA*, 282r: "El terzio officale e el thesaurero"; *DAR*, 60r (Ram, 287): "il terzo è il thesoriere." *CGA*, 417r: "como ipso compositore dice havere visto"; *DAR*, 86r (Ram, 413): "Et io viddi." Though "el" was a possible word for "the" in early sixteenth-century Italian and was surely used by some writers, it was rarely employed by Ramusio. According to Alberto Accarisio's 1543 book on spelling, which followed the preferred Tuscan style, "el" should be used for "the" only to replace "and the"—"et il" ("& il")—as in "il duca el sacretario" (*Vocabolario, Grammatica, et Orthographia de la Lingua Volgare* [Cento, 1543], 1). Yuhanna al-Asad, in contrast, uses "el" often and in cases where it is not replacing "and the." *CGA*, 354r, 361r–362r: repeated use of "dattoli"; *DAR*, 73r, 74v (Ram, 352, 359): "datteri" in all cases. Giuseppe Boerio, *Dizionario del dialetto veneziano* (Venice: Giovanni Cecchini, 1867), 220; Carlo Battisti and Giovanni Alessio, *Dizionario etimologico italiano* (Florence: G. Barbèra, 1968), 1215–16. On uneven spelling and "mixture of language" in port cities and elsewhere in Italy, see Trovato, *Lingua italiana*, 32–35, 61–64.

23. *CGA*, 464v: "ipso compositore per non recordarse piu per la label sua memoria . . . pero dunque pone silentio et fine al suo Parlare." Omitted in Ram, 460, and in Ép, 579. Robinson, *Islamic Historiography*, 174.

24. Ibid., 174–85. Johannes Pedersen, *The Arabic Book*, trans. Geoffrey French (Princeton, N.J.: Princeton University Press, 1984), 26–31. Al-Qasim al-Hariri, *Le livre des Malins: Séances d'un vagabond de génie*, trans. René R. Khawam (Paris: Phébus, 1992), 477: "I have written, then dictated these words." Ibn Battuta, *Voyages*, 1:65–75; Dunn, *Ibn Battuta*, 310–15. Ayman Fu'ad Sayyid, "Early Methods of Book Composition: al-Maqrizi's Draft of the 'Kitab al-Khitat,'" in Yasin Dutton, ed., *The Codicology of Islamic Manuscripts* (London: Al-Furqan Islamic Heritage Foundation, 1995), 98–101. Hajji, *Activité*, 145, 160. Joseph Schacht, "On Some Manuscripts in the Libraries of Morocco," *Hespéris Tamuda* 9 (1968): 45. Rauchenberger's statement that oral dictation was the "usual practice" for authors composing their books at this date is not supported by the evidence (Rauch, 128).

25. Letters of Alberto Pio, Lea MS 414, nos. 1–56, Special Collections, University of Pennsylvania Library. An example of a manuscript said to be in Egidio da Viterbo's hand: *Liber de Anima*, MS Lat. 1253, Biblioteca Angelica, Rome. Monfasani, "Sermons," in *Egidio da Viterbo*, 142–45; Martin, "Giles of Viterbo," ibid., 219.

26. On the emergence of the "author's book" or autograph manuscript in the later Middle Ages, see Armando Petrucci, *Writers and Readers in Medieval Italy. Studies in the History of Written Culture*, ed. and trans. Charles M. Radding (New Haven and London: Yale University Press, 1995), chaps. 8–9.

27. Rauchenberger has speculated that the scribe of Yuhanna al-Asad's manuscript was Elias bar Abraham, the Maronite (Rauch, 132–33). A comparison of Elias's Latin hand—which I have seen directly in MS Syriaque 44, BNF, and examples of which are reproduced by Levi Della Vida, *Ricerche*, plate 9, 1b (Vat. Sir. 9) and by Rauchenberger himself (113 , Vat. Sir. 15)—and the Italian hand of *CGA* makes it clear that this is impossible. Similar words and letters are written very differently.

28. For instance, marginal corrections on *CGA*, 47r, 130v, and 147r are clearly in the scribe's hand, those on 3r, 145r, and 149r in another hand. Yuhanna al-Asad's Latin hand is known only from the four words, *Jo. Leo servus medecis*, on the 1521 transcription of Saint Paul's Epistles (figure 4), and it does not resemble the corrections on 3r, 145r, and 149r. Of course Yuhanna al-Asad could have modified his handwriting in the Latin alphabet between 1521 and 1526.

29. *CGA*, 294r–295v.

30. Ram, 296–99. Ramusio's reordering of the description of Mazouna, Al-

giers, Tegdemt, and Médéa suggests guidance by a manuscript rather than editorial guessing. An impossible date for an event appears in *CGA*, 86r: 950 by the Muslim reckoning, which would be 1543 by the Christian dating. Ramusio gives it as 920 (1514), which suggests a manuscript source. Oumelbanine Zhiri is also convinced that MS V.E. 953 of the Biblioteca Nazionale Centrale was not the only manuscript copy of Yuhanna al-Asad's text, and that, whether or not MS V.E. 953 was available to him, Ramusio was working from a different copy (conversation of 23 May 2003; e-mail communication of 25 April 2005). In the eighteenth century, a copy of the manuscript was in the library of the Benedictine monastery of St. Michael in Venice (Giovanni Benedetto Mittarelli, *Bibliotheca codicum manuscriptorum Monasterii S. Michaelis Venetiarum prope Murianum* [Venice, 1779], 681). The colophon reproduced by Mittarelli has five differences in spelling from the colophon in *CGA*, 464v. Despite these variations, Rauchenberger has suggested that this could be the same as MS V.E. 953 at the Biblioteca Nazionale Centrale (Rauch, 138–39, 139 n.622), but it is also possible that this is a separate manuscript consulted by Ramusio.

31. Here are quotations from the manuscript and the printed version that illustrate syntactical, spelling, and stylistic changes made by Ramusio without affecting the content. Yuhanna al-Asad says that throughout Barbary most people live to sixty-five or seventy years, but in the mountains one can find men who live a hundred years and more and are still strong. *CGA*, 38r: "Per tutta la Barbaria le cipta de li Homini sonno o vero vanno fine ad 65 o 70 et sonno pochi che passano quella, ma pure se trovano in li monti de la Barbaria Homini che hanno 100 anni anchi li passano et sonno galiardi." *DAR*, 10r (Ram, 60): "Per tutte le città et terreni della Barberia le età de gli huomini aggiungono per insino a sessantacinque o a settanta anni, et v'hanno pochi che questo numero passino, ma pur si trovano ne monti della Barberia huomini che forniscono cento anni, et alcuni che ve gli passano. E sono questi d'una gagliarda e forte vecchiezza." Crofton Black gives some changes affecting the content in "Leo Africanus's *Descrittione dell'Africa* and its Sixteenth-Century Translations," *Journal of the Warburg and Courtauld Institutes* 65 (2002): 262–72, as does Rauchenberger in his replication of Yuhanna al-Asad's pages on sub-Saharan and Saharan Africa (Rauch, apps. 1–2). I shall be considering several important ones in the course of this book.

32. Marica Milanesi, "Introduzione," in Ram, xiii–xxi. Sanuto, *Diarii*, 54:144–48. Robert W. Karrow, Jr., *Mapmakers of the Sixteenth Century and Their Maps* (Chicago: Newberry Library, 1993), 216–17, 220–28.

33. Volume 1 of Ramusio's three-volume *Navigationi et Viaggi* first appeared in 1550, with a second edition in 1554, a posthumous edition in 1563 (Ramusio died in 1557), and later editions in 1588, 1606, and 1613. *La*

Descrittione dell'Africa of "Giovan Lioni Africano" opens volume 1 and is followed by accounts of other voyages, including one along the west coast of Africa, but they are all by Europeans. The Giunta firm was publishing its big edition of Aristotle, with the commentaries by Averroës translated by Jacob Mantino, during the same years that it began publishing Ramusio's *Navigationi et Viaggi*.

34. The major texts here are André Miquel, *La géographie humaine du monde musulman jusqu'au milieu du 11e siècle*, 4 vols. (Paris and The Hague: Mouton, 1973–88), especially volume 1, and J. B. Harley and David Woodward, eds., *The History of Cartography*, vol. 2, bk. 1: *Cartography in the Traditional Islamic and South Asian Societies*, ed. Ahmet T. Karamustafa, Joseph E. Schwartzberg, and Gerald Tibbetts (Chicago and London: University of Chicago Press, 1987), chaps. 1–14.

35. Ibid., 1:202–12. Houari Touati, *Islam et voyage*, 143–54. Al-Mas'udi, *Les prairies d'or*, trans. Barbier de Meynard and Pavet de Courteille, rev. Charles Pellat, 5 vols. (Paris: CNRS, 1965–97), 1:2–3, 84–85.

36. Miquel, *Géographie*, 1:313–30. Touati, *Islam et voyage*, 161–70. Al-Muqaddasi, *The Best Divisions for Knowledge of the Regions*, trans. Basil Anthony Collins and Muhammad Hamid al-Tai (London: Center for Muslim Contribution to Civilisation and Garnet Publishing, 1994), 2–8.

37. Ibid., 206.

38. Abu-'Ubayd al-Bakri, *Description de l'Afrique septentrionale*, trans. Mac Guckin de Slane (1913; repr., Paris: Librairie d'Amérique et d'Orient, 1965); Mac Guckin de Slane, "Préface" to *Description de l'Afrique septentrionale par Abou-Obeïd-el-Bekri. Texte arabe* (Paris: Librairie d'Amérique et d'Orient, 1965), 7–20. N. Levtzion and J.F.P. Hopkins, eds., *Corpus of Early Arabic Sources for West African History*, trans. J.F.P. Hopkins (Princeton, N.J.: Markus Wiener Publishers, 2000), 62–87, 384–87.

39. Harley and Woodward, eds., *History*, vol. 2, bk. 1, "Introduction," chaps. 4–5. J. Lennart Berggren and Alexander Jones, "Introduction," in *Ptolemy's Geography*, trans. J. Lennart Berggren and Alexander Jones (Princeton, N.J.: Princeton University Press, 2000), 10–14.

40. Henri Bresc and Annliese Nef, "Presentation," in al-Idrisi, *Première géographie*, 13–53, and al-Idrisi, "Prologue," ibid., 62–64, "Premier climat," ibid., 69. Mahamad Hadj Sadok, "Introduction. Vie et oeuvres d'al-Idrisi," in al-Idrisi, *Le Maghrib au 12e siècle*, trans. Mahamad Hadj Sadok (Paris: Publisud, 1983), 11–56. S. Maqbul Ahmad, "Cartography of al-Sharif al-Idrisi," in Harley and Woodward, eds., *History*, vol. 2, bk. 1, chap. 7.

41. Ibn Hawqal (late tenth century), *La configuration de la terre (Kitab Surat al-Ard)*, trans. J. H. Kramers and G. Wiet (Paris: Maisonneuve and

Larose, 2001), offers at least twenty-one maps for the different regions described. Al-Muqaddasi, *Best Divisions*, has twenty maps. Miquel, *Géographie*, 1:69–85; Harley and Woodward, eds., *History*, vol. 2, bk. 1, 7, 123–24.

42. CGA, 114r, 316v, 440r, 441r–v, 453r. Ram, 137, 317, 437–38, 449; Ép, 152, 376, 552–53, 565. VIA, 44v–45v; VIAHott, 267–68. Al-Idrisi's *Recreation* (*Nuzhat al-mushtaq fi-khtiraq al-afaq*) became known as *The Book of Roger* (*Kitab Rujar*), but Yuhanna al-Asad refers to it in a version of the original title (*Nushat al absar*).

43. The editions of Jacopo d'Angelo's translation of Ptolemy published in Bologna in 1475 and in Rome in 1478 were entitled *Cosmographia*, while those published in Rome in 1508 and Venice in 1511 were entitled *Geographia*.

44. CGA, 52v, 429r. Ram, 78, 425; Ép, 80, 532.

45. Ibn Khaldun, *The Muqaddimah. An Introduction to History*, trans. Franz Rosenthal, 2nd ed., 3 vols. (Princeton, N.J.: Princeton University Press, 1967), 1:frontispiece, 109; Ahmad, "Cartography," in Harley and Woodward, eds., *History*, vol. 2, bk. 1, 170. Piri Reis, *Kitab-I Bahriye* (*Book of Navigation*) (Ankara: Republic of Turkey, Prime Ministry, Undersecretaryship of Navigation, 2002).

46. *Cartographic Treasures of the Newberry Library* (Chicago: Newberry Library, 2001), no. 7. David Buisseret, *The Mapmakers' Quest. Depicting New Worlds in Renaissance Europe* (Oxford: Oxford University Press, 2003), 50–51. Karrow, *Mapmakers*, 216–28, 266–74, 604–5. Neither Alberto Pio nor Egidio da Viterbo figures in Karrow's extensive study as patrons of cartography or dedicatees of geographical works. Paolo Giovio, *De Legatione Basilii magni Principis Moscoviae ad Clementum VIII Pontificem Max. Liber*, in *Rerum Moscoviticarum Commentarii* (Basel: Johann Oporin, 1551), 159–75.

47. On the meanings of Muslim travel and travel writing, see the excellent work of Touati, *Islam et voyage*, chaps. 1–2, 5–7.

48. Ibn Jubayr, *The Travels of Ibn Jubayr*, trans. Ronald J. C. Broadhurst (London: Jonathan Cape, 1952), 321–22.

49. Ibn Battuta cited in Dunn, *Ibn Battuta*, 258–59. On the composition of rihlas in Morocco in the fifteenth and sixteenth centuries, see Benchekroun, *Vie*, 9–11; Hajji, *Activité*, 182.

50. CGA, 19r ("e meglio se ponno vedere le Hystorie de li Arabi di Ibnu Calden el quale fece quasi un grosso volume de li arbori et de le generatione de li Arabi imbarbarati"), 67r–74v, 178v ("opera de Ibnu Chaldun cronechista"), 317r–320v. Ram, 39 ([*DAR*, 5v] omits reference to Ibn Khaldun), 93–100, 195, 319–21; Ép, 34–35, 99–107, 219, 378–82. Ibn Khaldun, *Muqaddimah*. 1:lxxvii, xci–xcii. Robinson, *Islamic Historiog-*

raphy, 185. Recent important studies of Ibn Khaldun are Aziz al-Azmeh, *Ibn Khaldun. An Essay in Reinterpretation*, 2nd ed. (Budapest: Central European University Press, 2003) and Abdesselam Cheddadi, "Introduction," to Ibn Khaldun, *Le Livre des Exemples*, trans. Abdesselam Cheddadi, vol. 1: *Autobiographie. Muqaddima* (Paris: Gallimard, 2002), ix–liv. Oumelbanine Zhiri, "Jean Léon l'Africain lecteur de Ibn Khaldun: Les savants contre les charlatans," paper presented to the Colloque "Léon l'Africain" (EHESS, Paris, 22–24 May 2003), to be published in Pouillon and Zhiri, eds., *Léon l'Africain*. Another historical source for Yuhanna al-Asad was ʿAbd al-Wahid al-Marrakushi (thirteenth century), native of Marrakesh and author of a monumental work of biographies of scholars of al-Andalus and the Maghreb (*CGA*, 74r–v; Ram, 100; Ép, 109; *VIA*, 48r, *VIAHott*, 272; Benchekroun, *Vie*, 147–55; al-Qadi, "Biographical Dictionaries," in Atiyeh, ed., *Book*, 103–4).

51. *CGA*, 312v–313r (both Ram, 314 [*DAR*, 65v] and Ép, 372 give a somewhat different verse, and omit discussion of the verse form). Charles Pellat, "Hidjaʾ," *EI2*, 3:352–57; Trabulsi, *Critique poétique*, 228–30; G.J.H. Van Gelder, "Hijaʾ," *EAL*, 1:284–85; Benchekroun, *Vie*, 270.

52. Menocal et al., eds., *Literature*, 107–8. H. Kilpatrick, "Adab," *EAL*, 1:54–56. Peter Burke, *The Fortunes of the Courtier. The European Reception of Castiglione's "Cortegiano"* (University Park, Pa.: Pennsylvania State University Press, 1996), 23–40; Peter Burke, *The Italian Renaissance: Culture and Society in Italy* (Cambridge: Polity Press, 1986), 155–57.

53. *CGA*, 43v ("per essere necessario ad ciascuna Persona che compone narrare le cose como sonno"), 147r–v ("per essere obligato de dire la verita per ogni cuncto et como e il dovere che ciascuna persona debia fare"), 432v, 441r–v. Ram, 66, 169 [*DAR*, 34v] with different phrasing from Yuhanna al-Asad's, to be discussed below in chapter 8, 429, 438; Ép, 65, 191 (Épaulard follows the phrasing of Ramusio), 537, 553. Al-Masʿudi, *Prairies*, 2:334–36 (on the emeralds).

54. Ibn Khaldun, *Muqaddimah*, 1:6–65. Ibn Battuta, *Voyages*, 1:73. Robinson, *Islamic Historiography*, 143–55; Touati, *Islam et voyage*, 147–52; al-Azmeh, *Ibn Khaldun*, chap. 2. On the construction of geography as a form of adab by al-Jahiz (d. 254/868), see Miquel, *Géographie*, 1:35–56.

55. Badiʿ al-Zaman al-Hamadhani, *Le livre des vagabonds: Séances d'un beau parleur impénitent*, trans. René R. Khawam (Paris: Phébus, 1997); *The Maqamat of Badiʿ al-Zaman al-Hamadhani*, trans. W. J. Prendergast (London: Curzon Press, 1973). Al-Hariri, *Livre des Malins*; *The Assemblies of Al-Hariri*, trans. Thomas Chenery and F. Steingass, 2 vols. (1867–98; repr., Westmead, Hants.: Gregg International Publishers, 1969). Yuhanna al-Asad mentioned al-Hariri once: *CGA*, 182r ("in lo comento de la favola del hariri"); Ram, 197 ([*DAR*, 40v] reference to al-Hariri omitted), Ép, 222. On the *Maqamat* of al-Hamadhani and al-

Hariri, see Abdelfattah Kilito, *Les séances: Récits et codes culturels chez Hamadhani et Hariri* (Paris: Sindbad, 1983); Jaakko Hämeen-Anttila, *Maqama. A History of a Genre* (Wiesbaden; Harrassowitz Verlag, 2002); and Philip F. Kennedy, "The Maqamat as a Nexus of Interests: Reflections on Abdelfattah Kilito's *Les Séances* and Other Works," in Julia Ashtiany Bray, ed., *Muslim Horizons* (London and New York: Routledge Curzon, forthcoming). James T. Monroe, *The Art of Badiʿ az-Zaman al-Hamadhani as Picaresque Narrative* (Beirut: American University, 1983) is an important study, but like Kilito and Kennedy, I do not follow his highly moralistic reading of al-Hamadhani. For the *maqamat* in al-Andalus, see Rina Drory, "The maqama," in Menocal et al., eds., *Literature*, 190–210.

56. Ramusio claimed in his dedication that Giovanni Leone had "learned to read and write the Italian language, and had translated his book from the Arabic. This book, written by him himself, after many accidents which it would be too long to recount, came into our hands" (*Primo volume, et Seconda editione delle Navigationi et Viaggi . . . nella quale si contengono La Descrittione dell' Africa* [Venice: Giunti, 1554], *iiir, dedication to Hieronomo Fracastora; Ram, 6). Ramusio had never seen an Arabic manuscript, however, and it is more reasonable to assume that Yuhanna al-Asad was working from, recasting, and translating Arabic notes and perhaps partial drafts. Rauchenberger makes a plausible argument for an Arabic draft of the whole section on the kingdom of Marrakesh (Rauch, 133–34), but even here there would have to be many adjustments for Italian readers.

57. *CGA*, 6v, 19r, 28r, 458r (he cannot remember all he once knew about chameleons). Ram, 25 ([*DAR*, 2r] omits reference to his not having seen a history book for ten years), 39–40 ([*DAR*, 5v] omits reference to Ibn Khaldun), 50, 453; Ép 12 ("histoire sainte" instead of "histoire"), 35, 47, 570–71.

58. Ibn Khaldun, *Muqaddimah*, lxxi.

59. *CGA*, 1r, 184v, 441v. Ram, 19, 199, 439; Ép, 3, 224, 553. Some examples: "la Pascha" for "Ramadan" (22r); "populo" (10r, 22v) and sometimes "sterpe" (25v) for "qabila" or "tribe"; "signori" (165r among many places) and sometimes "gentilhomini" (61r) for notables and leaders, including the shaykh; "sacerdoti," that is, "priest" (380r, 382r), for prayer-leader or imam, an especially misleading equivalent; "el Judice" for "judge" or "qadi"; "Doctori" (165v, 380r, 382r, and many places) for "faqih" and more accurately "homini Docti in la lege" (53r); "Pontefece" (12v, 200v) for "caliph," "khalifa." For *waqf* (or *habus*, the special Maghreb term), that is, the pious foundation in perpetuity, which is the financial basis for numerous buildings and institutions mentioned throughout the book, he gave no word. He did define the word "sharif": "nobile de la casata de Mucametto" (62r), "noble of the house of Muhammad."

60. For example, Yuhanna al-Asad's interesting account of the foundation and early history of Qayrawan in Tunisia was much shortened by Ramusio (*CGA*, 333r–334r; Ram, 331–32; Ép, 394–95).

61. *CEI*, 93. Sanuto, *Diarii*, 24:190–91, 25:142; Lucette Valensi, *Venise et la Sublime Porte. La naissance du despote* (Paris: Hachette, 1987), 11–23; Setton, *Papacy*, 3:155–56; Daniel Goffman, *The Ottoman Empire and Early Modern Europe* (Cambridge: Cambridge University Press, 2002), 46. John E. Wansbrough, "A Moroccan Amir's Commercial Treaty with Venice of the Year 913/1508," *Bulletin of the School of Oriental and African Studies* 25 (1962): 449–71.

62. *VIA*, 45v; *VIAHott*, 268.

63. *CGA*, 432v–433r. Ram, 429; Ép, 537–38.

64. Al-Hamadhani, *Maqamat*, trans. Prendergast, no. 27, "Al-Aswad," 110; *Livre des vagabonds*, trans. Khawam, no. 8, "La famille Aswad," 139.

CHAPTER FOUR · BETWEEN AFRICA AND EUROPE

1. *CGA*, 43r–v ("narrare le cose como sonno"). Ram, 66 ([*DAR*, 11v] see below, chapter 8, on Ramusio's additions to this quotation); Ép, 65.

2. *CGA*, 43v ("*Lo Cento Novelle*"). Ram, 66 ([*DAR*, 11v] with ornamentation of the story: "una brieve novelletta" instead of "*Lo Cento Novelle*"); Ép, 65 ("une courte historiette" instead of "*Les Cent Nouvelles*").

3. *CGA*, 43v–44r ("nel libro del cento novelle"). Ram, 66–67 ([*DAR*, 11v]: "un' altra brieve et piacevole novelletta" instead of "libro del cento novelle"); Ép, 66 ("une courte et amusante historiette").

4. The closest I have come is *Les cent et une nuits*, trans. M. Gaudefroy-Demombynes (Paris: Sindbad, 1982). The stories include neither the executioner's tale nor the bird story. Rather they have much overlap with the *Thousand and One Nights*. Though they presumably go back to an old Arabic collection, this translation is drawn from four modern Maghrebi manuscripts at the Bibliothèque Nationale de France, with no indication of origin. Thus, it is difficult to know what title the collection was given in the early sixteenth century (*Cent et une nuits*, 15–18).

5. D. Pinault, "*Alf layla wa-layla*," *EAL*, 1:69–77; Eva Sallis, *Sheherazade through the Looking Glass: The Metamorphosis of the "Thousand and One Nights"* (Surrey: Curzon Press, 1999), chaps. 1–2. The first published European translation of the entire text was made in French by Antoine Galland and published between 1704 and 1717; it was based on a fourteenth-century Arabic manuscript of Syrian provenance, now in the library of the University of Leiden (ibid., 3, 145). Petrus Alfonsi grew up in al-Andalus as the Jewish Moses and wrote his collection of tales, the *Disciplina Clericalis*, and other works after his conversion to Christianity.

On him and this text, see the "Introduction" by Eberhard Hermes to *The "Disciplina Clericalis" of Petrus Alfonsi* (London and Henley, England: Routledge and Kegan Paul, 1977) and "Introduction" by Jacqueline-Lise Genot-Bismuth to *Moïse le Séfarade alias Pierre d'Alphonse. La Discipline de Clergie* (St. Petersburg: Editions Evropeiski Dom and Paris: Éditions de Paris, 2001).

6. *Le Ciento Novelle Antike*, ed. Carlo Gualteruzzi (Bologna: Girolamo Benedetti, 1525). *The Novellino or One Hundred Ancient Tales*, ed. and trans. Joseph P. Consoli (New York and London: Garland, 1997). The bird story and the executioner tale are not in the alternate manuscript collections of *Il Novellino*, as this collection is now called (Sebastiano lo Negro, ed., *Novellino e conti del Duecento* [Turin: Unione Tipografico, 1963], 57–209); nor is the bird story among the animal fables that appeared in Girolamo Morlini's Latin collection, published in Naples in 1520 (Girolamo Morlini, *Novelle e favole*, ed. Giovanni Villani [Rome: Salerno Editrice, 1983]). The fifteenth-century French collection entitled *Les Cent Nouvelles Nouvelles* also contains no stories like the executioner tale or the story of the amphibian bird; Yuhanna al-Asad would probably never have heard of this collection, dedicated by its unknown author to the duke of Burgundy.

7. Hasan M. El-Shamy, *Folk Traditions of the Arab World. A Guide to Motif Classification*, 2 vols. (Bloomington and Indianapolis: Indiana University Press, 1995), K512, K520–539. 'Abd al-Rahman al-Sulami, *La courtoisie en Islam: Pour une meilleure fréquentation des gens*, trans. Tahar Gaïd (Paris: Éditions IQRA, 2001), 84: execution stopped because of generous action by one of those sentenced. Stith Thompson, *Motif-Index of Folk Literature*, rev. ed. (Copenhagen: Rosenkilde and Bagger, 1957), K512–K513. D. P. Rotunda, *Motif-Index of the Italian Novella in Prose* (Bloomington: Indiana University Press, 1942), K512. Harriet Goldberg, *Motif-Index of Medieval Spanish Folk Narrative* (Tempe, Ariz.: Medieval and Renaissance Texts and Studies, 1998), K512.

8. Ibn al-Muqaffaʿ, *Le livre de Kalila et Dimna*, trans. André Miquel (Paris: Klincksieck, 1957), especially nos. 393–493, "Les hiboux et les corbeaux." Farid-ud-Din ʿAttar, *Le langage des oiseaux*, trans. Garcin de Tassy (Paris: Sindbad, 1982). Annemarie Schimmel, *The Triumphal Sun: A Study of the Works of Jalaloddin Rumi* (Albany: SUNY Press, 1993), 76–77, 111, 113–124. None of these texts has a tale like Yuhanna al-Asad's bird story, though see Rumi on the ostrich, to be discussed below. *Le livre des ruses*, trans. René R. Khawam (Paris: Phébus, 1976), 17, 33. This book is entitled *Raqaʾiq al-hilal fi Daqaiq al-hiyal*, that is, *Cloaks of fine cloth for subtle ruses*. The one known manuscript, at the Bibliothèque Nationale de France, has a full table of contents but includes only half the chapters, and the one on animals is among the missing.

9. The ethnographer Claude Lefébure has heard tales in present-day Mo-

rocco that have some connection with the bird story themes: "Au trébuchet de la Description: Léon l'Africain ethnographe des Berbères du Maroc," paper presented at the Colloque "Léon l'Africain," EHESS, Paris, 22–24 May 2003, forthcoming in Pouillon and Zhiri, eds., *Léon l'Africain.*

10. ʿAmr ibn Bahr al-Jahiz, *Kitab al-Hayawan,* ed. ʿAbd-al-Salam Muhammad Harun, 7 vols. (Cairo, 1930–45), 4:321–23. Hasan M. El-Shamy, *Types of the Folktale in the Arab World. A Demographically Oriented Tale-Type Index* (Bloomington and Indianapolis: Indiana University Press, 2004), 0207D: Task evaded by altering identity; H0954.1: Ostrich's excuse for not carrying. Al-Jahiz also referred to Aristotle's comments on the difficulty of classifying this winged animal, which had characteristics both of a bird and a quadruped (*On the Parts of Animals* 4:14:697b; al-Jahiz, *Livre des animaux,* ed. and trans. Mohamed Mestiri and Soumaya Mestiri [Paris: Fayard, 2003], 217).

11. Schimmel, *Triumphal Sun,* 122–23.

12. René Basset, ed., *Loqman berbère avec quatre glossaires et une étude sur la légende de Loqman* (Paris: Ernest Leroux, 1890), xi–lxix. The wise Luqman is the subject of Sura 31 of the Qurʾan. Fable 1, "A Lion and Two Bulls," a ruse that succeeds; Fable 5, "The Lion and the Bull," a ruse that fails (*Fables de Lokman,* trans. M. Cherbonneau [Paris: Librairie Orientaliste Paul Geuthner, 1925], 12–13, 18–20).

13. *The Medici Aesop. Spencer MS 50. From the Spencer Collection of the New York Public Library,* facsimile edition with a translation by Bernard McTigue (New York: Harry Abrams, 1989), 132. The illustrated manuscript, with text in Greek, was in the library of Piero de' Medici in 1495. It is copied from the printed edition of 1483, which includes a Latin translation of Aesop made by Ranutio d'Arezzo, *Vita Esopi una cum suis Fabulis a Graeco in latinum translata* (Rome, 1483): the printed edition is dedicated to Lorenzo de' Medici (Léopold Hervieux, *Les Fabulistes latins depuis le siècle d'Auguste jusqu'à la fin du Moyen Âge,* 2 vols. [Paris: Firmin Didot, 1884–99], 269). There are two bat stories found in different editions of Aesop, this one ("Vespertilio et mustela") where the bat gets away with its ruse, and another one ("De Avibus et quadrupedibus") where the bat has to pay a penalty for switching sides in a battle between the birds and the four-footed animals. Jonathan Burton discusses this second version in connection with "Leo Africanus" in "'A Most Wily Bird': Leo Africanus, *Othello* and the Trafficking in Difference," in Ania Loomba and Martin Orkin, *Post-colonial Shakespeares* (London and New York: Routledge, 1998), 43–63. For deceptive birds in the European tradition, see Thompson, *Motif-Index,* K233.1; his examples of amphibians concern frogs, turtles, and crocodiles, A2160, A2214.5, B245, B645, G211.6, G303.3.3.7.

14. Wehr, 253; Joseph Schacht, *"Hiyal,"* EI2, 3:110–13. A.-L. de Prémare, ed., *La tradition orale du Mejdub: Récits et quatrains inédits* (Aix-en-Provence: Édisud, 1986), 138, 174, 255 (an example of "hila" in the expression of a sixteenth-century Moroccan folk saint). Micheline Galley and Zakia Iraqui Sinaceur, eds., *Dyab, Jha, La'âba: Le triomphe de la ruse. Contes marocains du fonds Colin* (Paris: Les Belles Lettres, 1994), 51–59, 116–81. Enid Welsford, *The Fool. His Social and Literary History* (London: Faber and Faber, 1935), 29–33. Nasreddin Hodja, *La sagesse afghane du malicieux Nasroddine,* trans. Dider Leroy (La Tour d'Aigues: Éditions de l'Aube, 2002), 5–13, 103. A fool figure, with similar characteristics, appears across the Islamic world with the name Nasreddin Hodja (the Turkish spelling) and variants, and with the name Djia and variants such as Djoha, Djouha, and the like.

15. Arberry, 1:81 (Arabic: "makra"), 121 (Arabic: "khada'a"); 2:334 (Arabic: "kaid," "kaiada"). Other examples from the Qur'an: 7:99, 7:183, 8:30, 13:42, 27:50, 43:79, 68:45. *Livre des ruses,* trans. Khawam, 11–12; Wehr, 266, 995, 1076.

16. QAn, Sura "Vacca," 56b, verse 53 [for 3:54]; Sura "De Mulieribus," 99a, verse 141 [for 4:142]; Sura "De Divisionibus," 156b, verse 99 [for 7:99], 164b, verse 181 [for 7:183]; Sura "De Spoliis," 170a, verse 29 [for 8:30]; Sura "De Tonitruis," 234a, verse 42 [for 13:42]; Sura "De Formicis," 370a, verse 53 [for 27:50]; Sura "De Ornamentis," 478, verse 78 [for 43:79]; Sura "De Polo," 598a, verses unnumbered [for 86:15–16].

17. EpiP, 33a, 34b. In this manuscript, the chapters and verses of the second letter to the Corinthians are properly located after the first letter to the Corinthians, but the title of the second letter is incorrectly "to the Thessalonians." I am grateful to Dr. Stefania Dodoni for checking this section of the manuscript for me.

18. Baldassare Castiglione, *The Book of the Courtier,* trans. Charles S. Singleton (Garden City, N.Y.: Doubleday, 1959), 1:18, 2:40; Burke, *Fortunes,* 23: Castiglione redrafted the *Courtier* in Rome in the early 1520s. Niccolò Machiavelli, *The Prince,* trans. Luigi Ricci and E.R.P. Vincent (New York: Random House, 1940), chap. 18, 64–65. Machiavelli finished the manuscript of *The Prince* in 1514; during the years Yuhanna al-Asad was in Rome, he was writing his *History of Florence* for Cardinal Giulio de' Medici, who would become Pope Clement VII in 1523. Francesco Guicciardini, *Maxims and Reflections of a Renaissance Statesman,* trans. Mario Domandi (New York: Harper and Row, 1965), nos. 103–5, p. 67. Guicciardini had a role as papal administrator and diplomat under Leo X and Clement VII.

19. CGA, 176v–178v. Ram, 193–95; Ép, 218–20. *AM,* 59r–60r. Yuhanna al-Asad described the master in Tunis as the son of the commentator

al-Marjani. But since al-Marjani lived in the late fourteenth century, the Tunis master must have been a grandson or great-grandson of the commentator.

20. *CGA*, 178v–179r. Ram, 195; Ép, 219–20. On the prohibition of astrology in Malikite law, see al-Qayrawani, *Risâla*, chap. 44, 243: "On ne devra observer les astres que pour en tirer des indications sur la direction de la qibla [direction toward which Muslims turn while praying, toward the Kaʿba] et sur les diverses divisions de la nuit. On devra s'en abstenir dans toute autre intention."

21. Fahd, *Divination arabe*, 243–45. Ibn Khaldun, *Muqaddimah*, 1:238–45, especially 242–45; 3:182–214, especially 213–14. H.P.J. Renaud, "Divination et histoire nord-africaine au temps d'Ibn Khaldun," *Hespéris* 30 (1943): 213–21. Zhiri, "Léon l'Africain lecteur d'Ibn Khaldun," to be published in Pouillon and Zhiri, eds., *Léon l'Africain*.

22. *CGA*, 22v. Ram, 43; Ép, 40.

23. *CGA*, 227r–v ("il vulgo de Affrica et di Betteca tengono le sue baptaglie scripte in Hystorie parte in versi et parte in proso al modo de le cose de Orlando infra li latina vulgari"). Ram, 238; Ép, 272.

24. Ibn Khaldun, *Histoire des Berbères et des dynasties musulmanes de l'Afrique septentrionale*, ed. Paul Casanova, trans. Mac Guckin de Slane, 4 vols. (Paris: Librairie Orientaliste Paul Geuthner, 1925–56), 1:65, 2:232, 235; accounts of the battle by al-Marrakushi and Ibn Abi Zera, ibid., 2:224 nn.1–2, 223 nn.1–2. Nor is this Hilal mentioned in the account of the battle of Las Navas de Tolosa (as the Spaniards always called it) by the great seventeenth-century historian of al-Andalus al-Maqqari (*History*, bk. 8, chap. 30).

25. Ibn Khaldun, *Muqaddimah*, 3:415–420 and 415 n.1631; *Berbères*, 1:41–44 summarizes some of the stories in the *Sirat Bani Hilal*. Micheline Galley, "Introduction" to Galley and Sinaceur, eds., *Dyab*, 35–37. Lucienne Saada, ed., *La Geste Hilalienne: Version de Bou Thadi (Tunisie)* (Paris: Gallimard, 1985); Roselyne Layla Grech, *Indexation de la Geste des Banu Hilal* (Algiers: Publications Universitaire, 1989).

26. There is a small error of memory or of knowledge in Yuhanna al-Asad's account when he locates the battle site—Las Navas de Tolosa/al-ʿUqab—in Catalonia rather than much farther south (*CGA*, 227v; Ram, 238; Ép, 272), but the Hilal figure does not seem to be due to a fault of memory or mere confusion. In the introductory section of *CGA*, Yuhanna al-Asad describes the invasion of the Banu Hilal and other Arab tribes as violent and destructive, a characterization found in other literature as well (*CGA*, 11r–12v; Ram, 31–33; Ép, 21–23; Ibn Khaldun, *Berbères*, 1:32–45; Abun-Nasr, *Maghrib*, 69–71). Yuhanna al-Asad refers to poetry of the Banu Hilal and other tribes, each celebrating their noble qualities, *CGA*, 18v; Ram, 39; Ép, 34.

27. Al-Masʿudi, *Prairies*, 2:345, no. 915; Miquel, *Géographie*, 2:357–58. Charlemagne is not mentioned by Ibn Khaldun. Peter V. Marinelli, *Ariosto and Boiardo: The Origins of "Orlando Furioso"* (Columbia: University of Missouri Press, 1987), chap. 3. Among friends and acquaintances mentioned by Ariosto in his final canto are Alberto Pio, a former schoolmate of Ariosto, and Ercole Gonzaga, bishop of Mantua and a patron of Jacob Mantino in the early 1520s (ibid., 100; Kaufmann, "Mantino," 35, 40, 221–23). Weil, *Lévita*, 176–81.

28. CGA, 146v. Ram, 168; Ép, 190. Delumeau, *Rome*, 81–82.

29. CGA, 147r. Ram, 168–69; Ép, 191. Ramusio inserted a sentence on women in the Fez hostelries, changing Yuhanna al-Asad's comparison of the cross-dressed men to European female prostitutes to a comparison between women prostitutes in Fez and in Europe and thereby weakening the reference to male prostitution. See below, chapter 7, for fuller treatment of sexuality and homosexual practice.

30. CGA, 223v–224v. Ram, 235; Ép, 268. On al-Manzari, see Abun-Nasr, *Maghrib*, 208–9, and John D. Latham, "The Reconstruction and Expansion of Tetuan: The Period of Andalusian Immigration," in *From Spain to Barbary. Studies in the History and Culture of the Muslim West* (London: Variorum Reprints, 1986), no. 4.

31. CGA, 130r–132r ("li Mori . . . sonno gente bestiale"), 218r (Asila: "in lanno 882 Dalhegera fu assaltata et occupata da li Portughesi et li sos Habitatori furno tutti menati captivi ad Portogallo"; date of 882/1477 incorrect for 876/1471). Ram, 153–54 (*DAR*, 30r–v), 230; Ép, 173–74, 261. Ramusio and Épaulard, following him, embroider the battle of al-Maʿmura considerably so as to give more credit to the Portuguese and enhance the perfidy of the Muslims. Ahmed Boucharb, master of the sources on the Portuguese invasion of North Africa, also notes the "neutrality" in Yuhanna al-Asad's description of these battles, "une neutralité troublante." Boucharb, "Conquête ibérique," forthcoming in Pouillon and Zhiri, eds., *Léon l'Africain*. Robinson, *Islamic Historiography*, 147–48; J. R. Hale, *Machiavelli and Renaissance Italy* (New York: Collier Books, 1960), chaps. 9–10.

32. CGA, 164v–165r. Ram, 184–85; Ép, 208–9.

33. Al-Qayrawani, *Risâla*, chap. 42, 234–35. Miquel, *Géographie*, 4:275. Al-Jahiz, *Le livre des avares*, trans. Charles Pellat (Paris: Éditions Maisonneuve et Larose, 1997), especially 97–113, "Histoire d'al-Harithi."

34. Barbara Ketcham Wheaton, *Savoring the Past: The French Kitchen and Table from 1300 to 1789* (Philadelphia: University of Pennsylvania Press, 1983), 54–55; Sergio Bertelli and Giuliano Crifò, eds., *Rituale, cerimoniale, etichetta* (Milan: Bompiani, 1985), chaps. 2–4. Desiderius Erasmus, *On Good Manners for Boys (De civilitate morum puerilium)*, trans. Brian McGregor, in *Collected Works of Erasmus* (Toronto: University of Toronto

Press, 1985), 25:282–83. Disgusting comportment at the table, including inappropriate wiping with the napkin, is condemned by Giovanni Della Casa's much reprinted *Galateo* (1558): *Galateo of Manners and Behaviours (1576)*, trans. Robert Peterson (Bari: Adriatica Editrice, 1997), 26–29.

35. *CGA*, 99v–101v. Ram, 123–25; Ép, 136–38.

36. *CGA*, 137r–202v (on Fez), quotations on 139v, 161r, 190r; 405r–419v (Cairo), quotations on 405r, 407r. Ram, 158–214, quotations on 162, 181, 204; 402–16, quotations on 402, 404; Ép, 182–241, quotations on 184, 205, 230; 503–19, quotations on 503, 505.

37. Luigi Balsamo, "Alberto Pio e Aldo Manusio: Editoria a Venezia e Carpi Fra '400 e '500," in *Società*, 1:133–66. *Psalterium Hebraeum, Graecum, Arabicum*, 2r: dedication of Agostino Giustiniani to Leo X, Genoa, August 1516. *Sapientissimi Philosophi Aristotelis Stagiritae. Theologia sive mistica Phylosophia secundum Aegyptios noviter Reperta et in Latinum Castigatissime redacto* (Rome: Jacobus Mazochius, 1519), A2r–B2r: Dedication of Franciscus Roseus of Ravenna to Leo X, January 1519. Alastair Hamilton, "Eastern Churches and Western Scholarship," in Anthony Grafton, ed., *Rome Reborn. The Vatican Library and Renaissance Culture* (Washington, D.C.: Library of Congress, New Haven: Yale University Press, and Vatican City, Biblioteca Apostolica Vaticana, 1993), 235–39. Weil, *Lévita*, 95–101; David Amram, *The Makers of Hebrew Books in Italy* (London: Holland Press, 1963), 109, 169, 241; Martin, "Giles of Viterbo," 210–11; Kaufmann, "Mantino," 34–39, 221–23.

38. Robinson, *Islamic Historiography*, 172–74. Pedersen, *Arabic Book*, 131–34. Muhsin Mahdi, "From the Manuscript Age to the Age of Printed Books," in Atiyeh, ed., *Book*, 1–4; Jacques Berque, "The Koranic Text: From Revelation to Compilation," ibid., 17–29; Franz Rosenthal, "'Of Making Many Books There Is No End:' The Classical Muslim View," ibid., 33–55; Seyyed Hosein Nasr, "Oral Transmission and the Book in Islamic Education: The Spoken and the Written Word," ibid., 57–70; Geoffrey Roper, "Faris al-Shidyaq and the Transition from Scribal to Print Culture in the Middle East," ibid., 209. Bloom, *Paper*, 91–122. Annie Vernay-Nouri, "Livres imprimés," in Marie-Geneviève Guesdon and Annie Vernay-Nouri, eds., *L'art du livre arabe* (Paris: Bibliothèque Nationale de France, 2001), 162–75. Abraham Haberman, "The Jewish Art of the Printed Book," in Cecil Roth, ed., *Jewish Art* (Greenwich, Conn.: New York Graphic Society, 1971), 165, 171 (Istanbul). Karl Schaefer, "Arabic Printing before Gutenberg. Block-printed Arabic Amulets," in Hanebutt-Benz et al., eds., *Middle Eastern Languages*, 123–28; Hartmut Bobzin, "From Venice to Cairo: On the History of Arabic Editions of the Koran (16th–20th Century)," ibid., 152–55. Moshe N. Rosenfeld, "The Development of Hebrew Printing in the Sixteenth and Seventeenth Centuries," in Leonard Singer Gold, ed., *A Sign and a Witness: 2000 Years of Hebrew*

Books and Illuminated Manuscripts (New York: New York Public Library and Oxford: Oxford University Press, 1988), 92–94 (Fez, Istanbul, Safed). Amram, *Hebrew Books*, 136–37 (Salonika, Istanbul).

39. Weil, *Lévita*, 230. Levita, *Thisbites*, 67–68. Khatibi and Sijelmassi, *Islamic Calligraphy*, 6–33. Israel Abrahams, *Jewish Life in the Middle Ages*, ed. Cecil Roth (London: Edward Goldston, 1932), 239–40.

40. *CGA*, 267r; 382r. Ram, 274, 379; Ép, 316, 468–69; Rauch, 280.

CHAPTER FIVE · CONCEIVING AFRICA

1. *CGA*, 1r. Ram, 19; Ép, 3. Other accounts of Ifricos in al-Bakri, *Afrique*, 48–49; Ibn Khaldun, *Berbères*, 1:28, 168.

2. Miquel, *Géographie*, 2:44 n.5, 131. Ibn Hawqal, *Configuration*, 64–65, 80, 85. Al-Muqaddasi, *Best Divisions*, 198–200. Al-Idrisi, *Première géographie*, 180, 304–5; al-Idrisi, *Maghrib*, 127, 133, 147. Ibn Khaldun, *Muqaddimah*, 1:9, 9 n.19, 130. Quotation from the history of the conquest of Egypt by Ibn ʿAbd al-Hakam (ninth century), in Ibn Khaldun, *Berbères*, 1:306.

3. Ptolemy, *Ptolemy's Geography*, 145 n.1. Harley and Woodward, eds., *History*, vol. 1: *Cartography in Prehistoric, Ancient, and Medieval Europe and the Mediterranean*, 316. *In hoc opere haec Continentur Geographiae Cl. Ptolemaei*, trans. Jacopo d'Angelo (Rome: Evangelista Tosino, 1508), Liber Quartus: Expositionem totius Aphricae, followed by the names of different regions of Africa; bk. 8, Aphricae Tabulae. *Claudii Ptholemaei Alexandrini Liber Geographiae cum Tabulis*, ed. Bernardo Silvano (Venice: Jacopo Pencio, 1511), +2r, D6r, bk. 8.

4. *CGA*, 213r, 350r, 439v–440r. Ram, 224, 349, 437; Ép, 254, 419, 551. Harley and Woodward, eds., *History*, vol. 2, bk. 1, 10. Al-Khwarizmi, *Afrika nach der arabischen Bearbeitung der "Geographia" des Claudius Ptolemaeus*, trans. Hans von Mžik (Vienna: Kaiserliche Akademie der Wissenschaften, 1916). Similarly, the Yemenite geographer al-Hamdani (tenth century), summing up Ptolemy's teaching for astrological purposes, used Ifriqiya in a limited sense for the area around Tunis, and Lubiya for the region of Abyssinia and the Land of the Blacks (Miquel, *Géographie*, 2:34–48).

5. Ibid., 2:35, 60. Al-Idrisi, *Première géographie*, 372–73.

6. Harley and Woodward, eds., *History*, vol. 1, chap. 18, and plates 19–21. Martin W. Lewis and Kären E. Wigen, *The Myth of Continents. A Critique of Metageography* (Berkeley and Los Angeles: University of California Press, 1997), 25–26.

7. Harley and Woodward, eds., *History*, vol. 2, bk. 1, 5–7. Ibn Hawqal, *Configuration*, 8–16. Ibn Khaldun, *Muqaddimah*, 1:109–11, frontispiece.

8. *CGA*, 1v. Ram, 20; Ép, 4.

9. Al-Idrisi, *Première géographie*, 458–64; Ibn Khaldun, *Muqaddimah*, 1:128–39. Al-Muqaddasi, *Best Divisions*, xxiii, 177–97. On the Greek theory of "klimata" and the role of "aqalim" in Arabic geographical thought, see Miquel, *Géographie*, 2:56–60; Harley and Woodward, eds., *History*, vol. 2, bk. 1, 94, 102, 146.

10. *CGA*, 26v, 74v. Ram, 48, 100; Ép, 44–45. In one instance, he uses "Ifrichia"—that is, not "Affrica"—to refer specifically to the area around Tunis (12v).

11. *CGA*, 1v–5v. Ram, 20–23; Ép, 4–10.

12. Levtzion and Hopkins, eds., *Early Arabic Sources*, 366–67.

13. *CGA*, 1r–v, 3r, 393v, 397v–398r, 433r. Ram, 19, 21, 390, 394, 429; Ép, 3, 6, 489, 494, 537. Miquel, *Géographie*, 135. Ibn Hawqal, *Configuration*, 129–62; Al-Muqaddasi, *Best Divisions*, 177–79; al-Idrisi, *Première géographie*, 114, 117–24; Ibn Khaldun, *Muqaddimah*, 1:125–26. Zhiri, *Miroir*, 14. Harley and Woodward, eds., *History*, vol. 1, 328.

14. *CGA*, 5v ("Apresso de li cosmographi et Hystoriogrophi Affrica antiguamente gia fu deshabitata excepto la terra negresca ma la Barbaria et la Numidia e stata molti seculi deshabitata"), 9r, 378r. Ram, 23, 28, 374–75; Ép, 10, 16, 463–64; Rauch, 264.

15. *CGA*, 5v–8v. Ram, 23–27; Ép, 10–15. Ibn Khaldun, *Berbères*, 1:168–85. On the myths regarding the origin of the Berbers and their cultural and political function, see Maya Shatzmiller, *The Berbers and the Islamic State* (Princeton, N.J.: Markus Wiener Publishers, 2000), chap. 2.

16. *CGA*, 5v, 8v–9r, 28r–v. Ram, 24, 27–28, 50; Ép, 11, 15–16, 47–48. Ibn Khaldun, *Berbères*, 1:168: "the word *berbera* means a mixture of unintelligible cries." Al-Muqaddasi, *Best Divisions*, 217.

17. *CGA*, 9v–26v. Ram, 28–48; Ép, 17–44. Yuhanna al-Asad gave the three major tribes as the "Chachim," the "Hilal," and "Machil" (13v). Épaulard points out that the "Chachim" are difficult to identify as a major tribe (26 n.167), though perhaps this is his transliteration for "Sulaym." Ibn Khaldun listed the major Arab tribal groups migrating to North Africa as the banu Hilal, the banu Sulaym, and the banu al-Makil (*Berbères*, 1:28, 115). Ibn Khaldun also categorized Arab immigrants to North Africa as "aʿrab mustaʿjam" (1:7).

18. *CGA*, 394r–395v. Ram, 390–92; Ép, 490–91. Al-Muqaddasi, *Best Divisions*, 177, 186.

19. *CGA*, 26v–27r, 47v–48r, 52v–53r, 57r, 61r, 62v, 78r, 79v–80r, 82v, 90v, 94r, 104r, 110r, 111v, 194v–195r, 254r, 326v ("et lo dicto officio lo usano tenere certi Judei ricchi"), 353r, 357r, 363r–v, 396r, 407r. Ram, 48, 71–72, 78, 82, 104–5, 108, 115, 118, 127, 133–34, 207–8, 262, 325 ([*DAR*, 67v–68r] refer-

ence to rich Jewish official omitted), 351, 355, 361, 392, 404; Ép, 45, 74–75, 81, 85–86, 112, 114, 117, 126, 131, 142, 147, 149, 234, 303, 387, 423, 428, 436–37, 492, 505. On the Karaite Jews in the Islamic world, see David Biale, ed., *Cultures of the Jews. A New History* (New York: Schocken Books, 2002), 321–22. Modern scholarship accounting for the Jewish presence in Africa uses the same three processes as those given by Yuhanna al-Asad: an initial ancient immigration from Palestine, conversion of indigenous Berbers and black populations, and subsequent immigration movements (Brignon et al., *Histoire*, 52). For the status of dhimmis, see Mark R. Cohen, *Under Crescent and Cross: The Jews in the Middle Ages* (Princeton, N.J.: Princeton University Press, 1994), chap. 3.

20. CGA, 6v, 18v–19r, 395r, 429v. Ram, 25, 39–40, 391, 425; Ép, 12, 34–35, 491, 532. Ibn Khaldun, *Berbères*, 1:iii–vii, 4, 169–84.

21. Don Cameron Allen, *The Legend of Noah* (Urbana: University of Illinois Press, 1963), 77–78. David Woodward, "Medieval *Mappaemundi*," in Harley and Woodward, eds., *History*, vol. 1, chap. 18. Benjamin Braude, "The Sons of Noah and the Construction of Ethnic and Geographical Identities in the Medieval and Early Modern Periods," *William and Mary Quarterly* 54, no. 1 (Jan. 1997): 103–41. Suzanne Conklin Akbari, "From Due East to True North: Orientalism and Orientation," in *The Postcolonial Middle Ages*, ed. Jeffrey Jerome Cohen (New York: St. Martin's Press, 2000), 19–34. Miquel, *Géographie*, 2:60, 115, 142. Marcel Cohen, "Ham," *EI2*, 3:104–5. Jonathan Schorsch, *Jews and Blacks in the Early Modern World* (Cambridge: Cambridge University Press, 2004), chaps. 1, 6. Levtzion and Hopkins, eds., *Early Arabic Sources*, 20 (curse on Canaan, no mention of color, servitude), 31, 34 (curse on Ham of blackness and servitude), 50, 94, 172, 212 (mentions curse of blackness in regard to Ham but says not accurate; color due to clime in which people live; no mention of servitude), 332–33. Al-Tabari, *The History of al-Tabari*, vol. 2, *Prophets and Patriarchs*, trans. William M. Brinner (Albany: State University of New York Press, 1985), 11–12, 14, 19, 21; al-Tabari, *La Chronique, Histoire des prophètes et des rois*, trans. (from the Persian abridgment of al-Balʿami) Hermann Zotenberg (Arles: Actes Sud, 1984), 1:102, 107–8. Al-Masʿudi, *Prairies*, paras. 66–72 (para. 67: the curse of Ham, the blessing of Shem), 793, 806, 844, 910, 1103, 1167–69. Ibn Hawqal, *Configuration*, 150. Al-Idrisi, *Première géographie*, Al-Muqaddasi, *Best Divisions*, 177: "Misr, the son of Ham, the son of Noah (on whom be peace) colonized [Egypt]." Ibn Khaldun, *Muqaddimah*, 1:169–73 (refutation of blackness as due to curse of Ham); *Berbères*, 1:178 (quoting al-Bakri on the blackness of Ham). John Ralph Willis, "The Ideology of Enslavement in Islam," in Willis, ed., *Slaves*, 1:8–9; Akbar Muhammad, "The Image of Africans in Arabic Literature: Some Unpublished Manuscripts," ibid., 1:56; John Hunwick and Eve Trout Powell, eds., *The African Diaspora in the Mediterranean Lands of Islam* (Princeton, N.J.: Markus Wiener Publishers, 2002), xx, 37–40.

22. Hunwick and Powell, eds., *African Diaspora*, xviii, 40–42: the text of al-Suyuti (d. 911/1505) was entitled *Raising the Status of the Ethiopians*. Hunwick, "Islamic Law," in Marmon, ed., *Slavery*, 48–59; Willis, "Ideology," in Willis, ed., *Slaves*, 4–5.

23. *CGA*, 9r, 10r, 19r, 432r. Ram, 28–29, 39, 428; Ép, 16, 18, 34, 534. Ibn Khaldun, *Berbères*, 1:7. On the diverse meanings of "Chaldean" in the sixteenth century, see Levi Della Vida, *Ricerche*, 132 n.1.

24. *CEI*, 46–48. Blachère, *Histoire*, 1:70–82. Consuelo López-Morillas, "Language," in Menocal et al., eds., *Literature*, 37–40.

25. Al-Muqaddasi, *Best Divisions*, 186. Ibn Khaldun, *Muqaddimah*, 3:316–52.

26. Ibid., 3:414–80. *CGA*, 23v–24r. Ram, 44–45; Ép, 41.

27. Al-Qayrawani, *Risâla*, 139–41. Muhammad ibn Idris al-Shafiʿi, *La Risâla, les fondements du droit musulman*, trans. Lakhdar Souami (Paris: Sindbad, 1997), 239–41. Bouhdiba, *Sexualité*, 24–25. Cohen, *Under Crescent*, 133; Bruce Masters, *Christians and Jews in the Ottoman Arab World: The Roots of Sectarianism* (Cambridge: Cambridge University Press, 2001), 21–22. David Nirenberg, *Communities of Violence: Persecution of Minorities in the Middle Ages* (Princeton, N.J.: Princeton University Press, 1996), 136–37.

28. Cohen, *Under Crescent*, 34–35, 109, 129–30. Nirenberg, *Communities*, 136–39. Marmon, "Domestic Slavery," in Marmon, ed., *Slavery*, 4.

29. Nirenberg, *Communities*, 132–40, 150, 182–84. Meyerson, *Muslims*, 220–23.

30. Manuela Marín, *Mujeres en al-Ándalus* (Madrid: Consejo Superior de Investigaciones Científicas, 2000), 143–44, 425. On prostitutes in al-Andalus, ibid., 302, 673–74. On the Christian population, free and slave, of Granada, and the important Jewish population of Granada in the last centuries of Muslim rule, see Arié, *Espagne*, 314–38. On Granadan Muslims with Christian wives, see Gaignard, *Maures*, 121. On prostitution in Fez, *CGA*, 147r, 188r; Ram, 169; Ép, 191 (differs from *CGA*), 228, and chapter 7 below.

31. Mary Lindemann, *Medicine and Society in Early Modern Europe* (Cambridge: Cambridge University Press, 1999), 55–57. Jon Arrizabalaga, John Henderson, and Roger French, *The Great Pox. The French Disease in Renaissance Europe* (New Haven and London: Yale University Press, 1998), chap. 7.

32. *CGA*, 39r–v: "alcuni tristi de quilli Mori se mescolorono con le Femine de li ditz. Judei." Ram, 61–62 ([*DAR*, 10v] changes and omissions from *CGA*); Ép, 60–61.

33. Abraham ben Salomon Adrutiel, *Sefer ha-Kabbala*, in Yolanda Moreno Koch, trans. and ed., *Dos Crónicas Hispanohebreas del Siglo XV* (Barcelona: Riopiedras Ediciones, 1992), 107–9. Andres Bernaldez, *Memorias*

del reinado de los Reyes Catolics, ed. Manuel Gomez-Moreno and Juan de M. Carriazo (Madrid, 1962), chap. 113, especially p. 261. According to both accounts, a terrible fire broke out in the Jewish quarter some months after the refugees arrived, followed by famine and then the plague, which took the lives of both Jews and Muslims. Adrutiel stresses that in contrast with the Christian authorities along the African coast, the Wattasid sultan Muhammad al-Shaykh, "benevolent among the gentiles," had been welcoming to the Jews (*Sefer*, 70, 107).

34. Bernard Rosenberger and Hamid Triki, "Famines et épidémies au Maroc aux XVIe et XVIIe siècles," *Hespéris Tamuda* 14 (1973): 115.

35. Anna Foa, "The New and the Old: The Spread of Syphilis," in Edward Muir and Guido Ruggiero, eds., and Margaret Gallucci, trans., *Sex and Gender in Historical Perspective* (Baltimore and London: Johns Hopkins University Press, 1990), 35–37.

36. *CGA*, 432r–v. Ram, 428; Ép, 537.

37. Al-Qayrawani, *Risâla*, 140–41. R. Brunschvig, "ʿAbd," *EI2*, 1:25–30. Shaun E. Marmon, "Concubinage, Islamic," in Joseph Strayer, ed., *Dictionary of the Middle Ages*, 13 vols. (New York: Charles Scribner & Sons, 1982–89), 3:527–29. Marmon, "Domestic Slavery," in Marmon, ed., *Slavery*, 4. Baber Johansen, "The Valorization of the Human Body in Muslim Sunni Law," in Devin J. Stewart, Baber Johansen, and Amy Singer, *Law and Society in Islam* (Princeton, N.J.: Markus Wiener Publishers, 1996), 80, 84. Powers, *Law*, 27–28.

38. *CGA*, 354r. Ram, 352 ([*DAR*, 73r] omits reference to the marriage of the slaves, though slaves were allowed by law to marry in medieval Italy; Epstein, *Speaking of Slavery*, 64, 97); Ép, 424 (omits reference to marriage of slaves). Another example: *CGA*, 63v, from Tagowost in the Sus region of southern Morocco, a market town for trade with the Land of the Blacks: "the women there are very beautiful and charming and in the city are many brown men, born of the whites and the blacks." Ram, 89; Ép, 94.

39. *CGA*, 365r–v. Ram, 362; Ép, 439. Ibn Khaldun, *Muqaddimah*, 1:170–73.

40. Wehr, 294–96, 1062–63.

41. Al-Muqaddasi, *Best Divisions*, 153–54. See also his treatment of the "magnificence" of al-Fustat (Cairo), "the most important of the metropoles of the Muslims," along with its disagreeable qualities, including "their debased language" (183).

42. *CGA*, 324r–v. Ram, 324; Ép, 385. On homoerotic and lesbian "excess" in Fez, see chapter 4 above and especially chapter 7 below.

43. *CGA*, 416v. Ram, 413 ([*DAR*, 86r] omits most of the section on dishonest talk in Cairo); Ép, 516 (omits much of the original).

44. Johansen, "Valorization," in Stewart et al., *Law*, 79. Bouhdiba, *Sexualité*, 110–11. Roded, ed., *Women*, 161–67 (excerpt from al-Ghazali's recommendations on the "etiquette of marriage"). Yves Linant de Bellefonds, *Traité de droit musulman comparé*, 3 vols. (Paris and The Hague: Mouton, 1965–73), 2:297–99. Ibn Iyas, *Journal*, 318–24 (case of adultery). Al-Hamadhani, *Livre des vagabonds*, séance 26, "La Syrie," 127–29 (omitted from many Arabic editions of the text [127 n.1], and omitted from Prendergast's English translation). The wife accuses the vagabond poet of inadequate sexual performance as a ruse to goad him into admitting intercourse with her and thus marriage; her strategy shows that this argument could be used before the judge.

45. *CGA*, 52v–53v, 96r–v. Ram, 78–79, 120–21; Ép, 80–81, 133–34.

46. *CGA*, 362r. Ram, 359–60; Ép, 435.

47. *CGA*, 380r–v. Ram, 377; Ép, 466. The exact site of the seat of royal government is not surely known by scholars today (Dunn, *Ibn Battuta*, 301).

48. *CGA*, 114r–115v ("non hano ne Judice ne sacerdoti ne Persona che habbia virtu alcuna"), 390v. Ram, 136–38, 387; Ép, 152–53, 482; Rauch, 316.

49. *CGA*, 312v. Ram, 314; Ép, 372.

50. *CGA*, 19r–22r. Ram, 40–43; Ép, 35–39.

51. *CGA*, 18v, 22v, 23v–24r. Ram, 39, 43–45; Ép, 34, 40–41.

52. On Islamic traditions in regard to the Blacks and the Land of the Blacks, see Bernard Lewis, *Race and Color in Islam* (New York: Harper and Row, 1971); Willis, ed., *Slaves*; Miquel, *Géographie*, 2:140–47; Aziz al-Azmeh, "Barbarians in Arab Eyes," *Past and Present* 134 (1992): 3–18. Ibn Khaldun, *Muqaddimah*, 1:116–21, 167–76.

53. Arberry, 2:107, 232. QAn, Sura "De Roma," 398a, verse 20; Sura "De Cameris," 524a, verse 13 (with several corrections by Yuhanna al-Asad).

54. Ibn Ishaq (d. ca. 150/767), *La Vie du Prophète Muhammad, l'Envoyé d'Allah*, version of al-Bakka'i, ed. Ibn Hisham (d. ca. 218/833), trans. ʿAbdurrahman Badawi, 2 vols. (Beirut: Éditions Albouraq, 2001) 1:5. Lewis, *Race*, 6–7, 18–22. Hunwick, "Islamic Law," in Marmon, ed., *Slavery*, 51.

55. Al-Masʿudi, *Prairies*, paras. 170, 871–72 (among other negative comments about the Zanj: strong odor, large genitalia, brains "imperfectly organized, from which results the feebleness of their intellect." He does concede, however, that they express themselves with eloquence in their own language). Charles Pellat, *The Life and Works of Jahiz: Translations of Selected Texts*, trans. Charles Pellat and D. M. Hawke (London: Routledge and Kegan Paul, 1969), 195–97. Lewis, *Race*, 15–18. Miquel, *Géographie*, 2:143–46. Muhammad, "Image of Africans," in Willis, ed., *Slaves*, 1:48–51; Hunwick and Powell, eds., *African Diaspora*, xix–xx, citing other texts.

56. See, for instance, Levtzion and Hopkins, eds., *Early Arabic Sources*,

no. 22, 62–87 (Al-Bakri), no. 38, 181–94 (Ibn Saʿid), nos. 46–47, 252–76 (Al-ʿUmari), no. 53, 333–42 (Ibn Khaldun; the editors point to the enlarged description of Mali on the basis of oral evidence, given in the author's revised manuscript of 796/1393–94, pp. 317–18). Ibn Battuta, *Black Africa*.

57. Rauchenberger provides a useful introduction to and summary of the contents of all the sections on the Blacks (Rauch, 172–234) as well as a comparison of Giovanni Leone's text on the Blacks with Ramusio's edition (239–327).

58. CGA, 43r. Ram, 65–66; Ép, 65.

59. CGA, 376v–377r. Ram, 373–74; Ép, 461–62; Rauch, 258–61.

60. Ram, 373–74 (*DAR*, 77v); Ép, 461–62. *Historiale Description de l'Afrique, tierce partie du monde . . . Escrite de nôtre tems* [sic] *par Iean Leon, African*, trans. Jean Temporal (Lyon: Jean Temporal, 1556/1557), 321–22. *Ioannis Leonis Africani, De Totius Africae Descriptione Libri IX*, trans. John Florian (Antwerp: Jan de Laet, 1556), 247r–v. The English translation of this section puts several sentences in the past, which makes better sense in context, then moves into the present: *A Geographical Historie of Africa, Written in Arabicke and Italian by Iohn Leo a More, borne in Granada, and brought up in Barbarie*, trans. John Pory (London: George Bishop, 1600), 284–85.

61. CGA, 388v–389r. Ram, 386; Ép, 480; Rauch, 308–10.

62. CGA, 387r–v. Ram, 383–84; Ép, 477–78. On color prejudice, in addition to the sources cited in note 52 above, see John S. Trimingham, *A History of Islam in West Africa* (Oxford: Oxford University Press, 1959), 31 and app. 3; E. Lévi-Provençal, *Histoire de l'Espagne Musulmane*, 3 vols. (Paris: Maisonneuve, 1950, repr. 1967), 3:178. Elena Lourie, "Black Women Warriors in the Muslim Army Besieging Valencia and the Cid's Victory: A Problem of Interpretation," *Traditio* 55 (2000): 181–209.

63. Ibn Battuta, *Black Africa*, 59, 68–69. Dunn, *Ibn Battuta*, 304–6. Levtzion and Hopkins, eds., *Early Arabic Sources*, 47 ("very comely slave girls"), 153 ("God has endowed the slave girls there with laudable characteristics, both physical and moral . . . their bodies are smooth, their black skins are lustrous, their eyes are beautiful, their noses well shaped, their teeth white").

64. CGA, 63r–v, 354r, 381r. Ram, 89, 352, 378; Ép, 94, 424, 467; Rauch, 276. On the appearance of the slave woman and the examination of her body by potential buyers at the slave market, see Brunschvig, "ʿAbd," *EI2*, 1:32, and Johansen, "Valorization," in Stewart et al., *Law*, 80.

65. CGA, 383r ("homo nigrissimo ma valentissimo, savio, et justo"). Ram, 380; Ép, 470; Rauch, 284.

66. *CGA*, 41v. Ram, 64; Ép, 63.

67. *CGA*, 378r–382v. Ram, 375–79; Ép, 464–69; Rauch, 264–82.

68. Brunschvig, "ʿAbd," *EI2*, 1:26. Marmon, "Slavery, Islamic World," in Strayer, *Dictionary*, 11:332. Hunwick, "Islamic Law," in Marmon, ed., *Slavery*, 44–45.

69. *CGA*, 197r, 199r, 224r–v, 282r, 326v. Ram, 210–11, 235, 326, 287; Ép, 236, 238, 268, 335, 387.

70. *CGA*, 420r–v. Ram, 416; Ép, 520.

71. *CGA*, 376v–377r, 380r–v ("ingeniosi" is spelled "igneniosi"). Ram, 373–74, 377; Ép, 462, 466; Rauch, 258–60, 272. Levtzion and Hopkins, eds., *Early Arabic Sources*, 77–80; al-Bakri, *Afrique*, 324–28.

72. On European concepts of Africa in the opening decades of the sixteenth century, see the splendid pages of Zhiri, *Miroir*, 16–25. Strabo, *The Geography*, trans. H. L. Jones, 8 vols. (London: William Heinemann and Cambridge, Mass.: Harvard University Press, 1960–67), bk. 17 (on Egypt, Ethiopia, and regions of Libya). Pliny the Elder, *L'Histoire naturelle*, vol. 5, chaps. 1–46 (L'Afrique du Nord), trans. Jehan Desanges (Paris: Les Belles Lettres, 1980). Pliny the Elder, *Histoire naturelle*, trans. É. Littré, 2 vols. (Paris: Firmin Didot, 1865), 1:325, bk. 8, para. 17: "Aussi y voit-on se produire des formes diverses d'animaux, les femelles s'accouplant de gré ou de force avec des mâles de toute espèce; de là vient cette façon de parler proverbiale en Grèce: L'Afrique produit toujours quelque chose de nouveau." An example of the skimpy knowledge of Africa is Pierre d'Ailly's *Imago Mundi*, a text that much influenced Columbus: *Ymago Mundi*, trans. Edmond Buron, 3 vols. (Paris: Librairie Orientale et Américaine Maisonneuve, 1930), chaps. 21, 32–37. Joannes Boemus, *Gli Costumi, le Leggi et l'usanze di tutte le Genti*, trans. L. Fauno (Venice: Michele Tramezino, 1543 [1st ed. in Latin, Augsburg, 1520]),*viiir, 5r, 17r–v, 21v–22r, 26v. Dedication of Jean Temporal to François, Dauphin of France, *Historiale Description*, *2r–v: "choses nouvelles et non veües."

73. *CGA*, 378v (the Portuguese call the area "Ghenia"); Rauch, 266. Ram, 376; Ép, 464. Levtzion and Hopkins, eds., *Early Arabic Sources*, 366–67. Gregory C. McIntosh, *The Piri Reis Map of 1513* (Athens, Ga., and London: University of Georgia Press, 2000), 25, 50, 52, 174 n.5. In his *Book of Navigation*, completed in Istanbul in 931/1525, Piri Reis discusses at some length the Portuguese rounding of the Cape of Good Hope (*Kitab-I Bahriye*, 39–41). The sea route around the tip of Africa appeared on the Martin Behaim globe of 1492. Ptolemy had believed that Africa and Asia were connected by an unknown land bridge, and some Ptolemaic maps following his tradition in the early sixteenth century continued to show it, while also adding "tabulae novellae" (new maps) representing the discovery of open sea to the south of Africa. Claudius Ptolemy, *Geographicae*

enarrationis Libri Octo, ed. Wilibald Pirckheimer, with annotations and corrections by Joannes Regiomontanus (Strasbourg: Johann Grueninger and Johann Koberger, 1525), tabulae of Africa.

74. Further discussion on this matter is in François-Xavier Fauvelle-Aymar and Bertrand Hirsch, "Le 'pays des Noirs' selon Jean-Léon l'Africain: Géographie mentale et logiques cartographiques," Colloque "Léon l'Africain" (EHESS, Paris, 22–24 August 2003), forthcoming in Pouillon and Zhiri, eds., *Léon l'Africain*.

CHAPTER SIX • BETWEEN ISLAM AND CHRISTIANITY

1. *CGA*, 389r ("alcuni de li dicti Montanari non tengono Fedé alcuna ne christiana ne Judea ne Mucamottana"). Ram, 386 ([*DAR*, 80r] "sono huomini che non tengono fede alcuna, nè cristiana nè giudea nè macomettana"); *Historiale Description*, 330 ("ils n'ont aucune cognoissance de quelque Foy que ce soyt tant Chrétienne, Iudaïque que Mahommetane"); *Geographical Historie*, 293 ("they embrace no religion at all, being neither Christians, Mahumetans, nor Iewes, nor of any other profession"). Only the Latin translator, John Florian, could not bear to keep Christian in a series with the other two. *De Totius Africae Descriptione*, 441 ("Nullam omnino neque Mahumeticam neque Iudaicam neque aliam denique fidem habent"). Arberry, 1:139; QAn, Sura "De Mensa," 116b, verse 75 [for 5:59]; this verse is not well translated by Joannes Gabriel and is inadequately corrected by Yuhanna al-Asad. *CEI*, 27.

2. *CGA*, 26v–27v. Ram, 48–49; Ép, 44–47. The phrase "circa 10 anni do poi la morte di Mucametto tutta la Barbaria deventorono Mucamettani" is clear in *CGA*, but this is an impossible date, and in contradiction with what Yuhanna al-Asad goes on to say about Berber rebellion. Ramusio gives it as "doppo la morte di Maumetto cerca dugento anni," that is, "two hundred years" (*DAR*, 7v).

3. *CGA*, 27v. Ram, 49; Ép, 46–47. Ibn Khaldun, *Berbères*, 1:218, 224. Abun-Nasr, *Maghrib*, 26–50.

4. Julien, *Histoire*, 1:185–92.

5. Ram, 48–49. DAR, 8r.

6. *Historiale Description*, 29–30. Temporal also added anti-Islamic sentiment to Ramusio's rendering of the conversion of Berber and Black kingdoms at the opening of book 5 (321): "les peuples de Luntune et Libye par les paroles deceptives et hypocrisie dissimulee d'un predicateur furent tous subvertis et reduits à la pernicieuse et damnable secte de Mahommet" ("by the deceptive words and dissimulated hypocrisy of a preacher the peoples of Luntuna and Libya were all subverted and reduced to the pernicious and damnable sect of Muhammad"). Temporal began his career in the atelier of the publishing house of the Gabiano family, which

became one of the most important Reformed families in Lyon. In 1558, now a merchant-publisher on his own, Temporal published a French translation of Flavius Josephus's History, made by the then Protestant François Bourgoing. In 1564 and 1565 he was among the witnesses signing a Protestant will and a Protestant marriage contract, together with other loyal supporters of the Reformed Church (Archives départementale du Rhône, 3E6942, 468r–v; 3E5295, 1565).

7. *De Totius Africae Descriptione*, 22v–23r. *Geographical Historie*, 27–28.

8. Juan Andrés, *Opera chiamata Confusione della Setta Machumetana, composta in lingua Spagnola, per Giovan Andrea gia Moro et Alfacqui, della citta di Sciativa* [sic for *Játiva*], *hora per la divina bontà Christiano e Sacerdote*, trans. Dominco de Gaztelu (Seville, 1540), 4r–5r. The first Spanish edition was published in Valencia in 1515, the first edition in Italian in Venice in 1537. Juan Andrés may also be the reckonmaster who published *Sumario breve de la practica de la arithmetica* in Valencia in 1515, with a second edition at Seville in 1537 (Jochen Hoock and Pierre Jeannin, *Ars Mercatoria. Eine analytische Bibliographie*, vol. 1, *1470–1600* [Paderborn: Schöningh, 1991], A6.1). Hartmut Bobzin, "Juan Andrés und sein Buch *Confusion dela secta mahomatica* (1515)," in Martin Forstner, ed., *Festgabe für Hans-Rudolf Singer* (Frankfurt: Peter Lang, 1991), 528–48.

9. *CGA*, 464v, 468v.

10. Guillaume Postel, *De la Republique des Turcs: et . . . des meurs et loys de tous Muhamedistes, par Guillaume Postel Cosmopolite* (Poitiers: Enguilbert de Marnef, 1560), 56–65, 75–106. Similar expression is found in the *Cosmographie de Levant* by the Franciscan André Thevet: e.g., "The number of parishes of the devil [in Cairo], that is mosques, goes up to 1002, so has Satan multiplied his synagogues" (*Cosmographie de Levant . . . Revue et augmentee* [Lyon: Jean de Tournes and Guillaume Gazeau, 1556], 142, fascimile edition with an excellent introduction and notes by Frank Lestringant [Geneva: Librairie Droz, 1985]). The remarkable account of the naturalist Pierre Belon, rich in information about animals, plants, minerals, and human customs in the Levant, opens its chapter on the Qur'an: "Toutes les superstitions et foles cerémonies des Turcs proviennent des enseignements de l'Alcoran" (Pierre Belon, *Les observations de plusieurs singularitez et choses memorables, trouvées en Grece, Asie, Iudée, Arabie et autres pays estranges . . . Reveuz de nouveau* [Paris: Gilles Corrozet, 1555], 172v). On this literature, see Frédéric Tinguely, *L'Écriture du Levant à la Renaissance. Enquête sur les voyageurs français dans l'empire de Soliman le Magnifique* (Geneva: Librairie Droz, 2000).

11. Hoca Saduddin Efendi (1533–99), *Tac ul-Tevarih*, 3 vols. (Istanbul, 1862–64), 1:419; *Tacu't-Tevarih*, trans. Ismet Parmaksizoglu, 3 vols. (Istanbul,

1974–79), 2:273. Translation given by Bernard Lewis, *The Muslim Discovery of Europe* (London: Phoenix, 1994), 30–31.

12. Thomas D. Goodrich, ed. and trans., *The Ottoman Turks and the New World: A Study of "Tarih-I Hind-I Garbi" and Sixteenth-Centuy Ottoman Americana* (Wiesbaden: Otto Harrassowitz, 1990), 151–52.

13. *CGA*, 9v, 48r, 227v, 343r (the scribe, perhaps following Yuhanna al-Asad's manuscript, used an unconventional abbreviation for "Christo"—x with a superscript o). Ram, 28 ([*DAR*, 3r] by error says "400 de lhegira" instead of the correct 24), 72, 238, 340; Ép, 17, 75, 272, 406. A Muslim victory that took place during Yuhanna al-Asad's years in Italy and that was described to him when he was in Naples, he dates "in lanno 1520 millesimo de christiani," "in the year 1520 by the reckoning of the Christians" (*CGA*, 231r; Ram, 241; Ép, 275–76). In a colophon, Yuhanna al-Asad dates his work "in Roma alli 10 di Marzo 1516" (*CGA*, 464v); Ramusio adds "L'anno di Cristo" (*DAR*, 95v; Ram, 460). See figures 9–10.

14. *CGA*, 27r–v, 417v–418r; Ram, 48–49 ([*DAR*, 7v] "Maumetto" several times, "Maumettani," once "Macomettani"), 414 ([*DAR*, 86r] both "Macometto" and "Mahumetto"). Yuhanna al-Asad used both "Mucametto" and "Mucamed" ("Mucamet," "Muchamed") to refer to the Fez sultan Muhammad al-Burtughali and the Almohad caliph Muhammad al-Nasir (*CGA*, 73v, 91v, 216v, 218r–v, 221r, 319r); but the Prophet is always "Mucametto." Battisti and Alessio, *Dizionario*, 2301, 2357, 2395. Manlio Cortelazzo, Paolo Zolli, and Michele Cortelazzo, *Il Nuovo Etomologico: Dizionario Etimologico della Lingua Italiano* (Bologna: Zanichelli, 1999), 931, 950. Neither dictionary gives an entry for Mucametto.

15. Battisti and Alessio, *Dizionario*, 4:2538. Cortelazzo et al., *Dizionario*, 1020. Neither dictionary gives an entry for "mucamettani."

16. Cornell, *Realm*, xxxviii–xxxix, 199–217.

17. *CGA*, 26v, 27v, 376v, 417v. Ram, 48, 49, 373 ([*DAR*, 77v) "se fece Mahumettano," "si fecero Mahumettani"), 414. Ramusio ignored Yuhanna al-Asad's spelling and used "maumettani" or "mahumettani" and sometimes "macomettani." See note 14 above.

18. *CGA*, 173r ("in laude de Dio et de li soio Propheta Mucametto"), 180v ("la lege del Propheta"), 181r ("la lege et fede del Propheta"), 206r ("le parole de loro Propheti"). Ram, 191 ([*DAR*, 39r] "in lode di Dio et del propheta Maumetto"); 196 ([*DAR*, 40r–v] "della legge del propheta," section much shortened by Ramusio); 218 ([*DAR*, 45r] "col testimonio di Mahumetto" instead of "Propheta"); Ép, 216, 221, 246.

19. Al-Masʿudi, *Prairies*, 1:1, 9, 73, 248. Al-Idrisi, *Première géographie*, 57–58, 97, 108, 114, 124, 244, 351, 416, 457. Al-Muqaddasi, *Best Divisions*, 1, 31, 41, 63. Ibn Khaldun, *Muqaddimah*, 1:3–5, 14, 85, 245, 310, 351, 380, 414.

20. *CGA*, 44v, 432v, 455r ("regratiando Dio"), 468v. Ram, 68 ([*DAR*, 12r] changes text considerably, omits reference to God), 429, 450 ([*DAR*, 93r] changes crocodile story a little; omits "regratiando Dio"); omits table of contents and final colophon; Ép, 69, 538, 567, omits colophon. The final colophon in *CGA* reads: "Explicit tabula huius operis prefati Joannis Leonnis feliciter semper Deo optimo laus, Gloria, Decus, et honor, seculorum secula Amen." On the use of *Amin* in Muslim prayer, see *CEI*, 40–41.

21. *CGA*, 92v–93r. Ram, 117; Ép, 129. To live up fully to Islamic criteria, the prayer of Sultan Muhammad al-Burtughali would have included references to the greatness of God and other formulaic expressions not given by Yuhanna al-Asad.

22. *CGA*, 395v–396v: "et do poi la Nativita di christo li egiptiani pure deventorono christiani . . . et do poi la venuta de la Pestilentia di Mucametto el dicto Re fu preso di Mucamettani da un capitano chiamata Hamr." Ram, 392–93; Ép, 491–93. *Historiale Description*, 336.

23. *CGA*, 401r ("Propheta et Re secondo la pazia di Mucametto nel corano"). Ram, 398; Ép 498. Ramusio omits the offensive "folly"; *DAR*, 82v: "gran propheta et Re, si come essi leggono nell'Alcorano." Possibly the phrase did not appear in a second manuscript. See below, chapter 8, for further discussion of this matter.

24. *CGA*, 81r–v, 179v–181r, 185r ("uno setto per lo universo mundo"), 417v–418v. Ram, 107, 196–97, 200, 414–15; Ép, 116, 220–21, 225, 517–18.

25. *CGA*, 417v–418v. Ram, 414–15; Ép, 517–18. Yuhanna al-Asad described the Shafi'ite chief qadi as the most important in Mamluk times (418r), and the Shafi'ites had more judges appointed by the sultan for their school than the other rites. But all four chief qadis came together for the monthly reverence to the sultan (Ibn Iyas, *Journal*, 1:307, 329).

26. Ibn Iyas, *Journal*, 1:318–29, 2:176; Johansen, "Valorization," in Stewart et al., *Law*, 71.

27. Powers, *Law*, 11–12, 173.

28. Ibid., 16–17. Cornell, *Realm*, 67, 106–7, 197, 230.

29. *CGA*, 179r. Ram, 195; Ép, 220.

30. *CGA*, 181r–v. Ram, 197 ([*DAR*, 40v] several changes and omissions); Ép, 222. Ibn Khaldun, *Muqaddimah*, 2:295.

31. *CGA*, 179r–180r. Ram, 195–96; Ép, 220–21. In some of its features, the tale of the unnamed Sufi resembles an event in the life of al-Shadhili (d. 656/1258), born in the Rif Mountains, a descendant of the Prophet, and founder of an important Sufi order. Denounced by the chief qadi of Tunis and ordered arrested as a political threat to the Ayyubin sultan in Egypt, al-Shadhili uttered an imprecation before the sultan, who was struck dumb, sought his pardon, and became his supporter (Cornell,

Realm, 149). Yuhanna al-Asad sets his story earlier in time and in Baghdad. Ibn Khaldun, *Muqaddimah*, 3:76–103.

32. *VIA*, 41v–43r; *VIAIIott*, 262–65. *CGA*, 180r–181r. Ram, 196 ([*DAR*, 40r–v] omits the public reading and the banquet); Ép, 221. The vizier Nizam al-Mulk had been murdered by the Assassins in 485/1092, while al-Ghazali was still teaching law at the Nizamiyya in Baghdad, so al-Mulk could not possibly have organized the public reading of al-Ghazali's later works or this banquet. In his beautiful autobiography, al-Ghazali does not mention a public reading of his *Revival of the Religious Sciences*, which is surely the book Yuhanna al-Asad had in mind, or a banquet of reconciliation between lawmen and Sufis, but only that his *Revival* had received criticisms in Baghdad and elsewhere and that he had answered them in other books (al-Ghazali, *Deliverance from Error* in *The Faith and Practice of al-Ghazali*, trans. W. Montgomery Watt [London: George Allen and Unwin, 1970], 52; *Deliverance from Error and Mystical Union with the Almighty*, ed. George McLean, trans. Muhammad Abu-laylah [Washington, D.C.: Council for Research in Values and Philosophy, 2001], 88).

33. *VIA*, 33r–v; *VIAHott*, 249–51. Corbin, *Philosophie islamique*, 165–72. *CEI*, 51–52. Abu-l-Hasan ʿAli ibn Ismaʿil al-Ashʿari, *Highlights of the Polemic against Deviators and Innovators* in *The Theology of al-Ashʿari*, trans. Richard J. McCarthy (Beirut: Imprimerie Catholique, 1953), chap. 2, paras. 27–48.

34. *CGA*, 184v. Ram, 199; Ép, 225. Qurʾan, 6:145; Al-Qayrawani, *Risâla*, chap. 23; *CEI*, 133; Cornell, *Realm*, 82, 137.

35. *CGA*, 182r–v. Ram, 197–98; Ép, 222–23. On Shihab al-Din Yahya al-Suhrawardi, see Corbin, *Philosophie islamique*, 285–305, and Salvador Gómez Nogales, "Suhrawardi et sa signification dans le domaine de la philosophie," in Pierre Salmon, ed., *Mélanges d'Islamologie: Volume dédié à la mémoire de Armand Abel* (Leiden: E. J. Brill, 1974), 150–71.

36. *CGA*, 21r–22r, 100v, 151r, 168r–v, 173r–v, 322r, 406r. Ram, 42–43, 124, 172, 186–87, 191, 322, 403; Ép, 38–39, 137, 195, 211–12, 215–16, 383, 504.

37. *CGA*, 213v, 225r, 240v–241r. Ram, 225, 235, 251; Ép, 255, 269, 288. Al-Qayrawani, *Risâla*, chap. 44, 242. *CEI*, 418. Lagardère, *Histoire*, 51 no. 184s, 52 no. 188, 113 no. 4m–n, 125 no. 54, 138 no. 110, 308 no. 68h, 379 no. 10, 395 no. 84, 436 no. 54, 444 no. 91, 471 no. 36. Hajji, *Activité*, 259.

38. *CGA*, 35r, 39r, 160r, 188v–189r, 213v (in Azjen, a wealthy town on a Rif slope, the population had a centuries-old statute from a sultan of Fez permitting wine, and the people all imbibed it), 225r, 230r, 234r, 236r–241r, 254r. Ram, 57, 61, 180, 203, 225, 235, 240–41, 245, 247–51, 262; Ép, 55, 60, 203, 228–29, 255, 269, 275, 280, 283–88, 303.

39. Arberry, 2:221. QAn, Sura "Vacca," 34b–35a, verse 214 [for 2:219]; Sura "De Mensa," 120a, verses 96–97 [for 5:90–91]; Sura "De Bello" [Yuhanna al-Asad has added to the title the words "and also called Muhammad"], 512b–514a, verse 16 [for 47:15]; Sura "Cadentis," 542b, verses unnumbered [for 56:18–19], Yuhanna al-Asad adds the word "pure" to the description of the liquid drunk in Paradise; Sura "De Deceptoribus," 594b–596a, verses unnumbered [for 83:22–25]. Suzanne Pinckney Stetkevych, "Intoxication and Immortality: Wine and Associated Imagery in al-Maʿarri's Garden," in J. W. Wright and Everett K. Rowson, eds., *Homoeroticism in Classical Arabic Literature* (New York: Columbia University Press, 1997), 210–32.

40. *CGA*, 182v. Ram, 199; Ép, 223. ʿUmar ibn al-Farid, "Wine Ode (al-Khamriyah)," in *Sufi Verse, Saintly Life*, trans. and ed. Th. Emil Homerin (New York and Mahwah, N.J.: Paulist Press, 2001), 45–72; "L'Éloge du vin," in *Poèmes mystiques*, ed. and trans. Jean-Yves L'Hôpital (Damascus: Institut Français d'Études Arabes de Damas, 2001), 217–43. Elizabeth S. Cohen and Thomas V. Cohen, *Daily Life in Renaissance Italy* (Westport, Conn.: Greenwood Press, 2001), 228.

41. Fahd, *Divination arabe*, chap. 2. Al-Masʿudi, *Prairies*, 1:459–68, paras. 1217–42. Ibn Khaldun, *Muqaddimah*, 1:202–45, 2:200–202.

42. *CGA*, 174r–176r. Ram, 192–93 ([*DAR*, 39v] section on the women diviners shortened); Ép, 216–17. Yuhanna al-Asad also includes a few sentences on the widespread practice of geomancy. Fahd, *Divination arabe*, 98–104 (women diviners), 171–73 (ventriloquism), 196–294 (geomancy).

43. *CGA*, 184r–v. Ram, 199; Ép, 224–25. Fahd, *Divination arabe*, 219, 228–41. The literature on the Divine Names of God was in part a response to the Muʿtazilites, who denied names and attributes of God as suggesting anthropomorphism (234–35). Here again, as in his support of al-Ashʿari, Yuhanna al-Asad was showing his reservations about the strongly rationalist school.

44. *CGA*, 176v–179r. Ram, 193–95; Ép, 218–20.

45. Ibn Khaldun, *Muqaddimah*, 1:188–92. *CGA*, 323r. Ram, 323; Ép, 384. Another example of holy fools: a sect where the men go about naked and even copulate with women in public, as al-Wazzan had seen himself in Cairo. The crowd ran to touch the woman as an object of devotion (*CGA*, 183r–v; Ram, 198; Ép, 223–24).

46. *CGA*, 411r–411v. Ram, 408–9 [*DAR*, 84v–85r]; Ép, 510. Where Yuhanna al-Asad spoke simply of "li miracoli" at the tomb, Ramusio added "lying miracles," "mentiti miracoli"; Yuhanna al-Asad did, however, call the tomb "cursed," "maledicto." Ibn Iyas, *Journal*, 2:148, 223. Nafisa was not only "virtuous and chaste," she was also celebrated for her learning and was consulted by the great jurist al-Shafiʿi. She made many pilgrimages and was known also for her charity (Walther, *Women*, 109–10).

47. *CGA*, 125v–126r, 449v–450r. Al-Wazzan had also been present in 920/ 1514, when the sultan had sworn peace with his cousin over Abu Yaʿza's tomb (125n). Ram, 148–49 ([*DAR*, 29v] adds reference to vows), 446; Ép, 167–68, 562. On Abu Yaʿza, see Ferhat and Triki, "Hagiographie," 29–30; Halima Ferhat, *Le Soufisme et les Zaouyas au Maghreb. Mérite individuel et patrimoine sacré* (Casablanca: Éditions Toubkal, 2003), 102–10; and Émile Dermenghem, *Le culte des saints dans l'Islam maghrébin* (Paris: Gallimard, 1954), 59–70; Abu Yaʿza was included in al-Tadili's *Kitab al-tashawwuf* (617/1220) and al-ʿAzafi devoted an entire manuscript to him not long afterward, also widely read in the Maghreb in the next centuries. On the importance of taming wild beasts as evidence for sanctity among the holy men of Morocco, especially Berber holy men, see Cornell, *Realm*, 115, 120.

48. *CGA*, 185r, 418v. Ram, 200, 415; Ép, 225, 518.

49. *CGA*, 185r. Ram, 199–200; Ép, 225. The tradition assigned 70 sects to the Magians, 71 to the Jews, 72 to the Christians, and 73 to the Muslims. Either Yuhanna al-Asad misremembered or the 72 is a scribal error. Muhammad ibn ʿAbd al-Karim al-Shahrastani, *Muslim Sects and Divisions*, trans. A. K. Kazi and J. G. Flynn (London, Boston, Melbourne, and Henley: Kegan Paul International, 1984), 9–10, 12. On the "seventy-three sects of Islam" and the relatively tolerant tradition represented by al-Shahrastani, see the introductory chapters to al-Shahrastani, *Livre des religions et des sectes*, trans. Daniel Gimaret and Guy Monnot (Louvain: Peeters/UNESCO, 1986): "Shahrastani, la tolérance et l'altérité" and "L'Islam au 'soixante-treize sectes.'"

50. *CGA*, 184v–185r: "la opera de uno chiamato elacfani el quale narra tutte le diverse sette le quali procedono de la Fede de Mucametto." Ram, 199–200; Ép, 225. Muhammad ibn Ibrahim ibn al-Akfani and his book on the division of the sciences, *Irshad al-qasid li-asna al-maqasid*, are mentioned, along with al-Shahrastani and others, by the historiographer al-Sakhawi (d. 902/1497) in his section on historians of the sects and of innovators (*Open Denunciation of the Adverse Critics of the Historians*, trans. Franz Rosenthal, in *A History of Muslim Historiography* [Leiden: E. J. Brill, 1952], 356). Ibn al-Akfani was born in Iraq in the late thirteenth century and died in Cairo of the plague in 749/1348. On his work and on connections with al-Shahrastani, see J. J. Witkam, *De Egyptische Arts Ibn al-Akfani en zijn Indeling van de Wetenschappen* (Leiden: Ter Lugt Pers, 1989).

51. Al-Qayrawani, *Risâla*, chap. 30, 129. Muhammad ibn Yaggabsh al-Tazi, *Kitab al-jihad* as quoted in Cornell, *Realm*, 237–40; also in Hajji, *Activité*, 235–38. On earlier Moroccan texts on jihad, see Benchekroun, *Vie*, 90, 222–24.

52. In his chapter on Marrakesh in *CGA*, Yuhanna al-Asad did not mention

the conquest of the town by the Saʿdiyan sharif al-Aʿraj, though it had occurred several months before he put the finishing touches on his manuscript in March 1526. Yuhanna al-Asad carried the story of Marrakesh no later than the time of his own embassy to en-Nasir, the Hintata ruler of Marrakesh in 921/1515. He did promise, however, to say more about the town's history in his *Epitome of Muslim Chronicles*. CGA, 67r–74v, 89v–90r, 93r. Ram, 93–100, 114, 117; Ép, 99–108, 125, 130. The fall of Marrakesh is not mentioned in the correspondence collected by the Venetian secretary Sanuto, but given the presence of an Ottoman ambassador in Venice, and a Venetian ambassador in Istanbul in 1525, it is likely that the event became known in Italy (Sanuto, *Diarii*, vols. 39–40).

53. On the judicial opinions and events around al-Maghili's attack on the Jews of Tuwat, see the studies of John O. Hunwick, *Shariʿa*, 37–39; "Al-Maghili and the Jews of Tuwat: The Demise of a Community," *Studi islamica* 61 (1985): 157–83; "The Rights of *Dhimmis* to Maintain a Place of Worship: A 15th Century *Fatwa* from Tlemcen," *Al-Qantara* 12 (1991): 133–55. Sources and further discussion in Lagardère, *Histoire*, 44 no. 162; Amar, ed. and trans., *Consultations juridiques*, 244–65; Georges Vajda, "Un traité maghrébin 'Adversus Judaeos': 'Ahkam al al-Dhimma' du Shaykh Muhammad ibn ʿAbd al-Karim al-Maghili," in *Études d'orientalisme dédiées à la mémoire de Lévi-Provençal*, 2 vols. (Paris: G.-P. Maisonneuve et Larose, 1962), 2:805–12; Jacob Oliel, *Les Juifs au Sahara: Le Touat au Moyen Âge* (Paris: CNRS Éditions, 1994), 106–11. Rudolph Peters, *Jihad in Classical and Modern Islam: A Reader* (Princeton, N.J.: Markus Wiener Publishers, 1996), 2–7, 37–41 (translation from Ibn Rushd's legal handbook *Bidayat al-Mujtahid*). Al-Qayrawani, *Risâla*, chap. 30, 129.

54. Peters, *Jihad*, 7, 30 (translation from Ibn Rushd, *Bidayat*). Hamani, *Au carrefour*, 192. Al-Qayrawani, *Risâla*, chap. 44, 242.

55. CGA, 56v, 115r. Ram, 82, 137; Ép, 85, 153.

56. CGA, 32r–v, 57r ("sonno nel dicto monte grande quantita de Judei che cavaleano et portano Arme et combatrano in favore de loro Patroni cio et el Populo del dicto Monte"), 59r–v, 79v–80r ("sonno molti judei nel dicto Monte per Artesani quali pagano tributo al dicto signore, tutti tengono la opinione de le Carraimi et sonno valenti con le Arme in mano"), 84v–85v, 89v–90v, 194v–195r, 359v. Ram, 54, 82, 84, 105–6, 109–10, 114–15, 208, 357; Ép, 52, 85–86, 88, 114, 119–20, 125–26, 234, 431. Cohen, *Under Crescent*, 61–64; Israel Goldman, *The Life and Times of Rabbi David Ibn Abi Zimra* (New York: Jewish Theological Seminary, 1970), 52–56 (fulmination of the head rabbi of Cairo against the Karaites in the early sixteenth century). Nicole Serfaty, *Les courtisans juifs des sultans marocains: Hommes politiques et hauts dignitaires, XIIIe–XVIIIe siècles* (Saint-

Denis: Éditions Bouchène, 1999), 97, 97 n.2, 105, 105 n.3 (Jewish envoy to Portugal), 106. *SIHMP*, 1:16, 18 (Jewish interpreter for sultan of Fez). Yuhanna al-Asad also talked without judgment of Jews selling wine to Muslims in Badis, even though it was in violation of the dhimmi laws (*CGA*, 230v; Ram, 240–41; Ép, 275). Lagardère, *Histoire*, 44–45, no. 162.

57. *VIH*, 65v–68v; *VIHHott*, 286–91.

58. *VIH*, 68r–v; *VIHHott*, 290–91. Harun ben Shem Tov was also known as Harun ibn Batash. On the importance of astrologers to Muslim rulers, see also Ibn Khaldun, *Muqaddimah*, 2:201–2; Fahd, *Divination arabe*, 119–20.

59. In his *Geography*, Yuhanna al-Asad made brief references to the assassination of Sultan ʿAbd al-Haqq without mentioning his Jewish vizier: he had "been slain at the hands of his people and of the sharif, who was a great figure in Fez and of the lineage of the founders of Fez [the Idrisids], and the people elected the sharif for their ruler" (*CGA*, 218r, 223r–v; Ram, 230, 234; Ép, 261, 267). On this uprising, see Mercedes García-Arenal, "The Revolution of Fas in 869/1465 and the Death of Sultan ʿAbd al-Haqq al-Marini," *Bulletin of the School of Oriental and African Studies* 41 (1978): 43–66; Kably, *Société*, 330–34; Abun-Nasr, *Maghrib*, 115.

60. Excerpt from the *Raud* of ʿAbd al-Basit ibn Halil (844/1440–920/1514) in Robert Brunschvig, ed. and trans., *Deux récits de voyage inédits en Afrique du Nord au XVe siècle* (Paris: Maisonneuve and Larose, 2001), 63–65.

61. *CGA*, 279v (sacking of Jewish houses in Tlemcen, 923/1517), 363r–v (the Tuwat and Gurara pillage and massacre, 897–898/1492). Either the Gurara massacre occurred a year later than that at Tuwat, or Yuhanna al-Asad has moved the date forward to make these events simultaneous with the expulsion of the Jews from Spain. Ram, 285, 361; Ép, 333, 436–37.

62. Ibn Khaldun, *Muqaddimah*, 2:156–200. On eschatological thinking, the Mahdi, and the World Conqueror in Islamic and Ottoman thought, see the important essays by Cornell H. Fleischer, "The Lawgiver as Messiah: The Making of the Imperial Image in the Reign of Süleyman," in Gilles Veinstein, ed., *Soliman le Magnifique et son temps. Actes du Colloque de Paris, Galéries nationales du Grand Palais 7–10 mars 1990* (Paris: École de Louvre and EHESS, 1992), 159–77, and "Seer to the Sultan: Haydar-I Remmal and Sultan Süleyman," in Jayne L. Warner, ed., *Cultural Horizons. A Festschrift in Honor of Talat S. Halman* (Syracuse, N.Y.: Syracuse University Press, 2001), 290–99.

63. Ibid., 291–94; Fleischer, "Lawgiver," 162 and 175 n.15. Sartain, *Al-Suyuti*, 1:69–72.

64. Fleischer, "Lawgiver," 162–64; Fleischer, "Seer," 294–95. *CGA*, 402r–v. Ram, 399; Ép, 499.

65. Sanuto, *Diarii*, 26:195.

66. Ottavia Niccoli, *Prophecy and People in Renaissance Italy*, trans. Lydia G. Cochrane (Princeton, N.J.: Princeton University Press, 1990), chaps. 2, 7. Minnich, "Role of Prophecy," in Reeves, ed., *Prophetic Rome*, 111–20; Reeves, "Cardinal Egidio of Viterbo," ibid., 95–109. O'Malley, *Giles of Viterbo*, 115–16, 127–31. Kaufmann, "Mantino," 57.

67. *CGA*, 59r (Yuhanna al-Asad says "le scripture" here because the Mahdi prophecies are especially found in hadith, rather than in the Qur'an itself, *CEI*, 246–47). Ram, 84; Ép, 88.

68. Ibn Khaldun, *Muqaddimah*, 1:326–37, 2:196–97. Al-Bakri, *Afrique*, 306 ("Masset [*sic*] . . . est un *ribat* très fréquenté, où se tient une foire qui réunit beaucoup de monde. Cet établissement sert de retraite aux hommes qui veulent s'adonner à la dévotion"). On these Moroccan ribat and their holy men, see Cornell, *Realm*, 39–54. On the continued religious and eschatological importance of Massa, see Hajji, *Activité*, 272–73, 626–28.

69. *CGA*, 59r–v. Ram, 84; Ép, 88. On these beached whales, see above, chapter 1, p. 54.

70. Ibn Khaldun, *Muqaddimah*, 1:53–55, 273, 471–72; 12:57; *Berbères*, 1:252–64, 2:84, 161–73, 573–75. Abun-Nasr, *Maghrib*, 87–91. Powers, *Law*, 12; Mansour Hasan Mansour, *The Maliki School of Law: Spread and Domination in North and West Africa* (Lanham, Md.: Austin and Winfield, 1994), 91–96. Kably, *Société*, 20–21, 31. Cornell, *Realm*, 137.

71. *CGA*, 7v, 69v–70r, 79r. Ram, 26 ([*DAR*, 2v] adds favorable words about Ibn Tumart: "che un grande huomo nelle cose della lor fede et predicatore appresso loro molto estimato"), 95–96, 105; Ép, 14 (adds favorable words), 102–3, 113. Ibn Khaldun, *Berbères*, 162. Abun-Nasr, *Maghrib*, 89. Kably, *Société*, 20. Cornell, *Realm*, 194.

72. Abun-Nasr, *Maghrib*, 59–66. Al-Shahrastani, *Muslim Sects*, 309–14. Ibn Khaldun, *Muqaddimah*, 1:412–13. *CEI*, 194–96.

73. Ibn Khallikan and al-Suyuti were among those who considered ʿUbayd Allah as an impostor. Ibn Khaldun thought his genealogical claims legitimate but considered his views heretical (Hitti, *Arabs*, 617–18; Ibn Khaldun, *Muqaddimah*, 1:41–46).

74. *CGA*, 316v ("el Mahdi heretico Pontefece"), 331r–332r. Yuhanna al-Asad makes some errors in his account, attributing to the Mahdi the defeat of the Berber rebel Abu Yazid, but in fact the important battle at Mahdiyya took place in 336/947, thirteen years after ʿUbayd Allah's death, and the victor was his grandson (Ibn Khaldun, *Muqaddimah*, 2:210–11; Abun-Nasr, *Maghrib*, 65). Ram, 318, 330–31 ([*DAR*, 69r] omits some of the details given by Yuhanna al-Asad about the Sijilmasa rescue); Ép, 377, 392–93. Yuhanna al-Asad's reservations about eschatological leaders may also account for his silence about a tomb discovered in Fez in 841/1438

and claimed by some to be that of Idris II, founder of the city of Fez and a descendant of the Prophet. Idris's father had brought a version of Shi'ite ideas of the Imamate to the Maghreb—Yuhanna al-Asad called him a "schismatic"—and the Idrisid belief in an inherited "baraka" had nourished the long development of political sharifism in Morocco. The claim that a suddenly-discovered Fez tomb held the bones of Idris II was part of a sharifian movement for power in Fez in the mid-fifteenth century. Yuhanna al-Asad spoke only of the tomb of Idris I in the mountain town of Walila, where it was venerated and visited by Moroccans. *CGA*, 135v, 205v ("el Patre suo fu sepulto in la dicta cipta di Gualili"). Ram, 158, 217; Ép, 245. Abun-Nasr, *Maghrib*, 50–51; Kably, *Société*, 327–30; Cornell, *Realm*, 300–301; Jacques Berque, *Ulémas, fondateurs, insurgés au Maghreb au XVIIe siècle* (Paris: Sindbad, 1982), 28–32.

75. *CGA*, 401r. Ram, 395 ([*DAR*, 82v] omits phrase "la pazia di Mucametto"); Ép, 498.

76. Arberry, 327–28. Ibn Khaldun, *Muqaddimah*, 1:162–63, 3:473. Al-Mas'udi, *Prairies*, 2:274, para. 730. Miquel, *Géographie*, 2:497–511.

77. Ibn Khaldun, *Muqaddimah*, 1:162–63, 3:473. Al-Mas'udi, *Prairies*, 2:274, para. 730. Miquel, *Géographie*, 2:497–511. "Al-Iskandar," *EI1*, 2:533–34; W. Montgomery Watt, "Al-Iskandar," *EI2*, 4:127; *CEI*, 32, 107–8. Armand Abel, "Dhu'l Qarnayn, prophète de l'universalité," *Annuaire de l'Institut de Philologie et d'Histoire Orientales et Slaves* 11 (1951): 5–18.

78. Niccoli, *Prophecy*, 172–75; Sylvie Deswarte-Rosa, "L'Expédition de Tunis (1535): Images, interprétations, répercussions culturelles," in Bartolomé Bennassar and Robert Sauzet, eds., *Chrétiens et Musulmans à la Renaissance* (Paris: Honoré Champion, 1998), 99–102. Fleischer, "Lawgiver," 164; Sanuto, *Diarii*, 25:439.

79. *CGA*, 73v, 222v–224r. Ram, 99–100, 234–35; Ép, 107, 267–68. Abun-Nasr, *Maghrib*, 114; Kably, *Société*, 325 (according to a Portuguese chronicle, the sultan Abu Sa'id's failure to defend Ceuta was due to his quarrels with his brothers). Al-Qayrawani, *Risâla*, chap. 30, 129; Peters, *Jihad*, 1.

80. *CGA*, 48r, 51v, 73r–74r, 114r, 117r–124r (119v: "la dicta terra [of Anfa] fu bene destrutta; el capitano alhora con la sua armata ritorno a Portogallo et lasso la dicta terra per li lupi et civette. Dice il compositore essere stato in la dicta terra molte volte la quale fa piangere"), 126r–v, 130r–v, 209v–210r, 216v–218r, 232r–233r, 243r–244r. Ram, 72, 76, 98–99, 137, 140–44, 146, 149, 152–54, 221, 228–30, 243, 253–55; Ép, 75, 79, 106–7, 152, 158–63, 165–66, 169, 173–74, 251, 259–61, 277–78, 291.

81. *CGA*, 28v–29r. Ram, 51 (adds additional phrases on the anti-Christian viciousness of the Turks); Ép, 48. *CGA*, 29r: "li Turchi in le cose memorabili de li christiani guastano fine le figure depincte in li templi"; *DAR*, 8r: "i Turchi nè luoghi che prendono di Christiani, guastando non solamente

le belle memorie et gli honorati titoli, ma nelle chiese le imagini de santi et sante che vi trovano." In his comment on the recent popes, Yuhanna al-Asad may have been referring to the building projects of Leo X and their relation to those undertaken by Julius II (cf. Giovio, *Leon Decimo*, 94r).

82. *VIA*, 31r–33r; *VIAHott*, 246–49. On Yuhanna ibn Masawayh and the Nestorians, see Hitti, *Arabs*, 311–12, 363–64; *CEI*, 299–300. *CGA*, 27r, 401r, 429r, 430r–431r; Ram, 49, 397–98, 425–27; Ép, 46, 497–98, 532, 534.

83. *CGA*, 146r–v, 170r, 334r–v, 392r. Ram, 168, 188, 332, 388; Ép, 190, 212–13, 395–96, 484. The bejeweled table in the cathedral at Toledo was ordinarily described in Muslim and Christian literature as belonging to King Solomon (Hitti, *Arabs*, 497). On the Christmas/New Year's festivities and their condemnation, see H. R. Idris, "Les tributaires en occident musulman médiéval," in Salmon, ed., *Mélanges*, 173, no. 9.

84. *CGA*, 27r. Ram, 49; Ép, 46. To Yuhanna al-Asad's description of the city of Bône, called Hippo in Roman times, Ramusio added the fact that Augustine had been its bishop (Ram, 312; *DAR*, 65r). This is not found in *CGA*, 310r. Augustine, *The Confessions*, trans. John K. Ryan (New York: Image Books, 1960), bk. 9, chap. 7, 215. Peter Brown, *Augustine of Hippo. A Biography* (Berkeley and Los Angeles: University of California Press, 1969), 378, 422–26. William A. Sumruld, *Augustine and the Arians. The Bishop of Hippo's Encounters with Ulfilan Arianism* (Selinsgrove: Susquehanna University Press and London and Toronto: Associated University Presses, 1994), chaps. 4–5. Alberto Pio, Prince of Carpi, *Tres et viginiti Libri in locos lucubrationum variarum D. Erasmi Rhoterodami* (Venice: Luc-Antonio Giunta, 1531), 140v–143r.

85. *SIHME*, 3:213 n.4, 739; *SIHMP*, 1:489, 498, 498 n.2. Halima Ferhat, "Abu-l-ʿAbbas: Contestation et sainteté," *Al-Qantara* 13 (1992): 181–99; Cornell, *Realm*, 80–92. Yuhanna al-Asad said he had visited the first tomb of Ibn Rushd (Averroës) at Marrakesh; Abu-l-ʿAbbas Sabti was buried in the same tomb (*VIA*, 52r–v; *VIAHott*, 279; Cornell, *Realm*, 92).

86. EpiP, 1, 68 (colophon). Arabic transcription in Levi Della Vida, *Ricerche*, 105.

87. The standard salutation is "ar-Rahman ar-Rahim"; Yuhanna al-Asad has replaced ar-Rahman, "the merciful," with ar-Raʾuf, which means "merciful, compassionate, kind," but with a nuance toward kindliness, gentleness. Ibn Hawqal, *Configuration*, 1; Ibn Jubayr, *Travels*, 25; al-Idrisi, *Première géographie*, 57; Ibn Battuta, *Voyages*, 1:65.

88. Biblioteca Apostolica Vaticana, MSS Vat. Ar. 80, fol. 2. Arabic transcription in Levi Della Vida, *Ricerche*, 102; reproduced in Rauch, 68.

89. *CEI*, 161–62, 208–9. F. E. Peters, ed., *Judaism, Christianity, and Islam. The Classical Texts and Their Interpretation*, 3 vols. (Princeton, N.J.: Princeton University Press, 1990), 2:349–51.

90. Valeria Annecchino, *La Basilica di Sant'Agostino in Campo Marzio e l'ex complesso conventuale, Roma* (Genoa: Edizioni d'Arte Marconi, 2000), 8–9, 29–31.

91. Gaignard, *Maures*, 191. This is the view of him expressed by Muhammad Hajji in his introduction to the first Arabic translation of *The Description of Africa* (1400/1980): al-Wazzan was always fully a follower of the religion into which he had been born and had feigned conversion to be released from prison: *Wasf Ifriqiya*, 1:4–21. Hajji's views were discussed by Driss Mansouri at the Colloque "Léon l'Africain" (EHESS, Paris, 22–24 May 2003), forthcoming in Pouillon and Zhiri, eds., *Léon l'Africain.*

92. Arberry, 1:298–99. QAn, Sura "De Apibus," 258b, verse 106. *CEI*, 397. R. Strothmann and Moktar Djebli, "*Takiyya*," *EI2*, 10:134–36. Nikki R. Keddie, "Symbol and Sincerity in Islam," *Studia Islamica* 19 (1963): 27–63. Devin J. Stewart, "*Taqiyyah* as Performance: The Travels of Baha' al-Din al-ʿAmili in the Ottoman Empire (991–93/1583–85)," in Stewart et al., *Law*, 1–70. José Fernando García Cruz, "El *Disimulo* Religioso en el Ámbito Doctrinal y Legal Islámico," in *Actas del VIII Simposio Internacional de Mudejarismo. De mudéjares a moriscos: una conversión forzada. Teruel. 15–17 de septiembre de 1999* (Teruel: Centro de Estudios Mudéjares, 2002), 661–71.

93. L. P. Harvey, ed. and trans., "Crypto-Islam in Sixteenth-Century Spain," *Actas Primer Congreso de Estudios Arabes e Islamicos, Cordoba, 1962* (Madrid: Comité Permanante del Congreso de Estudios Arabes e Islamicos, 1964), 163–81. Monroe, "Morisco Appeal," 281–303. Al-Maqqari, *History*, 2:391.

CHAPTER SEVEN · CURIOSITY AND CONNECTIONS

1. Grassi, *Diarium*, 2:309r–v.

2. Levi Della Vida, *Ricerche*, 101. Juan de Torquemada (1388–1468), *De Plenitudine Potestatis Romani Pontificis in Ecclesia Dei Opusculum ex Operibus Io. De Turrecremata*, ed. Joannis Thomas Ghilardus (Turin: Marietti, 1870). The publication of this excerpt from Torquemada's larger text was timed to the 1870 decree of the Vatican Council on the infallibility of the pope. Medieval background to this controversy is found in Brian Tierney, *Origins of Papal Infallibility, 1150–1350* (Leiden: E. J. Brill, 1972).

3. Ibn Iyas, *Journal*, 2:179, 186. The title to the caliphate seems to have fallen into abeyance until the late eighteenth century, when a fictional translation from the ʿAbbasid caliph to the Ottoman emperor Selim was asserted. But Selim himself made no such claim (*CEI*, 305).

4. *CGA*, 200r. Ram, 212; Ép, 239.

5. *CGA*, 140r–v. Ram, 162–63; Ép, 184–85.

6. Al-Muqaddasi, *Best Divisions*, 2, 368–69.

7. Ibid., 2.

8. Weil, *Lévita*, 29–30, 75, 78, 83–85, 88. Elijah Levita's son Yehuda was still alive and a practicing Jew in Rome in 1557. His daughter Hannah married Isaac ben Yehiel Bohême. Her sons Elijah and Joseph helped their grandfather with the printing of his *Bovo Buch* in 1541. Later they converted to Catholicism. Other descendants of Elijah Levita remained Jewish (ibid., 108–9, 135, 153, 163–64). When Jacob Mantino moved to Venice in 1528, he lived in the Ghetto but repeatedly sought and sometimes got permission from the Signory to wear a black hat rather than the yellow headcovering required of the Jews (Kaufmann, "Mantino," 43, 228–32).

9. Secret, *Kabbalistes*, 108. Elijah Levita, *Accentorum Hebraicorum Liber Unus*, trans. Sebastian Münster (Basel: Heinrich Petri, 1539), second preface, 17–19. Elijah Levita, *The Massoreth Ha-Massoreth*, ed. and trans. Christian D. Ginsburg (London: Longmans, Green, Reader and Dyer, 1867), 92, 96–101. In addition to Psalm 147:20, the rabbis also cited Proverbs 26:8 in criticism of Levita ("As he that bindeth a stone in a sling, so is he that giveth honor to a fool").

10. Al-Qayrawani, *Risâla*, chap. 32, 142, 146 (four years of husband's disappearance required before marriage dissolved); Amar, ed. and trans., *Consultations juridiques*, 394; Linant de Bellefonds, *Traité*, 2:125–26, 457–58; David Santillana, *Istituzioni de Diritto Musulmano Malichita*, 2 vols. (Rome: Istituto per l'Oriente, 1925–1938), 1:169. Marriage and judicial dissolution of marriage would have been among the subjects covered in al-Wazzan's own lost treatise on "the faith and law of Muhammad according to the Malikite school of law."

11. Dunn, *Ibn Battuta*, 39. Reynolds, ed., *Interpreting the Self*, 78–79, 123–31. Al-Suyuti, however, did not mention his wife or wives in his autobiography (Sartain, *Al-Suyuti*, 1:23).

12. *CGA*, 24r–v, 416v. Ram, 45, 413; Ép, 41–42, 516.

13. *CGA*, 46v, 94v, 115r–v, 145v, 199r, 234r, 350v, 381r. Ram, 70, 118, 137–38, 167 ([*DAR*, 33v] omits reference to bathhouse women as "Blacks"), 211, 244 ([*DAR*, 50v] differs considerably from *CGA* and specifically leaves out women herding goats), 349, 378; Ép, 73, 131, 153, 189, 238, 280 (adds material not in *CGA* or Ram), 420, 467.

14. *CGA*, 110v, 153r, 204v, 234r, 259r, 321r, 362r. Ram, 133, 174, 216, 245, 268, 322, 359; Ép, 147, 197, 244, 280, 309, 382, 435. Maya Shatzmiller, *Labour in the Medieval Islamic World* (Leiden: E. J. Brill, 1994), 351–52.

15. *CGA*, 43r, 147r, 160v, 163r, 188r–v, 309r, 324r, 354r ("meretrice"), 403r. Ram, 66, 169, 180, 182, 311, 324, 352 ([*DAR*, 73r] instead of "meretrice," "molte ve ne sono da partito"), 400; Ép, 65, 191, 203, 206, 228, 368, 385, 424, 500. On prostitution in Islamic societies, see Ibn Iyas, *Journal*, 1:158, 284; Bouhdiba, *Sexualité*, 228–39; Walther, *Women*, 99; Leila Ahmed, *Women and Gender in Islam* (New Haven, Conn.: Yale University Press, 1992), 115; Rudi Matthee, "Prostitutes, Courtesans, and Dancing Girls: Women Entertainers in Safavid Iran," in Rudi Matthee and Beth Baron, eds., *Iran and Beyond: Essays in Middle Eastern History in Honor of Nikki R. Keddie* (Costa Mesa, Calif.: Mazda Publishers, 2000), 124–38.

16. *CGA*, 327v–328r. Ram, 326; Ép, 388. Ibn Iyas, *Journal*, 1:241, 267. Matthee, "Prostitutes," 138–44.

17. Ibn Battuta, *Voyages*, 2:75. Al-Bakri, *Afrique*, 201, 216.

18. *CGA*, 46v, 49r, 53v, 63v, 94v, 96v, 111r, 304r–v, 354r, 362v. Ram, 70, 74, 79, 89, 119, 120, 307, 352, 360, 400; Ép, 73, 77, 81, 94, 131, 133, 148, 363, 424, 435, 500. Rural women in the Maghreb were usually unveiled over the centuries (Mohamed Hobbaida, "Le costume féminin en milieu rural. Observations préliminaires sur le Maroc précolonial," in Dalenda Larguèche, ed., *Histoire des femmes au Maghreb* [Tunis: Centre de Publication Universitaire, 2000], 205–6).

19. *CGA*, 24r v, 134r, 164v, 324v, 381r, 415r. Ram, 45, 156, 183, 324, 378, 412; Ép, 42, 177, 208, 385, 467, 514–15.

20. *CGA*, 20v–21r, 40v, 49r, 53v, 66r, 94v, 238r, 256r. Ram, 41, 63, 74, 79, 91, 119, 249, 264 ([*DAR*, 55r] exaggerates character of jealousy of men); Ép, 37, 62, 77, 81, 97, 131, 285, 305 (exaggerates character of jealousy of men).

21. Bouhdiba, *Sexualité*, 24–25; Walther, *Women*, 61–64. Al-Shafi'i, *Risâla*, 121–23, nos. 375–83; Roded, ed., *Women*, 106–7. Ibn Hazm, *De l'amour et des amants. Tawq al-hamama fi-l-ulfa wa-l-ullaf (Collier de la colombe sur l'amour et les amants)*, trans. Gabriel Martinez-Gros (Paris: Sindbad, 1992), chap. 29. The whole subject of sexual discourse and practices in Islamic lands will be much enriched by the forthcoming publication of Dror Zeevi, *Producing Desire: Changing Sexual Discourse in the Ottoman Middle East 1500–1900* (Berkeley and Los Angeles: University of California Press, 2006).

22. *CGA*, 324r. Ram, 324; Ép, 385.

23. Charles Pellat, "*Liwat*," *EI2*, 5:776–79; James Bellamy, "Sex and Society in Islamic Popular Literature," in al-Sayyid-Marsot, ed., *Society*, 36–40; Malek Chebel, *L'esprit de sérail. Perversions et marginalités sexuelles au Maghreb* (Paris: Lieu Commun, 1988), 24–27; Jim Wafer, "Muhammad and Male Homosexuality," in Stephen O. Murray and Will Roscoe, eds.,

Islamic Homosexualities (New York and London: New York University Press, 1997), 87–96.

24. *CGA*, 175r–176r. Ram, 192–93; Ép, 217–18. Ibn Hazm, *De l'amour*, 216–17. Pellat, "*Liwat*," *EI2*, 5:777–78; Walther, *Women*, 174; Chebel, *Esprit*, 22–24; Camilla Adang, "Ibn Hazm on Homosexuality. A Case-Study of Zahiri Legal Methodology," *Al-Qantara* 24 (2003): 7–9, 25–29: the most serious Malikite punishment for sexual acts between women was one hundred lashes. Stephen O. Murray, "Woman-Woman Love in Islamic Societies," in Murray and Roscoe, eds., *Islamic Homosexualities*, 97–104. Interestingly enough, a 1948 field report from Libya described women offering themselves to possession by djinns and engaging in lovemaking with women on festive occasions (100). *Suhaqiyat* is related to the root "sahq," "to crush or pound" (Wehr, 466), rather than to the verb for rubbing as in the Italian "fregare," "to rub." See below, Note 45, on the significance of al-Wazzan's use of the slang term "fregatrice."

25. Bouhdiba, *Sexualité*, 44–45. Pellat, "*Liwat*," *EI2*, 5:776–77 (stresses severity of the law against sodomy, but notes that in fact the practices were tolerated); Bellamy, "Sex," in al-Sayyid-Marsot, ed., *Society*, 37–38; Adang, "Ibn Hazm," 7–15: the standard Malikite view was that *liwat* was the most serious form of zina², and that both male partners should be executed by stoning.

26. *CGA*, 90v, 147r–v, 170v. Ram, 115 ([*DAR*, 22r] elaborates on *CGA*), 168–69 ([*DAR*, 33v] adds more negative remarks to *CGA*), 188; Ép, 127, 191 (adds comments to *CGA*), 213. Wehr, 304; Pellat, "*Liwat*," *EI2*, 778; Stephen O. Murray, "The Will Not to Know: Islamic Accommodations of Male Homosexuality" and "The Sohari *Khanith*," in Murray and Roscoe, eds., *Islamic Homosexualities*, 24–32, 244–48. Al-Suyuti described a much frequented "house of dissipation" in Cairo in 886/1481, located right next to a mosque. Men gathered there for "adultery, sodomy, drinking, playing musical instruments, and so forth" and were seen there engaging in sex with young lads. As a legal scholar, al-Suyuti made the case for razing the building. Ultimately he won his argument, but it is interesting that razing was opposed by other judges and legal scholars of Cairo (al-Suyuti, "On How God Blessed Me by Setting Enemies Against Me," trans. Kristen Brustad, in Reynolds, ed., *Interpreting the Self*, 203–6).

27. *CGA*, 181v–182r. Ram, 197; Ép, 222. On the possible connection of Sufi love mysticism with the contemplation of beautiful young men, see Jim Wafer, "Vision and Passion: The Symbolism of Male Love in Islamic Mystical Literature," in Murray and Roscoe, eds., *Islamic Homosexualities*, 110–11. On the contrast between the highly ascetic path of early "classical Sufi conduct," including the renunciation of sex, and the Sufi embracing of various forms of sexual love, see Schimmel, "Eros," in al-Sayyid-Marsot, ed., *Society*, 119–28.

28. *CGA*, 181v ("pero che molte volte se e ritrovata alli dicti conviti"), 324r–v. Right after describing the male and female prostitutes of Tunis, Yuhanna al-Asad talks of the use there of the drug hashish ("el hasis") and its aphrodisiac qualities; Ramusio separates the two sections. Ram, 197 ([*DAR*, 40v] omits the phrase on his attendance at the banquets); 324 ([*DAR*, 67r] adds words about the infamy of the "fanciulli"); Ép, 222, 385 (in both cases follows Ramusio's additions and omissions).

29. Michael Sells, "Love," in Menocal et al., eds., *Literature*, 134–36. J. W. Wright, Jr., "Masculine Allusion and the Structure of Satire in Early ʿAbbasid Poetry," in Wright and Rowson, *Homoeroticism*, 1–23; Franz Rosenthal, "Male and Female: Described and Compared," ibid., 24–54; Everett Rowson, "Two Homoerotic Narratives from Mamluk Literature," ibid., 158–91. Al-Jahiz, *Kitab mufakharat al-jawari wa-l-ghilman*, translated as *Éphèbes et courtisanes*, ed. Malek Chebel, trans. Maati Kabbal (Paris: Rivages Poches, 1997). Schimmel, "Eros," in al-Sayyid-Marsot, ed., *Society*, 131–38. Ibn Hazm, *De l'amour*, 80, 84–85, 88–89, 192–97, 209–12. Adang's important article on Ibn Hazm's legal views makes clear that he viewed homosexual acts as a serious sin; but using a Zahirist rather than a Malikite approach to legal texts, he did not categorize it as zinaʾ and recommended a maximum of ten lashes and a prison term to reform behavior ("Ibn Hazm," 6–31).

30. *CGA*, 182r. Ram, 197 ([*DAR*, 40v] omits entire reference to al-Hariri); Ép, 222. Al-Hariri, *Livre des Malins*, Maqama 10, "La Séance d'Al-Rahba," 95–100; *Assemblies*, trans. Chenery and Steingass, Assembly 10, "Of Rahbah," 158–63.

31. *CGA*, 172r. Ram, 190; Ép, 214. *VIH*, 67r–68r; *VIHH*, 288–90 (leaves out the words "the young man whom he sodomized," "juvenis, quem pedamaverat," replacing them with dashes). Ibrahim ibn Sahl was born a Jew in Seville and wrote widely read love poetry in which Musa/Moses is the beloved figure. But Yuhanna al-Asad assigned him a life quite at odds with the contemporary evidence, saying nothing of the poet's conversion to Islam in the wake of the Christian conquest of Seville. Yuhanna al-Asad has him move to Córdoba, where the Jewish community protests to the qadi, Ibn Rushd (Averroës), that his poetry is corrupting the young. Ibn Sahl visited different parts of al-Andalus, but settled in Ceuta, not Córdoba (Teresa Garulo, "Introducción" to Ibrahim ibn Sahl, *Poemas*, ed. and trans. Teresa Garulo [Madrid: Hiperión, 1983], 7–32). In any case, Ibn Rushd died before Ibn Sahl was born. For legends about Ibn Sahl among the Jews of North Africa, see ibid., 25 n.55.

32. *CGA*, 182v. Ram, 198; Ép 223. Annemarie Schimmel, *As Through a Veil. Mystical Poetry in Islam* (New York: Columbia University Press, 1982), 42–44; Ibn Farid, *Poèmes*, trans. L'Hôpital, 15–16.

33. *CGA*, 449v–450r. Ram, 446 ([*DAR*, 92v] adds to the end of the story the

skeptical phrase, "each person will believe this as he wants to"); Ép, 562 (follows Ramusio's addition).

34. Delumeau, *Rome*, 37, 43, 49, 102.

35. Schimmel, "Eros," in al-Sayyid-Marsot, ed., *Society*, 122–24. CGA, 182r–v ("sue abstinentie"). Ram, 197–98; Ép, 222–23.

36. Ludwig Pastor, *History of the Popes from the Close of the Middle Ages*, 40 vols. (London: Routledge and Kegan Paul, 1898–1953), 8:406–7. Delumeau, *Rome*, 101–2. Guido Ruggiero, *Binding Passions. Tales of Magic, Marriage, and Power at the End of the Renaissance* (New York and Oxford: Oxford University Press, 1993), 33–48, 178. Monica Kurzel-Runtscheiner, *Töchter der Venus. Die Kurtisanen Roms im 16. Jahrhundert* (Munich: C. H. Beck, 1995), 46–51, 97–100. Margaret F. Rosenthal, *The Honest Courtesan: Veronica Franco, Citizen and Writer in Sixteenth-Century Venice* (Chicago and London: University of Chicago Press, 1992).

37. Delumeau, *Rome*, 102–3. Martin, "Giles of Viterbo," in *Egidio da Viterbo*, 198. Elizabeth S. Cohen, "Seen and Known: Prostitutes in the Cityscape of Late-Sixteenth-Century Rome," *Renaissance Studies* 12, no. 3 (1998): 392–401. Thomas V. Cohen and Elizabeth S. Cohen, *Words and Deeds in Renaissance Rome: Trials before the Papal Magistrates* (Toronto: University of Toronto Press, 1993), chap. 2. Romano Canosa and Isabella Colonello, *Storia della Prostituzione in Italia dal Quattrocento alla fine del Settecento* (Rome: Sapere, 1989), 43–53. Guido Ruggiero, *The Boundaries of Eros: Sex Crime and Sexuality in Renaissance Venice* (New York and Oxford: Oxford University Press, 1985), 41. Sherrill Cohen, *The Evolution of Women's Asylums Since 1500: From Refuges for Ex-Prostitutes to Shelters for Battered Women* (New York and Oxford: Oxford University Press, 1992), 43–44.

38. Bette Talvacchia, *Taking Positions. On the Erotic in Renaissance Culture* (Princeton, N.J.: Princeton University Press, 1999), chaps. 1, 4, 5. Giulio Romano, Marcantonio Raimondi, and Pietro Aretino, *I Modi. The Sixteen Pleasures. An Erotic Album of the Italian Renaissance*, ed. and trans. Lynne Lawner (Evanston, Ill.: Northwestern University Press, 1988).

39. Sheila S. Blair and Jonathan Bloom, *The Art and Architecture of Islam 1250–1800* (New Haven and London: Yale University Press, 1995), 24–35, for pictorial illustration in manuscripts in Baghdad and Persia and throughout the chapters on Islamic lands in the east. Dominique Clévenot, "Peintures," in Guesdon and Vernay-Nouri, *Art du livre*, 111. Rachel Arié, *Miniatures hispano-musulmanes. Recherches sur un manuscrit arabe illustré de l'Escurial* (Leiden: E. J. Brill, 1969), 9–12. Touati, *Armoire*, 113–19. Technical illustration (e.g., mathematical, surgical) in Andalusian manuscripts in *Les Andalousies de Damas à Cordoue. Exposition présentée à l'Institut du monde arabe du 28 novembre 2000 au 15*

avril 2001 (Paris: Hazan, 2000), nos. 237, 239, 240, 250, 251. The sexually explicit miniatures reproduced in Murray and Roscoe, eds., *Islamic Homosexualities* are from the Mughal and Ottoman empires and seem to date from later periods.

40. Francisco Delicado, *Retrato de la Lozana Andaluza*, ed. Claude Allaigre (Madrid: Cátedra, 1985), Mamotreto 24, pp. 298–99; Mamotreto 44, p. 387; *Portrait of Lozana, The Lusty Andalusian Woman*, trans. Bruno M. Damiani (Potomac, Md.: Scripta Humanistica, 1987), sketch 24, p. 114; sketch 44, p. 194. On Delicado's life, see Louis Imperiale, *La Roma clandestina de Francisco Delicado y Pietro Aretino* (New York: Peter Lang, 1997), 4–5; Folke Gernet, *Francisco Delicados "Retrato de la Lozana Andaluza" und Pietro Aretinos "Sei giornate": Zum literarischen Diskurs über die käufliche Liebe im frühen Cinquecento* (Geneva: Librairie Droz, 1999), 13–17.

41. Guy Poirier, *L'Homosexualité dans l'imaginaire de la Renaissance* (Paris: Honoré Champion, 1996), pt. 2. James Brundage, *Law, Sex, and Christian Society in Medieval Europe* (Chicago and London: University of Chicago Press, 1987), 533–35. Tamar Herzig, "The Demons' Reaction to Sodomy: Witchcraft and Homosexuality in Gianfrancesco Pico della Mirandola's *Strix*," *Sixteenth-Century Journal* 34 (2003): 52–72. ASR, Camerale I, Busta 1748, no. 8 (1518), 76v, 85r; no. 9 (1518), 6r, 15r, 54r, 57r.

42. Rowland, *High Renaissance*, 24 25, 213. Gouwens, *Remembering the Renaissance*, 17–18. Castiglione, *Courtier*, bk. 2, para. 61, 159; Burke, *Fortunes*, 23. Cellini, *Autobiography*, 33; *Vita*, bk. 1, chap. 23, 75–77. On the term "kinaidos," used in Athens to refer to male dancers, prostitutes, and finally to the passive homosexual, and the Latin term "cinaedus," see Will Roscoe, "Precursors of Islamic Male Homosexualities," in Murray and Roscoe, eds., *Islamic Homosexualties*, 58, 63–64.

43. Ruggiero, *Boundaries*, 109–45, 159–61; Ruggiero, *Binding Passions*, 175–76. Michael Rocke, *Forbidden Friendships: Homosexuality and Male Culture in Renaissance Florence* (New York and Oxford: Oxford University Press, 1996), especially pt. 1 and pt. 3 for the historical narrative; "abominable vice," 212.

44. *CGA*, 147r ("ciascaduno de quisti maladicti Hosti tene uno homo al modo del Marito"), 147v ("el Populo li desidera la morte alli prefati giottoni"), 306v ("do poi la dette ad un altro suo tignoso figliolo troppo giovene el quale era un cinedo et grande imbriaco et iniusto et cosi el Populo se rebello contra esso"). Ramusio changes all these phrases to omit the popular argot: Ram, 169, 309 (see above, p. 218, and below, note 73); Ép, 213, 366. Rocke, *Forbidden Friendships*, 90, 107–8.

45. *CGA*, 175r: "intitulate sahacat cio e le Fregatrice." Ramusio changes to "chiamano queste femine Sahacat, che tanto dinota quanto nella voce latina fricatrices" (*DAR*, 39v; Ram, 192). The word "fregare" was used for

sexual intercourse by Pietro Aretino in his *Ragiomento* of 1536, and "fre-gola" was already used in the late fifteenth century to refer to a state of sexual excitement. In regard to same-sex attachment, the only reference I have found is to male activity, the Latin "fregator sodomita" (1313). Thus, Yuhanna al-Asad seems to have picked up a term from local Italian slang, which would be used as an Italian literary term to denote sexual activities between women only toward the end of the sixteenth century.

46. Bellamy, "Sex," in al-Sayyid-Marsot, ed., *Society*, 35; Adang, "Ibn Hazm," 29. Vern Bullough and James Brundage, *Sexual Practices and the Medieval Church* (Buffalo, N.Y.: Prometheus Books, 1982), 60, 69; Brundage, *Law*, 400–401, 535. For a milder view in Venice, Ruggiero, *Boundaries*, 114–15, 190 n.26.

47. Cohen and Cohen, *Daily Life*, 95, 232–34.

48. *CGA*, 147r ("in li Bordelli de la europa"). Ram, 169 ([*DAR*, 34r] "le mere-trici ne i chiassi dell'Europa"); Ép, 191.

49. Delicado, *Retrato*, ed. Allaigre, "Cómo se escusa el autor," 484–85; *Por-trait*, ed. Damiani, vi–vii, "Apology," 279. Delicado explains that before she was given the name Lozana at the time of her life with her first lover Diomedes, her name had been "'Aldonza' or 'Alaroza' in the Arabic lan-guage." These names mean "something graceful or beautiful" (*Retrato*, "Explicit," 487; *Portrait*, "Explication," 282). The Arabic words for "beautiful" are in fact "hasan" or "jamil." Allaigre discusses the Spanish meanings of the term in "Introducción," *Retrato*, 80–84.

50. Delicado, *Retrato*, Mamotreto 2, pp. 177–79 ("alcuzcuzu con garban-zos"), Mamotreto 4, pp. 184–86, Mamotreto 7, p. 194, Mamotreto 11, p. 207, Mamotreto 49, p. 404; *Portrait*, sketch 2, p. 8 ("honey cakes" in-stead of couscous!), sketch 4, pp. 13–15, sketch 7, p. 22, sketch 11, p. 34, sketch 49, p. 210. *CGA*, 165r. Ram, 184; Ép, 208. On the Mediterranean lingua franca, see Wansbrough, *Lingua franca*; Lozana's milieu adds to the chancery and commercial milieux discussed in his book.

51. Delicado, *Retrato*, Mamotreto 9, p. 202, Mamotreto 34, p. 339, Mamotreto 37, p. 351, Mamotreto 56, p. 440 ("Mirá el al-faquí"); *Por-trait*, sketch 9, p. 28, sketch 34, p. 152, sketch 37, p. 162, sketch 56, p. 238 ("like a Moslem lawyer").

52. Delicado, *Retrato*, Mamotreto 29, p. 318; *Portrait*, sketch 29, p. 133.

53. Gnoli, ed., "Censimento," 423. In the Rione Campo Marzio, nine women are listed with "cortesana" as their official occupation (421–26). On Del-icado's effort "to have the voice of Rome enter into his relation," see Im-periale, *Roma*, 19–32. The 1559 testimony of Roman prostitute Camilla the Sienese, suspected of burning the door of a rival prostitute, and other prostitutes questioned in the inquiry, fit into the world and language of Lozana (Cohen and Cohen, *Words*, 49–52, 59–60, 89–91).

54. Gnoli, ed., "Censimento," 467. I examined the registers of four notaries for the 1520s, all of whom had some clients from the Rione Regula: ASR, Collegio dei Notai Capitolini, nos. 1704, 1706, 1709, 1710 (Nicolaus Straballatus); nos. 562–563 (Laurentius de Cinciis); nos. 823–853 (Evangelista Gorius); nos. 1871–72 (Felix de Villa). I looked for the names of the principal actors in the acts as well as the witnesses to wills. In addition, I looked through the following registers, whose acts all fell within the years 1520–27: ASR, Camerale I, Busta 1748 and Busta 1749; ASR, Mandati Camerali, 859A–B; ASV, Cam. Ap. Intr. et Ex., 559–561; ASV, Arch. Concist., Acta Consist., 2–3. "Jo. Leo venetus," in ASR, Camerale I, Busta 1748, no. 10, 14v, 22 Nov. 1522.

55. Gnoli, ed., "Censimento," 466–81. Out of 1,180 households in the Rione Regula, about 48 had only one male occupant.

56. Maalouf, *Léon l'Africain*, 399–407.

57. Brundage, *Law*, 244, 296, 340. Bono, *Schiavi*, 337–40; Epstein, *Speaking of Slavery*, 64, 97. Al-Qayrawani, *Risâla*, chap. 32, 142, 146.

58. Weil, *Lévita*, 7–8, 30, 62, 108–9; Kaufmann, "Mantino," 216–18; Stow, *Jews*, 1:329, no. 378; 1:779 no. 1787, 1:855 no. 1941.

59. Leon Modena, *The History of the Rites, Customes, and Manner of Life, of the Present Jews, throughout the World*, trans. Edmund Chilmead (London: John Martin and John Ridley, 1650), 171. Kenneth R. Stow, "Marriages Are Made in Heaven: Marriage and the Individual in the Roman Jewish Ghetto," *Renaissance Quarterly* 45 (1995): 445–91; Howard Tzvi Adelman, "Jewish Women and Family Life, Inside and Outside the Ghetto," in Robert C. Davis and Benjamin Ravid, eds., *The Jews of Early Modern Venice* (Baltimore and London: Johns Hopkins University Press, 2001), 149–56.

60. Kenneth Stow, *Theater of Acculturation. The Roman Ghetto in the 16th Century* (Seattle: University of Washington Press, 2001), 20. S. Simonsohn, *History of the Jews in the Duchy of Mantua* (Jerusalem: Kiryath Sepher, 1977), 526. Brian Pullan, *Rich and Poor in Renaissance Venice* (Cambridge, Mass.: Harvard University Press, 1971), 449, 556.

61. Levita considered that his Yiddish poetry and his *Bovo-Buch* were especially directed to women (Weil, *Lévita*, 146–47).

62. Ahmad ibn Qasim al-Hajari, *Kitab nasir al-din 'ala-l-qawm al-kafirin. The Supporter of Religion against the Infidel*, ed. and trans. P. S. Van Koningsveld, Q. al-Samarrai, and G. A. Wiegers (Madrid: CSIC/AECI, 1997), 138–44.

63. Stow, *Jews*, 1:46, no. 127; 1:57, no. 157; 1:141, no. 375. On Jewish dowries, see Stow, *Theater*, 74–76, 137. On Christian dowries in Italy, see Christiane Klapisch-Zuber, *Women, Family and Ritual in Renaissance Italy*, trans. Lydia G. Cochrane (Chicago: University of Chicago Press, 1985), chap. 10: "The Griselda Complex: Dowry and Marriage Gifts in Quattrocento."

64. *CGA*, 166r–167r ("una figlia femina e la ruina del Patre in ciascaduno Paese"); 364r (in Tichit, "usano dare Dote de Possessione alli Mariti de le figlie como se usano in molti Paesi et lochi de la Europa"). Ram, 185–86 ([*DAR*, 38r] modifies the direction of the Muslim dowry and confuses trousseau with dowry), 362 ([*DAR*, 75r] substitutes "alle lor figliuole" for "alli Mariti de le figlie"); Ép, 210 (follows Ramusio's confusion), 438. Maya Shatzmiller points out that the Muslim father sometimes paid for his daughter's trousseau from the first installment of the dowry (naqd) from the husband ("Women and Property Rights," 233). Likewise in Europe, husbands sometimes paid for the garments and jewels promised their wives from the dowry that they had received from those wives.

65. Gnoli, ed., "Censimento," 420–26, 466–81. On the formation of marriage and dowries in Florence and Rome, see the splendid studies of Klapisch-Zuber in *Women*, chaps. 9, 11 (195–196 especially on dowries and marriage ritual and contracts among the lower orders).

66. Harvey, ed., "Crypto-Islam," 169, art. 11.

67. *CGA*, 167r. Ram, 186 (reverses direction of dowry); Ép, 210 (follows Ramusio's error). Al-Hajari, *Kitab nasir*, 141, 144.

68. Weil, *Lévita*, 177–78. On Floripas, see the excellent doctoral dissertation of Kristina Gourlay, "'Faire Maide' or 'Venomous Serpente': The Cultural Significance of the Saracen Princess Floripas in France and England, 1200–1500," Ph.D. diss., University of Toronto, 2002. Marinelli, *Ariosto*, 64, 84, 135, 186, 189, 210.

69. Theodore Spandugino, *Petit Traicté de l'origine des Turcqz*, ed. Charles Schefer (Paris: Ernest Leroux, 1896), xxxviii–lxix, 77–80, 186–87, 189–90, 201, 229–38. Clarence Dana Rouillard, *The Turk in French History, Thought, and Literature (1520–1660)* (Paris: Boivin, 1940), 177; Tinguely, *Écriture*, 161, 177. The first French edition of Spandugino's work is *La Genealogie du grant Turc a present regnant*, trans. Balarin de Raconis (Paris: François Rengault, 1519). The Italian manuscript dedicated to Leo X is located at the library of the Faculty of Medicine of the University of Montpellier and bears the arms of the pope. The other Italian manuscript was presented to the papal datary Gian Giberti. The presentation to the pope was probably made when Spandugino came to Italy in 1516 (Schefer, xlii n.1; xlvii n.1).

70. *CGA*, 199r, 326v, 327v–328r. Ram, 211, 325–27; Ép, 238, 387–88.

71. *CGA*, 145r–146v. Ram, 166–67 ([*DAR*, 33v] "et le piu volte si sollazzano a varie guise"); Ép, 188–89 (follows Ramusio's addition). Spandugino, *Petit Traicté*, 232–33.

72. Spandugino, *Petit Traicté*, 201.

73. "Ciascaduno de quisti maladicti Hosti tene uno homo al modo del Marito" (*CGA*, 147r) becomes "Ciascuno di questi infami huomini si tiene

un concubino, et usa con esso lui non altrimenti che la moglie use co'l marito" (*DAR*, 34r; Ram, 169). "El Populo li desidera la morte alli prefati giottoni" (*CGA*, 147v) becomes "E tutto il populo grida loro la morte" (*DAR*, 34r; Ram, 169). "Do poi la dette ad un altro suo tignoso figliolo troppo giovene el quale era un cinedo et grande imbriaco et iniusto et cosi el Populo se rebello contra esso" (*CGA*, 306v) becomes "Finalmente l'assegnò al terzo: il quale essendo molto giovane, non prendeva vergogna di patire ciò che patono le femine, peril che il popolo, vergognandosi di servire a tal Signore, il volse uccidere" (*DAR*, 64v; Ram, 309). Also, see note 45 above: "le Fregatrice" (*CGA*, 175r) becomes the learned "nella voce latina fricatrices" (*DAR*, 39v; Ram, 192).

74. Ram, 266; Ép, 307. Not found in *CGA*, 257v. The story in Ramusio is at the end of a chapter; possibly the scribe just left it out as he copied this manuscript while the scribe included it in another one. The word "sirocchia" is an archaic word for "sister" and is used by Dante and Boccaccio (Dictionary of the Accademia della Crusca).

75. For the Arabic tradition, see ʿAbd al-Rahim al-Hawrani, *Kachf asrar al-muhtaline wa nawamis al-khayyaline* (Unveiling of the Ruses Woven by Women Who Spread Their Nets by Imagination and Its Codes), translated as *Les Ruses des femmes* by René R. Khawam (Paris: Phébus, 1994), "Un parangon de vertu," and "L'épouse récalcitrante," 27–30, 43–45; "L'écuyer et la dame" in *Les cent et une nuits*, 144–45; and especially El-Shamy, *Folk Traditions*, 1:K1500–1599, "Deceptions connected with adultery," 2:11; and the further treatments of these themes in El-Shamy, *Types of the Folktale*. For the Italian tradition, see Giovanni Boccaccio, *The Decameron*, trans. John Payne (New York: Modern Library, 1931), tales from the Seventh Day; Rotunda, *Motif-Index*, K1500–1599.

76. El-Shamy, *Types of the Folktale*, K1877, Z0105. Mohammed Mrabet, *M'hashish*, ed. Paul Bowles (City Lights Books, 1976), "The Lane Break." Al-Jahiz, *Kitab al-Hayawan*, 3:11–12; Hasan El-Shamy, "A Motif Index of Alf Layla wa Layla and Its Relevance to the Study of Culture, Society and the Individual," *Journal of Arabic Literature* (forthcoming). Deborah Kapchan, e-mail to author, 14 September 2004; Jamila Bargach, e-mail to author, 2 October 2004. I am grateful to Hasan El-Shamy, Hannah Davis Taïeb, Jamila Bargach, and Deborah Kapchan for their assistance.

77. Rotunda, *Motif-Index*, H451, K1858. Pietro Fortini, *Le giornate delle novelle dei novizi*, ed. Adriana Mauriello, 2 vols. (Rome: Salerno Editrice, 1988), Third Day, tale 18, 1:321–36 ("sorella" on 334); First Day, tale 4, 1:85 ("fratello" for penis). Aretino's verses for the *Positions* and his *Ragiomenti* are full of slang terms for the male and female genitalia, but not the two used by Fortini. I am grateful to Andrea Baldi, Elizabeth Cohen, and Sarah Matthews-Grieco for assistance.

78. Lagardère, *Histoire*, 3:99, 196, 285, 384, 387; 5:98, 336, 374. Shatzmiller,

Labour, 352–57. Roded, ed., *Women*, 131–58 (includes information about and excerpt from al-Sakhawi's biographical dictionary). Two of the biographical dictionaries from the Maghreb cited by Yuhanna al-Asad in his *Illustrious Men among the Arabs*—those authored by Ibn al-Abbar and by ʿAbd al-Wahid al-Marrakushi—included women in their pages (*VIA*, 48r–50r, *VIAHott*, 272–76; Victoria Aguilar, "Mujeres y Repertorios Biográficos," in Mariá Luisa Ávila and Manuela Marín, eds., *Biografías y género biográfico en el occidente islámico* [Madrid: Consejo Superior de Investigaciones Científicas, 1997), 131. Ibn Khaldun, *Muqaddimah*, 2:368–70. Amy Singer, *Constructing Ottoman Beneficence: An Imperial Soup Kitchen in Jerusalem* (Albany: State University Press of New York, 2002), chap. 3. Reynolds, ed., *Interpreting the Self*, 40; Benchekroun, *Vie*, 292. *AM*, 61v; *AMC*, 198; al-Maqqari, *History*, 1:44–45; Walther, *Women*, 144–48; Menocal et al., *Literature*, 308–10; Eric Ormsby, "Ibn Hazm," ibid., 238; Ormsby points out that Ibn Hazm's strong appreciation for women's capacities was a minority position among Islamic writers.

79. *CGA*, 67r–69v, 70v–71r, 83r–85v, 106v–107v, 117r–118r, 137v, 231r. Ram, 96–97 ([*DAR*, 18r] adds references to the popular belief as "magical" and "superstitious"); Ép, 100–102, 104, 118–20, 144–45, 158–59, 182, 275. Ibn Khaldun, *Berbères*, 2:71–72; Abun-Nasr, *Maghrib*, 81. The important paper by Jocelyne Dakhlia, "Jean-Léon et les femmes: Quand l'adultère fait l'histoire," presented at the Colloque "Léon l'Africain" (EHESS, Paris, 22–24 May 2003; forthcoming in Pouillon and Zhiri, eds., *Léon l'Africain*) especially stresses the sexualization of politics in the published text of Yuhanna al-Asad's *Description of Africa* and its long-term implications for European views of a hypersexualized Orient. While agreeing with the imbalance in his political narrative, I am arguing that in the short term the full body of his writing on women and sexuality put some limits to already existing European stereotypes of an Islamic world saturated with sexuality.

80. Christine de Pizan, *Le Livre de la Cité des Dames* in *La Città delle Dame*, ed. Patrizia Caraffi and Earl Jeffrey Richards (Milan: Luni Editrice, 1998); *The Boke of the Cyte of Ladyes*, trans. Brian Anslay (London: H. Pepwell, 1521). Cornelius Agrippa von Nettesheim, *De nobilitate et Praecellentia foeminei sexus*, 1st ed., 1509 (Antwerp: Michael Hillenius, 1529). Pompeo Colonna, *Apologiae Mulierum Libri Duo*, ed. Guglielmo Zappacosta in *Studi e ricerche sull'umanesimo italiano: Testi inediti del XV e XVI seculo* (Bergamo: Minerva Italica, 1972), 157–246. Roded, *Women*, 128–34. For an important discussion of the frame tale and Shahrazad's accomplishment in *The Thousand and One Nights*, see Fedwa Malti-Douglas, *Woman's Body, Woman's Word. Gender and Discourse in Arabo-Islamic Writing* (Princeton, N.J.: Princeton University Press, 1991), chap. 1.

81. Castiglione, *Courtier*, bk. 3; Burke, *Fortunes*, 23, 27–28. ʿAbd al-Rahim al-Hawrani, *Désirs de femme*, trans. René R. Khawam (Paris: Phébus, 1996), especially 108–84 on the court debate and Hurra's final tale.

82. Herzig, "Demons' Reaction," 54–61: the *Strix* was published in Latin by Hieronymus de Benedictis in Bologna in May 1523, with an Italian translation the following year. Kaufmann, "Mantino," 40, 221–23. Margaret L. King, *Women of the Renaissance* (Chicago and London: University of Chicago Press, 1991), 194–200.

CHAPTER EIGHT • TRANSLATION,
TRANSMISSION, AND DISTANCE

1. *CGA*, 419v. Ram, 415; Ép, 519. The necessity and extent of female circumcision in Islamic law is controversial. Circumcision is not mentioned in the Qurʾan in either its male or female form. Two hadiths attribute approval by the Prophet of limited female excision: in one, going back to ʿAʾisha and cited by Malik, the Prophet says, "When the circumcised part touches the circumcised part, *ghusl* [ablution] is necessary"; in the other, going back to Umm ʿAtiya al-Ansariyya, the Prophet says to a female circumciser of Medina, "Do not destroy it completely, for that is more favorable for the woman and preferable for the husband." The Egyptian al-Suyuti recommended limited female excision but did not require it and also described male activities to increase the pleasure of both man and woman. Whatever the range of legal opinion, female excision was practiced in only limited areas, of which (as Yuhanna al-Asad remarks) Egypt was the most important region in North Africa. See Jonathan Berkey, "Circumcision Circumscribed, Female Excision and Cultural Accommodation in the Medieval Near East," *International Journal of Middle East Studies* 28 (1996): 19–38; Roded, *Women*, 97–98.

2. *CGA*, 113v. Ram, 136; Ép, 151.

3. *AM*, 56r–v, 58r, 59r; *AMC*, 188, 191–92. Wehr, 102; Tova Rosen, "The Muwashshaw," in Menocal et al., eds., *Literature*, 167.

4. Umberto Eco, *Experiences in Translation*, trans. Alastair McEwen (Toronto: University of Toronto Press, 2001), 17–18, 92–94.

5. Dict, 6b, 7a, 36a, 38b, 39a. *CGA*, 139v, 140v, 379r, 380r, 382r. Ram, 162–63, 376–77, 379; Ép, 184–85, 465–66, 468; Rauch, 268, 272, 280.

6. Dict, 4a. Both the incorrect Hebrew Heh, Lamed, and the Latin "Deus" are clearly in a different hand from Mantino's Hebrew and Latin cursive. The Latin "Deus" is in the same hand as the Latin entries that start on 5b, after Mantino's have ended. (I am grateful to Moshe Sluhovsky for his advice on the Hebrew entry here.) On beliefs and practices in regard to the Names of God, see Joshua Trachtenberg, *Jewish Magic and Superstition:*

A Study in Folk Religion (New York: Atheneum, 1977), 90–97, 148–51. Yuhanna al-Asad included the word "rabb" in his text, which means "lord, master, owner," and can also refer to the Lord or God, and the word "rububiya," "divinity, deity" (Dict, 48b; Wehr, 370). The words were located well beyond the section annotated by Mantino but have entries written much later in Spanish.

7. Dict, 6a, 109b. A. J. Wensinck and L. Gardet, "*Iblis*," in *EI2*, 3:668–69. Trachtenberg, *Jewish Magic*, 15, 34–37, 56–57, 155. Moses Maimonides, *The Guide for the Perplexed*, trans. M. Friedländer (London: George Routledge, 1928), 2:30, 217; 3:32, 298–99. Gershom Scholem, *Origins of the Kaballah*, trans. Allan Arkush (Princeton, N.J.: Princeton University Press and Jewish Publication Society, 1990), 148–51. Raphael Patai, *On Jewish Folklore* (Detroit: Wayne State University Press, 1983), 51, 65. Mantino knew Maimonides's writings well and was to publish his Hebrew translation of Maimonides's *Ethics* in 1526 (see chapter 2, note 90, above).

8. Trachtenberg, *Jewish Magic*, 34–37, 101, 169, 227–28 n.33. Scholem, *Origins*, 235, 294–96. Patai, *Jewish Folklore*, 49–50.

9. Dict, 6a. The Qurʾan describes Iblis as a fallen angel, but there was much Islamic discussion about whether he was not also a djinn, or participated in both natures (*EI2*, 3:668–69). Qurʾan, 2:34–36, 7:11–18, 15:26–44, 17:61–65, 38:71–85. QAn, Sura "Vacca," 7b, verse numbers cut off; Sura "De Divisionibus," 146b–148a, verses 10–17; Sura "De Lapidibus," 242v–244a, verses 26–44; Sura "De Insomnio," 268a–b, verses 63–67; Sura "De Davide," 457a–b, verses 67–78. Joannes Gabriel, translator of the Qurʾan for Egidio da Viterbo, used "diabolus" in most instances, "daemon" in "De Lapidibus"; Yuhanna al-Asad let these stand. "Midrash of Shemhazai and Azael," translation from *Midrash Bereshit Rabbati*, ed. H. Albeck (Jerusalem: Mekitze Nirdamim, 1940), 29–31, in *www.uncc.edu/jcreeves/bereshit_rabbati_29–31.htm*. I am very grateful to Yossi Chajes for calling this reference to my attention and for information about the rabbinical tradition in regard to the name "Lucifer."

10. Dict, 4a, 6a, 7a, 12b, 29b, 30a, 41b, 80b, 87a, 88b.

11. Dict, 6a, 10b, 80b, 87a. Harvey, ed. and trans., "Crypto-Islam," 168, art. 4. On "zakat" and "ihsan," see Michael Bonner, Mine Ener, and Amy Singer, eds., *Poverty and Charity in Middle Eastern Contexts* (Albany: State University of New York Press, 2003), especially 1, 276–80.

12. EpiP, 1r. Harvey, ed. and trans., "Crypto-Islam," 169, arts. 16–17.

13. *CEI*, 167–68. Corbin, *Philosophie islamique*, 258, 358, 404–7, 424. William C. Chittick, *Imagined Worlds: Ibn al-ʿArabi and the Problem of Religious Diversity* (Albany: State University of New York Press, 1994), chap. 9, especially 145–46.

14. *VIA*, 43r (includes an Arabic verse by al-Ghazali in transliteration, but the space for the Arabic letters is blank); *VIAHott*, 264 (includes only the first word of the Arabic transliteration). Al-Ghazali, *Deliverance*, 91; also see *Le chemin assuré des dévots vers le Paradis (Minhaj al-ʿabidin ila al-jannah)*, ed. Yahya Cheikh, trans. Miguel Asin Palacios (Beirut: Éditions Al-Bouraq, 2000), 21–22.

15. Th. W. Juynboll, "*Hadith*," *EI1*, 2:189–94. Abdelfattah Kilito, *L'auteur et ses doubles: Essai sur la culture arabe classique* (Paris: Éditions du Seuil, 1985), chap. 4. Lucette Valensi, "Le jardin de l'Académie ou comment se forme une école de pensée," in *Modes de transmission de la culture religieuse en Islam*, ed. Hassan Elboudrari (Cairo: Institut Français d'Archéologie Orientale du Caire, 1992), 45–48. Wael B. Hallaq, *Authority, Continuity and Change in Islamic Law* (Cambridge: Cambridge University Press, 2001), 7–8, 23, 76 and chap. 6. Reynolds, ed., *Interpreting the Self*, 3–4, 37–38, 41–43. Robinson, *Islamic Historiography*, 15–16, 36, 38, 83–102. Jonathan Berkey, *The Transmission of Knowledge in Medieval Cairo* (Princeton, N.J.: Princeton University Press, 1992), 157–59. Ibn Khaldun, *Muqaddimah*, 1:6–14, 3:481; *Voyage*, 21, 45–71. Al-Azmeh, *Ibn Khaldun*, 107–19. Cheddadi, "Introduction" to Ibn Khaldun, *Livre des Exemples*, xxiii–xxxv.

16. *CGA*, 142r–v. Ram, 164; Ép, 186–87.

17. *CGA*, 1v ("appresso de li nostri doctori et cosmographi, Affrica e divisa in 4 parti"), 2v ("secundo li nostri cosmographi"), 3r ("apresso li nostri cosmographi"). Ram, 20–21; Ép, 4–5.

18. Ibn Khallikan, *Biographical Dictionary*, 1:90–91. Gerhard Wedel, "Lebensweg, Wissen und Wissensvermittlung. Arabische Biographik im 13. Jahrhundert," paper presented to the session on "Selbstzeugnisse in transkultureller Perspektive," Deutscher Historikertag, Aachen, 29 September 2000.

19. *VIA*, 37r, 43r, 44v, 52r, 63r. *VIAHott*, 256, 264, 267, 279, 283–84. On Ibn al-Khatib's correspondence, also praised by Ibn Khaldun, and its manuscripts, see Ibn Khaldun, *Voyage*, 104–11, 120–29, and Benchekroun, *Vie*, 271, 275 n.8.

20. *CGA*, 43v: "Ma per essere necessario ad ciascuna persona che compone narrare le cose como sono"; 147r–v: "El prefato compositore fu per ascondere alcuna cosa o per dire cose piu o mino et non dire tal mancamento o vergogna de la cipta dove el fu allevato et nutrito, Ma per essere obligato de dire la verita per ogni cuncto et come e il dovere che ciascuna persona debia fare." Cf. Ram, 66 (*DAR*, 11v): "ma faccia appresso tutti mia scusa *l'officio dell'historico*, il quale è tenuto à dire senza rispetto la verità delle cose, et non à compiacere al desiderio di niuno: di maniera che io sono necessariamente costretto à scriver quello che io scrivo, non

volendo io in niuna parte allontanarmi dal vero et lasciando gli ornamenti delle parole et l'artificio da parte" (italics mine); Ram, 169 (*DAR*, 34r): "io certamente se la legge, alla quale *é astretto l'historico*, non m'havesse sospinto a dir la verità, volentieri harei trapassa questa parte con silentio per tacere il biasimo della città, nella qual sono allevato et cresciuto" (italics mine); Ép, 65, 191 (follows Ramusio).

21. *CGA*, 4r ("li Cosmographi et Hystoriographi"), 8v ("Cronechista d'Affrica"), 18v, 62v, 156r. Ram, 22 ([*DAR*, 1v] leaves out "Hystoriographi"), 27 ([*DAR*, 2v] leaves out phrase), 39, 87 ([*DAR*, 16r] omits full title of the *Epitome*), 176; Ép, 7 (leaves out "historians"), 15, 34, 92, 199. *VIA*, 32v, 35r, 36r, 39v, 43v, 48r, 49v, 62v; *VIAHott*, 248, 253–54, 259, 265, 272, 275, 283. Robinson, *Islamic Historiography*, xii–xiii, 6, 55 143–55. Ibn Khaldun, *Muqaddimah*, 1:15–65.

22. For example, *CGA*, 5r, 19r, 21r, 23v, 25v, 28r, 31r, 34r, 36v, 43r, 44r, 142r, 144r, 177r, 184r, 191v, 402r, 407r, 416v, 432v, 433r, 448v, 449v, 454r, 455r–v, 459r, 461r, 464r, 464v. "Auctori": 7r, 28r (used to refer to others, ancient writers of history, in the same sentence that he refers to himself as "ipso compositore"). Battisti and Alessio, *Dizionario*, 1038–39; Manlio Cortelazzo and Paolo Zolli, *Dizionario etimologico della lingua italiana*, 5 vols. (Bologna: Zanichelli, 1979–88), 1:261–62. Dict, 74a: "mu'allif"; Wehr, 29. Robinson, *Islamic Historiography*, 94. Michael Cooperson, letter to author, 17 September 2001; I am grateful to Professor Cooperson for his assistance.

23. *VIA*, 33v, 37r, 43r, 44v, 52r, 63r; *VIAHott*, 250, 256, 264, 267, 279, 283. Reynolds, ed., *Interpreting the Self*, 42, 294. Dict, 16b, "turjuman"; Wehr, 112.

24. *CGA*, 43v. One of the few other examples: 48v, regarding a mountain town in the Haha region "nel tempo qui io fui in quelle Paese . . ." A single example from the *Illustrious Lives*: in the biography of the Baghdad Jacobite Christian Ibn Telmid, Yuhanna al-Asad says, "I believe his book was translated into Latin" (*VIA*, 34r; *VIAHott*, 251).

25. Examples of first-person use: al-Ghazali, *Deliverance*, trans. Watt, 19–30, *Deliverance*, trans. Abulaylah, 61–74; Al-Muqaddasi, *Best Divisions*, 4–8, 44–47; Ibn Khaldun, *Voyage*, 1, 72–73, 117, 132; Ibn Battuta, *Voyages*, 1:79–84, 2:83. On Mas'udi, see Touati, *Islam et voyage*, 145. Al-Harawi used "I" much of the time in his *Kitab az-Ziyarat*, *Guide to Pilgrimage Sites*, and in few instances used the third person together with his name: "The author of this work, 'Ali ibn Abi Bakr al-Harawi, says" (*Guide des lieux de pèlerinage*, trans. Janine Sourdel-Thomine [Damascus: Institut Français de Damas, 1957], 3, 113, 225). Robinson, *Islamic Historiography*, 96, 100. Reynolds, ed., *Interpreting the Self*, 42–45, 79–83, 180–86; of the ten examples given here of autobiographical writing before 911/1505, only the excerpt from Abu Shama (d. 666/1268) is in the third person. In the late sixteenth century, the anonymous Ottoman author of *Tarih-I*

Hind-i garbi (Fresh News: A History of the India of the West), written in Turkish, used "I" in his Preface and referred to himself in the text as "the humble writer" (Goodrich, *Ottoman Turks*, 71–75, 83, 97, 145). Dict, 4a, "ana," "ani," "ego." Malek Chebel, *Le Sujet en Islam* (Paris: Éditions du Seuil, 2002), 32–33.

26. Spandugino, *Petit Traicté*, 1–4. Hernando Cortés, *Praeclara Ferdinandi Cortesii de Nova Maris Oceani Hyspania Narratio*, trans. Petrus Savorgnanus (Nuremberg: Fridericus Peypus, 1524), 1r, 12r; *La preclara narratione della Nuova Hispagna*, trans. N. Liburnio (Venice: Bernardino Vercellese, 1524). The first Spanish edition of the *Second Letter* was published in Seville in 1522; Cortés is referred to as "el capitan general" on the title page, but the first person is used in the text (Anthony Pagden, "Translator's Introduction" to Cortés, *Letters from Mexico* [New Haven and London: Yale University Press, 1986], lviii, 49). Michel de Certeau, "Montaigne's 'Of Cannibals': The Savage 'I'," in *Heterologies: Discourse on the Other*, trans. Brian Massumi (Minneapolis: University of Minnesota Press, 1986), 68–74; Anthony Pagden, "*Ius et Factum*: Text and Experience in the Writings of Bartolomé de Las Casas," in Stephen Greenblatt, ed., *New World Encounters* (Berkeley and Los Angeles: University of California Press, 1993), 88. Giorgio Vasari's *Vite* of Italian architects, painters, and sculptors, first published in Florence in 1550, did use the third person to refer to himself when he entered another artist's story (e.g., when he came to study with Michelangelo and Andre del Sarto, *Lives of the Artists. A Selection*, trans. E. L. Seeley [New York: Noonday Press, 1958], 304).

27. For example, all the mentions of the "Compositore" given in note 22 are replaced by "io" or the first-person verb in Ramusio. Ram, 23, 39, 42, 44, 47, 50, 53, 56, 59, 66, 67, 164, 166, 193, 199, 204, 399, 404, 413 (omits sentence), 429, 445, 446, 450, 455, 460. Here are a few full examples: CGA, 5r: "Anchi ipso compositore dice esser stato in 15 Regni de terra negrasca." DAR 2r (Ram 23): "Nè voglio tacer d'esser stato in quindici regni di terra negra." CGA, 142r: "Dice il compositore havere audire da molti soi Maestri." DAR, 33r (Ram 164): "io ho udito dir da molti maestri." CGA, 402r–v: "in la qual cipta ipso compositore dice esser stato quando Silim gran Turcho passo per essa cipta." DAR, 82v (Ram, 399): "Io fui in questa città nel tempo, che Selim gran Turcho passà par lei." CGA, 448v–449r: "ipso compositore dice havere vista una coda de uno de dicti castroni." DAR, 92v (Ram, 445): "Io viddi una coda di questi castroni." Épaulard followed Ramusio's practice. A century later, Hottinger kept "interpres" for his publication of *De Viris Illustribus*, with a note saying—incorrectly—that this was the Arabic custom. VIAHott, 264 note a.

28. CGA, 401r: "Alexandro magno el quale fu propheta et Re secondo la pazia di Mucametto nel corano." Ram, 398 ([DAR, 82v] "Alessandro Magno, gran propheta et Re, si come essi leggono nell'Alcorano,"

"Alexander the Great, great prophet and king, as is read in the Qur'an"). Ép, 498, follows *CGA* rather than Ram. On the one hand, Ramusio would be expected to keep a phrase hostile to Islam in the book. On the other hand, Ramusio could have consulted the Latin translation of the Qur'an, published in Basel in 1543, or the Italian translation, published in his own Venice in 1547, and seen that "Alexander" appeared in the text with the Gog and Magog story (*L'Alcorano di Macometto*, 61r–v). Unaware of the conflict about Alexander's status within Islam and baffled by Giovanni Leone's statement, he could then have removed the phrase about the "folly of Mucametto." The other possibility is that Yuhanna al-Asad had second thoughts and had removed it from one of the manuscripts. Harvey, ed. and trans., "Crypto-Islam," 169, art. 15. On the allowable limits of taqiyya, Stewart, "*Taqiyyah*," in Stewart et al., *Law*, 35.

29. *CGA*, 398v. Ram, 395 ([*DAR*, 82r] "con colorita mezogna"); Ép, 495.

30. *CGA*, 401r.

31. Rhuvon Guest, "Al-Iskandar," *EI1*, 2:534; Andreas Schmidt-Colinet, "Das Grab Alexanders d. Gr. in Memphis?" in M. Bridges and J. C. Bürgel, eds., *The Problematics of Power: Eastern and Western Representations of Alexander the Great* (Berne: Peter Lang, 1996), 87–90: considers the stop of Alexander's corpse at Memphis before its removal to Alexandria. Al-Mas'udi, *Prairies*, chap. 25, para. 679, 2:24–559. Al-Harawi, *Guide*, 112. Doris Behrens-Abouseif, "Notes sur l'architecture musulmane d'Alexandrie," in Christian Décobert and Jean-Yves Empereur, eds., *Alexandrie médiévale 1* (Cairo: Institut Français d'Archéologie Orientale, 1998), 101. Alexander's grave is not mentioned in the Alexandria section of the accounts of Ibn Hawqal, al-Muqaddasi, Ibn Jubayr, or Ibn Battuta. In the twentieth century, E. M. Forster said the mosque of the Prophet Daniel had been built upon Alexander's mausoleum (*Alexandria: A History and a Guide* [originally published 1922; London: Michael Haag, 1982], 86).

32. *CGA*, 206r ("una scriptura de verbis Mucametti"). Ram, 217–18 ([*DAR*, 45r] "il Libro delle parole di Mahumetto"); Ép, 246. Abun-Nasr, *Maghrib*, 51.

33. *CGA*, 395r–v. Ram, 392, Ép, 491. On Hisham Ibn al-Kalbi, see *The Book of Idols*, trans. Nabih Amin Faris (Princeton, N.J.: Princeton University Press, 1952), vii–xii; *Les Idoles de Hicham Ibn al-Kalbi*, trans. Wahib Atallah (Paris: Librairie C. Klincksieck, 1969), xix–xxviii; and al-Nadim, *Fihrist*, 1:205–13. The text cited by Yuhanna al-Asad is one of the many that are lost. Al-Tabari, *History*, 2:50, 109–10.

34. "Al-Iskandar," in *EI1*, 2:533–34. "Iskandar Nama," in *EI2*, 4:127–29. A set of classic texts feeding the Islamic tradition are available in Ernest A. W. Budge, ed. and trans., *The History of Alexander the Great, Being the Syriac Version of the Pseudo-Callisthenes* (Cambridge: Cambridge University Press, 1889), see especially 176–200, and *The Life and Exploits of*

Alexander the Great, Being a Series of Ethiopic Texts, 2 vols. (repr., 1896; New York and London: Benjamin Blom, 1968). Charles Genequand, "Sagesse et pouvoir: Alexandre en Islam," in Bridges and Bürgel, eds., *Problematics*, 126–33; Caroline Sawyer, "Sword of Conquest, Dove of the Soul: Political and Spiritual Values in Ahmadi's *Iskandarnama*," ibid., especially 144–45; Claude-Claire Kappler, "Alexandre dans le *Shah Nama* de Firdousi: De la conquête du monde à la découverte de soi," ibid., 165–73.

35. On the debate about the identity of Iskandar as Dhu-l-Qarnayn, see "Al-Iskandar," in *EI1*, 2:534; Abel, "Dhuʾl Qarnayn," 5–16; Genequand, "Sagesse et pouvoir" in Bridges and Bürgel, eds., *Problematics*, 130; François de Polignac, "Cosmocrator: L'Islam et la légende antique du souverain universel," ibid., 150; Faustina Doufikar-Aerts, "Alexander the Great and the Pharos of Alexandria in Arabic Literature," ibid., 191–97. Ibn Khaldun, *Muqaddimah*, 1:163: "In the middle of the ninth section is the Dam [i.e., the wall against Gog and Magog] built by Alexander . . . Correct information about it is found in the Qurʾan." Al-Masʿudi, *Prairies*, chap. 25, para. 671, 2:251: describes disagreement about the identity of Iskandar and Dhu-l-Qarnayn. Al-Idrisi, *Première géographie*, 98–99, clime 2, pt. 1.

36. Al-Tabari, *History*, 2:107–9; Polignac, "Cosmocrator," in Bridges and Bürgel, eds., *Problematics*, 153–56, 162; Robert Hillenbrand, "The Iskandar Cycle in the Great Mongol *Shahnama*," ibid., 204–5: Hillenbrand calls Iskandar's status "ambivalent."

37. Quoted by Abel, "Dhuʾl Qarnayn," 15–16.

38. *VIA*, 33r–v; *VIAHott*, 250. Corbin, *Philosophie islamique*, 160, 170–71; *EI2*, 7:788.

39. Berque, "Koranic Text," in Atiyeh, ed., *Book*, 17–29. Primary texts in Peters, *Judaism, Christianity and Islam*, 2:29–57 (56: quotation from the Prophet from Baghawi, *Mishkat al-Masabih*, 8.3.1). *CEI*, 228–41, 324–25 ("Qiraʾah"). Abu Jaʿfar Muhammad ibn Jarir al-Tabari, *The Commentary on the Qurʾan. Being an abridged translation of Jami ʿal-bayan ʿan taʾwil ay al-Qurʾan*), trans. J. Cooper (Oxford: Oxford University Press, 1987), xxi–xxiii, 16, 25–31. Ibn Khaldun, *Muqaddimah*, 2:439–43.

40. Arberry, 1:73. QAn, Sura "Imrana," 49a, verse 6. Jane Dammen McAuliffe, Barry D. Walfish, and Joseph W. Goering, eds., *With Reverence for the Word: Medieval Scriptural Exegesis in Judaism, Christianity, and Islam* (Oxford: Oxford University Press, 2003), especially chap. 20, Jane Dammen McAuliffe, "An Introduction to Medieval Interpretation of the Qurʾan," and chap. 27, Stefan Wild, "The Self-Referentiality of the Qurʾan. Sura 3:7 as an Exegetical Challenge."

41. Imam al-Haramayn al-Juwayni (d. 478/1085), *The Noble Healing*, quoted in Peters, *Judaism, Christianity, and Islam*, 1:33–37. Muhammad Murtada

al-Kashi (d. ca. 911/1505), *The Pure in the Interpretation of the Qur'an*, quoted ibid., 1:57–59. Goldman, *Life and Times*, 62. Ibn Hazm, "On the Inconsistencies of the Four Gospels," excerpted from *Al-Fasl fi al-milal*, trans. Thomas E. Burman, in Olivia Remie Constable, ed., *Medieval Iberia. Readings from Christian, Muslim, and Jewish Sources* (Philadelphia: University of Pennsylvania Press, 1997), 81–83. *CGA* 185r, 418v. Ram, 200, 415; Ép, 225, 518. On Shi'ite commentary on the Qur'an, see Cooper, "Translator's Introduction" to al-Tabari, *Commentary*, xxvii–xxviii.

42. James A. Bellamy, "Some Proposed Emendations to the Text of the Koran," in Ibn Warraq, ed., *What the Koran Really Says: Language, Text, and Commentary* (Amherst, N.Y.: Prometheus Books, 2002), 489–90, 511 n.4. Other examples of commentators offering corrections for individual words are in J. Barth, "Studies Contributing to Criticism and Exegesis of the Koran," trans. G. A. Wells, ibid., 400, 427, 429. Andrew Rippin, "The Designation of 'Foreign' Languages in the Exegesis of the Qur'an," in McAuliffe et al., eds., *With Reverence*, chap. 28.

43. Egidio da Viterbo, *Scechina e Libellus de Litteris Hebraicis*, ed. François Secret, 2 vols. (Rome: Centro Internazionale di Studi Umanistici, 1959), 2:166. Valeriano, *Hieroglyphiques*, as World Conqueror: 189b, 236d–237a, 657d; 321b (prognostication regarding Alexandria); 420d (just); 41d and 64c (strength); 401a (image believed to bring good fortune); 440c (sexual control).

44. George Carey, *The Medieval Alexander*, ed. D.J.A. Ross (Cambridge: Cambridge University Press, 1956), 67, 260–72, 343: (Domenico Falugi, *Triompho magno nel qual si contiene le famose guerra d'Alexandro magno* [Rome: Marcello Silber, 1521]). Joachim Storost, *Studien zur Alexandersage in der älteren italienischen Literatur* (Halle: Max Niemeyer Verlag, 1935), 256–70. Niccolò Machiavelli, *The Art of War*, ed. Neal Wood, trans. Ellis Farneworth (New York: Bobbs-Merrill Co., 1965), 107, 128, 179, 193, 206, 211 (*Libro della arte della guerra* [Florence: Heirs Giunta, 1521]). Castiglione, *Courtier*, 1:18, 35; 1:43, 68; 1:45, 72–73, 75; 1:52, 81; 2:67, 166; 3:35, 239–40. Florens Deuchler, "Heldenkult im Mittelalter: Alexander der Grosse," in Bridges and Bürgel, eds., *Problematics*, 16–26.

45. "Alexander in Jerusalem," from *Josippon* in Micha Joseph Bin Gorin, *Mimekor Yisrael: Classical Jewish Folktales*, ed. Emanuel Bin Gorion and Dan Ben-Amos, trans. I. M. Lask (Bloomington and Indianapolis: Indiana University Press, 1990), 89–93.

46. Martin, "Giles," in *Egidio da Viterbo*, 205–15; Weil, *Lévita*, 301–22; Levita, *Massoreth*, 86–96. Crawford Howell Toy and Caspar Levias, "Masorah," JewishEncyclopedia.com.

47. Martin, "Giles," in *Egidio da Viterbo*, 205, 219. Roland H. Bainton, *Erasmus of Christendom* (New York: Charles Scribner's Sons, 1969), 133–40.

Erasmus called for an improved translation of the New Testament in the preface to his 1505 edition of Lorenzo Valla's *Adnotationes in Novum Testamentum* (Charles Trinkaus, *"In Our Image and Likeness": Humanity and Divinity in Italian Humanist Thought* [London: Constable, 1970], 572–73).

48. Ernesto Utrillas Valero, "Los Mudéjares Turolenses: Los Primeros Cristianos Nuevos de la Corona de Aragón," in *Actas del VIII Simposio Internacional de Mudejarismo*, 820, 823.

49. The full title for QAn is Alchoranus Arabico Latinus Transcriptus, Biblioteca Ambrosiana, Milan, MS D100 inf, 1a–2b: 1621 Latin preface by the Scotsman David Colville, in which he describes the manuscript he has copied from the Escorial and talks of the roles of Egidio da Viterbo, "Iohannes Gabriel Terrolensis," and "Iohannes Leo Granatinus"; reprinted by Löfgren and Traini, *Arabic Manuscripts*, 1:41–43. On this manuscript, see Bobzin, *Koran*, 84–88, and especially Thomas Burman, "Cambridge University Library MS Mm.v.26," in Thomas Burman, Mark D. Meyerson, and Leah Shopkow, eds., *Religion, Text, and Society in Medieval Spain and Northern Europe: Essays in Honor of J. N. Hillgarth* (Toronto: Pontifical Institute of Mediaeval Studies, 2002), 335–63. Burman has found a second and early copy of this Qur'an transcription and translation, and comments on its place in late medieval treatments of the text. He is discussing these texts at length in *Reading the Qur'an in Latin Christendom, 1140–1560* (Philadelphia: University of Pennsylvania Press, forthcoming).

50. Thomas Burman, "Polemic, Philology, and Ambivalence: Reading the Qur'an in Latin Christendom," *Journal of Islamic Studies* 15, no. 2 (2004): 181–209, and Burman's important forthcoming book *Reading the Qur'an*.

51. QAn, introductory pages by David Colville, in which he quotes directly the dedication of "Iohannes Leo Granatinus"; Löfgren and Traini, *Arabic Manuscripts*, 1:43.

52. Burman, "MS Mm.v.26," 344. The verse numbers already appear in this copy of Egidio's Qur'an, dating from the early sixteenth century. Al-Tabari, *Commentary*, 1:37–38: reflecting on the hadith derived from ʿAʾisha, "The Prophet would never comment on anything from the Qur'an except verses with a number," al-Tabari said. "These, no doubt, were verses with a number." But the actual numbering was not incorporated into the Qur'an until recent times (Guesdon and Vernay-Nouri, eds., *Art du livre*, 60–75; Khatibi and Sijelmassi, *Islamic Calligraphy*, 118). Biblical verse numbering was first instituted by the Protestant Robert Estienne in his Greek New Testament of 1551 and his French New Testament of 1552, both published in Geneva (Elizabeth Armstrong, *Robert Estienne Royal Printer* [Cambridge: Cambridge University Press, 1954], 226, 228).

53. QAn, opening Sura, 1a; Bobzin, *Koran*, 88. Commenting on the Ambrosiana manuscript, Thomas Burman notes the frequency of "simpl[e] paraphrases of the Latin text . . . clearly meant to make it more readable, or more faithful to the Arabic text literally understood, or both" (Burman, "MS Mm.v.26," 353–54). The numbering of the Suras in QAn differs from the classical system today: among other changes, the opening Sura is not given a name or number in QAn, and the Qurʾan's Sura 2, "The Cow," is numbered in QAn Sura 1. Thus, in citing QAn, I have been giving the Sura by the name used in QAn, the folio number, and the verse number. Present-day numbering is indicated in square brackets.

54. QAn, Sura "Vacca," 4b, verse number hidden; 21a, verse 133 [for 2:22, 135]. Sura "De Apibus," 248a, verses 1, 3; 250a, verse 27; 250b, verse 35 [for 16:1, 3, 27, 35]. Sura "De Gentibus," 314b, verse 17; 316a, verses 24, 29 [for 22:17, 26, 31]. Burman, "MS Mm.v. 26," 351–52; Bobzin, *Koran*, 87–88. Al-Tabari, *Commentary*, 76–78, 165–67. To give another example, for Qurʾan 108:1, where the translator simply gave up on the word "kawthar" ("abundance") and has God telling Muhammad that "we have given you *alcauthar*," Yuhanna al-Asad explains, again following an Islamic commentary, that the "abundance" referred to here was "a river of paradise" (QAn, Sura "De alcautar," 608a); Walid Saleh, *The Formation of the Classical "Tafsir" Tradition. The Qurʾan Commentary of al-Thalʿabi (d. 427/1035)* (Leiden and Boston: E. J. Brill, 2004), 119–24.

55. QAn, Sura "De Antro," 282b–284a, especially verse 76 [for 18:84]. Budge, *Life*, 2:14–26, 344, 347; Carey, *Medieval Alexander*, 110–16, 290–91; Deuchler, "Heldenkult," in Bridges and Bürgel, *Problematics*, 23; Polignac, "Cosmocrator," ibid., 149–51; Kappler, "Alexandre," ibid., 165.

56. Arberry, 1:82. QAn, Sura "Imrana," 53a (comments on verses 58–59 [for 3:59–61]); 57a, verse 58 [for 3:5.9].

57. QAn, Sura "De Apibus, 258b, verse 106 [for 16:106]. *Machumetis Saracenorum principis, Eiusque Successorum Vitae, ac Doctrina, Ipsique Alcoran*, ed. Theodor Bibliander, 3 vols. (Basel: Johann Oporinus, 1543), 1:90, 97. Bobzin, *Koran*, 232, 232 n.466.

58. Andrés, *Confusione*, 5r–v, 64r–v. Bobzin, "Juan Andrés," 537–48; Bobzin, *Koran*, 345. See chapter 6 above.

59. CGA, 433r. Ram, 429; Ép, 538.

CHAPTER NINE · THE RETURN

1. CGA, 43v–44r, 432v–433r. Ram, 66–67, 429; Ép, 65–66, 538.

2. For a general account, see Judith Hook, *The Sack of Rome, 1527*, 2nd ed. (London: Palgrave MacMillan, 2004), and Denis Crouzet, *Charles de*

Bourbon, Connétable de France (Paris: Fayard, 2003), chap. 5. Cellini, *Autobiography*, 59–69; *Vita*, 1:34–39, 127–51. Luigi Guicciardini, *The Sack of Rome*, trans. James H. McGregor (New York: Italica Press, 1993), especially 83–116; "All the sacraments of the modern Church were scorned and vilified as if the city had been captured by Turks or Moors or some other barbarous and infidel enemy" (115). Gouwens, *Remembering the Renaissance*, xvii–xix, 184 (Latin oration of Pietro Alcionio).

3. Guicciardini, *Sack*, 92–93. Hook, *Sack*, 61, 112, 136, 177, 182–83, 208. Emanuele Mattaliano, "L'autonomia del territorio di Carpi dagli inizi al passaggio sotto il dominio Estense," in *Società*, 393. Sanuto, *Diarii*, 44:545; 45:177, 210, 227. Weil, *Lévita*, 107. Though some sources say Egidio da Viterbo's library was "destroyed" during the sack, 809 manuscripts passed from his collection to Cardinal Niccolò Ridolfi after his death in 1532 (Roberto Ridolfi, "La Biblioteca del cardinale Niccolò Ridolfi, 1501–1550," *Bibliofilia* 31 [1929]: 176–77). Part of Egidio's collection may have been at Viterbo and/or the pillagers in Rome ran off with only some of his books.

4. Weil, *Lévita*, 107–8. Levita, *Massoreth*, 100.

5. Weil, *Lévita*, 110. Sanuto, *Diarii*, 45:364, 383, 408, 551. Secret, *Kabbalistes*, 117. Egidio da Viterbo, *Scechina*, 1:104–6.

6. Sanuto, *Diarii*, 46:135. *Alberti Pii Carporum Comitis ad Erasmi expostulationem responsio* (Paris: Josse Badius, 1529). *Alberti Pii Carporum Comitis . . . tres et viginti Libri in locos lucubrationum variarum D. Erasmi Rhoterdami* (Paris: Josse Badius, 1531). There was also a 1531 edition printed at Venice by the heirs of Luc-Antonio Giunta. Albondo Biondi, "Alberto Pio nella pubblicistica del suo Tempo," in *Società*, 124–25.

7. *Alcorano*, 22v–23r. Secret agrees that this is a garbled reference to "Leo Africanus," conjoining the Jew Michael ben Sabthai, known as Zematus, with al-Wazzan (Secret, *Kabbalistes*, 109, 126 n.89; F. Secret, "Guillaume Postel et les études arabes à la Renaissance," *Arabica*, 9 [1962]: 23 n.5). See on this edition of the Qur'an, chapter 2, note 71, above.

8. Widmanstadt, *Liber Sacrosancti Evangelii*, a***4a–4b.

9. Valeriano, *Hieroglyphiques*, 308–10. Book 25, which opens with the ostrich and the bat, is dedicated to Thomas Milario of Belluno, Valeriano's home town: Valeriano recalls the coronation festivities of Emperor Charles V at Bologna by Pope Clement in 1529–30, which Milario had witnessed not long before.

10. Ibid., 310–12.

11. Sanuto, *Diarii*, 26:195 (al-Wazzan is wrongly identified, however, as an ambassador for the sultan of Tlemcen); examples of ambassadorial exchange between Venice and Constantinople from October 1526 through

January 1527 are in 43:39–40, 44–45, 51–52, 67, 81, 101, 125, 132, 134, 150, 299, 322, 472, 596, 599, 687, 719, 725. Jacob Ziegler to Wilibald Pirckheimer, 3 calends February 1530, in Rauch, 457.

12. Robert Ricard, "Moulay Ibrahim, Caïd de Chechaouen (circa 1490–1539)," in *Études*, 261–80. Luiz de Sousa, *Les Portugais et l'Afrique du Nord de 1521 à 1557*, trans. Robert Ricard (Lisbon: Livraria Portugália and Paris: Société d'Éditions "Les Belles Lettres," 1940), 44–45. Abun-Nasr, *Maghrib*, 208–9; Cornell, *Realm*, 243–44. *CGA*, 235r. Ram, 246; Ép, 281.

13. "Les Relations du martyre d'André de Spolète," in *SIHME*, 1:6–40. Al-Hasan al-Wazzan was not mentioned in this account, nor in the report of the French expedition to the sultan and vizier of Fez in 1533 (*SIHMF*, 1:1–46).

14. Abun-Nasr, *Maghrib*, 210–13; García-Arenal, "Sainteté," 1021–24; Cornell, *Realm*, 255–63. Al-Ghazwani died in 935/1528–29, but the Jazulite tradition continued in the south, and most often in support of the Saʿdiyan cause.

15. *Libro Sacrosancti Evangelii*, dedication of Johann Widmanstadt to Emperor Ferdinand, a***4b.

16. *CGA*, 178r–v, 306v, 320r–327v. Ram, 194–95, 309, 321–26; Ép, 219, 366, 381–88.

17. Giovio, *Elogia virorum bellica virtute*, 313–15; *Gli Elogi Vite . . . d'Huomini Illustri di Guerra*, 404–6; *La Seconda Parte dell'Historie del suo tempo*, trans. Lodovico Domenichi (Venice: Bartolomeo Cesano, 1554), bk. 34, 371r–v. Matteo Bandello, *Le Novelle*, ed. Delmo Maestri, 4 vols. (Alessandria: Edizioni dell-Orso, 1995), vol. 4, "La Quarta Parte de le Novelle," novella 4, 39. Deswarte-Rosa, "Expédition," in Bennassar and Sauzet, eds., *Chrétiens*, 126. Abun-Nasr, *Maghrib*, 150–51, 168–69; Julien, *Histoire*, 2:256–57.

18. Amar, ed. and trans., *Consultations juridiques*, 394–95; Lagardère, *Histoire*, 102, no. 155.

19. Farhat Dachraoui, "À propos de la réalité culturelle des Morisques en Tunisie," in Haddad-Chamakh and Baccar-Bournaz, eds., *Écho*, 57–63. Bono, *Schiavi*, 461–74.

20. Jean de Thevenot, *Relation d'un Voyage fait au Levant* (Paris: Louis Billaine, 1665), 522–26.

21. Nicolas Clenardus, *Correspondance de Nicolas Clénard*, ed. Alphonse Roersch, 3 vols. (Brussels: Palais des Académies, 1940), 3:120, 125, 135–36. According to a fatwa in al-Wansharisi's *Miʿyar*, there were some jurists who said one should not take the Qurʾan with one when passing through

the lands of enemies, lest it be touched by the hands of infidels and thereby insulted (Amar, ed. and trans., *Consultations juridiques*, 200–201).

22. Biondi, "Alberto Pio," in *Società*, 128. François I's efforts to establish trading and diplomatic ties with the sultan of Fez date from 1533 (*SIHMF*, 1:1–46), but Alberto Pio's advice earlier may have prepared the way.

23. Julien, *Histoire*, 2:257–58. Deswarte-Rosa, "Expédition," in Bennassar and Sauzet, eds., *Chrétiens*, 97–113.

24. Ibid., 81–94. Paolo Giovio to Francesco II Sforza, Duke of Milan, Rome, 6 June 1535, in Paolo Giovio, *Lettere*, ed. Giuseppe Guido Ferrero, 2 vols. (Rome: Istituto Poligrafico dello Stato, 1956), no. 52, 1:153–56. *CGA*, 322v.

25. Paolo Giovio to Federico Gonazaga, Duke of Mantua, 14 July 1535, and Paolo Giovio to Rodolpho Pio di Carpi, 28 December 1535, in *Lettere*, no. 52, 1:156–60; no. 59, 1:171. Deswarte-Rosa, "Expédition," in Bennassar and Sauzet, eds., *Chrétiens*, 121–23. Cornelius Scepper, ed., *Rerum à Carolo V Caesare augusto in Africa bello gestarum Commentarii* (Antwerp: Jean Bellère, 1554).

26. Deswarte-Rosa, "Expédition," in Bennassar and Sauzet, eds., *Chrétiens*, 126. Giovio, *Seconda Parte dell'Historie*, bk. 34, 371r–372r. Erika Spivakovsky, *Son of the Alhambra: Diego Hurtada de Mendoza, 1504–1575* (Austin and London: University of Texas Press, 1970), 38–39, 52–57, 105.

27. Joannes Etrobius, *Commentarium seu potius Diairium Expeditionis Tunetanae a Carolo V*, in Scepper, ed., *Rerum*, 51v–52v.

28. Julien, *Histoire*, 2:270. The conspiracy against and blinding of Sultan al-Hasan are described by Giovio in *La Rimanente della Seconda Parte dell'Historie de suo tempo*, trans. Lodovico Domenichi (Venice: Comin da Trino, 1555), bk. 44, 334v–344r; Matteo Bandello devoted an entire novella to the episode (*Novelle*, 4:38–48). Deswarte-Rosa, "Expédition," in Bennassar and Sauzet, eds., *Chrétiens*, 129.

29. Clenardus, *Correspondance*, 3:101, 123. See above in my Introduction, p. 8, and note 11 for the first biographical notice of al-Hasan al-Wazzan in Arabic in the 1930s and the first Arabic translation of his work by Muhammad Hajji in 1980. Hajji includes him in his *L'activité intellectuelle au Maroc* (28, 35, 61, 64, 402), but only for the works written in Italy.

30. On the importance of networks, social and familial, for the Christian or Jewish convert to Islam, see Jocelyne Dakhlia, "'Turcs de profession'? Réinscription lignagères et redéfinitions sexuelles des convertis dans les cours maghrébines XVIe–XIXe siècles)," in Mercedes García-Arenal, ed., *Conversions islamiques. Identités religieuses en Islam méditerranéen* (Paris: Maisonneuve et Larose, 2001), 151–71. Such insertion would be equally or more important for an "apostate" like al-Wazzan.

31. Hajji, *Activité*, 180–83. Al-Hajari, *Kitab nasir*. McIntosh, *Piri Reis Map*,

6–7; Reis, *Kitab-I Bahriye*, 50–55, 75–78. Goodrich, *Ottoman Turks*, 7–11. Bernadette Andrea, "Columbus in Istanbul: Ottoman Mappings of the 'New World,'" *Genre* 30 (Spring/Summer 1997), 135–65. For the later period, see Nabil Matar, ed. and trans., *In the Lands of the Christians: Arabic Travel Writing in the Seventeenth Century* (London: Routledge, 2003).

32. Ibn ʿAskar, *Dawhat-an-Nasir. Sur les vertus éminentes des Chaiks du Maghrib au dixième siècle*, trans. A. Graulle, *Archives marocaines* 19 (1913): 35–37. Lévi-Provençal, *Historiens*, 231–37. Similarly in the important biographical compendium of scholars by Ibn Maryam of Tlemcen (d. ca. 1602/1011), the voyages (rihalat) mentioned are all within the abode of Islam for study and spiritual development (Ibn Maryam, *El Bostan ou jardin des biographies des saints et savants de Tlemcen*, trans. F. Provenzali [Algiers: Imprimerie Orientale Fontana, 1910], 238).

33. Reynolds, ed., *Interpreting the Self*, 56–58.

34. Goodrich, *Ottoman Turks*, 35–38, 110.

35. Widmanstadt, *Libro Sacrosancti Evangelii*, a***4b. Dict, 117b. Perles, *Beiträge*, 158–62, 161 n.1. Kaufmann, "Mantino," 37, 213. Spivakovsky, *Son*, 105, 121, 147. "La biblioteca de Don Diego Hurtado de Mendoza (1576)," in P. Gregorio de Andrés, *Documentos para la historia del Monasterio de San Lorenzo el Real de El Escorial* (Madrid: Imp. Saez, 1964), 7:291. Elijah Levita, *Nomenclatura Hebraica* (Isny: Paul Fagius, 1542). Bobzin, *Koran*, 292.

36. Spivakovsky, *Son*, 401–4. QAn, introductory pages: the Scotsman David Coville made his copy of Egidio da Viterbo's Qurʾan from the original at the Escorial; the Escorial Qurʾan is now lost; Burman, "MS Mm.v.26," 336, 340–41. Levi Della Vida, *Ricerche*, 311.

37. Levi Della Vida, *Ricerche*, 311–13, 321 (Postel sends the Arabic grammar of "Leo Africanus" to his friend Andreas Masius, city councillor of Kleve, on the German-Dutch border, and student of Arabic); Bobzin, *Koran*, 450 n.458. F. Secret, "Filippo Archinto, Girolamo Cardano et Guillaume Postel," *Studi Francesi* 13 (1969): 73–76. F. Secret, "Postel et Jean Léon l'Africain," in *Postel revisité. Nouvelles recherches sur Guillaume Postel et son milieu* (Paris: SÉHA and Milan: Arché, 1998), 149–56: Secret shows the influence of al-Wazzan's Africa book on Postel's *Admirabilis Judaeorum clausorum seu decem tribuum Israel, sub Turcarum et Ismaelitarum potentia redactarum historia, atque ipsa Ismaelitarum origo*, written in 1548. On Postel's universal vision, see William Bouwsma, *Concordia Mundi: The Career and Thought of Guillaume Postel (1510–1581)* (Cambridge, Mass.: Harvard University Press, 1957).

38. *VIA* and *VIH* are part of Antonio Petrei's collection of manuscripts at the Biblioteca Medicea Laurenziana in Florence. Petrei was in the circle of Cardinal Niccolò Ridolfi, who had acquired Greek, Latin, Hebrew, and

Arabic manuscripts from Egidio da Viterbo's library after the latter's death in 1532. Perhaps this was the path by which al-Wazzan's manuscripts passed into Petrei's hands (*AMC*, 181–82; Roberto Ridolfi, "Antonio Petrei letterato e bibliofilo del Cinquencento," *Bibliofilia* 48 [1947]: 53–70; Ridolfi, "Biblioteca," 176). Johann Heinrich Heidegger, *Historia vitae et obitus I. Henrici Hottinger* (Zurich, 1667). Hottinger had studied Arabic at the University of Leiden and was the author of a multivolumed *Historiae Ecclesiasticae* (1651), with parallel histories of Christianity, Judaism, and Islam; a bibliography of books in Hebrew, Arabic, Syriac, and Coptic, where among other things, he mentioned Arabic manuscripts in the Laurenziana (*Promptuarium, sive Bibliotheca Orientalis* [Heidelberg, 1658], 211–12); and *Historia Orientalis* (1660), a book on the history of Islam. *VIAHott*, 262 (omits most of 41r and top of 41v); *VIHHott*, 290 (replaces *VIH*, 290, "quod Iuvenis, quem pedamaverat" with dashes).

39. *Ioannis Leonis Africani, De Totius Africae descriptione, Libri IX* (Antwerp: Jan de Laet, 1556), copy at the Biblioteca Nacional Madrid, R-25410, title page: "Prohibido in totium" in a seventeenth-century hand, 36v–37r. A mysterious "Ioannes Leonis Nardi" appeared for the first time on a Roman index of 1596, with all his books to be condemned, but without further identification or book titles (J. M. de Bujanda et al., *Index de Rome 1590, 1593, 1596* [Sherbrooke: Éditions de l'Université de Sherbrooke and Geneva: Librairie Droz, 1994], 600, no. 593). In 1667 Antonio de Sotomayor, inquisitor-general of Spain, added after that name "Perhaps the same as Ioannes Leo Africanus, who wrote *de Lege Mahometana* and *Descriptionem Africae*, published at Antwerp by Joannes Latius and at Zurich by the Gesner brothers." *Index Librorum Prohibitorum et Expurgandorum Novissimus* (Madrid: Didaci Diaz, 1667), 631, column 2.

EPILOGUE · AFFINITIES

1. François Rabelais, *Oeuvres complètes*, ed. Mireille Huchon, with the collaboration of François Moreau (Paris: Gallimard, 1994), 239 (*Pant* 7), 988–92, 1051–55, 1212, 1748–49. Richard Cooper, *Rabelais et l'Italie* (*Études rabelaisiennes* 24) (Geneva: Librairie Droz, 1991), 22–30, 79–85, 99–103.

2. Rabelais, *Oeuvres*, 989, 1748–49. Cooper, *Rabelais*, 33–41.

3. Kaufmann, "Mantino," 47–57, 207–9. Rabelais, *Oeuvres*, 1017; Cooper, *Rabelais*, 157. J. J. Scarisbrick, *Henry VIII* (Harmondsworth, Middlesex: Penguin Books, 1971), 434–37.

4. Ibid., 23; Jean du Bellay had already met Rodolfo Pio in Paris in 1530, the year of Alberto Pio's death. Du Bellay was surely aware of Alberto Pio's role in preparing the way for François I's alliance with Sultan Suleyman. Svalduz, *Carpi*, 371 (will of 21 July 1530). *Società . . . a Carpi*, 170. During Rabelais's second visit to Rome, August 1535 to May 1536, Rodolfo

Pio was probably away much or all of the time in Paris, where he had been named papal nuncio.

5. Giovio, *Lettere*, 1:163, 171, 173. Cooper, *Rabelais*, 25, 31, 38–39, 114–16, 119–20, 133–34. Rabelais, *Oeuvres*, 1000–1017. Deswarte-Rosa, "Expédition," in Bennassar and Sauzet, eds., *Chrétiens*, 82–83, 90–91.

6. Rabelais, *Oeuvres*, 1012; Cooper, *Rabelais*, 143.

7. Rabelais, *Oeuvres*, 703, 1456. Ptolemy, *Continentur Geographiae* (Rome: Evangelista Tosino, 1508), tabula 4 of Africa; *Liber Geographiae* (Venice: Jacopo Pencio, 1511), fourth map of Africa; *Geographicae enarrationis Libri Octo*, ed. Wilibald Pirckheimer (Strasbourg: Johann Grieninger and Johann Koberger, 1525), tabula 4 of Africa; *Geographicae Enarrationis Libri Octo*, trans. Wilibald Pirckheimer, ed. Michael Servetus (Lyon: Melchior and Gaspard Trechsel, 1535), index, map.

8. Ibn Khaldun, *Muqaddimah*, 1:119, 168. CGA, 388v–389r. Ram, 386; Ép, 480; Rauch, 310–11.

9. Rabelais, *Oeuvres*, 709. Ibn Hawqal, *Configuration*, 1:143–44; al-Idrisi, *Première géographie*, 89–90; Ibn Khaldun, *Muqaddimah*, 1:120–21; Michel, *Géographie*, 2:135–36. CGA, 432r–v, 440v–441r. Ram, 428, 437–38; Ép, 536, 552–53. Al-Wazzan explains the lack of commercial navigation south of Aswan by the shallowness of the river rather than by the impact of the cataracts upstream. Ibn Hawqal and al-Idrisi describe how cargo is taken off boats and carried by camel to Aswan.

10. In his questioning of the deaf-mute Nazdecabre by signs, Panurge placed his hand "above his buttocks in the place the Arabs call Al-Katim" ("au dessus des fesses on lieu que les Arabes appellent Al Katim"). This was the medical Latin rendering of the Arabic for "qatan," "small of the back," and the physician Rabelais could readily pick that up (Rabelais, *TL*, 20, in *Oeuvres*, 413 [editor wrongly translates as "sacrum"]; A. Fonahn, *Arabic and Latin Anatomical Terminology chiefly from the Middle Ages* [Oslo: Jacob Dybwad, 1922], 79, no. 1765). In contrast, when Rabelais writes, "*Teleniabin et Geleniabin*, Arabic sayings, manna, rose honey" (*QL*, in *Oeuvres*, 707), he is simply concocting definitions.

11. Rabelais, *Oeuvres*, 46 (*Garg* 16); 437 (*TL* 27); 734 (*CL* 3). The saying "Africa always produces things new" also appeared as the last line of a French dedicatory poem in the French translation of al-Wazzan's *Geography* (*Historiale Description*, *5r–v).

12. Rabelais, *Oeuvres*, liii, lv–lvi. Cooper, *Rabelais*, 80; J. Lesellier, "Deux enfants naturels de Rabelais légitimés par le Pape Paul III," *Humanisme et Renaissance* 5 (1938): 549–70.

13. Rabelais, *Oeuvres*, 833–37 (*CL* 45–46).

14. Ibid., 6 (*Garg* Prologue), 1050–51, 1456–57. M. A. Screech, *Rabelais*

(London: Duckworth, 1979), 111–14, 203–4, 208–9, 313, 321. J. M. De Bujanda, Francis M. Higman, and James K. Farge, *Index de l'Université de Paris, 1544, 1545, 1547, 1549, 1551, 1556* (Sherbrooke: Éditions de l'Université de Sherbrooke and Geneva: Librairie Droz, 1985), 63, 359 (no. 428), 381–83 (nos. 464–465).

15. Ibid., 213–14 (*Pant* Prologue), 315 (*Pant* 28); Huchon's important discussion and bibliography, 1213–17.

16. Ibid., 272–76 (*Pant* 16), 281–91 (*Pant* 18–20), 321–22 (*Pant* 30), 1221–24. Marcel Detienne and Jean-Pierre Vernant, *Cunning Intelligence in Greek Culture and Society*, trans. Janet Lloyd (Chicago: University of Chicago Press, 1991), introduction, chaps. 1–2.

17. Rabelais, *Oeuvres*, 263–67 (*Pant* 14).

18. For an important reading of this chapter, somewhat different from my own, see Timothy Hampton, "'Turkish Dogs': Rabelais, Erasmus, and the Rhetoric of Alterity," *Representations* 41 (Winter 1993): 58–82.

19. Rabelais, *Oeuvres*, 91–95 (*Garg* 33), 319 (*Pant* 29), 1044–45.

20. Ibid., 124 (*Garg* 46), 132–36 (*Garg* 50), 481–82 (*TL* 41).

21. Ibid., 219–21 (*Pant* 1), 244 (*Pant* 8), 246–47 (*Pant* 9), 264–66 (*Pant* 14), 336 (*Pant* 34).

22. Ibid., 232–35 (*Pant* 6), 246–50 (*Pant* 9).

23. Ibid., 669–70 (*QL* 56).

24. Ibid., 1217–20, 1223. Claude Gaignebet, *A plus hault sens. L'esotérisme spirituel et charnel de Rabelais*, 2 vols. (Paris: Maisonneuve et Larose, 1986), pt. 2. Edwin M. Duval, *The Design of Rabelais's "Pantagruel"* (New Haven: Yale University Press, 1991), chap. 2.

25. Rabelais, *Oeuvres*, lxv, 1472–73. Herodotus, *The Persian Wars*, trans. George Rawlinson (New York: Modern Library, 1947), multiple gods in bk. 2, chap. 4, 118; chap. 18, 124–25; chaps. 42–43, 137–39; chap. 48, 141. Jan Assmann, *Moses the Egyptian: The Memory of Egypt in Western Monotheism* (Cambridge: Harvard University Press, 1997), 18–19, 55.

26. *CEI*, 160, 244, 318–19, 349. J. Horovitz, "Nabi," *EI1*, 3:802–3; A. J. Wensinck, "Rasul," *EI2*, 8:454–55. Qurʾan, 11: Hud; 31: Luqman. Muhsin Mahdi, *La cité vertueuse d'Alfarabi: La fondation de la philosophie politique en Islam* (Paris: Albin Michel, 2000), 282–308.

27. Fahd, *Divination*, 92–104. W. P. Heinrichs and Afif ben Abdesselem, "Sadjʿ" in *EI2*, 8:732–35.

28. Arberry, 1:39.

29. QAn, 13a–b, Sura "Vacca," verse 84.

30. Ibn al-ʿArabi, *Al-Futuhat al-makkiyya*, as quoted in Chittick, *Imagined Worlds*, 160.

Glossary of Arabic Words

adab: decorous manners, rules for good conduct, witty cultivated literary expression including instructive anecdotes, knowledge and writing outside the sphere of theology and law

ahbas: see *habus*

akhbari: transmitter of past events, historian

amir: prince, provincial governor

aqalim: see *iqlim*

awqaf: see *waqf*

baraka: spiritual blessing sent down from God

basmala: Muslim formulaic prayer used to consecrate an action, open a text

bid'a: an innovation in Muslim law or practice, not found in the Qur'an or early tradition, and suspect as contrary to Islamic spirit

Dar al-'Ahd: the abode of treaty, territories which have treaties or contractual relations with Islamic lands

Dar al-Harb: the abode of war, territories in which Islam does not prevail

Dar al-Islam: the abode of peace, lands in which Islam prevails *dhimmi*: a person belonging to one of the Peoples of the Book—primarily Jews and Christians—living as "protected" in Islamic lands and subject to a special tax and requirements for dress and conduct

faqih: a learned scholar trained in the law

fatwa: legal opinion from a jurist

fiqh: jurisprudence, judicial theology of Islam

habus, pl. *ahbas*: charitable endowment of inalienable land, Maghrebi term for *waqf*

hadith: report or reports of words or deeds of the Prophet Muhammad, supported by trustworthy transmitters

Hajj: pilgrimage to Mecca, one of the Five Pillars of Islam, required once in a lifetime for those able to manage it

halal: lawful food, especially meat ritually slaughtered

*hija*ʾ: poetry of invective

Hijra: the Prophet Muhammad's migration from Mecca to Medina in 622 C.E., which became the first year of the Muslim calendar

hila: ruse, artifice, stratagem, ingenious device, trick

ʿId al-Adha: an important feast commemorating Abraham's sacrifice of a ram, brought to him by an angel as substitute for his son

ijaza: certificate from a teacher affirming that one has read certain books with him and is qualified to teach them

imam: prayer leader

iqlim, pl. *aqalim*: latitudinal climatic zones dividing the world in Greek, Arabic, and western geography

isnad: a chain of trustworthy authorities transmitting reports about the Prophet Muhammad and by extension about other major figures, events, scholarly information

jihad: from "struggle" or "effort." External jihad is Holy War

jizya: special tax required of people with *dhimmi* status *kafir*: nonbeliever in the divine revelation and in Muhammad as Messenger, infidel

kahin, kahina: diviner, male and female

kaid: ruse, stratagem

khanith, mukhannath (adj.): said of a man who acts like a woman; effeminate

khitan: circumcision

kitab: piece of writing, record, book

liwat: sexual or sodomitic practices between men

al-madh: panegyric poem

madhhab, pl. *madhahib*: School of Islamic Law. Among the Sunnis, there are four Schools, of which the Malikite School was dominant in the Maghreb

madrasa: college, school for advanced learning

Mahdi: "the guided one," a figure bringing spiritual and political renewal at the end of time; a title claimed by historical religious/political reformers

mahr: dowry given by the Muslim husband to his wife

makr, makra, adj. *makir*: ruse, artifice, trick; cunning, wily

maqama, pl. *maqamat*: literally assembly, assemblies; a genre in rhymed prose involving a narrator and an eloquent wandering hero

Mawlid an-Nabi: the feast day for the birthday of the Prophet Muhammad

mizaj: mixture, blend, medley

mu'aliff: compiler, writer, author

mu'arrikh: chronographer, historian

mufti: jurist

muhtasib: officer supervising activities and conduct at the market

mujun: ribald, brazen, clowning, used for a genre of erotic and hedonistic poetry and prose *mukhannath,* see *khanith*

mukhtasar: abridgment, epitome of an earlier text

murabit, pl. *murabitun:* holy man, saintly man, leader of a ribat

mutarjim: translator, interpreter, biographer

nisba: adjective ending in an i, placed at the end of name to indicate relation to a place, occupation, idea, etc.

qadi: judge

qaʾid: leader, local governor

Qibla: direction faced by Muslims during ritual prayer, toward the Kaʿba in Mecca

qutb: pole or axis; used for a holy man thought to be the center of sanctity of his time

Ramadan: the ninth month of the Islamic calendar in which Muslims are required to fast from daybreak until the setting of the sun

ribat: a Sufi religious community

rihla: travel, voyage; also a travel account

sadaqa: charitable gifts or alms beyond one's required annual *zakat*

sadjʿ: rhymed alliterative prose

shahada: literally "witness," the creed affirming acceptance of Islam

shariʿa: the holy law of Islam

sharif: a descendant of the Prophet Muhammad

shaykh: chief, elder, leader; sometimes used for religious leader

sudan, Bilad al-Sudan: Blacks, Land of the Blacks

suhaqiyat: women who perform sexual acts with each other

Sunna: the words and actions of the Prophet Muhammad as a standard for living and values

tabaqat: a compendium of biographies organized by entries, often linked to people in a specified field or fields *takhlit*: a confused and disordered mixture

taqiyya: dissimulation of one's true heartfelt religious beliefs under circumstances of coercion

tarjama: a biography, an entry in a biographical compendium

al-tawil: a prized poetic meter

ʿulamaʾ: religious scholars

waqf, pl. *awqaf*: charitable endowment

zaʾiraja: a form of learned divination using complex patterns of letters, numbers, and symbols

zakat: annual fixed charitable donation, required of all Muslims

zawiya, pl. *zawaya*: Sufi communities and confraternities, term especially used in sixteenth century and afterward

zinaʾ: sinful, illicit sexual activity

Bibliography

MANUSCRIPTS AND ARCHIVES

Egidio da Viterbo. *Dichionarium sive liber radicum Aegidio Viterbien. Card. Interprete.* MS 3. Biblioteca Angelica, Rome.

———. *Aegidio Viterbiensis Historia viginiti seculorum.* MS 351. Biblioteca Angelica, Rome.

Elias bar Abraham, the Maronite, copyist. *Liber quatuor Evangelistarum Caldaice Scriptus Anno incar. 1521.* MS Syriaque 44. Bibliothèque Nationale de France, Paris.

Grassi, Paride. *Diarium An. 1513 ad 1521.* MS E53. Department of Special Collections, Spencer Research Library, University of Kansas Libraries, Lawrence, Kansas.

al-Hariri, al-Qasim. *Maqamat,* illustrated, copied ca. 619/1222. MS arabe 6094. Bibliothèque Nationale de France, Paris.

———. *Maqamat,* with illustrations by Yahya al-Wasiti, copied Ramadan 634/1237. MS arabe 5847. Bibliothèque Nationale de France, Paris.

Pio, Alberto, Prince of Carpi. Correspondence, 1512–23. MS Lea 414, nos. 1–56. Special Collections, University of Pennsylvania Library, Philadelphia.

al-Wazzan, al-Hasan. *De Arte Metrica Liber.* MS Plut. 36.35, 54r–61v. Biblioteca Medicea Laurenziana, Florence.

———. *De Viris quibusdam Illustribus apud Arabes.* MS Plut. 36.35, 31r–53v, 62r–65r. Biblioteca Medicea Laurenziana, Florence.

———. *De quibusdam Viris Illustribus apud Hebraeos.* MS Plut. 36.35, 65v–69v. Biblioteca Medicea Laurenziana, Florence.

———. *Libro de la Cosmogrophia [sic] et Geographia de Affrica.* V. E. MS 953. Biblioteca Nazionale Centrale, Rome.

————. *Al-Qur'an* in Arabic and Latin, translated and annotated by Joannes Gabriel of Teruel (1518); corrected and annotated by al-Hasan al-Wazzan (1525); copied by David Colville (1621). MS D100 inf. Biblioteca Ambrosiana, Milan.

————, transcriber. The Epistles of Saint Paul in Arabic. MS Orientale 16-alfa.J.6.3. Biblioteca Estense Universitaria, Modena.

————, Jacob Mantino et al. Arabic-Hebrew-Latin-Spanish dictionary. MS 598, Manuscritos árabes 16. Real Biblioteca del Escorial, Spain.

Archivio Segreto Vaticano. Archivio Concistoriale, Acta Vicecancellerii. Vol. 2. Camera Apostolica, Introitus et Exitus, nos. 559–61.

Archivio di Stato di Roma. Camerale I, Busta 1748, 1749. Camerale I, Mandati Camerali 859 A–B. Collegio dei Notai Capitolini 562–63, 852–53, 1704, 1706, 1709–10, 1871–72.

Biblioteca Apostolica Vaticana, Vatican City. MSS Vat. Ar. 80, 115, 357, with reader's signatures of al-Hasan al-Wazzan.

PRINTED PRIMARY SOURCES

Adrutiel, Abraham ben Salomon. *Sefer ha-Kabbala*. In *Dos Crónicas Hispanohebreas del Siglo XV*. Edited and translated by Yolanda Moreno Koch. Barcelona: Riopiedras Ediciones, 1992.

Aesop. *The Medici Aesop. Spencer MS 50. From the Spencer Collection of the New York Public Library*. Facsimile. Edited and translated by Bernard McTigue. New York: Harry Abrams, 1989.

Alcala, Pedro de. *Arte para ligeramente saber la lengua araviga* and *Vocabulista aravigo en letra castellana*. Granada: Juan Varela, 1505.

L'Alcorano di Macometto, Nel qual si contiene la Dottrina, la Vita, I Costumi, et le Leggi sue. Tradotto nuovamente dall'Arabi in lingua Italiana. N.p. (Venice): Andrea Arrivabene, 1547.

Amar, Émile, ed. and trans. *Consultations juridiques des faqihs du Maghreb* [translations of selected fatwas and juridical opinions from the *Mi'yar* of Ahmad al-Wansharisi]. *Archives marocaines* 12 (1908).

Andrés, Juan. *Opera chiamata Confusione della Setta Machumetana, composta in lingua Spagnola, per Giovan Andrea gia Moro et Alfacqui, della citta di Sciativa* [sic for *Játiva*], *hora per la divina bontà Christiano e Sacerdote*. Translated by Dominco de Gaztelu. Seville, 1540.

al-Ash'ari, Abu-l-Hasan 'Ali ibn Isma'il. *Highlights of the Polemic against Deviators and Innovators*. Translated by Richard J. McCarthy. In Richard J. McCarthy, *The Theology of al-Ash'ari*. Beirut: Imprimerie Catholique, 1953.

ʿAttar, Farid-ud-Din. *Le langage des oiseaux*. Translated by Garcin de Tassy. Paris: Sindbad, 1982.

al-Bakri, Abu-ʿUbayd. *Description de l'Afrique septentrionale*. Translated by Mac Guckin de Slane. 1913. Reprint, Paris: Librairie d'Amérique et d'Orient, 1965.

Boccaccio, Giovanni. *The Decameron*. Translated by John Payne. New York: Modern Library, 1931.

Budge, Ernest A. W., ed. and trans. *The History of Alexander the Great, Being the Syriac Version of the Pseudo-Callisthenes*. Cambridge: Cambridge University Press, 1889.

————, ed. and trans. *The Life and Exploits of Alexander the Great, Being a Series of Ethiopic Texts*. 2 vols., 1896. Reprint, New York and London: Benjamin Blom, 1968.

Carvajal, Bernardino López de. *La Conquista de Baza*. Translated by Carlos de Miguel Mora. Granada: Universidad de Granada, 1995.

————. *Epistola ad invictissimum Carolum in Imperio E. super declaratione M. Suae contra Lutherum facta*. N.p.: n.d. [1521].

Castiglione, Baldassare. *The Book of the Courtier*. Translated by Charles S. Singleton. Garden City, N.Y.: Doubleday, 1959.

Castries, Henry de, ed. *Les sources inédites de l'histoire du Maroc. Archives et bibliothèques d'Espagne*. 1st series. 3 vols. Paris: Ernest Leroux and Paul Geuthner and Madrid: Ruiz Hermanos, 1921–61.

————, ed. *Les sources inédites de l'histoire du Maroc de 1530 à 1845. Archives et bibliothèques de France*. 1st series. 4 vols. Paris: Ernest Leroux, 1905–26.

Cellini, Benvenuto. *La vita*. Edited by Lorenzo Bellotto. Parma: Ugo Guanda, 1996.

————. *Autobiography*. Translated by George Bull. London: Penguin, 1998.

Cenival, Pierre de, and Robert Ricard, eds. *Les sources inédites de l'histoire du Maroc. Archives et bibliothèques de Portugal*. 1st series. 5 vols. Paris: Paul Geuthner, 1934–53.

Les cent et une nuits. Translated by M. Gaudefroy-Demombynes. Paris: Sindbad, 1982.

Chronique de Santa-Cruz du Cap de Gué (Agadir). Edited and translated by Pierre de Cenival. Paris: Paul Geuthner, 1934.

Clenardus, Nicolas. *Correspondance de Nicolas Clénard*. Edited by Alphonse Roersch. 3 vols. Brussels: Palais des Académies, 1940.

David Reuveni. *The Story of David Hareuveni* (in Hebrew). Edited by Aaron Zeev Aescoly. Jerusalem: Bialik Institute, 1993.

Delicado, Francisco. *Portrait of Lozana, The Lusty Andalusian Woman.* Translated by Bruno M. Damiani. Potomac, Md.: Scripta Humanistica, 1987.

———. *Retrato de la Lozana Andaluza.* Edited by Claude Allaigre. Madrid: Cátedra, 1985.

Della Casa, Giovanni. *Galateo of Manners and Behaviours (1576).* Translated by Robert Peterson. Bari: Adriatica Editrice, 1997.

Dorado, Bernardo. *Compendio Historico de la Ciudad de Salamanca.* Salamanca: Juan Antonio de Lasanta, 1776.

Egidio da Viterbo. *Scechina e Libellus de Litteris Hebraicis.* Edited by François Secret. 2 vols. Rome: Centro Internazionale di Studi Umanistici, 1959.

Erasmus, Desiderius. *On Good Manners for Boys (De civilitate morum puerilium).* Translated by Brian McGregor. Volume 25 of *Collected Works of Erasmus.* Toronto: University of Toronto Press, 1985.

Fagnan, E., ed. and trans. *Extraits inédits relatifs au Maghreb (Géographie et histoire).* Algiers: Jules Carbonel, 1924.

al-Farabi, Abu Nasr. *Aphorismes choisis.* Translated by Soumaya Mestiri and Guillaume Dye. Paris: Fayard, 2003.

Ferrajoli, Alessandro. *Il ruolo della corte di Leone X.* Edited by Vincenzo de Caprio. Rome: Bulzoni, 1984.

Fortini, Pietro. *Le giornate delle novelle dei novizi.* Edited by Adriana Mauriello. 2 vols. Rome: Salerno Editrice, 1988.

Furtu, Ahmad. *A Sudanic Chronicle: The Borno Expeditions of Idris Alauma (1564–1576) according to the Account of Ahmad B. Furtu.* Translated by Dierk Lange. Stuttgart: Franz Steiner Verlag, 1987.

Galley, Micheline, and Zakia Iraqui Sinaceur, eds. *Dyab, Jha, La'âba: Le triomphe de la ruse. Contes marocains du fonds Colin.* Paris: Les Belles Lettres, 1994.

al-Ghazali, Abu Hamid Muhammad. *Le chemin assuré des dévots vers le Paradis (Minhaj al-'abidin ila al-jannah).* Edited by Yahya Cheikh and translated by Miguel Asin Palacios. Beirut: Éditions Al-Bouraq, 2000.

———. *Deliverance from Error.* Translated by W. Montgomery Watt. In W. Montgomery Watt, *The Faith and Practice of al-Ghazali.* London: George Allen and Unwin, 1970.

———. *Deliverance from Error and Mystical Union with the Almighty.* Edited by George F. McLean and translated by Muhammad Abulaylah. Washington, D.C.: Council for Research in Values and Philosophy, 2001.

Giovio, Paolo. *Commentario de le cose de' Turchi.* Rome: Antonio Blado, 1532.

———. *Elogia Doctorum Virorum.* Antwerp: Jean Bellère, 1557.

————. *Elogia virorum bellica virtute illustrium veris imaginibus supposita.* Florence: Lorenzo Torrentino, 1551.

————. *Gli Elogi Vite Brevemente Scritti d'Huomini Illustri de Guerra, Antichi et Moderni.* Translated by Lodovico Domenichi. Florence: Lorenzo Torrentino, 1554.

————. *Lettere.* Edited by Giuseppe Guido Ferrero. 2 vols. Rome: Istituto Poligrafico dello Stato, 1956.

————. *La Prima Parte delle Historie del suo tempo.* Translated by Lodovico Domenichi. Venice: Domenico de' Farri, 1555.

————. *La Seconda Parte dell'Historie del suo tempo.* Translated by Lodovico Domenichi. Venice: Bartolomeo Cesano, 1554.

————. *La Rimanente della Seconda Parte dell'Historie de suo tempo.* Translated by Lodovico Domenichi. Venice: Comin da Trino, 1555.

————. *Le Vite di Leon Decimo et d'Adriano Sesto Sommi Pontefici.* Translated by Lodovico Domenichi. Venice: Giovanni de' Rossi, 1557.

————. *Turcarum rerum commentarius.* Translated by Francesco Negri. Paris: Robert Estienne, 1539.

Gnoli, D., ed. "Descriptio urbis o censimento della popolazione di Roma avanti il Sacco Borbonica." *Archivio della R. Società Romana di Storia Patria* 17 (1894): 375–520.

Góis, Damião de. *Crónica do Felicissimo Rei D. Manuel.* Edited by J. M. Teixeira de Carvalho and David Lopes. 4 vols. Coimbra: Universidade de Coimbra, 1926.

Goodrich, Thomas D., ed. and trans. *The Ottoman Turks and the New World: A Study of "Tarih-I Hind-I Garbi" and Sixteenth-Century Ottoman Americana.* Wiesbaden: Otto Harrassowitz, 1990.

Guicciardini, Francesco. *Maxims and Reflections of a Renaissance Statesman.* Translated by Mario Domandi. New York: Harper and Row, 1965.

Guicciardini, Luigi. *The Sack of Rome.* Translated by James H. McGregor. New York: Italica Press, 1993.

al-Hajari, Ahmad ibn Qasim. *Kitab nasir al-din ʿala-l-qawm al-kafirin. The Supporter of Religion against the Infidel.* Edited and translated by P. S. Van Koningsveld, Q. al-Samarrai, and G. A. Wiegers. Madrid: CSIC/AECI, 1997.

al-Hamadhani, Badiʿ al-Zaman. *Le livre des vagabonds. Séances d'un beau parleur impénitent.* Translated by René R. Khawam. Paris: Phébus, 1997.

————. *The Maqamat of Badiʿ al-Zaman al-Hamadhani.* Translated by W. J. Prendergast. London: Curzon Press, 1973.

al-Harawi, ʿAli ibn Abi Bakr. *Guide des lieux de pèlerinage.* Translated by Janine Sourdel-Thomine. Damascus: Institut Français de Damas, 1957.

al-Hariri, al-Qasim. *Le livre des Malins: Séances d'un vagabond de génie.* Translated by René R. Khawam. Paris: Phébus, 1992.

———. *The Assemblies of Al-Hariri.* Translated by Thomas Chenery and F. Steingass. 2 vols., 1867–98. Reprint, Westmead, Hants.: Gregg International Publishers, 1969.

Harvey, L. P., ed. and trans. "Crypto-Islam in Sixteenth-Century Spain." [Transcription in Latin alphabet of the 910/1504 fatwa in *aljamiado* of al-Wahrani]. In *Actas. Primer Congreso de Estudios Arabes e Islamicos, Córdoba, 1962,* 163–81. Madrid: Comité Permanente del Congreso de Estudios Arabes e Islamicos, 1964.

al-Hawrani, ʿAbd al-Rahim. *Les Ruses des femmes.* Translated by René R. Khawam. Paris: Phébus, 1994.

———. *Désirs de femme.* Translated by René R. Khawam. Paris: Phébus, 1996.

Heidegger, Johann Heinrich. *Historia vitae et obitus I. Henrici Hottinger.* Zurich, 1667.

Hodja, Nasreddin. *La sagesse afghane du malicieux Nasroddine.* Translated by Dider Leroy. La Tour d'Aigues: Éditions de l'Aube, 2002.

Hunwick, John O., ed. and trans. *Shariʿa in Songhay: The Replies of al-Maghili to the Questions of Askia al-Hajj Muhammad.* Oxford: Oxford University Press, 1985.

———. *Timbuktu and the Songhay Empire: Al-Saʿdi's Taʾrikh al-Sudan down to 1613 and Other Contemporary Documents.* Leiden: Brill, 1999.

Ibn ʿAskar. *Dawhat-an-Nasir. Sur les vertus éminentes des Chaiks du Mahgrib au dixième siècle.* Translated by A. Graulle. *Archives marocaines* 19 (1913).

Ibn Battuta, Abu ʿAbdallah. *Ibn Battuta in Black Africa.* Translated by Said Hamdun and Noël King. Princeton, N.J.: Markus Wiener Publishers, 1994.

———. *Voyages.* Edited by Stéphane Yerasimos and translated by C. Defremery and B. R. Sanguinette. 3 vols. Paris: Librairie François Maspero and Éditions La Découverte, 1982–97.

Ibn Halil, ʿAbd al-Basit. *Ar-Raud.* Translated by Robert Brunschvig. In Robert Brunschvig, *Deux récits de voyage inédits en Afrique du Nord au XVe siècle,* 17–84. Paris: Maisonneuve et Larose, 2001.

———. "El Reino de Granada en 1465–66." In *Viajes de estranjeros por España y Portugal.* Edited and translated by J. Garcia Mercadel, vol. 1. Madrid: Aguilar, 1952.

Ibn Hawqal. *La configuration de la terre (Kitab Surat al-Ard).* Translated by J. H. Kramers and G. Wiet. Paris: Maisonneuve and Larose, 2001.

Ibn Hazm. *De l'amour et des amants. Tawq al-hamama fi-l-ulfa wa-l-ullaf (Collier de la colombe sur l'amour et les amants).* Translated by Gabriel Martinez-Gros. Paris: Sindbad, 1992.

Ibn Ishaq. *La Vie du Prophète Muhammad, l'Envoyé d'Allah*. Edited by Ibn Hisham and translated by ʿAbdurrahman Badawi. 2 vols. Beirut: Éditions Albouraq, 2001.

Ibn Iyas, Muhammad ibn Ahmad. *Journal d'un bourgeois du Caire: Chronique d'Ibn Iyas*. Edited and translated by Gaston Wiet. 2 vols. Paris: Librairie Armand Colin and SEVPEN, 1955–60.

Ibn Jubayr. *The Travels of Ibn Jubayr*. Translated by Ronald J. C. Broadhurst. London: Jonathan Cape, 1952.

Ibn Khaldun, ʿAbd-ar Rahman. *Histoire des Berbères et des dynasties musulmanes de l'Afrique septentrionale*. Edited by Paul Casanova and translated by Mac Guckin de Slane. 4 vols. Paris: Librairie Orientaliste Paul Geuthner, 1925–56.

———. *Le Livre des Exemples*. Vol. 1: *Autobiographie. Muqaddima*. Translated by Abdesselam Cheddadi. Paris: Gallimard, 2002.

———. *The Muqaddimah. An Introduction to History*. Translated by Franz Rosenthal. 2nd ed., 3 vols., Princeton, N.J.: Princeton University Press, 1967.

———. *Le Voyage d'Occident et d'Orient. Autobiographie*. Translated by Abdesselam Cheddadi. 2nd ed. Paris: Sindbad and Arles: Actes Sud, 1995.

Ibn Khallikan. *Biographical Dictionary*. Translated by Mac Guckin de Slane. 4 vols., 1842–72. Reprint, New York and London: Johnson Reprint, 1961.

Ibn Maryam. *El Bostan ou jardin des biographies des saints et savants de Tlemcen*. Translated by F. Provenzali. Algiers: Imprimerie Orientale Fontana, 1910.

Ibn al-Muqaffaʿ. *Le livre de Kalila et Dimna*. Translated by André Miquel. Paris: Klincksieck, 1957.

Ibn Sahl, Ibrahim. *Poemas*. Edited and translated by Teresa Garulo. Madrid: Hiperión, 1983.

al-Idrisi. *Le Maghrib au 12e siècle*. Translated by Mahamad Hadj Sadok. Paris: Publisud, 1983.

———. *La Première géographie de l'Occident*. Edited by Henri Bresc and Annliese Nef and translated by Jaubert and Annliese Nef. Paris: Flammarion, 1999.

al-Jahiz, ʿAmr ibn Bahr. *Éphèbes et courtisanes* (A translation of *Kitab mufakharat al-jawari wa-l-ghilman*). Edited by Malek Chebel and translated by Maati Kabbal. Paris: Rivages Poches, 1997.

———. *Kitab al-Hayawan*. Edited by ʿAbd-al-Salam Muhammad Harun. 7 vols. Cairo, 1930–45.

———. *The Life and Works of Jahiz: Translations of Selected Texts*. Translated from the Arabic by Charles Pellat; translated from the French by D. M. Hawke. London: Routledge and Kegan Paul, 1969.

————. *Livre des animaux*. Selections edited and translated by Mohamed Mestiri and Soumaya Mestiri. Paris: Fayard, 2003.

————. *Le livre des avares*. Translated by Charles Pellat. Paris: Éditions Maisonneuve et Larose, 1997.

Kati, Mahmud. *Tarikh el-Fettach ou Chronique du chercheur pour servir à l'histoire des villes, des armées et des principaux personnages du Tekrour*. Translated by O. Houdas and M. Delafosse. Paris: Librairie d'Amérique et d'Orient, 1964.

al-Khwarizmi. *Afrika nach der arabischen Bearbeitung der "Geographia" des Claudius Ptolemaeus*. Translated by Hans von Mžik. Vienna: Kaiserliche Akademie der Wissenschaften, 1916.

The Koran Interpreted. Translated by Arthur J. Arberry. 2 vols. New York: Macmillan, 1955.

Leo X. *Bando de le Processioni per la unione di Principi Christiani contra Turchi*. Rome, 1518.

Levita, Elijah. *Accentorum Hebraicorum Liber Unus* (Hebrew and Latin). Translated by Sebastian Münster. Basel: Heinrich Petri, 1539.

————. *Capitula Cantici . . . et officiorum* (Hebrew and Latin). Translated by Sebastian Münster. Basel: J. Froben, 1527.

————. *Grammatica Hebraica Absolutissima* (Hebrew and Latin). Translated by Sebastian Münster. Basel: J. Froben, 1525.

————. *Lexicon Chaldaicum*. Edited by Paul Fagius. Isny: Paul Fagius, 1541.

————. *The Massoreth Ha-Massoreth*. Edited and translated by Christian D. Ginsburg. London: Longmans, Green, Reader and Dyer, 1867.

————. *Nomenclatura Hebraica*. Isny: Paul Fagius, 1542.

————. *Opusculum Recens Hebraicum . . . cui titulum fecit . . . Thisbites, in quo 712 vocum quae sunt partim Hebraicae, Chaldaicae, Arabicae, Graecae et Latinae quaeque in Dictionariis non facilè inveniuntur* (Hebrew and Latin). Translated by Paul Fagius. Isny: Paul Fagius, 1541.

————. *Sefer Ha-Buohur . . . Liber Electus complectens in Grammatica quatuor orationes*. Basel: J. Froben, 1525.

————. *Vocabula Hebraica irregularia*. Translated by Sebastian Münster. Basel: Heinrich Petri, 1536.

Levtzion, N., and J.F.P. Hopkins, eds. *Corpus of Early Arabic Sources for West African History*. Translated by J.F.P. Hopkins. Princeton, N.J.: Markus Wiener Publishers, 2000.

Le livre des ruses. Translated by René R. Khawam. Paris: Phébus, 1976.

Luqman. *Fables de Lokman*. Translated by M. Cherbonneau. Paris: Librairie Orientaliste Paul Geuthner, 1925.

————. *Loqman berbère avec quatre glossaires et une étude sur la légende de Loqman.* Edited by René Basset. Paris: Ernest Leroux, 1890.

Machiavelli, Niccolò. *The Art of War.* Edited by Neal Wood and translated by Ellis Farneworth. New York: Bobbs-Merrill Company, 1965.

————. *The Prince.* Translated by Luigi Ricci and E.R.P. Vincent. New York: Random House, 1940.

Machumetis Saracenorum principis, Eiusque Successorum Vitae, ac Doctrina, Ipsique Alcoran. Edited by Theodor Bibliander. 3 vols. Basel: Johann Oporinus, 1543.

Madelin, Louis, ed. "Le journal d'un habitant français de Rome au XVIe siècle." *Mélanges d'archéologie et d'histoire* 22 (1902): 251–300.

Maimonides, Moses. *Ethical Writings of Maimonides.* Edited by Raymond L. Weiss and Charles Butterworth. New York: New York University Press, 1975.

Mantino, Jacob, trans. *Avicennae Arabis Medicorum . . . principis. Quarta fen, primi. De universali ratione medendi nunc primum M. Iacob. Mantini, medici hebraei, latinitate donata.* Ettlingen: Valentinus Kobian, 1531.

————, trans. *Averois Cordubensis Paraphrasis in Librum Poeticae Aristotelis, Iacob Mantino Hispano Hebraeo, Medico interprete.* In Aristotle, *Omnia quae extant Opera,* 2:89r–94r. Venice: Giunti, 1550–52.

————, trans. *Averois Paraphrasis Super libros de Republica Platonis, nunc primum latinitate donata, Iacob Mantino Medico Hebraeo Interprete.* Rome: Valerio and Luigi Dorici, 1539.

Manuel I. *Epistola Invictissimi Regis Portugalliae ad Leonem X.P.M. Super foedore inito cum Presbytero Joanne Aethiopiae Rege.* N.p. [Strasbourg], n.d. [1521].

al-Maqqari, Ahmad. *The History of the Mohammedan Dynasties in Spain.* Translated by Pascual de Gayangos. 2 vols. London: W. H. Allen, 1840–43.

Martire d'Anghiera, Pietro. *Una Embajada de los Reyes Católicos a Egipto según la "Legatio Babylonica" y el "Opus Epistolarum de Pedro Mártir de Angleria."* Edited in Latin and translated by Luis García y García. Valladolid: Consejo Superior de Investigaciones Científicas, 1947.

al-Mas'udi. *Les prairies d'or.* Translated by Barbier de Meynard and Pavet de Courteille; revised by Charles Pellat. 5 vols. Paris: CNRS, 1965–97.

Monroe, James T., trans. "A Curious Morisco Appeal to the Ottoman Empire," *Al-Andalus* 31 (1966): 281–303.

Münzer, Hieronymus. *Viaje por España y Portugal (1494–1495).* Translated by José López Toro. Madrid: Ediciones Polifemo, 1991.

al-Muqaddasi. *The Best Divisions for Knowledge of the Regions.* Translated by Basil Anthony Collins and Muhammad Hamid al-Tai. London: Centre for Muslim Contribution to Civilisation and Garnet Publishing, 1994.

Muradi. *La vida, y historia de Hayradin, llamado Barbarroja: Gazavat-I Hay-reddin Paşa.* Edited by Miguel A. de Bunes and Emilio Sola; translated by Juan Luis Alzamora. Granada: Servicio de Publicaciones de la Universidad de Granada, 1997.

al-Nadim. *The Fihrist of al-Nadim: A Tenth-Century Survey of Muslim Culture.* Translated by Bayard Dodge. 2 vols. New York and London: Columbia University Press, 1970.

Novellino e conti del Duecento. Edited by Sebastiano lo Negro. Turin: Unione Tipografico, 1963.

The Novellino or One Hundred Ancient Tales. Edited and translated by Joseph P. Consoli. New York and London: Garland, 1997.

Palmer, H. R., trans. *Sudanese Memoirs. Being mainly translations of a number of Arabic Manuscripts relating to the Central and Western Sudan.* 3 vols. London: Frank Cass, 1967.

Peters, F. E., ed. *Judaism, Christianity, and Islam. The Classical Texts and Their Interpretation.* 3 vols. Princeton, N.J.: Princeton University Press, 1990.

Pio, Alberto, Prince of Carpi. *Tres et viginiti Libri in locos lucubrationum variarum D. Erasmi Rhoterodami.* Venice: Luc-Antonio Giunta, 1531.

Piri Reis. *Kitab-I Bahriye (Book of Navigation).* Ankara: Republic of Turkey, Prime Ministry, Undersecretaryship of Navigation, 2002.

Pliny the Elder. *L'Histoire naturelle.* Vol. 5. Translated by Jehan Desanges. Paris: Les Belles Lettres, 1980.

Postel, Guillaume. *De la Republique des Turcs: et . . . des meurs et loys de tous Muhamedistes, par Guillaume Postel Cosmopolite.* Poitiers: Enguilbert de Marnef, 1560.

Prémare, A.-L. de, ed. *La tradition orale du Mejdub: Récits et quatrains inédits.* Aix-en-Provence: Édisud, 1986.

Psalterium Hebraeum, Graecum, Arabicum, Chaldeum cum tribus latinis interpretationibus et glossis. Edited by Agostino Giustiniani. Genoa: Petrus Paulus Porrus, 1516.

Ptolemy, Claudius. *Claudii Ptholemaei Alexandrini Liber Geographiae cum Tabulis.* Edited by Bernardo Silvano. Venice: Jacopo Pencio, 1511.

———. *In hoc opere haec Continentur Geographiae Cl. Ptolemaei.* Translated by Jacopo d'Angelo. Rome: Evangelista Tosino, 1508.

———. *Geographicae enarrationis Libri Octo.* Edited by Wilibald Pirckheimer, annotated by Joannes Regiomontanus. Strasbourg: Johann Grueninger and Johann Koberger, 1525.

———. *Ptolemy's Geography*. Translated by J. Lennart Berggren and Alexander Jones. Princeton, N.J.: Princeton University Press, 2000.

Pucci, Antonio. *Sanctissimi Domini nostri Papae Leonis Decimi, una cum coetu cardinalium, Christianissimorum que regum, et principum oratorum consultationes, pro expeditionem contra Thurcum*. N.p [Basel?], n.d. [1518].

al-Qayrawani, Ibn Abi Zayd. *La Risâla, Ou Epître sur les éléments du dogme et de la loi de l'Islam selon le rite Mâlikite*. Translated by Léon Bercher. Paris: Éditions IQRA, 1996.

Al-Quran: A Contemporary Translation. Translated by Ahmad Ali. Princeton, N.J.: Princeton University Press, 2001.

The Qur'an. A new translation. Translated by M.A.S. Abdel Haleem. Oxford: Oxford University Press, 2004.

Rabelais, François. *Oeuvres complètes*. Edited by Mireille Huchon, with the collaboration of François Moreau. Paris: Gallimard, 1994.

Ramusio, Giovanni Battista, ed. *Primo volume, et Seconda editione delle Navigationi et Viaggi . . . nelle quale si contengono La Descrittione dell'Africa*. Venice: Giunti, 1554.

———, ed. *Primo volume, et Terza editione delle Navigationi et Viaggi*. Venice: Giunti, 1563.

———, ed. *Navigazioni e Viaggi*. Edited by Marica Milanesi. 6 vols. Turin: Giulio Einaudi, 1978.

Rodrigues, Bernardo. *Anais de Arzila*. Edited by David Lopes. 2 vols. Lisbon: Academia des Ciências de Lisboa, 1915.

Romano, Giulio, Marcantonio Raimondi, and Pietro Aretino. *I Modi. The Sixteen Pleasures. An Erotic Album of the Italian Renaissance*. Edited and translated by Lynne Lawner. Evanston, Ill.: Northwestern University Press, 1988.

Saada, Lucienne, ed. *La Geste Hilalienne: Version de Bou Thadi (Tunisie)*. Paris: Gallimard, 1985.

Saduddin Efendi, Hoca. *Tac ul-Tevarih*. 3 vols. Istanbul, 1862–64.

Sanuto, Marino. *I Diarii di Marino Sanuto*. 58 vols. 1879–92. Reprint of the Venice 1879–92 edition. Bologna: Forni Editore, 1969.

Scepper, Cornelius, ed. *Rerum à Carolo V Caesare Augusto in Africa bello gestarum Commentarii*. Antwerp: Jean Bellère, 1554.

Sepúlveda, Juan Ginés de. *Ad Carolum V. Imperatorem ut bellum suscipiat in Turcas cohortatio*. Bologna: Giovanni Battista di Phaelli, 1529.

al-Shafi'i, Muhammad ibn Idris. *La Risâla, les fondements du droit musulman*. Translated by Lakhdar Souami. Paris: Sindbad, 1997.

al-Shahrastani, ʿAbd al-Karim. *Livre des religions et des sectes*. Translated by Daniel Gimaret and Guy Monnot. Louvain: Peeters/UNESCO, 1986.

————. *Muslim Sects and Divisions*. Translated by A. K. Kazi and J. G. Flynn. London, Boston, Melbourne, and Henley: Kegan Paul International, 1984.

Spandugino, Theodore. *Petit Traicté de l'origine des Turcqz*. Edited by Charles Schefer. Paris: Ernest Leroux, 1896.

Strabo. *The Geography*. Translated by H. L. Jones. 8 vols. London: William Heinemann and Cambridge, Mass.: Harvard University Press, 1960–67.

al-Sulami, ʿAbd al-Rahman. *La courtoisie en Islam: Pour une meilleure fréquentation des gens*. Translated by Tahar Gaïd. Paris: Éditions IQRA, 2001.

al-Tabari, Abu Jaʿfar Muhammad ibn Jarir. *La Chronique, Histoire des prophètes et des rois*. Abridgment by al-Balʿami. Translated by Hermann Zotenberg. 2 vols. Arles: Actes Sud, 1984.

————. *The Commentary on the Qurʾan. Being an abridged translation of Jamiʿ al-bayan ʿan taʾwil ay al-qurʾan*. Translated by J. Cooper. Oxford: Oxford University Press, 1987.

————. *The History of al-Tabari*. 39 vols. Vol. 1: *From the Creation to the Flood*, translated by Franz Rosenthal; vol. 2: *Prophets and Patriarchs*, translated by William M. Brinner. Albany: State University of New York Press, 1985–98.

Thenaud, Jean. *Le voyage d'outremer (Égypte, Mont Sinay, Palestine) de Jean Thenaud, suivi de la Relation de l'ambassade de Dominico Trevisan auprès du Soudan d'Égypte, 1512*. Edited by Charles Schefer. Paris: Ernest Leroux, 1884.

Thevenot, Jean de. *Relation d'un Voyage fait au Levant*. Paris: Louis Billaine, 1665.

Valeriano, Pierio. *Amorum Libri V*. Venice: G. Giolito, 1549.

————. *Hexametri, Odae et Epigrammata*. Venice: G. Giolito, 1550.

————. *Hieroglyphica seu De Sacris Aegyptiorum aliarumque Genium Literis Commentarii*. Lyon: Paul Frellon, 1602.

————. *Les Hieroglyphiques*. Translated by Jean de Montlyart. Lyon: Paul Frellon, 1615.

Vatin, Nicolas, ed. *Sultan Djem. Un prince ottoman dans l'Europe du 15e siècle d'après deux sources contemporaines: "Vakiʿat-I Sultan Cem," "Oeuvres" de Guillaume Caoursin*. Ankara: Imprimerie de la Société Turque d'Histoire, 1997.

al-Wazzan, al-Hasan ibn Muhammad. *Description de l'Afrique*. Translated by Alexis Épaulard; annotated by Alexis Épaulard, Théodore Monod, Henri Lhote, Raymond Mauny. New ed. Paris: Librarie d'Amérique et d'Orient, 1980–1981.

————. *Historiale Description de l'Afrique, tierce partie du monde . . . Escrite de nôtre tems* [sic] *par Iean Leon, African.* Translated by Jean Temporal. Lyon: Jean Temporal, 1556/1557.

————. *La Descrittione dell'Africa.* In *Primo volume, et Seconda editione delle Navigationi et Viaggi,* edited by Giovanni Battista Ramusio, 1r–103r. Venice: Giunti, 1554.

————. *La Descrittione dell'Africa.* In *Primo volume, et Terza editione delle Navigationi et Viaggi,* edited by Giovanni Battista Ramusio, 1r–95v. Venice: Giunti, 1563.

————. *La descrizione dell'Africa di Giovan Lioni Africano.* In Giovanni Battista Ramusio, ed., *Navigazioni e Viaggi,* edited by Marica Milanesi, 1:19–460. Turin: Giulio Einaudi, 1978.

————. *A Geographical Historie of Africa, Written in Arabicke and Italian by Iohn Leo a More, borne in Granada, and brought up in Barbarie.* Translated by John Pory. London: George Bishop, 1600.

————. *Ioannis Leonis Africani, De Totius Africae Descriptione, Libri IX.* Translated by John Florian. Antwerp: Jan de Laet, 1556.

————. "Il Trattato dell'Arte Metrica di Giovanni Leone Africano." Edited by Angela Codazzi. In *Studi orientalistici in onore di Giorgio Levi Della Vida,* 1:180–98. Rome: Istituto per l'Oriente, 1956.

————. *Waṣf Ifrīqiya.* Translated by Muhammad Hajji. Rabat, 1980.

————. *De Viris quibusdam Illustribus apud Arabes, per Johannem Leonem Affricanum* [sic] *ex ea Lingua in maternam traductis* and *De quibusdam Viris Illustribus apud Hebraeos per Joannem Leonem Africanum.* In *Bibliothecarius Quadripartitus,* edited by Johann Heinrich Hottinger, 246–91. Zurich: Melchior Stauffacher, 1664.

Weiditz, Christoph. *Authentic Everyday Dress of the Renaissance: All 154 Plates from the "Trachtenbuch."* Edited by Theodor Hampe. New York: Dover Publications, 1994.

Widmanstadt, Johann Albrecht. *Liber Sacrosancti Evangelii de Iesu Christo Domino et Deo nostro . . . characteribus et lingua Syra.* Vienna: Michael Zymmerman, 1562.

————, ed. *Mahometis Abdallae Filii Theologia Dialogo explicata, Hermanno Nellingaunense interprete. Alcorani Epitome Roberto Ketense Anglo interprete. Iohannis Alberti Widmestadii Iurisconsulti Notationes falsarum impiarumque opinionum Mahumetis, quae in hisce libris occurrunt.* N.p. [Nuremberg], 1543.

SECONDARY SOURCES

Abel, Armand. "Dhu'l Qarnayn, prophète de l'universalité." *Annuaire de l'Institut de Philologie et d'Histoire Orientales et Slaves* 11 (1951): 5–18.

Abun-Nasr, Jamil M. *A History of the Maghrib in the Islamic Period.* Cambridge: Cambridge University Press, 1987.

Actas del VIII Simposio Internacional de Mudejarismo (1999). De mudéjares a moriscos: una conversión forzada. 2 vols. Teruel: Centro de Estudios Mudéjares, 2002.

Adang, Camilla. "Ibn Hazm on Homosexuality. A Case-Study of Zahiri Legal Methodology." *Al-Qantara* 24 (2003): 5–31.

Ahmed, Leila. *Women and Gender in Islam.* New Haven, Conn.: Yale University Press, 1992.

Akbari, Suzanne Conklin. "From Due East to True North: Orientalism and Orientation." In *The Postcolonial Middle Ages,* edited by Jeffrey Jerome Cohen, 19–34. New York: St. Martin's Press, 2000.

Alberto Pio III, Signore di Carpi (1475–1975). Modena: Aedes Muratoriana, 1977.

Allen, Don Cameron. *The Legend of Noah.* Urbana: University of Illinois Press, 1963.

Amram, David. *The Makers of Hebrew Books in Italy.* London: Holland Press, 1963.

Andrea, Bernadette. "Columbus in Istanbul: Ottoman Mappings of the 'New World.'" *Genre* 30 (Spring/Summer 1997): 135–65.

Annecchino, Valeria. *La Basilica di Sant'Agostino in Campo Marzio e l'ex complesso conventuale, Roma.* Genoa: Edizioni d'Arte Marconi, 2000.

Arié, Rachel. *L'Espagne musulmane au temps des Nasrides (1232–1492).* Paris: Éditions de Boccard, 1973.

———. *Études sur la civilisation de l'Espagne musulmane.* Leiden: E. J. Brill, 1990.

———. *Miniatures hispano-musulmanes. Recherches sur un manuscrit arabe illustré de l'Escurial.* Leiden: E. J. Brill, 1969.

Arrizabalaga, Jon, John Henderson, and Roger French. *The Great Pox. The French Disease in Renaissance Europe.* New Haven and London: Yale University Press, 1998.

Atiyeh, George N., ed. *The Book in the Islamic World: The Written Word and Communication in the Middle East.* Albany: SUNY Press, 1995.

al-Azmeh, Aziz. "Barbarians in Arab Eyes." *Past and Present* 134 (1992): 3–18.

———. *Ibn Khaldun. An Essay in Reinterpretation.* 2nd ed. Budapest: Central European University Press, 2003.

Bedini, Silvio A. *The Pope's Elephant.* London: Carcanet, 1997.

Benchekroun, Muhammad B. A. *La vie intellectuelle marocaine sous les Mérinides et les Wattasides.* Rabat, 1974.

Bennassar, Bartolomé, and Lucile Bennassar. *Les Chrétiens d'Allah: L'histoire extraordinaire des renégats, XVIe–XVIIe siècles.* Paris: Perrin, 1987.

Bennassar, Bartolomé, and Robert Sauzet, eds. *Chrétiens et Musulmans à la Renaissance. Actes du 37e colloque international du CESR (1994).* Paris: Honoré Champion, 1998.

Berkey, Jonathan. *The Transmission of Knowledge in Medieval Cairo.* Princeton, N.J.: Princeton University Press, 1992.

Bernheimer, Carlo. *Catalogo dei Manoscritti Orientali della Biblioteca Estense.* Modena: Libreria dello Stato, 1960.

Blachère, Régis. *Histoire de la littérature arabe des origines à la fin du XVe siècle.* 3 vols. Paris: Librairie d'Amérique et d'Orient, 1964–66.

Black, Crofton. "Leo Africanus's *Descrittione dell'Africa* and its Sixteenth-Century Translations." *Journal of the Warburg and Courtauld Institutes* 65 (2002): 262–72.

Blair, Sheila S., and Jonathan Bloom. *The Art and Architecture of Islam 1250–1800.* New Haven and London: Yale University Press, 1995.

Bloom, Jonathan. *Paper Before Print: The History and Impact of Paper in the Islamic World.* New Haven and London: Yale University Press, 2001.

Bobzin, Hartmut. "Juan Andrés und sein Buch *Confusion dela secta mahomatica* (1515)." In *Festgabe für Hans-Rudolf Singer,* edited by Martin Forstner, 528–48. Frankfurt: Peter Lang, 1991.

———. *Der Koran im Zeitalter der Reformation: Studien zur Frühgeschichte der Arabistik und Islamkunde in Europa.* Beirut and Stuttgart: Franz Steiner Verlag, 1995.

Bonner, Michael, Mine Ener, and Amy Singer, eds. *Poverty and Charity in Middle Eastern Contexts.* Albany: SUNY Press, 2003.

Bono, Salvatore. *Corsari nel Mediterraneo: Cristiani e Musulmani fra guerra, schiavitù e commercio.* Milan: Arnoldo Mondadori, 1993.

———. *Schiavi musulmani nell'Italia moderna.* Naples: Edizioni Scientifiche Italiane, 1999.

Bouhdiba, Abdelwahab. *La sexualité en Islam.* Paris: Quadrige/Presses Universitaires de France, 1998.

Bovill, Edward William. *The Golden Trade of the Moors.* 2nd ed. Princeton, N.J.: Markus Wiener Publishers, 1995.

Braude, Benjamin. "The Sons of Noah and the Construction of Ethnic and Geographical Identities in the Medieval and Early Modern Periods." *William and Mary Quarterly* 54, no. 1 (January 1997): 103–41.

Braudel, Fernand. *La Méditerranée et le monde méditerranéan.* 2 vols. Paris: Armand Colin, 1966.

Bridges, M., and J. C. Bürgel, eds. *The Problematics of Power: Eastern and Western Representations of Alexander the Great*. Berne: Peter Lang, 1996.

Brignon, Jean, Abdelaziz Amine, Brahim Boutaleb, Guy Martinet, and Bernard Rosenberger. *Histoire du Maroc*. Paris: Hatier and Casablanca: Librairie Nationale, 1994.

Brundage, James. *Law, Sex, and Christian Society in Medieval Europe*. Chicago and London: University of Chicago Press, 1987.

Brunschvig, Robert. *La Berbérie orientale sous les Hafsides des origines à la fin du XVe siècle*. 2 vols. Paris: Librairie d'Amérique et d'Orient, 1940–47.

Buisseret, David. *The Mapmakers' Quest. Depicting New Worlds in Renaissance Europe*. Oxford: Oxford University Press, 2003.

Bullard, Melissa Meriam. *Filippo Strozzi and the Medici: Favor and Finance in Sixteenth-Century Florence and Rome*. Cambridge: Cambridge University Press, 1980.

Burke, Peter. *The Fortunes of the Courtier. The European Reception of Castiglione's "Cortegiano."* University Park, Pa.: Pennsylvania State University Press, 1996.

Burman, Thomas. "Cambridge University Library MS Mm.v.26 and the History of the Study of the Qur'an in Medieval and Early Modern Europe." In *Religion, Text, and Society in Medieval Spain and Northern Europe: Essays in Honor of J. N. Hillgarth*, edited by Thomas Burman, Mark D. Meyerson, and Leah Shopkow, 335–63. Toronto: Pontifical Institute of Mediaeval Studies, 2002.

———. "Polemic, Philology, and Ambivalence: Reading the Qur'an in Latin Christendom." *Journal of Islamic Studies* 15, no. 2 (2004): 181–209.

Burnett, Charles. "Learned Knowledge of Arabic Poetry, Rhymed Prose and Didactic Verse, from Petrus Alfonsi to Petrarch." In *In the Middle Ages: A Festschrift for Peter Dronke*, edited by John Marenbon. Leiden: E. J. Brill, 2001.

Burnett, Charles, and Anna Contadini, eds. *Islam and the Italian Renaissance*. London: Warburg Institute, 1999.

Carey, George. *The Medieval Alexander*. Edited by D.J.A. Ross. Cambridge: Cambridge University Press, 1956.

Casiri, Miguel. *Bibliotheca Arabico-Hispana Escurialensis*. 2 vols. Madrid: Antonius Perez de Soto, 1760–70.

Certeau, Michel de. "Montaigne's 'Of Cannibals': The Savage 'I'." In *Heterologies: Discourse on the Other*, 67–79. Translated by Brian Massumi. Minneapolis: University of Minnesota Press, 1986.

Chebel, Malek. *L'esprit de sérail. Perversions et marginalités sexuelles au Maghreb*. Paris: Lieu Commun, 1988.

Chittick, William C. *Imagined Worlds: Ibn al-ʿArabi and the Problem of Religious Diversity*. Albany: State University of New York Press, 1994.

Cissoko, Sékéné Mody. *Tombouctou et l'Empire Songhay*. Paris and Montréal: L'Harmattan, 1996.

Codazzi, Angela. "Leone Africano." In *Enciclopedia italiana*, 20:899. Rome, 1933.

———. "Dell'unico manoscritto conosciuto della *Cosmografia dell'Africa* di Giovanni Leone l'Africano." In *Comptes rendus du Congrès international de géographie. Lisbonne 1949*, 4:225–26. Lisbon, 1952.

Cohen, Elizabeth S. "Seen and Known: Prostitutes in the Cityscape of Late-Sixteenth-Century Rome." *Renaissance Studies* 12, no. 3 (1998): 392–401.

Cohen, Elizabeth S., and Thomas V. Cohen. *Daily Life in Renaissance Italy*. Westport, Conn.: Greenwood Press, 2001.

Cohen, Mark R. *Under Crescent and Cross. The Jew in the Middle Ages*. Princeton, N.J.: Princeton University Press, 1994.

Cohen, Thomas V., and Elizabeth S. Cohen. *Words and Deeds in Renaissance Rome: Trials before the Papal Magistrates*. Toronto: University of Toronto Press, 1993.

Cook, Jr., Weston F. *The Hundred Years War for Morocco: Gunpowder and the Military Revolution in the Early Modern Muslim World*. Boulder, Colo.: Westview Press, 1994.

Cooper, Richard. *Rabelais et l'Italie*. Études rabelaisiennes 24. Geneva: Librairie Droz, 1991.

Corbin, Henry. *Histoire de la philosophie islamique*. Paris: Gallimard, 1986.

Cornell, Vincent J. *Realm of the Saint: Power and Authority in Moroccan Sufism*. Austin: University of Texas Press, 1998.

———. "Socioeconomic Dimensions of Reconquista and Jihad in Morocco: Portuguese Dukkala and the Saʿdid Sus, 1450–1557." *International Journal of Middle East Studies* 22 (1990): 383–92.

Corriente, Federico. *Árabe andalusí y lenguas romances*. Madrid: Editorial Mapfre, 1992.

Cruz Hernández, Miguel. *Abu-l-Walid ibn Rushd (Averroës): Vida, obra, pensamiento, influentia*. Córdoba, 1986.

D'Amico, John F. *Renaissance Humanism in Papal Rome: Humanists and Churchmen on the Eve of the Reformation*. Baltimore and London: Johns Hopkins University Press, 1983.

Delumeau, Jean. *Rome au XVIe siècle*. Paris: Hachette, 1975.

Dermenghem, Émile. *Le culte des saints dans l'Islam maghrébin*. Paris: Gallimard, 1954.

Detienne, Marcel and Jean-Pierre Vernant. *Cunning Intelligence in Greek Culture and Society*. Translated by Janet Lloyd. Chicago: University of Chicago Press, 1991.

D'Onofrio, Cesare. *Castel S. Angelo*. Rome: Cassa di Risparmio di Roma, 1971.

Dunn, Ross. *The Adventures of Ibn Battuta, a Muslim Traveler of the 14th Century*. Berkeley and Los Angeles: University of California Press, 1986.

Eco, Umberto. *Experiences in Translation*. Translated by Alastair McEwen. Toronto: University of Toronto Press, 2001.

Egidio da Viterbo, O.S.A. e il suo tempo. Atti del V convegno dell' Istituto Storico Agostiniano, Roma-Viterbo, 20–23 ottobre 1982. Rome: Ed. "Analecta Augustiniana," 1983.

Eliav-Feldon, Miriam. "Invented Identities: Credulity in the Age of Prophecy and Exploration." *Journal of Early Modern History* 3 (1999): 203–32.

El-Shamy, Hasan M. *Folk Traditions of the Arab World. A Guide to Motif Classification*. 2 vols. Bloomington and Indianapolis: Indiana University Press, 1995.

———. *Types of the Folktale in the Arab World. A Demographically-Oriented Tale-Type Index*. Bloomington and Indianapolis: Indiana University Press, 2004.

The Encyclopaedia of Islam. Leiden, 1913–1936; supplement, 1938. New ed., 1954–2001.

Epstein, Steven. *Speaking of Slavery: Color, Ethnicity and Human Bondage in Italy*. Ithaca, N.Y.: Cornell University Press, 2001.

Esposito, John L., ed. *The Oxford Encyclopedia of the Modern Islamic World*. 4 vols. New York and Oxford: Oxford University Press, 1995.

Fahd, Toufic. *La divination arabe. Études religieuses, sociologiques et folkloriques sur le milieu natif de l'Islam*. Paris: Sindbad, 1987.

Fakhry, Majid. *Averroës (Ibn Rushd). His Life, Works and Influence*. Oxford: One World, 2001.

Ferhat, Halima. "Abu-l-ʿAbbas: Contestation et sainteté." *Al-Qantara* 13 (1992): 181–99.

———. *Le Soufisme et les Zaouyas au Maghreb. Mérite individuel et patrimoine sacré*. Casablanca: Éditions Toubkal, 2003.

Ferhat, Halima, and Hamid Triki. "Hagiographie et religion au Maroc médiéval." *Hespéris Tamuda* 24 (1986): 17–51.

Fisher, Humphrey J. "Leo Africanus and the Songhay Conquest of Hausaland." *International Journal of African Historical Studies* 11 (1978): 86–112.

Fleischer, Cornell H. "The Lawgiver as Messiah: The Making of the Imperial Image in the Reign of Süleyman." In *Soliman le Magnifique et son temps*.

Actes du Colloque de Paris, Galéries nationales du Grand Palais 7–10 mars 1990, edited by Gilles Veinstein, 159–77. Paris: École du Louvre and EHESS, 1992.

————. "Seer to the Sultan: Haydar-I Remmal and Sultan Süleyman." In *Cultural Horizons. A Festschrift in Honor of Talat S. Halman*, edited by Jayne L. Warner, 290–99. Syracuse, N.Y.: Syracuse University Press, 2001.

Frede, Carlo de. *La prima traduzione italiana del Corano*. Naples: Istituto Universitario Orientale, 1967.

Gaignard, Catherine. *Maures et chrétiens à Grenade, 1492–1570*. Paris: Éditions L'Harmattan, 1997.

Gaignebet, Claude. *A plus hault sens. L'esotérisme spirituel et charnel de Rabelais*. 2 vols. Paris: Maisonneuve et Larose, 1986.

Gaisser, Julia Haig. "The Rise and Fall of Goritz's Feasts." *Renaissance Quarterly* 48 (1995): 41–57.

Galán Sánchez, Ángel. *Los mudéjares del reino de Granada*. Granada: Universidad de Granada, 1991.

Gams, Pius Bonifacius, ed. *Series episcoporum ecclesiae catholicae*. Leipzig: Karl Hiersemann, 1931.

García-Arenal, Mercedes. "The Revolution of Fas in 869/1465 and the Death of Sultan ʿAbd al-Haqq al-Marini." *Bulletin of the School of Oriental and African Studies* 41 (1978): 43–66.

————. "Sainteté et pouvoir dynastique au Maroc: La résistance de Fès aux Saʿdiens." *Annales.ESC* 45 (1990): 1019–42.

————, ed. *Conversions islamiques. Identités religieuses en Islam méditerranéen*. Paris: Maisonneuve et Larose, 2001.

García-Arenal, Mercedes, and María J. Viguera, eds. *Relaciones de la península Ibérica con el Magreb siglos XIII–XVI. Actas del Coloquio (Madrid, 17–18 diciembre 1987)*. Madrid: CSIC, 1988.

García-Arenal, Mercedes, and Gerard Wiegers. *A Man of Three Worlds: Samuel Pallache, a Moroccan Jew in Catholic and Protestant Europe*. Translated by Martin Beagles. Baltimore, Md.: Johns Hopkins University Press, 2003.

Gattoni, Maurizio. *Leone X e la Geo-Politica dello Stato Pontificio (1513–1521)*. Vatican City: Archivio Segreto Vaticano, 2000.

Goffman, Daniel. *The Ottoman Empire and Early Modern Europe*. Cambridge: Cambridge University Press, 2002.

Gold, Leonard Singer, ed. *A Sign and a Witness: 2000 Years of Hebrew Books and Illuminated Manuscripts*. New York: New York Public Library and Oxford: Oxford University Press, 1988.

Goldman, Israel. *The Life and Times of Rabbi David Ibn Ali Zimra*. New York: Jewish Theological Seminary, 1970.

Gouwens, Kenneth. *Remembering the Renaissance: Humanist Narratives of the Sack of Rome.* Leiden, Boston, and Cologne: E. J. Brill, 1998.

Grabar, Oleg. *The Illustrations of the Maqamat.* Chicago and London: University of Chicago Press, 1984.

Guesdon, Marie-Geneviève, and Annie Vernay-Nouri, eds. *L'art du livre arabe.* Paris: Bibliothèque nationale de France, 2001.

Haddad-Chamakh, Fatma, and Alia Baccar-Bournaz, eds. *L'écho de la prise de Grenade dans la culture européene aux XVIe et XVIIe siècles. Actes du Colloque de Tunis 18–21 novembre 1992.* Tunis: Cérès, 1994.

Hajji, Muhammad. *L'activité intellectuelle au Maroc à l'époque Sa'dide.* 2 vols. Rabat: Dar El-Maghrib, 1976–77.

al-Hajwi, Muhammad al-Mahdi. *Hayat al-Wazzan al-Fasi wa-atharuh.* Rabat, 1935.

Hale, J. R. *Machiavelli and Renaissance Italy.* New York: Collier Books, 1960.

Hallaq, Wael B. *Authority, Continuity and Change in Islamic Law.* Cambridge: Cambridge University Press, 2001.

Hama, Boubou. *Histoire du Gobir et de Sokoto.* Paris: 1967.

Hamani, Djibo Mallal. *Au carrefour du Soudan et de la Berberie: Le sultanat touareg de l'Ayar.* Niamey: Institut de Recherches en Sciences Humaines, 1989.

Hamilton, Alastair. "Eastern Churches and Western Scholarship." In *Rome Reborn. The Vatican Library and Renaissance Culture,* edited by Anthony Grafton, 225–49. Washington, D.C.: Library of Congress, New Haven: Yale University Press, and Vatican City, Biblioteca Apostolica Vaticana, 1993.

Hampton, Timothy. "'Turkish Dogs': Rabelais, Erasmus, and the Rhetoric of Alterity." *Representations* 41 (Winter 1993): 58–82.

Hanebutt-Benz, Eva, Dagmar Glass, Geoffrey Roper, and Theo Smets, eds. *Middle Eastern Languages and the Print Revolution. A Cross-Cultural Encounter.* Westhofen: WVA-Verlag Skulima, 2002.

Harley, J. B., and David Woodward, eds. *The History of Cartography.* Vol. 1: *Cartography in Prehistoric, Ancient, and Medieval Europe and the Mediterranean;* vol. 2, bk. 1. *Cartography in the Traditional Islamic and South Asian Societies.* Chicago and London: University of Chicago Press, 1987.

Haywood, John A. *Arabic Lexicography. Its History, and its Place in the General History of Lexicography.* Leiden: E. J. Brill, 1960.

Herzig, Tamar. "The Demons' Reaction to Sodomy: Witchcraft and Homosexuality in Gianfrancesco Pico della Mirandola's *Strix.*" *Sixteenth-Century Journal* 34 (2003): 52–72.

Hirst, Michael. *Sebastiano del Piombo.* Oxford: Clarendon Press, 1981.

Hitti, Philip K. *History of the Arabs from the Earliest Times to the Present.* 10th ed. New York: St. Martin's Press, 1996.

Holl, Augustin F. C. *The Diwan Revisited: Literacy, State Formation and the Rise of Kanuri Domination (AD 1200–1600).* London and New York: Kegan Paul International, 2000.

Hook, Judith. *The Sack of Rome, 1527.* 2nd ed. London: Palgrave Macmillan, 2004.

Hunwick, John. "Al-Maghili and the Jews of Tuwat: The Demise of a Community." *Studi islamica* 61 (1985): 157–83.

———. "The Rights of *Dhimmis* to Maintain a Place of Worship: A 15th Century *Fatwa* from Tlemcen." *Al-Qantara* 12 (1991): 133–55.

Hunwick, John, and Eve Trout Powell, eds. *The African Diaspora in the Mediterranean Lands of Islam.* Princeton, N.J.: Markus Wiener Publishers, 2002.

Imperiale, Louis. *La Roma clandestina de Francisco Delicado y Pietro Aretino.* New York: Peter Lang, 1997.

Jansky, H. "Die Eroberung Syriens durch Sultan Selim." *Mitteilungen zur osmanischen Geschichte* 2 (1923–26): 173–241.

Jardine, Lisa, and Jerry Brotton. *Global Interests: Renaissance Art between East and West.* Ithaca, N.Y.: Cornell University Press, 2000.

Jomier, Jacques. *Le mahmal et la caravane égyptienne des pèlerins de La Mecque, XIIIe–XXe siècles.* Cairo: Institut Français d'Archéologie Orientale, 1953.

Julien, Charles-André. *Histoire de l'Afrique du Nord (Tunisie, Algérie, Maroc) de la conquête arabe à 1830.* 2nd ed., 2 vols. Paris: Payot, 1964.

Kably, Muhammad. *Société, pouvoir et religion au Maroc à la fin du Moyen-Âge (XIVe–XVe siècle).* Paris: Maisonneuve and Larose, 1986.

Kalck, Pierre. "Pour une localisation du royaume de Gaoga." *Journal of African History* 13 (1972): 520–40.

Karrow, Robert W., Jr. *Mapmakers of the Sixteenth Century and Their Maps.* Chicago: Newberry Library, 1993.

Kaufmann, David. "Jacob Mantino. Une page de l'histoire de la Renaissance." *Revue des études juives* 27 (1893): 30–60, 207–38.

Kennedy, Philip F. "The Maqamat as a Nexus of Interests: Reflections on Abdelfattah Kilito's *Les Seánces* and Other Works." In *Muslim Horizons,* edited by Julia Ashtiany Bray. London and New York: Routledge Curzon, forthcoming.

Khatibi, Abdelkebir, and Muhammad Sijelmassi. *The Splendor of Islamic Calligraphy.* London and New York: Thames and Hudson, 2001.

Khoury, Philip S., and Joseph Kostiner, eds. *Tribes and State Formation in the Middle East.* Berkeley and Los Angeles: University of California Press, 1990.

Khushaim, Ali Fahmi. *Zarruq the Sufi*. Tripoli: General Company for Publication, 1976.

Kilito, Abdelfattah. *Les séances: Récits et codes culturels chez Hamadhani et Hariri*. Paris: Sindbad, 1983.

———. *L'auteur et ses doubles: Essai sur la culture arabe classique*. Paris: Éditions du Seuil, 1985.

Klapisch-Zuber, Christiane. "L'adoption impossible dans l'Italie de la fin du Moyen Âge." In *Adoption et fosterage*, edited by Mireille Corbier, 321–37. Paris: De Boccard, 1999.

———. *Women, Family and Ritual in Renaissance Italy*. Translated by Lydia G. Cochrane. Chicago: University of Chicago Press, 1985.

Kuehn, Thomas. "L'adoption à Florence à la fin du Moyen-Âge." *Médiévales* 35 (Autumn 1998): 69–81.

Kurzel-Runtscheiner, Monica. *Töchter der Venus. Die Kurtisanen Roms im 16. Jahrhundert*. Munich: C. H. Beck, 1995.

Ladero Quesada, Miguel Ángel. *Granada después la conquista: Repobladores y mudéjares*. Granada: Diputación Provincial de Granada, 1988.

Lagardère, Vincent. *Histoire et société en Occident musulman au Moyen Âge. Analyse du "Mi'yar" d'al-Wansharisi*. Madrid: Casa de Velázquez, 1995.

Larguèche, Dalenda, ed. *Histoire des femmes au Maghreb*. Tunis: Centre de Publication Universitaire, 2000.

Le Tourneau, Roger. *Fez in the Age of the Marinides*. Translated by Besse Albert Clement. Norman: University of Oklahoma Press, 1961.

Levi Della Vida, Giorgio. *Ricerche sulla formazione del più antico fondo dei manoscritti orientali della Biblioteca Vaticana*. Vatican City: Biblioteca Apostolica Vaticana, 1939.

———. *Elenco dei manoscritti arabi islamici della Biblioteca Vaticana*. Vatican City: Biblioteca Apostolica Vaticana, 1935.

Lévi-Provençal, E. *Les historiens des Chorfa: Essai sur la littérature historique et biographique au Maroc du XVIe au XXe siècle*. Paris: É. Larose, 1922.

Lewis, Bernard. *Race and Color in Islam*. New York: Harper and Row, 1971.

Lewis, Martin W., and Kären E. Wigen. *The Myth of Continents. A Critique of Metageography*. Berkeley and Los Angeles: University of California Press, 1997.

Linant de Bellefonds, Yves. *Traité de droit musulman comparé*. 3 vols. Paris and The Hague: Mouton, 1965–73.

Löfgren, Oscar, and Renato Traini. *Catalogue of the Arabic Manuscripts in the Biblioteca Ambrosiana*. 2 vols. Milan: Neri Pozza Editore, 1975.

Losada, Angel. *Jean Ginés de Sepúlveda a través de su "Epistolario" y nuevos documentos*. Madrid: Consejo Superior de Investigaciones Científicas, 1973.

Maalouf, Amin. *Léon l'Africain*. Paris: J. C. Lattès, 1986.

Malti-Douglas, Fedwa. *Woman's Body, Woman's Word. Gender and Discourse in Arabo-Islamic Writing*. Princeton, N.J.: Princeton University Press, 1991.

Marín, Manuela. *Mujeres en al-Ándalus*. Madrid: Consejo Superior de Investigaciones Científicas, 2000.

Marinelli, Peter V. *Ariosto and Boiardo: The Origins of "Orlando Furioso."* Columbia: University of Missouri Press, 1987.

Marmon, Shaun, ed. *Slavery in the Islamic Middle East*. Princeton, N.J.: Markus Wiener Publishers, 1999.

Le Maroc Andalou: À la découverte d'un art de vivre. Casablanca: EDDIF and Aix-en-Provence: Édisud, 2000.

Martin, Francis X. *Friar, Reformer, and Renaissance Scholar: Life and Work of Giles of Viterbo, 1469–1532*. Villanova, Pa.: Augustinian Press, 1992.

Masonen, Pekka. *The Negroland Revisited: Discovery and Invention of the Sudanese Middle Ages*. Helsinki: Finnish Academy of Science and Letters, 2000.

Massignon, Louis. *Le Maroc dans les premières années du 16e siècle. Tableau géographique d'après Léon l'Africain*. Algiers: Typographie Adolphe Jourdan, 1906.

Matthee, Rudi. "Prostitutes, Courtesans, and Dancing Girls: Women Entertainers in Safavid Iran." In *Iran and Beyond: Essays in Middle Eastern History in Honor of Nikki R. Keddie*, edited by Rudi Matthee and Beth Baron. Costa Mesa, Calif.: Mazda Publishers, 2000.

Mazzuchelli, Giammaria. *Gli Scrittori d'Italia*. 3 vols. Brescia, 1753.

McAuliffe, Jane Dammen, Barry D. Walfish, and Joseph W. Goering, eds. *With Reverence for the Word: Medieval Scriptural Exegesis in Judaism, Christianity, and Islam*. Oxford: Oxford University Press, 2003.

McIntosh, Gregory C. *The Piri Reis Map of 1513*. Athens, Ga., and London: University of Georgia Press, 2000.

Mediano, Fernando Rodriguez. *Familias de Fez (SS. XV–XVII)*. Madrid: Consejo Superior de Investigaciones Científicas, 1995.

Menocal, María Rosa, Raymond P. Scheindlin, and Michael Sells, eds. *The Literature of al-Andalus*. Cambridge: Cambridge University Press, 2000.

Meyerson, Mark. *The Muslims of Valencia in the Age of Fernando and Isabel: Between Coexistence and Crusade*. Berkeley and Los Angeles: University of California Press, 1991.

Minnich, Nelson. "Raphael's *Portrait of Leo X with Cardinals Giulio de' Medici and Luigi de' Rossi*: A Religious Interpretation." *Renaissance Quarterly* 56 (2003): 1005–46.

————. *The Catholic Reformation: Council, Churchmen, Controversies*. Aldershot: Variorum, 1993.

Miquel, André. *La géographie humaine du monde musulman jusqu'au milieu du 11e siècle*. 4 vols. Paris and The Hague: Mouton, 1973–88.

Monroe, James T. *The Art of Badiᶜ az-Zaman al-Hamadhani as Picaresque Narrative*. Beirut: American University, 1983.

Murray, Stephen O., and Will Roscoe, eds., *Islamic Homosexualities*. New York and London: New York University Press, 1997.

Niccoli, Ottavia. *Prophecy and People in Renaissance Italy*. Translated by Lydia G. Cochrane. Princeton, N.J.: Princeton University Press, 1990.

Nirenberg, David. *Communities of Violence: Persecution of Minorities in the Middle Ages*. Princeton, N.J.: Princeton University Press, 1996.

Odier, Jeanne Bignami. *La Bibliothèque Vaticane de Sixte IV à Pie XI*. Vatican City: Biblioteca Apostolica Vaticana, 1973.

Oliel, Jacob. *Les Juifs au Sahara: Le Touat au Moyen Âge*. Paris: CNRS Éditions, 1994.

O'Malley, John W. *Giles of Viterbo on Church and Reform: A Study in Renaissance Thought*. Leiden: E. J. Brill, 1968.

Partner, Peter. *The Pope's Men: The Papal Civil Service in the Renaissance*. Oxford: Clarendon Press, 1990.

————. *Renaissance Rome. 1500–1559*. Berkeley and Los Angeles: University of California Press, 1976.

Pasquier, Jules. *Jérôme Aléandre de sa naissance à la fin de son séjour à Brindes*. Paris: E. Leroux, 1900.

Pastor, Ludwig. *History of the Popes from the Close of the Middle Ages*. 40 vols. London: Routledge and Kegan Paul, 1898–1953.

Pedersen, Johannes. *The Arabic Book*. Translated by Geoffrey French. Princeton, N.J.: Princeton University Press, 1984.

Peirce, Leslie. *The Imperial Harem: Women and Sovereignty in the Ottoman Empire*. New York and Oxford: Oxford University Press, 1993.

Perles, Joseph. *Beiträge zur Geschichte der hebräischen und aramäischen Studien*. Munich: Theodor Ackermann, 1884.

Peters, Rudolph. *Jihad in Classical and Modern Islam. A Reader*. Princeton, N.J.: Markus Wiener Publishers, 1996.

Petrucci, Armando. *Writers and Readers in Medieval Italy. Studies in the History of Written Culture*. Edited and translated by Charles M. Radding. New Haven and London: Yale University Press, 1995.

Petry, Carl F. *Protectors or Praetorians? The Last Mamluk Sultans and Egypt's Waning as a Great Power*. Albany: SUNY Press, 1994.

Pouillon, François, and Oumelbanine Zhiri, eds. *Léon l'Africain*. Paris: Institut d'Étude de l'Islam et des Sociétés du Monde Musulman (EHESS), forthcoming.

Powers, David S. *Law, Society, and Culture in the Maghrib, 1300–1500*. Cambridge: Cambridge University Press, 2002.

Racine, Matthew T. "Service and Honor in Sixteenth-Century Portuguese North Africa: Yahya-u-Ta'fuft and Portuguese Noble Culture." *Sixteenth-Century Journal* 32 (2001): 67–90.

Rauchenberger, Dietrich. *Johannes Leo der Afrikaner. Seine Beschreibung des Raumes zwischen Nil und Niger nach dem Urtext*. Wiesbaden: Harrassowitz Verlag, 1999.

Reeves, Marjorie, ed. *Prophetic Rome in the High Renaissance*. Oxford: Clarendon Press, 1992.

Reynolds, Dwight F., ed. *Interpreting the Self: Autobiography in the Arabic Literary Tradition*. Berkeley and Los Angeles: University of California Press, 2001.

Ricard, Robert. *Études sur l'histoire des portugais au Maroc*. Coimbra: Universidade da Coimbra, 1955.

Robinson, Chase F. *Islamic Historiography*. Cambridge: Cambridge University Press, 2003.

Rocke, Michael. *Forbidden Friendships: Homosexuality and Male Culture in Renaissance Florence*. New York and Oxford: Oxford University Press, 1996.

Roded, Ruth, ed. *Women in Islam and the Middle East. A Reader*. London and New York: I. B. Tauris, 1999.

Rosenberger, Bernard, and Hamid Triki. "Famines et épidémies au Maroc aux XVIe et XVIIe siècles." *Hespéris Tamuda* 14 (1973): 109–75.

Rosenthal, Franz. *A History of Muslim Historiography*. Leiden: E. J. Brill, 1952.

Rotunda, D. P. *Motif-Index of the Italian Novella in Prose*. Bloomington: Indiana University Press, 1942.

Rowland, Ingrid. *The Culture of the High Renaissance. Ancients and Moderns in Sixteenth-Century Rome*. Cambridge: Cambridge University Press, 1998.

Ruderman, David, ed. *Essential Papers on Jewish Culture in Renaissance and Baroque Italy*. New York and London: New York University Press, 1992.

Ruggiero, Guido. *The Boundaries of Eros: Sex Crime and Sexuality in Renaissance Venice*. New York and Oxford: Oxford University Press, 1985.

Saad, Elias. *Social History of Timbuktu: The Role of Muslim Scholars and Notables, 1400–1900*. Cambridge: Cambridge University Press, 1983.

Sabattini, Alberto. _Alberto III Pio: Politica, diplomazia e guerra del conte di Carpi_. Carpi: Danae, 1994.

Safran, Janina M. _The Second Umayyad Caliphate. The Articulation of Caliphal Legitimacy in al-Andalus_. Cambridge, Mass.: Harvard University Press, 2000.

Sallis, Eva. _Sheherazade through the Looking Glass: The Metamorphosis of the "Thousand and One Nights."_ Surrey: Curzon Press, 1999.

Salmon, Pierre, ed. _Mélanges d'Islamologie: Volume dédié à la mémoire de Armand Abel_. Leiden: E. J. Brill, 1974.

Sartain, E. M. _Jalal al-din al-Suyuti. Biography and Background_. 2 vols. Cambridge: Cambridge University Press, 1975.

Sayyid, Ayman Fu'ad. "Early Methods of Book Composition: al-Maqrizi's Draft of the 'Kitab al-Khitat.'" In _The Codicology of Islamic Manuscripts_, edited by Yasin Dutton. London: Al-Furqan Islamic Heritage Foundation, 1995.

al-Sayyid-Marsot, Afaf Lutfi, ed. _Society and the Sexes in Medieval Islam_. Malibu, Calif.: Undena Publications, 1979.

Schimmel, Annemarie. _As Through a Veil. Mystical Poetry in Islam_. New York: Columbia University Press, 1982.

———. _The Triumphal Sun. A Study of the Works of Jalaloddin Rumi_. Albany: SUNY Press, 1993.

Secret, F. _Les Kabbalistes chrétiens de la Renaissance_. Paris: Dunod, 1964.

———. _Postel revisité. Nouvelles recherches sur Guillaume Postel et son milieu_. Paris: SÉHA and Milan: Arché, 1998.

Serfaty, Nicole. _Les courtisans juifs des sultans marocains: Hommes politiques et hauts dignitaires, XIIIe–XVIIIe siècles_. Saint-Denis: Éditions Bouchène, 1999.

Setton, Kenneth M. _The Papacy and the Levant (1204–1571)_. 4 vols. Philadelphia: American Philosophical Society, 1976–84.

Shatzmiller, Maya. _The Berbers and the Islamic State_. Princeton, N.J.: Markus Wiener Publishers, 2000.

———. _Labour in the Medieval Islamic World_. Leiden: E. J. Brill, 1994.

———. "Women and Property Rights in al-Andalus and the Maghrib: Social Patterns and Legal Discourse." _Islamic Law and Society_ 2 (1995): 219–57.

Signorelli, Giuseppe. _Il Card. Egidio da Viterbo: Agostiniano, umanista e riformatore, 1464–1532_. Florence: Libreria Editrice Fiorentina, 1924.

Silverberg, Robert. _The Realm of Prester John_. Athens: Ohio University Press, 1972.

Società, politica e cultura a Carpi ai tempi di Alberto III Pio. Atti del Convegno Internazionale (Carpi, 19–21 Maggio 1978). 2 vols. Padua: Editrice Antenore, 1981.

Spaulding, J. L. "Comment: The Geographic Location of Gaoga." *Journal of African History* 14 (1973): 505–8.

Spivakovksy, Erika. *Son of the Alhambra: Diego Hurtado de Mendoza, 1504–1575*. Austin and London: University of Texas Press, 1970.

Stewart, Devin J., Baber Johansen, and Amy Singer. *Law and Society in Islam*. Princeton, N.J.: Markus Wiener Publishers, 1996.

Stow, Kenneth. *The Jews in Rome*. 2 vols. Leiden: E. J. Brill, 1997.

———. "Marriages Are Made in Heaven: Marriage and the Individual in the Roman Jewish Ghetto." *Renaissance Quarterly* 45 (1995): 445–91.

———. *Theater of Acculturation. The Roman Ghetto in the 16th Century*. Seattle: University of Washington Press, 2001.

Sumruld, William A. *Augustine and the Arians. The Bishop of Hippo's Encounters with Ulfilan Arianism*. Selinsgrove: Susquehanna University Press and London and Toronto: Associated University Presses, 1994.

Svalduz, Elena. *Da Castella a "città": Carpi e Alberto Pio (1472–1530)*. Rome: Officina Edizioni, 2001.

Talvacchia, Bette. *Taking Positions. On the Erotic in Renaissance Culture*. Princeton, N.J.: Princeton University Press, 1999.

Temimi, Abdejelil, ed. *Las practicas musulmanas de los moriscos andaluces (1492–1609). Actas del III Simposio Internacional de Estudios Moriscos*. Zaghouan, 1989.

Thompson, Stith. *Motif-Index of Folk Literature*. Rev. ed. Copenhagen: Rosenkilde and Bagger, 1957.

Tinguely, Frédéric. *L'Écriture du Levant à la Renaissance. Enquête sur les voyageurs français dans l'empire de Soliman le Magnifique*. Geneva: Librairie Droz, 2000.

Touati, Houari. *L'armoire à sagesse: Bibliothèques et collections en Islam*. Paris: Aubier, 2003.

———. *Islam et voyage au Moyen Âge*. Paris: Éditions du Seuil, 2000.

Trabulsi, Amjad. *La critique poétique des Arabes jusqu'au Ve siècle de l'Hégire (XIe siècle de J. C.)*. Damascus: Institut Français de Damas, 1955.

Trachtenberg, Joshua. *Jewish Magic and Superstition: A Study in Folk Religion*. New York: Atheneum, 1977.

Triki, Hamid. "L'oiseau amphibie." In *Fez dans la Cosmographie d'Al-Hassan*

Bibliography

ben Mohammed al-Wazzan az-Zayyat, dit Léon l'Africain, 13–47. Mohammedia, Morocco: Senso Unico Editions, 2004.

Trimingham, John S. *A History of Islam in West Africa.* Oxford: Oxford University Press, 1959.

Trinkaus, Charles. *"In Our Image and Likeness": Humanity and Divinity in Italian Humanist Thought.* London: Constable, 1970.

Trovato, Paolo. *Storia della lingua italiana: Il primo Cinquecento.* Bologna: Il Mulino, 1994.

Ugr, Ahmet. *The Reign of Sultan Selim in the Light of the Selim-Name Literature.* Berlin: Klaus Schwarz Verlag, 1985.

Vajda, Georges. "Un traité maghrébin 'Adversus Judaeos': 'Ahkam ahl al-Dimma' du Shaykh Muhammad ibn 'Abd al-Karim al-Maghili." In *Études d'orientalisme dédiées à la mémoire de Lévi-Provençal,* 805–13. Paris: G.-P. Maisonneuve et Larose, 1962.

Valensi, Lucette. "Le jardin de l'Académie ou comment se forme une école de pensée." In *Modes de transmission de la culture religieuse en Islam,* edited by Hassan Elboudrari, 41–64. Cairo: Institut Français d'Archéologie Orientale du Caire, 1992.

———. *Venise et la Sublime Porte. La naissance du despote.* Paris: Hachette, 1987.

Vergé-Franceschi, Michel, ed. *Guerre et commerce en Méditerranée.* Paris: Éditions Veyrier, 1991.

Vidal Castro, Francisco. "Ahmad al-Wansharisi (m. 914/1508). Principales Aspectos de su Vida." *Al-Qantara* 12 (1991): 315–52.

Walther, Wiebke. *Women in Islam from Medieval to Modern Times.* Translated by C.S.V. Salt. Princeton, N.J.: Markus Wiener Publishers, 1999.

Wansbrough, John E. *Lingua Franca in the Mediterranean.* Richmond, Surrey: Curzon Press, 1996.

———. "A Moroccan Amir's Commercial Treaty with Venice of the Year 913/1508." *Bulletin of the School of Oriental and African Studies* 25 (1962): 449–71.

Weil, Gérard E. *Élie Lévita, humaniste et massorète (1469–1549).* Leiden: E. J. Brill, 1963.

Welsford, Enid. *The Fool. His Social and Literary History.* London: Faber and Faber, 1935.

Willis, John Ralph, ed. *Slaves and Slavery in Muslim Africa.* 2 vols. London: Frank Cass, 1985.

Winspeare, Fabrizio. *La congiura dei cardinali contro Leone X.* Florence: Leo S. Olschki, 1957.

Wright, J. W., and Everett K. Rowson, eds. *Homoeroticism in Classical Arabic Literature*. New York: Columbia University Press, 1997.

Yahya, Dahiru. *Morocco in the Sixteenth Century: Problems and Patterns in African Foreign Policy*. London: Longman, 1981.

Zhiri, Oumelbanine. "'Il compositore' ou l'autobiographie éclatée de Jean Léon l'Africain." In *Le voyage des théories*, edited by Ali Benmakhlouf, 63–80. Casablanca: Éditions Le Fennec, 2000.

———. *L'Afrique au miroir de l'Europe: Fortunes de Jean Léon l'Africain à la Renaissance*. Geneva: Librairie Droz, 1991.

———. *Les sillages de Jean Léon l'Africain: XVIe au XXe siècle*. Casablanca: Wallada, 1995.

Zimmerman, T. C. Price. *Paolo Giovio: The Historian and the Crisis of Sixteenth-Century Italy*. Princeton, N.J.: Princeton University Press, 1995.

Acknowledgments

TRICKSTER TRAVELS took me into parts of the world and bodies of scholarship that I had not known before, so I have many guides to thank. My daughter Hannah Davis Taïeb first introduced me to Morocco during her field work there and has made important suggestions throughout my research and writing. Together with Jill Ker Conway I took a second trip, where we followed several of al-Hasan al-Wazzan's paths. Among those who made that visit especially fruitful were Professor Brahim Boutaleb of the Faculty of Letters at the University Muhammad V in Rabat, Dr. Armand Guigui of Fez, and Touria Haji Temsamani of the Librairie des Colonnes in Tangier. My son-in-law André Taïeb showed me around the Tunisia he knows so well, helping me to imagine how its sights might have appeared to al-Wazzan's eyes.

The example of Robert Tignor, distinguished Africanist and my colleague at Princeton, made me understand how important it is for a historian of Europe to venture beyond its borders. My agent Anne Engel gave me much needed support and guidance throughout the years it took to accomplish my task. Along the way, the assistance of my translators from the Arabic was essential: Mustapha Kamal and Andrew Lane helped me early in my research; Michael Marmura took time from his busy schedule to read a text for me; Stefania Dodoni checked a manuscript in Italy toward the end of my work. Muhammad Sid-Ahmad has patiently reviewed all my texts and translations and answered my many queries about Arabic vocabulary; I am very grateful to him. Moshe Sluhovsky and Benjamin Fisher translated some correspondence in Hebrew for me; Gabriel Piterberg assisted me with a text in Turkish.

Lucette Valensi kindly read a draft of the entire manuscript of *Trickster Travels*; I am fortunate, indeed, to have had suggestions from a scholar of such wide and deep learning in the world of North Africa and Islam. Elisabeth Sifton's attentive and wise editing of my text made the book an added joy to finish.

Many scholars, colleagues, and friends were generous in giving me advice about sources to consult and paths to follow. Conversations and exchange with Michael Bonner, Michael Cooperson, Hasan El-Shamy, Philip F. Kennedy, Abdelfattah Kilito, Shaun Marmon, and Ingrid Rowland were especially important to the shape of my argument. I was glad to have the opportunity to interview Amin Maalouf about his interest in "Léon l'Africain." For assistance on different features of this book, I want to thank Renata Ago, Suzanne Conklin Akbari, Svetlana Alpers, James Amelang, Nadia al-Baghdadi, Andrea Baldi, Paola Banchetti, Jamila Bargach, Ali Benmakhlouf, Margarita Birriel, Ross Bran, Thomas Burman, Charles Burnett, Massimo Ceresa, Yossi Chajes, Elizabeth Cohen, Thomas Cohen, Denis Crouzet, Sylvie Deswarte-Rosa, Stephen Epstein, Anna Esposito, Cornell Fleischer, Mercedes García-Arenal, Xavier Gil, Daniel Goffman, Kenneth Gouwens, Anthony Grafton, Michael Harbsmeier, Holland Lee Hendrix, Diane Owen Hughes, Lisa Jardine, Deborah Kapchan, Nikki Keddie, Philip S. Khoury, Christiane Klapisch-Zuber, Thomas Kuehn, Claude Lefébure, Carla Marcato, Sarah Matthews-Grieco, Jane McAuliffe, Alexander Nagel, Laurie Nussdorfer, Lauren Osborne, Olga Pugliese, Miri Rubin, Teofilo Ruiz, Janina Safran, Paula Sanders, Lucienne Senocak, Maya Shatzmiller, Amy Singer, Randolph Starn, Esther Stebler, Brian Stock, Kenneth Stow, Muhammad Tavakoli-Targhi, Houari Touati, Avram Udovitch, Germaine Warkentin, Gerhard Wedel, Gillian Weiss, and Oumelbanine Zhiri. I am grateful to all of these colleagues for their generous assistance, though the responsibility for any errors in my book rests on me alone.

Five conferences in which I participated helped me learn much about the worlds of al-Hasan al-Wazzan: "Poverty and Charity in Middle Eastern Contexts," held at the University of Michigan Center for Middle Eastern and North African Studies (2000); "The Impact of the Ottoman Empire on Early Modern Europe," held at the Folger Shakespeare Library (2002); "Léon l'Africain," held at the École des Hautes Études en Sciences Sociales (2003); "Frontières religieuses. Rejets et passages, dissimulation et contrebande spirituelle," held at the Centre Culturel Calouste Gulbenkian and the Université de Paris 4–Sorbonne (2003); and "La Méditerranée dans l'Histoire," sponsored by Les Rendezvous de l'Histoire at Rabat (2005). I would especially like to thank Professors Abdelmajid Kaddouri and Abdesselam Cheddadi for their warm welcome at this last event.

Over the years of research on al-Wazzan, I had the opportunity to present my findings to diverse university communities, learning much from questions, criticisms, and advice proffered by my listeners. Among those visits were Bir Zeit University, Bryn Mawr College, the City University of New York Graduate School, Concordia University, Cornell University, the Einstein Forum Potsdam, Koç University, the New York Public Library at which I gave the Toynbee Lecture, New York University, the Pontifical Institute for Mediaeval Studies at Toronto, Ritsumeikan University, Smith College, the Technische Universität Berlin, Tel Aviv University, the Universidad Autónoma de Madrid, the Université de Lyon 2, the Université de Paris 7–Denis Diderot, the University of California at Berkeley, the University of California at Los Angeles, the University of Edinburgh, the University of Illinois at Chicago, the University of Illinois at Urbana-Champaign, the University of Massachusetts at Amherst, the University of Michigan, the University of Pennsylvania, the University of Toronto, and the University of Vermont.

My research took me to numerous libraries and collections, each one remembered along with the delight of discovery. Among them, I thank here especially the staff at the Real Biblioteca del Escorial, the Biblioteca Ambrosiana in Milan, the Biblioteca Angelica in Rome, the

Biblioteca Nazionale Centrale in Rome, the Archivio di Stato di Roma, the Rare Book Collection of the Hungarian Academy of Sciences, the Oriental Manuscripts Division of the Bibliothèque Nationale de France, the Rare Books Reading Room of the British Library, the Newberry Library, the Thomas Fisher Rare Book Library at the University of Toronto, and the Houghton Library of Harvard University. I am grateful to Professor Ulrich Gäbler for opening to me the library at the Frey-Grynaeischen Institut at Basel, on whose shelves I could track seventeenth-century interest in Joannes Leo Africanus and Christian study of Arabic and Islam more generally. As I was building up my own library collection, I also got excellent guidance from learned book dealers in Paris, among whom I especially want to thank the staff of the Librairie Avicenne.

The photographer Michael van Leur put his remarkable skills to work to prepare the illustrations for this book. I am grateful to Charles Battle, Susan Goldfarb, and Abby Kagan at Farrar, Straus and Giroux for all they have done in the production of *Trickster Travels*. I also extend my thanks to Chika Azuma for designing the handsome cover, Janet Biehl for her observant copyediting, Elizabeth Schraft for her careful proofreading, and Daniel Liebman for preparing the index.

This book is dedicated to Chandler Davis in appreciation for his innumerable discussions with me about its themes and his tireless reading of drafts, and even more in tribute to all he has done over the decades to help our earth become a place where peoples can live together in peace. Whether traveling the globe or locked in a prison cell, he has never lost faith in a future in which greed, violence, and political repression might give ground to justice, negotiation, and an unhindered quest for truth.

Index

Illustration Credits

1. Biblioteca Vaticana, Vatican City. MS Vat. Ar. 115 (four Arabic texts by Nestorian and Jacobite Christians), 295v. © Biblioteca Apostolica Vaticana (Vaticano).

2. Paride Grassi, *Diarium An. 1513 ad 1521:* MS E53, vol. 2, 310v. Department of Special Collections, Spencer Research Library, University of Kansas Libraries.

3. Biblioteca Vaticana, Vatican City. MS Vat. Ar. 357 (Tha'lab, *Qawa'id as-si'r,* a book on the Art of Poetry), 1a. © Biblioteca Apostolica Vaticana (Vaticano).

4. Biblioteca Estense Universitaria, Modena. MS Orientale 16-alfa.J.6.3 (Epistles of Saint Paul in Arabic), 1r. Su concessione del Ministero per i Beni e le Attività Culturali.

5. Real Biblioteca del Escorial, Spain. Esc. MS árabe 598 (Arabic-Hebrew-Latin-Spanish Dictionary), 3a. Copyright © Patrimonio Nacional.

6. *Al-Qur'an,* in Arabic and Latin: MS D100 inf., 316a. Biblioteca Ambrosiana, Milan. Diritti Biblioteca Ambrosiana. Vietata la riproduzione. Aut. No. F 99/05.

7. Al-Hasan al-Wazzan, *De Arte Metrica Liber:* MS Plut. 36.35, 60r. Biblioteca Medicea Laurenziana, Florence. Su concessione del Ministero per i Beni e le Attività Culturali. E'vietata ogni ulteriore riproduzione con qualsiasi mezzo.

8. Al-Hasan al-Wazzan, *De Viris quibusdam Illustribus apud Arabes:* MS Plut. 36.35, 33r. Biblioteca Medicea Laurenziana, Florence. Su concessione del Ministero per i Beni e le Attività Culturali. E'vietata ogni ulteriore riproduzione con qualsiasi mezzo.

9. Al-Hasan al-Wazzan, *Libro de la Cosmographia [sic] et Geographia de*

Affrica: V.E. MS 953, 464v. Biblioteca Nazionale Centrale di Roma. Vietata di ulteriori riproduzioni effettuate senza autorizzazione.

10. Al-Hasan al-Wazzan, *La Descrittione dell'Africa*, in Giovanni Battista Ramusio, ed., *Primo volume, et Terza editione delle Navigationi et Viaggi* (Venice: Giunti, 1563), 95v: Courtesy of the Thomas Fisher Rare Book Library, University of Toronto.

11. Ibn Khaldun, *Kitabu'l-Mukkaddime* (804/1402): Atif Efendi Library 1936. Süleymaniye Kütüphanesi, Istanbul.

12. Ptolemy, *Liber Geographiae*, ed. Bernardo Silvano (Venice: Jacopo Pencio, 1511), facsimile edition, "Quarta Africae Tabula": Courtesy of the Thomas Fisher Rare Book Library, University of Toronto.

13. Topkapi Palace Museum Library, Istanbul. MS 642 reproduced in Piri Reis, *Kitab-I Bahriye (Book of Navigation)* (Ankara, 2002), 469–71.

14. Giovanni Battista Ramusio, ed., *Primo volume, et Terza editione delle Navigationi et Viaggi* (Venice: Giunti, 1563), Primo Tavola: Courtesy of the Thomas Fisher Rare Book Library, University of Toronto.

15. Christoph Weiditz, *Authentic Everyday Dress of the Renaissance: All 154 Plates from the "Trachtenbuch"* (New York: Dover Publications, 1994), pl. 84.

16. Charles Terrasse, *Médersas du Maroc* (Paris: Éditions Albert Morance, 1928), pl. 38.

17. Sheila S. Blair and Jonathan Bloom, *The Art and Architecture of Islam 1250–1800* (New Haven and London: Yale University Press, 1995), fig. 158.

18. *Kitab al-sulwanat*: Esc. MS árabe 528, 15r. Real Biblioteca del Escorial, Spain. Copyright © Patrimonio Nacional.

19. *Kitab al-sulwanat*: Esc. MS árabe 528, 79v. Real Biblioteca del Escorial. Copyright © Patrimonio Nacional.

20. Shukri Bey Bitlisi, *Selim Name*: Yah. MS. Ar. 1116, 122v. Jewish National and University Library, Jerusalem.

21. Loqman, *Shahnama-yi Salim Khan* (1581): MS A. 3595, 54r. Topkapi Palace Library, Istanbul.

22. Al-Hariri, *Maqamat*, with illustrations by Yahya al-Wasiti, 634/1237: MS arabe 5847, 84v, 86. Bibliothèque Nationale de France, Paris.

23. Giovanni Antonio Dosio, *Urbis Romae aedificiorum illustriumque supersunt reliquiae* (1569), 224. Courtesy of the Thomas Fisher Rare Book Library, University of Toronto.

24. Valeria Annecchino, *La Basilica di Sant'Agostino in Campo Marzio* (Genoa: Edizioni d'Arte Marconi, 2000), fig. 3.

25. Bernardino Loschi (attributed to), Portrait of Alberto Pio, 1512. Oil on wood, 58.4 x 49.5 cm. © National Gallery, London, NG3940.